THE PARALLEL UNIVERSES OF DAVID SHRAYER-PETROV

A COLLECTION PUBLISHED ON THE OCCASION OF THE WRITER'S 85TH BIRTHDAY

Jews of Russia and Eastern Europe and Their Legacy

Series Editor
Maxim D. Shrayer (Boston College)

Editorial Board
Karel Berkhoff (NIOD Institute for War, Holocaust and Genocide Studies)
Jeremy Hicks (Queen Mary University of London)
Brian Horowitz (Tulane University)
Luba Jurgenson (Universite ParisIV—Sorbonne)
Roman Katsman (Bar-Ilan University)
Dov-Ber Kerler (Indiana University)
Vladimir Khazan (Hebrew University of Jerusalem)
Alice Nakhimovsky (Colgate University)
Antony Polonsky (Brandeis University)
Jonathan D. Sarna (Brandeis University)
David Shneer (University of Colorado at Boulder)
Anna Shternshis (University of Toronto)
Leona Toker (Hebrew University of Jerusalem)
Mark Tolts (Hebrew University of Jerusalem)

THE PARALLEL UNIVERSES OF DAVID SHRAYER-PETROV

A COLLECTION PUBLISHED ON THE OCCASION OF THE WRITER'S 85TH BIRTHDAY

Edited by
Roman Katsman,
Maxim D. Shrayer,
Klavdia Smola

BOSTON
2021

Acknowledgements
The editors gratefully acknowledge the support of Boston College.

Library of Congress Cataloging-in-Publication Data
Names: ShraYer-Petrov, David, honouree. | Katsman, Roman, editor. | Shrayer, Maxim D., 1967- editor. | Smola, Klavdiīa, editor.
Title: The parallel universes of David Shrayer-Petrov : a collection published on the occasion of the writer's 85th birthday / edited by Roman Katsman, Maxim D. Shrayer, Klavdia Smola.
Other titles: Jews of Russia & Eastern Europe and their legacy.
Description: Boston : Academic Studies Press, 2021. | Series: Jews of Russia & Eastern Europe and their legacy | Includes bibliographical references and index.
Identifiers: LCCN 2020050411 (print) | LCCN 2020050412 (ebook) |
ISBN 9781644695265 (hardback) | ISBN 9781644695272 (paperback) |
ISBN 9781644695289 (adobe pdf) | ISBN 9781644695296 (epub)
Subjects: LCSH: Shraer-Petrov, David--Criticism and interpretation. |
Russian literature--Jewish authors--20th century--History and criticism. | Russian literature--Jewish authors--21st century--History and
criticism. | Russian literature--United States--20th century--History and criticism. | Russian literature--United States--21st century--History and criticism.
Classification: LCC PG3549.S537 Z84 2021 (print) | LCC PG3549.S537 (ebook) | DDC 891.73/44--dc23
LC record available at https://lccn.loc.gov/2020050411
LC ebook record available at https://lccn.loc.gov/2020050412

Copyright © 2021 by Roman Katsman, Maxim D. Shrayer, Klavdia Smola.
Individual contents copyright © 2021 by the contributors.
Works by David Shrayer-Petrov copyright © 1956-2021 by the author.

Book design by Lapiz Digital Services
Cover design by Ivan Grave

Published by Academic Studies Press
1577 Beacon St.

Brookline, MA 02446, USA
www.academicstudiespress.com

Contents

Preface — vii
   Roman Katsman, Maxim D. Shrayer, Klavdia Smola

A Note on Transliteration and Spelling of Names

PART ONE David Shrayer-Petrov: Life, Art, and Thought — 1

David Shrayer-Petrov, Russian-Jewish Writer — 3
   Klavdia Smola

The Nonconformist Poetics of David Shrayer-Petrov — 25
   Roman Katsman

David Shrayer-Petrov's Exilic Voices — 59
   Maxim D. Shrayer

PART TWO Studies of David Shrayer-Petrov's Poetry — 93

Drums of Fate: David Shrayer-Petrov's Poetics of Fractured Wholeness — 95
   Ian Probstein

Voice of Destiny: Notes in the Margins of David Shrayer-Petrov's Poems — 132
   Oleg Smola

Italy in the Poetry of David Shrayer-Petrov — 155
   Stefano Garzonio

David Shrayer-Petrov's Poem "Friend's Illness": An Approach to Reading — 173
   Andrei Ranchin

David Shrayer-Petrov and Genrikh Sapgir: Feasts of Friendship — 198
   Evgeny Ermolin

PART THREE David Shrayer-Petrov's Refusenik Novels — 219

David Shrayer-Petrov's *Aliyah* Novels and the Epistemology of the Jewish Soviet Cultural Revival — 221
   Klavdia Smola

Doctor Levitin by David Shrayer-Petrov and the Theme of Jewish Revenge Joshua Rubenstein	239
On Literary Tradition and Literary Authority in David Shrayer-Petrov's *Doctor Levitin* Brian Horowitz	259
Leaving Home Is for the Brave: A Reading of David Shrayer-Petrov's *Doctor Levitin* Monica Osborne	270
PART FOUR Approaches to David Shrayer-Petrov's Prose	**283**
Who is Grifanov? David Shrayer-Petrov's Dialogue with Yuri Trifonov Marat Grinberg	285
The Birth of a Novel from the Spirit of Contradiction: The Jewish Theologeme in David Shrayer-Petrov's Novel-Fantella *Yudin's Redemption* Leonid Katsis	305
To Kill the Leader: The Morphology of David Shrayer-Petrov's Novella "Dinner with Stalin" Boris Lanin	332
POST SCRIPTUM	**347**
"Each writer has his or her own Jewish secret. . . .": A Conversation in Three Parts Conducted on the Occasion of the Publication of David Shrayer-Petrov's Collection *Dinner with Stalin and Other Stories* (2014) David Shrayer-Petrov and Maxim D. Shrayer	349
David Shrayer-Petrov: A Pictorial Biography Maxim D. Shrayer	**360**
David Shrayer-Petrov (Давид Шраер-Петров): A Bibliography of Works Maxim D. Shrayer	403
Index of Names and Places	**425**
Contributors	**437**
Praise for *The Parallel Universes of David Shrayer-Petrov*	443

Preface*

Roman Katsman, Maxim D. Shrayer, Klavdia Smola

This volume celebrates the literary oeuvres of David Shrayer-Petrov (Давид Шраер-Петров)—poet, fiction writer, memoirist, playwright, essayist, and literary translator (and medical doctor and researcher in his parallel career).

David Shrayer-Petrov is one of the most important representatives of the Jewish-Russian literature that gained its shape and form during the post-Stalin years, developed in both officially sanctioned and underground conditions, subsequently emigrated from the USSR along with its creators, and is presently dispersed across many countries and five continents. A product of three historical epochs and a bearer of three dimensions—Soviet, émigré, and transnational—Jewish-Russian culture has transcended national boundaries. Once vibrantly alive, it is starting its descent into the depths of history and memory. This is why the task of studying and documenting its rich and diverse legacy has become especially urgent today.

Published in the year of David Shrayer-Petrov's eighty-fifth birthday, almost thirty-five years after the writer's emigration from the former USSR, this is the first volume to gather materials and investigations that examine his writings from various literary-historical and theoretical perspectives. By focusing on many different aspects of Shrayer-Petrov's multifaceted and eventful literary career, the volume brings together some of the leading

---

* Copyright © 2021 by Roman Katsman, Maxim D. Shrayer, Klavdia Smola.

American, European, Israeli, and Russian scholars of Jewish poetics, exilic literature, and Russian and Soviet culture and history.

* * *

Born on January 28, 1936 in Leningrad (now St. Petersburg), David Shrayer-Petrov entered the Soviet literary scene in the late 1950s as a poet and translator. He published a collection of poetry, many literary translations, and two books of essays in the 1960s and 1970s. Exploration of Jewish themes put Shrayer-Petrov in conflict with the Soviet authorities, limiting publication of his work and prompting him to emigrate. A Jewish refusenik in 1979–1987, Shrayer-Petrov lived as an outcast in his native country but continued to write prolifically, despite expulsion from the Union of Soviet Writers and persecution by the KGB. "Jews and Russians are the two peoples . . . closest to me in flesh (genes) and spirit (language),"[2] Shrayer-Petrov wrote in early 1986, less than two years before emigrating from Russia. He was finally allowed to emigrate in 1987, settling in the United States. Since emigrating, Shrayer-Petrov has published ten books of poetry, ten novels, six collections of short stories, two plays, and four volumes of memoirs. He is best known for the trilogy of novels about refuseniks and the exodus of Jews from the USSR. The English translation of *Doctor Levitin*, the first part of the trilogy, was published in 2018. In a 2014 interview, Shrayer-Petrov commented on his experience as an immigrant writer: "Most of my recent stories fashion Russian—Jewish-Russian—characters living in America. In this sense, I've become an American writer. . . . I think that I've rooted myself in New England. It has become my second—now my main—habitat."[3]

* * *

Our volume consists of four sections and an addendum. Essays in the first section offer overarching views of David Shrayer-Petrov's life and works. Klavdia Smola considers the question of the writer's place in Jewish-Russian

---

2   David Shraer-Petrov, *Druz'ia i teni. Roman s uchastiem avtora* (New York: Liberty Publishing House, 1989), 9.
3   Maxim D. Shrayer and David Shrayer-Petrov, "Dinner with Stalin: A 3-Part Conversation with David Shrayer-Petrov," *Jewish Book Council / My Jewish Learning*, July 8–10, 2014, https://www.jewishbookcouncil.org/pb-daily/crypto-jews-and-autobiographical-animals-part-3-of-a-3-part-conversation.

culture, Roman Katsman analyzes the distinct features of Shrayer-Petrov's poetics in the context of late Soviet artistic nonconformism, while Maxim D. Shrayer offers a panoramic view of the writer's literary biography in dialogue with Jewish, Russian and American exilic literature.

The second section gathers together studies of David Shrayer-Petrov's poetry. Ian Probstein casts a long glance at Shrayer-Petrov's collections and cycles of poetry, written both in Russia and in America, while also identifying leitmotifs and prosodic trends. In his "notes in the margins," Oleg Smola regards such key terms of Shrayer-Petrov's poetry as fate and destiny, Jewishness, and Russianness, as well as his (neo-)futurist poetics and love lyric. Stefano Garzonio devotes his essay to the Italian themes and motifs in Shrayer-Petrov's poetic oeuvres. Andrei Ranchin contributes a detailed reading and analysis of one poem, thereby delving deep into Shrayer-Petrov's poetic laboratory. Finally, Evgeny Ermolin investigates one of the central literary-biographical lifelines in Shrayer-Petrov's career—his friendship with the "avant-garde classic" Genrikh Sapgir.

The third section of the volume focuses its attention on the refusenik trilogy, which has brought Shrayer-Petrov the most recognition. Klavdia Smola examines Shrayer-Petrov's writings in the context of the Jewish renaissance and the "*aliyah* literature" of the late Soviet period. Joshua Rubenstein zooms in on the theme of Jewish revenge as a psychocultural phenomenon in Shrayer-Petrov's refusenik fiction. Brian J. Horowitz considers the interrelationship of the author and his protagonist in *Doctor Levitin*—the first part of the refusenik trilogy. In her essay, Monica Osborne reads the novel as a reflection of the changing Jewish identity and of the relations between the Jewish community and power—both in the USSR of the late 1970s and early 1980s and in the present-day diaspora.

Essays, collected in the volume's fourth section, contribute to the study of Shrayer-Petrov's artistic prose. Marat Grinberg leans upon the figure of the writer "Grifanov" in Shrayer-Petrov's refusenik trilogy and draws far-reaching parallels between the writings of David Shrayer-Petrov and Yuri Trifonov. Leonid Katsis pursues various textual and cultural sources of Shrayer-Petrov's historical novel *Yudin's Redemption*, and in doing so unearths evidence of the spiritual quest that was characteristic of Soviet Jewish intelligentsia of the late Soviet period. Boris Lanin anatomizes the novella "Dinner with Stalin"—one of Shrayer-Petrov's best known works of short fiction—and also steeps it in the context of Russian-language prose, both Soviet and émigré, about the mythologization of Stalin.

The four sections of this volume reflect some, albeit not all, of the principal vectors of David Shrayer-Petrov's creativity. It is our hope that this book will serve as a catalyst for further study of his life and work. The addendum (Post Scriptum) is comprised of materials that could serve as a foundation for further study. Those include a long conversation with Maxim D. Shrayer, which raises a number of new and relevant questions, many of them related to the writer's "Jewish secret." The addendum also includes a curated pictorial biography, which highlights David Shrayer-Petrov's literary and professional formation and development. A detailed bibliography of the writer's publications concludes the volume.

August 2020
Giv'at Shmuel, Israel—South Chatham, MA—Dresden, Germany

A Note on Transliteration and Spelling of Names

A modified version of the Library of Congress system for transliterating the Russian alphabet is used throughout the text of the essays included in this volume. Exceptions are Russian words and geographical and personal names that have gained a common spelling in English, such as Joseph Brodsky instead of "Iosif Brodskii," Osip Mandelstam instead of "Osip Mandelshtam," Vladimir Jabotinsky instead of "Vladimir Zhabotinsky," Babi Yar instead of "Babii Iar," and so forth. Bibliographical references, including authors' names and titles of Russian-language periodicals, in the footnotes and the bibliography are rendered in the standard Library of Congress system of transliterating the Russian alphabet, without diacritical marks.

Part One

David Shrayer-Petrov: Life, Art, and Thought

David Shrayer-Petrov, Russian-Jewish Writer*

Klavdia Smola

In 2021, David Shrayer-Petrov, poet, fiction writer, and memoirist, physician and medical scientist, former refusenik, turns eighty-five. Among the Russian-Jewish intelligentsia, Shrayer-Petrov had already become a legend: a man who, having experienced and described the history of the Jewish *aliyah* movement in the Soviet Union, became one of the most outstanding chroniclers of the late Soviet period and of the Jewish-Soviet diaspora. Shrayer-Petrov has been a medical scientist for most of his professional career, both in Russia and in America; he made some notable scientific discoveries in the fields of microbiology and cancer research.[1] Like one of his favorite authors, Anton Chekhov, with whom he carries on a creative dialogue in many of his texts (see Maxim D. Shrayer's essay in this volume), for many years Shrayer-Petrov worked as a practicing physician.[2] For students of Slavic literature and for those studying Jewish history and

---

*Copyright © 2021 by Klavdia Smola. English translation copyright © 2021 by Dobrochna Fire.

An earlier version of this essay appeared in Russian as: "O proze russko-evreiskogo pisatelia Davida Shraera-Petrova," in *Russkie evrei v Amerike*, ed. Ernst Zal´tsberg, vol. 15 (St. Petersburg: Giperion, 2017), 135–150.

1 About Shrayer-Petrov's medical and scientific career, see his book *Okhota na ryzhego d'iavola. Roman s mikrobiologami*, ed. Maxim D. Shrayer (Moscow: Agraf, 2010).
2 About the parallels in the literary and medical biographies of Chekhov and Shrayer-Petrov, see also Maxim D. Shrayer, "Afterword: Voices of My Father's Exile," in David Shrayer-Petrov, *Autumn in Yalta: A Novel and Three Stories*, ed., co-tr., and with an afterword by Maxim D. Shrayer, Library of Modern Jewish Literature (Syracuse, NY: Syracuse University Press, 2006), 224–225.

culture, Shrayer-Petrov is a classic of the literature of the late Soviet exodus and an important figure in the Third Wave of Russian émigré literature. Until quite recently, his creative and academic biography, many of his texts, and his role in the intellectual history of Russian Jewry and Russian culture as a whole have not received sufficient attention. David Shrayer-Petrov's writings await further investigation. This essay—and this entire volume—seeks to close the gap while offering directions for further study.

"I feel that I am an American, a Russian writer, and a Jew, that is, three hypostases are now already conjoined within me: America, my Jewishness, and, of course, Russia, because language is the only weapon a writer has at his disposal," said Shrayer-Petrov in January 2016 during an interview with the St. Petersburg poet Tatyana Voltskaya on Radio Liberty (Radio Svoboda).[3] The question of the writer's identity that this self-characterization leads us to think about is as complex and, at the same time, as simple as it is for many writers of the transnational Jewish diaspora, going back to the period of the Haskalah (the Jewish Enlightenment) in Europe and the rise of Jewish assimilation. In many instances, it is precisely in artistic texts that this identity is best manifested through the syncretism of various cultural traditions at the level of imagery, style, themes, and authorial perspective. Toward the beginning of the second half of the twentieth century—the time of Shrayer-Petrov's adolescence and youth—the process of the Russification and Sovietization of Jews had been effectively accomplished.[4] At the same time, the awareness of their nationality by Soviet Jews—and the re-acquisition of ethnic knowledge that in many cases was already absent—was a symptom not so much of the cultural as of the political climate of the late Stalin years. Like many of his peers, Shrayer-Petrov experienced the state and popular antisemitism of the Stalinist and post-Stalinist period.

---

3   David Shraer-Petrov and Tat′iana Vol′tskaia, "Mertsanie zheltoi zvezdy," Radio Liberty, January 28, 2016, http://www.bigbook.ru/articles/detail.php?ID=25001, accessed June 3, 2020.

4   Cf. Zvi Gitelman, *A Century of Ambivalence. The Jews of Russia and the Soviet Union, 1881 to the Present* (Schocken: New York, 1988); Ludmila Tsigel′man, "The Impact of Ideological Changes in the USSR on Different Generations of the Soviet Jewish Intelligentsia," in *Jewish Culture and Identity in the Soviet Union*, ed. Yaacov Ro'i and Avi Beker (New York and London: New York University Press, 1991), 42–72; Igor Krupnik, "Soviet Cultural and Ethnic Policies toward Jews: A Legacy Reassessed," in *Jews and Jewish Life in Russia and The Soviet Union*, ed. Yaacov Ro'i (Routledge: Ilford, 1995), 67–86; Theodore H. Friedgut, "Nationalities Policy, the Soviet Regime, the Jews, and Emigration," in *Jewish Life after the USSR*, ed. Zvi Gitelman, Musya Glants, and Marshall I. Goldman (Bloomington-Indianapolis: Indiana University Press, 2003), 27–45.

In his autobiographical prose, notably in the short novel *Strange Danya Rayev* (*Strannyi Dania Raev*),⁵ he frequently depicts this reawakening—a forcible reminder of the young Jewish protagonist's own descent. In the novel's first chapter, from the mouth of Dodonov, formerly a frontline soldier and now a local law-enforcement officer in the Uralian village where Danya and his mother had been evacuated from the besieged Leningrad, the seven-year-old Jewish boy hears a typical set of insults and insinuations aimed at an elderly evacuee (actually a Karaite whom Dodonov presumed, based on phenotypical characteristics, to be a Jew): "Понаехали сюда горбоносые да картавые и свои порядки устанавливают. Я кровь рабоче-крестьянскую проливал, а вы, гады ползучие, по тылам отсиживаетесь. [. . .] Видишь, Владимировна, за какую мразь мы с немцем воюем" ("All of you hooked noses, you can't even roll your r's properly, and now you've descended on us and try to install your way of life. I spilled my peasant-worker's blood for the Motherland, while you, creeping reptiles, were lounging around behind the lines. [. . .] See, Vladimirovna, what scum we defend from the Germans?"⁶).

Judging by much evidence of this kind, the Jewishness of David Shrayer-Petrov and his texts was both nourished and reinforced against the backdrop of the Soviet discrimination. This connects him to a broad range of Russian-Jewish writers born in the 1930s and 1940s and their stories about a Jewish childhood in the Soviet Union: Aleksandr Melikhov, Mark Zaichik, David Markish, Izrail Metter, Yulia Shmukler, Lyudmila Ulitskaya, Yury Karabchievsky, and Boris Khazanov (penname of Gennady Faibusovich), to name a few. Both Jewish ethnic renaissance and the struggle for repatriation to Israel (*aliyah*), which began in the second half of the 1960s, stemmed from these experiences: a negatively formed Jewish identity, fomented by antisemitism, turns into one of the strongest emancipatory, anti-assimilationist movements of ethnic minorities in Russian and Soviet history—indeed, into one of the most interesting phenomena of the European cultural and political underground. Like Eli Lyuksemburg, Efrem Baukh, or Felix Kandel, Shrayer-Petrov becomes

---

5   David Shraer-Petrov, *Strannyi Dania Raev*, in *Eti strannye russkie evrei* (Moscow: Raduga, 2004), 5–92; English translation, David Shrayer-Petrov, *Strange Danya Rayev*, tr. Arna B Bronstein and Aleksandra I. Fleszar, in *Autumn in Yalta: A Novel and Three Stories*, ed., co-tr., and with an afterword by Maxim D. Shrayer, Library of Modern Jewish Literature (Syracuse: Syracuse University Press, 2006), 1–101.

6   Shraer-Petrov, *Strannye russkie evrei*, 55; idem, *Autumn in Yalta*, 57–58.

a writer of the exodus in the biblical sense of this word. Thus the novel *Doctor Levitin* (*Doktor Levitin*, 1979–1980), the first part of the refusenik trilogy and an exemplary work of Russian prose of the second half of the twentieth century, draws its imagery (albeit in a pointillistic fashion) from the many centuries of Judaic culture while at the same time tapping into the traditions of the world literature of Zionism.

Shrayer-Petrov's biography offers keys to some aspects of his poetics and the circle of his literary interests, which come vibrantly alive in his literary memoirs of Leningrad and Moscow,[7] in the scientific memoir *Hunt for the Red Devil* (*Okhota na ryzhego d'iavola*, 2010). Some information about Shrayer-Petrov's biography and creativity can also be gathered from his essays dispersed across collections of his works and anthologies or still uncollected. Finally, and insofar as a writer's life may be read through the prism of his poetry, some of Shrayer-Petrov's shorter and longer lyrical poems with Jewish and Judaic themes, such as "My Slavic Soul" ("Moia slavianskaia dusha," 1975) and *Villa Borghese* (1987–1990), or longer narrative poems, such as *Flying Saucers* (*Letaiushchie tarelki*, 1981) and *Runner Begoon* (*Begun*, 1987), offer powerful interpretive tools for an interdisciplinary study of his life and art.

Shrayer-Petrov's literary debut was connected with his studies in medical school: "I met the future outstanding film director Ilya Averbakh. And together with him and Vasya [Vasily] Aksyonov, we founded a literary seminar. Later it became the literary seminar at the Palace of Culture of Industrial Cooperation (*lito Promkooperatsii*, or Promka), frequented by such future important writers as [Evgeny] Reyn, [Sergei] Volf, [Dmitry] Bobyshev, [Anatoly] Nayman, [Aleksandr] Kushner, [Mikhail] Eremin, and [Viktor] Sosnora."[8] Shrayer-Petrov organically entered the cohort of young Leningrad poets of the late 1950s and early 1960s, who sought to resurrect the Petersburg school of the Silver Age while also capitalizing on the great accomplishments of early Soviet poetry. Like other poets of the postwar Soviet period, very often of Jewish heritage, who existed entirely or partially in the space of unsanctioned culture, in the 1960s and the

---

7   David Shraer-Petrov, *Druz'ia i teni. Roman s uchastiem avtora* (New York: Liberty Publishing House, 1989); idem, *Moskva zlatoglavaia. Literaturnye vospominaniia* (Baltimore: Vestnik Information Agency, 1994); idem, *Vodka s pirozhnymi. Roman s pisateliami*, ed. Maksim D. Shraer (St. Petersburg: Akademicheskii Proekt, 2007).

8   David Shraer-Petrov and Gennadii Katsov, "Ia dumaiu, chto my vse drug druga chemu-to nauchili . . . ," RYNYweb.com, May 17, 2011, http://www.runyweb.com/articles/culture/literature/david-shayer-petrov-interview.html, accessed June 3, 2020.

1970s Shrayer-Petrov mainly published poetry translations.[9] His original poetry appeared in print in 1959 in the monthly magazine *Young Pioneer* (*Pioner*), not long before he left for Belarus to serve as an army physician (about Shrayer-Petrov's poetic debut, see Stefano Garzonio's essay in this volume). In 1967 some of his earlier poems were collected in *Canvasses* (*Kholsty*), the only book of poetry he would publish in the Soviet Union.[10] In his literary publications of the Soviet 1950s–1970s, the writer used a Russianized penname, David Petrov, which the authorities often pressured him to shorten to "D. Petrov," so as to obliterate the non-Russian, and likely Jewish, first name.

Before emigrating to the United States in 1987 with his family—his wife Emilia and son Maxim—the writer spent over eight years as a refusenik. The conflict with the regime began with Shrayer-Petrov's decision to read his poems with Jewish themes in public. "I suddenly understood that, of course, I was obligated to write about Jews. This is the main line of my life. Who if not I?" he stated in a 2011 interview.[11] Shrayer-Petrov's living testimony of the scope of the Jewish movement and of the punitive actions taken by the Soviet authorities contradicts the fairly widespread opinion (including on the part of some Western historians) about the relative insignificance of the refusenik community and the alleged elitism of the interests of the participants in the Soviet *aliyah* movement:

> It was a lesser form of genocide [*malyi genotsid*; малый геноцид] that the Soviet authorities committed. In Moscow alone there were fifty thousand Jewish refuseniks, and moreover, which is the most important thing, they for the most part let people with [less education or blue collar workers] and filtered out and mostly kept as refuseniks the intelligentsia. And the intelligentsia was being degraded. For example, I know that one Artist of Merit of the Russian Federation, a violinist, his name escapes me now, worked as a custodian in an underpass on Smolenskaya Square.

---

9   On the phenomenon of Jewish translators during the Soviet period, see the novels *Stop the Plane—I'm Getting Off!* (*Ostanovite samolet—ia slezu!*) by Efraim Sevela (1975), *A Certain Finkelmeyer* (*Nekto Finkel'maier*) by Felix Roziner (1975), and *Decade* (*Dekada*) by Semyon Lipkin (1980).
10 David Petrov, *Kholsty*, poetry collection published as part of the collective volume *Pereklichka* (Moscow: Molodaia gvardiia, 1967), 116–160.
11 Shraer-Petrov and Katsov, "Ia dumaiu, chto my vse drug druga chemu-to nauchili. . . .."

> There was a plethora of such examples; all of our friends essentially worked as manual laborers, electricians, boiler-room attendants, although these were doctors, engineers, and so forth. Although doctors had it a little easier in that I went from being a "senior research investigator" down to the position of a rank-and-file physician, but at least I was working, this was my profession, while very many suffered. During the time we were refuseniks, our whole family started intersecting very rigorously with such activists as Slepak, Begun, and others. [The authorities] warned me many times, snatched up and arrested me several times, took me in to the station, conducted intimidating interrogations, and so on and so forth. It culminated in essence with a trial that was publicly staged by the newspaper *Arguments and Facts*, in which a lengthy article appeared [. . .].
>
> They sent me subpoenas to the prosecutor's office. I decided I would not go. As a result I ended up in the hospital; I collapsed with a heart attack, after which [the persecution campaign] suddenly went away. They left me alone.[12]

Despite the injustice and suffering, the experience of being a refusenik, the expulsion from the Union of Soviet Writers and the persecution by the authorities became a powerful creative impulse, which fueled many of Shrayer-Petrov's works composed not only before but also after emigration, and led him to identify himself as a refusenik writer.

We should note that the style, artistic texture, and intellectual basis of Shrayer-Petrov's writings were formed in his pre-emigration period and subsequently enriched in the United States—above all, by his experience of the life and anxieties of Russian Jews abroad, especially in America. In this sense, Shrayer-Petrov is specifically an émigré and exilic writer and not a representative of the newer Russian-Jewish literature, transnational in spirit, problematics, and geography, which gives evidence of the open and polyvalent identity of the young authors of Russian-Jewish (or Soviet-Jewish) origin who not infrequently write in two languages. This is not surprising if one takes into account that Shrayer-Petrov, born in 1936, left for the West in 1987 at the age of fifty-one. By that time, he had already created a large corpus of lyrical and narrative poetry, his main novels (the first two parts of his refusenik trilogy, which I examine in a separate essay in this volume) as well as a memoir, a body of short stories, nonfiction, and literary criticism. During his Russian (Soviet) decades he had imbibed the

---

12 Shraer-Petrov and Katsov, "Ia dumaiu, chto my vse drug druga chemu-to nauchili . . ." (transcription errors in the publication have been corrected in the English translation).

unique multi-layered atmosphere of Jewish culture in late Soviet Russia with its exceptional hybridity, its (anti-)Soviet Jewish self-awareness, with the memory of the Shoah that had been suppressed by the authorities, and with the official obfuscation of various historical stages of Soviet antisemitism. Moreover, prior to emigration Shrayer-Petrov had reflected intensively on the cultural and political Zionism of *aliyah*, his attitude to which appears ambiguous. Finally, still prior to becoming an émigré and an immigrant, Shrayer-Petrov had already displayed a double stylistic and intertextual orientation—both towards Russian and towards Western European and American literature. However, the question of the possible development of Shrayer-Petrov's poetics compared to other Jewish writers of this same generation who live or have lived in the United States, Canada, Germany, and other countries outside Russia (such as Grigory Svirsky or Friedrich Gorenstein) calls for a separate investigation.

During his American years, Shrayer-Petrov has published more than twenty books. While publishing his pre-emigration poetry and prose, some of it revamped and revised, he has created a large body of new shorter and longer poems, short stories and novellas, novels, literary memoirs, as well as essays and criticism (see Shrayer-Petrov's Bibliography in this volume). To date, four books of his fiction have appeared in English, edited and co-translated by his son, Maxim D. Shrayer, a literary scholar and author in his own right; among Shrayer-Petrov's translators, his wife of over fifty-five years, Emilia Shrayer, deserves a special mention. In collaboration with his son, Shrayer-Petrov wrote the first book monograph about the leading poet of the postwar avant-garde, Genrikh Sapgir, with whom the writer was close for many years.[13]

Of the works of fiction written by Shrayer-Petrov in the United States, I have a special appreciation for the two novels *Strange Danya Rayev* (*Strannyi Dania Raev*, 2001) and *Savely Ronkin* (*Savelii Ronkin*, 2004) published under the same cover in the volume *These Strange Russian Jews* (*Eti strannye russkie evrei*, 2004), as well as some of the short stories and novellas included in the collection *Carp for the Gefilte Fish* (*Karp dlia farshirovannoi ryby*, 2005). Shrayer-Petrov's selected works of shorter fiction

---

13 Maksim D. Shraer and David Shraer-Petrov, *Genrikh Sapgir: Klassik avangarda* (St. Petersburg: Dmitrii Bulanin, 2004). Two more editions have since appeared. Shrayer-Petrov and Shrayer also edited the first academic edition of Genrikh Sapgir's poetry, published in 2004 by the "New Poet's Library" series; see Genrikh Sapgir, *Stikhotvoreniia i poemy*, ed., introduction, and commentary by Maksim D. Shraer and David Shraer-Petrov, Novaia biblioteka poeta, Malaia seriia (St. Petersburg: Akademicheskii proekt, 2004).

were subsequently reprinted in the volume *Round-the-Globe Happiness* (*Krugosvetnoe schast´e*), published in Moscow in 2016.

As a work of autobiographical fiction, *Strange Danya Rayev* encompasses the prewar childhood years of the main character in Leningrad and the wartime years spent in evacuation in a remote village in the Northern Ural region. The short novel culminates with the hero's return to Leningrad in 1944 and ends in the summer of 1945 following the defeat of Nazi Germany. The artful simplicity and organicism of this novel's language, the deliberate choice of recollected and narrated impressions and experiences, and the humor and quaintness characteristic of "infantile" storytelling reveal a kinship not only with classical works about children by Lev Tolstoy (*Detstvo* [*Boyhood*, 1852]) or Anton Chekhov (such as "Grisha," 1886), but also with the Soviet- and post-Soviet-era works by such writers as Anatoly Pristavkin (*Nochevala tuchka zolotaia* [*A Golden Cloud Spent the Night*, 1987]) or Aleksandr Chudakov (the novel *A Gloom Is Cast upon the Ancient Steps* [*Lozhitsia mgla na starye stupeni*, 2012]). As in the best examples of literature about childhood, the limited scope and the estrangement of the child's perception paradoxically give the most accurate portrait of a historical period. A vibrant picture emerges first of prewar life in Leningrad and of the Uralian village during the war. Shrayer-Petrov's narrator converts the memories into an artistic narrative—an adult's correlation of facts is woven into the poetics of a child's perspective: short sentences, the present tense (the time of the hero's outlook) interlaced with the past tense, the concreteness of the optics, the gradually expanding space of perception:

> Помню деда Вульфа. Он старый. У него белая борода. Он почему-то в полушубке. Значит была зима? Да, зима. Он сидит у окна кухни. За окном улица. Сугробы. Крыши деревянных домов покрыты снегом. Дым идёт из бурых кирпичных труб. Я сижу на коленях у деда Вульфа. Он кормит меня сладкой булкой и дает запивать молоком из кружки. «Это Полоцк, сынок, — говорит дед Вульф. — А когда-то мы жили в золотой Литве, в Шауляе». Из маминых рассказов я знаю, что дедушка Вульф, бабушка Ева, мамины сестры Ривочка и Маня, брат Митя и моя мама бежали из Литвы от белополяков. Поляки убили Ривочку. Бабушка Ева умерла от горя и от тифа. Дедушка с остальными детьми поселился в Полоцке. Он стал учителем еврейского языка. Тогда в Белоруссии ещё были еврейские школы.[14]

---

14 Shraer-Petrov, *Strannyi Dania Raev*, 17.

I do remember Grandpa Wolf. He's old. He has a white beard. For some reason he's wearing a sheepskin jacket. Does that mean it was winter? Yes, winter. He's sitting by the kitchen window. You can see the street through the window. Snow drifts. The roofs of the wooden houses are covered in snow. Smoke billows out of sooty-brown, brick chimneys. I'm sitting on Grandpa Wolf's lap. He's feeding me a sweet roll and milk from a mug. "This is Polotsk, son," says Grandpa Wolf. "But there was a time when we lived in golden Lithuania, in Shavel." From what mama told me, I know that Grandpa Wolf, Grandma Eva, mama's sisters Rivochka and Manya, brother Mitya and my mother ran away from Lithuania fleeing the White Poles. The Poles killed Rivochka. Grandma Eva died from sorrow and typhus. Grandpa settled in Polotsk with the rest of the children. He used to be a rabbi. He became a teacher in a Jewish school. At that time there were still Jewish schools in Belarus.[15]

The reaction of an urban child to the everyday language of the Uralian village causes something of culture clash:

— Меня зовут Пашка, — говорит мне подросток. —А тебя?

— А меня Даник, — отвечаю я. — А это моя мама, Стэлла Владимировна.

— Мудрёно! — изумляется Пашка. — Вы кто будете?

— Ленинградцы! —с гордостью и даже с хвастовством говорю я.

— А люди бают «выковыренные»!

Не вдруг осознаю, что баять значит «говорить». А «выковыренные» — искажённое слово эвакуированные.

Пашка станет моим старшим товарищем и учителем деревенской жизни.

Мама между тем начинает переносить вещи в избу. Ей помогает пожилая тётенька, Елена Матвеевна. Мне Елена Матвеевна велит называть её: баба Лена. Она — хозяйка избы. Андрей Михеевич, которого я буду называть дед Андрей, её муж. Пашка их сын. Через некоторое время хозяева начинают называть маму: Владимировна, а она их: Матвеевна и Михеич.[16]

"My name is Pashka," says the teenager. "And you?"

"And my name is Danik," I answer. "And this is my mother, Stella Vladimirovna."

---

15 Shrayer-Petrov, *Autumn in Yalta*, 13.
16 Shraer-Petrov, *Strannyi Dania Raev*, 24.

"That's a hard one!" Pashka says in amazement. "So, who would you be?"
"We're from Leningrad!" I say with pride and even with some boasting.
"And they say you're the vacated ones!"
I don't immediately get it that "vacated" is a distortion of the word "evacuated." Pashka is to become my older friend and teacher of village life.

In the meantime mama begins to bring our things inside the *izba*. An older woman, Elena Matveevna, helps her. Elena Matveevna tells me to call her *Baba* (Grandma) Lena. She's the owner of the *izba*. Andrey Mikheich, whom I will call *Ded* (Grandpa) Andrey, is her husband. Pashka is their son. In time these hosts start to refer to mama as Vladimirovna and she calls them Matveevna and Mikheich—by patronymic, after the village fashion. [17]

Here the Russian peasant milieu meets Russian-Jewish urban culture, or, to augment the sociological aspects of the story, the Russian folk culture interacts with the culture of the intelligentsia. (David Markish depicts something similar in the early autobiographical novel *Story Embellishment* [*Priskazka*, 1971].) Unlike the neighbors in his building in Leningrad, where Danya lives with his parents before the war, his host family—the Terekhins—show not a shadow of Judeophobia. Instead, the evacuated Jews experience human all-inclusiveness. It was no accident that during these wartime years spent in evacuation Danya forgets about his Jewishness and becomes a part of the ethnic Russian and the Orthodox Christian communities. He celebrates Shrovetide, Easter, Trinity Sunday, Nicholas's Day, and Christmas along with his host family. It is true that the narrator notes that the Terekhins have a vague idea of the identity of their tenants and guilelessly propose that Danya and his mother get a pig—which they do, so as not to die of hunger:

> И вот наш собственный поросёнок Нюф хрюкает в сарайчике и, чавкая, нетерпеливо лопает варёную и толчёную с крапивой и лебедой картошку. А там и два гуся, переваливаясь, шагают под моей неусыпной заботой на луг к речке и обратно. У нас с мамой большое хозяйство: огород, поросёнок, гуси. Мы совсем деревенские.

And here we have our very own piglet, Fifer, snorting in the shed, and smacking with impatience, devouring potatoes boiled and mashed with

---

17 Shrayer-Petrov, *Autumn in Yalta*, 20–21.

nettle and goosefoot. And also we have two geese, waddling and walking back and forth between the meadow and the river, under my unremitting care. Mama and I have a large dominion: a garden, a piglet, geese. We are real villagers.[18]

Danya reads Russian folk tales and later short novels by Pushkin, Gogol, and Kuprin, but also such masterpieces of Soviet literature for the adolescents as Lev Kassil's *Konduit and Shvambrania* (1931) and Yury Tynyanov's *Kyukhlya* (1925). And he is ashamed of the fact that Yiddish, which his great-aunt Tyotya Enya tells him about, resembles the language of Germans—of the enemy.

Adroitly and unpretentiously, Shrayer-Petrov shows the conflagration of the various shades and nuances forming the unique, heterogeneous environment for the "newcomer" Jews into the Russian provinces of the 1940s: the folk cosmopolitism of Grandpa Andrey and Grandma Lena; the assimilation of the child from a Jewish family with an already "thin"[19] ethnic affiliation. At the same time, the novel depicts Danya's lively interaction with the members of his own *meshpocha*; the everyday antisemitism of local rural authorities (see above about law enforcement officer Dodonov). Meanwhile, Shrayer-Petrov underscores the syncretism of the primordial Russian culture itself: the men are fighting at the war front, while their families, celebrating the victory at Stalingrad, are praying and crossing themselves before the icon of St. Nicholas the Wonderworker, some of them out of faith, others out of habit.[20] In Leningrad, his dying grandfather gives Danya Chanukah *gelt*, while in another episode Danya's family celebrates Shabbat and buries a relative according to Jewish rites. This syncretism, the variety of traditions set against the background of Communist (half-)taboos, the young Jewish boy's absorption of this essentially contradictory reality, is testimony to Shrayer-Petrov's unique art of the literary and factographical storytelling.

Strange Danya Rayev is an example of the artistic-documentary writing characteristic of the majority of Shrayer-Petrov's literary texts. But in terms of the genealogy of the "strange," hybrid Soviet Jewry, perhaps the most interesting feature of Shrayer-Petrov's fiction is the countering of all attempts at essentializing the concept of ethnic culture. Among all else, his

---

18 Shraer-Petrov, *Strannyi Dania Raev*, 36–37; Shrayer-Petrov, *Autumn in Yalta*, 36.
19 Mikhail Krutikov, "The Jewish Future in Russia: Trends and Opportunities," *East European Jewish Affairs* 1 (2002): 5.
20 Shraer-Petrov, *Strannyi Dania Raev*, 62.

writings, both prose and poetry, capture the naissance of the image of the Jew of the late Soviet type, one who has grown up with a fragmentary memory and knowledge of Jewish customs and of Yiddish, with a grandfather or grandmother who still carries on the tradition, and with a powerful experience of antisemitism (this is also the case with the characters of Yury Karabchievsky, Aleksandr Melikhov, and other Russian-Jewish writers born in the 1930s and 1940s). Shrayer-Petrov admitted that in the 1970s he wanted to write "about those Jews who still existed, not Sholem Aleichem types, *schlimazels*, but about the real Jewish intelligentsia."[21] The juxtaposition of the "folkloric" Jews of Sholem Aleichem and the "real" Soviet ones is significant as a marker of the writer's simultaneous self-identification and self-distancing. To begin with, the somewhat stereotypical portrait of the "classic" literary Jew betrays a certain limitedness of the Jewish literary education in late Soviet times, this also being true of Shrayer-Petrov's target reader. But much more important is the perceived difference between the Jew of the Imperial Russian past (essentially unknown and unknowable to the majority) and the Jew of the present—the Russian (Soviet) intellectual with a self-awareness that is totally unlike that of Tevye the Dairyman but, conversely, rather like that of Lev Odoevtsev, protagonist of the celebrated novel *Pushkin House* (1878) by Shrayer-Petrov's close contemporary and fellow Leningradian Andrey Bitov. Moreover, striving to avoid the widespread Soviet stereotype of the "weak" Jews who genealogically belong to the ranks of well-known *schlimazels* and *schlemiels*, the writers of the *aliyah* drew inspiration from completely different sources. Their Jewish characters are not comic and often heroic and tragic, based on the biblical figures. (Here the exception is Efraim Sevela, who, after the fashion of Ilya Ehrenburg's Lazik of the *Stormy Life of Lazik Roitschwantz*, transferred the image of the *schlimazel* from Yiddish culture onto the Soviet present.)

After he became an émigré and an American, Shrayer-Petrov created the figure of a Jewish intellectual with qualities of the *schlimazel* in the novel *Savely Ronkin* (2004), which was a contender for the 2004 Russian Booker Prize. In terms of genre, *Savely Ronkin* conflates elements of immigrant fiction, adventure-erotic *belle-lettres*, and literary memoirs. It is a hybrid novel, simultaneously an engaging, often even piquant, and intellectually demanding. A chronicle of the everyday lives of young Russian bohemians in America, it combines features of a psychological, confessional narrative

---

21   Shraer-Petrov and Katsov, "Ia dumaiu, chto my vse drug druga chemu-to nauchili. . . ."

and literary-critical reflections. The novel, which can be read in one breath, derives its captivating quality in no small part from the creative alternation of setting and scenery: in the novel's pages, the late Soviet literary bohemian milieu in the restaurant of the Central House of Writers (TsDL) is succeeded by the lush décor of the suburban house of Paul and Sabina Rothman on Cape Cod; Genrikh Sapgir's dacha outside Moscow is counterbalanced by Boston apartments; Moscow streets neighbor American beaches. In *Savely Ronkin* and elsewhere, Shrayer-Petrov brings together elements that may strike one as not compatible. This artistic syntheticism is typical of Shrayer-Petrov, a writer who is not afraid of heterogeneous storylines that span various tiers of narration.

The poet Savely Ronkin emigrates to the United States along with his wife, Wanda, and her close friend (and cousin) Sabina, who obtains a visa by marrying the millionaire financier Paul Rothman, a passionate admirer of Russian literature and a generous patron of Russian underground poets. The amorous relations of the heroes are complicated because the two women are connected by an erotic relationship, and Savely not only has to reconcile himself to this but is himself drawn into the sexual orbits of the two women. The talented Russian-American translator Greta Dimer is Englishing Savely's poems. At the same time, she is, apparently, an intimate friend of Paul Rothman. As the plot progresses, she becomes a temporary wife of the expatriate poet Gorokhovsky, whose works she also translates and whom she most certainly idolizes. Savely both likes and envies his friend, the genius Gorokhovsky, who is gradually becoming famous both in emigration and in Russia and receives a Pulitzer Prize. Known in literary circles so far "only" as a poet-translator, Ronkin suffers from his own lack of success and nurtures the cherished thought of publishing a collection of poems, which indeed comes out at the end of the novel under the title *Waves*. Ronkin starts to feel more and more hatred toward the benevolent, practical, and at the same time slightly starry-eyed Paul Rothman. Most of all, Ronkin abhors his own material dependence and creative inferiority. As a tormented, insecure, addicted poet, he feels some primal alienation from the successful educated banker who knows no want.

Notable is Paul's characterization—a stereotypical portrait of an American, which deserves a place of honor in the Russian writers' gallery of different national images (the dumb German in Chekhov, the frivolous Frenchman in Tolstoy, the narrow-minded Pole in Dostoevsky, and so forth): "Now a bit about Paul Rothman's smile. He was well-mannered. It was instilled in him since childhood that it is natural to greet good events with a smile. And how it is also much more fitting to greet with a smile events or words that are dubious or even negative (a smile that is is circumspect, not mocking, sad, reproachful, or even sarcastic) rather than with an angry or distressed face."[22]

Ronkin sometimes earns money by working at a car wash, and at one point he manages, thanks to Paul's intercession and Gorokhovsky's recommendation, to get a position as an academic associate in the Linguistics Department of Boston College, located in one of Boston's suburbs. But his academic career soon ends because he goes on a drinking bender and loses his interest not only in work but in the external world altogether. Ronkin's latest binge is triggered by the scandalous unsuccess of his new book, *Memoirs of a Literary Horse*, released by a Russian émigré publisher. With bitter sarcasm and a masterful eye for literary polemics, Shrayer-Petrov depicts the biased reaction of critics and "educated" émigré readers to the sometimes unflattering but essentially objective, or at least controversial, opinions and facts Ronkin divulged in his memoirs. The "partisanship" and aggressively amateurish judgments of the public, which in the novel likely stem from the author's autobiographical experiences, are transmitted with particularly poignant irony in Savely's dialogues with his fellow émigrés at a party. The physicians Mark and Nina Shuster are shocked by the close acquaintance of Ronkin with the "Stalinist" writer Konstantin Simonov; the mathematician Yuly Okun is insulted by the alleged "denigration" of the "Orthodox Jewish refusenik Tsukerman";[23] the former refusenik activist and dissident Volodya Gopak is distressed by Ronkin's perceived sympathy for Muslims, whom Gopak considers enemies of the Jewish nation; and the host, Gena Gofman, is astounded that Ronkin does not consider the poet-songwriter Bulat Okudzhava to be a "great" poet.[24] In an almost poster-like manner, like Goncharov's succession of neighboring landowners in the beginning of *Oblomov* (1859), Shrayer-Petrov parades representatives of the émigré reading public in front of the reader.

The cultural significance and historical veracity of the unacknowledged Jewish poet-translator who suffers from unemployment is validated by its serious literary genealogy, which includes Felix Roziner's *A Certain*

---

22 David Shraer-Petrov, *Savelii Ronkin*, in his *Eti stranye russkie evrei* (Moscow: Raduga, 2004), 119.

23 The grotesque figure of the religious refusenik Tsukerman is depicted in Shrayer-Petrov's story "Tsukerman and His Children" (*Tsukerman i ego deti*, 1989), in his *Karp dlia farshirovannoi ryby. Rasskazy* (Moscow: Raduga, 2006), 65–73.

24 Shraer-Petrov, *Savelii Ronkin*, 292–295.

Finkelmayer (*Nekto Finkel'maier*, 1975), Semyon Lipkin's *Decade* (*Dekada*, 1980), and, to a degree, David Markish's *Dog* (*Pes*, 1984). Only the last of these texts is about an émigré cultural space (Israel) and the narrowness of its publishing and readership politics. Along with Roziner and Lipkin, Shrayer-Petrov explores the topic of creative failure and creative secondariness of translation work, but does so in the post-Soviet period. Along with Markish, he connects the literary dots of Russia and the West in an rather unflattering manner. Yet, the publication of Ronkin's book of poems at the end and his return to Russia augur a new beginning for him.

Several individual fragments of *Savely Ronkin* are taken, in a modified form, from Shrayer-Petrov's earlier texts. For example, the episode with Karaites in Trakai hearkens back to *Doctor Levitin*. The novel also reveals a literary kinship with Shrayer-Petrov's literary memoirs (especially *The Gold-Domed Moscow*) and with his short stories. A version of the short story "The Old Writer Forman" ("Staryi pisatel´ Forman," 1995) appears in *Savely Ronkin* as a text within a text. Tsukerman also appears as the title character in another of Shrayer-Petrov's post-emigration stories. These connections bring us back to Shrayer-Petrov's creativity as a writer of shorter fiction.

David Shrayer-Petrov can justly be called a master of short fiction ("мастер рассказа"). His stories and novellas are characterized by everyday realism combined with elements of mysticism and surrealism; a poetic polysemy and semantics of subtexts; grotesquerie but also, simultaneously, precision and fullness of details; the development of the plot toward unexpected and contrasting endings. While Shrayer-Petrov's short fiction touches upon some of the most complex and tragic themes—the Shoah, Jewish emigration, Jewish identity over the course of centuries of the diaspora, Judaism as a worldview—it is totally devoid of dogmatism or attempts to lead the reader by the hand. In several stories, dogmatism of views—especially Jewish dogmatism—forms an important theme. Shrayer-Petrov inherits from Chekhov the imaginative candor and open-mindedness, as well as the soberly ironic portrayal of his misfit heroes—which Maxim D. Shrayer first observed in connection with Shrayer-Petrov's story "Autumn in Yalta" ("Osen´ v Ialte," 1992) and further explores in the essay included in this volume.[25] Above all, Shrayer-Petrov's stories

---

25 Maxim D. Shrayer, "Afterword: Voices of My Father's Exile," in David Shrayer-Petrov, *Autumn in Yalta: A Novel and Three Stories*, ed., co-tr., and with an afterword by Maxim D. Shrayer, Library of Modern Jewish Literature (Syracuse: Syracuse University Press, 2006), 205–234.

abunduntly illustrate the transformation of documentary writing into the artistic fabric of prose with its ambiguous appraisal of historical facts.

Chekhov's universal oneness and tragedy of existence, that in "Rothchild's Fiddle" ("Skripka Rotshil'da," 1894) opens up the path to mutual reconciliation and washes away the distinctions separating a Jew and a non-Jew, also finds an embodiment in Shrayer-Petrov's Russian-Jewish short fiction. The "ethnic" point of view and historical backdrop change, but the artistic philosophy remains. Shrayer-Petrov echoes Chekhov's poetics of relegating ethnic or cultural conflict to the deep foundations of being, and explores these conflicts in his own time period in his stories and novellas.

This is what happens in "Mimicry" ("Mimikriia," 1996),[26] in which the writer analyzes one of the themes central to his artistic universes—the theme of accommodation, self-concealment, and hyperassimilation of Jews in the diaspora. Mimicry is a concept whose many meanings Shrayer-Petrov the natural scientist verifies on the human species, and the writer-philosopher transforms and converts to a symbol of human life. In the plot, the mimicry of chameleons and moths is studied by Michael Kaminski, an American academic of Jewish-Polish origin, and by his colleague, the émigré professor of biology Viktor Turkin, in whose New England home the characters socialize. "Mimicry" is also the name of the puppet theater organized by the professor's wife, Rita; the puppets are archetypal reflections of the national types of different characters. The casual conversation of the guests about the dispersion and cultural influence of Jews in Europe first turns into a dispute and then devolves into an argument. Kaminski contends that the role of Jews in historical progress is greatly exaggerated, and Jews themselves, especially in Russia, have become something like a fashion ("Judeomania"). The narrator, a Russian Jew and an émigré himself, also participates in the discussion. He gets more and more annoyed, as he sees in Kaminski's arguments a desire to disavow his own apparent Jewishness. The conversation moves to subjects that feel complicated to most of the guests: the genocide of the Armenians in Turkey (among the guests are a young Armenian woman, Astrid, a visiting historian at the local university, and a neurosurgeon of Turkish descent, Doctor Stephen Akhmet) and the complicity of the Eastern European populations in the Shoah. The conflict between the narrator and Kaminski the "chameleonologist," made more acute by a love rivalry (they are both courting the beautiful Armenian

---

26 David Shraer-Petrov, "Mimikriia," in his *Karp dlia farshirovannoi ryby*, 147–150.

woman), turns the denouement into a kind of a duel. The whole group goes to a rocky New England beach, and, in spite of the upcoming bad weather, compete with each other in a swimming race. When Kaminski hits his head on a rocky reef, the narrator suddenly forgets about everything: "I completely forgot about Astrid, about the competition, about our arguments over lunch. Everything was erased by these mad waves that could kill a man."[27] As they manage to reach the shore, Kaminski scornfully admits that he was one of the children that the Germans "did not succeed" in incinerating in the gas chambers: "And forgive me my cynicism. That is probably also an attempt to wear a mask. Someone else's mask."[28] The narrator attempts to understand himself, to find the root of his sudden hatred, as well as his writer's rebelliousness, "the tooth-gnashing lines of my truth-seeking writings."[29] An episode from his Russian—Soviet—childhood emerges in his consciousness, offering both the motive and the solution; he leaves the recollection of the lack of solidarity among Jews where it lives in his memory—in the world of Judeophobia.

As in many of Chekhov's prose masterpieces—most articulately revealed in the short story "Enemies" ("Vragi," 1887) and the novella "The Duel" ("Duel'," 1891)—Shrayer-Petrov studies the enmity of ideas as a symptom of underlying psychological processes. In late Chekhov (and, one might add, in some of Nabokov's short stories), the ideological conflict often resolves not by the characters' insight but only by their departure from a previously unshakeable conviction. Their subjective pictures of the world change and become more complex, but the process of cognition remains uncompleted: "No one knows the real truth," says Layevsky to von Koren in the denouement of "The Duel." The conflict in "Mimicry" is similar but slightly different: the clash becomes a kind of therapy and leads to catharsis, to an inner liberation.

In the story "Tsukerman and His Children" (1989), which caused something of a polemic in the Russian-Jewish communities of the United States and Israel,[30] Shrayer-Petrov transplants the typical Chekhovian hero

---

27 Ibid., 147.
28 Ibid., 147.
29 Ibid., 149; Shrayer-Petrov, *Jonah and Sarah: Jewish Stories of Russia and America*, ed. Maxim D. Shrayer, Library of Modern Jewish Literature (Syracuse: Syracuse University Press, 2003), 78.
30 See Lev Katsin, "Kogo razdrazhaet boroda Tsukermana i pochemu . . . ?," *Evreiskii mir*, January 31, 1997.

to late Soviet times and, specifically, into the community of those seeking to emigrate. The refusenik Tsukerman is a bore and moralizer whose maladroitness is revealed on the level of human and family relations. "He was fanatically, fervently loyal to the letter of Judaism, I'm fantastically hapless in viscous conversations,"[31] the autobiographical narrator explains. Shrayer-Petrov depicts the contemporary Jewish Pecheneg from the refusenik milieu (compare Chekhov's story "Pecheneg," 1897), the modern Doctor Lvov (compare Chekhov's play *Ivanov*, 1887), the modern Belikov (compare Chekhov's "A Man Encased" ["Chelovek v futliare," 1898]) as various hypostases of the inwardly shriveled and cocooned, limited in his convictions, and also pathetic, inadequate bearer of an idea. Tsukerman judges the narrator for being a writer; literature, after all, draws one away from the only worthy source—the Bible. It seems strange in the face of such moral rigor that, when leaving for Israel with his family, Tsukerman leaves behind in Moscow the preteen daughter of his wife from her first marriage (the girl's non-Jewish father, whom Tsukerman deems a "barbarian," does not give his permission for her to leave). Shrayer-Petrov masterfully employs a system of (crooked, grotesque) portrait reflections—be it a boorish drunk or another "obsessed" Jew, Monya Kalman—for a multidimensional characterization of the human type. But Tsukerman's most accurate mirror is his poor, misfortunate, inarticulate family. Here is the final scene at the airport: "On the other side of the turnstile stood Tsukerman's wife, hardly recognizable in a thick black shawl concealing her head. Baby Samuil slept in the arms of Tsukerman's wife. In one hand she clutched the handle of a green suitcase on wheels, and to the other Boris-Barukh had attached himself, playing choo-choo train."[32]

This short essay cannot do justice to David Shrayer-Petrov's rich and varied writings, as his creativity attracts increasing attention from researchers in Russia, the United States, Europe, and Israel.[33] Shrayer-Petrov's oeuvres may be called a monument to Russian Jews of the transitional and, in a broader sense, syncretic cultural type—both Soviet

---

31 Shraer-Petrov, *Karp dlia farshirovannoi ryby*, 65; Shrayer-Petrov, *Jonah* and *Sarah*, 78

32 Tr. Maxim D. Shrayer, in Shrayer-Petrov, *Jonah and Sarah: Jewish Stories of Russia and America*, edited by Maxim D. Shrayer, Library of Modern Jewish Literature (Syracuse: Syracuse University Press, 2003), 73.

33 See, for instance, Maksim Kyrchanoff, "'Dark Shadows of the Past Will Forever Remain with Us,' or Fathers and Sons: Boundaries and Frontiers, Walls and Bridges in Soviet and Post-Soviet Literature," *Zhurnal frontirnykh issledovanii* 2 (2019): 11–33.

and émigré, far from the communal practices of Judaism and yet reflecting the history of its existence and survival under Communism; a monument to the Jewishness of memory and self-analysis. Of the three hypostases David Shrayer-Petrov identified—the American, the Jewish, and the Russian—the last two undoubtedly define his writing even today, after three and a half decades without Russia.

Translated from the Russian by
Dobrochna Fire

Works Cited

Friedgut, Theodore H. "Nationalities Policy, the Soviet Regime, the Jews, and Emigration." In *Jewish Life after the USSR*, edited by Zvi Gitelman, Musya Glants, and Marshall I. Goldman, 27–45. Bloomington: Indiana University Press, 2003.

Gitelman, Zvi. *A Century of Ambivalence. The Jews of Russia and the Soviet Union, 1881 to the Present.* New York: Schocken, 1988.

Katsin, Lev. "Kogo razdrazhaet boroda Tsukermana i pochemu . . .?" *Evreiskii mir*, January 31, 1997.

Krupnik, Igor. "Soviet Cultural and Ethnic Policies toward Jews: A Legacy Reassessed." In *Jews and Jewish Life in Russia and The Soviet Union*, edited by Yaacov Ro'i, 67–86. Ilford: Routledge, 1995.

Krutikov, Mikhail. "The Jewish Future in Russia: Trends and Opportunities." *East European Jewish Affairs* 1 (2002): 1–16.

Kyrchanoff, Maksim. "'Dark Shadows of the Past Will Forever Remain with Us,' or Fathers and Sons: Boundaries and Frontiers, Walls and Bridges in Soviet and Post-Soviet Literature." *Zhurnal frontirnykh issledovanii* 2 (2019): 11–33.

Sapgir, Genrikh. *Stikhotvoreniia i poemy*. Introduction, edited, and commentary by Maksim D. Shraer and David Shraer-Petrov. Novaia biblioteka poeta, Malaia seriia. St. Petersburg: Akademicheskii proekt, 2004.

Shrayer, Maxim D. [Maksim D. Shraer], and David Shrayer-Petrov [David Shraer-Petrov]. *Genrikh Sapgir: Klassik avangarda*. St. Petersburg: Dmitrii Bulanin, 2004.

Shrayer, Maxim D. "Afterword: Voices of My Father's Exile." In David Shrayer-Petrov, *Autumn in Yalta: A Novel and Three Stories*, edited, co-translated, and with an afterword by Maxim D. Shrayer, 205–234. Library of Modern Jewish Literature. Syracuse: Syracuse University Press, 2006.

———, ed. *An Anthology of Jewish-Russian Literature: Two Centuries of Dual Identity in Prose and Poetry, 1801–2001.* 2 vols. Armonk, NY: M. E. Sharpe, 2007.

———, ed. *Voices of Jewish-Russian Literature: An Anthology*. Boston: Academic Studies Press, 2018.

Shrayer-Petrov, David [David Petrov]. *Kholsty*. In *Pereklichka*, 116–160. Moscow: Molodaia gvardiia, 1967.

―――― [David Shraer-Petrov]. *Druz´ia i teni. Roman s uchastiem avtora.* New York: Liberty Publishing House, 1989.

―――― [David Shraer-Petrov]. *Frantsuzskii kottedzh.* Edited by Maksim D. Shraer. Providence, RI: APKA Publishers, 1999.

――――. *Jonah and Sarah: Jewish Stories of Russia and America.* Edited by Maxim D. Shrayer. Library of Modern Jewish Literature. Syracuse: Syracuse University Press, 2003.

―――― [David Shraer-Petrov]. *Forma liubvi. Izbrannaia lirika.* Moscow: Izdatel´skii dom "Iunost´," 2003.

―――― [David Shraer-Petrov]. *Savelii Ronkin.* In his *Eti strannye russkie evrei,* 93–317. Moscow: Raduga, 2004.

―――― [David Shraer-Petrov]. *Strannyi Dania Raev.* In his *Eti strannye russkie evrei,* 1–93. Moscow: Raduga, 2004.

―――― [David Shraer-Petrov]. *Karp dlia farshirovannoi ryby. Rasskazy.* Moscow: Agraf, 2005.

――――. *Autumn in Yalta: A Novel and Three Stories.* Edited, co-translated, and with an afterword by Maxim D. Shrayer. Library of Modern Jewish Literature. Syracuse: Syracuse University Press, 2006.

―――― [David Shraer-Petrov]. *Vodka s pirozhnymi. Roman s pisateliami.* Edited by Maksim D. Shraer. St. Petersburg: Akademicheskii proekt, 2007.

―――― [David Shraer-Petrov]. *Okhota na ryzhego d´iavola. Roman s mikrobiologami.* Edited by Maksim D. Shraer. Moscow: Agraf, 2010.

――――. *Dinner with Stalin and Other Stories.* Edited, with notes, and commentary by Maxim D. Shrayer. Library of Modern Jewish Literature. Syracuse: Syracuse University Press, 2014.

―――― [David Shraer-Petrov]. *Gerbert i Nelli.* Moscow: Knizhniki, 2014.

―――― [David Shraer-Petrov]. *Krugosvetnoe schast´e. Izbrannye rasskazy.* Moscow: Knizhniki, 2016.

――――. *Doctor Levitin.* Edited and with notes by Maxim D. Shrayer, translated by Arna B. Bronstein, Aleksandra I. Fleszar, and Maxim D. Shrayer. Detroit: Wayne State University Press, 2018.

Shraer-Petrov, David, and Gennadii Katsov. "Ia dumaiu, chto my vse drug druga chemu-to nauchili…." RUNYweb.com, May 17, 2011. http://www.runyweb.com/articles/culture/literature/david-shayer-petrov-interview.html. Accessed June 3, 2020.

Shraer-Petrov, David, and Tat′iana Vol′tskaia. "Mertsanie zheltoi zvezdy." Radio Liberty, January 28, 2016. http://www.bigbook.ru/articles/detail.php?ID=25001. Accessed June 3, 2020.

Ludmila Tsigel′man. "The Impact of Ideological Changes in the USSR on Different Generations of the Soviet Jewish Intelligentsia." In *Jewish Culture and Identity in the Soviet Union*, edited by Yaacov Ro'i and Avi Beker, 42–72. New York and London: New York University Press, 1991.

The Nonconformist Poetics of David Shrayer-Petrov*

Roman Katsman

Some critics note that there are no more lacunae on the map of late Soviet unofficial or nonconformist literature.[1] In this extensively developed field of study, however, too little attention has been devoted to the work of the Leningrad and Moscow—and since 1987 American—poet, prose writer, playwright and literary translator David Shrayer-Petrov. This has partly to do with the fact that nonconformist literature has long since developed its own unofficial but fully hegemonic canon. On the other hand, this is related to the question of how the national, particularly the Jewish, component should be related to the discourse on Soviet nonconformism. The theoretical interpretation of the latter is far from completed, nor is the interpretation of the cultural-anthropological motifs at the foundation of nonconformist literature. This essay focuses on the writings of David Shrayer-Petrov, mostly those created while he was a refusenik. I will attempt to show that the arena of the conflict lying at the root of the nonconformist imagination, represented symbolically and aimed at mobilizing a Jewish identity, can be described in terms of the generative anthropology of Eric Gans as the scene of blocking

---

* Copyright © 2021 by Roman Katsman. English translation copyright © 2021 by Dobrochna Fire.
I would like to thank David Shrayer-Petrov and Maxim D. Shrayer for the materials they provided and for their help in my work on this essay. An original version was published in Russian as "Parallel′nye vselennye Davida Shraera-Petrova," *Wiener Slawistischer Almanac* 79 (2017): 255–279.

1   Galina El′shevskaia, "Neskol′ko geniev v ogranichennom prostranstve: k istorii odnogo samooshchushcheniia," *Novoe literaturnoe obozrenie* 100 (2009), http:// magazines.russ.ru/nlo/2009/100/el32.html, accessed October 13, 2016.

the gesture of appropriation directed at the victim.² Jewish nonconformism thereby assimilates and overcomes the victimary state of mind characteristic of the post-Holocaust period and possibly of modern times in general. Let us begin by examining the concept of nonconformism.

Nonconformism may be described as a kind of homonym with diverse but similar meanings on the artistic, social, and socio-psychological planes. In sociology and rhetoric, nonconformism is reduced to protest and disagreement and is also sometimes included in manifestations of anarchism; it is, however, apparent that these concepts are not exhausted by each other. In its most general sense, nonconformism is understood as resistance to forms of thinking, writing, behavior, and so forth that are in effect and imposed by the authorities, the hegemony, or the government, but also by generally accepted opinions, stereotypes, and prejudices, that which is outside the mold, or, as Lidiya Ginzburg put it, "that which is dissimilar."³

As regards Soviet literature, nonconformism becomes an even more opaque concept because the Soviet authorities, like no other, bestowed a huge significance on the adoption of any form, be it in the aesthetic or in the sociocultural sphere, thereby leaving no room outside the bounds of its scene of appropriation. Analyzed by Alexei Yurchak as one of the sociocultural possibilities of "late socialism,"⁴ the naïve fantasy of existing "outside" this scene cultivated in certain circles, from Thaw-era hipsters (Russian: "стиляги," *stiliagi*) to Russian rock, could not be realized. Even those who were "simply" "creative people, not fitting into the system," who "were not active soldiers but simply wanted to be left in peace and not prevented from self-expression,"⁵ inevitably turned out to be in conflict with the Soviet system.⁶

---

2   Eric Gans, *A New Way of Thinking: Generative Anthropology in Religion, Philosophy, Art* (Aurora: The Davies Group, 2011).
3   Boris Ivanov, "Evoliutsiia literaturnykh dvizhenii v piatidesiatye–vos′midesiatye gody," in *Istoriia leningradskoi nepodtsenzurnoi literatury, 1950-e–1980-e*, ed. B. Ivanov and B. Roginskii (St. Petersburg: DEAN, 2000), 21.
4   Alexei Yurchak, *Everything Was Forever, Until It Was No More: The Last Soviet Generation* (Princeton and Oxford: Princeton University Press, 2006), 126–157.
5   Tat′iana Nikol′skaia, "Krug Alekseia Khvostenko," in Ivanov and Roginskii, *Istoriia leningradskoi nepodtsenzurnoi literatury*, 93.
6   For further research into the subject, see the selection of articles recently curated by Klavdia Smola, "Nonkonformizm kak performativnoe zerkalo rezhima," *Novoe literaturnoe obozrenie* 155 (2019), https://www.nlobooks.ru/magazines/novoe_literaturnoe_obozrenie/155_nlo_1_2019/, accessed August 15, 2020.

As a result, Soviet nonconformism could exist only in conflictual spaces and in a battle for possession of these very spaces. In this battle, an imagined, hypothetical, but at the same time tangible scene of conflict was created, in which the victim of the system (political or aesthetic) ceased to be a victim and became an active force—that is to say, historical consciousness stepped outside the boundaries of the victimary paradigm. The basic effort of being outside the mold was applied to a mutual symbolic recodification of the political, religious, social, metaphysical, folkloric, national, and other "forms." This method was directed at blocking the gestures of appropriation and at deferring violence, which generated new signs and a new, nonconformist culture. Its rhetorical instrument was "fearless speech,"[7] consisting of individual, sometimes minimalist and fragmented utterances. Such utterances embodied the essence of nonconformism: the transformation of helplessness and weakness into strength (aesthetic, cultural, and political) and the formation of a new identity outside the bounds of the victimary paradigm.

When such utterances generate signs with a Jewish character, it makes sense to talk of a specifically Jewish component of nonconformism. Alek Rapoport wrote, "Being a nonconformist artist is already critical. Being at the same time also a 'Jewish artist' is a simply scandalous situation for the USSR."[8] Thus Joseph Brodsky develops the space of conflict formation outside the fence of a Jewish cemetery, mobilizing the readers of the *samizdat* publication *Sintaksis* in 1960 to the perception of "jurists, merchants, musicians, and revolutionaries" as idealists and interpreters of the Talmud—and their self-sacrifice, depicting them as a tenacious seed that has fallen into the soil.[9]

Natalia Ivanova wrote about the violation of the triple taboo of Soviet literature in the writing of some Jewish authors: they wrote about Jews, they were Jews writing about Russia, and they wrote about Russian Orthodoxy (and more broadly about Christianity) while being Jews.[10] Can this be applicable to all Jewish nonconformists? Ivanova's diagnosis may be too

---

7   Michel Foucault, *Fearless Speech* (Los Angeles: Semiotext[e], 2001).
8   Alek Rapoport, *Nonkonformizm ostaetsia* (St. Petersburg: DEAN, 2003), 28–29.
9   Iosif Brodskii, "Evreiskoe kladbishche okolo Leningrada" ("Jewish Cemetery near Leningrad"), *Sintaksis* 3 (1960), http://rvb.ru/np/publication/05supp/syntaxis/3/brodsky.htm, accessed October 14, 2016.
10 Natalia Ivanova, "Skvoz' nenavist'—k liubvi, skvoz' liubov'—k ponimaniiu," in Fridrikh Gorenshtein, *Psalom* (Moscow: Eksmo, 2001).

essentialist and somewhat inaccurate. It was not so much the artist, the literature, or the writing as the utterance itself that was "Jewish," in the artistic sense. Commenting on the literary situation of the second half of the 1950s, David Shrayer-Petrov wrote: "We were not divided into Jews and non-Jews,"[11] and more often than not there was no place for "Jewish problems"[12] in Jewish friendships and conversations. This situation later underwent something of a change, and thoughts about "Jewish writers who shied away from the topic that was most difficult for us: assimilation in Russia or emigration to Israel" acquired a significant meaning.[13] And yet these changes had little influence on the poetic tastes and habits of the ones whose creative output was formed in those years. For that reason, the Jewish component of nonconformism should be sought not so much on the social and political plane as on the symbolic plane, in spite of the fact that the social sphere plays a huge role in everything that concerns the relations between the official sphere and unofficial literature, which is framed and defined in in relation to the former.

Regardless of how the complex issue of the interrelation between official and unofficial literature is resolved, the latter, as Stanislav Savitsky rightly noted, cannot be reduced to the social, "even when it is understood in the context of action theory."[14] Jews who were nonconformists did not join poetic associations as Jews, and thus the key to understanding their work should be not so much the sociology of communities of writers as the hermeneutics of imagined and symbolic "communities of utterances." Such an approach does not contradict an understanding of a "unified nonconformist cultural movement," of "unofficial culture as an integral phenomenon,"[15] but it seems more productive in this case.

I will now attempt to formulate the theoretical premises on which an analysis of a nonconformist utterance can be built. As a discursive formation, nonconformism (both sociopolitical and poetical) is a sincere,

---

11 David Shraer-Petrov, *Druz'ia i teni. Roman s uchastiem avtora* (New York: Liberty, 1989), 112. See also idem, *Vodka s pirozhnymi. Roman s pisateliami*, ed. Maksim D. Shraer (St. Petersburg: Akademicheskii proekt, 2007), 65.
12 Ibid., 167.
13 Ibid., 203.
14 Stanislav Savitskii, *Andegraund: istoriia i mify leningradskoi neofitsial'noi literatury* (Moscow: Novoe literaturnoe obozrenie, 2002), 89.
15 Viacheslav Dolinin, "Nepodtsenzurnaia literatura i nepodtsenzurnaia pechat' (Leningrad 1950–1980 godov)," in Ivanov and Roginskii, *Istoriia leningradskoi nepodtsenzurnoi literatury*, 13–14.

just, and adequate[16] utterance in the face of danger (to success, one's career, fame, well-being), that is, "fearless speech," a risky project with a conflicted preamble, and risk consists not only in the interaction with government institutions but also in the search for new forms, truths, and self-identification. It is not enough to not be a conformist in order to be a nonconformist; for literature to be nonconformist it is not enough for it to be unofficial, underground, "second literature."[17] Nonconformism must be understood not as a negative theoretical characteristic but as a positive, active deed, which takes place not in the context of an isolated subculture but in answer to the challenges of the dominant culture and for the sake of solving spiritual and pragmatic problems spawned by this culture.

The cultural-pragmatic components of nonconformism are the following: (1) the perception of conflict as a given; (2) the symbolic design of a project as possible/new; (3) the economy of risk/danger as the only real/true/genuine one.[18] In this configuration, the structure of myth is easy to infer: (1) the discovery/creation of the conflict; (2) the elimination of the conflict with the aid of a risky/transgressive project (war, a journey, a metamorphosis, a crime, a sacrifice); (3) the realization of one's personality as transcendental/numinous. Thus, the writing of nonconformism is homologous to mythopoesis. In it, as in myth, the possible and the impossible merge in order to allow the subject to transcend from the conflict into the real (for example, into a consciousness of their own authentic identity). Thanks to the primal conflict, this writing becomes, in Eric Gans's terms, the generative scene of sign- and culture-creation.[19] In this light, the essence of the conflict itself emerges as a consequence of the triangle of the mimetic desire[20] to possess symbols, while thanks to the risk connected with this conflict, the nonconformist utterance acquires a performative character and turns into a kind of cultural, ritual, magical formula, irreversibly changing

---

16 Jürgen Habermas, *The Theory of Communicative Action*. Volume 1: *Reason and the Rationalization of Society*, tr. Thomas McCarthy (Boston: Beacon, 1984), 275.
17 Boris Ivanov and Boris Roginskii, "Ot sostavitelei," in *Istoriia leningradskoi nepodtsenzurnoi literatury*, 4–5.
18 The structure of conflict as the problematization of the relationship "I—other" reproduces Jacques Lacan's psychoanalytical structure. See Jacques Lacan, *R.S.I. Séminaire 1974–1975*, tr. Cormac Gallagher (Paris: A.L.I., 2002).
19 Gans, *A New Way of Thinking*.
20 René Girard, *Violence and the Sacred*, tr. Patrick Gregory (Baltimore: Johns Hopkins University Press, 1979).

the cultural and sometimes social status of the author[21] and, as a result, also changing the state of cultural, intellectual, social, and possibly political reality. In addition, this transformation has a mythical nature, even an epic-heroic one: the author symbolically becomes a cultural hero, often a martyr of culture, independently of his or her personal motives and relationships with the official institutions.

In the words of Viktor Krivulin, nonconformists thus "lived what they said," "built their lives according to the word" in a unique "social-cosmic protest," and "any life circumstance [. . .] was perceived symbolically."[22] And finally, by virtue of the communicative mechanisms that start working (the implementation of unofficial or underground measures), the performative change in the author's status extends to the public sphere as well. Nonconformist literature is not necessarily a minor one, in Gilles Deleuze's terminology, but it is always mythopoetic, conceptual, and performative in its essence, outside a dependence on the concrete style and genre of one or another work. In other words, Joseph Brodsky did not at all need to read Paul Tillich in order to see a manifestation of the "courage to be" in poetry.[23] Nonconformism is an act that makes the persona of the author a "public sign."[24] Moreover, even falling out of the space of minority and political conflict formation (as in the case of emigration), true nonconformism "remains," in the words of Alek Rapoport; and nonconformist literature often remains, for example in the case of Ilia Bokstein, a "way of life."[25]

Now we can point to what forms the specifically Jewish utterance within the framework of the nonconformist discourse in accordance with its three pragmatic components or dimensions specified here. In the Jewish nonconformist utterance (1) the imagining of conflict has a Jewish character (the incorporation of Jews into the conflict is a necessary but not a sufficient condition); (2) the project of the possible/new is constructed with the aid of

---

21 See Marcel Moss [Marsel' Moss], *Sotsial'nye funktsii sviashchennogo*, tr. I. Utekhin (St. Petersburg: Evraziia, 2000); John L. Austin, *How to Do Things with Words* (Cambridge, MA: Harvard University Press, 1975).
22 Viktor Krivulin, "Peterburgskaia spiritual'naia lirika vchera i segodnia (k istorii neofitsial'noi poezii Leningrada 60–80-kh godov," in *Istoriia leningradskoi nepodtsenzurnoi literatury*, 103–104.
23 Iakov Gordin, *Rytsar' i smert', ili Zhizn' kak zamysel: O sud'be Iosifa Brodskogo* (Moscow: Vremia, 2010), 85–101.
24 Boris Ivanov, "Rid Grachev," in *Istoriia leningradskoi nepodtsenzurnoi literatury*, 49.
25 Naum Vaiman, "Poeziia kak obraz zhizni: Il'ia Bokshtein," *Open Space*, October 12, 2010, http://os.colta.ru/literature/events/details/18665/, accessed October 14, 2016.

Jewish themes, images, and symbols; (3) the revealed and embodied "real" touches upon the Jewish identity or other aspects of the individual. In other words, what is "Jewish" in this discourse is a specifically Jewish (culturally, nationally, or religiously conditioned) recodification of the economy of the risk of "fearless" sign creation in the above-described mythopoesis. Such a formally pragmatic configuration inevitably also influences the ideological content of the utterance. Thanks to the transition from a conflictual arena of meaning-creation, where the "sacred" object of violence, that is, the victim, is a Jew, to the real scene of self-awareness, where the Jew becomes an equal participant in the struggle for the appropriation of the real "sacred," a new, non-victim or, in Gans's terms, originary paradigm of Jewish existence is born.

The vector of overcoming victimhood appears in Soviet literature at the end of the 1960s and the beginning of the 1970s, in many ways in connection with the Israeli wars and at the same time almost simultaneously with the intensification of the manifestation of the paradigm of Soviet-Jewish victimhood itself (outside the context of the Shoah [Holocaust], acknowledged and assimilated as early as the 1940s–1950s).[26] That is to say, Jews are writing more and more about themselves as the victims of the system, but they are also aware of themselves as being capable of not being victims. This dynamic would intensify with time, up to the refusenik literature of the 1970s–1980s, to which the writings of David Shrayer-Petrov, which I will be examining below, testify and bear witness.

* * *

David Shrayer-Petrov (David Peysakhovich [Petrovich] Shrayer) was born in 1936 in Leningrad. In his memoirs, he writes about the circle within which his literary path was initiated. He became acquainted with the would-be film director Ilya Averbakh in 1955 and entered the literary seminar (*lito*) of the First Leningrad Medical School, in which Vasily Aksyonov also participated. In 1959, David Dar, through Lev Ozerov, showed Shrayer-Petrov's poems and those of Aleksandr Kushner to Boris Pasternak, who, according to Shrayer-Petrov, responded favorably to them, "gave some good advice," and wanted to meet the young poets personally.[27] In the literary seminar (*lito*) at the Palace of Culture of Industrial Cooperation (later renamed Lensovet Palace

---

26 Maxim D. Shrayer, *I Saw It: Ilya Selvinsky and the Legacy of Bearing Witness to the Shoah* (Boston: Academic Studies Press, 2013).
27 Shraer-Petrov, *Druz´ia i teni*, 252.

of Culture), he became closely acquainted with fellow young poets Dmitry Bobyshev, Aleksander Kushner, Anatoly Naiman, Mikhail Eremin, Evgeny Reyn, and others.[28] A few years later, Shrayer-Petrov met and befriended the fiction writer and Sinologist Boris Vakhtin (David Dar's stepson and son of Vera Panova), and participated in Vakhtin's literary "Thursdays."[29] He more than once fell within the gravitational pull of Anna Akhmatova and her intimates and acquaintances, but stayed his own course. Shrayer-Petrov was professionalized as a literary translator of poetry under the patronage of Efim Etkind and participated in his oral "almanacs," as well as in the translation seminar of Tatiana Gnedich.[30] He admired the poems of the young Joseph Brodsky; a friendship and meetings with him in Leningrad in the early 1960s left an indelible mark on his soul,[31] comparable perhaps only with his literary friendship with Genrikh Sapgir, subsequently crowned by his book (together with his son Maxim D. Shrayer) about Sapgir.[32] Shrayer-Petrov moved to Moscow in 1964.

The writer reminisced about the fact that in the winter of 1977–1978 Aksyonov proposed that he participate in the unofficial "grand almanac," but he refused: barely a year earlier, in early 1976, he "sweated blood" to be accepted into the Writers Union, and "he didn't want to risk it."[33] In 1979, however, the same year that he and his family applied for emigration to Israel, he supported the position of the *Metropol* contributors. He was expelled from the Union of Soviet Writers in 1980. During the time he was a refusenik, until late spring of 1987, Shrayer-Petrov wrote a great deal and conducted a literary seminar-salon for refuseniks. During the years of the seminar-salon's existence such then underground authors as Genrikh Sapgir and Yury Karabchievsky gave readings.[34] Shrayer-Petrov also socialized with foreign diplomats; participated in the screenings of films in the British

---

28 Ibid., 103. See also Shraer-Petrov, *Vodka s pirozhnymi*, 64–81, 90–99, 167–176.
29 Ibid., 249.
30 Ibid., 259, 268.
31 Ibid., 273–283.
32 Maksim D. Shraer and David Shraer-Petrov, *Genrikh Sapgir. Klassik avangarda* (St. Petersburg: Dmitrii Bulanin, 2004). See also the chapter about Sapgir, "Tigr snegov," in Shraer-Petrov, *Vodka s pirozhnymi*, 177–217.
33 Shraer-Petrov, *Druz'ia i teni*, 143.
34 Shraer-Petrov, *Vodka s pirozhnymi*, 212–213. See also Maxim D. Shrayer, ed., *An Anthology of Jewish-Russian Literature*, vol. 2 (Armonk, London: M. E. Sharpe, 2007), 1056–1057.

embassy;³⁵ protested against the drafting into the army of his student who as a member of the Evangelical Baptist Church opposed to bearing arms;³⁶ participated in protest demonstrations of refuseniks; gave interviews to ABC and CBS; passed on letters of protest through foreign journalists;³⁷ wrote and submitted open letters of protest (in particular, to the congress of the Union of Soviet Writers in 1986)³⁸—in a word, he combined within himself the features of a Zionist-refusenik and a dissident. Shrayer-Petrov was subjected to persecution, punitive arrests, and ostracism in the Soviet press. His works appeared in the Jewish *samizdat*. In 1985, a microfilm of the first part of his refusenik trilogy was illegally taken out of the USSR to Israel and formed the bulk a collection of materials about refuseniks published by Biblioteka-Aliia in 1986.³⁹ The first two parts of the future refusenik trilogy would be first published in Moscow in 1992 under the title *Gerbert i Nelli* (*Herbert and Nelly*) and subsequently reprinted twice in Russia. The refusenik novel, and specifically its first publication in Israel, gave a powerful boost to the development of the Jewish theme in Shrayer-Petrov's work, a development that had started much earlier.

The writer's son, the literary scholar and author Maxim D. Shrayer, writes, "Starting with his earliest poems, which became known in *samizdat* since the 1950s and 1960s, Shrayer-Petrov examined the nature of the Jewish consciousness, antisemitism, and the relations between Jews and Russians under the Soviet totalitarian regime."⁴⁰ Shrayer-Petrov's Jewish identity formed under the influence of his family. His "Jewish genes," according to him, prevented him from living "normally" all his life.⁴¹ In his grandmother's house, he read the "Jewish Bible with a parallel Russian translation" voraciously,⁴² while the image of his Uncle Moisey (Moshe Sharir), who had left home in 1924 for the British Mandate of Palestine to build a Jewish state,⁴³ brought to this identity a warm attachment to Israel

---

35 Shraer-Petrov, *Okhota na ryzhego d'iavola. Roman s mikrobiologami* (Moscow: Agraf, 2010), 216.
36 Ibid., 228.
37 Ibid., 253.
38 Shraer-Petrov, *Druz'ia i teni*, 208.
39 Shraer-Petrov, *V otkaze. Roman*, in *V otkaze* (Jerusalem: Biblioteka-Aliia, 1986), 147–242.
40 Shraer, "Posleslovie," 384.
41 Shraer-Petrov, *Druz'ia i teni*, 11.
42 Shraer-Petrov, *Okhota na ryzhego d'iavola*, 12. See also Shrayer-Petrov, *Frantsuzskii kottedzh* (Providence, RI: APKA Publishers, 1999), 173.
43 Shraer-Petrov, *Okhota na ryzhego d'iavola*, 66, 200.

along with the longing for truth, justice, and freedom.[44] Shrayer-Petrov's father "dreamed of one day walking down the ramp of an airplane that had landed in Israel."[45] In talking about the "happy" 1960s, Shrayer-Petrov writes:

> Life seemed fairly interesting and very promising. If it weren't for the constant anguish characteristic of my generation's young intelligentsia! The anguish was probably connected with thoughts of our possible emigration. However I might convince myself that everything was going well for my "albeit little family," the literary events of the past decade could never ever vanish from memory: the public rout of Vladimir Dudintsev's *Not by Bread Alone* (1956), the civil execution of Boris Pasternak for publishing *Doctor Zhivago* abroad (1958), the trial and [punitive] exile of Joseph Brodsky (1964), and much else. The catalyst for these secret subversive thoughts was the meeting with Tsilya Poliak, my wife Mila's aunt, who had come to Moscow from Israel [in the midle 1960s] to visit her family.[46]

Thus finally, in 1979, the Shrayer family started to live the life of activist refuseniks: "We met constantly with other refuseniks and dissidents (Vladimir Slepak, Josef Begun, Yuri Medvedkov, Aleksander Lerner, and others), we extended the hospitality of our home to representatives of Jewish organizations from the United States, Canada, England, and France, who fought actively for our liberation from this 'new Egyptian captivity.'"[47]

It is therefore no surprise that the vast majority of Shrayer-Petrov's prose and poetry was not published in the Soviet Union. In his memoirs, he writes that his first book of poetry was withdrawn from publication in Leningrad "for his friendship with Joseph Brodsky"; in 1979–1980, for the attempt to emigrate, his collection of poetry *Winter Ship* (*Zimnii korabl'*), his book of translations from Lithuanian, and his book of prose *Hunt for the Red Devil* (*Okhota na ryzhego d'iavola*) were steamrolled, the latter already in galleys.[48] (See also Maxim D. Shrayer's and Ian Probstein's essays in this volume.) Toward the end of the 1970s, his "conflict with official Soviet

---

44 See also the version of this family story in "Mimosas for Grandmother's Grave" (1984), Shraer-Petrov, "Mimozy na mogilu babushki," in his *Krugosvetnoe schast'e. Izbrannye rasskazy* (Moscow: Knizhniki, 2016), 183, and in the novel *Frantsuzskii kottedzh*, 166.
45 Shraer-Petrov, *Okhota na ryzhego d'iavola*, 123.
46 Ibid., 82–83.
47 Ibid., 242.
48 Shraer-Petrov, *Druz'ia i teni*, 57–58.

culture"⁴⁹ had intensified. As previously mentioned, from 1979, when he applied for and refused permission to emigrate, up to his emigration in early June 1987, Shrayer-Petrov wrote a great deal, and some of his prose works of this period are vivid examples of refusenik literature. To this period belong, first of all, the refusenik trilogy, the first part of which was written in 1979–1980,⁵⁰ and the second part in 1982–1984;⁵¹ and the "novel-fantella" *Yudin's Redemption* (*Iskuplenie Iudina*), which Shrayer-Petrov started while a refusenik (1981–1982) and subsequently revised for the original publication in the United States (1992–1993).⁵² (About *Yudin's Redemption*, see Leonid Katsis's essay in this volume.) The book-length cycle *Nevan Poems* (*Nevskie stikhi*), poems on Jewish themes, short stories, the play in verse *Ed Tenner* (titled *Vaktsina* [Vaccine] in the revised edition), and *Friends and Shadows* (*Druz´ia i teni*), a book of memoirs about Leningrad and Leningrad writers of the 1950s and early 1960s, were also written during these years. I shall dwell here in greater detail primarily on the texts of the refusenik period, in the hope that Shrayer-Petrov's work will be examined in all its breadth and fullness in subsequent studies.

Refusenik literature recodes the conflict with the authorities from the political to the cultural and spiritual spheres. Applying to OVIR (Section of Visas and Registrations) for emigration to Israel was already in and of itself an act-utterance of "fearless speech" that irrevocably changed the social status of the applicant, initiated his new identity, and transcended him beyond the bounds of Soviet reality, and reality in general, to that primal scene of generative conflict where new signification was born and the battle for meaning was waged. Not so much the desire to leave, accompanied by the government's refusal to grant permission and refusal of freedom, as the refusal of the individual to come to terms with the refusal, the protest constitutes a nonconformist element in this act-utterance.⁵³ It was a protest against Jewish humility and helplessness, dependence, and secondariness, the symbolic embodiment of which the heroes of Shrayer-Petrov's refusenik trilogy see in Eastern European grasses "stretching out under the peasant's scythe," or in the tree mushrooms (conks) "on a Russian trunk": the trunk

---

49 Shraer-Petrov, *Okhota na ryzhego d´iavola*, 175.
50 Shraer-Petrov, *V otkaze*, 242.
51 Shraer-Petrov, *Gerbert i Nelli* (Moscow: Poliform, 1992), 588.
52 Shraer-Petrov, *Iskuplenie Iudina*, *Mosty* 5 (2005): 5–61; 6 (2005): 21–116; 7 (2005): 11–88.
53 Shraer-Petrov, *Gerbert i Nelli*, 154.

"nourished us and allowed us to develop."[54] Even more so, the foundation of nonconformism here is not only a protest against the decision of the Soviet authorities but also a protest against the rules of the game, the "laws of the genre" according to which this drama was being played out. In Shrayer-Petrov's short novel *Strange Danya Rayev* (*Stannyi Dania Raev*), the events of which unfold during the evacuation to the Urals during World War II, a Jewish woman bravely stands up to an anti-Semite in front of everyone at the marketplace. Her young son shouts "words of justice, fidelity, and protest" into the face of another offender, who happens to be a Jew and who is attempting to take the place of the boy's father, an officer at the war front, and humiliating both the mother and the boy, calling the military uniform, which the father had sent his son from the front, a "masquerade."[55]

And yet it was not the protesting subjects but the Soviet authorities that were performing a sinister carnival. The refuseniks were turning the Soviet carnival on its head, straightening what was twisted, and staging a true drama. The carnival was depriving everything that was individual of meaning, was appropriating and ravaging the present moment by filling it with phantoms and nightmares, was wiping out all that was culturally significant, unique, and meaningful. The activity of refuseniks was aimed at the diametrically opposite side—on the restoration of the mechanisms of culture creation and the establishment of a true being of the individual in the "now" of history, with its, in Bakhtin's terms, consciousness of a task and responsibility of the writing-action.[56] In this connection, the particular attachment of refuseniks to a celebration of Purim and the Purim spiel (Purim play) is telling. In spite of its external, subsequently acquired masquerade appearance, this traditionally subversive holiday of the victory over tyranny is not carnivalesque in essence: its content has no relation to the Bakhtinian "popular culture of laughter," and at its foundation lies not in the act of forgetting oneself but, on the contrary, a nation's recollection of its own roots.

David Shrayer-Petrov's refusenik texts convincingly demonstrate this common and shared direction. His creation of a Purim spiel script[57] and his

---

54 Ibid., 381–382.
55 David Shraer-Petrov, *Eti strannye russkie evrei. Romany: Savelii Ronkin. Strannyi Dania Raev* (Moscow: Raduga, 2004).
56 Mikhail Bakhtin, *Towards a Philosophy of the Act*, tr. Vadim Liapunov, ed. Vadim Liapunov and Michael Holquist (Austin: University of Texas Press, 1993).
57 See Shraer-Petrov, *Vodka s pirozhnymi*, 208, and idem [author of the play], *Purimshpil'* (Purim spiel), dir. Roman Spektor, video recording (Moscow, 1987), https://www.youtube.com/watch?v=CxW_RNscgTQ, viewed October 14, 2016.

(jointly with his wife Emilia Shrayer) leadership of a literary seminar-salon were in themselves acts of "fearless speech" for him and his family, as well as for many other refuseniks. Later, when he was already living in the United States and reflecting on the past, the writer pointed to the fact that one can consider the image-event of the death of Stalin to be the meaning-creating event of his life, the foundational myth, "when, as in a fairytale, the Evil Sorcerer dies and Justice triumphs."[58] In the eyes of Shrayer-Petrov, Stalin died during Purim, before he could realize his worst plans regarding the Jews (the "doctors' plot" and mass deportation), and the victory of Justice acquired a personal, national, mythological meaning.[59] It is for this reason that the Purim spiel for Shrayer-Petrov is a celebration of the initiation and realization of the individual in history. Stalin's death became the symbol of the resolution of a conflict, the deferral of violence, even if only temporarily, and the birth of a new life and a new kind of consciousness. For Shrayer-Petrov, as for many of his contemporaries, re-Stalinization,[60] the resurrection of Stalin, was the worst nightmare, the symbol of violence, the loss of their individuality and humanity.[61]

The symbol as self-awareness through another is the central component of the structure of nonconformism; the symbol conjoins two other aspects: imagining the conflict, and the "real" of true identity. As Shrayer-Petrov's works testify, this central component can be completely minimalistic. This feature is manifest already in the poems of the late 1950s and 1960s, about which Lev Ozerov wrote, "He [Shrayer-Petrov] lives in the search for precision."[62] This is all the more true in relation to the poems of the 1970s, which touch to one

---

58 Shraer-Petrov, *Okhota na ryzhego d´iavola*, 8.
59 See Maxim D. Shrayer, "A Purim 'Shpil' in Soviet Moscow," *Mosaic*, February 29, 2016, http://mosaicmagazine.com/observation/2016/02/a–purim–shpil–in–soviet–moscow/, accessed June 22, 2016.
60 The fear of re-Stalinization was one of the basic topoi, above all, of the dissident movement. See, for example, "Ot izdatelei," in Alexander Ginzburg, *Belaia kniga po delu A. Siniavskogo i Iu. Danielia* (Frankfurt am Main: Posev, 1967); Pyotr Yakir, Yuly Kim, and Ilya Gabai's letter "To the Leaders of Science, Culture, and Art" (January 1968); Ilya Gabai, "Ilya Gabai's Final Speech in His January 19–20, 1970, Trial at the Tashkent Municipal Court," in his *Pis´ma iz zaklucheniia (1970–1972)* (Moscow: Novoe literaturnoe obozrenie, 2015), 8. See also the numerous materials on this subject in the samizdat information bulletin *Chronicle of Current Events* (*Khronika tekushchikh sobytii*), which appeared in 1968–1983 (for the digital resourse see: http://hts.memo.ru/).
61 See, for example, Shrayer-Petrov's late novella "Dinner with Stalin" ("Obed s vozhdem," 2008), in his *Krugosvetnoe schast´e*, 196–215.
62 Lev Ozerov, "Ob avtore" ("About the Author"), in David Petrov, *Kholsty*, in *Pereklichka* (Moscow: Molodaia gvardiia, 1967), 116.

degree or another upon Jewish themes and the author's search for his identity; even in this alone the poems are nonconformist. Shrayer-Petrov writes, "At the Spring of Poetry celebrations [Poezijos pavasaris] in 1978 in Vilnius, to which I took Maxim, I read the poem 'My Slavic Soul' ['Moia slavianskaia dusha']. The transmission was broadcast live. In Moscow, I was summoned to the secretariat of the Union of Writers, and for the first time I was chastised for a public reading of a poem that 'smelled of Zionism.'"[63] This poem, written in 1975, is a fantasy, surrealistic and grotesque, about the lyrical hero's loss of his (Slavic) soul. This loss is only partially and implicitly motivated by Zionism,[64] and in the poem even Jewishness remains nothing more than an empty and useless form: "[...] What shall I do alone amid this grove of birches/ In my perennial, banal, so typically Jewish wrapping?" ("[...] Что делать мне среди берёзок/ С моей еврейскою пустой, такой типичной упаковкой?").[65] And yet, one cannot but note that the apparatchiks of the Union of Soviet Writers "worked over" the poet for his not yet realized, imaginary conflict, only symbolically sketched as the flight of a Slavic soul from a Jewish body ("I don't have the wild expanse of those generous Slavic cheeks" ["мне не дана славянских ликов широта"]) and as a possible realization of this body as a reality, what will replace Slavic "birches," "dips and ditches" ("рытвины и канавы"), and "haylofts."[66]

The imagination of conflict, of the generative scene of violence, appears very expressively in the 1976 poem "Early Morning in Moscow" ("Rannee utro zimoi"), which unexpectedly explodes with the theme of antisemitism and the Holocaust, when "the deadening wooden sound" ("деревянный мертвеющий звук") of a woodpecker is echoed by the muttering of a janitor:

Это дворник лопатой шуршит,

Повторяя, как будто во сне:

Жид–жид–жид,

Жид–жид–жид,

Жид–жид–жид,

Ты попался бы в лагере мне.

---

63 Shraer-Petrov, *Okhota na ryzhego d'iavola*, 160.

64 At that time, official Soviet discourse used the term "Zionist" to label everything that was consciously or manifestly Jewish and did not fit into the mold of Soviet ideology.

65 Shrayer-Petrov, "My Slavic Soul," tr. Maxim D. Shrayer, in *Voices of Jewish Russian Literature*, ed. Maxim D. Shrayer (Boston: Academic Studies Press, 2018), 831; cf. Shraer-Petrov, "Moia slavianskaia dusha," in his *Pesnia o golubom slone* (Holyoke, MA: New England Publishing House), 40–41.

66 Ibid.

The janitor shovels the street,
rehearsing his snowy reverie:
dirty Jew dirty Jew
dirty Jew
In the camps
I'd break your head in two.[67]

The word *zhid* (yid, Kike, "dirty Jew"), repeated nine times in the Russian original, makes the identification undeniable, traumatic, and potentially dangerous: the janitor's words sound as a missed opportunity in the past or perhaps the promise of its realization in the future.

The poems written during Shrayer-Petrov's refusenik years are endowed with these same qualities. In *Nevan Poems* there are not many articulated, strictly Jewish motifs. (For a close reading of one text from *Nevan Poems*, see Andrei Ranchin's essay in this volume). However, in the Soviet-Jewish symbolic world, one Jewish word or even just the word "Jew" or "Jewish" was enough to elicit an outburst of emotions rife with the national memory and self-identification.[68] The hero of the refusenik trilogy explains this by an inferiority complex of small nations forced to live under the authority of a "great nation."[69] Thus the Kaddish is mentioned in the poem "Mother's Grave" ("Mogila mamy").[70] In the poem "Gypsy Encampment in Ozerki" ("Tsyganskii tabor v Ozerkakh"), a "little Yid" ("жидёнок") is mentioned, and also a paraphrase of Tsvetaeva's maxim is echoed, "we are all eternal Yids."[71] According to the principle of minimal foundations of Jewish philology[72] or in line with Mandelstam's thought about the all-infusing scent of the smallest drop of the "musk of Judaism,"[73] this is quite enough for the keen and eager eyes and ears of Soviet Jews. Throughout the majority

---

67 Shraer-Petrov, "Rannee utro zimoi," in his *Pesnia o golubom slone*, 41–42; cf. Shrayer-Petrov, "Early Morning in Moscow," tr. Edwin Honig and Maxim D. Shrayer, in Shrayer, *An Anthology of Jewish-Russian Literature*, vol 2, 1059.
68 Shrayer, *I Saw It*.
69 Shraer-Petrov, *Gerbert i Nelli*, 274.
70 Shraer-Petrov, *Nevskie stikhi*, 33.
71 Ibid., 39.
72 Roman Katsman, "Boris Pasternak's *Doctor Zhivago* in the Eyes of the Israeli Writers and Intellectuals (A Minimal Foundation of Multilingual Jewish Philology)," in *Around the Point: Studies in Jewish Multilingual Literature*, ed. Hillel Weiss, Roman Katsman, and Ber Kotlerman (Newcastle: Cambridge Scholars Publishing, 2014), 643–686.
73 See a detailed development of this principle in Leonid Katsis, *Osip Mandel´shtam: Muskus iudeistva* (Moscow: Mosty kul´tury, 2002).

of Soviet epochs, in particular during the difficult pre-perestroika 1980s, such mentioning served as a latent form of nonconformist Jewish utterance since they were designators of the tabooed Jewish presence, doomed to invisibility by the authorities.

The nonconformist nature of the poems of this cycle is expressed in full measure not so much in their themes as in the form, which stands the closest to the poetry of Genrikh Sapgir and in general to the first and second Russian avant-garde. Exceedingly elliptical and at the same time impressionistic; rooted in the concrete and bodily and at the same time metaphysical; full of the traditions of Russian folkloric *skaz* while at the same time loftily elitist—this poetry shuns not only any closed forms but also any coherent hermeneutics. It is precisely in form that the conflict with the hegemony of the form is embodied, as is its overcoming (if not resolution) in the project of the unlimitedly free, disconnected poetic discourse on the verge of muteness. Equally embodied is the risky flight to the real—to the archetypal identification that dialectically joins the primal violence and its transcendence:

    циганёнок ли
    жидёнок ли
    перевив
    сосновых корневищ
    кнутовище
    удавить поджечь утопить разлить
    кровь
    по песку
    желчь
    вскипает
    желваками щёк
    кнутовища щёлк
    кровь
    на песке
    роспись
    все мы
    вечные
    жиды[74]

---

74 Shraer-Petrov, *Nevskie stikhi*, 38–39.

("whether a dirty little gypsy or/ a dirty little Jew/ having woven/ pine rootstock/ into a bullwhip/ strangle torch drown spill/ blood/ on the sand/ bile/ boils/ with the jaw muscles/ bullwhip snaps/ blood/ on the sand/ a mural/ we are all/ eternal/ Yids")

This painting in blood on the sand is, of course, not simply an ornament but the poet's personal signature as he prepares for the role of a nomad, an exile, a vagabond—a paradigmatic nonconformist. The last poem in the book-length cycle, "Peter's Oak" ("Petrovskii dub"), is permeated with the premonition of the road:

обронен я
недоброй волей
на
стынь дорог

("I am [accidentally] dropped/ by an unkind will/ onto/ the iciness of roads")

The native land already appears from afar as a not fully defined scorched place, the relation to it being a priori noted by the dichotomy of leaving and returning:

но
я
зачем
тянусь
из стыни
дальних
к заброшенному пепелищу
погоди
роняй листы
летите
облака и тучи
с силуэтами листов
я возвращаюсь[75]

("but/ I/ why/ reach out/ from the iciness/ of the distant/ to the abandoned scorched hearth/ just wait/ shed leaves/ fly/ wisp and rain clouds/ with the silhouettes of leaves/ I am coming back")

---

75 Ibid., 56–57.

Thus oak leaves transform into pages ("leaves") of poetry, having been imbibed "into the contortions / of the roads / of my losses and enticements" ("в извивы / дорог / моих утрат и обольщений"). The poet grows anew, like an acorn, like an oak, into the native—new—earth and sky, and the conflict of exile is a priori transcended by poetry itself, not yet having been reached in reality. This unresolvable, logically not fully precise duality of the native and new also sets in motion the mechanisms of recodification in the works to be considered below, particularly in *Herbert and Nelly*, as the first two parts of the refusenik trilogy are known to the Russian-language reader.

Thematically, *Herbert and Nelly* is close to the voluminous corpus of Jewish literature about Spanish Jews, Marranos or their descendants, who have preserved or newly acquired a national self-awareness.[76] In the essay included in this volume, Klavdia Smola notes that the novel "draws its imagery (albeit in a pointillistic fashion) from the many centuries of Judaic culture while at the same time tapping into the traditions of the world literature of Zionism."[77] The changes taking place within the heroes are all the more significant in that the author employs specifically Jewish cultural codes, intertexts, and stylistics with a great economy of means. The transition from the imagining of conflict to the risky process of becoming oneself as the only reality takes place via a thin and subtle layer of the symbolic order, in Lacan's terms.[78] And it is precisely for this reason that the introduction of the few key symbols, as, for example, the image of the old woman-owl, a nightmarish personification of Soviet authority, which appears in Doctor Levitin's visions, is so significant. Moreover, the novel incorporates, in the author's own words, "a mosaic of [his] own life," so that "what resulted was a novel-autobiography within the novel's own narrative plot."[79] In this way the novel and its main heroes are tangibly drawn to Jewishness but do not merge with it, like Genrikh Sapgir as he appears in

---

76 See also, for example, Shrayer-Petrov's later story "White Sheep on a Green Mountain Slope" ("Belye ovtsy na zelenom sklone gory," 2003), in *Krugosvetnoe schast'e*, 5–21, where a family in Azerbaijan, descended from Mountain Jews, was "forcibly Muslimized," but "still remained Jews." At the center of the story is the minimalist symbol, the mention of which takes only several lines: the family chapel with a Tanakh and a menorah, locked behind seven bolts, located in the basement of the house, deep underground.

77 Klavdia Smola, "O proze russko-evreiskogo pisatelia Davida Shraera-Petrova," in *Russkie evrei v Amerike*, vol. 15 (St. Petersburg: Giperion, 2017), 135–150; in English, see Klavdia Smola's essay "David Shrayer-Petrov, Russian-Jewish Writer," in this volume.

78 Lacan, *R.S.I. Séminaire*.

79 Shrayer-Petrov, *Vodka s pirozhnymi*, 412.

Shrayer-Petrov's memoirs[80]—that is, they retain a nonconformist view both of the Russian intelligentsia and of the Jewish-national poles.[81]

Herbert and Nelly is devoted to the Jewish theme of the refusenik movement, but it retains the characteristic symbolic minimalism that makes the transition from conflict to the realization of a new identity very fragile. Here, one does not encounter Jewish words and diglossia very frequently, such as, for example, in the "traditional Passover toast," which is offered by Doctor Levitin: *"l'shana haba'ah b'Yerushalayim!"*—Hebrew words that are not translated in the novel and mean "Next year in Jerusalem!" Unlike his poetry, the author here avoids extended or unexpected images-concepts; his symbolism is precisely targeted and conventional, as, for example, the picture of Moscow streets strewn with "Magen Davids [Stars of David] of maple leaves"[82] or the comparison of the tearing away of Jews from Russia with the separation of the placenta.[83] The narrator endows the symbols with great meaning, but, as it seems, he understands them as a set of conventions: "We live in a world of symbols. In a world of Chinese theater. In a world of conventions and gestures."[84]

At the same time, the entire novel is built on one hypersymbol, on one main gesture-myth—on what Bertold Brecht calls the *Gestus*:[85] the act of protest as self-sacrifice. The loudly protesting refuseniks are turned into the players in a game that recodes itself from a political to an ethical

---

80 Ibid., 211.
81 In Shrayer-Petrov's *The French Cottage*, one of the heroes even prophesies the existence of Russian Jews as a "separate tribe," a kind of "leaven" without which the rotting of the "great nation" might begin (Shraer-Petrov, *Frantsuzskii kottedzh*, ed. Maksim D. Shraer [Providence, RI: APKA Publishers, 1999], 84). Another character even muses about "Jewish Slavs" (ibid., 235).
82 Shraer-Petrov, *Gerbert i Nelli*, 148. In the published English translation: "like Jewish stars, maple leaves spread out on the passes and on the grass" (Shrayer-Petrov, *Doctor Levitin*, tr. Arna B. Bronstein, Aleksandra I. Fleszar, and Maxim D. Shrayer [Detroit: Wayne State University Press, 2018], 184). See also the long poem "Yellow Star" ("Zheltaia zvezda"), built on the metaphoric comparison of Brodsky with a reddish-yellow maple leaf that had come off a tree amidst a snowy winter night, in Shraer-Petrov, *Propashchaia dusha* (Providence, RI: APKA Publishers, 1997), 87–95. Already in the early collection *Canvases*, the color of red hair is associated with light, the sun, spring, and love (see David Petrov, "Zimnie stikhi o ryzhem lyzhnike" ["Winter Poems about a Red-Headed Skier"], in *Pereklichka*, 151–152).
83 Shraer-Petrov, *Gerbert i Nelli*, 69. See also Shrayer-Petrov, *Doctor Levitin*, 81.
84 Shraer-Petrov, *Gerbert i Nelli*, 245.
85 Brigid Doherty, "Text and Gestus in Brecht and Benjamin," *MLN* 115, no. 3 (2000): 442–481.

and metaphysical one, a game in which they have a priori won: "you are successful and are sacrificing this—what can match such a sacrifice?"[86] And even though Doctor Levitin does not agree with the words of the chess grandmaster Balayan and does not agree to participate in the suicidal protest, a protest that has already killed all that he held most dear, the concept expressed in Balayan's words lies at the base of both the refusenik movement and nonconformism in general. And although Doctor Levitin uses "the spirit of Judaism" to justify his refusal to assist Balayan in his hunger strike, "his [Doctor Levitin's] soul, diluted by a Russian propensity to self-contradict, did not give him peace or rest."[87] However, the contradiction here is only external, for even the words mentioned above, *"L'shanah haba'ah b'Yerushalayim!"* are the final phrase of the two most important rituals, at the center of which is sacrifice: the Passover Seder and the prayer Neilah, which ends Yom Kippur (Day of Atonement).

Other such words-codes are *aliyah, Eretz Israel, Shalom, bekitzer*, and the names of Jewish holidays.[88] They mark the coordinates of a "parallel universe," "a universe of a native nation," "universe of Jews," the yearning for which causes so much suffering. But the yearning and longing is mentioned in the context of other suffering—the yearning of Uncle Moisey (Moses), who lives in Israel, for Russia, for another "Universe of the soul—the world of the native language."[89] Refuseniks, *gebeshniks* (KGB personnel), Jews, Russians, Israelis, émigrés, "official Jews," anti-Semites, religious believers, Zionists, *inakomysliashchie* (literally: "people who think differently"; heterodoxies), dissidents—all of these are not social groups, as Doctor Levitin's other interlocutor, the refusenik Misha Gaberman, maintains, but rather parallel universes, other dimensions, even though with the passage of time, in the refusenik community an "atmosphere of family, brotherhood, unity" develops.[90] This multiplicity of worlds and histories constitutes the polyphony of the novel, a polyphony that becomes evident not only in the narrative voices but also in the composition, deliberately "fractured"[91] and

---

86   Shraer-Petrov, *Gerbert i Nelli*, 247.
87   Ibid., 253.
88   Ibid., 277.
89   Ibid., 277–278.
90   Ibid., 289.
91   Shrayer-Petrov recasts Shklovsky's "art as device" into "art as fracture [or rupture]," having in mind the downfall of the unity of the device and the aesthetic and social awareness standing behind it, see David Shraer-Petrov, "Iskusstvo kak izlom," *The New Review / Novyi zhurnal* 196 (1995): 245–256.

multicomponent. And although among the participants of the dialogue within this multiplicity there are both Jews and Russians, it has a vividly expressed character, "if not of scandal," then of Russian intelligentsia's polyglossia.[92] All these universes exist within the very same spaces and personalities; they attract and repel but do not unite. So, for example, the main female character of the second part of the refusenik trilogy, Nelly Shamova, feels that she's a "a Russian young woman" and at the same time feels an "inner attraction to what is Jewish, Semitic, Oriental."[93] In time, she learns to "live like a Jew," endowing this with one main meaning—a yearning for Israel.

Learning and the accompanying debating of fundamental problems constitute an important part of any protest movement as one of the means of forming an identity and socializing. In Shrayer-Petrov's novel, which fictionally describes such a movement, these elements fulfill several functions. The learning process serves to construct a narrative time and gives the plot a shade of the *Bildungsroman*. This is particularly characteristic for the depiction of Nelly. The scenes of discussion and debate raise the degree of dramatism, and they are in equal degree characteristic of Nelly's story and of Herbert's story, although the latter is much less inclined toward the polemical heat. And finally, the polemical, didactic, ritual, and performative functions are intrinsic to such activity, which can be called "protest simulacra": being traditional activites of social life, they also serve the goals of the protest movement, as Christian Lahusen put it, "on the symbolic level through the encoding and enactment of a protest oratory and organizational paraphernalia."[94]

An example of such activities in the novel is the wedding of Mira and Naum, which coincides with the holiday of Simchat Torah. At the wedding the guests dance Jewish dances and sing Jewish songs, while Nelly gives a speech that symbolically unites all this into a performance of what it means to "live like Jews," lifting routine to the level of fearless nonconformist religious-political utterance: "May the joy of the most joyous and fun-filled Jewish holiday of Simchat Torah shed light on their lives and lead to the gates of the destroyed Temple. And if each of us comes to these gates with joy in our souls and determination in our hands, the Temple will be rebuilt.

---

92 Shraer-Petrov, *Gerbert i Nelli*, 288.
93 Ibid., 311–312.
94 Christian Lahusen, *The Rhetoric of Moral Protest* (Berlin, New York: Walter de Gruyter, 1996), 366.

The Bright Kingdom of the Third Temple will begin, when everything that is alive will sing, rejoice, and praise the joy of life."[95] Here the cultural and the spiritual are translated into the political.[96] What they have in common, however, is symbolic recoding. It is the recoding itself, not its direction, that is essential for true risky exposure of the real order that is characteristic of nonconformism. We will consider an example of this in Shrayer-Petrov's novel-fantella *Iskuplenie Iudina* (*Yudin's Redemption*). While a draft of the novel was composed when the author was still a refusenik, it was revised and published during his American years. Moreover, for this novel as for nonconformism in general, a complex and multi-stage recoding is characteristic, allowing one to act against the hegemony simultaneously on several generative scenes of the appropriation of meanings and forms.

The genre of the *fantella* that Shrayer-Petrov invented both for shorter fiction and for novels allows the author to fantasize on one topic or another without limiting himself within the framework of the conventions of existing genres, discourses, and poetics; as a result, the new fantasy becomes hyper-conventional. In it, the actual signified does not hide behind the decorations of historical allegory but merges deliberately with it, fills the convention with the real (a device that is reminiscent of the theatre philosophy of Yuri Lyubimov at the Taganka Theater in the 1970s Moscow). This kind of literary and intellectual Brechtian phantasmagoria serves as a double for social protest, only without the seriousness of the latter. The novel *Yudin's Redemption* is deliberately replete with motifs and devices that are maximally distant from Soviet literature, such as Christianity, historical Zionism, carnal sensuality approaching (or at times going beyond) scenic eroticism. The turn toward erotica in Shrayer-Petrov is motivated by what in his novel *The Story of My Beloved, or the Spiral Staircase* (*Istoriia moei vozliublennoi, ili vintovaia lestnitsa*, 2013) is called the "ultimate merging

---

95 Shraer-Petrov, *Gerbert i Nelli*, 410–411.
96 Shrayer-Petrov's novel *The French Cottage* includes a philosophical-poetic study of temples, which "hold the dual unity of beauty and community" and in which is preserved the memory of the pre-verbal unity of "politics and prayer"; the narrator dreams of "reviving a time of a unified temple of primal glosso-emotions giving birth to unified feelings and unified words" (Shraer-Petrov, *Frantsuzskii kottedzh*, 101). This philosophical parable of the half-destroyed temple as of the Tower of Babel justifies, from the opposite political context and as if outside the bounds of it, the necessity of mutual translation of the political and the spiritual. In fact, such a translation means, in Jacques Derrida's terms, in his thoughts on the essence of translation, going outside the meaning (Jacques Derrida, *Vokrug vavilonskikh bashen*, tr. V. Lapitskii [St. Petersburg: Akademicheskii proekt, 2002], 76), that is, in our terms, extreme nonconformism.

of ecstasy and spirituality" ("наслаждения и духовности") and the "achievement of the moment of truth," and also "sexual dissidence."[97] The writer creates an underground historical and philosophical parable, a priori not intended for publication in the Soviet Union.

The core of the plot of *Yudin's Redemption* is a kind of new gospel: the story of the life, death, and resurrection of Evsey, a doctor/healer and miracle worker; his betrayal by his disciple Yudin; their love for each other and for a woman; and also the relationship they both have with other disciples, with various communities, and with the central power. Evangelical events are transported from Judea to the diaspora, to the shores of the Black Sea, and hence the theological-historical transformation: the Jewish dispersion is presented not as a result of events depicted in the gospels but as their cause—that is, Evsey emerges as a Zionist—spiritual and political—leader, guiding his people back to the Temple, to Israel, and at the same time to the heavenly kingdom. He is actually condemned and crucified not so much for organizing a spiritual-political exodus as for a protest against the omnipotence of the Empire—the Roman empire as an allegory of the Soviet empire. Thus, the struggle for an exodus does not crowd out dissidence; political and religious (or, more broadly, spiritual) conflicts recodify each other mutually, without neutralizing each other.

Shrayer-Petrov's pseudohistorical fantasy combines such an improbable number of irreconcilable cultural elements that the main culturological conclusion of the novel comes to the surface: the conflict in the center of which the Jews find themselves is never only cultural or sociopolitical but always was and remains metaphysical. The central sacred object of the novel is not Evsey himself but myrrh—the miracle-working oil with the power to resurrect; its secret is carefully guarded by the Empire. It is myrhh that resurrects Evsey, who has died on the cross, and it is also serves as a symbol of messianism, the rebuilding of the Temple and of the Kingdom. Myrrh, being the basic symbol of the novel, embodies the struggle for possessing the key to the kingdom of truth and to the earthly kingdom. However, this symbol translates the imagined conflict into the dimension of the real, when at the end of the novel the paths diverge: the resurrected Evsey remains on the shore of the Black

---

97 Shraer-Petrov, *Istoriia moei vozliublennoi, ili vintovaia lestnitsa* (Moscow: Vest-Konsalting, 2013), 72–73.

Sea, while the Jews return to Israel without the myrrh and without Evsey and Yudin, leaving behind the story of their love and betrayal.

The working symbolism of myrrh as a mechanism of revealing the real is manifested in the fact that the figure of Evsey is taken outside the bounds of the victimary paradigm—that is, the concept of sacrifice as the center of culture. Evsey is not an a priori designated victim but rather one of the participants in the scene of conflict, in which the roles are not distributed in advance and all the characters stand before the eye of the reader as pure possibilities, singularities, still steeped in the chaos of unpredictability and chance. It is possible that this revision of Jewish victimhood that constitutes the main nonconformist Jewish utterance of Shrayer-Petrov's novel-fantella. His protest is directed not against the authorities, against ideology, or against the psycho-cultural complexes of the relationships between them and the individual, but rather against the mental paradigm in which these complexes are born. The writer's vision comprises, as is the case with other nonconformists, both Christianity and Judaism within a single spiritual quest. But he goes deeper and turns to the generative scene of culture that precedes sacrifice. The Jew appears in this scene as an equal participant in the struggle, without the characteristics of helplessness. Overcoming the Jewish "conformist" complex of victimhood yet without discrediting the idea of spiritual self-sacrifice strikes us as the highest task of *Yudin's Redemption* and perhaps of Jewish "fearless utterance" as such. One of the main components of this utterance, more precisely, of the individual capable of such an utterance, in Shrayer-Petrov is the profession of doctor/healer. The medical theme becomes central in his tragicomedy *Vaccine. Ed Tenner*. Let us examine it in greater detail.

The prototype of the main hero of *Vaccine. Ed Tenner* is "Edward Jenner—the great English doctor and smallpox vaccinator (1749–1823)."[98] At the center of the plot is the "experiment" proving the effectiveness of the vaccine, in which the experimental subject, revealed to be Tenner's son, almost dies. According to the author's dating, it was written in 1974–1984–1998–2009–2020, that is, initially conceived and written in draft form still in the USSR.[99] And although

---

98   David Shraer-Petrov, *Ed Tenner (Tragikomediia v dvukh deistviiakh i shesti kartinakh)* [2009], http://www.mromm.com/p/ShrayerDavid-03.htm, accessed October 14, 2016. Shraer-Petrov. *Vaksina. Ed Tenner*, edited by Maksim D. Shraer (Moscow: Tri Kvadrata, 2021 forthcoming).

99   In *The Story of My Beloved, or The Spiral Staircase*, the narrator recalls his "failure to stage the biographical novel in which the main hero was the inventor of the vaccine against smallpox, the English doctor of the beginning of the nineteenth century, Edward Jenner. The play was written for the theater affiliated with the House of

it was originally published only in 2009, the first three dates indicate that while at least in concept it appeared before the refusenik period, during relatively peaceful years, the play was developed during the refusenik years, and it was completed in emigration. Such a dating places in doubt the possibility of contextualizing this text and likewise forbids its reading as a straightforward ideological allegory. At the same time, it makes possible seeing a kind of a through line in the play connecting almost all the stages of the writer's creative output, including his novels and stories, as well as his memoirs.

A common theme unifies *Vaccine. Ed Tenner*, the refusenik trilogy, and *Yudin's Redemption*: medical science and biology, quite widespread in Soviet literature in the 1950s–1980s, for example, in the novels of Vasily Aksyonov and Vladimir Dudintsev, both of whom are highly regarded by Shrayer-Petrov and are often mentioned in his fiction and memoirs. Numerous variations of the medical theme also appear in his later works, all the way to his most recent novel, *The Story of My Beloved, or The Spiral Staircase* (2013). The novel *The French Cottage* (*Frantsuzskii kottedzh*) also fits in with this theme; it was conceived, in the words of the author, as early as 1977 as the "story of the life in Georgia of the great microbiologist Félix d'Hérelle and the death of Professor Georgi Eliava."[100] These are books about doctors, and not only in the meaning of the professions of their protagonists but in the deeper, metaphysical meaning.[101] Ed Tenner, Herbert Levitin, and Evsey are not only healers but searchers for truth, sacrificing themselves for the sake of a great goal. They are all intentional or, as in the case of Doctor Levitin, unintentional enlighteners. Medicine appears, as in Shrayer-Petrov's memoirist novel *Hunt for the Red Devil*, as the path of spiritual salvation, liberation, and self-realization, and in its scientific aspect as a mythical quest, a heroic-epic journey, with battles, victories, and defeats in the war between life and death.[102]

Medical Workers, which was at that time headed by Mark Rozovsky. It was written but not accepted" (Shraer-Petrov, *Istoriia moei vozliublennoi*, 120–121). In this same novel, Jenner is mentioned again, when the narrator meets his childhood friend, who is engaged in "hunting" for the bacteria causing listeric infections in animals and preoccupied with inventing a vaccine (ibid., 226).

100 Shraer-Petrov, *Frantsuzskii kottedzh*, 349.
101 Cf. also David Shrayer-Petrov, "Autumn in Yalta," in his *Autumn in Yalta. A Novel and Three Stories* (Syracuse: Syracuse University Press, 2006).
102 See Shraer-Petrov, *Frantsuzskii kottedzh*, 127. In *The French Cottage*, one of the characters argues, having in mind both microbiology and culture, that "if there is a vector of strength directed against human civilization, there should also be a defensive anti-vector" (ibid., 287).

In 2009 (the penultimate date for the play *Vaccine. Ed Tenner*), David Shrayer-Petrov taught a course on "Medicine and Literature" at Boston College. The three works mentioned above point to what in the syllabus of this course is called the "intimate connections between artistic creativity and the challenges of medicine and healing."[103] In 1974 (the first date for the play about Ed Tenner), Shrayer-Petrov's short book *Poetry and Science: Notes and Reflections* (*Poeziia i nauka: Zametki i razmyshleniia*) was published by the Moscow publisher Znanie. In this book, the theme announced in the title is examined from various points of view: what is common and dissimilar in scientific and artistic inspiration or intuition; the reflection of scientific knowledge in poetry; the scientific nature of poetic thinking itself.[104] However, most important of all from my point of view is what lies behind all this and what may be formulated in the terminology of Bruno Latour: the concept that scientific creativity of the modern age is directed toward the creation of "hybrids" of human and nonhuman beings, as, for example, in microbiology, and at the same time toward concealing this hybridization and toward the "cleansing" of the natural and social in the eyes of all who may be outside the boundaries of the scientific community.[105] From Shrayer-Petrov's thinking it follows that not only anthropology, as in Latour, but literature as well can be an effective method of detecting and describing this dual process. It is crucial to understand the essence of these hybrids, because hidden in them is a key to saving life. That is how the author sees the computer ("electronic counting machine"), in the spirit of the cybernetic ideas of the 1960s: "Thought splashes out in columns of numbers and ornaments of equations. Only a minute—and hundreds of animals are be saved from senseless death. O machine! extend your hand! Take the animal that is flailing in fear and anguish. Heal, heal, heal our smaller brothers so as then to heal Man."[106] There is no doubt that these

---

103 David Shraer-Petrov. "Medicine and Literature: Syllabus," Boston College, Spring Semester, 2009.

104 See also the comparison of the poet and the biologist: "Khlebnikov worked on the word like a cytologist, manipulating the cell-letter (sound) and creating wondrous chimeras of words (organs) that give rise to poetry (organisms)" (Shraer-Petrov, *Vodka s pirozhnymi*, 59).

105 Bruno Latur [Bruno Latour], *Novogo vremeni ne bylo. Esse po simetrichnoi antropologii*, tr. D. Ia. Kalugin (St. Petersburg: Izdatel´stvo Evropeiskogo universiteta v Sankt-Peterburge, 2006), 64–98.

106 David Shraer-Petrov [D. Petrov], *Poeziia i nauka. Zametki i razmyshleniia* (Moscow: Znanie, 1974), 54.

words refer, as does all of Shrayer-Petrov's work, not only to the physical but also to the social and spiritual healing of man and society.

The play lays bare the three coordinates within which the medical theme evolves: the victory over death, the struggle with authority (or hegemony, obscurantism, fanatical orthodoxy), and overcoming victimhood. Like Doctor Herbert Levitin, the hero of the refusenik trilogy, Ed Tenner loses his wife and son, yet, like Job, he acquires a new family. And finally, an archetypal scene is built into the play of Abraham's representative sacrifice of Isaac. Tenner, a hero of science, like the hero of faith Abraham, fearlessly realizes his *credo*. In the contemporary scientific experiment, as in the ancient testing of faith, truth is revealed, which is guaranteed by the purity of heart of its witness and by the purity of the experiment. The scene of the experiment, being, in Gans's terms, a scene of an aborted gesture of violence (experiment-torture), a replacement of the victim, and a transformation of a gesture into representation, becomes the scene of culture-creation. A deep conviction lies at the foundation of both narrations: the same force that requires the conduct of a trial-experiment will lead the experimenter to a moral and cultural elevation, to a progress— all the more so that conceptually the experiment almost merges with healing, and healing merges with salvation and heroism,[107] "'healing' the World Ocean" merges with "restoring the lost links of civilization."[108] In one instance, this force is the Almighty and in another, Nature, but it is endowed in both instances with rationality, either given through revelation or through cognition. The irrationality of everyday human consciousness is thereby overcome—be it the idolatry surrounding Abraham, the crude ignorance of English farmers, the distrust of official science surrounding Tenner, or the powerfulness of the Empire and its ideologies surrounding Doctor Levitin and Evsey.

Such an overriding or transformation of the given (that is, the conflict as a given) into the possible (cognition of the real) can be interpreted, as has already been mentioned, in the terms of Gans's generative anthropology: it takes place with the aid of blocking the gesture of violence-appropriation and the transformation of the representation of the image itself of this unrealized gesture into a sign of the origination of a new language (a new culture, religion, science). A new language of science is thus born on the

---

107 Cf. also Shraer-Petrov, *Frantsuzskii kottedzh*, 239–240.
108 Ibid., 253.

scene of an unrealized gesture of violence in which the trial-torture of the object is recoded into the representation of knowledge about a fact of reality.[109] It is the recoding of the victim of reality into a sign of reality, which takes advantage of the status of irrefutable certainty and credibility, that embodies the deep nonconformism leading the philosophical anthropology of the work outside the bounds of the victimary paradigm. Understanding this dynamic is particularly essential for the first two books of the refusenik trilogy, in which at first glance violence remains unblocked and all the people close to Doctor Levitin become its victims. *Vaccine. Ed Tenner* can serve as the prism through which this novel, and more precisely the refusenik movement presented in it, may be seen as a grandiose scientific or, as in *Yudin's Redemption* and Isaac's binding, spiritual experiment. Doctor Levitin, in all his fearless defenselessness, becomes the symbol of protest against the rigidity of exile given as a curse, and thus he turns from a victim into a hero of the exodus and of return to the homeland as a quest of truth, similar to Tenner's experiment leading him to truth as to the homeland.

Summarizing the analysis of some of David Shrayer-Petrov's nonconformist and refusenik texts, it is essential to note, above all, the variety of their genres and styles. The author freely crosses any canonical boundary, as if striving to exhaust all possible languages in order to form his Jewish "fearless utterance," retaining his right to maximal allowable freedom under the given circumstances. Speaking of the content of this "fearless utterance," one can delineate two competing and interconnected lines: the realization of Jewish victimhood and the overcoming of Jewish victimhood. Both goals are achieved through an in-depth experimentation at the scene of the conflict, as in a laboratory, where the observer becomes the witness of the *aletheia*—disclosure—of the Jewish as the "real." In this laboratory, the symbolic plays the role of the experimental equipment and thus has a minimalist character. Seeing himself and his heroes as the research subjects or even the tortured ones, the author has the certainty that behind the visible senselessness of what is taking place there is nonetheless preserved a certain meaningfulness. This meaningfulness consists, as in science, in intelligible human observation and notation of traces left by nonhuman forces. It may be posited that this philosophy of David Shrayer-Petrov's literature was formed under the influence of his scientific thinking

---

109 For the conception of the trial-torture of the object, see Latour, *Novogo vremeni ne bylo*, 77–85.

and that these literary and scientific aspects—parallel universes—of his personality must be inseparably joined. This question, however, goes outside the bounds of this essay and will be examined, one must hope, in other works.[110]

Translated from the Russian by
Dobrochna Fire

---

110 See the essay by Leonid Katsis in this volume.

Works Cited

Austin, John L. *How to Do Things with Words*. Cambridge, MA: Harvard University Press, 1975.

Bakhtin, Mikhail. *Towards a Philosophy of the Act*. Translated by Vadim Liapunov. Edited by Vadim Liapunov and Michael Holquist. Austin: University of Texas Press, 1993.

Brodskii, Iosif. "Evreiskoe kladbishche okolo Leningrada." *Sintaksis* 3 (1960). http://rvb.ru/np/publication/05supp/syntaxis/3/brodsky.htm. Accessed October 14, 2016.

Derrida, Jacques. *Vokrug vavilonskikh bashen*. Translated by V. Lapitskii. St. Petersburg: Akademicheskii proekt, 2002.

Doherty, Brigid. "Text and Gestus in Brecht and Benjamin." *MLN* 115, no. 3 (2000): 442–481.

Dolinin, Viacheslav. "Nepodtsenzurnaia literatura i nepodtsenzurnaia pechat´ (Leningrad 1950–1980 godov)." In *Istoriia leningradskoi nepodtsenzurnoi literatury. 1950–1980 gody*, edited by B. Ivanov and B. Roginskii, 10–16. St. Petersburg: DEAN, 2000.

El´shevskaia, Galina. "Neskol´ko geniev v ogranichennom prostranstve: k istorii odnogo samooshchushcheniia." *Novoe literaturnoe obozrenie* 100 (2009). Accessed October 13, 2016. http:// magazines.russ.ru/nlo/2009/100/el32.html.

Foucault, Michel. *Fearless Speech*. Los Angeles: Semiotext(e), 2001.

Gabai, Il´ia. *Pis´ma iz zakliucheniia (1970–1972)*. Moscow: Novoe literaturnoe obozrenie, 2015.

Gans, Eric. *A New Way of Thinking: Generative Anthropology in Religion, Philosophy, Art*. Aurora: The Davies Group, 2011.

Ginzburg, Alexander. *Belaia kniga po delu A. Siniavskogo i Iu. Danielia*. Frankfurt am Main: Posev, 1967.

Girard, René. *Violence and the Sacred*. Translated by Patrick Gregory. Baltimore: Johns Hopkins University Press, 1979.

Gordin, Iakov. *Rytsar´ i smert´, ili Zhizn´ kak zamysel: O sud´be Iosifa Brodskogo*. Moscow: Vremia, 2010.

Habermas, Jürgen. *The Theory of Communicative Action*. Volume 1: *Reason and the Rationalization of Society*. Translated by Thomas McCarthy. Boston: Beacon, 1984.

Ivanov, Boris. "Evoliutsiia literaturnykh dvizhenii v piatidesiatye-vos´midesiatye gody." In *Istoriia leningradskoi nepodtsenzurnoi literatury.*

1950s–1980s, edited by B. Ivanov and B. Roginskii, 17–28. St. Petersburg: DEAN, 2000.

———. "Rid Grachev." In *Istoriia leningradskoi nepodtsenzurnoi literatury. 1950–1980*, edited by B. Ivanov and B. Roginskii, 49–59. St. Petersburg: DEAN, 2000.

Ivanov, Boris, and Boris Roginskii. "Ot sostavitelei." In *Istoriia leningradskoi nepodtsenzurnoi literatury. 1950s–1980s*, edited by B. Ivanov and B. Roginskii, 4-5. St. Petersburg: DEAN, 2000.

Ivanova, Natalia. "Skvoz´ nenavist´—k liubvi, skvoz´ liubov´—k ponimaniiu." In Fridrikh Gorenshtein, *Psalom*, 5-10. Moscow: Eksmo, 2001.

Katsis, Leonid. *Osip Mandel´shtam: Muskus iudeistva*. Moscow: Gesharim / Mosty kul´tury, 2002.

Katsman, Roman. "Boris Pasternak's Doctor Zhivago in the Eyes of the Israeli Writers and Intellectuals (A Minimal Foundation of Multilingual Jewish Philology)." In *Around the Point: Studies in Jewish Multilingual Literature*, edited by Hillel Weiss, Roman Katsman, and Ber Kotlerman, 643–686. Newcastle: Cambridge Scholars Publishing, 2014.

———. "Parallel´nye vselennye Davida Shraera-Petrova." *Wiener Slawistischer Almanac* 79 (2017): 255–279.

Krivulin, Viktor. "Peterburgskaia spiritual´naia lirika vchera i segodnia (k istorii neofitsial´noi poezii Leningrada 60–80-kh godov)." In *Istoriia leningradskoi nepodtsenzurnoi literatury. 1950s–1980s*, edited by B. Ivanov and B. Roginskii, 99–109. St. Petersburg: DEAN, 2000.

Lacan, Jacques. *R.S.I. Séminaire 1974–1975*. Translated into English by Cormac Gallagher. Paris: A.L.I., 2002.

Lahusen, Christian. *The Rhetoric of Moral Protest*. Berlin, New York: Walter de Gruyter, 1996.

Latour, Bruno [Bruno Latur]. *Novogo vremeni ne bylo. Esse po simetrichnoi antropologii*. Translated by D. Ia. Kalugin. St. Petersburg: Izdatel'stvo Evropeiskogo universiteta v Sankt-Peterburge, 2006.

Moss, Marcel. *Sotsial´nye funktsii sviashchennogo*. Translated by I. Utekhin. St. Petersburg: Evraziia, 2000.

Nikol´skaia, Tat'iana. "Krug Alekseia Khvostenko." In *Istoriia leningradskoi nepodtsenzurnoi literatury. 1950s–1980s*, edited by B. Ivanov and B. Roginskii, 92–98. St. Petersburg: DEAN, 2000.

Ozerov, Lev. "Ob avtore." In David Petrov [David Shrayer-Petrov], *Kholsty*. In *Pereklichka*, 116-117. Moscow: Molodaia gvardiia, 1967.

Rapoport, Alek. *Nonkonformizm ostaetsia*. St. Petersburg: DEAN, 2003.

Savitskii, Stanislav. *Andegraund: istoriia i mify leningradskoi neofitsial'noi literatury*. Moscow: Novoe literaturnoe obozrenie, 2002.

Shraer, Maksim D. [Maxim D. Shrayer], and David Shraer-Petrov [David Shrayer-Petrov]. *Genrikh Sapgir. Klassik avangarda*. St. Petersburg: Dmitrii Bulanin, 2004.

Shrayer, Maxim D, ed. *An Anthology of Jewish–Russian Literature: Two Centuries of Dual Identity in Poetry and Prose, 1801–2001*, 2 volumes. Armonk and London: M. E. Sharpe, 2007.

——— [Maksim D. Shraer]. "Posleslovie." In David Shraer-Petrov, *Okhota na ryzhego d'iavola*, 383–388. Moscow: Agraf, 2010.

———. *I Saw It: Ilya Selvinsky and the Legacy of Bearing Witness to the Shoah*. Boston: Academic Studies Press, 2013.

———. "A Purim 'Shpil' in Soviet Moscow." *Mosaic*, February 29, 2016. http://mosaicmagazine.com/observation/2016/02/a–purim–shpil–in–soviet–moscow/. Accessed June 22, 2016.

———, ed. *Voices of Jewish Russian Literature: An Anthology*. Boston: Academic Studies Press, 2018.

Shrayer-Petrov, David [David Petrov]. *Kholsty*. In *Pereklichka*, 116–160. Moscow: Molodaia gvardiia, 1967.

——— [D. Petrov]. *Poeziia i nauka. Zametki i razmyshleniia*. Moscow: Znanie, 1974.

——— [David Shraer]. *V otkaze (roman)*. In *V otkaze. Sbornik.*, 147–242. Jerusalem: Biblioteka-Aliia, 1986.

——— [David Shraer-Petrov]. *Druz'ia i teni. Roman s uchastiem avtora*. New York: Liberty, 1989.

——— [David Shraer-Petrov]. *Pesnia o golubom slone*. Holyoke, MA: New England Publishing Co, 1990.

——— [David Shraer-Petrov]. *Gerbert i Nelli*. Moscow: Poliform, 1992.

——— [David Shraer-Petrov]. "Iskusstvo kak izlom." *The New Review / Novyi zhurnal* 196 (1995): 245–256.

——— [David Shraer-Petrov]. *Propashchaia dusha*. Providence, RI: APKA Publishers, 1997.

——— [David Shraer-Petrov]. *Frantsuzskii kottedzh*. Providence, RI: APKA Publishers, 1999.

——— [David Shraer-Petrov]. *Eti strannye russkie evrei. Romany: Savelii Ronkin. Strannyi Dania Raev*. Moscow: Raduga, 2004.

——— [David Shraer-Petrov]. "Iskuplenie Iudina." *Mosty* 5 (2005): 5–61; 6 (2005): 21–116; 7 (2005): 11–88.

———. "Autumn in Yalta." In David Shrayer-Petrov, *Autumn in Yalta. A Novel and Three Stories*, edited, co-translated, and with an afterword by Maxim D. Shrayer. Library of Modern Jewish Literature. Syracuse: Syracuse University Press, 2006.

——— [David Shraer-Petrov]. *Vodka s pirozhnymi. Roman s pisateliami.* Edited by Maksim D. Shraer. St. Petersburg: Akademicheskii proekt, 2007.

——— [David Shraer-Petrov]. *Ed Tenner. Tragikomediia v dvukh deistviiakh i shesti kartinakh.* 2009. http://www.mromm.com/p/ ShrayerDavid–03.htm. Accessed October 14, 2016.

——— [David Shraer-Petrov]. *Vaksina. Ed Tenner*, edited by Maksim D. Shraer. Moscow: Tri Kvadrata, 2021 (forthcoming).

———. "Medicine and Literature: Syllabus." BI 226/SL 290: Boston College. Spring Semester. 2009.

——— [David Shraer-Petrov]. *Okhota na ryzhego d'iavola. Roman s mikrobiologami.* Moscow: Agraf, 2010.

——— [David Shraer-Petrov]. *Nevskie stikhi.* Edited by Maksim D. Shraer. St. Petersburg: Ostrovitianin, 2011.

———. *Istoriia moei vozliublennoi, ili Vintovaia lestnitsa.* Moscow: Vest-Konsalting, 2013.

——— [David Shraer-Petrov]. *Gerbert i Nelli.* Moscow: Knizhniki, 2014.

——— [David Shraer-Petrov]. "Belye ovtsy na zelenom sklone gory." In David Shrayer-Petrov, *Krugosvetnoe schast'e*, edited by Maksim D. Shraer, 5–21. Moscow: Knizhniki, 2016.

——— [David Shraer-Petrov]. "Mimozy na mogilu babushki." In David Shraer-Petrov, *Krugosvetnoe schast'e*, 180–195. Moscow: Knizhniki, 2016.

——— [David Shraer-Petrov]. "Obed s vozhdem." In David Shrayer-Petrov, *Krugosvetnoe schast'e*, 196–215. Moscow: Knizhniki, 2016.

——— [David Shraer-Petrov]. *Purimshpil'* [stsenarii]. Directed by Roman Spektor. Video recording. Moscow, 1987. https://www.youtube.com/watch?v=CxW_RNscgTQ. Accessed October 14, 2016.

———. *Doctor Levitin.* Edited and with notes by Maxim D. Shrayer, translated by Arna B. Bronstein, Aleksandra I. Fleszar, and Maxim D. Shrayer. Detroit: Wayne State University Press, 2018.

Smola, Klavdia. "O proze russko-evreiskogo pisatelia Davida Shraera-Petrova." In *Russkie evrei v Amerike*, vol. 15, 135–150. St. Petersburg: Giperion, 2017.

———, ed. "Nonkonformizm kak performativnoe zerkalo rezhima." *Novoe literaturnoe obozrenie* 155 (2019). https://www.nlobooks.ru/magazines/novoe_literaturnoe_obozrenie/155_nlo_1_2019/. Accessed August 15, 2020.

Vaiman, Naum. "Poeziia kak obraz zhizni: Il´ia Bokshtein." *Open Space*, October 12, 2010. http://os.colta.ru/literature/events/details/18665/. Accessed October 14, 2016.

Yurchak, Alexei. *Everything Was Forever, Until It Was No More: The Last Soviet Generation*. Princeton and Oxford: Princeton University Press, 2006.

David Shrayer-Petrov's Exilic Voices*

Maxim D. Shrayer

For many Anglo-American readers, the word "Yalta" in the title of "Autumn in Yalta" ("Osen′ v Ialte," 1992)—one of David Shrayer-Petrov's most celebrated works of fiction—also the title story of his second collection in English translation—readily suggests the Yalta Conference. In February 1945, the defeat of Nazism nearing, the "Big Three" allied leaders, Churchill, Roosevelt, and Stalin, gathered in Crimea to redraw the map of postwar Europe. Already in Yalta of 1945 both the Eastern Bloc and the Cold War—which surrounded David Shrayer-Petrov during the first three decades of his literary career—became a looming reality. But for many readers with Russian connections, Yalta is above all Chekhov's Yalta. Writing to his sister Mariya on 14 July 1888, Anton Chekhov (1860–1904) described his first impressions of Yalta, which never fully abandoned him:

> Looking at the shore from aboard the ship, I realized why it hasn't yet inspired a single poet or given a plot to any decent artist-belletrist. Doctors and wealthy ladies advertise it, and that's its main strength. Yalta is a cross of something European, resembling pictures of Nice, with something tacky and country-fairish [. . .].[1]

---

* Copyright © 2021 by Maxim D. Shrayer. An early version of several sections of this essay appeared as "Afterword: Voices of My Father's Exile," in David Shrayer-Petrov, *Autumn in Yalta: A Novel and Three Stories*, ed., co-tr., and with an afterword by Maxim D. Shrayer, Library of Modern Jewish Literature (Syracuse: Syracuse University Press, 2006), 205–234. Unless noted otherwise, all translations from the Russian are my literal translations—M.D.S.

Chekhov kept returning to Yalta, also spending time in other Crimean coastal resorts in its environs. To the poet and translator Aleksey N. Pleshcheev, Chekhov wrote these aphoristic lines on August 3, 1889: "In Yalta there are many young ladies, but not a single pretty one. Many littérateurs, but not one talented person. Much wine, but not a drop of decent one. The only good things here are the sea and the ambling horses."[2] In Yalta a number of women, including younger and older actresses, passed though the pages of Chekhov's life, some vanishing in the blank margins, others resurfacing in the black print of his stories and plays. Known for their mild and dry Mediterranean-like climate, Yalta and its environs (Simeiz, Alupka, Gurzuf) have been a traditional destination for those suffering from respiratory and lung ailments—something David Shrayer-Petrov notes in several of his shorter and longer fictions, including the novel *The French Cottage* (*Frantsuzskii kottedzh*, pub. 1999). Yalta's evanescent mix of "something European" and something of the Orient (which also distinguishes the atmosphere of many Mediterranean resorts) did inspire Russia's greatest master of shorter fiction, as it has also inspired other Russian authors, providing them with a vibrant setting and an evocative place of composition.

"I've been writing this story my whole life," states Shrayer-Petrov in the opening sentence of the story "The Bicycle Race" ("Velogonki"), which he finally penned down in November 2004 in Providence, Rhode Island. Set in the postwar Leningrad and featuring the autobiographical protagonist Daniil (Danya), this story is a satellite on one of the orbits of Shrayer-Petrov's novel *Strange Danya Rayev* (*Strannyi Dania Raev*, 2001), to which I will turn in the pages below. (See also Klavdia Smola's essay in part one of this volume.) For now, take note of the Yalta setting of the finale of "The Bicycle Race," in which Chekhovian motifs entertwine with autobiographical echoes:

> I got married and moved to Moscow. One time, Mira and I were vacationing in the Crimea. We were staying in Yalta. There we quickly rented an old shanty, dropped off our suitcases, and went to catch some evening sea air at the embankment, there where Chekhov's young lady with a white Pomeranian

---

1   "To M. P. Chekhova," July 14, 1988, in A. P. Chekhov, *Polnoe sobranie sochinenii i pisem v tridtsati tomakh* (Moscow: Nauka, 1974–1985), *Pis´ma*, vol. 2, 295–296.

2   "A. N. Pleshcheevu," August 3, 1889, in Chekhov, *Polnoe sobranie sochinenii i pisem v tridtsati tomakh*, *Pis´ma*, vol. 3, 233–234.

used to take her strolls. That same Anna Sergeevna, whom Gurov met in Yalta and fell in love with. In short, one day, about fifty to seventy years later, that is already in our time and, quite possibly, on the first evening when Mira and I set out for a stroll on the Yalta embankment, at one of the tables of an open-air café there sat Shvarts and Natasha. They were sipping wine and kissing.³

* * *

Anton Chekhov in Fiume and Genoa, Ivan Bunin in Grasse and Juan-les-Pins, Vladimir Nabokov in Cannes and Menton . . . Whenever I have the good fortune to find myself on the Riviera, voices of Russian writers reach me there, dispatching long trains of biographical and literary associations. Illness and love, war and exile have chased Russian writers and their fictional representatives to the Mediterranean and Crimean shores. In Yalta, Abbazia (Opatija), Ospedaletti, Nice, and other Rivierized resorts, the very air conjures up a sense of unrecognizable, foreboding familiarity that so nurtures a literary imagination . . .

In October–November 2004 I spent five weeks at an artists' and authors' colony in Bogliasco, a Ligurian fishing village east of Genoa. It was a different world: before the ascent of the Trump, before COVID-19, before the wave of protests against racism and the bacchanalia of monument-beheadings that set aflame the very country my parents and I had made our own after emigrating from the USSR in 1987. While hindsight corrects for what it fails to acknowledge, back in 2004 life our immigrant life in America seemed so much more seamless than it does today, in the summer of 2020, to the one writing these lines . . . Despite the charming distractions of a small Italian town still unspoiled by the development and wealth of Northern Italy, despite the view of Golfo Paradiso from my studio, I managed to work hard at Bogliasco. I was finishing a project of many years: an anthology of Jewish-Russian literature from the early 1800s to the late 1990s. I faced a deadline. And I lived for the first ten days in anticipation of my wife's visit.

Karen could only come for two weeks; practicing primary care doctors have a difficult time leaving their patients. She arrived during the fourth week in October, and the next day we walked from our villa down to the

---

3   Tr. Margaret Godwin-Jones, in David Shrayer-Petrov, *Dinner with Stalin and Other Stories*, ed., notes, and commentary by Maxim D. Shrayer, Library of Modern Jewish Literature (Syracuse: Syracuse University Press, 2014), 221.

pocketsize Bogliasco train station. On a misty late October morning a commuter train—graffiti, Roma women with infants, and truant Italian school children—zipped us through Genoa'a densely populated suburbs, each of them with a smattering of clothing boutiques, gelatterias, and tobacconist shops visible from the train. On the right, we saw mountains, smoke rising from the middle, olive-green parts of the slopes, and the barren tops with the occasional pyramidal tree. On the left, when we were not caught in the tunnel's throat, it was the sea, beige and salmon villas, toothy cliffs, umbrella pines. I remembered myself as a teenage refusenik reading about and imagining all the places a Soviet—especially a Jew—could only dream of visiting: the Italian Riviera, Venice, Capri. And when I saw—through the dusty windows of the train pulling into Stazione Brignole—the hilly horizon of Genoa studded with towers, domes, and palazzos, like a gilded chessboard of another life, I told my American-born wife that the odd moments of happiness come from knowing one's destiny.

The subject of a writer's destiny was still on my mind the next day, as Karen and I walked from Bogliasco to its fancier neighbor Nervi, Genoa's easternmost suburb. We descended Via Aurelia past an empty Pit Bar. Bearing to the left, we passed a small baroque church. We left behind a dilapidated grand villa sunk in a shady park. Turning left toward the water, we strolled past a former train station, now a private residence with an overgrown back garden, where overripe persimmons and a couple of bursting, forgotten aubergines hung from their burdened branches and vines. We passed a little harbor with a pebbly beach, reliquary boats, and a boarded-up café. Enthroned on a bench, two swarthy keepers of the vessels were so engrossed in solving the affairs of the world that they barely responded to our cautionary greetings. Karen and I climbed a sequence of steps, and there it was, the locally famed boardwalk, the *passagiata al mare*.

The *passagiata* stretches along the water for about a mile, ending in the old Nervi seaport. When we first walked there, the sun was setting over the sea to our left. Elegantly dressed Italians, many of them with lapdogs of various breeds, sizes, and shapes, sauntered back and forth or congregated around benches facing the water. Trains whooshed by, the mercurial intercity trains and the slower commuter ones. The *passagiata* was built on ledges of the cliffs and probably on remains of medieval fortresses and walls. Narrow steps with rope railings went down to pools of azure water, whose color, I have heard, owes its intense blueness to the pollution level of the Mediterranean. Using bread as bait, fishermen with long poles cast their lines from the flat platforms in the cliffs. Exhausted-looking Berber peddlers offered their wares, leather goods, and music CDs. Ancient pines hung over the water, the cliffs, and the villas. The cafés with pink tablecloths and woven chairs looked more Viennese than Genoese. On our right we left behind an underground passage to the Nervi train station and on our left—Hotel Ristorante Marinella, a lovers' escape right on the boardwalk. It was hot, despite the early evening hour in late October. Sheltered from the winds by the surrounding cliffs and the maritime pines, perched betwixt the sun and the cliff wall, the *passagiata* was a greenhouse by the sea, a northerner's overheated dream.

We were approaching the spot where the road curves sharply before it drops into the seaport. "Look, Sholem Aleichem," Karen exclaimed. And she pointed to a plaque immured in a concave cliff wall. Taking in so much else and happy to be reunited with my wife, I probably would not have noticed the plaque, had it not caught Karen's eye. Right above the plaque stood an elegant peach-color stucco building. I took out a notebook to write down the commemoration: "A ricordo dei lunghi anni di soggiorno a Nervi del brilliante scrittore in lingue Yiddish Shalom Rabinovitz in arte 'Sholem Alejchem' (1859–1916)." The plaque had only been put up in February 2003. As I stood in the middle of the boardwalk, a small crowd of onlookers gathered around me: two disheveled mothers with stray strollers and screaming babies, a group of older bejeweled ladies in fur coats and two elderly distinguished gentlemen wearing fine-tailored sport coats and cravats, and also a dreamy young woman with an anxious Pomeranian on a long leash. I copied the plaque slowly, trying not to introduce any errors in the Italian, and I had a chance to see that the onlookers were equally bemused by the plaque itself, which they clearly had not noticed before, and by the peculiar foreigner studiously writing down what was written on the plaque. In "memory of the long years" that a "brilliant writer in the Yiddish language" spent . . . in Nervi?

It did not take me long to discover that Nervi had been an important coordinate in the life of Sholem Aleichem, just as the Ligurian coast, where I was a lucky resident during the autumn of 2004, has been for many other writers who came from Russia. In the autumn of 1908, after being diagnosed with pulmonary TB, Sholem Aleichem moved to Italy with his wife Olga and their daughters. At the time, because of its climate and location, Nervi was considered an ideal place for pulmonary patients to winter. From 1908 until 1913, when doctors pronounced Sholem Aleichem "recovered," he would spend the colder months in Nervi, dividing the rest of the year between the "magic" mountains of Switzerland and spas of Germany's Black Forest.

Genoa's Jewish community was small and Sephardic. During the Nervi months Sholem Aleichem lived in isolation from his native Yiddish-speaking milieu. The Italians identified Sholem Aleichem and his family as "Russians." A Jew in Russia and a Russian abroad, despite the remoteness of home, Sholem Aleichem worked prolifically during his European exile. Those were the years of his growing fame and international reputation, especially in Russian translation and among Russia's mainstream readers and writers. The "good years" lasted until the outbreak of World War I and Sholem Aleichem's move to America, where he died in 1916.

Although Sholem Aleichem was fond of Nervi and the Ligurian vistas outside his windows, he did not take well to the contrast of warm sunny days and cold windy nights. In *My Father, Sholom Aleichem* (1968), Marie Waife-Goldberg recalled her father's first winter in Nervi:

> The nights in Nervi were agonizing, for he could not sleep for coughing. [. . .] On a small table near his bed lay the book which was placed there each evening and a chair for the watcher to sit down and read to him until he fell asleep. The book was usually a collection of short stories by my father's favorite author, Chekhov, in the original Russian.[4]

A "Yiddish Chekhov," they called him at home, and Sholem Aleichem was not unaware of this comparison. He wrote perfect literary Russian and like his junior contemporaries such as David Aizman (1869–1922) or Semyon Yushkevich (1868–1927), Sholem Aleichem might have become an important Jewish author in the Russian language if he had not chosen—had not been destined—to be a great Yiddish writer. Sholem Aleichem imbued his works with the best contributions of Russian writers, past and present, especially Gogol and Chekhov. By the time Sholem Aleichem had gained a broad Russian-language audience in Russia, Anton Chekhov, a peer in years, was gone. He died at a German spa town, of the same lung ailment that later brought Sholem Aleichem to Italy . . .

I kept pondering the fact that we were living in such physical proximity to the place where Sholem Aleichem spent a total of several years. Karen went back to Boston, and I stayed for two more weeks at Bogliasco.

---

4   Marie Waife-Goldberg, *My Father, Sholom Aleichem* (New York: Simon and Schuster, 1968), 247.

I focused on the editing and co-translating of *Autumn in Yalta: A Novel and Three Stories*, the second book of David Shrayer-Petrov's works that I have helped to English. One of my tasks was to check the translated texts against the author's Russian originals. A product of exile and a casualty of translingualism, I could not help thinking that the Sholem Aleichem plaque, which my wife had discovered in Nervi, was a fatidic clue. The clue applied to my own life as David Shrayer-Petrov's son and translator, to Jewish-Russian writers' dialogue with Chekhov, and to the tales of exile that were gaining their final English-language contours under my laptop-tapping fingers.

* * *

A dual name, David Shrayer-Petrov (Давид Шраер-Петров), betokens the writer's literary career. Born in 1936 in Leningrad (St. Petersburg), he descends, on his father's side, from Podolian millers, and from Lithuanian rabbis on his mother's side. As young people, both of Shrayer-Petrov's parents (father an engineer, mother a chemist) made the transition, tantamount to immigration, from the former Pale of Settlement to Leningrad in the 1920s. Growing up, Shrayer-Petrov heard Yiddish in the home of his paternal grandparents. Evacuated from Leningrad as the Nazi siege closed in, he spent three years in a remote Russian village in the Urals, over a thousand miles away from Moscow and Leningrad and from the frontlines (the experience permeates the short novel *Strange Danya Rayev*). A Jewish youth coming of age in postwar Leningrad, he formulated the questions, which his writings probe to this day: *Do Jews belong in Russia? Is assimilation (im)possible?*

Starting medical school in 1953, the year of the antisemitic "doctors' plot," whose paranoid mechanics were interrupted by Stalin's death, Shrayer-Petrov entered the literary scene as a poet and translator in the middle-to-late 1950s, during Khrushchev's Thaw. In 1958, on the advice of the influential Jewish-Russian poet Boris Slutsky (1919–1986), he adopted the penname "David Petrov," the last name derived from his father's Russianized first name Pyotr (Peysakh).[5] This assimilatory gesture hardly facilitated the publication Shrayer-Petrov's poetry in the Soviet Union; his first poetry collection was

---

5   About this, see David Shraer-Petrov, "Ierusalimskii kazak. Slutskii," in David Shraer-Petrov, *Vodka s pirozhnymi. Roman s pisateliami*, ed. Maksim D. Shraer (St. Petersburg: Akademicheskii proekt, 2007), 232.

derailed in 1964 in Leningrad, following the trial of the poet Joseph Brodsky, with whom Shrayer-Petrov was friendly at the time. During his Soviet years he made a name for himself mainly as a literary translator, especially from the Lithuanian and the South-Slavic languages.

After graduating from Leningrad's Pavlov Medical School in 1959, Dr. Shrayer-Petrov served as a military physician in Belarus. Two years after his marriage in 1962 to the phililogist and translator Emilia Shrayer (neé Polyak, born 1940), he completed a PhD at the Leningrad Institute of tuberculosis (defended in 1966). His PhD (candidate's) dissertation studied the impact of staphylococcal infections on the occurrence of TB in white mice, and its echoes can be heard in the story "Autumn in Yalta," in the medical experiments of its protagonist Doctor Samoylovich, as well as in the earlier story "Mimosas for My Grandmother's Grave" ("Mimozy na mogilu babushki," 1984; pub. 1997). In 1964 Shrayer-Petrov moved to his wife's native Moscow, where their son Maxim was born in 1967. In 1967–1978 Shrayer-Petrov worked as a medical scientist at the Gamaleya Research Institute of Epidemiology and Microbiology in Moscow. His research focused on the treatment of mixed infections, on bacteriophages, and, after immigration to the United States, on oncological immunology. As a medical researcher, he published almost one hundred articles as well as the monograph *Staphylococcal Disease in the USSR* (1989).

From his earliest verses, and to some extent from his earliest attemps at fiction (of which little survives[6]), Shrayer-Petrov explored the dual nature of Jewish identity in diaspora. Although he managed to publish a collection of poems (*Canvasses*, 1967) and two books of essays in the 1970s, most of his writings were too controversial for Soviet officialdom to allow their publication. His occasional flights into prescribed Soviet subjects (such as space exploration or the construction of the Baikal-Amur railroad), in poetry, essays, and song lyrics, did not earn him the trust of the regime. Despite recommendations by such prominent writers as Viktor Shklovsky, Lev Ozerov and Andrei Voznesensky, Shrayer-Petrov only became a member of the Union of Soviet Writers in 1976, after a protracted battle.[7] The manuscript of what would have been his second poetry collection,

---

6   A draft of an unpublished story about the shock of antisemitism as experienced by a young Jewish man, titled "Solntse upalo v shakhtu" ("The Sun Fell into the Mineshaft," 1960s), has survived in the papers of David Shrayer-Petrov.

7   See David Shrayer-Petrov's file at the Union of Soviet Writers, Russian State Archive for Literature and the Arts (RGALI), f. 631, op. 41, d. 404.

Winter Ship (*Zimnii korabl'*),[8] moved up the frozen straits of "Soviet Writer" publishing house with discouraging slowness and was finally scheduled to appear in 1979-1980. It was never published.

By the early 1970s the relations between Jews and Gentiles became a principal concern for Shrayer-Petrov's as his writings turned increasingly nonconformist. (See Roman Katsman's essay in this volume.) In 1978, a scandal erupted following a spring Poetry Festival in Vilnius, Lithuania, where he recited a poem of protest, "My Slavic Soul" ("Moia slavianskaia dusha," 1975). In the poem, the poet's "Slavic" soul abandons his "Jewish" body to hide in a hayloft: "I'll chase her: Wait! What shall I do alone amid this grove of birches/ In my perennial, banal, so typically Jewish wrapping."[9] Immediately after Shrayer-Petrov's return from Lithuania to Moscow, officials of the Union of Soviet Writers threatened him with blacklisting. Ostracism for having transgressed the unspoken taboo on the treatment of Jewish subjects weaned the writer from his last illusions, pushing him to emigrate. In the summer of 2019, Shrayer-Petrov commented on his conflict with the regime and decision to emigrate:

> And then I understood: that's it, I cannot do it. They are tempting me, like Satan tempted Adam, that I will be a successful poet-translator if I concoct a few conformist poems about my . . . how shall I put it . . . my relationship with Russia. And instead I began to write about Jewish themes . . . I also told them I would now sign my work "Shrayer-Petrov," that's my literary name, and I won't have it otherwise. Then they started putting my readings on hold, stopped commissioning translations . . . Everything started coming to a halt. My poetry collection . . . [the book of] stories for young readers. I came to a dead end and decided to leave. And so we applied for exit visas.

In January 1979, Shrayer-Petrov and his family submitted the paperwork to the OVIR (Section of Visas and Registrations). Their application for exit visas was denied and they joined tens of thousands of other refuseniks—Jews and their families who were de facto disenfranchised and ghettoized. Their academic careers were mutilated. Dr. Shrayer-Petrov's innovative research

---

8   See the file on Shrayer-Petrov's *Zimnii korabl'* in the papers of the publishing house Sovetskii pisatel' ("Soviet Writer") at the Russian State Archive for Literature and the Arts, f. 1234, op. 23, d. 1436.
9   See David Shrayer-Petrov, "My Slavic Soul," tr. Maxim D. Shraer, in *Voices of Jewish-Russian Literature: An Anthology*, ed. Maxim D. Shrayer (Boston: Academic Studies Press, 2018), 831.

on staphylococcal infections, which had helped save peoples' lives, no longer mattered to the Soviet state. Following Shrayer-Petrov's expulsion from the Union of Soviet Writers, galleys of three of his forthcoming books were broken (he had already corrected the proofs of one of them and seen the the commissioned illustrations). The three books never appeared. The writer was banned from publishing in the Soviet Union. In 1979-80, while driving an illegal cab at night and working at an emergency room lab, he conceived of a panoramic novel about the destinies of Jewish refuseniks, eventually to become a trilogy of novels about the exodus of Soviet Jews and the mutilated destinies of refuseniks. The protagonist, Doctor Herbert Levitin, is a Moscow professor of medicine. His Jewishness evolves in the course of the novel from a prohibitive ethnic garb to a historical and spiritual mission. Levitin is married to Tatyana Levitina (née Pivovarova), a Russian woman of peasant stock from the Pskov Province. In documenting with anatomical precision the mutually unbreachable contradictions of a mixed Jewish-Russian marriage, Shrayer-Petrov also treats the story of Doctor Levitin as an allegory of Jewish-Russian history. *Doctor Levitin*, part one of the refusenik saga, ends with killing of the Letivins' son, Anatoly, in Afghanistan, Tatyana's death of grief, and Doctor Levitin's phantasmogoric revenge. (On Jewish revenge, see Joshua Rubenstein's essay in this volume.) Shrayer-Petrov completed the composition of *Doctor Levitin* in the autumn of 1980, an author-doctor stuck in refusenik's limbo, living out the destinies of his own fictional characters. Over the next three years he completed the second novel about refuseniks. In part two of Shrayer-Petrov's trilogy, a novel in its own right titled *Cursed Be You… Just Don't Die*, refusenik activists, Palestinian drug lords, and Soviet chess masters share the stage as Doctor Levitin himself finds transcendent love in his new beloved Nelly. In 1984 the manuscript of part one and part two was clandestinely photographed, and the negatives were smuggled out of the USSR. Shrayer-Petrov's persecution by the KGB intensified in 1985, when the publication of part one was announced in Israel. In 1986 an abridged text appeared in Jerusalem under the title *V otkaze* (*Being a Refusenik*), in a volume of the same title, comprised of writings by and about refuseniks and published by Biblioteka-Aliia ("*Aliyah* Library"). The earliest critical references to Shrayer-Petrov's refusenik trilogy go back to the late 1980s and early 1990s, when it was still known under the provisional title, *Being a Refusenik* or *Being Refused*.[10]

---

10 In 1991, as the USSR was heading towards dissolution, Shrayer-Petrov, already an immigrant living in the United States, submitted part one (*Doctor Levitin*) and part two (*Cursed Be You… Just Don't Die*) for publication in Moscow. They were published

After Shrayer-Petrov and his family requested permission to emigrate, the KGB unleashed persecutory measures against them, ranging from physical harassment to a smear campaign in the press. The persecution intensified in 1985. In Soviet newspapers Shrayer-Petrov was labeled a "Zionist" author and accused of "infecting" Jews with a "hostile" ideology. A real threat of being charged with anti-Soviet activity and imprisoned hung over his head; for parts of the autumn of 1985 he was evading arrest. The mounting pressures of being hunted by the Soviet secret police brought on a heart attack and subsequent hospitalization. Plainclothes KGB thugs waited for Shrayer-Petrov outside the hospital ward.

A refusenik's isolation, coupled with the absurdity of being a Jewish writer who is both silenced by and shackled to Russia, made Shrayer-Petrov's last Soviet decade prolific in spite of persecution. "You see, all Soviet poets, even the most talented ones, always played this game, in which on their desk a cup of poison stood side by side with the sweet nectar of official court poetry," Shrayer-Petrov said in an interview in July 2019. "Which is why there were cases when I wrote weak and not very sincere poems. What is the point of poetry, of lyrical poetry, as I see it? It is in being absolutely honest with oneself. And so if you no longer look back and take cues... And as a refusenik I no longer looked back when I wrote. I only took cues from myself, ... I no longer cared."[11] In 1979–1987 he wrote three novels, several plays, a memoir, and many stories and verses. In a long interiew, occasioned by the publication of *Dinner with Stalin and Other Stories* and conducted

---

in the spring of 1992—the first post-Soviet spring—under the same cover, in a single volume titled *Herbert and Nelly*—Herbert after the protagonist, Herbert Levitin, Nelly after Nelly Shamova, the heroine of part two. In 2006 Shrayer-Petrov embarked on the third novel, in which Doctor Levitin finally emigrates from the USSR, spends the transit months in Austria and Italy, and then settles in the Boston area. An early version of part three, the final part of his trilogy, was published in 2009 under the title *The Third Life* (*Tret′ia zhizn′*) and subsequently revised as *The Third Life of Doctor Levitin* (*Tret′ia zhizn′ doktora Levitina*, currently being prepared for publication). As Shrayer-Petrov worked on *The Third Life*, he also revised the text of the first two parts, and it subsequently appeared in two different editions, first in 2009 in St. Petersburg, then in 2014 in Moscow. The 2014 Moscow edition came out in the series "Prose of Jewish Life," an imprint of Knizhniki, the world's leading publisher of Jewish books in the Russian language.

11 Maxim D. Shrayer, "A Russian Typewriter Longs for Her Master: A portrait of my father, the refusenik writer and medical scientist David Shrayer-Petrov, as a New England poet, on his 84th Birthday," *Tablet Magazine*, January 28, 2020, https://www.tabletmag.com/sections/arts-letters/articles/maxim-shrayer-david-shrayer, accessed January 29, 2020.

in 2014 (it is reprinted in this volume), Shrayer-Petrov commented on becoming a self-consious writer of short fiction:

> I hadn't fully fathomed how to write short stories until I became a Jewish refusenik living like a literary hermit, in total isolation from the official Soviet culture. And already as a writer-refusenik I had suddenly understood that there is a magic trick, a device of fiction-making, which one needs to realize in order to compose a short story—to make it up as opposed to merely copying it from so-called real life. This magic fictional quality—that inimitable vibration of feeling—is something Chekhov's stories exhibit in the fullest sense.[12]

Chekhov's double tuning fork—that of a writer-doctor—would stand on Shrayer-Petrov desk throughout the refusenik years. In *Doctor Levitin*, the protagonist Herbert Anatolyevich says this to his wife Tatyana, punctuating the change he has been experiencing since they applied for exit visas: "You're right, Tanyusha. Our family's life has moved on into a new, still unchartered, difficult phase. A period of self-reflection has begun, when we shouldn't be reflecting, just acting. Time's running out. I'm turning into Chekhov's character, Ionych, the old doctor."[13] The day Doctor Levitin and his family received a "refusal" from the Section of Visas, he followed his usual route around the old center of Moscow:

> Ahead lay the usual path, which he measured out daily with his lean legs. He ran. Others may have taken his running for fast jogging, but his was actually an unhurried running along Tsvetnoy Boulevard toward Trubnaya Square, which rolled down and crossed over the circles of other boulevards. Then Herbert Anatolyevich would reach Pushkin Square. The area in front of "Russia" cinema house would still be empty of people. Without stopping he perused the film posters and then turned onto Chekhov Street, heading toward the city's main artery, Garden Ring, humming with early morning traffic. And then he turned back home.[14]

From 1944 until 1993, Chekhov Street (Ulitsa Chekhova) was the name of Malaya Dmitrovka in the center of Moscow, a street running from Pushkin

---

12 Maxim D. Shrayer and David Shrayer-Petrov, "A Fictional Model of the Former USSR: Part 1 of a 3Part Conversation," Jewish Book Council, https://www.jewishbookcouncil.org/pb-daily/a-fictional-model-of-the-former-ussr-part-1-of-a-3-part-conversation, accessed June 20, 2020.
13 David Shrayer-Petrov, *Doctor Levitin*, ed. and with notes by Maxim D. Shrayer, tr. Arna B. Bronstein, Aleksandra I. Fleszar, and Maxim D. Shrayer (Detroit: Wayne State University Press, 2018), 140.
14 Ibid., 186.

Square to the Garden Ring. Shrayer-Petrov's short stories written in 1985–1987 on the brink of emigration include "Rusty" ("Ryzhukha"), a dog story gently nodding to Chekhov's "Kashtanka" (1887). Also notable for it Chekhovian oscillations is "Apple Cider Vinegar" ("Iablochnyi uksus"), originally composed in Moscow and revised already in America. In this story about a woman's unexplained infertility, the female protagonist, Sashenka, gets briefly involved with one Doctor Pekhov:

> Sashenka began to frequent the Ksyondzov's evening gatherings. Lusya, a kind and sociable person who liked to do nice things in that simple, ingenious Russian fashion, began to introduce Sashenka to Vasya's friends. There was a succession of three or four of them. The sculptor Abkin was a burly lover of fun and drink, with curly black hair; Sashenka spent about two months with him. Alik was a designer at the auto works, scrawny, sinewy, and silent; she went away with him for a vacation on Lake Seliger. Then there was Droctor Pekhov from the Artists' Fund Clinic, whom we all, of course, called "Doctor Chekhov"; Doctor Pekhov announced that he was going out of town on business, but what he really did was hide out at Sashenka's apartment for the whole week. And, finally, there was Kurt Schneider, a graphic artist from East Germany who came to Moscow to draw churches and immediately fell in love with Sashenka Brodsky.[15]

Chekhov would continue to inspire Shrayer-Petrov after emigration—not so much through literary style as such, but as the highest standard of poetic perfection of prose. (Robert Louis Jackson, America's great interpreter of Chekhov, taught his students that Chekhov ought to be read as poetry, where "every word, every comma counts."[16]) For example, in the story "Behind the Zoo Fence" ("Za ogradoi zooparka," 1987–2007), dedicated to the writer's wife, Emilia (Mila) Shrayer, Shrayer-Petrov revisited the middle 1960s—the time when he, a young writer and medical scientist, was getting intimately familiar with Moscow. Even though telltale signs indicate that the protagonist, Dr. Boris Erastovich Garin, is Jewish, Shrayer-Petrov has given him a name loaded with rich Russian cultural baggage. The writer Nikolai Garin-Mikhailovsky (1852–1906) is remembered for his popular autobiographical tetralogy, *Tyoma's Childhood, Pupils, University Students,*

---

15 David Shrayer-Petrov, *Jonah and Sarah: Jewish Stories of Russia and America*, ed. Maxim D. Shrayer, Library of Modern Jewish Literature (Syracuse: Syracuse University Press, 2003), 6–7.
16 A personal recollection from having taken R. L. Jackson's Chekhov seminar at Yale University in the Fall of 1991.

and *Engineers* (*Detstvo Temy, Gimnazisty, Studenty, Inzhenery*). Erast Garin (1902–1980) was a well-known Soviet stage and screen actor, director and screenwriter. As a literary character, Garin appears in Aleksey Tolstoy's science-fiction novel *The Hyperboloid of Engineer Garin* (*Giperboloid inzhenera Garina*, 1927). Last but not least, the spirit of Anton Chekhov hovers over the story, and Shrayer-Petrov tips his hat off to the great doctor-author in a number of ways. To name just four: the last name of Doctor Garin is a perfect anagram of Doctor Ragin, the protagonist of "Ward 6" (1892), arguably Chekhov's most famous short story about medicine, madness, and society, while Doctor Garin's patient, Natasha Altman, is placed in Ward 7 at the Filatov Children's Hospital (where the author himself worked after moving to Moscow in 1964); the lucky number hints at Natasha's miraculous recovery. Furthermore, the last name of the Garins' friend, the Gurovs, is the same as that of Gurov, the protagonist of "Lady with a Lapdog" (1899). Finally, Doctor Garin and his family live on Chekhov Street—yet another instance of Shrayer-Petrov's Chekhovian "signs and symbols."

The permission to emigrate finally came in April 1987 as the sluices of Jewish emigration were starting to reopen. After a forced long goodbye, the leave-taking was short. Their whole lives packed in five suitcases and two typewriters, the writer and his family left the Soviet Union on June 7, 1987. After a summer in Austria and Italy, they arrived in the United States on August 26, 1987. Providence, Rhode Island, the petite capital of the smallest American state, became Shrayer-Petrov's new home. Both the writer and his wife were professionally affiliated with Brown University. Emigration and unturbulent life in New England accorded Shrayer-Petrov both distance from and perspective on his Soviet—Russian and Jewish—past. His arrival in the West brought forth new publications, including ten novels and about fifty shorter fictions. For the first twenty of his nearly thirty-five American immigrant years Shrayer-Petrov divided his time between writing and doing cancer research (experimental therapy). In many of his works, both pre- and post-emigration David Shrayer-Petrov's medical interests overlap with those of a fictionist.

* * *

Before turning to the subject of Shrayer-Petrov's exilic dialogue with Chekhov, both a doctor and a belletrist, and also with the magisterial Russian-American writer Vladimir Nabokov (1899–1977), I would like to take a step back and revisit the years of World War II, Shrayer-Petrov's formative years. It was then the future writer experienced the unspoiled dialectal richness of the Russian language as the peasants in the Urals still spoke it. Shrayer-Petrov depicted the naissance of a dual, Jewish-Russian identity, in *Strange Danya Rayev*. Set in Stalinist Russia in the late 1930s–1940s, the novel focuses on the wartime childhood experiences of Danya (Daniil) Rayev, its Jewish-Russian protagonist and storyteller. Danya and his mother Stella are evacuated from the besieged Leningrad to Siva, a village in the Ural Mountains. In Siva, far away from the war front and the life he knew as a small child, Danya nearly forgets about his otherness, assimilating after a Russian peasant fashion. Returning to the destroyed city of Leningrad in 1944, Danya confronts the challenges of his dual identity while also learning that his father, a decorated naval officer, has a "field wife" and started a new family. Told in a confessional voice, the novel ends as its young protagonist regains the bitter knowledge of antisemitism while celebrating the Soviet victory over Nazism on the ruins of his native city and family.

The short story "Autumn in Yalta" may be considered a satellite on one of the orbits of the novel *Strange Danya Rayev*. Danya Rayev and Samoylovich of "Autumn in Yalta" are in essence the same Jewish boy from the author's native city of Leningrad or, to put it differently, Samoylovich is a projection of Danya Rayev onto the axis of postwar Jewish-Soviet history.

By reading *Strange Danya Rayev* and "Autumn in Yalta" in succession (or, in English, under the same cover), one best experiences the exilic transposition of the theme of Jewish-Russian identity in both texts. Danya spends the war years away from Leningrad and the Nazi siege, which scythed almost a million lives. While the episode with the police officer Dodonov lashing out at the mysterious Karaite Babukh offers an early warning, Danya first consciously suffers from visceral, still incomprehensible antisemitism, soon after his return home in 1944. The languid antisemitism of an adult (the woman-baker at the bread factory) shocks and literally nauseates him; the furtive, malicious baiting of a peer (his classmate Mincha) hardens Danya, transforming him into a Jewish fighter. Recall the episode in which the adult Samoylovich, himself a survivor of the siege of Leningrad, remembers his first day in elementary school, when a group of other hungry children surrounds him, asking for food. Nowhere in the story does Shrayer-Petrov identify his protagonist as "Jewish"—although the reader notes his last name and such cultural markers as the occasional Yiddish expression, which his grandmother would drop, *sotto voce*, behind the narrative stage, or the Jewish chopped herring, *farhsmak*, which she prepares for Samoylovich. I brought up Samoylovich's memories of his first day of school because in this brief recollection, occurring in a moment of his desperate reckoning with the past, the reader faces the habitual antisemitism of a group of Russian, non-Jewish children who stereotypically believe that their Jewish classmate has more food than they do, that his family (Samoylovich has lost both parents in the war) is richer, more fortunate, better-off than theirs. The adult Samoylovich is only a partial extension of Danya Rayev. Samoylovich never learns to fight back, to be tough, to suspect malice in others. (Or, as Shrayer-Petrov explained in December 2004, responding to my e-mail query, "Samoylovich becomes Danya—the fighter—too late.") A Jewish doctor in post-Stalinist Soviet Union, one who has lived as a young man through the darkest years for Soviet Jewry, Samoylovich continues to cure those around him with love, with his "soul," and regardless of their origins. A writer-doctor, Shrayer-Petrov creates a privileged protagonist in Doctor Samoylovich. Having sacrificed ten years of freedom for his beloved, the actress Polechka who is not Jewish, Samoylovich returns to Moscow from a prison camp in Siberia, seeking—or not seeking—to settle scores with his ruptured past. Judging by the reference to the re-renaming of Leningrad, which occurred in 1991, the story ends during the liminal years 1991-1992. Formerly a doctor and a medical researcher, the Soviet Jew Samoylovich has been reduced to an underground man of sorts, a nighttime driver of an illegal cab. Yet the flourishing of Samoylovich's love for Polechka dates to the Leningrad of the late 1960s, when he was still a successful academic, and she a "promising" young actress and a TB patient. The story culminates in the 1970s, on the location of a TB sanatorium in the resort of Simeiz, south of Yalta. Which brings us back to the tubercular Doctor Chekhov, his Yalta, and the biographical and historical background behind the composition of "Autumn in Yalta."

* * *

A deterioration of Chekhov's health in 1897 led to his permanent move to Yalta, where he was based during the last five years of his life. In Yalta in 1899-1904, Chekhov wrote *Three Sisters* and *The Cherry Orchard*, as well as a number of his greatest stories, among them "Lady with a Lapdog." In October 1898 Chekhov started building a house in a suburb of Yalta. One of Doctor Chekhov's contributions was his well-publicized 1899 appeal to the public to donate funds for the construction of a charity TB sanatorium in Yalta. Lung ailments and stories where vectors of desire extend from doctors to their TB patients are a notable subject of Chekhov's fiction and drama, from the early "Belated Flowers" (1882) with its Doctor Toporkov and the dying Princess Priklonskaya to *Ivanov* (1887) with the "kikess" (*zhidovka*) Anna Petrovna, born Sara Abramson, and the compassionate if judgmental Doctor Lvov, who carries something of the Tolstoyan mantle.

At the turn of the century, Chekhov's presence had energized Yalta's provincial cultural life. The Moscow Art Theater gave performances in Yalta in April 1900. Some of Russia's best writers walking in Chekhov's footsteps visited him in Yalta: Maxim Gorky, Ivan Bunin, Aleksandr Kuprin. And so did Olga Knipper-Chekhova, an actress at the Moscow Arts Theater, both before and after she and Chekhov were married in 1901. Sometimes feeling like an exile in Yalta, Chekhov longed to see Knipper-Chekhova and pined after Moscow and Central Russia. Yalta's cold, stormy winter weather was hardly beneficial for Chekhov's TB. Chekhov left Yalta in May 1904, never to see it again.

Incidentally in Yalta, perhaps more so than elsewhere, Chekhov socialized with a number of Jewish (and Karaite) acquaintances, including Jewish doctors. In the autumn of 1898 Chekhov stayed in Yalta at the dacha of Dr. Isaak Altshuller. Another colorful Jewish acquaintance was Isaak Sinani, owner of a local book and tobacco shop, which was a meeting place of Yalta's tubercular exiles. In the 1880s–1900s Chekhov observed and recorded the thirst with which the acculturated Jews consumed Russian literature. In "My Life" (1896) Chekhov wrote about a southern provincial town where "only Jewish adolescents frequented the local . . . libraries." In "Ionych" (1898) Chekhov stressed again that "the people in S. read very little, and at the local library they said that if it hadn't been for unmarried ladies and young Jews, one might as well close the library. . . ." The Jewish question certainly preoccupied the creator of *Ivanov*, "Mire" (1886), "Steppe" (1888), and "Rothschild's Fiddle" (1894), and during his final years in Yalta Chekhov was likely to hear from his acquaintances among the Jewish-Russian intelligentsia about the birth of Zionism. Be it as it may, as Chekhov's life and art demonstrate, his personal and literary relationship with Jewishness and the Jewish question was never simple or unambiguous.

Like a watermark, Chekhov's Yalta bleeds through the pages of several works of fiction by Shrayer-Petrov. Reading "Autumn in Yalta," one comes across various telltale signs of its author's dialogue with Chekhov's masterpiece "Lady with a Lapdog." In "Lady with a Lapdog," Anna and Gurov, the lovers, first meet in autumnal Yalta. In a meaningful structural reversal of Chekhov's narrative, the last amorous meeting of Polechka and Samoylovich, which leads to Samoylovich's "crime," occurs during the so-called *barkhatnyi sezon* ("velvet season") in the Crimean resort. This fateful meeting brings the story to the brink of a Chekhovian adultery narrative: just as Anna in Yalta, Polechka (as she is quick to inform Samoylovich) is a "married lady." Indicators of this literary dialogue—occurring almost a century later and across the Atlantic—are numerous in Shrayer-Petrov's story. Consider, for instance, the scene in a Yalta café where Polechka asks if she is "contagious," and Samoylovich replies, in a seemingly non-sequitur fashion, "I love you, Polechka." The scene recalls both Gurov and Anna's first meeting in a café on the Yalta embankment and a following episode with the arrival of a steamship and a festive crowd of vacationers, where in a bout of hyperrealism Chekhov planted more generals than one expects to see on one particular day on a waterfront in one Riviera resort. Even Sazonova (note the Sazonova-Casanova translingual anagram), the name of the fictitious, ageless stage diva in "Autumn in Yalta," hints at a real-life contemporary of Chekhov, the writer Sofia Smirnova-Sazonova (1852–1921), who recorded in her diary for July 1899: "I saw Chekhov on the promenade. He sits [like an orphan] on a little bench."[17]

"Autumn in Yalta" might not have become an exilic—and a Russian-American—story if besides Chekhov's Yalta it had not also dialogued with Nabokov's Fi(Y)alta. The epigraph comes from "Spring in Fialta" ("Vesna v Fial′te," 1936), Nabokov's fabled tale of love and exile: "Every time I had met her during the fifteen years of our—well, I fail to find the precise term for our kind of relationship—she had not seemed to recognize me at once...."[18] Through the epigraph, Shrayer-Petrov signals not only his debt to Nabokov, but also his awareness that Chekhov's "Lady with a Lapdog" had served as a major point of departure for Nabokov's story. Composed in Berlin in 1936 and published the same year in Paris, "Spring in Fialta" belonged—by

---

17 Quoted in Donald Rayfield, *Chekhov: A Life* (Evanston: Northwestern University Press, 2000), 493.
18 Vladimir Nabokov, *The Stories of Vladimir Nabokov*, ed. Dmitri Nabokov (New York: Alfred A. Knopf, 1995), 410–411.

Nabokov's own admission—to "the leading troika" of his stories.[19] Nabokov referred to "Spring in Fialta" as an "exemplary" short story such as Chekhov's "Lady with a Lapdog" and Kafka's "The Metamorphosis."[20] (In 1956 the New York-based Chekhov Publishing House issued Nabokov's third collection of Russian stories under the title *Spring in Fialta*). Mindful of his "predecessor" Chekhov (Nabokov's expression), Nabokov set his story in interwar Europe and created a fictional resort. Nabokov's composite Mediterranean town with echoes of the Dalmatian Fiume (now Rijeka) and the Crimean Yalta, Fialta hosted exiles, whose lives conflated lofty memories of Russia and the quotidian *realia* of early 1930s Europe.[21]

Nabokov's "Spring in Fialta" (the *spring* season, the *spring* of memories, and the narrative *spring*) resonates through Shrayer-Petrov's "Autumn in Yalta," inviting a comparatist to investigate a three-generational literary dynamic. In the limited space of this essay, I will point out that in Chekhov's love story, omission and silence are the chosen devices to depict sexuality. The next thing Chekhov shows the reader after Gurov and Anna disappear to her hotel room (to make love) is that Gurov is eating watermelon to the accompaniment of Anna's sobs and self-flagellation as a "bad . . . woman." In Nabokov's covertly modernist text, sex is partly metaphorized, partly alluded to, and partly silenced. Consider this recollection by the narrating protagonist Vasenka (Victor in the English version of the story, published in 1947):

> [Nina] turned and rapidly swaying on slender ankles led me along the sea-blue carpeted passage. A chair at the door of her room supported a tray with the remains of breakfast . . . and because of our sudden draft a wave of muslin embroidered with white dahlias got sucked in, with a shudder and knock, between the responsive halves of the French window, and only when the door had been locked did they let go that curtain with something like a blissful sigh; and a little later I stepped out on the diminutive cast-iron balcony beyond to inhale a combined smell of dry maple leaves and gasoline.[22]

---

19 Stephen Jan Parker, "Vladimir Nabokov and the Short Story," *Russian Literature Triquarterly* 24 (1991): 68.
20 Ibid., 69.
21 For a detailed discussion of Nabokov's dialogue with Chekhov, see Maxim D. Shrayer, *The World of Nabokov's Stories* (Austin: University of Texas Press, 1998), 191–238.
22 Tr. Vladimir Nabokov and Peter A. Pertzoff, in Nabokov, *The Stories of Vladimir Nabokov*, 415–416.

Even though in Shrayer-Petrov's love story, the Russian classical chastity of Chekhov's art yields to Nabokov's more nuanced and liberal portrayal of sexuality and lovemaking, even though Shrayer-Petrov adds a medical researcher's eye to Nabokov's eye of a lepidopterist, Doctor Samoylovich still refuses to clinicize Polechka's sexual numbness. *It*, he calls her unresponsiveness, perhaps forgetting to consider his own lovemaking of an "eternal student" (*pace* Chekhov). It is Polechka, not Samoylovich, who resorts to medical terminology and yet suggests, as both Chekhov and Nabokov do in their own ways, a fundamental divide between the world of sexuality and the world of romantic fulfillment. "Maybe my own exalted imagination or how much I was actually driven to him stood in the way of my normal sensations?" Polechka confesses to Samoylovich after the New Year's party and her "rendezvous" with the actor Kaftanov. "You know, don't you, Samoylovich, what I mean? You doctors call it frigid. I would call it 'waiting for a miracle.' I've been waiting for it my whole life."[23]

Thus writing at the shores of New England and modeling a life in his former homeland, Shrayer-Petrov returns from the fictionality of Nabokov's locale (Fialta) to the reality of Chekhov's Yalta. This re-fictionalized space of the resort blends the Jewish-Russian writer's own exilic recollections with layers of collective memory stored in the Russian language he has brought with him to America. When Samoylovich waits for Polechka at his Crimean seaside cottage, finally prepared to "believe" that "Polechka had deceived him," does he also recall, as I do when I reread Shrayer-Petrov's story, this episode from the middle of "Lady with a Lapdog"?

> In Oreanda they [Anna and Gurov] sat on a bench, not far from the church, looking silently at the sea down below. Yalta was hardly visible through the morning fog; white clouds stood motionless upon the mountain peaks. Leaves didn't stir on the trees, crickets screamed, and the monotonous, hollow sound of the sea coming up from below, spoke of quietude, of the eternal sleep awaiting us all. The same sound could be heard from down below when there was no Yalta or Oreanda, and it was still heard now and would continue with the same indifference and hollowness when we were no longer around. And in this permanence, this sheer indifference to the life and death of each one of us, there lies, perhaps, the promise of our eternal

---

23 Shrayer-Petrov, *Autumn in Yalta*, 116.

salvation, of life's uninterrupted stride on earth, of continuous movement towards perfection.[24]

Does Samoylovich the Jewish idealist turned illegal cab driver still believe, however faintly, in this Chekhovian "movement towards perfection" when he encounters his past after having returned from the labor camp? (Shrayer-Petrov suggested to me on New Year's morning of 2005 that, perhaps, the character of Doctor Samoylovich has a close antecedent in the self-sacrificing Doctor Dymov of Chekhov's "The Grasshopper" [1892].) "Autumn in Yalta" ends by bringing the reader back to its establishing scene, where Samoylovich recognizes his beloved Polechka in one of the "classy" ladies (the other one, perhaps, is Nina, whom Samoylovich had met at a wintry dacha outside Moscow, and the men are the actor Kaftanov, once Samoylovich's rival and now Nina's husband, and the astrophysicist Murov, Polechka's husband). Clashing with the expeditiousness of Soviet historical time, this almost miraculous stoppage of character time cannot but hint at a possibility of death or revenge beyond the story's ending (Ivan Bunin's exemplary story "Genrikh," composed in 1940 in Grasse and culminating in Nice, comes to mind as Samoylovich strokes his jacket pocket, where he keeps a gun). Such an artistic choice on Shrayer-Petrov's part takes stock both of Chekhov's open ending, rife with tremulous possibilities, and of Nabokov's decision to kill Nina, the female protagonist of "Spring in Fialta," in a banal car crash. Shrayer-Petrov's Polechka takes not after Chekhov's Anna but mainly after Nina of Nabokov's "Spring in Fialta" (Shrayer-Petrov purposely gave the markedly Chekhovian name and something of the aura of Nabokov's heroine to an episodic character in his story). And yet, no matter what outcome the reader may project beyond the physical end of Shrayer-Petrov's text, in the triangulating composition of "Autumn in Yalta" it is Polechka who belongs with "those salamanders of fate, those basilisks of good fortune," as Nabokov labeled Nina's belletrist husband Ferdinand and his cohort Segur who survive the car crash that claims Nina's life in Fialta. Shrayer-Petrov's consumptive Polechka will probably live on, whereas her driver Samoylovich . . . Venturing beyond the physical ending, the reader will speculate for herself or himself.

And finally, in assessing the Jewish-Russian writer's double homage to Chekhov and Nabokov, one might consider the impact of Shrayer-Petrov's

---

24 A. P. Chekhov, *Polnoe sobranie sochinenii i pisem v tridtsati tomakh* (Moscow: Nauka, 1974–1985), vol. 10, 133.

medical experiences upon the making of "Autumn in Yalta." This is not only Chekhov's and Nabokov's (pre-Soviet) Yalta but also Soviet Yalta, where Doctor Shrayer-Petrov worked during a cholera epidemic.[25] In the summer of 1970 a large territory in Ukraine and Southern Russia was struck by cholera. It was part of the seventh world pandemic of cholera, spread to the former USSR from the South-East Asia. Soviet newspapers, radio, and TV preferred not to tell the people about the dangerous situation at home. A small piece of information concerning "sporadic cases" of gastroenteritis of "unknown" bacterial origin was published in the Moscow-based *Medical Gazette*. Eventually, more and more residents of the stricken areas became gravely ill. The symptoms of the disease were typical for cholera. The outbreaks occurred in Astrakhan (the Caspian Sea), Kerch (the Black Sea and the Sea of Azov), Feodosiya and Yalta (both on the Black Sea). In September 1970, soon after the outbreak had been registered, a small group of microbiologists from Moscow's Gamaleya Research Institute of Epidimeology and Microbiology was dispatched to Yalta. As a member of this group, Doctor Shrayer-Petrov worked in Yalta for a month in the midst of the cholera epidemic. The purpose of their mission was to find the best ways to prevent the spread of cholera, to provide treatment to the deathly sick patients, and to study the biology and molecular genetics of the causative agent, *Vibrio cholerae*. Less than a year later, in the summer of 1971, Shrayer-Petrov's article on cholera appeared in the Soviet magazine *Nature* (*Priroda*). It was possibly the first Soviet academic publication where the 1970 epidemic was discussed in no uncertain terms.[26]

Many years thence, first still in Russia and then in America, Shrayer-Petrov revisited the subject in his novel *The French Cottage* (*Frantsuzskii kottedzh*, 1999), started in the 1970s in the USSR and revampled and completed in America. The protagonist of *The French Cottage*, Daniil Geyer, shares much in common not only with Samoylovich of "Autumn in Yalta," but also with Daniil Rayev of *Strange Danya Rayev*. In going back to the wartime past and his character's childhood, Shrayer-Petrov rehearses aspects of the future Danya Rayev not only in Samoylovich, whose fictional existence stops in 1991 or 1992, but also in the famous scientific journalist Daniel Geyer, who becomes a refusenik and immigrates to America

---

[25] For details, see David Shrayer-Petrov's memoir of working at the 1970 Yalta cholera outbreak, "Osen´ v Ialte," in *Okhota na ryzhego d´iavola. Roman s mikrobiologami*, ed. Maksim D. Shraer (Moscow: Agraf, 2010), 103–123.

[26] D. P. Shraer, "Izmenchivost´ vozbuyditelia kholery," *Priroda* 6 (1971): 43–50.

in the late 1980s. The authorial chosenness of and deep connections between Daniil Rayev [Даниил Раев] and Daniel Geyer [Даниэль Гаер] are augmented not only by the way their last names echo the last name of their creator: Shrayer-Rayev-Geyer [Шраер-Раев-Гаер], but also by the virtual sameness of the characters' first names and by a certain Biblical and prophetic complementarity between the first names of the characters and the first name of their creator: Daniel-David. (Additionally, the spelling of the first name of the protagonist of *The French Cottage* hints at the last name of the writer and translator Yuly Daniel [Юлий Даниэль], the codefendant of Andrey Sinyavsky at the famous Moscow trial of 1966; Sinyavsky was sentenced to seven, Daniel to five years of hard labor.)

Because Shrayer-Petrov's artistic method privileges Nabokov's combination of the *eye*-narrator with the *I*-storyteller over Chekhov's dispassionate omniscience, Shrayer-Petrov's semiautobiographical narrators both look out from within and stare in from without. "How difficult it is," the adult Danya Rayev remarks, "to separate those sixty-year-old impressions from my present memories of those impressions!"[27] This statement not only explains Shrayer-Petrov's deliberate blurring of the traditional borderlines of fiction and memoir, but also helps Shrayer-Petrov's readers make sense of his renewed dialogue with Nabokov and Chekhov—across the boundaries of time, language, and exile.

Like many other authors and intellectuals in the Soviet 1970s, Shrayer-Petrov first tasted of Nabokov's prose by reading smuggled *tamizdat* editions and unsanctioned bound copies of those *tamizdat* books. In the middle part of *The French Cottage*, the principal characters read, reread and discuss *Lolita*. In chapter seven, "Yalta," set in Yalta before and during the 1970 cholera epidemic, the protagonist Geyer has the following exchange with Ilya Bukhman, a successful film director who collaborates with Geyer's beloved, Valya, and also drops sardonically sallacious hints about Geyer and Sonechka, Valya's teenage daughter:

"Вот именно, кто знает? Разве предполагал Набоков, что его «Лолита» станет так патологически знаменита!"

"Почему же патологически?"

"Потому что её бешеный успех — не что иное, как выражение несокрушимой страсти цивилизованного общества к сексуальной патологии."

---

27 Shrayer-Petrov, *Autumn in Yalta*, 23.

"Я как-то по другому воспринимал этот роман. Искусство — да! Эротика — несомненно! Но никак не патология. Впрочем, надо перечитать. Мне «Лолиту» давали на одну ночь."

"Вот вы и перечитайте, Гаер. Я вам пришлю с Валей. Полезное и *поучительное* чтение. Особенно для тех, кто оказывается в сходных ситуациях."[28]

"Exactly, who knows. Did Nabokov even imagine, that his *Lolita* would become so pathologically famous?"

"And why pathologically?"

"Because its rabid success is nothing else but an expression of the civilized society's unvanquishable passion for sexual pathology."

"I must have perceived the novel differently. Art—yes indeed! Eroticism—undoubtedly! But nothing like pathology. Actually I must reread it. I only had *Lolita* for one night."

"Why don't you reread it, Geyer. I'll send it over with Valya. A useful and *instructing* read. Especially for those who find themselves in similar circumstances."

In chapter eight, which opens in Moscow in 1977, the reader learns that Bukhman has uprooted himself and made *aliyah*, but the germs of his earlier insinuations have infected Valya's inflamed imagination. The marriage ripping at its seams, Valya throws angry words at Geyer:

"И что же? Я её люблю, как родную дочь. При чём тут твои страхи и предчувствия, Валя?"

"При том, что для Сонечки ты не отец и не отчим. Ты для неё метафора мужчины. То есть её влечение к тебе вполне естественно. Да и по возрасту она давно не Лолита. Хотя ты вполне подходишь на роль Гумберта. Ведь всё это началось ещё в Ялте. Я помню отлично, как она была возбуждена. И это был как раз возраст Лолиты. Бухман предсказывал . . ."

"Послушай, Валя, всё, что угодно, но не оракулства этого пончика с говном!" — взорвался Гаер.

"Да ты, Гаер, просто-напросто завидуешь Бухману. Завидуешь и трусишь. Завидуешь его решительности и трусишь говорить о нём

---

28 David Shrayer-Petrov, *Frantsuzskii kottedzh*, ed. Maksim D. Shraer (Providence, RI: APKA Publishers, 1999), 204.

хорошо, потому что он бросил всё: свою блистательную карьеру, квартиру, связи и уехал в Израиль!" — выкрикнула Валя.[29]

"So what's the problem? I love her like my own daughter. Valya, what do your fears and premonitions have to do with us?"

"What do they have to do with us? To Sonechka you're neither father not stepfather. You to her are a metaphor of manhood. That is, her attraction to you is quite natural. And she's long past the age of Lolita. But you actually fit the part of Humbert Humbert pretty well. This all had started in Yalta. I remember perfectly well how excited she was. And that was exactly Lolita's age. Bukhman predicted..."

"Listen, Valya, anything but the oracular pronouncements of this donut with shit," Geyer exploded.

"You, Geyer, you're simply jealous of Bukhman. You're jealous and act like a coward. You're jealous of his decisiveness and you're too much of a coward to speak well of him, because he dropped averything: his brilliant career, apartment, connections—and moved to Israel," Valya screamed out.

In the final chapter of the novel, set on Cape Cod during Hurricane Bob and the Moscow putch of 1991, Geyer is living in America and finishing the nonfiction book of his life—which in a sense destroyed his marriage and Soviet career. Is Geyer's book also to to be named *The French Cottage*? The gratified reader wonders as he or she recognizes echoes of both Russian (*The Gift*) and American (*Lolita* and *Pnin*) Nabokov in the final design of the novel.

* * *

Jews and Russians are the "two peoples ... closest to me in flesh (genes) and spirit (language),"[30] Shrayer-Petrov wrote in early 1986, a year a a half before emigration, in *Friends and Shadows* (*Druz'ia i teni*), a memoir-novel of the 1950s and early 1960s Leningrad. Over fifteen years later, in the preface to the collection *Jonah and Sarah*, he commented: "These fourteen stories bear testimony to over fifteen years of setting roots in my new country. Whether they feature characters still living in the old country or having

---

29 Shraer-Petrov, *Frantsuzskii kottedzh*, 256–257.
30 David Shraer-Petrov, *Druz'ia i teni. Roman s uchastiem avtora* (New York: Liberty Publishing House, 1989), 9.

already arrived in the New World, these stories are a record of a Jewish writer's separation from his Russian homeland."[31]

In a number of stories written after coming to America, love between Jews and Gentiles fuels Shrayer-Petrov's imagination. Some of the stories are gently ironic; others, like the story "Hände Hoch!" (1999) about the legacy of the Shoah in modern America, are sharply polemical, going against the grain of commonly maintained stereotypes. Such is also the case of the story "Carp for the Gefilte Fish" ("Karp dlia farshirovannoi ryby"), where the love of a non-Jewish, Belarusian man for his Jewish wife endures over the boundaries of time, language, and country, whereas hers for him fissures (or at least it seems so at first glace). Exile and its many forms and varieties has become a focus of Shrayer-Petrov's writing. The author's own Jewish experience provides a point of calibration when he writes of other, non-Jewish immigrants to America, such as the Japanese protagonist of "The Love of Akira Watanabe" ("Liubov´ Akiry Vatanabe").

Characters in the novel *Strange Danya Rayev*, in "Autumn in Yalta," and other longer and shorter fictions written in America struggle with the dilemmas of their dual Jewish-Russian selves. These fictions not infrequently depict Soviet immigrants interacting with and confronting native-born Americans—as coworkers, intellectual and romantic rivals, as lovers and non-lovers. In the American landscape, the newcomers from the dominantly Jewish, 1970s–1980s wave of emigration from the former Soviet Union ("Third Wave") are habitually subsumed into two categories: Jews as "Russians" and Russians as "Jews"—either based on country of origin and its main language or based on communal religious identity.

Shrayer-Petrov's shorter fiction reveals the author's obsession with identity markers, and his self-conscious adherence to the canons of the European love story of Guy de Maupassant, Anton Chekhov, Thomas Mann, Ivan Bunin, Vladimir Nabokov, and Isaac Bashevis Singer. A characteristic example of Shrayer-Petrov's imperative to explore the parameters of identity by constructing variations of the traditional love story is "The Love of Akira Watanabe." In this story, told in first person, Shrayer-Petrov creates an alternative model of exile and alienation. A Jewish-Russian scientist, inspired and informed by the author's own biography, meets and befriends a Japanese professor as they both take English as a Second Language at an American university, in the company of other campus-based immigrants.

---

31 Shrayer-Petrov, *Jonah and Sarah*, ix.

The Japanese professor, an estranged scion of a samurai family, and hardly a man of his time either at home or abroad, falls in love with Margaret, their ESL teacher, only to learn that she shares her life with a female partner. In taking an epigraph from Nabokov's story for "Autumn in Yalta," Shrayer-Petrov fondly acknowledges a literary master. Conversely, in drawing an epigraph from "A Story about the Creation of Stories" ("Rasskaz o tom, kak sozdaiutsia rasskazy," 1926) by Boris Pilnyak (1894–1937), Shrayer-Petrov polemically sets "The Love of Akira Watanabe" against fictions of stereotyping. Naturally, fiction writers play with various perceptions (and misperceptions) of stereotypes. What distinguishes Pilnyak's portrayal of a Japanese officer married to a Russian woman in "A Story about the Creation of Stories" is the degree to which Pilnyak adheres to a simplistic and negative stereotype of a Japanese man dating to the turn of the twentieth century and the Russo-Japanese War. (In his portrayal of Jewish characters, the talented writer Pilnyak likewise clung to offputting if stylistically accomplished stereotypes). As drawn by the Jewish-Russian narrator, the character of Akira Watanabe serves to undermine stereotypes. To phrase this differently, Akira Watanabe is a stereotype debunking stereotypes. Ironically, the storyteller readily lends himself to stereotyping by Akira's rival in the story's love triangle, Margaret's partner Leslie: "Like all Russians, you probably drink your vodka *straight*?"[32]

We create our own, unique diasporas by undoing stereotypes, be they ethnic, religious, or sexual, suggests this story with a surprisingly lyrical ending. The undoing of stereotypes culminates in the story "Carp for the Gefilte Fish." Set in Rhode Island, Shrayer-Petrov's home in 1987–2007, and nurtured by memories of his military service in Belarus in 1959–1960, this story features a tetrangle of desire linking an émigré couple, Fyodor and Raya Kuzmenko, and their American employers, a widowed furniture store owner Harry Kapler and his daughter Rachel. Hailing from a provincial Belarusian town in the heart of the former Pale of Settlement, the Kuzmenkos bring to America the contrapuntal contradictions of a mixed marriage; Raya is Jewish, Fyodor is not. The couple is without children, and Fyodor periodically goes on drinking binges. The Kuzmenkos distance themselves from Raya's *meshpocha* in Providence (Fyodor has no living blood relatives), moving to a small town where no other "Russians" live, but where a small Jewish community has established itself. At the end of

---

32 Shrayer-Petrov, *Autumn in Yalta*, 148.

the story, a turn of events, involving Raya's adulterous adventure with their Jewish-American employer, Fyodor's fishing expedition and eschewing of temptation, and an old Ashkenazi cooking recipe, brings the émigré couple back together. Or does it?

A volume of Shrayer-Petrov's selected stories, published in Moscow in 2005, bears the title *Carp for the Gefilte Fish*, portentous of a privileged place the author assigns the title story. The story's debunking of stereotypes functions as an admonition to the kind of self-righteous Jewish reader who appreciates only the tales where exclusively Jews emerge as positive characters. Rather than create a fictional hierarchy of ethics, Shrayer-Petrov examines his subjects from many different ethical, aesthetic, and metaphysical angles, often presenting conflicting and incongruous points of view. Coupled with the conviction that the author does not know much more than do his characters, this (Dostoevskian?) quality of non-narrative analysis of the narrative events is distinctly manifest in modern Jewish writing.

"Literature can very well describe the absurd, but it should never become absurd itself," stated Isaac Bashevis Singer (1904–1991) in the "Author's Note" to his *Collected Stories* (1982).[33] Whether or not one agrees with Bashevis Singer's dictum, one observes that in some of the most dramatic points of Shrayer-Petrov's fiction (such as the drunk Samoylovich's "escape" attempt, where a boat transmogrifies into a yard dog) Shrayer-Petrov places his characters on the brink of the absurd. This teetering on the verge, a *dybbuk* dancing on the author's humanist imagination, brings to mind not only the traditions of what Ken Frieden calls "classic Yiddish fiction" (S. Y. Abramovitsh, Sholem Aleichem, and I. L. Peretz forming the triumvirate), but also the fiction of Bashevis Singer. To the career of David Shrayer-Petrov in general and to his immigrant fiction in particular, I find especially pertinent the novels *Enemies: A Love Story* (1966) and *Shosha* (1974), Bashevis Singer's post-Shoah exilic tales—one of America and maturity, the other of Poland and youth. In Bashevis Singer's fiction—as in much of Shrayer-Petrov's—encounters between Jews and non-Jews (Slavs) prompt the workings of the "love story."

In 1975–1976, already gearing up for an open challenge to Soviet officialdom, Shrayer-Petrov composed poems where disharmonies of his Russian and Jewish selves adumbrated a conflict with the regime. Earlier

---

33 Isaac Bashevis Singer, "Author's Note," in *The Collected Stories of Isaac Bashevis Singer* (New York: Farrar, Straus and Giroux, 1982), viii.

I discussed the poem "My Slavic Soul," and here I will quote another poem, "Early Morning in Moscow" ("Rannee utro zimoi," literally "Early Morning in Winter," 1976), in its entirety. Published in English in 1993, it originally appeared in Shrayer-Petrov's first American collection of Russian verse, *Song of a Blue Elephant* (1990):

Раннее утро зимой

Это дятел стучит на сосне,
Повторяя, как будто во сне:
Тук-тук-тук,
Тук-тук-тук,
Тук-тук-тук —
Деревянный мертвеющий звук.

Это дворник лопатой шуршит,
Повторяя, как будто во сне:
Жид-жид-жид,
Жид-жид-жид,
Жид-жид-жид,
Ты попался бы в лагере мне.

Это доктор стучит в мою грудь,
Повторяя, как будто во сне:
Как-нибудь,
Как-нибудь,
Как-нибудь,
Мы ещё запоем по весне.

Эти звуки наполнили рань,
Повторяясь слезами во мне:
Жизни грань,
Жизни грань,
Жизни грань,
И Москва в снеговой пелене.[34]

---

34 David Shraer-Petrov, "Rannee utro zimoi," in *Pesnia o golubom slone. Liubovnaia lirika* (Holyoke, MA: New England Publishing House, 1990), 41-42; in *Forma liubvi. Izbrannaia lirika* (Moscow: Izdatel′skii dom "Iunost′," 2003), 52.

Early Morning in Moscow

The woodpecker knocks on the pine tree
rehearsing his wooden reverie
knock-knock-knock
knock-knock-knock
On the ground
falls the deadening wooden sound.

The janitor shovels the street
rehearsing his snowy reverie
dirty Jew dirty Jew
dirty Jew—
In the camps
I'd break your head in two.

The doctor knocks on my chest
rehearsing his wishful reverie
one day we'll
one day we'll
one day we'll
be free to sing in the spring.

Sounds filling the dawn
keep time with my salt tears
on the verge of life
on the verge of life
on this low verge lies
Moscow muffled in snow.[35]

Commenting on the translation, a product of my collaboration with the American poet and translator Edwin Honig, Shrayer-Petrov wrote in 1992: "this poem of mine in English translation (I almost wrote in 'American translation') acquired a particularly revelatory and lament-like intonation, akin to what I hear in the character of the writer Robert Cohn in

---

35 David Shrayer-Petrov, "Early Morning in Moscow," tr. Edwin Honig and Maxim D. Shrayer, in *An Anthology of Jewish-Russian Literature: Two Centuries of Dual Identity in Prose and Poetry, 1801–2001*, ed. Maxim D. Shrayer (Armonk, NY: M. E. Sharpe, 2007), vol. 2, 1059.

Hemingway's novel *The Sun Also Rises* [1926]."³⁶ (Published in 1935 in Vera Toper's fine translation and better known in Russian as *Fiesta*, Hemingway's novel had been immensely popular in the USSR of Shrayer-Petrov's youth.)

I confess that as I read "Carp for the Gefilte Fish" in English, I hear in the emergent translated voice of the narrator echoes of Bernard Malamud's novel *The Assistant* (1957). Hear or want to hear? And in the character of Fyodor Kuzmenko there is perhaps something of Frank Alpine, Malamud's archetypal American *goy* who takes upon himself the great burden of Jewishness, driven to it by a mixture of desire, love, guilt, and self-hatred. Frank Alpine, the Italian-American Catholic "holdupnik" of a measly Jewish grocery store, identifies with St. Francis of Assisi, and Malamud engages him in an *imitatio* of Morris Bober the old Jewish grocer. Answering Alpine's question what it means to be a Jew, Morris first tells him this: "My father used to say to be a Jew all you need is a good heart."³⁷ Only later does Bober share with Alpine his justification of not following *koshrut*, his notion of Jewish Law, and his idea of Jewish suffering. Referring to Alpine's circumcision, Malamud ends his great American novel with one of the most enigmatic sentences composed by a Jewish writer: "The pain enraged and inspired him. After Passover he became a Jew."³⁸ The "he" refers to Frank Alpine. Marking the protagonist of "Carp for the Gefilte Fish" with the name Fyodor (from the Greek *Theodoros*, "Gift of God"), Shrayer-Petrov remarks in the middle of the story: "He [Fyodor] had lived among Jews for many years but could never really understand them completely."³⁹ Fyodor may not have "become a Jew," but he stays with them his whole life, loving Raya more than anything, more than his Belarusian homeland.

Almost twenty years ago, in the afterword to *Jonah and Sarah: Jewish Stories of Russia and America*, I speculated about the trajectory of my father's writing career, which had led him to writing about the Jewish-, the Russian-, and—increasingly—the unhyphenated America. My father's fictions of the immigrant years can be claimed not only by the Jewish-Russian but increasingly the Jewish-American literary canon,⁴⁰ particularly

---

36 David Shrayer-Petrov, "Edwin Honig as a Translator of Russian Verse," in *A Glass of Green Tea with Edwin Honig*, ed. Susan Brown et al. (Providence, RI: Alephoe Books, 1994), 238.
37 Bernard Malamud, *The Assistant* (New York: Macmillan, 1957), 124.
38 Ibid., 246.
39 Shrayer-Petrov, *Autumn in Yalta*, 163.
40 See Marc Shechner, A Review of *Dinner with Stalin and Other Stories*, by David Shrayer-Petrov, erikadreifus.com, August 17, 2014, https://www.erikadreifus.com/2014/08/mark-shechner-david-shrayer-petrov/, accessed June 18, 2020.

so in its multiplicity of cultural perspectives, its diversity of subjects, in seeking to overcome stereotypes, but also in its insistence on getting over the traumas of the past. Furthermore, I can hardly imagine his writing works such as "Autumn in Yalta" or "Dinner with Stalin" (see Boris Lanin's essay in this volume) not in America but in post-Soviet Russia. Consider this passage from the ending of "Carp for the Gefilte Fish":

> He [Fyodor] drove on thinking what a happy guy he really was. There he was, in a new country, where he came not like some sort of a loser but a married man. Both he and Raya have jobs. They have their own house and a garden. And they haven't hit old age. It's too bad, of course, that they don't have a boy or a girl. But who knows, maybe they'll get lucky? Here in America, even worse kinds of ailments get cured. If it's all from his drinking, then he's practically on the wagon. And what if?[41]

What if? One of the things that have always sustained me as my father's reader, translator and commentator is his belief in a form of universal harmony, in a "saving proportionality" ("спасительная соразмерность") as he termed it first in *Doctor Levitin*, in one of the key authorial digressions, and subsequently reformulated in the preface to *Jonah and Sarah*: "Не гармония в высоком пантеистическом смысле, а соразмерность, предназначенная для того, чтобы распределить между людьми счастье и несчастье" ("Not a harmony in the grand poetic [pantheistic] sense of the word, but a proportionality, intended for the purpose of distributing happiness and unhappiness among people").[42]

---

41 Shrayer-Petrov, *Autumn in Yalta*, 181.
42 David Shraer-Petrov, *Gerbert i Nelli* (Moscow: Knizhniki, 2014), 155; cf. Shrayer-Petrov, *Doctor Levitin*, 142; Shrayer-Petrov, *Jonah and Sarah*, xix.

Works Cited

Chekhov, A. P. *Polnoe sobranie sochinenii i pisem v tridtsati tomakh*. Edited by N. I. Sokolov. Moscow: Nauka, 1974–1985.

Malamud, Bernard. *The Assistant*. New York: Macmillan, 1957.

Nabokov, Vladimir. *The Stories of Vladimir Nabokov*. Edited by Dmitri Nabokov. New York: Alfred A. Knopf, 1995.

Parker, Stephen Jan. "Vladimir Nabokov and the Short Story." *Russian Literature Triquarterly* 24 (1991): 63–72.

Rayfield, Donald. *Chekhov: A Life*. Evanston: Northwestern University Press, 2000.

Shrayer, Maxim D., and David Shrayer-Petrov. "A Fictional Model of the Former USSR: Part 1 of a 3-Part Conversation." Jewish Book Council. 8 July 2014. https://www.jewishbookcouncil.org/pb-daily/a-fictional-model-of-the-former-ussr-part-1-of-a-3-part-conversation. Accessed June 20, 2020.

Shrayer, Maxim D. *The World of Nabokov's Stories*. Austin: University of Texas Press, 1998.

———. "Afterword: Voices of My Father's Exile." In David Shrayer-Petrov, *Autumn in Yalta: A Novel and Three Stories*, edited, co-translated, and with an afterword by Maxim D. Shrayer, 205–234. Library of Modern Jewish Literature. Syracuse: Syracuse University Press, 2006.

———, ed. *An Anthology of Jewish-Russian Literature: Two Centuries of Dual Identity in Prose and Poetry, 1801–2001*. 2 vols. Armonk, NY: M. E. Sharpe, 2007.

———, ed. *Voices of Jewish-Russian Literature: An Anthology*. Boston: Academic Studies Press, 2018.

———. "A Russian Typewriter Longs for Her Master: A Portrait of my Father, the Refusenik Writer and Medical Scientist David Shrayer-Petrov, as a New England poet, on his 84th Birthday." *Tablet Magazine*, January 28, 2020. https://www.tabletmag.com/sections/arts-letters/articles/maxim-shrayer-david-shrayer. Accessed January 29, 2020.

Shrayer-Petrov, David [David Shraer-Petrov]. *Druz′ia i teni. Roman s uchastiem avtora*. New York: Liberty Publishing House, 1989.

———. *Pesnia o golubom slone. Liubovnaia lirika*. Holyoke, MA: New England Publishing House, 1990.

———. "Edwin Honig as a Translator of Russian Verse." In *A Glass of Green Tea with Edwin Honig*, edited by Susan Brown et al., 236–238. Providence, RI: Alephoe Books, 1994.

——— [David Shraer-Petrov]. *Frantsuzskii kottedzh*. Edited by Maksim D. Shraer. Providence, RI: APKA Publishers, 1999.

———. *Jonah and Sarah: Jewish Stories of Russia and America*. Edited by Maxim D. Shrayer. Library of Modern Jewish Literature. Syracuse: Syracuse University Press, 2003.

——— [David Shraer-Petrov]. *Forma liubvi. Izbrannaia lirika*. Moscow: Izdatel´skii dom "Iunost´," 2003.

———. *Autumn in Yalta: A Novel and Three Stories*. Edited, co-translated, and with an afterword by Maxim D. Shrayer. The Library of Modern Jewish Literature. Syracuse: Syracuse University Press, 2006.

——— [David Shraer-Petrov]. *Vodka s pirozhnymi. Roman s pisateliami*. Edited by Maksim D. Shraer. St. Petersburg: Akademicheskii proekt, 2007.

———. *Dinner with Stalin and Other Stories*. Edited, with notes and commentary, by Maxim D. Shrayer. The Library of Modern Jewish Literature. Syracuse: Syracuse University Press, 2014.

——— [David Shraer-Petrov]. *Okhota na ryzhego d´iavola. Roman s mikrobiologami*. Edited by Maksim D. Shraer. Moscow: Agraf, 2010.

——— [David Shraer-Petrov]. *Gerbert i Nelli*. Moscow: Knizhniki, 2014.

———. *Doctor Levitin*. Edited and with notes by Maxim D. Shrayer, translated by Arna B. Bronstein, Aleksandra I. Fleszar, and Maxim D. Shrayer. Detroit: Wayne State University Press, 2018.

Singer, Isaac Bashevis. *The Collected Stories of Isaac Bashevis Singer*. New York: Farrar, Straus and Giroux, 1982.

Waife-Goldberg, Marie. *My Father, Sholom Aleichem*. New York: Simon and Schuster, 1968.

Part Two

Studies of David Shrayer-Petrov's Poetry

Drums of Fate: David Shrayer-Petrov's Poetics of Fractured Wholeness*

Ian Probstein

Big, eventful, filled with journeys, quests, and self-questioning, the life of David Shrayer-Petrov—poet, translator, fiction writer, essayist, physician, medical researcher—does not fit within straight biographical borders, spills out of the conventional genres of the novel, biography, travelogue, love lyric, and civic poetry. The author's eye takes in the surrounding world, to be imprinted on the retina and subsequently—years or decades later—extracted from the storerooms of memory.

Born on the historically working-class Vyborg Side of Leningrad/St. Petersburg ("Я родился в Ленинграде, в Петрограде, в Петербурге,/ Там, где скачет Медный Всадник над Невою в сизой бурке" ["I was born in Leningrad, Petrograd, Petersburg,/ There where the Bronze Horseman gallops in a slate-gray cloak over the Neva"]),[1] he spent three wartime years evacuated to a village in the Urals. Shrayer-Petrov would keep going back to this formative period of his childhood in prose, poetry, and poems in prose, such as "Ivan Terekhin Returns from the Front to the Village of Siva, Molotov Province in 1943" ("Ivan Terekhin vozvrashchaetsia s fronta

---

* Copyright © 2021 by Ian Probstein. English translation copyright © 2021 by Daria Sadovnichenko and Maxim D. Shayer.
1 David Shraer-Petrov, "Moi gorod," in his *Propashchaia dusha* (Providence, RI: APKA Publishers, 1997), 17. Here and hereafter, unless noted otherwise, all poetry translations from the Russian are literal, not literary translations (tr.).

v selo Siva Molotovskoi oblasti, 1943 god") or "Wanderings across the Urals" ("Bluzhdaniia po Uralu"), both from the book-length cycle *Travels from the Banks of the Neva* (*Puteshestviia ot beregov Nevy*), composed in Moscow in 1986.[2] Memories of a postwar childhood and youth do not so much contain observations of an eyewitness as lead to a ruthless portrayal of those who decided the people's fate throughout the greater part of the twentieth century. This is the case of the paradoxical poem "During a Flood in Leningrad in the Late Fifties" ("Vo vremia navodneniia v Leningrade v kontse piatidesiatykh") from the cycle *Oddities* (*Strannosti*, circa 1986):

Дочь бывшего начальника тюрьмы
Выходит замуж за реабилитанта
Соединяются житейские таланты
И сверхинтеллигентные умы.[3]

("Daughter of a former prison warden/ Marries a rehabilitated victim of repressions./ Worldly talents are conjoined/ With superintelligent minds.")

Further in the poem, the implied author, an eyewitness, who was part of the "rescue team," describes events that words can explain, "how beasts were leaving the Zoo . . . / obedient like people," yet speaks of a supposedly "unexplainable" incident with a retired KGB general, who had once been "in charge of the arts in Leningrad," and who lost all his acquired (looted?) property during the flood:

"Всё кончено" заплакал генерал
"Он отомстить приплыл"
Осиплым басом
Размазывая слезы по щекам
Наш генерал твердил одно и то же имя "Осип Осип Осип"[4]

("It's over," the general started weeping/ "He sailed [swam] here to have his revenge"/ In a hoarse basso voice/ Smearing tears over his cheeks/ Our general kept repeating the same name "Osip Osip Osip")

The epithet *osiplyi* ("hoarse") is menacingly echoed by the first name "Osip," thus emphasizing the theme of retribution. Osip is certainly Mandelstam

---

2   David Shraer-Petov, *Villa Borgeze* (Holyoke, MA: New England Publishing, 1992), 51 and 53.
3   Ibid., 14.
4   Ibid., 14.

(and against the ideas, popular in today's Russia, that everything is supposedly relative, and that Stalin indeed built socialism and won World War II, it is necessary to note that just the deaths of the genius Mandelstam, of Nikolay Klyuev, of members of the OBERIU group are alone a verdict to Stalinism). Those poems reflect the mindset of the 1960s (even though David Shrayer-Petrov was not a member of the *shestidesyatniki*), the years that witnessed the Twentieth Congress of the Communist Party of the Soviet Union and subsequent rehabilitation of the victims of terror—not only juridical, but also providential—as Shrayer-Petrov has it in the finale of his poem. A tribute to memory for some is the scourge of memory for others. In another poem-reminiscence about Moscow, "In Front of the Synagogue at Simchat Torah" ("Pered sinagogoi v prazdnik Simkhat-Tora"), the story is about a certain "young man in a purple cap . . . / [who] enjoys life he is selling off/ the Jewish religious calendar" ("Юноша в шапочке лиловой . . . / Радуется жизни он распродаёт/ Еврейский календарь религиозный"), while being a KGB informant, in simple terms—a snitch:

> Змеёнком зреет плёнка в магнитофоне
> Он выполнил финплан и план Лубянки
> Он ждёт полуночи когда б в квартале пустынном Свиблова
> Ново-Гиреева или Перова
> Ему откроет двери заспанная девка
> Он выставит на столик кухонный водку колбасу и шпроты
> Он позабудет те и эти вожделенные широты
> Он не удавится
> Как тот несчастный Идеалист.[5]

("Like a snakelet a tape is ripening in the recorder/ He carried out the business plan and Lubyanka's plan/ He waits for midnight when in deserted city block of Sviblovo/ Novogireyevo or Perovo/ A sleepy wench will open the door for him/ He will put vodka sausage and sprats on the kitchen table/ He will forget these and those desirable latitudes/ He won't hang himself/ Unlike that miserable Idealist.")

However, poems written *in* Russia and poems written *about* Russia—are different poems not only in form, but also in their worldview. At first, the career of David Shrayer (Petrov is a penname, taken on the advice of Boris Slutsky from Shrayer's Russified patronymic Peysakhovich [Petrovich],

---

5   Shraer-Petrov, *Villa Borgeze*, 15.

following the same formative principle as in the case of David Samuilovich Samoylov [Kaufman]) was fairly successful.[6] He entered the Pavlov First State Medical University of Leningrad (St. Petersburg) in 1953—soon after the death of Stalin, "doctors' plot" of 1952–1953, and the anti-cosmopolitan campaign (during which my own father, a singer, was banned from performing solo on the radio), following the dark period when a Soviet Jew could not even dream of medical or literary activity. Nonetheless, after Stalin's death the situation changed dramatically. In medical school, David Shrayer-Petrov became friends with fellow students Ilya Averbakh, the future film director, and Vasily Aksyonov, the future fiction writer, and they both introduced the twenty-year-old Shrayer-Petrov to the literary environment—first at the medical school, which had an active literary seminar (*lito*). In collaboration with Dmitry Bobyshev, Mikhail Eremin, Anatoly Naiman, Evgeny Reyn, Viktor Sosnora, Vladimir Uflyand, Sergei Volf and many other would-be outstanding poets, fiction writers, and literary translators, they formed a literary seminar at the Palace of Culture of Industrial Cooperation (Dvorets Kul´tury Promyshlennoi Kooperatsii, subsequently renamed Dvorets Kul´tury Lensoveta); in the history of Leningrad poetry, the seminar became known by its abbreviation, *promka*. The first nominal leader of the seminar was the poet Vsevolod Azarov; the critics Zelik Shteynman and Aleksandr Ninov succeeded him. However, as Dmitry Bobyshev, one of *promka*'s most fervent participants in 1956–1958, notes in the *Dictionary of Poets of Russia Abroad*, the seminar was "essentially self-governed" by its participants.[7]

Shrayer-Petrov's first publications appeared in the late 1950s and early 1960s in periodicals—the newspaper of the First Medical University *Pulse* (*Pul´s*), in the magazines *Young Pioneer* (*Pioner*) and *Neman*, and in collectives such as *Young Leningrad* (*Molodoi Leningrad*). However, his poems much more daring both in content and in form (including some of his first blues verses, to which I will turn later) were circulating in *samizdat*. Already then, Shrayer-Petrov's poems were marked by keen attention to detail, loosened assonance-consonance rhymes, and experiments with rhythm. From the very beginning, the poet was drawn to the poetics of the avant-garde, which explains his further rapprochement

---

6 See David Shraer-Petrov, "Ierusalimskii kazak. Slutskii," in his *Vodka s pirozhnymi. Roman s pisateliami*, ed. Maksim D. Shraer (St. Petersburg: Akademicheskii proekt, 2007), 232.
7 Dmitrii V. Bobyshev, "Shraer-Petrov, David," in *Slovar´ poetov russkogo zarubezh´ia*, ed. Vadim Kreid (St. Petersburg: RKhGI, 1999), 432.

with one of the leaders of the Lianozovo school, Genrikh Sapgir, whom Shrayer-Petrov had befriended still before moving to Moscow in 1964. (See Evgeny Ermolin's essay in this volume.) But at first, after graduating from medical school in 1959 and serving as a military doctor in Belarus, he completed a graduate course of studies in microbiology at the Leningrad Institute of Tuberculosis and defended his *kandidat meditsinskikh nauk* (PhD equivalent) degree; subsequently, in Moscow, Dr. Shrayer-Petrov would defend his higher *doctor meditsinskikh nauk* (habilitation equivalent) degree. For most of his life, he would combine medical and scientific work with literary work. Already in Moscow, Shrayer-Petrov became an active contributor to periodicals—both as a literary translator and a poet, and later as an essayist. In 1967 David Shrayer-Petrov's collection of twenty-nine poems *Canvases (Kholsty)* came out in a volume comprised of works by seven younger poets.[8] It was furnished with an elegant foreword by Lev Ozerov, in which the older poet and translator, known for his poetic aphorism "Талантам надо помогать,/ Бездарности пробьются сами" ("Talents must be helped,/ Mediocrities will succeed on their own"), noted Shrayer-Petrov's diverse life experience, extensive education, close attention to life, when "the feeling can and should be filled with thought, and the thought—alive with feeling."[9] Knowing full well that Shrayer-Petrov's neo-avant-garde writing style might have been rejected by this fairly conservative publishing house affiliated with the Central Committee of the Young Communist League (Komsomol), Ozerov diplomatically wrote: "One can argue about certain images or stanzas of David Petrov, but one thing is indisputable: he carefully, persistently, unhurriedly studies life. Many of his peers already have two, or even three or four books to their credit, and he is only now publishing the first one. Not a problem! There is no need to hurry, the matter is serious: his microscopes study the finest living cells."[10] It is important to note that the author, along with some very stylistically audacious texts also included some poems that in the Soviet context could be deemed "locomotives" and helped push the collection towards publication while still retaining the poets avant-garde quest for form. The latter included "Members of the

---

8 Shrayer-Petrov's first collection, which was supposed to have come out in Leningrad, had been knocked out of the publishing plans following the 1964 trial of Joseph Brodsky, with whom Shrayer-Petrov was friendly in Leningrad.
9 Lev Ozerov, "Ob avtore," in David Petrov [David Shrayer-Petrov], *Kholsty*, in *Pereklichka* (Moscow: Molodaia gvardiia, 1967), 116.
10 Ibid., 117.

Italian Komsomol in a Young Pioneer Camp" ("Ital′ianskie komsomol′tsy v pionerskom lagere," for a discussion of Shrayer-Petrov's Italian theme, see Stefano Garzonio's essay in this volume); "On Our Way to Serve" ("Edem sluzhit′," which opens the collection); "Poems about Loyalty" ("Stikhi o vernosti"); "Cottage of Yanka Kupala" ("Domik Ianki Kupaly"). At the same time, in his first published book David Shrayer-Petrov already showed himself to be a fine love lyricist, capable of expressing a deepmost feeling. Such are the dedications to *EP*, Emilia Shrayer (née Polyak), his wife since 1962 (thus, they celebrated their fiftieth, golden wedding anniversary in 2012). The flow of lyrical poetry, backed by a golden reserve of feelings, has not run out to this day:

Одиночество

 Э. П.
Одиночество.
Ты одна
от меня заслонила дно.
Ты — морская голубизна,
и тебе возвратить дано
всё, что я на земле терял,
что мелькало в слоях воды.
Стань моей глубиной!
Войди
в то, за чем я на дно нырял.

Станешь всем. Но когда-нибудь
одиночеством ты побудь,
чтоб сама ты открылась мне
в голубой своей глубине.[11]

("Loneliness": "*To E. P.* You alone/ shielded the bottom from me./ You— are the sea blueness,/ and you're destined to return/ everything I lost in the world,/ what sparkled in the layers of water./ Become my depth!/ Enter/ that for which I dived to the bottom. || You'll become everything. But one day/ try being loneliness,/ so that you would open up to me/ in your blue depth.")

---

[11] Petrov, *Kholsty*, in *Pereklichka*, 143.

At first, the Moscow life of David Shraer-Petrov was relatively successful: the collection of poems *Kholsty*, as noted above, was published in 1967. Although he struggled to place his original poems in magazines and collectives, his literary translations, on which he had started working professionally back in Leningrad, as a participant of Efim Etkind's and Tatiana Gnedich's seminars, garnered prizes and appeared in magazines and newspapers. In 1977, he received the prize jointly awarded by the monthly magazine *People's Friendship* (*Druzhba narodov*) and the weekly *Literary Gazette* (*Literaturnaia Gazeta*). His translations were regularly commissioned by the leading publishing houses Khudozhestvennaia literatura and Sovetskii pisatel´, and he also collaborated with publishing houses Vaga (Lithuania), Merani (Georgia), and others. In 1974 he published a book-essay, *Poetry and Science* (*Poeziia i nauka*), in the publishing house Znanie, and in January 1976 Shrayer-Petrov was finally accepted into the Union of Soviet Writers on the recommendations of Lev Ozerov, Viktor Shklovsky, and Andrei Voznesensky. The process, which Shrayer-Petrov describes in his memoir *Gold-Domed Moscow* (*Moskva zlatoglavaia*, 1994), parts of it subsequently reprinted in *Vodka and Pastries* (*Vodka s pirozhnymi*),[12] had taken a number of years and had been difficult because of the resistance of some members of the governing board of the Union of Soviet Writers. Becoming a member of the Union facilitated the acceptance of a large book of poetry, to be titled *Winter Ship* (*Zimnii korabl´*), for publication in Sovetskii pisatel´ publishing house.[13] The book was never published. In the meantime, within D. Petrov, if one may say so, David Shrayer was coming to life more and more, the greater awakening propelled by the desire to absorb, realize, and translate his own Jewishness into the sphere of words—to express the Jewish part of his soul. Therefore, he was turning more and more to Jewish themes and even began to read in public poems infused with Jewish motifs. At the concluding evening event of the 1978 spring poetry festival in Lithuania (*Poezijos pavasaris*), Shrayer-Petrov recited the poem "My Slavic Soul" ("Moia slavianskaia dusha"), for which "he was subjected to an administrative rebuke."[14] After several years

---

12 David Shraer-Petrov, *Moskva zlatoglavaia* (Baltimore: Vestnik, 1994); idem, *Vodka s pirozhnymi. Roman s pisateliami*, ed. Maksim D. Shraer (St. Petersburg: Akademicheskii proekt, 2007).
13 See the file on Shrayer-Petrov's *Zimnii korabl´* in the papers of Sovetskii pisatel´ at The Central Russian Archive for Literature and the Arts (RGALI), f. 1234, op. 23, d. 1436 (tr.).
14 Bobyshev, "Shraer-Petrov, David," 433.

of indecision, in early January 1979 Shrayer-Petrov and his family applied for exit visas to Israel, which in those days was regarded as an act of betrayal. Shrayer-Petrov's conflict with the authorities and leaders of the Union of Soviet Writers had escalated; he was expelled from the Union, three of his books, accepted for publication, were derailed in 1979–1980: the collection of poems *Winter Ship*; a book of poetry translations from Lithuanian, and a book of fiction for young adults (the latter already in galleys and with original illustrations).[15]

In the anthology *Samizdat of the Century* (1997), in a foreword to the selection of Shrayer-Petrov poetry, Genrikh Sapgir commented on this rupture in his career:

> A mature poet, who once was among Soviet poets and translators, but found the strength to get out of this swamp. Well, of course, his fate also turned that way. David decided to emigrate, became a refusenik. But these are, as I far as I understand, external events. For a long time already, he had been thinking and writing differently than that whole gang ("The People—the winner! The nation—the builder! BAM! BAM! BAM!"[16] And all this falsehood was considered to be an unquestionable truth!
>
> When David came to see me, he read something completely different. . . . He had lived in Moscow for a long time, and we regularly met. It happened that David was able to publish his real, original poems only in emigration, in America.[17]

Already after emigration, Shrayer-Petrov, in collaboration with his son, literary critic and author Maxim D. Shrayer, would edit and write a commentary to a volume of Sapgir's shorter and longer poems for the "New Poet's Library"(Novaia biblioteka poeta) series; they would also co-author the first book about this classic of the second Russian avant-garde.[18] Shrayer-Petrov dedicated several poems to his friend, such as "Skating on the Ice of the Gulf of Finland in a Finnish Sleigh ("Katanie po l´du Finskogo zaliva v

---

15 David Shraer-Petrov, *Druz´ia i teni. Roman s uchastiem avtora* (New York: Liberty, 1989), 57–58.
16 The abbreviation of the Baikal-Amur Railroad is BAM. *Bam* in Russian also means a banging sound (tr.).
17 Anatolii Strelianyi, Genrikh Sapgir, Vladimir Bakhtin, Nikita Ordynskii, eds., *Samizdat veka* (Minsk-Moscow: Polifakt, 1997), 468; cf. Genrikh Sapgir, "David Shraer-Petrov," in *Neofitsial´naia poeziia: antologiia poeticheskogo samizdata sovetskoi epokhi*, https://rvb.ru/np/publication/sapgir4.htm#58, accessed August 22, 2019.
18 Maksim D. Shraer and David Shraer-Petrov, *Genrikh Sapgir. Klassik avangarda* (St. Petersburg: Dmitrii Bulanin, 2004).

finskikh saniakh").[19] He mourned Sapgir and dedicated verses to his memory, such as "In the Memory of Genrikh" ("Pamiati Genrikha"):

Памяти Генриха

молчу хотя сказать хочу
так много что слова толпятся
как хохотушки смехачу
в стогу посеявшие святцы
валятся не могу прорваться
какую кнопочку нажать
мне от себя к тебе бежать
иль тело к твоему прижать
чтоб отцепились муть и гать
и братья заорали братцы[20]

("silent even though I want to say/ so much that the words keep crowding/ like laughing ladies near the source of laughter/ after they've lost the list of saints' names in a haystack/ falling down I cannot break through/ which little button to press/ for me to run from myself to you/ or press my body to yours/ so that opacity and balderdash would snap off/ so that brothers would yell bro")

The critic Eduard Mikhailov even wrote this about the poet's path: "The fate of Shrayer-Petrov is so typical of the Russian-Jewish intelligentsia living in the Russian capital during the second half of the twentieth century, that Pasternak's textbook formulation comes to mind: 'I speak for the whole milieu' ['Я говорю про всю среду']."[21] I would caution against such generalizations and would rather quote Osip Mandelstam: "Do not compare: the living is incomparable" ("Не сравнивай: живущий несравним," from the untitled poem of 1937). In particular, the difference between the typical fate of the "Russian-Jewish intelligentsia living in the Russian capital during the second half of the twentieth century" and the fate of David Shrayer-Petrov expressed itself in his works written during the years of refusal, such as the book of poems *Nevan Poems* (*Nevskie stikhi*, 1984–1985; see

---

19 David Shraer-Petrov, *Barabany sud'by* (Moscow: Argo-risk, 2002), 13.
20 David Shraer-Petrov, *Linii-figury-tela: Kniga stikhotvorenii* (St. Petersburg: Biblioteka Aesthetoscope, 2010), 9.
21 Eduard Mikhailov, "Sud'ba-sinekdokha," *Lekhaim* 226 (February 2, 2011), https://lechaim.ru/ARHIV/226/mihailov.htm. This line from Boris Pasternak's poem "Lofty Malady" ("Vysokaia bolezn'," 1923–1928) is misquoted in Mikhailov's article (tr.).

also Andrei Ranchin's and Roman Katsman's essays in this volume) or the political poem *Begun* (*Runner Begoon*, 1987), which I will analyze below, or Shrayer-Petrov's Purim spiel (Purim play) in verse, written in 1987 on the commission of an unsanctioned Moscow theater troupe.[22]

In Moscow, prior to becoming a refusenik, Shraer-Petrov worked as a senior investigator at the Gamaleya Research Institute of Microbiology of the Russian Academy, from where he was dismissed at the end of 1978 due to his intention to submit documents to OVIR (Section of Visas and Registrations). Despite having been castigated from scientific research and academic medicine, throughout the open conflict and struggle with the Soviet authorities that lasted for over eight years, Shrayer-Petrov insisted on remaining a part of the medical profession. He worked as a physician in a local clinic near the Voykovskaya Metro station, and, as Shrayer-Petrov writes in his memoir *Hunt for the Red Devil: A Novel with Microbiologists* (*Okhota na ryzhego d´iavola. Roman s mikrobiologami*), there was such a shortage of rank-and-file medical practitioners in the country that the clinic's director managed to shield him from further employment troubles.[23] In contrast to his famous fellow writers and great Russian predecessors—Anton Chekhov and Mikhail Bulgakov—Shrayer-Petrov, like the great American poet and prose writer William Carlos Williams, combined medical work with literary work throughout most of his life, without neglecting either. In the United States, from 1987 until his retirement in 2007, he worked as a research professor at the medical schools of Brown University and Boston University, pursuing research on the immunology of cancer. In this regard, it is important to note that the nostalgic motives in the poetry of Shrayer-Petrov, especially in 1987–1992, do not stem from an unsettled state and anxiety for the future, as is common among older immigrant writers, but rather betoken a spiritual and existential quest.

The longing for the Messiah breaks into Shrayer-Petrov's "Russian" poems (one of his books is called *A Certain Degree of Longing for the Messiah* (*Nekotoraia stepen´ toski po Messii*, 2005–2006);[24] while the longing for Russia takes hold of his "American" poems. Nostalgia is particularly

---

22 See Maksim D. Shraer, "Moskovskii purimshpil´—1987," *Lekhaim* 3 (2019): 37–41. See the recording of the performance based on Shrayer-Petrov's original play: "Purimshpil´ 1987/5747," https://youtu.be/CxW_RNscgTQ.
23 David Shraer-Petrov, *Okhota na ryzhego d´iavola. Roman s mikrobiologami*, ed. Maksim D. Shraer (Moscow: Agraf, 2010), 207–255.
24 In David Shraer-Petrov, *Dve knigi* (Philadelphia: Poberezh´e, 2009), 41–71.

evident in the poems of 1987-1992, especially in the cycle "Six American Blues on Russian Themes" ("Shest´ amerikanskikh bliuzov na russkie temy," 1992, in the collection *Lost Soul*), which I will consider in detail; in the poems of this period dedicated to Emilia Shrayer, and, of course, in the often-anthologized long poem *Villa Borghese*, which gave the title to Shrayer-Petrov's book of 1992 and which the poet has included in other collections of his poems:

Случались собаки на Вилле Боргезе,
Случались в том смысле, что обитали.
Случались, собачью трубя бордельезу,
Случались, хвостами трубя. О, детали!

Конкретная музыка тел шелестящих,
Балетная — пляска собачьего тела,
Конкретная — плачь по России, болящей,
Балетная — плач. Унеслась, улетела.[25]

These dogs copulating at Villa Borghese,
Copulating, the casual bitches and males,
Taking over the place, blaring out Brothellaise,
Blatantly wagging their tails—oh, details!

The concrete music of dog bodies rustling,
Of dogs' scrawny bodies, a low street ballet.
The concrete tears for the anguish of Russia.
The weeping ballet has flown, rushed away.[26]

In a review of the collection *Villa Borghese* (1992), Victor Terras, the distinguished American Slavic of Estonian origin, who has written about Shrayer-Petrov on a number of occasions and also translated his short stories into English, noted that such poems as *Villa Borghese* and "Hospital Garden" ("Bol´nichnyi sad") recall the poetics of Boris Pasternak "with their rapidly advancing amphibrachs and refraction of thought through the bizarre strangeness of the poetic hero's consciousness."[27] Furthermore, Terras notes the dialogue of Shrayer-Petrov's poems with Mikhail Kuzmin's

---

25 Shraer-Petrov, *Villa Borgeze*, 57.
26 David Shrayer-Petrov, "Villa Borghese," tr. Dolores Stewart and Maxim D. Shrayer, *Salmagundi* 101–102 (Winter–Spring 1994): 151–153; cf. Maxim D. Shrayer, ed., *Voices of Jewish-Russian Literature* (Boston: Academic Studies Press, 2018), 831–833.
27 Viktor Terras, "Villa Borgeze," *Novoe russkoe slovo*, July 3, 1992.

Alexandrian Songs (*Aleksandriiskie pesni*, 1908) and observes poetic devices kindred to Marina Tsvetaeva's "technique of composition," such as, for instance, "homonymy, paronomasia, and other figures based on sound association and creating a stream of poetic thought." Reflecting on the poems of Shrayer-Petrov that were written during the first five years of emigration, Terras questions whether Russian free verse ("русский верлибр") is possible and productive, or as Terras puts it, "is pure free verse even possible in Russian?" Terras believes that it would require overcoming the propensity of Russian verse to syllabo-tonic versification, especially to iambs.[28] In my view, Shrayer-Petrov's poetry of the American years provides an answer to this question by demonstrating both a return to traditional meters and verse forms, and as an overcoming of the latter in the poems written at the end of the twentieth and the beginning of the twenty-first century, to which I will also turn in the pages that follow.

To come back to the poem *Villa Borghese*, it is noteworthy that in one of its first publications, the poem carries an epigraph from Vladimir Nabokov's essay "Jubilee" ("Iubilei," 1927), which was written on the tenth anniversary of the Bolshevik revolution and made a big impact on Nabokov's contemporaries because of the historical parallels it drew:

> And at the same time, we celebrate ten years of freedom. The kind of freedom that we know, perhaps, no other nation has ever known. [. . .] These days, when the ussr-gray jubilee is celebrated, we celebrate ten years of contempt, loyalty and freedom. Let us not blame the exile. Let us repeat in these days the words of the ancient warrior of whom Plutarch writes: "At night, in empty fields, far away from Rome, I pitched my tent, and my tent was Rome to me."[29]

Be it as it may, in this poem, which Shrayer-Petrov had started in Rome in the summer of 1987 and completed already in the capital of Rhode Island, Providence, one feels a fair share of nostalgia, and the famous Roman park merges in the mind of the poet with St. Petersburg's Summer Garden, exposing the wound that is yet unhealed:

---

28 Ibid.
29 Vladimir Nabokov, "Iubilei," *Rul'*, November 18, 1927. Reprinted in Vladimir Nabokov, *Sobranie sochinenii russkogo perioda*, ed. N. I. Artemenko-Tolstaia, vol. 2 (St. Petersburg: Simpozium, 1999), 647. In a slightly shortened and modified form, the epigraph appears in David Shraer-Petrov, *Villa Borgeze* (Holyoke, MA: New England Publishing, 1992), 57.

Когда умирать мне придется, чуть живы,
Прошепчут мои полумертвые губы:
Мы стали чужими, Россия, чужими,
А были своими сыны Иегуды.

Как это забавно валяться в обнимку
С последней бутылкой, с последним приветом
На Вилле Боргезе, как старому снимку,
На свалке истории вместе с конвертом.

На Вилле Боргезе якшаться с трубящей
Компанией псов, абсолютно античных.
О, Боже! Ну что же Тебе до болящей
Души и до мраморных анемичных

Созданий, наставленных между стволами,
Как в Летнем Саду, где когда-то ночами
Гуляли по стежкам-дорожкам, стояли
Ночами под бледными небесами.[30]

When my time comes to die, when I'm barely alive,
Half-dead lips will whisper, like never before:
For you and us, Russia, no closeness survives,
We sons of Yehudah who used to be yours.

To lie here embracing—perhaps it's a laugh—
Last bottle, last letter, whatever remains.
At Villa Borghese, like an old photograph
On history's dump. Along with the frame.

At Villa Borghese, hang out with the gang
Of roaming wild dogs, an antique mosaic.
How much can you care, oh my Lord, for the paining
Soul and how much for the marble, anemic

Creatures arranged among columns of wood.
Like Petersburg's Summer Gardens. We walked
A sweet winding path, lovers' lane, and we stood
All night beneath skies that would never grow dark.[31]

---
30 Shraer-Petrov, *Villa Borgeze*, 57–58; idem, *Propashchaia dusha*, 6–7.
31 Shrayer-Petrov, "Villa Borghese."

Thus, in *Villa Borghese*, the theme of nostalgia is intertwined with the theme of love, forming an existential texture. Many critics have pointed out that in the poetic works of David Shrayer-Petrov love poems occupy a privileged position, sustaining the refusenik writer and giving him strength to survive during his open confrontation with the system; subtitled "love lyric," Shrayer-Petrov's collection *Song of a Blue Elephant* was named by Encyclopedia Britannica among the best Russian émigré books for 1990. But do not be mistaken: these lyrical poems are far from pastoral idylls; they are filled with pain, uncertainty, and in the first years of emigration, cut with nostalgia and guilt:

> Дорогая моя, дорогая моя,
> Дорогая моя, дорогая,
> Я привёз тебя за леса, за моря.
> А что делать с тобой не знаю.
>
> Там, в далёкой степи, где ямщик замерзал,
> Знал и я, как тебя приголубить,
> Знал секрет про большой голубой минерал
> Где-то между Москвой и Калугой[32]

("My dear, my dear,/ My dear, dear,/ I brought you here over forests and seas,/ But I don't know what to do with you. || There, in a faraway steppe, where a coachman was freezing,/ I still knew how to comfort you,/ I knew the secret of a big blue rock/ Somewhere half the distance between Moscow and Kaluga")

In the cycles "Lost Soul" ("Propashchaia dusha") and "Winter Song" ("Zimniaia pesnia"), similar feelings imbue such texts as "White City" ("Belyi gorod"), "My Soul Is Done Aching" ("Otbolela dusha"), "To My [Old] Female Friend" ("Moei podruzhke") "You Said: I Love You" ("Ty govorila: Ia tebia liubliu"), "Lift Me Up" ("Podnimi menia") and other poems of that period. Back in 2010, the émigré critic Irina Chaikovskaya wrote about the conflation of Hellenism, Judaism, and Russian motifs in Shrayer-Petrov's love poems, comparing them to the Song of Songs of Solomon.[33] These same themes are heard in the cycle "Six American Blues

---

32 Shraer-Petrov, *Propashchaia dusha*, 49.
33 Irina Chaikovskaia, "Po napravleniiu k zhenshchine. O stikhakh Davida Shraera-Petrova," *Krugozor* (February 2010), http://www.krugozormagazine.com/show/Shraer-Petrov.640.html, accessed August 22, 2019.

on Russian Themes," although the cultural framework here is expanded beyond Russian literary or historical references. Shrayer-Petrov's blues are filled with allusions to Pushkin's *Eugene Onegin* and Blok's *The Twelve*, and they contain, if one may say so, Russian verse music from Pushkin and Blok to Mandelstam and Pasternak. This is "Blues of the January Snowfall" ("Bliuz ianvarskogo snegopada"):

Чёрный камень, белый снег.
Чёрный камень, белый снег.
Чёрный камень, белый снег.
Что ж, прекрасно, дорогая, наши звёзды догорают,
Убивают наши звёзды
Белый смех,
Чёрный камень,
Белый снег.
[. . .]
Белый снег на всём бульваре,
Вдоль кладбищенской ограды.
Белый — грамотой охранной,
Чёрный — белкой-похоронкой,
Чёрный камень,
Белый снег.[34]

("Black stone, white snow./ Black stone, white snow./ Black stone, white snow./ Well, just beautiful, my darling, our stars are burning out,/ They are killing our stars/ White laugh,/ Black stone,/ White snow. [. . .] White snow is all over the boulevard/ Along the cemetery's fence./ White—like a safe conduct,/ Black—like a squirrel-death notice/ Black stone, white snow.")

Even with all their keenness, without music, poems, even in free verse, often turn into poetic prose, or even just prose. But in Shrayer-Petrov's blues, the verses give a performance. In the preface to his later collection of blues *Barabany sud'by* (2002, the cogent title can be variously translated as "Drums of Fate" and "Prayer Wheels"), David Shrayer-Petrov writes that he became interested in the blues form at the age of twenty. Such was the air of time in the middle 1950s: "We were all mad about American jazz. Especially Vasily Aksyonov and Sergei Volf, both of whom started their

---

34 Shraer-Petrov, *Propashchaia dusha*, 41.

ascent to avant-garde prose. . . . Jazz music primed my rhythmic drafts."[35] (In a memoir essay about Aksyonov, Shrayer-Petrov called him "the king of swing in Russian prose.")[36]

It is understood that American jazz came to the USSR from later musical sources, not directly from the African-American blues form. From the general musical perspective, jazz exhibits common principles of development of musical themes, such as syncopation, repetition, and free development of themes, based on rhythm. During the Khrushchev Thaw, the culture of American blues began to seep into the Soviet mainstream in a variety of ways. While in the beginning, in the late 1950s and early 1960s, the principal source was American jazz, in literary terms, as David Shrayer-Petrov noted himself in connection with his earliest experiments with blues verses, "the writer David Dar revealed to us an extraordinary richness of *Alexandrian Songs* by Mikhail Kuzmin, which were true Russian blues."[37]

While the rhythm of the Blok's *The Twelve* still resonates within his syncopations and repetitions, in Shrayer-Petrov's blues verses composed in America, the musical and thematic subtext has become more complex. In "Idiopathic Blues" ("Idiopaticheskii bliuz") one finds nuggets of Russian literature laced with Russian history. The name itself, *idiopathic*, is derived from the medical term "idiopathy," in other words, an illness that develops independently, without being caused or accompanied by other conditions. It is some sort of a special tendency, the origin of which is difficult to understand, which probably implies not only a longing for Russian culture, but also a disease afflicting society:

> Марфа Борисовна, это князь.
>
> Ваше превосходительство, ваше сиятельство,
>
> Марфа Борисовна, грязь, грязь, грязь.
>
> Чёрная лестница — мышки за кошками.
>
> Иволгой стонет грязный матрац.
>
> Марфа-посадница, Марфа-развратница,
>
> Генерал Иволгин, мразь, мразь, мразь.

> ("Marfa Borisovna, here is the Prince./ Your excellency, your grace,/ Marfa Borisovna, dirt, dirt, dirt/ Stairway is black—cats after mice./ A black

---

35 David Shraer-Petrov, *Barabany sud´by* (Moscow: Argo-risk, 2002), 3.
36 David Shraer-Petrov, "Korol´ svinga v russkoi proze. Aksenov," in his *Druz´ia i teni. Roman s uchastiem avtora* (New York: Liberty, 1989), 135–136.
37 Shraer-Petrov, *Barabany sud´by*, 3.

mattress moans like an oriole./ Marfa the Mayoress, Marfa the licentious one,/ General Ivolgin, scum, scum, scum [in the Russian the last name Ivolgin derives from 'иволга,' 'oriole'].")

And in the final round of this blues it is already difficult to distinguish Lev Nikolayevich Myshkin from Lev Nikolayevich Tolstoy:

Лев Николаевич достопочтеннейший,
Лев Николаевич достоевгеннейший.
Фёдор Михайлович, плац, плац, плац.
Лев Николаевич, плач, плач, плач.
Генерал Иволгин и князь Мышкин
Поднимаются по черной лестнице к.
Марфа Борисовна, Анна Аркадьевна,
Анна Андреевна, Настасья Филипповна,
Анна Аркадьевна, Марфа Борисовна,
Анна Андреевна, Анна Андреевна,
Лев Николаевич, Лев Николаевич,
Анна Андреевна, Лев Николаевич . . .[38]

("Lev Nikolaevich the most honorable,/ Lev Nikolaevich the most noble./ Fyodor Mikhailovich, *platz, platz, platz*./ Lev Nikolaevich, lament, lament, lament./ General Ivolgin and Prince Myshkin/ Climb the black staircase to./ Marfa Borisovna, Anna Arkadievna,/ Anna Andreevna, Nastasya Filippovna,/ Anna Arkadievna, Marfa Borisovna,/ Anna Andreevna, Anna Andreevna,/ Lev Nikolaevich, Lev Nikolaevich/ Anna Andreevna, Lev Nikolaevich . . .")

The verses of trisyllabic (triple meter), underscored by caesura, amplify this growing cadence of pain, while the triple "плац" ("platz"), an allusion to the near-execution of Fyodor Dostoevsky in April 1849, corresponds to the triple "плач" (*plach*, "lament") not only for the protagonist of *Idiot* Prince Lev Nikolayevich Myshkin, who was powerless to resist the selfish and base interests of society and was swept and carried away by the maelstrom of evil. However, perhaps this also hints at the later tragedy, the departure from home and the death of Lev Tolstoy. The blues repetitions unite even more dizzyingly the plot of the historical Marfa the Mayoress with Marfa Borisovna Terentieva, mother of Ippolit and intimate friend of General Ivolgin; Nastasya Filippovna Barashkova is linked with Anna Arkadievna

---

38 Shraer-Petrov, *Propashchaia dusha*, 43-44.

Karenina, both of them women with a tragic fate, while the rhythm and confluence of names carries the blues up to Anna Andreevna Akhmatova, her son Lev Nikolayevich Gumilev—and back to Lev Nikolaevich Tolstoy, thus closing the blues poem with a sound endowed with deliberate meaning.

In "The Blues of the Yellow River in New Orleans" ("Bliuz zheltoi reki v Novom Orleane"), built on the same metrical principle of repetition-permutation and unity of the triple meter (amphibrachic dimeters and trimeters with a caesura after the second foot, as per Pushkin), the author nevertheless "deceives" both musical and geographical associations. This is not the famous blues *Deep River*, and certainly not the rock song "Yellow River," the performance of which in 1970 made the English rock band Christie famous. A blue pheasant nearly turns into a stork (which, according to the legend, brings babies, and in this blues carries Moses in its beak); the river is not in the deep American South, but in Egypt:

По жёлтой реке	в корзинке плывёт Моисей
Фараонова дочка	корзинку в руки берёт
[...]	
Голубые глаза	глядят из жёлтой реки
По жёлтой реке	плывёт голубой фазан,
По жёлтой реке	в корзинке плывёт Моисей.

Along the yellow river	in a basket Moses floats
Pharaoh's daughter	picks up the basket
[...]	
Blue eyes	gaze from the yellow river
Along the yellow river	floats a blue pheasant
Along the yellow river	in a basket Moses floats.

Later on, the story of the rescue of Moses, who will become the deliverer of his people, is further transformed. Musical and semantic repetitions-substitutions shift the meaning and turn the well-known Biblical story into an avant-garde one, in which reality is deformed, and a fair dose of surrealism is combined with pain and compassion that are *made strange* (defamiliarized):

Фараонова дочка	голубого фазана берёт
Из жёлтой реки	голубого к лону несёт,
Голубого фазана	к царскому трону несёт.

По жёлтой реке	пустая корзинка плывёт.
Голубой фазан	к лону пустому плывёт,
Голубой фазан	клюв еврейский несёт,
Голубой фазан	к лону царевны несёт,
Фараоновой дочке	глаза и сердце клюёт.

Pharaoh's daughter	takes a blue pheasant
From the yellow river	presses a blue one to her lap,
She takes a blue pheasant	to the royal throne.
Along the yellow river	an empty basket floats.
A blue pheasant	to the empty lap floats,
A blue pheasant	carries a Jewish beak,
A blue pheasant	carries to the princess's lap,
He pecks the eyes and heart	of the pharaoh's daughter.

However, the poem does not end with the menacing omen, and the river in the poem takes another unexpected turn:

По жёлтой реке	жёлтый народ плывет,
По жёлтой реке	мёртвый народ плывет,
По жёлтой реке	плывёт голубой фазан,
По жёлтой тоске	плывут голубые глаза.
Та-да-да-да-та-та	та-да-да-да-та-та-та-та-та
Та-да-да-да-та-та	та-да-да-да-та-та-та-та-та
Голубой фазан	плывёт по жёлтой реке,
По жёлтой реке	плывёт голубой фазан.[39]

Along the yellow river	a yellow nation floats,
Along the yellow river	a dead nation floats,
Along the yellow river	a blue pheasant floats,
Along the yellow sorrow	blue eyes float.
Ta-da-da-da-ta-ta	ta-da-da-da-ta-ta-ta-ta-ta
Ta-da-da-da-ta-ta	ta-da-da-da-ta-ta-ta-ta-ta
A blue pheasant	along the yellow river floats
Along the yellow river	a blue pheasant floats.

Repetitions are akin to incantations or prayers; repetitions with displacement and substitution, as in this blues, perhaps spell out a terrible

---

39 Shraer-Petrov, *Propashchaia dusha*, 45–46.

omen or a warning: "корзинка" ("basket") is transformed into "жёлтый народ/мёртвый народ" ("yellow people/dead people"). Is this an echo of the Shoah? This way the flow of the river brings space, time, and history together. No less saturated and transformed is "The Blues of a Jewish Organist in a Harlem Church" ("Bliuz evreiskogo organista v garlemskoi tserkvi"), in which repetitions/substitutions evoke both Pushkin and Mandelstam, and strict alexandrines (iambic hexameters) are further molded into a modified Onegin stanza:

Еврейский органист играет в черной церкви,
Еврейский органист играет в черной церкви.
Еврейский гармонист играл когда-то в цирке,
Еврейский гармонист в гастрольном шапито.
Он жмёт на клавиши и напевает шепотком:
О, никогда не повторится
Та белобрысая девица,
Циркачка, неженка, блудница,
С которой я во снах кружу,
Которой я принадлежу.
Как никогда не повторится
Та златоглавая столица,
Дней отгремевших колесница,
В которых я во снах кружу,
Которым я принадлежу.
Еврейский органист, Аве Мария, Фруктус.
Еврейский органист, жми клавиши до хруста,
Еврейский гармонист, наяривай по-русски,
Еврейский органист, Аве Мария, Фруктус.
Прошу тебя, пожалуйста, без грусти.[40]

("A Jewish organist plays in a black church,/ A Jewish organist plays in a black church./ A Jewish accordion player once used to play in the circus,/ A Jewish accordion player—in a touring chapiteau circus./ He presses the keys and sings *sotto voce*:/ Oh, it will never happen again/ That blondish chick,/ Circus girl, sweetie, harlot,/ With whom I spin in my dreams,/ To whom I belong./ As will never happen again/ That gold-domed capital,/ The chariot of bygone days,/ In which I spin in my dreams,/ To which I belong./

---

40 Shraer-Petrov, *Propashchaia dusha*, 46–47.

A Jewish organist, Ave Maria . . . fructus./ O Jewish organist, press the keys until they crunch,/ Jewish accordion player, play one in the Russian style,/ Jewish organist, Ave Maria . . . fructus./ I beg you, please, without sadness.")

Shrayer-Petrov weaves into his nostalgic Jewish-American-Russian blues an allusion to Mandelstam's "Girl, upstart, proud" ("Devchonka, vyskochka, gordiachka") from the poem "After the long-fingered Paganini…" ("Za Paganini dlinnopalym …," 1935) with an allusion to the aphoristic lines from the first chapter of *Eugene Onegin*:

Людей, о коих не сужу

Затем, что к ним принадлежу.

("Of people whom I do not judge/ Because I'm one of them myself.")

Overcoming the inertia of writing leads to overcoming nostalgia. In his essay "Art as Fracture [or 'Rupture']" ("Iskusstvo kak izlom," 1992–1993), written in the same years as the "Six American Blues on Russian Themes" and polemically developing Viktor Shklovsky's "Art as Device," David Shrayer-Petrov writes not only about formal devices called for in order to "make strange" (defamiliarize) the tired and clichéd forms, but also about feelings, "the broken fates of Russian émigré writers": "the prose, written according to the method of *art as fracture* also ends with suchlike tragedies."[41] Art is born as a shock, as an overcoming. This is clearly audible in the twenty-six blues collected in Shrayer-Petrov book *Drums of Fate*. Those blues are often built on the same rhythmic principle of repetition/substitution, but now an elegiac note dominates, as in the poem "Girl in a Straw Hat" ("Devochka v solomennoi shliape"): "это фонтана старого круг/ это мозаика детства мой друг" ("this is the fountain's old circle/ this is a childhood mosaic my friend") or in the poem "A Walk on the Wintry Nevsky Prospect" ("Progulka po zimnemu Nevskomu prospektu"): "был невский мороз курчав/ был твой поцелуй горчав" ("the Nevan frost was kinky-haired/ your kiss was bitter-flavored"). Even nostalgia here gains an elegiac, defamiliarized sound, even though the pain remains:

и зачатый помимо воли

фотомиг

проявился в давнишней боли

фантом-миф

---

[41] David Shraer-Petrov, "Iskusstvo kak izlom," *Novyi Zhurnal/ The New Review* 196 (1995): 255.

кто там бродит в такую погоду
средь зимы
в прошлом веке по мертвому городу
это мы[42]

("and conceived against its will/ photomoment/ appeared in the lingering old pain/ phantom-myth/ who is wandering in such weather/ in the midst of winter/ in the past century across the city /it is us")

The pain is defamiliarized by sadness and sorrow, as in "Once in Petersburg" ("Kogda-to v Pitere"), "White Night" ("Belaia noch′"), and in the blues "To Part before Love Has Faded Away" ("Proshchat′sia poka ne ugasla liubov′), in contrast to the four blues verses from the earlier collection *Lost Soul*, the stretched and elongated rhythm is combined with the refrain "proshchat'sia poka ne ugasla liubov'" ("to part before love has faded away"). Turned inside out in the last, final chords, the refrain mutes the longing, thereby exposing the subtext of parting:

щенячью любовь не ценила ты смешить убивать влюблять ворожить
хвостом за баржой уплывает река щенячьим хвостом за тобой тоска
смешать голоса побольше льда глотнуть и память не ворошить
щенячью любовь не ценила ты чужую любовь не умела прощать
едва ли не самый испытанный ход прощаться пока не угасла любовь.[43]

("puppy love you didn't appreciate to amuse kill enchant conjure/ like a tail after a barge the river flows away like puppy tail longing follows you/ to mix voices more ice to gulp and not to stir up memories/ puppy love you didn't appreciate love of others you couldn't forgive/ perhaps the most proven move to part before love has faded away.")

Sometimes memories are defamiliarized by irony, or even sarcasm, as in the poem "In the Bar" ("V bare"), in which irony is already embedded in the incorporated motif of the Russian acrobatic folk dance "Kamarinskaya":

в этом баре все бутылки одинаково пьянят
в этом баре все затылки одиноки и готовы
на пол каменный свалиться как уроненный гранат
кем уронен неизвестно и совсем неинтересно
потому что в этом баре о любви не говорят.[44]

---

42 Shraer-Petrov, *Barabany sud′by*, 29.
43 Ibid., 33.
44 David Shraer-Petrov, "V bare," in *Barabany sud′by*, 35.

("in this bar all the bottles intoxicate the same/ in this bar all napes of the head are lonely and ready/ to tumble on the stone floor like a dropped pomegranate/ it's unknown who dropped it and of no interest at all/ because in this bar they don't talk about love.")

Conflated with "Kamarinskaya," the refrain "because in this bar they don't talk about love" defamiliarizes both sadness and nostalgia. However, in such poems as "A Donkey Named Jacques" ("Oslik po imeni Zhak"), the pain in which one hears "a lament for the killed walls" ("плач по убитым стенам") comes to life with a new force. Memories of visiting the Caucasus no longer sound somewhat abstract and philosophical, as is perhaps the case in the blues "Synagogue in Tbilisi" ("Sinagoga v Tbilisi") from the same book, but are filled with anger, which the dactylic trimeter, sustained on male rhymes, powerfully augments:

господи я не один
ослик по имени жак
между взбесившихся псин
я осязаю твой знак
дядя снимите пиджак
в землю упрятанный злак
вашей погибели знак

о не упорствуй палач
ты закатай рукава
топчет пески караван
ослик понуро бредёт
в храм никогда не придёт
мальчик поскольку полёт
господу посланный плач
[. . .]

ослик по имени жак
мальчик по имени сим
дядя по имени хам
город ерусалим
наша империя рим
наш император дурак
мы за толпой семеним[45]

---

45 Shraer-Petrov, *Barabany sud'by*, 27.

("god I am not alone/ donkey named Jacques/ amid dogs gone rabid/ I perceive your sign/ uncle take off your jacket/ a stalk of cereal hidden in the soil/ it's a sign of your death || o executioner do not persist/ roll up your sleeves/ a caravan tramples the sands/ donkey forlornly plods along/ will never reach the temple/ the boy because [of] the flight/ a lament sent to god || [. . .] donkey named Jacques/ boy named shem/ uncle named ham/ the city of yerushalaim/ our empire is rome/ our emperor is a fool/ we follow the crowd we roam")

The poet links centuries, epochs, and countries with the rhymes "сим-ерусалим-рим-семеним," "Shem-Jerusalaim-Rome-roam," blurring the boundaries of space and time—"chronotope of history," to use Mikhail Bakhtin's term[46]—as is the case in the poem "Synagogue in Tbilisi." He also stands next to the outcasts of all ages, eliminating the emotional boundary, and becomes a co-participant in their fate. From a witness he turns into a participant of the described events. All these themes—childhood memories, love, jealousy, being a pariah, overcoming nostalgia, gaining wisdom, contemplating one's destiny—are embodied in the last blues, "Drums of Fate" (or "Prayer Wheels"), which gave the title to the entire collection:

крутите вертите вращайте желтые барабаны судьбы
крутите потому что волчок желтые потому что будда
вертите потому что ветер вращайте потому что в радость
крутите вертите вращайте барабаны под деревом будды
крутите вертите вращайте будите свою судьбу
[. . .]

крутите вертите вращайте желтые барабаны судьбы
желтые потому что жадность желтые потому что ревность
желтые потому что жестокая желтые потому что будда
желтые барабаны судьбы под вечным деревом будды
желтое потому что солнце вечное потому что будда

крутите вертите вращайте желтые барабаны судьбы
желтые потому что солнце вечные потому что будды
избушка потому что детство монах потому что молитва
вечное дерево будды дерево потому что девочка
вечное потому что будда девочка потому что ты.[47]

---

46 M. M. Bakhtin, "Formy vremeni i khronotopa v romane. Ocherki po istoricheskoi poetike," in *Voprosy literatury i estetiki* (Moscow: Khudozhestvennaia literatura, 1975), 235.

47 Shraer-Petrov, *Barabany sud'by*, 41.

("spin turn rotate the yellow prayer wheels/ spin because it's a top yellow because buddha/ turn because the wind rotate because it's joyful/ spin turn rotate the wheels under the tree of buddha/ spin turn rotate awaken your fate [. . .] || spin turn rotate the yellow prayer wheels/ yellow because greed yellow because jealousy/ yellow because cruel yellow because buddha/ the yellow prayer wheels under the eternal tree of buddha/ yellow because the sun eternal because buddha || spin turn rotate the yellow prayer wheels/ yellow because the sun eternal because buddha/ hut because childhood monk because prayer/ the eternal tree of buddha tree because girl/ eternal because buddha girl because you.")

The color scheme, with its preponderance of yellow (the color of jealousy, Buryat tea, Buddha, sun, being an outcast, including one forced to wear the yellow star), combined with the sound orchestration ("желтые потому что жадность желтые потому что ревность/ желтые потому что жестокая желтые потому что будда," "yellow because greed yellow because jealousy/ yellow because cruel yellow because buddha") and with the rotational movement result in the circular thematic outcome. The poem outlines its circle of themes and brings to the fore the theme of fate, consonant with Buddha and turning the great prayer wheel. The color yellow is also important in another poem by Shrayer-Petrov, which he started in 1961, after meeting Joseph Brodsky, and completed in America after Brodsky's death. Titled *Yellow Star* (*Zheltaia zvezda*) and completed in 1996, this long poem is dedicated to Brodsky's memory. The title, *Yellow Star*, bears symbolic significance, and both at the beginning and at the end the poet deploys the motif of yellowness: "Understand, I am a yellow blindfold/ On my own eyes" ("Пойми, я жёлтая повязка/ На собственных моих глазах").[48] The color yellow and the yellow star first serves as a terrible omen, and then as a commemoration:

Что же касается *его*, то на исходе столетья,
Возвращаясь из траурного Нью-Йорка,
Я опять увидел над шоссе лучи раскалённые эти
Жёлтой звезды, припавшей к вершинке придорожной ёлки.[49]

("As far as *he* is concerned, at the exodus of the century,/ when I was returning from the mournful New York,/ I saw once again over the highway

---

48 David Shraer-Petrov, *Derevenskii orkestr. Shest' poem* (St. Petersburg: Ostrovitianin, 2016), 46.
49 Ibid., 54.

these red-hot rays/ of a yellow star, pressed to the slender top of a roadside fir tree.")

In further collections of poems by Shrayer-Petrov, and especially in the book *Some Degree of Longing for the Messiah* (*Nekotoraia stepen′ toski po Messii*, 2005–2006), Jewish themes (the name speaks for itself), literary themes ("Tolstoy, Dostoevsky, Chekhov," in which one can hear the echo of "Idiopathic Blues," albeit arranged already in a firmer and more free verse key), and musical themes of the blues verses are further developed. However, the later verses are now devoid of repetitions-refrains, and even in such poems about music as "The Concert of Schoenberg's Music" ("Kontsert muzyki Shenberga") or "Trio of Shostakovich" ("Trio Shostakovicha"), reality is defamiliarized, both by musical and linguistic means, the latter deliberately hearkening back to futurism[50] and *zaum* (transsense):

> Наскандалить балетом «барышня и хулиган»,
> «нагилух и яншыраб»,
> нагл и глух яныш раб,
> «барышня и хулиган»,
> «нагилух яншыраб»,
> нагл и глух ятаган.[51]

("scandalize with a ballet "young lady and hooligan",/ "nagilooh dna ydal gnuoy",/ nag and loose goy lad,/ "young lady and hooligan",/ "nagilooh dna ylad gnuoy",/ nag and loose the naked blade" [this translation seeks to capture the wordplay and paronamastic devices of the original—tr.].)

The title of Shostakovich's ballet, "Young Lady and Hooligan," is read backwards, palindromically as nonsense, transsense, *zaum*. Then *zaum* takes on a new meaning, which is also infused with the personal motif of the poet-refusenik (which is also confirmed by the final of the poem, to which I will turn shortly): "нагл и глух яныш раб" (literally: "arrogant and deaf is the ianush the slave"). Once again, the title of the ballet is read backwards so as to reveal a new meaning: "нагл и глух ятаган" (literally: "arrogant and deaf is the yatagan [Ottoman short saber]"). The poem's rhythmic structure varies as well: a trochaic tetrameter ("барышня и хулиган") is followed by a line that, due to the omission of one stressed syllable and the strong caesura in the middle, can be read as an anapestic dimeter with an extra

---

50 About Shrayer-Petrov and Futurism, see also Oleg Smola's essay in this volume.
51 David Shraer-Petrov, "Trio Shostakovicha," in *Dve knigi. Stikhi* (Philadelphia: Poberezh′e, 2009), 64.

stress on the first syllable of the first foot ("нагл и глух ятаган"), which, in turn, is followed by an iambic pentameter ("порвать с властями с самого начала"). The next line, "попасть в число 'проклятых формалистов, которые отвернулись от народа,'" contains a prosaic imitation of a Soviet newspaper's front page denunciation:

> порвать с властями с самого начала,
> попасть в число
> "проклятых формалистов, которые отвернулись от народа".
>
> ("To break with the authorities from the very beginning,/ to become one of the/ 'cursed formalists who have turned away from the people.'")

Musical themes coalesce with political ones; variations on the themes of Russian folk songs ("среди долины ровныя,/ на гладкой высоте" ["in the middle of the plain valley/ on a smooth high plain"]) morph into a Jewish theme that precedes the finale:

> ну что поборолся, видишь:
> с дымом отечества улетел идиш,
> с пеплом освенцима улетел идиш.
> слышишь? видишь?
> в трепете нот передай
> или навек пропадай!
>
> ("well, you have fought enough, now you see/ with the smoke of the fatherland yiddish flew away/ with the ashes of auschwitz yiddish flew away/ you hear? you see?/ convey with the shudder of notes/or just disappear forever!")

In the finale, an allusion to Exodus from Egypt rings in the voice of the refusenik author (an allusion which also appears in the finale of Shrayer-Petrov's long narrative poem *Yuri the Long-Armed* [*Iurii Dolgorukii*], 1985–1986):

> отпусти-прости нас,
> матерь русь![52]
>
> ("let us go—forgive us/ mother-rus´!")

Art is born at the intersection, in the struggle of two beginnings (recall "Art as Fracture"). In the works of David Shrayer-Petrov, written in Russia, the theme of the struggle for Jewish self-expression is not only found in his

---

52 Shraer-Petrov, "Trio Shostakovicha," 66.

best-known refusenik novels and short stories, but also in a many poems. These two stanzas from "Chimney Sweep" are filled with bitter irony:

В черной фетровой ермолке,
С поварешкой, помелом —
Ряженый с районной ярмарки,
Дьявол, негр иль костолом,

Или жид под псевдонимом
Негритянского лица
На велосипеде мимо
Убегает без конца?[53]

("In a black felt yarmulke,/ With a ladle, on a stoop—/ A mummer from the district fair/The devil, a Negro or a bonecracker,| Or a Yid under the pseudonym/ of a Negroid person/ On a bicycle past us/ Keeps running away?")

"Chimney Sweep" ("Trubochist") is the third part of the long poem *Flying Saucers* (*Letaiushchie tarelki*). Written in 1976 in Pärnu and dedicated to Shrayer-Petrov's close friend, the Estonian artist Jüri Arrak, *Flying Saucers* in fact became the poem of fracture and of the painful decision to emigrate and leave behind ancestral graves. Almost a decade later, in the poem "Mother's Grave" ("Mogila mamy") from *Nevan Poems* (1984–1985), Shrayer-Petrov would recite a post-modernist Kaddish, which I will quote in its entirety:

Могила мамы

... карельский
гранит в кровавых каплях
товарняк под мостом
спасибо вам ребята
канавка уходящая в Неву
или
Нева текущая к
кровавым
пой
последний кадиш
паровоз
космополит угарный
приложился к груди

---

53 Shraer-Petrov, *Derevenskii orkestr*, 14–15.

растоптанной
спасибо вам ребята
притормозил
транзитный товарняк
правительственной дачи
Херсонес в обломанных колоннах
от стены остзейского замка
или
от зубьев ледника
кровавый камень отделён
я опоздал
ладонь рябины
утешает.⁵⁴

("... karelian/ granite in bloody drops/ freight train before the bridge/ thank you pals/ the ditch that falls into the Neva/ or/ the Neva flowing to/ the bloody/ sing/ the last kaddish/ locomotive/ the suffocating cosmopolitan/ pressed himself to the breast / trampled/ thank you pals /slowed down/ the transit freight train/ of the governmental dacha/ Chersonesus of broken columns/ from the wall of a Baltic German castle/ or/ from the glacier's teeth/ the blood stone is detached/ I am late/ a rowanberry hand/ consoles.")

This text from *Nevan Poems*, which Genrikh Sapgir so highly valued (he selected poems from it for *Samizdat of the Century* anthology and wrote about them in the preface), written during the refusenik middle 1980s, is not only an elegy or a Kaddish, but also a historical memento. The "blood stone" is perhaps an echo of the unfulfilled plans for the forcible resettlement of the Jews to "faraway places," which in 1952–1953 would have solved the Jewish question in a Stalinist fashion. These plans were terminated with the death of the tyrant, he whom today's Russian pseudopatriots miss so very much. That is why the poem's backdrop is bloody.

Central to the poetics of the long poem *Runner Begoon* (1987), dedicated to the prisoner of Zion Iosef Begun, in whose release from prison in the spring of 1987 the poet's wife, Emilia Shrayer, played a role, is the wordplay on the last name of a leading activist in the Soviet *aliyah* movement. "Begun" (pronounced "begoon") in Russian means "runner," while the movement itself, which pressured the Soviet regime to allow

---

54 David Shraer-Petrov, *Nevskie stikhi* (St. Petersburg: Ostrovitianin, 2011), 33-34.

Jewish emigration, was regarded as anti-Soviet activity (the notorious article 58 of the Russian penal code comes to mind):

> [...] Грозятся высшей карою и праведной:
> Зачем рукой нечистой ты коснулся русских струн
> БЕГУН, БЕГУН, БЕГУН, БЕГУН, БЕГУН, БЕГУН?..
>
> Он, проходя смертельные спирали,
> Ловя частички Божьего дыханья,
> Засыпанный осколками, окурками, оскалистою бранью,
> Стирая пот кровавый ангельскою дланью,
> Им выдыхает:
> Русских струн я не касался,
> Чужие мы, родным я не казался,
> Хоть с вами я в обнимку и валялся
> На плахах нар, в промежностях канав,
> Хоть пот у нас подобно вышиблен, кровав,
> Я — иудей
> И русским не казался![55]

> [...] They threatened with supreme and righteous penance:
> How dare you touch Russian strings, your hands unclean,
> BEGOON, RUNNER BEGOON, BEGOON, BEGOON, BEGOON...
>
> Passing through death's final spiral,
> Catching particles of God's breath,
> Showered with shards of glass, cigarette butts and slurs,
> Wiping off bloody sweat with his angelic palm,
> He gasps out:
> I didn't touch Russian strings. We're strangers.
> I never tried to pass for one of you,
> Though I've embraced you as we wallowed together
> In prison bunks, in perineums of ditches;
> Though our sweat is equally bloody, spelled out likewise,
> I'm a Jew,
> I never tried to pass for a Russian.[56]

---

55 Shraer-Petrov, *Derevenskii orkestr*, 34–35.
56 David Shrayer-Petrov, *Runner Begoon*, tr. Maxim D. Shrayer, *Four Centuries: Russian Poetry in Translation* 7 (2014): 55, https://perelmuterverlag.de/FC72014.pdf, accessed July 5, 2020.

Later in the poem, the logic of the developing imagery leads the poet to archetypal and eschatological insights:

Я — Вечный Жид российский,
Я — БЕГУН, БЕГУН, БЕГУН, БЕГУН, БЕГУН, БЕГУН...[57]

I am the Wandering Jew of Russia.
I am BEGOON, RUNNER BEGOON, BEGOON, BEGOON, BEGOON...[58]

In the works written in America, Shrayer-Petrov exhibits a desire to preserve Russia, the Russia of memory, as in the poems "Once in Petersburg" ("Odnazhdy v Pitere") and "Moscow March ("Moskovskii mart"). These poems are also characterized by the poet's desire to render new images in a new form, a form which becomes the content itself and defines the poem's content. In its turn, the form of the poem endows the soul of the lyrical hero with its own form, as in the poem titled "The Form of the Soul" ("Forma dushi"):

если ты теряешь форму
самого себя
ты даешь большую фору
тем кого беся
полстолетия тревожил
непохожестью
помни ты талант и все же
чувствами шестью
ухватись за край обрыва
карточной судьбы.[59]

("if you are losing the form/ of yourself/ you give a big head start/ to those whom you enrage/ for half a century disturbing/ with being unlike them/ remember you have talent and yet/ with all the six senses/ grab the edge of the cliff/ of your card fortune.")

In the poem "Coolidge Corner," unexpected enjambments, where the words are either "cut off" or missing, make the imagery more tangible, visible, while also shifting the familiar spatial relations:

---

57 Shraer-Petrov, *Derevenskii orkestr*, 38.
58 Shrayer-Petrov, *Runner Begoon*, 57.
59 Shraer-Petrov, *Linii-figury-tela*, 26.

кулидж корнер это угол на пере
сечении бикон стрит и гарвард стрит
дело приближается к ночной поре
темнота городской стеной стоит
но оказывается не угол а углы
все четыре подпирают остановку трам
две аптеки банк и по утрам
место где народ над рельсами гудит

("coolidge corner—it is a corner at the inter/ section of beacon street and harvard street/ it's getting closer to nighttime/ darkness stands like a city wall/ but it turns out to be not a corner, but corners/ all four shore up the tram sta/ two pharmacies bank and in the morning/ place where people buzz over the rails")

Then the author rips apart the canvas of space and time, going from the intersection of Beacon and Harvard streets in the Boston near suburb of Brookline, where Shrayer-Petrov and his wife have lived since 2007, straight to Liteynyi Prospect in his native Leningrad/St. Petersburg:

две аптеки банк трамвай и все
что соединяет быт работу семью [...]
лестничными клетками литейный где
забежать на часик а потом к воде
от моста литейного рукой подать кресты
за какой из четырёх свернуть на ты
ног секущих линии биллиард фонарь
осыпает лилия золотую гарь[60]

("two pharmacies bank tram and everything/ that unites everyday living work family [...]/ with staircases where the liteynyi is where/ to stop by for an hour and then towards the water/ from the liteynyi bridge a stone's throw to the kresty [crosses] prison/ to which one of the four to turn to you/ legs dissecting lines of the billiards streetlight/ lily showers gold cinder")

Many poems are based on a similar shift of space and time (in the book *Lines—Shapes—Bodies*, in my view, space shifts are of the foremost importance). Such is the case with "Coolidge Corner" but also "The Shifted World" ("Sdvinutyi mir"), "Memories of Eastern Siberia" ("Vospominaniia

---

60 Ibid., 10.

o Vostochnoi Sibiri"), "The Crowd in Boston" ("Tolpa v Bostone") and the final poem, "Return from a Journey" ("Vozvrashchenie is puteshestviia"). The poem "Shifted World" deliberately starts with a shift in space:

> роща двинулась на асфальт
> рельсы съехали в чарльз-реку
> синагога сдвинув кипу
> минаретом играет в бейсбол
> кулидж корнер разинув рот
> шлет машины за поворот
> президент идёт на восток
> мусульманский закрыть роток
> говорков невозможно пусть
> президент торит звёздный путь

("grove moved onto the pavement/ rails slid into the charles river/ synagogue pulling down its kippah/ plays baseball with a minaret/ coolidge corner gaping-mouthed/ sends cars around the turn/ the president is going east/ that muslim mouth/ of dialects cannot be closed let/ the president drill through the trek of stars")

The three-ictus trimeters create an additional tension, but it turns out that it is not about a shift of space, but about a shift of ideas; wise with his life experience, the poet unerringly draws historical parallels, shifting historical time and remaining true to the personal time of his poetry. At the same time, the rhythmic repetition, akin to the blues, emphasizes this shift of time and space, revealing a falsity (initially, this appears to be about the Iraq War of 2003, but the logic of the poem takes the reader even further):

> роща двинулась на асфальт
> рельсы съехали в чарльз-реку
> новый путь да старая фальшь
> дайте въехать броневику
> дайте влезть поближе к броне
> витой башне и руку поднять
> чтоб ему ей тебе и мне
> президентскую правду понять
> вся загадка которой в том
> кто придёт когда мы уйдём[61]

---

61 Ibid., 27.

("the grove moved onto the pavement/ rails slid into the charles river/ the path is new but the falsity is old/ let the armored car drive in/ let me get closer to the armor/ to the twisted tower and raise my hand/ for him her you and me/ to understand the presidential truth/ the whole riddle of which is in/ he who will come when we are gone")

It is noteworthy that the poet is attuned to the details of his American surroundings (and, specifically, life in New England) yet conveys them in a hyperbolized, surrealist manner. Familiar reality is made strange so as to reveal the disturbing omens of time right there in the places of fractured meaning. In the poem "Wild Turkeys in Boston" ("Dikie indeiki v Bostone"), dedicated to his son Maxim D. Shrayer, his close collaborator and a poet in his own right, Shrayer-Petrov again begins with the external signs of time:

куда девались дикие индейки
они бродили в роще по утрам
меня терзали дивные идейки
с вполне реальной мыслью пополам
я понимал что подступила осень
а я к зиме бесплодной не готов
и что обманчива безоблачная просинь
все больше голых веток без листов[62]

what happened to the wild turkeys
they used to wander in the morning grove
wasn't i thinking such pure malarkey
enmeshed with something so morose
i realized autumn had approached
i wasn't prepared for the fruitless frost
the cloudless blue sky was treacherous
bare branches without leaves the yellow froth[63]

Then, after jokingly comparing himself to "ostrich-like birds" ("ptits strausopodobnykh"), the poet proceeds to a not humorous reflection about his own life and his creative work:

но собеседницы мои тянулись следом
за тем кто не дошел в мечтаньях до

---

62 Ibid., 22.
63 David Shrayer-Petrov, "Wild Turkeys in Boston," tr. Maxim D. Shrayer, *Four Centuries: Russian Poetry in Translation* 11 (2015): 19, https://perelmuterverlag.de/FC112015.pdf, accessed July 5, 2020.

таких как мне придумалось миражных
картин в которых с горем пополам
смешались и находки и пропажи
веселье со слезами пополам
но так недалеко до исаковских
твардовских матусовских добрести
был день осенний бостонских таковский
что я не знал в какую даль брести[64]

alas the pretty ones who could've shared my sorrow
followed not me but the fellow who was next
to me though not a crazy dreamer
he swept aside my fanciful mirage
in which the losses and the gains aren't real
in which the joy and tears are enmeshed
but wait this way i could end up like
isakovsky tvardovsky matusovsky
composers of lyrics for the crowd
it was a luminous autumn day in Boston
i wasn't sure which path i should try[65]

The mention of Soviet poets Mikhail Isakovsky, Mikhail Matusovsky, and Aleksandr Tvardovsky sounds like a warning—first of all to the poet himself—not to descend into traditionalism and banality, which, unfortunately, has happened to some well-known poets in exile. It is a poet's call not to freeze in place and to continue to break—not the soul, but the form. Hence, in the end, art is about hiding the fractured soul, about defamiliarizing emotional pain and anxiety without turning one's soul inside out; art is about celebrating winter without falling into sentimentality and turning back at his path while fearlessly looking ahead to the future. David Shrayer-Petrov persevered and succeeded both as a person and as a writer, and his poems—perhaps even more than prose, show how challenging and full of self-doubts this path has been.

*Translated, from the Russian, by
Daria Sadovnichenko with Maxim D. Shrayer*

---

64 Shraer-Petrov, *Linii-figury-tela*, 23.
65 Shrayer-Petrov, "Wild Turkeys in Boston."

Works Cited

Bakhtin, M. M. "Formy vremeni i khronotopa v romane. Ocherki po istoricheskoi poetike." In M.M. Bakhtin, *Voprosy literatury i estetiki*, 234–407. Moscow: Khudozhestvennaia Literatura, 1975.

Bobyshev, Dmitrii. "Shrayer-Petrov David." In *Slovar´ poetov russkogo zarubezh´ia*, edited by Vadim Kreid, 432–434. Saint Petersburg: RKhGI, 1999.

Chaikovskaia, Irina. "Po napravleniiu k zhenshchine. O stikhakh Davida Shraera-Petrova." *Krugozor* (February 2010). http://www.krugozormagazine.com/show/Shraer-Petrov.640.html. Accessed August 22, 2019.

Mikhailov, Eduard. "Sud´ba-sinekdokha." *Lekhaim* 226, February 2, 2011. https://lechaim.ru/ARHIV/226/mihailov.htm. Accessed January 2, 2020.

Nabokov, Vladimir. *Sobranie sochinenii russkogo perioda*. Edited by N. I. Artemenko-Tolstaia. Vol. 2. St. Petersburg: Simpozium, 1999.

Ozerov, Lev. "Ob avtore." In David Petrov, *Kholsty*. In *Pereklichka*, 116–117. Moscow: Molodaia gvardiia, 1967.

Sapgir, Genrikh. "David Shraer-Petrov." In Genrikh Sapgir, *Neofitsial´naia poeziia: antologiia poeticheskogo samizdata sovetskoi epokhi*. https://rvb.ru/np/publication/sapgir4.htm#58. Accessed August 22, 2019.

Shraer, Maksim D. [Maxim D. Shrayer], and David Shraer-Petrov [David Shrayer-Petrov]. *Genrikh Sapgir. Klassik avangarda*. St. Petersburg: Dmitrii Bulanin, 2004.

———. "Moskovskii purimshpil'—1987." *Lekhaim* 3 (2019): 37–41.

David Shrayer-Petrov [David Petrov]. *Kholsty*. In *Pereklichka*, 116–160. Moscow: Molodaia gvardiia, 1967.

——— [David Shraer-Petrov]. *Poeziia i nauka (zametki i razmyshleniia)*. Moscow: Znanie, 1974.

———[David Shraer-Petrov]. *Druz'ia i teni. Roman s uchastiem avtora*. New York: Liberty, 1989.

——— [David Shraer-Petrov]. *Villa Borgeze*. Holyoke, MA: New England Publishing, 1992.

——— [David Shraer-Petrov]. *Moskva zlatoglavaia*. Baltimore: Vestnik Information Agency, 1994.

———. "Villa Borghese." Translated by Dolores Stewart and Maxim D. Shrayer. *Salmagundi* 101–102 (Winter/Spring 1994): 151–153.

——— [David Shraer-Petrov]. "Iskusstvo kak izlom." *Novyi Zhurnal/ The New Review* 196 (1995): 245–256.

——— [David Shrayer-Petrov]. *Propashchaia dusha. Stikhotvoreniia i poemy. 1987–1996.* Providence, RI: APKA Publishers, 1997.
——— [David Shrayer-Petrov]. *Barabany sud´by.* Moscow: Argo-risk, 2002.
———[David Shrayer-Petrov]. *Vodka s pirozhnymi. Roman s pisateliami.* Edited by Maksim D. Shraer. St. Petersburg: Akademicheskii proekt, 2007.
——— [David Shrayer-Petrov]. *Dve knigi. Stikhi.* Philadelphia: Poberezh´e, 2009.
——— [David Shrayer-Petrov]. *Linii-figury-tela: Kniga stikhotvorenii.* St. Petersburg: Biblioteka Aesthetoscope, 2010.
——— [David Shrayer-Petrov]. *Okhota na ryzhego d´iavola. Roman s mikrobiologami.* Edited by Maksim D. Shraer. Moscow: Agraf, 2010.
——— [David Shrayer-Petrov]. *Nevskie stikhi.* St. Petersburg: Ostrovitianin, 2011.
——— [David Shrayer-Petrov]. *Derevenskii orkestr. Shest´ poem.* St. Petersburg: Ostrovitianin, 2016.
———. "Villa Borghese." In *Voices of Jewish-Russian Literature*, edited by Maxim D. Shrayer, 831–833. Boston: Academic Studies Press, 2018.
———. *Runner Begoon.* Translated by Maxim D. Shrayer. *Four Centuries: Russian Poetry in Translation* 7 (2014): 55–58. https://perelmuterverlag.de/FC72014.pdf. Accessed July 5, 2020.
———. "Wild Turkeys in Boston." Translated by Maxim D. Shrayer. *Four Centuries: Russian Poetry in Translation* 11 (2015): 19. https://perelmuterverlag.de/FC112015.pdf. Accessed July 5, 2020.
"Shraer-Petrov, David Petrovich." *Wikipedia.* https://ru.wikipedia.org/wiki/Шраер-Петров,_Давид_Петрович. Accessed August 22, 2019.
Strelianyi, Anatolii, Genrikh Sapgir, Vladimir Bakhtin, and Nikita Ordynskii, eds. *Samizdat veka.* Minsk-Moscow: Polifakt, 1997.
Terras, Viktor. "Villa Borgeze." *Novoe russkoe slovo.* July 3, 1992.

Voice of Destiny: Notes in the Margins of David Shrayer-Petrov's Poems*

Oleg Smola

They once asked Aleksandr Blok what he wanted to say in his long poem *The Twelve*. "I don't know," the poet replied. Korney Chukovsky, who was standing next to Blok and heard the reply, notes: "He indeed did not know, his lyrical poetry was wiser than him."[1]

I also found myself in the role of a simple-hearted man. As I was reading David Shrayer-Petrov's poems—by no means transparent, and in some places downright cryptic—I kept stumbling over every other step, and now and then I wanted to ask the poet for clarification. For instance, the poems "Pushkin's Gravestone" or "Anna Akhmatova in Komarovo," are they results of an immediate impression or is pure fiction at work here? But in all honesty I stop myself right away as I know: it is wrong to demand from the author something he himself does not have—an exhaustive and "correct" understanding of his own literary progeny.

Having detached itself from its creator, a completed literary work starts its own open voyage. It does not belong to him any longer. However, it was not completely his even throughout the process of creation. To return to Blok's *The Twelve*, the drafts are strewn with numerous corrections that

---

* Copyright © 2021 by Oleg Smola. English translation copyright © 2021 by Daria Sadovnichenko and Maxim D. Shrayer.

1 Kornei Chukovskii, *Aleksandr Blok kak chelovek i poet* (Petrograd: A. F. Marks, 1924), 27. Unless noted otherwise, here and hereafter all translations from the Russian, including verse translations, are the translators' own literal translations (tr.).

testify to the poet's uneven, draining struggle with himself. That is perhaps the only way to explain such revelations, which at first glance appear strange: Evgeny Baratynsky's "Не властны мы в самих себе..." ("We have no power within ourselves")² or Fyodor Tyutchev's "Поэт всесилен, как стихия,/ Не властен лишь в себе самом" (The poet is omnipotent, like the elements,/ Yet powerless only within himself")³.

I gained these thoughts upon my first acquaintance with the poetry of Shrayer-Petrov. I am still only gliding on the surface of his poems, but what immediately strikes me is the magnitude of the poet's personality and destiny. One may envy the students of his creative work. Ahead of them lies the task of an uninterrupted exploration of Shrayer-Petrov's entire life and artistic path with the purpose of determining his place in the history of Russian literature.

* * *

Could one judge a poet's real biography on the basis of his poems? Stéphane Mallarmé claimed that in poetry there are flowers that cannot be found in any other bouquet.⁴ Viktor Shklovsky thought along similar lines: "life, transfiguring itself into verses, is no longer life."⁵ Illustrating the incongruity between the words and the meaning one want to convey, Afanasy Fet goes to the very extreme and declares (echoing Tyutchev) that "поэзия есть ложь и поэт, который с первого же слова не начинает лгать без оглядки, никуда не годится" ("poetry is a lie and the poet, who from the first words does not start lying indiscriminately, is worthless").⁶ It is hard to disagree with these judgments, and yet one would be sinning against the truth if one made them an absolute. Fet was entitled to such thinking. Turgenev perceived some of his poems as "темнота, от которой волки взвоют" ("darkness at which the wolves start howling").⁷

---

2 E. A. Baratynskii, "Priznanie," in his *Polnoe sobranie sochinenii* (Leningrad: Sovetskii pisatel', 1957), 101.
3 F. I. Tiutchev, "Ne ver', ne ver' poetu, deva . . ." in his *Lirika* ed. K.V. Pigarev, Vol. 1 (Moscow: Nauka, 1966), 99.
4 Stefan Mallarme [Stéphane Mallarmé], *Sochineniia v stikhakh i proze* (Moscow: Raduga, 1995), 343.
5 Viktor Shklovskii, *Gamburgskii shchet (stat'i—vospominaniia—esse, 1914-1933)* (Moscow: Sovetskii pisatel', 1990), 143.
6 A. A. Fet, *Vechernie ogni* (Moscow: Nauka, 1979), 561.
7 Quoted in ibid., 558.

The poetry of David Shrayer-Petrov is of a different kind. The biographical "I" of the poet and the "I" of his lyrical character are, certainly, not the same. However, key words, motifs, themes, traveling from one literary work to another, tell us more about real biography than would some other events or facts.

In the USSR Shrayer-Petrov lived with a chokehold (literally: "with a compressed carotid artery," "с пережатой главной артерией").[8] After over eight years as a refusenik he immigrates to America, finally finding his much-desired freedom. He writes and publishes a lot. But even there, as a thinking being, he does not experience happiness: "Я слышу тоски бесконечной вопль./ — Нерв оголённый . . ." ("I hear the cry of endless anguish./ — The bare exposed nerve . . .").[9] This is far from the poet's only admission of this kind. Increasingly in his poems words set the tone; as Vladimir Mayakovsky would put it, the words "ache." And I would add: the words mourn, suffer, complain, communicating the feeling that life, if it has not yet fluttered away, is fading already, leaving behind everything that binds us to it: "О, как мне забыться, напиться, забиться" ("Oh how can I forget myself, get drunk, get lost")[10] or "Отболела душа, отлюбила, отпела свое" ("The soul is done hurting, done loving, done singing").[11] In the poem "To My [Old] Female Friend" (1995) he confesses, not without sorrow:

Много лет мы вместе пили,
Пили время, как вино,
А куда теперь приплыли,
Если вправду — всё равно![12]

("For many years we drank together/ We drank time, like wine,/ But where have we sailed to,/ If truth be told—what does it matter!")

Relentless summing-up, honest and uncompromising self-analysis inevitably leads to reflections about one's path. In Shrayer-Petrov's poetic lexicon, fate and destiny become key notions. No matter what is happening

---

8   David Shraer-Petrov, "Vnutrenniaia emigratsiia," in his *Dve knigi. Stikhi* (Philadelphia: Poberezh´e, 2009), 11.
9   David Shraer-Petrov, "Mirazh," in his *Forma liubvi. Izbrannaia lirika* (Moscow: Izdatel´skii dom "Iunost´," 2003), 105.
10 David Shraer-Petrov, "Stikhi iz romana 'Iona-strannik,'" in his *Propashchaia dusha. Stikhotvoreniia i poemy. 1987–1996* (Providence, RI: APKA Publishers, 1997), 9.
11 David Shraer-Petrov, "Otbolela dusha," in *Forma liubvi*, 101.
12 David Shraer-Petrov, "Moei podruzhke," in *Propashchaia dusha*, 70.

within him or without him, he treats the present state as preordained from above, something one has to obey: "праведность и путаницу/ Своей судьбы как воду хлеб и соль своей строки я пью и ем" ("righteousless and mayhem/ Of my fate like water bread and salt of my verse I drink and eat").[13] In these words one senses a shade of obedience. Nevertheless, this point calls for clarification. First, the summing-up and the accompanying motifs of fate came to the fore in Shrayer-Petrov's later oeuvre, and especially during his American period, when new "charms" of life—those of aging— were added to the earlier ones. Second, neither the "black square" ("chernyi kvadrat") of life, nor its equivalent "black abyss"[14] deprived him of his will. Moreover, in "Drums of Fate" (the original Russian title of the poem, "Barabany sud'by," literally means "drums of fate" while referring to prayer wheels in Tibetan Buddhism; also see Ian Probstein's essay in this volume), a poem which exhibits Buddhist awareness, the poet transforms into the oracle of fate, calling for people's awakening:

> крутите вертите вращайте желтые барабаны судьбы
> крутите потому что волчок желтые потому что будда
> вертите потому что ветер вращайте потому что в радость
> крутите вертите вращайте барабаны под деревом будды
> крутите вращайте будите свою судьбу[15]

("spin turn rotate the yellow prayer wheels/ spin because it's a top yellow because buddha/ turn because the wind rotate because it's joyful/ spin turn rotate the wheels under the tree of buddha/ spin turn rotate awaken your fate")

* * *

For Shrayer-Petrov the phenomenon of Jewish identity is not merely a theme to which one turns on occasion. For him it is both a personal destiny and the colossal destiny of his people—tragic, inescapable, extended in time and space starting with the Exodus of Jews from Egypt all the way to

---

13 David Shraer-Petrov, "Otkrovennyi razgovor na Braiton-biche," in *Villa Borgeze. Stikhotvoreniia* (Holyoke, MA: New England Publishing, 1992), 61-61.
14 David Shraer-Petrov, "Zheltyi kvadrat v chernom kvadrate," in *Barabany sud'by* (Moscow: Argo-risk, 2002), 32.
15 Shraer-Petrov, "Barabany sud'by," 41. The original's play on *budda* (Buddha) and *budit'* (to awaken) resists a literal translation (tr.).

their mass escape from the USSR. In many of his works Jewishness defines everything—content, the dominant tonality, the threshold of pain. The poet's "lost soul" (see the title of his 1997 collection), once condemned to live in the zone of exclusion and enmity, at times lets words of bitterness and pain come through. "Motherland," "Mother Russia," "Rus´—my wife," "My Darling Rus´"—all that is not about the hero of my essay. His Russia is a stepmother. From the poet's soul, from the depth of the subconscious the words break out, thus illustrating Marina Tsvetaeva's adage from *Poem of the End* (*Poema Kontsa*, 1924): "Life is a place, where it is impossible to live: a Jewish quarter. . . ."[16] In order to substantiate my observation, I will offer a few of the poet's own characterizations of his past life in Russia. This is the life that people flee to save themselves—and they were not only Jews:

Нас унижали, топтали в грязи. (They humiliated us, stomped us in mud.)[17]

. . . это наши скитанья с тобою/ по житейской пустыне. (. . . those are your and my wanderings/ across the desert of life.)[18]

. . . с той поры бредем в пустыне, / ноги в синяках. (. . . since that time we've been roaming in the desert, / our feet all bruised.)[19]

Забыть, как доили, давили, травили?
Забыть окаянную ласку Державы?[20]
Forget the purging, the crushing, the spilling,
Forget the evil caress of the empire?[21]

...Какие опричники-псы нас губили,
Какие иуды в любви нас топили,
А мы все равно эту землю любили

Она отвергала нас, отторгала,
Она изводила, греховно зачатых,

---

16 Marina Tsvetaeva, *Sobranie sochinenii v semi tomakh*, vol. 3 (Moscow: Ellis Lak, 1994), 48.
17 David Shraer-Petrov, "Esli pereshchitat´," in his *Piterskii dozh. Stikhotvoreniia i poema (1995–1998)* (St. Petersburg: Izdatel´stvo Fonda Fusskoi poezii, 1999), 12.
18 David Shraer-Petrov, "V restorane nad okeanom," in *Dve knigi*, 48-49.
19 David Shraer-Petrov, "Novogodnee," in *Dve knigi*, 47.
20 David Shraer-Petrov, "Villa Borgeze," in *Propashchaia dusha*, 6-7.
21 Quoted here and hereafter is the English translation of "Villa Borghese" by Dolores Stewart and Maxim D. Shrayer. See David Shrayer-Petrov, "Villa Borghese," *Salmagundi* 101–102 (Winter-Spring 1994): 151–153; and Maxim D. Shrayer, ed., *Voices of Jewish-Russian Literature* (Boston: Academic Studies Press, 2018), 831–833.

А нам не хватало, нам все было мало,
Пока нас не сжили со света, проклятых[22]

... Those animals hounding us, shunned and banned,
Those judases killing with kindness and smiles.
And yet, despite all, we still loved that land

That cast us away like inferior stuff,
Aborted like something conceived out of error,
All that wasn't all, it was never enough,
Until they were rid of us cursed ones forever

гетто "отказа" (refusenik ghetto)[23]
страна-тюрьма (country-prison)[24]

Judeophobia drove out, drives out and, unfortunately, will continue to drive out the Jews from Russia. Among the detractors there were sometimes the so-called theory scholars. The jesuitical activism of Vadim Kozhinov offers a striking example. He and I did not work side by side, but we did work in the same institution, the Institute of World Literature of the Soviet Academy of Sciences. An austere appearance. Well read. Prolific. A stern proponent of strong power of the state, he took upon himself the burden of a warrior and martyr for the Russian idea. I do not wish to be exceedingly biased, and so I will draw Kozhinov's portrait with the help of his own statements:

> At the head of the Union of the Russian People stood non-Russian people [apparently, the Jews—O.S.].
>
> The ongoing talk about Jewish pogroms in Russia is all a bluff.
>
> It is an absolute lie that the pogroms were allegedly supported by the state.
>
> They keep reiterating this stuff about "state-sponsored antisemitism" ... Not only had it not taken place, but it could not have taken place.

---

22 Ibid., 7.
23 David Shraer-Petrov, "Solomon Novosel´tsev," in *Dve knigi*, 10.
24 David Shraer-Petrov, "Tenitsy," in *Piterskii dozh*, 45.

I am sure that, if many centuries from now they will be talking about the twentieth century, the history of our country will appear as one of its most beautiful pages.

For us the danger of Jewish nationalism became particularly strong during this period [the establishment of the state of Israel—O.S.].

With regard to the deportation of the Jews—it is a complete and total myth.

For Russia not Zionists, but assimilationists pose a greater danger, they in whom the destructive and provocative gene of Jewry inevitably survives.[25]

And on and on he goes…

While gathering material for an article on Andrei Voznesensky, I asked the poet if he was really hurt by the criticism from the "extreme right" (Vadim Kozhinov, Igor Zolotussky, Anatoly Lanshchikov, and others). Voznesensky answered: "At first I was upset, then I began to get used to it, and now I do not notice it. At one time I even wrote an epigram directed at Kozhinov." Here is the text of that unpublished epigram:

Владимир Владимирович, милый,
Срок травли не истёк,
На Вас стучал Ермилов,
На нас — его зятёк.[26]

("Vladimir Vladimirovich, dear,/ The term of ostracism hasn't expired,/ Ermilov informed on you,/ And now his dear son-in-law informs on us.")

Vladimir Vladimirovich refers to Mayakovsky, whom the orthodox Soviet critic Vladimir Ermilov attacked and denounced in the 1920s. Kozhinov, who harassed Andrei Voznesensky, Vasily Aksyonov, Evgeny Evtushenko, Bella Akhmadulina, and others in print, was married to Ermilov's daughter.

* * *

---

25 Quotes taken from: *Vadim Kozhinov v interv´iu, besedakh, dialogakh i vospominaniiakh sovremennikov* (Moscow: Algoritm, 2005); Vadim Kozhinov, *Krasnaia sotnia* (Moscow: Algoritm, 2009). Union of the Russian People was the leading organization among the so-called Black Hundreds (eds.).

26 The epigram remained unpublished; the original is in the archive of Oleg Smola.

Voice of Destiny: Notes in the Margins of David Shrayer-Petrov's Poems

I would be doing David Shrayer-Petrov a grave injustice if I only observed in his lyric poetry damnations directed at Russia. There is also a mournful note of deep compassion resounding through his soul:

> Когда умирать мне придется, чуть живы,
> Прошепчут мои полумертвые губы:
> Мы стали чужими, Россия, чужими,
> А были своими сыны Иегуды.²⁷

> When my time comes to die, when I'm barely alive,
> Half-dead lips will whisper, like never before:
> For you and us, Russia, no closeness survives,
> We, sons of Yehudah, who used to be yours.

Countless are the lines of bitter sorrow in Shrayer-Petrov's poems, bemoaning the loss of Russia. Still in Italy en route to America, he cries for the "aching Russia."²⁸ Already in emigration, addressing his son, he states:

> Мы с тобой познаем вселенское братство,
> Да без России жить не с руки.²⁹

("You and I now will know universal brotherhood,/ But it doesn't suit us to live without Russia.")

Once, while taking a walk in a cemetery in a New England town, he read an inscription on a monument with a six-pointed star: "Прощай, моя Россия, навсегда,/ Тебя я не увижу никогда" ("Farewell, my Russia, now forever/ Alas I won't ever see you").³⁰ These unadorned lines moved the poet and brought to his mind reflections about his own destiny:

> Так почему, гонимый и бесправный,
> Мой соплеменник свой последний, главный
>
> Привет к стране рожденья обращал?
> Ужели, умирая, завещал
> Мне эту связь духовную продолжить,
> Чтоб передал ее все дальше, дольше,

---

27 Shraer-Petrov, "Villa Borgeze," 7.
28 "O Rossii boliashchei," ibid. 7.
29 David Shraer-Petrov, "Vnutrenniaia emigratsiia," in *Dve knigi*, 11.
30 David Shraer-Petrov, "Amerikanskoe kladbishche," in *Dve knigi*, 12.

Чтобы диковинный и несуразный плод
Любви и ненависти, языка и сердца
Родил в стране приобретенной скерцо,
Которое и плачет и поет?[31]

("So why did he, persecuted and discriminated,/ My fellow member of the tribe address his last, his final/ Farewell to the country of his birth?/ Did he really bequeath me in his dying hour/ To continue this spiritual bond,/ So I would pass it on further, for a longer time,/ So that this wondrous and outlandish fruit/ Of love and hatred, of language and heart/ Would give birth, in the adopted country, to a new scherzo/ That both cries and laughs?")

An old man like me finds these verses especially heart-warming, not so much because of the meaning they carry, but more so because of their dolorous melody.

In our hands lies a wealth of material for a scholar of Jewish-Russian literature. The Jewish fate of a Russian poet is the most heart-rending note of all in the poetry of David Shrayer-Petrov.

* * *

Try to determine to whom these fragments of three different texts belong:

1. По-прежнему шипят взоры вечноты картавой
   Два глаза вымена оной лукавой
   Четыре глаза ножки венского стула
   Вечерком ветерком она дула
   Град наступил бесчеловечно ты

("As ever hiss gazes of burring youternity/ Two eyes udders of that wily her/ Four eyes legs of a Viennese chair/ In the gentle evening a light wind she was blowing/ Hailstorm came inhumanely you")

2. вокруг этих кругов пчелиный рой мелодии убивает
   цвет разрывает уколами воздушный шар надутый
   надвигающейся грозой и в распростертом
   клочьями свете парит пространный аромат ее образа

("around these circles bee swarm of melodies kills/ the color pricks rips apart air balloon inflated/ with the approaching storm and in tattered/ sprawling light soars strange fragrance of her image")

---

31 Ibid.

3. летят осколки желтые стол озером поблескивает карты
осколки жизни угольки судьбы шипят в пространстве три
ноги железных страсть отгорающую принимают вот вод
погибельный итог туз пик иль уголек мой славный уголок
полати с печкою скрестились дама крести треножник

("yellow shards flying table cards glistening lakelike/ shards of life embers of fate hissing in the space three/ iron legs receive the burning out passion their waters'/ ruinous result ace of spades or little ember my glorious corner abode/ sleeping planks crossed with the oven dame of clubs tripod")

Is it not true that one could suppose these texts share the same author? In fact, the first one, from 1915, belongs to the futurist Roman Aliagrov (penname of Roman Jakobson);[32] the second one, from 1936, to the surrealist Pablo Picasso;[33] the third one, from the 1980s, to David Shrayer-Petrov.[34]

Indeed, during the time of Soviet punitive censorship, Shrayer-Petrov was among the few artists, whose quest to develop the mainlines of twentieth-century poetry continued at the time when, as he writes in the programmatic essay "Art as Fracture" (also "Art as Rupture"—tr.) "a fracture of all traditional lines" occurred in avant-garde art, represented by Shklovsky, Picasso, and Shostakovich.[35] Many of Shrayer-Petrov's poems, such as "Anna Akhmatova in Komarovo," "Shostakovich at the Dacha in Komarovo," "Pushkin's Gravestone," "Moses—Erzia's Sculpture in Saransk," and others hearken back to the poetics of Russian futurism.

Consider this emblematic text:

2 нижнии юбки . . .   60 к.
2 крыхма рубахи . . . 20 к.
5 воротничков . . .   30 к.
2 пары манжет . . .   20 к.

---

[32] Roman Aliagrov [Roman Jakobson], "Skol´ko rassypal oskolkov (ekstrakt)," in Roman Iakobson, *Budetlianin nauki. Vospominaniia, pis´ma, stat´i, proza*, ed. Bengt Iangfeldt (Moscow: Gileia, 2012), 192.

[33] Pablo Pikasso [Pablo Picasso], "10–12 fevralia 1936," in his *Stikhotvoreniia*, tr. from French and afterword by Mikhail Iasnov (Moscow: Tekst, 2008), part 4, 45; cf. the original French: "si autour des cercles que la couleur assassine l'essaim d'abeilles/ de l'air du disque rompt de ses piqûres le ballon gonflé de/ l'orange naissant flotte dans la lumière étendue en lambeaux le/ parfum éperdu de son image," in Pablo Picasso, *Poèmes*, ed. Androula Michael (Paris: Le Cherche Midi, 2005), 41.

[34] David Shraer-Petrov, "Gadanie pri luchine," in *Villa Borgeze*, 47.

[35] David Shraer-Petrov, "Iskusstvo kak izlom," *Novyi zhurnal/ The New Review* 196 (1995): 249.

| 3 навлычки ... | 9 к. |
| 1 куфайка ... | 5 к.³⁶ |

("2 under skirt . . . 60 k./ 2 starc shirts . . . 20 k. / 5 collars . . . 30 k./ 2 pairs of cuffs . . . 20 k./ 3 pillacases . . . 9 k/ 1 weatshirt . . . 5 k.")

The first thing that comes to mind is a laundry receipt. And it is in fact "Mr. Krysiun's laundry bill," which, as Aleksey Kruchenykh claims, constitutes a complete work of art, "the style of which [is] higher that Pushkin's."

I did not find either collars or cuffs in Shrayer-Petrov's poems, but I sense that the futuristic rebellion is dear to him in some very significant way.[37] Most likely, this is due to the mesmerizing audacity and disdain of common sense, which were characteristic of the avant-garde art. From the perspective of common sense, claiming that "a laundry receipt" is a poem amounts to an act of absurdity, a hooligan's outburst. Yet, according to the philosophy of *budetliane* (futurists), it represents a fundamental discovery. A fracture. An explosion that cleared the way to the art of the future. Osip Mandelstam was not a futurist in the obvious sense of the term, but in the spirit of the new thinking, he, too, considered the hole in the bagel to be more important that the bagel itself.[38] Is this a paradox? Vasilisk Gnedov "composes" "The Poem of the End" (1915), which constitutes a blank piece of paper.[39] Is this absurd?

I quoted the fragments from the texts of Jakobson, Picasso, and Shrayer-Petrov in order to demonstrate the latter's apparent kinship with the formal and structural quest of twentieth-century art. Russian futurism, along with Western European surrealism, had undoubtedly been of use for the poet. The question is to what extent and how exactly. The poem in prose "Pushkin's Gravestone" from the cycle "Travels from the Banks of

---

36 Aleksei Kruchenykh, *Apokalipsis v russkoi literature.* (*Chort i rechetvortsy. Tainye poroki akademikov. Slovo kak takovoe. Deklaratsii*) (Moscow: n.p., 1923), 32.

37 It is the testimony of one of this volume's co-editors, Maxim D. Shrayer, that once, at the Central House of Writers, his father ran into the poet Mikhail Lukonin and shared with him a poem by the then six-year-old Maxim: "Муха-муха,/ дам тебе в ухо" ("Fly o fly,/ I'll shut your open fly"; literally: "I'll whack you in the ear"), to which Lukonin replied: "Такой же футурист как и его отец" ("A futurist just like his father").

38 Osip Mandelstam, *Sobranie sochinenii v dvukh tomakh*, vol. 2: *Stikhotvoreniia. Proza* (Washington, DC: Inter-Language Literary Associates, 1969), 229.

39 Vasilisk Gnedov, "Poema kontsa," in his *Smert' iskusstvu: piatnadtsat' poem* (St. Petersburg: Peterburgskii glashatai, 1915); rpt. in V. Gnedov, *Smert' iskusstvu: piatnadtsat' poem*, ed. Dm. Kuz'min (Moscow: Arho-risk, 1996).

the Neva" (circa 1986) serves as a wonderful illustration of Shrayer-Petrov's poetics:

> ... туман курчавится холодный мрамор чело монастыря
> Святые горы туманы часты и звезда понадобится навсегда
> и посох о Господи пути твои на Север дальний звёздочку
> Давида принёс и положил чело монастыря на посох
> упираются креста во лбу курчавится туман звезда Давида
> детишки собирают землянику среди травы пасётся конь
> на склоне белее мрамор караваны паломники приходят
> в Мекку лоб монастыря и мрамор северной Каабы вот
> Слово Божие куда занесено[40]

("... the fog spreads curls cold marble the brow of the monastery/ Holy Mountains fogs are frequent and the star will be forever needed/ and the staff o Lord your ways to the far North the little star/ of David he brought and placed the brow of the monastery on the staff/ they abut the cross on the forehead curls the fog the star of David/ kiddies picking wild strawberries in the grass a gelding grazing/ on the slope whiter the marble caravans pilgrims arrive/ to Mecca the forehead of the monastery and the marble of the northern Kaaba here/ the Word of God has been dispersed")

Vladimir Nabokov's witty remark that an ellipsis ("suspension dots") "represents the footprints of words that have departed on tiptoe,"[41] resonates with the futurists' trend of seeing the text as a fragment. A poem for Velimir Khlebnikov is only a part of a total and boundless whole. For this great Russian futurist, poetry and life do not exist separately. Totality is not a principle for Khlebnikov, not an "aesthetic," but a state of living matter, that is, the only possible form of being in which the poetic and the epic, the past, present, and future, the real and the fantastic fluidly interact with and flow into each other. Thence the principle of the openness of the futuristic text, its particular receptiveness that allows us to regard all the poet's compositions as one larger work containing moving parts, and each separate poem is a continuation of the one preceding or following it.

---

40 David Shraer-Petrov, "Nadgrobie Pushkina," in *Villa Borgeze*, 50; cf. idem, *Forma liubvi*, 77.
41 Vladimir Nabokov, *The Complete Stories of Vladimir Nabokov*, ed. Dmitri Nabokov (New York: Knopf, 1995), 364; cf. the original in Vladimir Nabokov, "Pamiati L. I. Shigaeva," in his *Sobranie sochinenii russkogo perioda*, ed. N. I. Artemenko-Tolstaia, vol. 3 (Saint Petersburg: Simpozium, 2000), 648.

Shrayer-Petrov's "Pushkin's Gravestone" opens with an ellipsis. The first word is written with a lowercase letter. There is no period at the end of the poem. It does not really have either a beginning or an end—like any part ripped out of the whole. Ripped out but connected to the whole by invisible threads.

In its extreme, the poetics of Shrayer-Petrov strives toward absolute disentanglement and simplification, if not asceticism. In "Pushkin's Gravestone" there are essentially no punctuation marks, conjunctions, or prepositions. The poem is constructed as a chain of short nominal sentences, operating without supports or crutches, such as introductory phrases, participial or adverbial clauses. There are few words, but in each of them, as Gogol would put it, there is an abyss of space. Genrikh Sapgir, a poet with whom Shrayer-Petrov was close, composed a mantra to which, I have no doubt, Shrayer-Petrov would subscribe:

> случайные слова возьми и пропусти
> возьми случайные и пропусти слова
> возьми слова и пропусти случайные
> возьми «слова слова слова»
> возьми слова и пропусти слова
> возьми и пропусти «возьми» —
> и слова пропусти[42]

("take random words and skip/ take random ones and skip words/ take words and skip random ones/ take 'words words words'/ take words and skip words/ take and skip 'take'—/and skip words")

Skipping "random words" and seeking for words that have no substitution unites Sapgir and Shrayer-Petrov. Surely, both of them would be ready to agree with the paradoxical assertion of Osip Mandelstam that the best words in any poem remain unspoken, that they must be discovered by the listener.[43] The nature of the avant-garde text, both unpredictable and immanent, creates the protean illusion that the poem is able to take on all different kinds of shapes. No matter how many times one rereads the

---

42 Genrikh Sapgir, "Metod," in his *Stikhotvoreniia i poemy*, ed. and commentary by David Shraer-Petrov and Maksim D. Shraer (St. Petersburg: Akademicheskii proekt, 2004), 316.
43 Mandelstam, *Sobranie sochinenii v dvukh tomakh*, vol. 2, 507.

poems "Anna Akhmatova in Komarovo," "Fencing Lessons," "Variety Show in Tallinn," or "Pushkin's Gravestone," every time it feels like the first time.

Of all elements of play ("игровые элементы") in the poetics of Shrayer-Petrov I would highlight one that, I believe, is the favorite of the poet himself—the sound metaphor. Futurists were, of course, the unsurpassed masters of writing sound (звукопись; *zvukopis'*) in Russian poetry. Nikolai Aseev stood out among all during the period of his preoccupation with trans-sense (заумь, *zaum*).[44] But I do not believe Shrayer-Petrov is second to Aseev. Without making a judgment, I will simply provide a few examples from his poems. Taken out of context, they demonstrate even more forcefully the poet's interest in the theoretical advances of the Formalist School, particularly in their famous techniques such as defamiliarization (остранение; *ostranenie*), resurrection of the word (воскрешение слова; *voskreshenie slova*), laying bare the literary device (обнажение приёма; *obnazhenie priema*) and so forth: "Бродский бродит брагой" (literally: "Brodsky's fermenting brew");[45] "стол скоблёный оскоплён огнём" (literally: "the scraped table is emasculated by fire");[46] "катами казни катам заказывались" (literally: "headsmen executed ordered executions from headsmen");[47] «па-ры па-ришь Па-риж» (literally: "ste-ams stre-am Pa-ris");[48] "Невы/ но и не мы/ мы немы" (literally: "the Neva/ but us neither/ mute are we";[49] "маздой вмазываешь хайвею" (literally: "with your Mazda you hit the highway on the muzzle");[50] "там-там сердец/ то тут/ то там" ("tam-tam of hearts/ now here/ now there");[51] "до утра/ утрата" (literally: "till morning/ loss").[52]

Shrayer-Petrov's sound metaphors may be classified under two types: ones that obscure an author's thought ("нелюбимы неумолимы полукруглых арок гроты готы тоги гады таты гоги годы ига гои" ["unloved implacable arch's

---

44 See, for example, his line "Осень семенами мыла мили" (literally: "Autumn washed miles with seeds"). Nikolai Aseev, *Stikhotvoreniia i poemy*, Biblioteka poeta, Bol´shaia seriia (Leningrad: Sovetskii pisatel´, 1967), 113.
45 David Shraer-Petrov, "Stihi po knige Tikhonova 'Orda i braga,'" in *Villa Borgeze*, 59.
46 David Shraer-Petrov, "Gadanie pri luchine," in *Villa Borgeze*, 47.
47 David Shraer-Petrov, "Zakat na petrogradskoi storone godu v piat´desiat chetvertom," in *Villa Borgeze*, 13.
48 David Shraer-Petrov, "Sauna v Litve," in *Villa Borgeze*, 52-53.
49 David Shraer-Petrov, "Isaakievskii sobor," in *Villa Borgeze*, 27.
50 Shraer-Petrov, *Propashchaia dusha*, 56.
51 David Shraer-Petrov, "Rozovye sotsvetiia v botanicheskom sadu," in *Villa Borgeze*, 37.
52 David Shraer-Petrov, "Bolezn´ druga," in *Villa Borghese*, 42; also see Andrei Ranchin's essay in this volume.

semicircular grottos goths togas reptiles tats gogs yoke years goyim"])[53], and the ones that clarify it ("Бродский бросил бремя братства" ["Brodsky abandoned the burden of brotherhood"]).[54] Shrayer-Petrov the realist favors the second type. Shrayer-Petrov the avant-gardist prefers the first one. As Pasternak would have it, they carve out the author's unintended meaning:

И, чем случайней, тем вернее
Слагаются стихи навзрыд.[55]

("And the more random the more true it is/ Poems compose themselves through tears.")

* * *

It is impossible to imagine David Shrayer-Petrov outside the rich and varied legacy of the Russian and world avant-garde. And yet, his lyrical creativity is not "words in a top hat," nor is it automatic writing that permits free association of any words without exception. A poet of reflection, Shrayer-Petrov ponders many different things and life issues, both ordinary and fateful. Staying within the realm of futurist poetics, delving into the depths of the irrational and subconscious, he knows how to convey this or that content through an exquisitely short form.

What is "Pushkin's Gravestone," which we quoted earlier? To put it simply, what is it about?

I am going to venture a retelling of this small masterpiece.

The poet visits Svyatogorsky Monastery ("The Holy Mountains" cloister) in the Pskov Province, now called Pushkinskiye Gory (Pushkin Hills), where Pushkin is buried. From the very first words the poet shows the image by means of close and distant associations, so that it nearly turns into a religious sacrament. The initial notion of the Holy Mountains creates an atmosphere of adoration, which, in its turn, gives birth to such words and phrases as "cold marble" (associated with death), the poetic "brow" (and not "forehead"), "monastery," "Star of David," "pilgrims," "staff," "Mecca," "Kaaba," "the word of God."

---

53 David Shraer-Petrov, "Letnii Kaunas," in *Villa Borgeze*, 50.
54 David Shraer-Petrov, "Stihi po knige Tikhonova 'Orda i braga,'" in *Villa Borgeze*, 59.
55 Boris Pasternak, *Stikhotvoreniia i poemy*, edited by Lev Ozerov, Biblioteka poeta, Bol'shaia seriia (Leningrad: Sovetskii pisatel', 1965), 65.

Pushkin for Shrayer-Petrov, as for all of Russia, is a guiding star, he who had divined the future development of Russian poetry. The magnitude of Pushkin's creations is on par with the all-encompassing spiritual trends and practices in the history of humanity. Shrayer-Petrov's poem is a testimony to the cult of Pushkin in Russian culture. The lofty meaning of the poem is also underscored by the many symbolic details. This symbolism imbues the emerging picture with philosophical significance. "Holy Mountains..." Here, indeed, "the Word of God has been dispersed."

What else? For some reason, upon reading "Pushkin's Gravestone" Fyodor Tyutchev's lines come to mind: "Как океан объемлет шар земной,/ Земная жизнь кругом объята снами . . ." ("As the ocean encompasses the globe/ Life on Earth is all encompassed by dreams . . .").[56] The reason for that is, probably, that in this poem, as in all of Shrayer-Petrov's best creations, there is an elusive spirit of a mystery, which does not succumb to rational comprehension. This mystery makes craft into true art.

Even though plain retelling kills artistic content, it can nonetheless demonstrate that Shrayer-Petrov is a poet of thought—of thought often hidden behind a thick fence of associative images, sound metaphors, allusions, literary echoes, ellipses, and "footprints of words that have departed…"

* * *

I really like the artfully angular saying of the great humanist Albert Schweitzer: "I am life which wills to live, in the midst of life which wills to live."[57]

I regard the love poetry of David Shrayer-Petrov as nothing short of veneration of vibrant life itself. In the afterword to the poetry collection *Song of a Blue Elephant* (1990) he writes:

> . . . как влюбленный голубой слон в непролазных джунглях страсти, я трубил моими стихами, пробиваясь к единственной, самой прекрасной, самой нежной, самой жестокой и самой желанной — к

---

56 F. I. Tiutchev, "Kak okean ob''emlet shar zemnoi . . ." in *Lirika* Vol. 1, 29.
57 Albert Schweitzer, *Civilization and Ethics*, 3rd ed. (London: Adam & Charles Black, 1949), 242; cf. the Russian translation quoted in Al'bert Shveitser [Albert Schweitzer], *Kul'tura i etika* (Moscow: Progress, 1973), 306.

моей женщине . . . пробивался, как голубой слон сквозь джунгли жизни, где переплетаются лианы любви и нелюбви. . . .[58]

("... like a blue elephant in the impassible jungle of passion, like an elephant in love I was blaring my poems, fighting my way to that only one, the most beautiful, the most tender, the most cruel and the most desirable—to my beloved woman . . . fighting my way, like a blue elephant, through the jungle of life, where lianas of love and nonlove interlace. . . .")

This is a key to understanding not only Shrayer-Petrov's philosophy of love, but also—more broadly—his philosophy of being, at the center of which, inevitably, the question of fate arises again. Drawing on the love poetry alone, one can recreate the psychological portraits of the poet's lyrical addressee and the poet himself—a man driven by passions.

As I see it, the long poem *Tenitsy* (literally *Shadowmaidens*; Shrayer-Petrov's neologism, likely derived from "тени," "shadows" + "девицы," "maidens"—tr.)[59] is to a large degree autobiographical. Its protagonist is the author's alter ego. If this is true, then the poet, like his poetic character, literally fights his way through the jungle of life, through "данаек дары" ("Danaan women's gifts")[60]; through "метельных ночей угар" ("the frenzy of the blizzardy nights"),[61] though caresses and love of "полуодетых companion" ("half-clothed shadowy maidens").[62] Such definitions and assessments as "the most tender and the most cruel," "love and nonlove," "fighting my way to that only one," and "предан тебе, но предан тобой" ("dedicated to you yet betrayed by you")[63] show that the shared path of poem's characters is not only radiant, but also hurtful and often complicated. Similar motives appear in other poems by David Shrayer-Petrov, supporting the autobiographical associations.

Why am I indifferent to Valery Bryusov, while, for instance, I love Aleksandr Blok and Vladimir Mayakovsky? Is it because, for some reason, one is not inclined to love prosperous poets? In the poetry of Shrayer-Petrov there is a lot of love—for his wife, his son, his friends, and for the natural manifestations of life in general, but there is not a shade of coziness or contentment.

---

58 David Shraer-Petrov, *Pesnia o golubom slone. Liubovnaia lirika* (Holyoke, MA: New England Publishing, 1990), 45.
59 David Shraer-Petrov, "Tenitsy," in *Piterskii dozh*, 38.
60 Ibid., 40; cf. "Timeo Danaos et dona ferentes" ("beware Danaans [Greeks] bearing gifts") in Virgil's *Aeneid* (II, 49) (tr.).
61 Shraer-Petrov, "Tenitsy," 42.
62 Ibid., 38.
63 Ibid., 43.

Shrayer-Petrov calls his beloved woman "горчинка в отраве сладчайшей" ("bud of bitterness in the sweetest of poisons");[64] he confesses: "Все обрыдло, осточертело./ Некому слово родное сказать" ("Everything sickens, disgusts/ No one to say a dear native word to"),[65] or even "Отболела душа, отлюбила, отпела свое" ("My soul is done hurting, done loving, done singing").[66] In these lamentations, I believe, there is more than the torments of love:

> Никому не нужны мы, родная,
> Да и нету вокруг ни души.
> Только в небе вороньего грая
> Похоронная нота страшит.[67]

("Nobody needs us, my love,/ Not a soul around,/ Only in the sky of crows' grating/ The funeral note terrifies.")

Here, again, I see a conversation with Marina Tsvetaeva's *Poem of the End*: "Жизнь — это место, где жить нельзя . . ." ("Life is a place where one cannot live . . .")[68] And I would not be surprised if the Shrayer-Petrov, like Chekhov's character in the 1898 story "Gooseberries," would claim that "happiness does not exist as it should not exist, and if there is a meaning and purpose to life, then this meaning and purpose it is not in our happiness, but in something higher and more intelligent."[69]

Still more evident in Shrayer-Petrov's love poetry is a dialogue with the late poetry of Aleksandr Mezhirov. The motifs of fading, fatigue from life, and "the end" resonate in both poets with a tragic force, creating, I would venture to say, a new poetic genre that Mezhirov defined as "prose in poetry":

> Не впопыхах,
> А трудно и медленно, в муках —
> Проза в стихах,
> В чуждых поэзии звуках . . .[70]

---

64 David Shraer-Petrov, "Komnata proshchaniia." in *Pesnia o golubom slone. Liubovnaia lirika*, 31.
65 David Shraer-Petrov, "Sneg v Novoi Anglii," in *Dve knigi*, 12; also an allusion to Lermontov's poem "I skuchno i grustno" ("Bored and Sad") (tr.)
66 David Shraer-Petrov, "Otbolela dusha," in *Forma liubvi*, 101.
67 Shraer-Petrov, "Sneg v Novoi Anglii," in *Dve Knigi*, 12.
68 Tsvetaeva, *Sobranie sochinenii v semi tomakh*, vol. 3, 48.
69 A. P. Chekhov, *Polnoe sobranie sochinenii i pisem v tridtsati tomakh*, vol. 10 (Moscow: Nauka, 1986), 64.
70 Aleksandr Mezhirov, "Proza v stikhakh," in his *Proza v stikhakh* (Moscow: Sovetskii pisatel´, 1982), 92.

("Not hastily,/ But labored and slow, tortuous/ Prose in poetry,/ In sounds alien to poetry...")

To a degree, prose in poetry is characteristic of a number of poets of there same generation, including Aleksandr Mezhirov, Yuri Levitansky, Boris Slutsky, and David Samoylov.

I confess that the "senilia" of Shrayer-Petrov and Aleksandr Mezhirov warm my heart more than other older poets' verses.

* * *

Shrayer-Petrov's important, brilliantly written essay "Art as a Fracture" compelled me to reflect on the ontological nature of the poetry in general and Shrayer-Petrov's lyric poetry in particular.

Something new, primordial, and thus vibrantly alive in poems germinates at tension points, at any joints—of the earthly and the heavenly, quotidian and existential, the reality and the dreams, reveries, mirages, delusions, of self-conscious verbal gestures and ecstatic divination. I will not be substantiating this point with the oft-quoted comment about poems growing from litter.[71] I will, however, suggest that Shrayer-Petrov is prone to "pure poetry" that transports the reader to a transcendental state. See his numerous blues poems, such as his "Drums of Fate"/"Prayer Wheels." His essay "Art as a Fracture" (or "Art as Rupture"; Russian "Iskusstvo kak izlom")[72] directs the scholars of prose and poetry, to what is, perhaps, the most distinct principle of his creative process.

Furthermore, after reading Shrayer-Petrov's essay I was personally tempted to interpret its meaning expansively. If we proceed from the everyday meaning of the word *izlom* ("fracture" or "rupture"), then each sharp turn, each steep change of polarities, perspectives, directions could be linked to the general theory of conflict studies. And then formulations kindred to "fracture" start popping up: art as explosion, art as collapse, art as apocalypse, art as *epatage*, art as death, art as a change of milestones. And so forth.

---

71 "If you only knew from what litter/ Verses grow, without experiencing shame," from part 2 of Anna Akhmatova's cycle "Tainy remesla" ("Secrets of the Craft," 1936–1960). See Anna Akhmatova, "Tainy remesla," in *Stikhotvoreniia i poemy* (Leningrad: Sovetskii pisatel´, 1976), 201–206 (tr.).

72 David Shraer-Petrov, "Iskusstvo kak izlom," *Novyi zhurnal/ The New Review* 196 (1995): 245.

Taking into account my right of choice, I would first undertake an investigation under the working title "Fractures of David Shrayer-Petrov's Destiny."

* * *

Both in general and in particular, Shrayer-Petrov's lyrical poetry, including his avant-garde verse, strives to fathom manifestations and objects of physical reality. However, as a true poet, endowed with the gift of transfiguration, he knows how to find the specific words and to arrange them in such a special way that many things in his poems do not yield to rational explanation. There always remains something undecoded, enigmatic, and magical, which impacts the reader much as music does. As an example, I will take the poem "Novogodnee" ("New Year Poem")—short in length, but spacious and deep in meaning. With this poem I shall end my notes in the margins on the Shrayer-Petrov's pages.

Testing fate, with hope and longing for the Messiah, believing and unbelieving Jews wander in the "desert" of life. With them wanders the poet, novelist, and citizen of the world—David Petrovich Shrayer-Petrov:

Новогоднее

Мы с тобой родили сына
в давнем городе, в хлеву.
сеном хрупала скотина
и звезда зажглась во лбу.
три служаки появились:
шамес, кантор и раввин,
Божьим именем божились:
будет Божьим светом сын!
он укажет вам дорогу
за моря и за леса.
привыкайте понемногу
верить в чудеса.
город, хлев, друзей, скотину
кинув,
мы с тобой

побрели вдогонку сыну
с голубой звездой.
с той поры бредем в пустыне,
ноги в синяках.
я взываю: где мы, сыне?
небо в облаках.⁷³

("New Year Poem": "To you and me a son was given/ in a faraway city, in a cowshed,/ the cattle loudly chewed on their cud/ and in [his] forehead a star was lit./ three loyal servants then appeared:/ shames, cantor and rabbi/ they swore in God's name:/ your son will be God's own light!/ he will show you the passage/ over the forests and seas./ slowly start getting used to/ having faith in miracles./ city, cowshed, friends and cattle/ we abandoned,/ you and I,/ making our way after our firstborn/ with a blue star./ since that time we have been roaming/ in the desert, our feet bruised./ I call out: My son, where are we?/ sky is covered in white clouds.")

Translated, from the Russian, by
Daria Sadovnichenko and Maxim D. Shrayer

---

73 David Shraer-Petrov, "Novogodnee," in *Dve knigi*, 47. Note the echo of Marina Tsvetaeva's "New Year Poem" (1927) in the title: Marina Tsvetaeva, "Novogodnee," in *Sobranie sochinenii v semi tomakh*, vol. 3, 132–136 (tr.).

Works Cited

Akhmatova, Anna. *Stikhotvoreniia i poemy*. Edited by V. M. Zhirmunskii. Leningrad: Sovetskii pisatel´, 1976.

Aseev, Nikolai. *Stikhotvoreniia i poemy*. Biblioteka poeta. Bol´shaia seriia. Edited by A. Urban and R. Val'be. Leningrad: Sovetskii pisatel´, 1967.

Baratynskii, E. A. *Polnoe sobranie sochinenii*. Edited by E. N. Kupreianova. Leningrad: Sovetskii pisatel´, 1957.

Chekhov, A. P. *Polnoe sobranie sochinenii i pisem v tridtsati tomakh*. Edited by N. I. Sokolov. Volume 10. Moscow: Nauka, 1986.

Chukovskii, Kornei. *Aleksandr Blok kak chelovek i poet*. Petrograd: A. F. Marks, 1924.

Fet, A.A. *Vechernie ogni*. Edited by D. D. Blagoi and M. A. Sokolova. Moscow: Nauka, 1979.

Gnedov, Vasilisk. *Smert´ iskusstvu: piatnadtsat´ poem*. St. Petersburg: Peterburgskii glashatai, 1915.

———. *Smert´ iskusstvu: piatnadtsat´ poem*. Edited by Dm. Kuz´min. Moscow: Argo-risk, 1996.

Iakobson, Roman. *Budetlianin nauki. Vospominaniia, pis´ma, stat´i, proza*. Edited by Bengt Iangfeldt. Moscow: Gileia, 2012.

Kozhinov, Vadim. *Vadim Kozhinov v interv´iu, besedakh, dialogakh i vospominaniiakh sovremennikov*. Edited by S. V. Marshkov. Moscow: Algoritm, 2005.

———. *Krasnaia sotnia*. Moscow: Algoritm, 2009.

Kruchenykh, Aleksei. *Apokalipsis v russkoi literature. Chort i rechetvortsy. Tainye poroki akademikov. Slovo, kak takovoe. Deklaratsii*. Moscow: n.p., 1923.

Mallarme, Stefan [Mallarmé, Stéphane]. *Sochineniia v stikhakh i proze*. Moscow: Raduga, 1995.

Mandelstam, Osip. *Sobranie sochinenii v dvukh tomakh*. Edited by G. P. Struve and B. A. Filippov. Vol. 2: *Stikhotvoreniia. Proza*. Washington, DC: Inter-Language Literary Associates, 1969.

Mezhirov, Aleksandr. *Proza v stikhakh*. Moscow: Sovetskii pisatel´, 1982.

Nabokov, Vladimir. *The Complete Stories of Vladimir Nabokov*. Edited by Dmitri Nabokov. New York: Knopf, 1995.

———. *Sobranie sochinenii russkogo perioda*. Edited by N. I. Artemenko-Tolstaia. Vol. 3 St. Petersburg: Simpozium, 2000.

Pasternak, Boris. *Stikhotvoreniia i poemy*. Edited by Lev Ozerov. Biblioteka poeta. Bol'shaia seriia. Leningrad: Sovetskii pisatel´, 1965.

Picasso, Pablo. *Poèmes*. Edited by Androula Michael. Paris: Le Cherche Midi, 2005.

——— [Pablo Pikasso]. *Stikhotvoreniia*. Translated from French and afterword by Mikhail Iasnov. Moscow: Tekst, 2008.

Sapgir, Genrikh. *Stikhotvoreniia i poemy*. Edited and commentary by David Shraer-Petrov and Maksim D. Shraer. Novaia biblioteka poeta. St. Petersburg: Akademicheskii proekt, 2004.

Schweitzer, Albert. *Civilization and Ethics*. Edited by Lilian M. Rigby Russell, translated by Charles Thomas Campion. 3rd edition. London: Adam & Charles Black, 1949.

——— [Shveitser, Al´bert]. *Kul´tura i etika*. Edited by V. A. Karpushin, translated by N. A. Zakharchenko and G. V. Kolshanskii. Moscow: Progress, 1973.

Shklovskii, Viktor. *Gamburgskii schet (stat´i—vospominaniia—esse, 1914-1933)*. Edited by A. Galushkina. Moscow: Sovetskii pisatel´, 1990.

Shrayer, Maxim D. *Voices of Jewish-Russian Literature. An Anthology*. Boston: Academic Studies Press, 2018.

Shrayer-Petrov, David [David Shraer-Petrov]. *Pesnia o golubom slone. Liubovnaia lirika*. Holyoke: New England Publishing, 1990.

———. "Villa Borghese." Tr. Dolores Stewart and Maxim D. Shrayer. *Salmagundi* 101–2 (Winter–Spring 1994).

———. *Villa Borgeze. Stikhotvoreniia*. Holyoke: New England Publishing, 1992.

———. *Propashchaia dusha. Stikhotvoreniia i poemy. 1987-1996*. Providence: APKA Publishers, 1997.

———. *Piterskii dozh. Stikhotvoreniia i poema (1995-1998)*. St. Petersburg: Izdatel'stvo Fonda Russkoi poezii, 1999.

———. "Iskusstvo kak izlom." *Novyi Zhurnal / The New Review* 196 (1995): 245-256.

———. *Barabany sud'by*. Moscow: Argo-risk, 2002.

———. *Forma liubvi. Izbrannaia lirika*. Moscow: Izdatel'skii dom "Iunost'", 2003.

———. *Dve knigi. Stikhi*. Philadelphia: Poberezh'e, 2009.

Shveitser, Al'bert [Schweitzer, Albert]. *Kul'tura i etika*. Moscow: Progress, 1973.

Tiutchev, Fedor Ivanovich. *Lirika*. Edited by K.V. Pigarev. 2 vols. Moscow: Nauka, 1966.

Tsvetaeva, Marina. *Sobranie sochinenii v semi tomakh*. Volume 3. Moscow: Ellis Lak, 1994.

Italy in the Poetry of David Shrayer-Petrov[*]

Stefano Garzonio

In his preface to *Canvasses* (*Kholsty*, 1967), David Shrayer-Petrov's first published collection of poems, Lev Ozerov noted that the poet "meticulously, persistently, unhurriedly studies life" ("… пристально, настойчиво, неторопливо изучает жизнь").[1] In fact, it would be fair to suggest that a double sensitivity, of a writer and of a scientist, gave David Shrayer-Petrov's work a particular acuteness, a kind of "harmonic precision," which endows his verses with an almost southern "sunniness" (or, as one might put it in Italian, "una solarità quasi 'meridionale'"). It is no coincidence that the Italian and, more generally, the Mediterranean or Levantine theme, could be traced in Shrayer-Petrov's verses long before his destiny-arranged sojourn in Italy as a refugee and a former Jewish refusenik who was finally allowed to emigrate from the USSR in 1987.[2]

---

[*] Copyright © 2021 by Stefano Garzonio. English translation copyright © 2021 by Stefano Garzonio and Maxim D. Shrayer.
[1] Lev Ozerov, "Ob avtore," in David Petrov, *Kholsty*, in *Pereklichka* (Moscow: Molodaia gvardiia, 1967), 117.
[2] The concept of "Italian text" (Russian: итальянский текст) is to be related to the historical-typological category of "Petersburg text" (Russian: петербургский текст) in Russian literature, which was first identified and described by Vladimir Toporov. Toporov defined it as a hypertext, functioning as an organic thematic system of linguistic, literary, and cultural references. In 1990 Toporov also dedicated a pioneering article to the Italian theme in St. Petersburg culture: V. N. Toporov, "Italiia v Peterburge," in *Italiia i slavianskii mir. Sovetsko-ital´ianskii simpozium* (Moscow: Institut slavianovedeniia i balkanistiki, 1990), 49–81; see also V. N. Toporov, "Peterburg i 'peterburgskii tekst' russkoi literatury," in V. N. Toporov, *Mif. Ritual. Simvol. Obraz: Issledovaniya v oblasti mifopoeticheskogo. Izbrannoe* (Moscow: Progress-Kul´tura, 1995), 259–367. Other scholars subsequently proposed such specific concepts as "Roman text," "Venetian text," or "Florentine text" in Russian literature. See N. E. Mednis, *Sverkhteksty v russkoi literature* (Novosibirsk: Izdatel´stvo Novosibirskogo pedinstituta, 2003).

Already among the verses included in Shrayer-Petrov's first published collection, we immediately find an "Italian text." I am referring to the poem "Members of the Italian Komsomol [Young Communist League] in a Young Pioneer Camp" ("Ital′ianskie komsomol′tsy v pionerskom lagere"). This poem was young Shrayer-Petrov's debut publication in a major Soviet monthly magazine in 1959.³ It is certainly a text with a noticeable political orientation, which can be linked to the postwar Soviet rhetoric of people's friendship and internationalism. At the same time, the young poet here overcomes stereotypes and Soviet formulas in order to give the readers a faithful picture of reality. The poem depicts a meeting between Soviet young pioneers and a delegation of young people from the FGCI (Federazione della Gioventù Comunista Italiana; Federation of Italian Communist Youth). The poem describes singing performances by the two groups, and, specifically, points to an Italian partisan song:

> На могилах героев,
> Партизан героев
> Расцветают ромашки
> Каждой весною⁴

("On heroes' graves/ Partisan graves/ Daisies bloom/ Each spring")

Given the mention of the flowers on the partisans' graves, Shrayer-Petrov's poem most probably refers to verse four of "Bella ciao!" ("Goodbye, Beautiful"), the famous Mondine folk song, which during World War II became the anthem of anti-Fascism and anti-Nazism sung by Italian partisans (and, one might add, was quite popular in the postwar Soviet Union):

> E seppellire lassù in montagna
> o bella ciao bella ciao
> bella ciao ciao ciao
> e seppellire lassù in montagna
> sotto l'ombra di un bel fior.⁵

---

3   See David Petrov, "Ital′ianskie komsomol'tsy v pionerskom lagere," *Pioner* 5 (1959), 30; David Petrov, *Kholsty*, 118–119. Note that in the magazine publication, the cover illustrates the poem.
4   Here and hereafter, unless noted otherwise, all verse translations into English are literal.
5   For the full text, see "Bella ciao," https://en.wikipedia.org/wiki/Bella_ciao, accessed March 27, 2020.

("Lay me to rest in the mountain, / goodbye o beautiful goodbye beautiful/ goodbye beautiful/ lay me to rest in the mountain/ in the shade of a beautiful flower.")

In *Canvasses*, one also finds lyrical poems dedicated to Georgia, "Tbilisi" and "V sadakh iuga" ("In the Orchards of the South"). In their tone and imagery, these texts hearken back to the tradition of "southern poetry" from Konsantin Batyushkov and Aleksandr Pushkin all the way up to Maximillian Voloshin and to Osip Mandelstam's Tauric and Armenian verses, a tradition that subsequently spread widely across Soviet poetry of the 1920s.

As we know, following *Canvasses*, Shrayer-Petrov was unable to publish other collections of his poetry at home until the post-Soviet years; his collection *Winter Ship* (*Zimnii korabl´*), which showcased many of his poems from the 1970s, was derailed after the poet's expulsion from the Union of Soviet Writers and public ostracism. As a refusenik and banished writer, Shrayer-Petrov was unable to publish in the Soviet Union. In 1987 Shrayer-Petrov and his family were finally allowed to emigrate. Prior to arriving in the United States, they had spent most of the summer of 1987 in Italy, first in Rome, then in the small town of Ladispoli on the Tyrrhenian coast. As a result, a hiatus of over twenty years separates the Moscow-published *Canvasses* and *Song of a Blue Elephant* (*Pesnia o golubom slone*, 1990), which appeared in Holyoke, Massachusetts, already after the writer made New England his new home.

The long poem *Villa Borghese*, one of Shrayer-Petrov's best known works, as well as other poems in the eponymous collection published in Massachusetts in 1992, are linked to the writer's short stay in Italy en route to America. Next to the lyrical, self-denuding poem *Villa Borghese* we find another text with Italian themes. Dated December 8, 1990, the poem "Podvig" ("Exploit"; "Act of Heroism") is dedicated to the memory of V. N. (Vladimir Nabokov) and takes its title from Nabokov's fourth Russian novel *Podvig* (known in English as *Glory*). Both texts are included in the "Novyi svet" ("New World") cycle of the collection.[6] The poem *Villa Borghese* subsequently appeared in the Shrayer-Petrov's collection *Propashchaia dusha* (*Lost Soul*, 1997). There it gave its name to

---

6   See David Shraer-Petrov, *Villa Borgeze* (Holyoke, MA: New England Publishing Co., 1992), 57–58; 65.

a cycle of poems, which also features the poem "Exploit."[7] Shrayer-Petrov also included "Villa Borghese" in his retrospective collection *Forma liubvi* (*Form of Love*, 2003),[8] and, finally, in the most recent edition of selected long and longer poems *Derevenskii orkestr* (*Village Orchestra*), published in St. Petersburg in 2016.[9]

In Shrayer-Petrov's collection *Dve knigi* (*Two Books*, 2009) we find the poems "Bibleiskie siuzhety" ("Biblical Plots") and "Vernut′sia v Sorrento" ("Come Back to Sorrento"), both of them linked to Italy and the poet's Italian experience, and the poem "Zakat na beregu Tirrenskogo moria" ("Sunset at the Shore of the Tyrrhenian Sea").[10] These texts contain Italian themes and motifs with distinct autobiographical references, which is evident in many of David Shrayer-Petrov's poems. The poet's peregrinations from Soviet Russia to Italy and then to the United States provide the setting, while the cultural and autobiographical theme of Jewishness and Judaism looms large on the horizon of many of his poems.

Shrayer-Petrov started *Villa Borghese* during the 1987 Italian transit and completed it in 1990, already in Providence, Rhode Island, where he lived for almost twenty years.[11] Certainly, given its numerous reprintings in the poet's collections and anthologies,[12] the poem *Villa Borghese* occupies a central position among David Shrayer-Petrov's "Italian" poems, and becomes the Jewish-Russian poet's exilic lamentation par excellence. (Also see Ian Probstein's and Oleg Smola's essays in this volume.) Let us therefore take a closer look at this work. I will quote the text in its entirety, first in the original, then in the English translation by Dolores Stewart and Maxim D. Shrayer:

---

7   See David Shraer-Petrov, *Propashchaia dusha. Stikhotvoreniia i poemy 1987–1996* (Providence, RI: APKA Publishers, 1997), 6-8; 18-19.
8   David Shraer-Petrov, *Forma liubvi* (Moscow: Izdatel′skii dom "Iunost′," 2003), 84–85.
9   David Shraer-Petrov, *Derevenskii orkestr: Shest′ poem* (St. Petersburg: Ostrovitianin, 2016), 57–60.
10 David Shraer-Petrov, *Dve knigi* (Philadelphia: Poberezh′e, 2009), 44; 45–46; 56–57.
11 For biographical information, see Maxim D. Shrayer, "David Shrayer-Petrov," in *Voices of Jewish-Russian Literature: An Anthology*, ed. Maxim D. Shrayer (Boston: Academic Studies Press, 2018), 827–830.
12 See, for instance, Mikhail Grozovskii, comp., Evgenii Vitkovskii, ed., *Svet dvuedinyi. Evrei i Rossiia v sovremennoi poezii* (Moscow: Kh.G.S., 1996), 445; Rika Katsova and Gennadii Katsov, eds., *70: Mezhdunarodnaia poeticheskaia antologiia, posviashchennaia 70-letiiu Izrailia* (New York: KRiK, 2018), 292–294.

Вилла Боргезе

Случались собаки на Вилле Боргезе,
Случались в том смысле, что обитали.
Случались, собачью трубя бордельезу,
Случались, хвостами трубя. О, детали!

Конкретная музыка тел шелестящих,
Балетная — пляска собачьего тела,
Конкретная — плачь по России болящей,
Балетная — плач. Унеслась, улетела.

Собакою с римскими псами на Вилле,
Скользучею рыбой из Тибра — по травам.
Забыть, как доили, давили, травили?
Забыть окаянную ласку Державы?

На Вилле Боргезе в ночи итальянской,
На самой роскошной окраине Рима
Бездомной собакою выть по российским,
Навеки потерянным, неповторимым.

В траве, перепутанной с волосами,
Очнуться прижатым хвостами к ограде,
Очнуться под римскими небесами,
Твердя полоумно: ах, Наденька-Надя,

Ах, Вера-Верунчик, ах, Любушка-Люба,
Валюша, Марина, Катюша и Зина.
Здесь тянут ко мне пуританские губы
Трезвейшие новоанглийские зимы.

Когда умирать мне придётся, чуть живы,
Прошепчут мои полумёртвые губы:
Мы стали чужими, Россия, чужими,
А были своими сыны Иегуды.

Как это забавно валяться в обнимку
С последней бутылкой, с последним приветом
На Вилле Боргезе, как старому снимку —
На свалке истории вместе с конвертом.

На Вилле Боргезе якшаться с трубящей
Компанией псов, абсолютно античных.
О, Боже! Ну что же Тебе до болящей
Души и до мраморных анемичных

Созданий, наставленных между стволами,
Как в Летнем саду, где когда-то ночами
Гуляли по стёжкам-дорожкам, стояли
Ночами под бледными небесами.

Какие архангелы в трубы трубили!
Какие опричники-псы нас губили!
Какие иуды в любви нас топили,
А мы все равно эту землю любили.

Она отвергала нас, отторгала,
Она изводила, греховно зачатых,
А нам не хватало, нам всё было мало,
Пока нас не сжили со света, проклятых,

Пока не добрёл я до варварской Виллы,
Где псы и античные девы толпою
По стёжкам-дорожкам гуляют, как, милый,
Помнишь, гуляли дома с тобою...[13]

Villa Borghese

These dogs copulating at Villa Borghese,
Copulating, the casual bitches and males,
Taking over the place, blaring out Brothellaise,
Blatantly wagging their tails—oh, details!

The concrete music of dog bodies rustling,
Of dogs' scrawny bodies, a low street ballet.
The concrete tears for the anguish of Russia.
The weeping ballet has flown, rushed away.

Like a stray with the Roman dogs of the Villa,
Like a gasping fish on the banks of the Tiber,

---

13 Shraer-Petrov, *Villa Borgeze*, 57–58.

Forget the purging, the crushing, the spilling,
Forget the evil caress of the empire.

At Villa Borghese, on Italianate evenings,
In grandeur, the lap of luxurious Rome,
A stray is still howling for his Russian leavings,
The lost, irretrievable things of his home.

To wake and feel pressed by tails to the railing,
To wake and feel grass intertwining with hair,
Beneath skies of Rome, to go madly on mumbling
Oh, Nádenka, Nádya—a stumbling prayer—

Oh Véra, Verúnchik . . . Oh, Lyúbushka, Lyúba,
Valyúsha, Marína, Katyúsha, and Zína.
Here the soberest New England winters
Offer their lips to me, cool and serene.

When my time comes to die, when I'm barely alive,
Half-dead lips will whisper, like never before:
For you and us, Russia, no closeness survives,
We, sons of Yehudah, who used to be yours.

To lie here embracing—perhaps it's a laugh—
Last bottle, last letter, whatever remains.
At Villa Borghese, like an old photograph
On history's dump. Along with the frame.

At Villa Borghese, hang out with the gang
Of roaming wild dogs, an antique mosaic.
How much can you care, oh my Lord, for the paining
Soul and how much for the marble, anemic

Creatures arranged among columns of wood.
Like Petersburg's Summer Gardens. We walked
A sweet winding path, lovers' lane, and we stood
All night beneath skies that would never grow dark.

Those archangels blaring their trumpets of exile,
Those animals hounding us, shunned and banned,
Those judases killing with kindness and smiles.
And yet, despite all, we still loved that land

That cast us away like inferior stuff,
Aborted like something conceived out of error,
All that wasn't all, it was never enough,
Until they were rid of us cursed ones forever,

Until I came here to this barbarous Villa
Where statuesque maidens and dogs crowd my sight,
Out walking the dear little paths, like my darling
Remember, back home, how we walked those white nights?[14]

This poem is a plaintive, confessional text, in which the theme of exile and the theme of memory are deeply intertwined. Also central to the design of *Villa Borghese* is the theme of the painfully liberating expulsion from the "earthly paradise of socialism," which is, at the same time, presented as the expulsion from the poet's Leningrad youth and the Russian cultural past. The poem deploys and brings together autobiographical recollections and literary allusions. Its use of the adjective *italiiskii* (Italianite) appears, perhaps paradoxically, to be a reference to "Rim" ("Rome"), Mandelstam's 1937 anti-totalitarian poem, in which hints at Stalin's Moscow are superimposed upon visions of ancient and Renaissance Rome during Mussolini's rule:

Итальянские черборубашечники,
Мертвых цезарей злые щенки . . .[15]

("Italianate blackshirts/ vicious pups of dead ceasars . . .")[16]

Mandelstam's image from the poem "Ariost" ("Ariosto," 1933–1936), "В Европе холодно. В Италии темно./ Власть отвратительна, как руки брадобрея"[17] ("It's cold in Europe. Dark in Italy./ Power is repugnant like

---

14 David Shrayer-Petrov, "Villa Borghese," tr. Dolores Stewart and Maxim D. Shrayer, in *Voices of Jewish-Russian Literature: An Anthology*, ed. Maxim D. Shrayer (Boston: Academic Studies Press, 2018), 831–833.

15 O. E. Mandel´shtam, *Sobranie sochinenii v chetyrekh tomakh*, ed. G. P. Struve and B. A. Filippov, vol. 1 (Moscow: Terra, 1991), 260.

16 At the same time, in the context of Acmeist poetics the adjective *italiiskii* (Italianate) could also be an allusion to the line "Смыкает Италийские врата" from Dante's *Divine Comedy* in Mikhail Lozinski's translation (*Inferno*, 9:114); see Dante Alig´eri, *Bozhestvennaia komediia*, tr. Mikhail Lozinskii (Moscow: Pravda, 1982), http://lib.ru/POEZIQ/DANTE/comedy.txt , accessed April 17, 2020.

17 Mandel´shtam, *Sobranie sochinenii v chetyrekh tomakh*, vol. 1, 193.

the barber's hands"), hangs in the air of Shrayer-Petrov's poem. With a reference to Russian history, Shrayer-Petrov transforms stray Roman dogs into *oprichniki*, a special bodyguard force established by Ivan the Terrible and now nearly synonymous with members of special security corps, with its characteristic emblem of a dog's head. Shrayer-Petrov further extends the canine imagery to the representation of the dogs in the ancient world. The verse "Компанией псов, абсолютно античных" (literally: "the gang of wild dogs, [who are] completely from the antiquity") possibly refers to the images of ancient *canes pugnantes* ("fighting dogs") and also, perhaps, to the famous mosaic "Cave Canem" ("Beware of the Dog") in Pompeii's House of the Tragic Poet, which Shrayer-Petrov visited in July 1987.

On a separate note, the verse "Твердя полоумно: ах, Наденька, Надя" (literally "Repeating madly: oh, Naden′ka, Nadia") points directly to a well-known song by Bulat Okudzhava, "Iz okon korochkoi neset podzharistoi . . ." ("From the windows the smell of deep-fried crust is wafting in . . .," 1958), usually remembered for the repetition of the words "Ах, Надя, Наденька . . ." ("Oh, Nadya, Naden′ka . . .") in four of its five quatrains. Shrayer-Petrov's incorporation of this reference to the Okudzhava song was, perhaps, a tacit acknowledgment of their shared literary and personal past.[18]

The result is an articulated interweaving of epochs, settings, and destinies: the exilic present and the life story of Shrayer-Petrov's lyrical "I" are merged and later dissolved in the different planes of history and individual experiences of the past. Thus, a shared history is formed, in which ancient Rome converges with Rus′, Russia, and the Soviet Union. And yet, the defamiliarized Roman night of *Villa Borghese*, as perceived by the poet, becomes distinctly Jewish with the line "А были своими сыны Иегуды" ("We, sons of Yehudah, who used to be yours"). The concept and

---

18   See Bulat Okudzhava, "Iz okon korochkoi neset podzharustoi . . .," http://www.bards.ru/archives/part.php?id=17941, accessed April 2, 2020. Okudzhava's song is dedicated to the poet Evgeny Reyn, a friend of Shrayer-Petrov's Leningrad youth. On Shrayer-Petrov and Okudzhava, see Dmitrii Bykov, *Bulat Okudzhava* (Moscow: Molodaia gvardiia, 2009), 349–350. According to Bykov, Okudzhava was exposed to and influenced by Shrayer-Petrov's early poetry. The history of Shrayer-Petrov's personal and literary relations with Okudzhava in the 1950s–1970s is described in Shrayer-Petrov's literary memoir "Gusar s gitaroi" ("A Hussar with a Guitar"); see David Shraer-Petrov, "Gusar s gitaroi. Okudzhava," in his *Vodka s pirozhnymi. Roman s pisateliami*, ed. Maksim D. Shraer (St. Petersburg: Akademicheskii proekt, 2007), 218–230.

image of a Jewish night polemically evokes the opening of another famous poem by Mandelstam, this one from 1916:

> Это ночь непоправима,
> А у вас ещё светло.
> У ворот Ерусалима
> Солнце чёрное взошло.[19]

("This night is irreparable,/ Where you are it's still light out./ At the gates of Jerusalem/ A black sun has risen.")

Ultimately, the poem *Villa Borghese* conjures up a desperate yet disempowered declaration of the Jewish-Russian exile's love for mother—stepmother—Russia, a declaration that is made explicit, intertextually, by a series of references to and echoes of the poetic imagery of forced exile (Ovid; Dante; Mandelstam), and spatially, by the contrasting parallels between the park of Villa Borghese and the Summer Gardens in St. Petersburg/Leningrad. The fact that the poet has included *Villa Borghese* in many of his collections testifies to its privileged status in the poetic experience of Shrayer-Petrov as taken in its entirety.

We have already seen that Shrayer-Petrov's "Italian" text interweaves several dimensions of culture and existence, some Russian and some Italian, all belonging to different time periods. Moreover, references to Judaism are added into the texture of these poems, creating a Jewish-Italian encounter. In connection with this topic, the poem "Bibleiskie siuzhety" ("Biblical Plots") calls for attention. Here Shrayer-Petrov highlights the Judaic traits and features in the religious iconography of Italian and, more specifically, of Florentine painting. While wandering the streets of Florence for the first time, the poet encounters old Italian men who, presumably, look Jewish. The poet is reminded of the "three hundred thousand first Christians [who] carried/ Jewish genes to Italy from Palestine."[20] At the same time, this encounter also reminds the poet (a little bit like it does Isaac Babel's narrator in the short story "Pan Apolek," included in the collection *Red Cavalry*) that biblical faces in Christian religious paintings are inspired by the local Jews and their descendants. The biblical—Jewish—faces of the old Florentine men highlight the very essence of Florentine religious portraiture, and the poet can only wonder if their distant ancestors had been Jews. The lyrical

---

19 Mandel´shtam, *Sobranie sochinenii v chetyrekh tomakh*, vol. 1, 63.
20 Shraer-Petrov, *Dve knigi*, 44.

hero poses as a Messiah for the old Florentine men: "мне поручено вывезти его в палестину?/ он столько веков тосковал по мне, молясь в церкви"[21] ("am I charged with the task of leading him to palestine?/ for so many centuries he has longed for me while praying in church"). This imagined predicament far from the Promised Land is the poet's a doleful reinterpretation of the theme of exile and detachment, especially considering Shrayer-Petrov's own exile from Russia. But it is also a reimagining of the Jewish exodus and the return to the ancestral homeland.

Another poem on the Italian theme, "Vernut′sia v Sorrento" ("Come Back to Sorrento") validates the continuous perception of exile as a prominent part of one's life experience. Here, the obvious and deliberate reference to the famous song "Torna a Surriento" (1902, music by Ernesto De Curtis; lyrics by Giambattista De Curtis) underlines the poem's central theme: that of recovering lost time. The poet's attitude towards the days he and his family spent in Italy as refugees, waiting for the entry visa to the United States, is twofold. On the one hand, the lyrical hero has made a new life for himself in the New World; on the other, he experiences nostalgia for the unstable status of being in Italy in transit, still physically tied to a heroic period of his life before the emigration from the Soviet Union. "But the little song is over" ("но песенка спета"),[22] speaks/sings the hero, as if he were a character in the opera. This echoes both the famous Neapolitan song, and the carefree and, to some extent, irresponsible life in Italy following the escape from the Soviet Union. At the end he wonders if the song is really finished, sung to the end, or if life still offers the opportunity of escaping to Sorrento, "где каждая крыша/ бездельем согрета" ("where every roof/ is warmed by idling [perhaps a reference to the Italian *dolce far niente*]"). The nostalgic sense of Italian languor suddenly accompanies the treasured memory of the Peterhof palace and fountains outside Leningrad (St. Petersburg). It also evokes the supernatural images of *leshii*, the Russian wood-sprite, and *rusalka*, the undine of the Russian folklore, but also the *sirena* ("mermaid") from the Neapolitan song: "Vide attuorno sti Sirene,/ ca te guardano 'ncantate,/ e te vonno tantu bene . . ." ("Look at the mermaids/ that look at you with amazement/ and love you so much"). In this Italian-Russian-American song, memories of Italy ultimately give some hope that

---

21 Ibid., 44.
22 Ibid., 45–46.

the love will go on: "Is our little song really over?" ("Ужель наша песенка спета?").

Quite different, both in its atmosphere and its textual references, is the poem "Zakat na beregu Tirrenskogo moria" ("Sunset at the Shore of the Tyrrhenian Sea"):

Закат на берегу Тирренского моря

Максиму

Наша компания собралась полуслучайно:
двое из России, трое из Персии, трое с Украины.
а до этого мы зашли в "супермаркет"
и купили бутылку "кьянти",
огромную, как пизанская башня.
в определенном смысле наша полуслучайная компания
была не так уж категорически случайна,
не более, чем случайны сироты в детском доме,
или женщины в родильном отделении больницы,
или солдаты в одной роте.
всех объединяет какое-то похожее несчастье,
похожая повинность,
похожая мечта,
похожий страх.
мы все были беженцами-евреями.
это нас объединяло.
мы все бежали в Америку,
спасаясь от русских, персов, украинцев.
мы все бежали в Америку, как будто бы там обитал мессия.
это нас объединяло, но не роднило,
потому что у каждого были свои претензии к мессии.
мы пили вино из бумажных стаканчиков:
евреи всегда евреи,
сохраняют благообразие,
хотя нам — русским евреям — приходилось в прежней жизни
пить прямо из бутылки.
то же самое с украинскими евреями, которые за границей
          немедленно начинают сходить за русских евреев.
иранцы держались степенно,

каждый раз после очередного стаканчика,

вытирая носовыми платками рты и пальцы.

чёрный приморский песок терял свою черноту

по мере того, как красное солнце тонуло за линией горизонта.

"а что, если мы приедем в Америку и достигнем счастья? —

                  спросил один из иранцев.

— тогда нам больше не понадобится мессия,

мечта о мессии?"

"реальное счастье лучше прекрасной мечты!"

                  сказал кто-то из русских.

"у счастья нет будущего, ибо оно проходит" — сказал ещё кто-то.

было так темно, что бутылка пошла по кругу.

"зачем же мы уехали?" — спросил один из нас.

"чтобы узнать", — ответил кто-то.[23]

("Sunset at the Shore of the Tyrrhenian Sea": "Our group was assembled partly by accident,/ two from russia, three from persia, three from ukraine./ and before that we had stopped by the 'supermarket'/ and picked up a bottle of 'chianti,'/ huge, like the tower of pisa./ in a certain sense our group, assembled partly by accident,/ wasn't so categorically accidental,/ no more, than orphans are accidental in a children's home,/ or women in a hospital's maternal ward,/ or soldiers in the same company./ some sort of a similar misfortune unites all,/ a similar servitude,/ a similar dream,/ a similar fear./ we were all refugees-jews./ This united us./ We were all escaping to america,/ fleeing from russians, persians, ukrainians./ we were all escaping to america, as if the messiah were living there./ this united us, but didn't make us kin,/ because each of us had his own issues with the messiah./ we drank wine from paper cups;/ jews are always jews,/ retaining their respectability,/ even though we—russian jews—in the previous life had had the occasion/ to drink straight from the bottle./ the same with ukrainian jews, who once abroad/ immediately begin to pass for russian jews./ iranians conducted themselves measuredly,/ each time after the next little cup,/ wiping their mouths and fingers with handkerchiefs./ the black seaside sand was losing its blackness/ as the red sun sank behind the line of the horizon./ 'and what if we come to america and fail to attain happiness?'/ asked one of the iranians,/ 'would we no longer need the messiah,/ the dream of the messiah?'/ 'real happiness is better than a beautiful dream,'/ one of the russians said./ 'happiness has no future, for it passes,' said another person./

---

23 Ibid., 56–57.

it was so dark that the bottle was now passed around the circle./ 'why then did we leave?' one of us asked./ 'in order to know,'/ somebody replied.")

This lyrical poem has a distinct connection to the events in Shrayer-Petrov's biography, as it develops the texture of the exiles' everyday life in Italy without offering a mythical reinterpretation—as *Villa Borghese* does. The reference to the land of the exiles' destination, America, is decisive. If the poem *Villa Borghese* was, so to speak, turned towards the past, suspended between regret and reproach, "Sunset at the Shore of the Tyrrhenian Sea" extends its existential trajectory into the future, a future certainly full of uncertainty and mystery, but focused on the theme of immigrant "happiness." Both the departure from Italy and the detachment from Russia are therefore linked to a Jewish desire to learn ("чтобы узнать," "in order to know"), to a knowledge that alone can reveal the mystery of happiness.

Perhaps happiness is given only by the act of composing poetry, and the poet reaffirms the redeeming power of creativity in the short and loaded poem dedicated to the memory of Vladimir Nabokov (V. N. in the original publication). While the opening of the poem, "Vernut´sia v Pompei, na Kapri . . ." ("To come back to Pompeii, to Capri . . .") also echoes the Neapolitan song "Come Back to Sorrento," in this poem Shrayer-Petrov makes references to Pompeii and Capri as places of eternity and of the flow and ebb of human life.[24] Additionally, the poem also dialogues with *Villa Borghese* in the way it constructs a return to Italy and to the poetically imagined Russia. Creation of poetry by its very nature constitutes a true heroic act, a *podvig*:

Подвиг

Памяти В. Набокова

Вернуться в Помпеи, на Капри, вернуться отсюда
В такие места запредельные, в щёлочку их пролетел.

---

24 In the Russian cultural imagination, Pompeii is mostly known through Karl Briullov's classical painting "The Last Day of Pompeii" (1830–1833). David Shrayer-Petrov and his family visited Naples, Sorrento, Pompeii, and Capri in the summer of 1987 while staying in Italy. For details, see Maxim D. Shrayer, *Waiting for America: A Story of Emigration* (Syracuse: Syracuse University Press, 2007), 206–207; 215–225. In Russian literature, Capri was made famous by Ivan Bunin's novella "The Gentleman from San Francisco" (1915) and by Maxim Gorky's lengthy stay on the island.

Вернуться. В траттории быть половым или драить посуду,
И с берега камушки в синее. Ты не у дел.

Ты больше не лорд захудалой предместной усадьбы,
В которой от дивных соседских собак затерялся забор.
Ты больше не горд, ты случайность, ты свары и свадьбы,
Собачьей пирушки звонарь, органист и собор.

В такие места запредельные: Капри, Помпеи иль Бухта-Барахта
Бежать и утапливать камушки-рифмы солёной тоски.
Из самой цветущей, куда занесло тебя дьявольским фрахтом,
Затеянным в городе-бухте родном — до могильной тоски.[25]

("Exploit": "To come back to Pompeii, to Capri, to come back from here/ To such faraway unreachable places, you fly there though a chink./ To come back. To be a server in a trattoria or to scrub dishes,/ And from the shore [to toss] pebbles into the blue. You are no longer occupied./ You are no longer the master of a decaying manor house in a far suburb.||/ In which from the wondrous neighborhood dogs the fence is hidden./ You are no longer proud, you are a matter of chance, you are swarms of dogs, you are weddings,/ The bell-ringer, organist and cathedral of the dogs' little feast. ||/ To such faraway unreachable places, Capri, Pompeii or Frolic Bay/ To escape and to down the pebble-rhymes of salt longing./ From the most lush [bay] where a devilish boat journey has carried you,/ [a journey] conceived in your native city-bay—all the way to the gravestone.")

Shrayer-Petrov builds the themes and references to Italy into a homogeneous textual complex that brings together the most significant elements of what has been described as the "Italian text" of Russian literature. Shrayer-Petrov's Italian poems reveal layers of culture and civilization, from Classical antiquity to the world of the Renaissance. Such an intimate awareness of different tiers of the Italian past is interlaced in his poems with other key elements, such as the theme of the South and the Mediterranean, the theme of Catholicism and Judaism, but also the more recent and contemporary themes of Italian history, including Mussolini's rule and the influx of Jewish refugees to Italy after World War II and the Shoah and later in the 1970s–1980s. Shrayer-Petrov develops all these

---

25 Shraer-Petrov, *Propashchaia dusha*, 18–19.

themes and references in an original fashion, reinterpreting them through the prism of his own cultural, ethnoreligious, and biographical experience.

Poetic speech, as well as a poetic message, has no borders or barriers. Shrayer-Petrov's poetry is a "heroic exploit" of a true, genuine Jewish-Russian-American poet, a resident of the whole world.

Translated, from the Italian, by
the author with Maxim D. Shrayer

Works Cited

"Bella ciao." https://en.wikipedia.org/wiki/Bella_ciao. Accessed March 27, 2020.

Dmitrii Bykov. *Okudzhava*. Moscow: Molodaia gvardiia, 2009.

Grozovskii, Mikhail, comp., and Evgenii Vitkovskii, ed. *Svet dvuedinyi. Evrei i Rossiia v sovremennoi poezii*. Moscow: Kh.G.S., 1996.

Katsova, Rika, and Gennadii Katsov, eds. *70: Mezhdunarodnaia poeticheskaia antologiia, posviashchennaia 70-letiiu Izrailia*. New York: KRiK, 2018.

Mandel´shtam, O. E. *Sobranie sochinenii v chetyrekh tomakh*. Edited by G. P. Struve and B. A. Filippov. Vol. 1. Moscow: Terra, 1991.

Mednis, N. E. *Sverkhteksty v russkoi literature*. Novosibirsk: Izdatel'stvo Novosibirskogo pedinstituta, 2003.

Ozerov, Lev. "Ob avtore." In David Petrov, *Kholsty*. In *Pereklichka*, 116–117. Moscow: Molodaia gvardiia, 1967.

Shrayer-Petrov, David [David Petrov]. "Ital´ianskie komsomol´tsy v pionerskom lagere." *Pioner* 5 (1959): 30.

——— [David Petrov]. *Kholsty*. In *Pereklichka*, 116–160. Moscow: Molodaia gvardiia, 1967.

——— [David Shraer-Petrov]. *Villa Borgeze*. Holyoke, MA: New England Publishing Co., 1992.

——— [David Shrayer-Petrov]. *Propashchaia dusha. Stikhotvoreniia i poemy 1987–1996*. Providence, RI: APKA Publishers, 1997.

——— [David Shrayer-Petrov]. *Forma liubvi*. Moscow: Izdatel´skii dom "Iunost´," 2003.

——— [David Shrayer-Petrov]. *Dve knigi*. Philadelphia: Poberezh´e, 2009.

——— [David Shrayer-Petrov]. *Derevenskii orkestr: Shest´ poem*. St. Petersburg: Ostrovitianin, 2016.

———. "Villa Borghese." Translated by Dolores Stewart and Maxim D. Shrayer. In *Voices of Jewish-Russian Literature: An Anthology*, edited by Maxim D. Shrayer, 831–833. Boston: Academic Studies Press, 2018.

Shrayer, Maxim D. "David Shrayer-Petrov." In *Voices of Jewish-Russian Literature: An Anthology*, edited by Maxim D. Shrayer, 827–830. Boston: Academic Studies Press, 2018.

———, ed. *Voices of Jewish-Russian Literature: An Anthology*. Boston: Academic Studies Press, 2018.

Toporov, V. N. "Italiia v Peterburge." In *Italiia i slavianskii mir. Sovetsko-ital'ianskii simpozium*, 49–81. Moscow: Institut slavianovedeniia i balkanistiki, 1990.

———. "Peterburg i 'peterburgskii text' russkoi literatury." In V. N. Toporov, *Mif. Ritual. Simvol. Obraz: Issledovaniia v oblasti mifopoeticheskogo. Izbrannoe*, 259–367. Moscow: Progress-Kul´tura, 1995.

David Shrayer-Petrov's Poem "Friend's Illness": An Approach to Reading*

Andrei Ranchin

Болезнь друга

. . . проснулся
руку протянуть
в окно
свист
глаз нацелен
улица полна
его всегдашностью
площадка лестничная
преданность лица
расстались до утра
утрата
невозможна
нет
дня
нет
месяца
нет

---

* Copyright © 2021 by Andrei Ranchin. English translation copyright © 2021 by Daria Sadovnichenko and Maxim D. Shrayer.
  The author would like to thank Maxim D. Shrayer, Klavdia Smola, and Roman Katsman for a number of comments and suggestions he has taken into consideration during the composition of this essay.

года
нет
его
с утра до вечера
пустынен двор
колодец
подмигивает
глазом стрекозы
шуршат
с утра до ночи
облака
крыл слюдяных
дверей фанерных
нервно
просовываю
руку
в щель окна
оставлен
для общения
почтовый
молчит
пустынен провод телефонный
колодец входов и уходов
глаз фасетчатый
я вижу
каждый день
с тобой
мой
друг
я ухожу
твоя пустынна форточка
свистят мои глаза
шуршит
воспоминаний пепел[1]

---

1   David Shraer-Petrov, "Bolezn′ druga," in his *Nevskie stikhi*, ed. Maksim D. Shraer (St. Petersburg: Ostrovitianin, 2011), 50–52. The poem was originally published as part of the book-length cycle *Nevskie stikhi* (*Nevan Poems*) within Shrayer-Petrov's collection *Villa Borgeze* (*Villa Borghese*) (Holyoke, MA: New England Publishing Company, 1992), and subsequently reprinted as part of a selection from *Nevan Poems* in his book *Forma*

("Friend's Illness":[2] ". . . woke up/ to reach [my] hand/ toward the window/ whistling/ eye aimed/ street filled/ with his everpresentness/ staircase landing/ face's loyalty/ parted till morning/ [mourning] loss/ impossible/ no/ day/ no/ month/ no/ year/ no/ him/ from morning to evening/ the courtyard deserted/ the well/ winks/ dragonfly eye/ rustle/ from morning till night/ clouds [of]/ mica wings/ plywood doors/ anxiously [I]/ stick/ my hand/ through the chink in the window/ left/ for communication/ mail/ silent/ deserted telephone cord/ well of entrances and departures/ compound eye/ I see/ each day/ with you/ my/ friend/ I'm leaving [departing]/ your [ventilation] window is deserted/ my eyes whistle/ rustle/ ashes of memories")

David Shrayer-Petrov's poem "Friend's Illness" reveals a complex mechanism of creating meaning. Its semantics and its poetics are obscured, at least, at the first glance: it is not entirely clear which predicament the poem presents, how the metaphorical threads are woven, or how the individual lines of verse connect with each other.

The biographical subtext is only a partial help in understanding this poem. I quote from a letter by Maxim D. Shrayer, the poet's son, dated June 22, 2019, along with an addendum, dated January 26, 2020, both sent to me via email:

> Regarding the poem "Friend's Illness" from the book *Nevan Poems*: it was composed in late 1985 or early 1986. The "friend" is my father's closest Leningrad friend, the late Boris Smorodin. He was born in 1935 [and] survived the siege [of Leningrad] (my father was evacuated on one of the last trains—my late grandfather Peysakh Shrayer, a frontline officer, had managed to arrange for his family members to be evacuated). From 1944 until my father's departure for Borisov to serve as a military physician following his graduation from medical school, Boris and my father lived in the same building in Lesnoe [neighborhood of St. Petersburg's Vyborg Side] and were inseparable. Borya Smorodin (whom I knew well) was an engineer, but adored poetry. In the 1950s and early 1960s he accompanied my father to literary gatherings, witnessed many literary events, knew many poets, with whom my father was friendly at the time. Sometimes he served as a kind of representative of my father, if my father was unable to attend something. . . . Boris Smorodin appears in the pages of my father's literary

---

Liubvi (Form of Love) (Moscow: Izdatel´skii dom "Iunost´," 2003). *Nevan Poems* was published as a separate book in 2011 in St. Petersburg. On *Nevan Poems*, see also Ian Probstein's essay in this volume.

2   Here and hereafter, unless noted otherwise, the translations of Russian literary texts are are literal, some are annotated (tr.).

memoirs ("Bor'ka"; "Smoroda"), as well as in authorial digressions in the refusenik trilogy. . . . He had a bad heart. I saw him in 1993 and later in 1995, when I came to M[oscow] and P[etersburg]. He had preserved a small part of my father's archive, some of the early poems, which I took back to America. Boris left this world, if I'm not mistaken, in [late] 1995 or [early] 1996. He went to Moscow to undergo surgery and died under the surgeon's knife. Much later, in America, my father wrote the long poem *Tenitsy* [*Shadowmaidens*, 1997–1998], which, I believe, speaks of Boris's death and of my father's coming back too late. In 1998, when [my father] first visited Russia [after emigration], Boris was no longer alive. The said long poem was included in the collection *Piterskii dozh* [*Doge of Petersburg*, 1999], which is connected with Brodsky's death.[3]

In his memoir *Friends and Shadows* (*Druz´ia i teni*, pub. 1989), in the chapter titled "A Trolley in the Forestry Academy Park" ("Vagonetka v Lesotekhnicheskom parke"), David Shrayer-Petrov wrote about his friend as follows: "One can tell numerous stories that we lived through together. Not once had he double-crossed me or betrayed me. My whole life from the age of eight (1944) to twenty-three (1959) was always with Smoroda. He's like a hand. Both left and right."[4] While recalling his university years, Shrayer-Petrov adds: "He's loyal to me beyond measure, unconditionally, to the end."[5] Boris Smorodin was the only one to visit his poet-friend during his military service. "And he was the first," Shrayer-Petrov writes, "who greeted me when I returned home from the army. And the one who kept a watchful eye on me in the empty rooms, where my mother had recently died."[6]

The biographical context allows us to understand why the friend's illness caused such an anguished poetic response. The reasons are the heart condition of the poem's addressee and the author's very close attachment to him. But these strands of information do not add up to form a key to the poem's semantics.

One would think that the poem's title would serve as a key to the text. The title leads the readers to expect that what follows is some sort of a poetical message concerning precisely the illness of a friend. For some poems, such

---

3 The author thanks Maxim D. Shrayer for this information.
4 David Shraer-Petrov, *Druz´ia i teni. Roman s uchastiem avtora* (New York: Liberty Publishing House, 1989), 37–38.
5 Ibid., 38.
6 Ibid., 39.

a direct connection is valid. For example, several poems titled "Death of a Poet" speak precisely of a poet's death, be it Mikhail Lermontov's 1837 text about Pushkin's death after a duel or Anna Akhmatova's 1960 poem about Pasternak's departure. Joseph Brodsky's verses "On the Death of a Friend" ("Stikhi na smert′ druga," 1973) are indeed a poetic epitaph (even though the rumors about the death of the addressee, Sergey Chudakov, turned out to be false), while his "On the Death of Zhukov" ("Na smert′ Zhukova," 1974), written in emulation of Derzhavin's "Bullfinch" ("Snegir′," 1800), are about Marshal Zhukov's death and funeral.

In contrast, in Shrayer-Petrov's "Friend's Illness" the word "illness" is only present in the title. The theme set by the title unfolds in the text not through a sequence of direct meanings of lexemes, but through associations and allusions to literary subtexts. The first two verses, "... проснулся/ руку протянуть" ("... woke up/ to reach [my] hand"), are deliberately wrong from the semantic perspective ("I woke up in order to reach my hand"—the desire to see the friend is so strong that it becomes the reason for waking up).[7] These two verses apparently lead to the theme of friendship through the focus on a hand shake, or, to put it more accurately, through the impossibility of a hand shake because of the friend's illness and his absence. The poetic subtext here is the line "And there is no one to give a hand to" ("И некому руку подать") from Lermontov's "Both bored and sad ..." ("I skuchno i grustno...," 1840),[8] even though the motivation of impossibility in Lermontov's poem is different. The next two verses, "В окно/ свист" ("toward the window/ whistling") become clear with the help of another pretext, Sergei Yesenin's long poem *The Black Man* (*Chernyi chelovek*, 1926), which starts with these lines:

Друг мой, друг мой,
Я очень и очень болен.
Сам не знаю, откуда взялась эта боль.
То ли ветер свистит
Над пустым и безлюдным полем,
То ль, как рощу в сентябрь,

---

7   However, these verses can also be interpreted as two separate sentences, the second of which is incomplete: "Woke up. [I want] to reach [my] hand."
8   M. Iu. Lermontov, *Stikhotvoreniia i poemy, 1837–1841*, vol. 2 of *Polnoe sobranie stikhotvorenii*, 2 vols., introduction by D. V. Maksimov, comp. and commentary by E. E. Naidich (Leningrad: Sovetskii pisatel′, 1989), 41.

Осыпает мозги алкоголь.⁹

("My friend, my friend,/ I am very very sick./ I don't know myself where this pain comes from./ It is either the wind whistling/ Over an empty and deserted field,/ Or like a grove in September,/ Alcohol is shedding my brains.")

In the following fragment the motif of meetings with the friend is expressed through the possessive pronoun *his*:

улица полна
его всегдашностью
площадка лестничная
преданность лица
расстались до утра

("street filled/ with his everpresentness/ staircase landing/ face's loyalty/ parted till morning").

It is not clear whether the predicate "полна" ("full") modifies only "the street" or also "the staircase landing." Most likely, this one and the next verse should be understood as two nominal sentences describing a recent farewell that took place on the staircase. The unexpected "преданность лица" ("face's loyalty") is probably a transformation of the set phrase "личная преданность" ("personal [literally: facial] loyalty") into a configuration built on the principle of word subordination. However, other interpretations are quite tenable as well. In any case, the friendship here is given a deeply intimate and almost religious characteristic: the Russian word "лицо" is semantically paired by the word "лик," which is reserved for saints. At the same time, the poem does not clarify whose face embodies or expresses this loyalty and devotion: that of the lyrical subject (in the poem directly designated twice by the anaphoric I, but only closer to the end) or the poem's addressee (whose designations, "with you," and "you," also appear only in the final part of the text). "I" and "you" are here as if fused into a united whole, and this motif is contained in the very grammatical structure of the poem.

With the principle of paronomastic attraction, "до утра" ("till morning") gives rise to the next line, "утрата" ("loss"): "do utra/ utrata."

---

9   Sergei Esenin, *Stikhotvoreniia i poemy*, introduction by I. S. Eventov, comp. I. S. Eventov and I. V. Aleksakhina, commentary by I. V. Aleksakhina (Leningrad: Sovetskii pisatel´, 1986), 370.

When the next line appears, the words "till morning," which presuppose the possibility of an early meeting (as in "parted till morning"), appear fraught, pregnant with a terrible "loss"—a lexeme that indicates the danger that the most recent meeting may be the last one, that the illness is severe, dangerous. (Boris Smorodin's serious heart condition seems to be the real explanation behind this motif.)

The predicate "невозможна" ("impossible") is cut off from the subject "утрата" ("loss") by the boundary separating the lines[10] and is perceived as a kind of incantation or a denial in the interior dialogue of the lyrical "I" with himself: "Loss!?—Impossible!"

The next fragment contains the motif of time, stopped, frozen for the "I" because of the separation with the friend: "нет/ дня/ нет/ месяца/ нет/ года/ нет/ его/ с утра до вечера" ("no/ day/ no/ month/ no/ year/ no/ him/ from morning to evening"). The mysterious image of the dragonfly in the following verses calls for a special interpretation:

пустынен двор
колодец
подмигивает
глазом стрекозы.[11]

("the courtyard deserted/ the well/ winks/ dragonfly eye")

Why does the "dragonfly eye" of the courtyard (the Petersburg/Leningrad enclosed well-like courtyard) "wink" ("подмигивает глазом стрекозы")? What is the essence of this metaphor? The first meaning is on the surface: the courtyard has many windows ("eyes"). The metaphor of the "eye socket" ("глазница") connoting "window" is found in David Shrayer-Petrov's poem "In Leningrad after the Siege" ("V Leningrade posle blokady"), which is also included in his book *Nevan Poems* (*Nevskie stikhi*): ". . . копоть на камнях/ зияют глазницы/ где дом/ куда игрушки/ как жить дальше"[12] (". . . soot on stones/ gaping eye orbits/ where the house/ where the toys/ how to go on living").

---

10 It would be possible to say this word was cut off by enjambment, if such segmentation of the poem's lines would not have been a regular feature of its versification.
11 The text might have also been divided into sentences differently: "с утра до вечера пустынен двор" ("from morning to evening the courtyard is deserted").
12 Shraer-Petrov, *Nevskie stikhi*, 8–9.

One of the pretexts of "A Friend's Illness" is Boris Pasternak's poem "Spring has been simply you . . ." ("Vesna byla prosto toboi . . .," 1917) with its metaphor of a window as a dragonfly eyes:

> Не спорить, а спать. Не оспаривать,
> А спать. Не распахивать наспех
> Окна, где в беспамятных заревах
> Июль, разгораясь, как яспис,
> Расплавливал стекла и спаривал
> Тех самых пунцовых стрекоз,
> Которые нынче на брачных
> Брусах — мертвей и прозрачней
> Осыпавшихся папирос.[13]

("Not to argue, but to sleep. Not to dispute,/ But to sleep. Not to open up hastily/ The windows, where in heedless glowings of the sky/ July, catching up on fire like jasper,/ Melted the glass and paired up/ Those very crimson dragonflies,/ That now on the nuptial/ Beams—deadlier and more transparent/ Than crumbling *papirosy*.")

Yet the poem "Friend's Illness" is characterized not only and not so much by being a successor of Pasternak's poem, but rather by a polemical detachment from it. "Spring has been just you . . ." is a kind of spell, an invocation to dive into sleep where the character can return to harmony with the beloved woman and with the state of being in general. (All of these are invariant motifs of Pasternak's poetry.) Pasternak's poem is a memory of a union: see the metaphorical epithet *nuptial* and the association between the coming together of closing windows and the union of those in love. "Friend's Illness" is about a separation that can turn into a loss. And the connotations suggested by the image of the windows are different there, related to anxiety and misfortune.

Besides that, I would venture to suggest the possibility of a different, more complex interpretation, based on a symbolic, and not an object-oriented interpretation of the image. The image of the dragonfly in this section of the poem seems to be endowed with a negative significance, which is expressed by the following lines: "шуршат/ с утра до ночи/

---

13 Boris Pasternak, *Polnoe sobranie stikhotvorenii i poem*, introduction by V. N. Al´fonsov, comp. and commentary by V. S. Baevskii and E. V. Pasternak (St. Petersburg: Akademicheskii proekt, 2003), 177.

облака/ крыл слюдяных/ дверей фанерных" ("rustle/ from morning till night/ clouds [of]/ mica wings/ plywood doors"). There is something ominous in this rustling; the wings, like clouds, appear to engulf the entire sky. Compared to plywood doors, they resemble a barrier, a boundary between the "I" and the outside world, where the sick friend was left.

As far as the friend's illness in the poem develops as one fraught with death, a dragonfly with its "compound eye" (about this see below) calls to mind the many-eyed angel of death, described by Lev Shestov in the book *Na vesakh Iova (Stranstvovanie po dusham)* (*On Job's Balance* [*A Wandering across Souls*], 1929) in the chapter "Overcoming the Self-Evident (On the Centenary of F. M. Dostoevsky's Birth)," included into the first part of the book, which is titled "Revelations of Death." Consider this passage:

> They might remind me what one wise book states: the one who wants to know what was and will be, what is below the earth and what is above the sky, is better-off not to be born at all. But I will reply that the very same book tells how the angel of death flying down to a man to separate a man's soul from his body is all completely covered with eyes. Why so, why did the angel need so many eyes—he, who saw everything too early, that the man's time to leave the earth has not come. He can see everything in the sky and has nothing to observe on earth? And so I think that those eyes he has are not for himself. It sometimes happens that the angel of death coming down for a human's soul understands that he came too early, that the time has not yet come for one to leave the earth. He does not touch his soul, does not even reveal himself to it; but, before he goes, he clandestinely leaves the man two more eyes out of his own countless eyes. And then a man suddenly starts seeing more than everyone sees and what he used to see with his old eyes, [and can see] something completely new. And he sees the new in a novel way, not as people see, but as beings of "other worlds" see, so that it is not "necessary," but "free," i.e. at the same time it is and is not there, that it appears when it vanishes, and vanishes when it appears. The earlier, natural "like everyone else's" eyes testify to this "novel [vision]" what is exactly the opposite of what the eyes, left by the angel, can see.[14]

---

14 Lev Shestov, *Sochineniia*, 2 vols., ed. and introduction by A. V. Akhutin, annotation by A.V. Akhutin and E. V. Patkosh (Moscow: Izdatel′stvo "Nauka," 1994), vol. 2, 27. The first reference to the "wise book" has been traced to the Talmud. But the second reference "could not be found," see A. V. Akhutin and E. V. Patkosh, "Primechaniia," ibid., 511.

In Lev Shestov's book the many-eyed angel is an image of revelation, given by the approaching death, and not a sign of a possible misfortune. But even the fear of loss, related to a dragonfly-like creature, contains a revelation—a discovery of the special value of friendship, of the friend's presence.

Additionally, the dragonfly from David Shrayer-Petrov's poem resembles the many-eyed Argus Panoptes from Greek mythology (the ominous guard, thus a negative parallel). Another potential source are the many-eyed cherubim from the Book of Ezekiel: "Their entire bodies—backs, hands, and wings—and the wheels, the wheels of the four of them, were covered all over with eyes"[15] (Ezekiel 10:12). This image was later repeated in *The Exposition of the Orthodox Faith* (Book II, Chapter 3) by John of Damascus (Russian: Ioann Damaskin).[16]

Furthermore, the proximity of the "dragonfly" to the "well," even if a metaphorical one, recalls Alexey K. Tolstoy's poem "Where the vines bend over the whirlpool . . ." ("Gde gnutsia nad omutom lozy . . . ," 1840s), in which dragonflies, connected with the water element and with death, lure a child into a deadly whirlpool.[17]

The rustle of windows and doors most probably indicates the sensory tuning-in of the lyrical "I." The poet wonders whether the window/door will open, whether the long-awaited friend will look in/stop by.

The fragment that follows indicates that communication has been broken off:

нервно
просовываю
руку
в щель окна
оставлен
для общения
почтовый

("anxiously [I]/ stick/ [my] my hand/ through the chink in the window/ left/ for communication/ mail")

---

15 *Tanakh: A New Translation of the Holy Scriptures According to the Traditional Hebrew Text* (Philadelphia: Jewish Publication Society, 1995), 904.
16 Cf. Ioann Damaskin, *Tochnoe izlozhenie pravoslavnoi very* (St. Petesburg: Izdanie knogoprodavtsa I. L. Tuzova, 1894), 120.
17 See A. K. Tolstoi, *Polnoe sobranie stikhotvorenii i poem*, comp., introduction, and commentary by I. G. Iampol′skii (St. Petesburg: Akademicheskii proekt, 2004), 147-148, 577 [text of an earlier version].

The expression "the chink in the window" associatively anticipates the appearance of a "mailbox." Yet, its use in the poem is not transparent. On the one hand, the window can be interpreted as a metaphor for the mailbox, a window that is connected to the outside world. In this case, the chink in the window is a slot, a slit for letters. On the other hand, we can assume that we are looking at a metaphor of a window that is becoming overgrown, covered in. Following the topic of the previous lines, this image signifies troubled communication, a rising barrier.

The decision to exclude the lexeme "box" (as in "mailbox") is striking. Apparently, it is an act of tabooing the speculation about death: compare the idiom "сыграть в ящик," which literally means "to play into the box" and refers to the "game"—act—of dying.

The verses "молчит/ пустынен провод телефонный/ колодец входов и уходов" ("silent/ deserted telephone cord/ well of entrances and departures") exemplify an "exchange" of attributes between a mailbox that may be "empty" and a "telephone" that may be "silent." Depending on the syntagmatic breakdown, we either assume that the mailbox is "silent" and, probably, also "deserted," whereby a "telephone cord" is designated by the lexeme-metaphor "well,"[18] or we assign all these predicative functions to the telephone cord.[19]

A literary pretext here is Osip Mandelstam's "I came back to the city familiar to the point of tears ..." ("Ia vernulsia v moi gorod, znakomyi do slez ...," 1930):

Петербург! я ещё не хочу умирать:
У тебя телефонов моих номера.

Петербург! у меня ещё есть адреса,
По которым найду мертвецов голоса.
Я на лестнице чёрной живу ...

---

18 This is a play on the homonymy of the word "провод" (wire [of a telephone]), derived from "проводить" (to conduct—"to let through," "be a conductor of something"), and "провожать" ("to see off"). Thus, the courtyard-well, which is the space of the friend's comings and goings, is linked to the telephone wire, by which the friend's voice comes and goes.

19 Cf. the nominative usage of the phrase "провод телефона" ("telephone wire") in David Shrayer-Petrov's poem "O my peri, Queen Tamara" ("O moia peri, tsaritsa Tamara," 1977): "wire of a snaking phone" ("провод змеящийся телефона"), in Shraer-Petrov, *Forma liubvi*, 40.

("Petersburg! I do not want to die yet:/ You have my telephone numbers./ Petersburg! I still have the addresses,/ By which I'll find dead people's voices./ I live on the black stairway...")[20]

The lines "глаз фасетчатый/ я вижу/ каждый день" ("compound eye/ I see/ each day") show the lyrical "I" peering into the many-windowed courtyard-well: Will the friend finally appear? In this interpretation, a compound eye is an attribute of the lyrical "I." It is also worth remembering that a dragonfly (or rather, a chimerical insect that combines the characteristics of a dragonfly and a grasshopper/cicada), possesses a compound eye vision, and in Russian literature is associated with the poet.[21] At the same time, a different understanding is possible: every day I see the compound eye of the courtyard-well.

In the end, the perspective of vision, of seeing space, is suddenly changed. Previously the observer appeared to be in his own space, taking it in, and waiting for/not expecting the friend. But now he is gazing into the friend's ventilation window ("форточка"). Only a small part is left from the whole window; the window as a channel of visual communication looks contracted, shrunk. Now, the observer is not seeing his friend behind the window (is the friend at the hospital?):

с тобой

мой

друг

я ухожу

твоя пустынна форточка

свистят мои глаза

шуршит

воспоминаний пепел.

("with you/ my/ friend/ I'm leaving/ your [ventilation] window is deserted/ my eyes whistle/ rustle/ ashes of memories.")

---

20 Osip Mandel'shtam, *Polnoe sobranie stikhotvorenii*, introduction by M. L. Gasparov and A. G. Mets, comp. and commentary by A. G. Mets (St. Petersburg: Akademicheskii proekt, 1995), 194.

21 See F. B. Uspenskii, "Habent sua fata libellulae: k istorii russkikh literaturnykh nasekomykh," *Vestnik PSTGU*, seriia 3: "Filologiia" 2 (2008): 60-80. Reprinted in F.B. Uspenskii, *Tri dogadki o stikhakh Osipa Mandel'shtama* (Moscow: Iazyki slavianskoi kul'tury, 2008).

The locution "with you/ my/ friend/ I'm leaving" is paradoxical; after all, the context of the poem as a whole speaks of a non-meeting, and not of a joint leaving. One might, of course, suppose that "I'm leaving" and "my friend" belong to different sentences, but it does not seem possible to embed this "with you" into any other statement. However, another interpretation is also tenable: "I see [recollect] every day with you [through your eyes; spent with you]. My friend, "I'm leaving." In this version, the lyrical subject or the author himself appears to be leaving in the final lines—leaving first, so as to displace the unbearable nature of his friend's departure.

Most likely, a joint leaving must be interpreted as an imaginary one, as the departure of the lyrical "I" alone, which appears to be taking his friend with him. It is no accident that the poem's last verse contains the metaphor "воспоминаний пепел" ("ashes of memories"). Earlier in the poem, the "whistle" is associated with the lyrical "I." It is a metaphor for illness ("my eyes whistle"), which at the end strikes the lyrical subject. He now appears as a dead man, a skull: eyes cannot whistle, but empty eye sockets can, or rather, it is the wind that blows through them. In this case, "I'm leaving" can also be interpreted as a readiness to share death with the friend and enter the other world with him. The whistle can also be understood as a metaphor that expresses the idea of "calling," "urging." Finally, consider this alternative interpretation: the eye-windows whistle, the wind whistles though the windows. Memories disappear, they cannot replace a living person.

The poem "Friend's Illness" is a remarkable example of a poetic text in which the dismissal of punctuation marks creates a semantic multidimensionality. The text embraces different interpretations of its syntax and, accordingly, various and sometimes even mutually exclusive interpretations of its semantics. No less fascinating are the poem's unique development of the theme and its correlation with its literary pretexts. The poem never emphasizes the references to its pretexts, but they are traceable through the use of specific lexemes: for example, "whistle," "whistling," and "illness" are allusions to Yesenin's *The Black Man*. The pretexts are also visible through the metaphors that overlap in their semantics: for instance, the dragonfly's "window-eyes" in "Friend's Illness" recall Pasternak's "Spring has been just you. . . ." The reader must discover these hidden, unforced allusions in the text, so as to identify connections among them, and to reconstruct the pretexts.

Free verse usually presupposes a minimizing of the familiar signs of "poeticity," for instance, it often rejects poetic tropes. Instead, it is oriented toward what Yuri Lotman called "minus-devices."²² As an example of the development of free verse, "Friend's Illness"—and other texts in *Nevan Poems*—invite us to revise this point of view substantially. (On *Nevan Poems*, alse see Roman Katsman's and Ian Probstein's essays in this volume.)

It is very original free verse. Indeed, *vers libre* is usually created by a segmentation of lines, which produces pauses that do not match the pauses dictated by syntax and meaning in prose texts. The classical examples of Russian free verse are based on the departure from prose. In contrast, the basis of "Friend's Illness" is not prosaic, but syllabo-tonic. It is obvious in such lines as "пустынен провод телефонный/ колодец входов и уходов" ("deserted telephone cord/ well of entrances and departures"): both lines are iambic tetrameters (Ia4) with a pyrrhic on the third ictus (hereafter Ia=iamb; Tr=trochee).

If one were to break up the text of the poem into verses differently from the way the author did it, and with an emphasis on metrical unity, it would appear as:

... проснулся руку протянуть (Ia4)

в окно свист глаз нацелен (Ia3)

улица полна (Tr3 with a pyrrhic and a truncated final syllable)

его всегдашностью (Ia2 with a dactylic clausula)

площадка лестничная (Ia2 with a hyperdactylic clausula)

преданность лица (Tr3 with a pyrrhic with a truncated final syllable)

расстались до утра (Ia3 with a truncated final syllable)

утрата невозможна (Ia3)

нет дня нет месяца нет года нет его (Ia6)²³

с утра до вечера пустынен двор (Ia5)

колодец подмигивает глазом стрекозы (Dol'nik based on iamb)

шуршат с утра до ночи облака (Ia5)

---

22 Cf. Iu. M. Lotman, "Lektsii po struktural′noi poetike," in *Iu. M. Lotman i tartusko-moskovskaia semioticheskaia shkola* (Moscow: Gnozis, 1994), 71–83; Iu. M. Lotman, *Struktura khudozhestvennogo teksta* (Moscow: Iskusstvo, 1970), 120–132; Efim Etkind, *Razgovor o stikhakh* (Moscow: Detskaia literatura, 1970), 115–117. The poem is also interesting as an example of a "short-line" free verse: most of its lines consist of one or two words. Classical Russian free verse (Alexander Blok, Mikhail Kuzmin) is characterized by the preponderance of longer lines.

23 If separated into two lines: "нет дня нет месяца/ нет года нет его," it will be Ia3 with a dactylic ending in the first verse and with the final truncated syllable in the second verse.

крыл слюдяных дверей фанерных нервно (Ia5)[24]
просовываю руку в щель окна (Ia5)
оставлен для общения почтовый (Ia5)
молчит пустынен провод телефонный (Ia5)
колодец входов и уходов (Ia5)
глаз фасетчатый я вижу каждый день (Tr6)
с тобой мой друг я ухожу (Ia4)
твоя пустынна форточка (Ia3 with a dactylic clausula)
свистят мои глаза (Ia3 with the truncated final syllable)[25]
шуршит воспоминаний пепел (Ia3)

The verse theorist and historian Mikhail Gasparov, who studied poems with a similar rhythmic structure, suggested a special term to describe it: "Such a polymetry with unmotivated shifts of short segments could be termed *micropolymetry* ('fractional polymetry')."[26] As proposed by the scholar Yuri Orlitsky, if the text written in free verse contains more than 25% of syllabic lines, it should be considered a "transitional metrical form" rather than pure free verse.[27]

In verse theory, there is a notion that free verse is not devoid of features typical of other systems of versification. Rather, it is a peripheral phenomenon in relation to traditional forms of verse, a phenomenon marked by a certain rhythmic-syntactical order.[28] Within this framework, the polymetrical basis of David Shrayer-Petrov's poem can be considered not a unique, rare occurrence for free verse, but rather one of the many possible variations of *vers libre*. I have a greater affinity for Yuri Orlitsky's understanding of free verse: "After Mikhail Gasparov, we understand free

---

[24] The placement of the line break here depends on whether we recognize the adverb "нервно" as modifying "шуршат" or "просовываю." However, one can also see an enjambment here. In any case, when we assign "нервно" to the verse "просовываю руку в щель окна," the iambic nature of these verses is preserved, only the spondee appears in the first syllable of the second verse.

[25] If we see an enjambment here, the verses should be broken up differently: "свистят мои глаза шуршит" (Ia4) and "воспоминаний пепел" (Ia3).

[26] M. L. Gasparov, *Russkii stikh nachala XX veka v kommentariiakh*, 4th ed. (Moscow: Fortuna Limited, 2001), 138.

[27] See Iu. B. Orlitskii, *Stikh i proza v russkoi literature* (Moscow: RGGU, 2002), 325.

[28] See, for instance, Aleksandr Kviatkovskii, "Russkii svobodnyi stikh," *Voprosy literatury* 12 (1963): 60–77; A. L. Zhovtis, "Granitsy svobodnogo stikha," *Voprosy literatury* 3 (1966): 113–124; V. S. Baevskii et al., "K istorii russkogo svobodnogo stikha," *Russkaia literatura* 3 (1975): 101–102; Ol′ga Ovcharenko, *Russkii svobodnyi stikh* (Moscow: Sovremennik, 1984).

verse as a verse without meter and rhyme, which differs from prose only by its division into lines," that is, a system of versification that fundamentally rejects all secondary versification features such as rhyme, syllabo-tonic meter, isotonic and isosyllabic features, and regular stanzaic forms—and relies solely on the primary rhythm, the rhythm of verse lines, or, as Boris Bukhshtab termed it, "double segmentation of the text."[29] In Maksim Shapir's formulation, "in free verse different lines relate to each other as do different syllables in syllabic verse, different tacts in tonic versification, different feet—in syllabo-tonic verse."[30]

Since in "Friend's Illness" the number of metrically "correct" lines significantly exceeds 25%, from Yuri Orlitsky's point of view this text should not be classified as free verse, but should instead be recognized as an example of the transitional metrical form. Nevertheless, in this case such an interpretation is unacceptable. The reason for this is that the syllabo-tonic (mostly iambic) basis of the poem becomes apparent only when the division into lines is altered, that is, in a certain sense, when the author's purposeful design is violated. While free verse typically distances itself from prose by the segmentation of lines—and this segmentation is usually the only distinctive feature of texts written in free verse—in "Friend's Illness" there is a pushing away, a distancing not from prose, but from traditional syllabo-tonic verse, primarily free iambs with the dominance of the pentameter. Rather than repudiate the familiar features of poetic texts, as poets usually do when they write in free verse, Shrayer-Petrov, apparently, uses free verse to mask these features. In "Friend's Illness"—and other texts in *Nevan Poems*—free verse is positioned not as an alternative to traditional systems of versification, but as their disintegration. A hint about the metrical basis of "Friend's Illness" is visible only in two adjacent lines out of fifty-two: "пустынен провод телефонный/ колодец входов и уходов" ("deserted telephone cord/ well of entrances and departures"). These lines are long enough to be perceived as well-ordered in metrical terms, as composed in iambic tetrameter. In shorter iambic lines, the signs of metrical organization might be considered accidental. The reader must reconstruct this form in the same way as he or she reconstructs the poem's system of allusions to pretexts. Yet the purpose

---

29 See B. Ia. Bukhshtab, "Ob osnovakh i tipakh russkogo stikha," *International Journal of Slavic Linguistics and Poetics* 16 (1973): 110–111; cf. Orlitskii, *Stikh i proza v russkoi literature*, 322.

30 M. I. Shapir, "O predelakh dliny stikha v verlibre (D. A. Prigov i drugie)," *Philologica* 6, nos. 14–16 (1999–2000): 117–142.

of this reconstruction is not to prove that "Friend's Illness" is fundamentally a polymetrical or a iambic poem from the beginning. Instead, the quest is to determine which metrical system is being *destroyed* here. At the same time, this interesting phenomenon may be described in a different way: as the creation of a new—mobile and fluid—form, the perception and reconstruction of which depends on the interaction of the text and the reader.

The closest analog and a partial model for "Friend's Illness" can perhaps be found among Genrikh Sapgir's poems, which are also characterized by "micropolymetry," but in a hidden form, due to Sapgir's line divisions and splits, which destroy or camouflage the metrical or tonic base of the verse. David Shrayer-Petrov and Maxim D. Shrayer called this phenomenon in Sapgir's poetry "the disintegration [splitting] of the meter" ("распад размера"): "The disintegration of the meter [...] presupposes a structure of the poem in which Sapgir focuses on specified syllabo-tonic (and sometimes tonic) meters and their combinations, clearly stated at the beginning of the text, and subsequently deconstructs them. In many texts one observes a frequent, sometimes as often as in every line, change of meter."[31] But in order to reveal the metrical or tonic organization of verses, "a different division into lines" is necessary. As in "Friend's Illness," these verses can be written (graphically displayed) in different ways—which is important for the reconstruction of their metric system.[32] Earlier experiments in this direction go back to Velimir Khlebnikov and Nikolai Zabolotsky.[33] However, in all the above cases, and in contrast to the work of David Shrayer-Petrov, the "verslibration/liberation" of traditional forms of versification does not blur the links between the lexemes in the text. In Shrayer-Petrov's text, this blurring yields many different versions of the text's division into sentences.

In David Shrayer-Petrov's work the author's breakdown of the text into lines does not reveal, but instead conceals or destroys their metrical substratum. Therefore, we must recognize that "Friend's Illness" is not a transitional metrical form and not a polymetrical poem, but, conversely, an example of free verse. Usually in free verse, to quote Vladislav Kholshevnikov, the "graphic division into lines is an essential condition for

---

31 Maksim D. Shraer and David Shraer-Petrov, *Genrikh Sapgir. Klassik avangarda*, 3rd ed. (Ekaterinburg: Ridero, 2017), 36. The examples are from ibid., 33–37.
32 Ibid., 33.
33 Ibid., 38–39.

the correct perception of free verse,"³⁴ that is, its perception as verse, not as prose. In "Friend's Illness" this division is a condition for the perception of this poem as *free* verse, and not as polymetrical verse.

Describing the development of free verse in Russian poetry of the second half of the twentieth century, Mikhail Gasparov noted, that at that time "only a prosaized type of free verse [was] developing, one that emphasize[d] the syntactic partition of the text. Sometimes syntax groups are joined into lines of two or more groups, but never one group is split between two lines."³⁵ Enjambment appears rarely: "until recently, verses that violate[d] the syntactic breakdown of enjambment [were] in fact used only in translations."³⁶ Gasparov summarized his observations: "There is an easier free verse, with syntactic breakdowns into lines, and a more difficult kind, with anti-syntactic breakdowns and sharp enjambments; in Russia, the simplest, syntactic one prevails. More complex experiments are singular and individual."³⁷ David Shrayer-Petrov's poem "Friend's Illness" is one of such highly individual cases. Enjambment here is a means of destroying syntactic and semantic connections between phrases and sentences. Thanks to it, the text acquires a special semantic multidimensionality, which, it seems, has practically no equivalents in Russian free verse.³⁸

"Friend's Illness" can be understood more deeply in the context of the entire book *Nevan Poems*, which was composed in 1985–1986 in Moscow and published as a separate book in 2011 in the poet's native St. Petersburg. This book is indeed unique in many ways. Its title and the themes of most of its poems all indicate that it belongs to the St. Petersburg/Leningrad tradition. The composition of the book stresses this point by emphasizing

---

34 V. E. Kholshevnikov, *Osnovy stikhovedeniia: Russkoe stikhoslozhenie. Uchebnoe posobie. Dlia studentov filologicheskikh fakul´tetov*, 4th ed. (St. Petersburg: Filologicheskii fakul´tet SPbGU; Moscow: Izdatel´skii tsentr "Akademiia," 2002), 83.

35 Gasparov, *Ocherk istorii russkogo stikha*, 295.

36 Ibid., 295.

37 Ibid., 308.

38 For instance, see the free verse of Gennadii Alekseev ("pure" at their foundation rather than departing from metric versification). Alekseev is considered to be one of the masters of the so-called St. Petersburg's *vers libre* (see, for example, Iurii Orlitskii, "Gennadii Alekseev i peterburgskii verlibr," *Novoe literaturnoe obozrenie* 14 [1995]: 284–292). Alekseev's free verses are deprived of such syntactical ambiguity and therefore devoid of such semantic multidimensionality. This seems to be the case for most free verse in Russian. In this connection, see G. F. Chernikova's analysis of Russian free verse: G. F. Chernikova, "Poetika russkogo verlibra vtoroi poloviny XX veka," (Dissertatsiia na soiskanie uchenoi stepeni kandidata filologicheskikh nauk [PhD equivalent thesis], Astrakhanskii gosudarstvennyi universitet, 2005).

two key figures in this tradition: the opening poem of the collection, "Anna Akhmatova in Komarovo" ("Anna Akhmatova v Komarovo"), is dedicated to the poet who became the voice and symbol of St. Petersburg poetry, and the last poem, "Peter's Oak" ("Petrovskii dub"), is about the founder of the city. The collection also includes the programmatic poem "St. Isaac's Cathedral" ("Isaakievskii sobor"), with a dedication to the poet Dmitry Bobyshev, a friend of Shrayer-Petrov's poetic youth. The poem contains this emblematic image: "высокое стояние над градом/ перепоясанным Андреевскою лентой" ("standing high over the city/ girded with St. Andrew's ribbon").[39]

However, Shrayer-Petrov's poems contrast with a mainstream trend in St. Petersburg/Leningrad poetry. The "St. Petersburg poetics," as the first-wave émigré critic Vladimir Veidle termed it, is marked by "rootedness in the subject [предметность, materiality], and, along with it, a greater precision, a stricter balance, and, thus, a greater austerity of the word": an orientation towards classical clarity[40]. "Friend's Illness," as well as other poems from *Nevan Poems* are written exclusively in free verse (sometimes with a single metrical base;[41] sometimes polymetrical[42]) and break, through their division into individual lines, into syntactic and semantic multidimensionality. Deliberately disharmonious, these poems represent a distinct challenge to the St. Petersburg poetic tradition.

It is noteworthy that Joseph Brodsky, a poet who in a way became a later symbol of St. Petersburg poetry, repeatedly declared that the "classical character" of his own poetics was a product of the place of his birth and formation. Brodsky did not accept free verse, especially in Russian poetry, treating it if not with hostility, then at least with alienation and skepticism. In his essay "Poetry as a Form of Resistance to Reality," he bluntly stated:

> As far as literature (and poetry in particular) is concerned, any attempt to use the two world wars, thermonuclear weapons, social upheaval, or the apotheosis of methods of oppression to justify (or explain) the erosion of forms and genres is simply ludicrous, if not outrageous, in its disproportion.

---

39 Shraer-Petrov, *Nevskie stikhi*, 15.
40 Vladimir Veidle, "Peterburgskaia poetika," in his *Umiranie iskusstva*, comp. and afterword by V. M. Tolmachev (Moscow: Respublika, 2001), 314.
41 For example, the iambic foundation is clearly visible in Shrayer-Petrov's poem "Shostakovich at the Dacha in Komarovo" ("Shostakovich na dache v Komarovo").
42 Such is the case, among others, for "Leningrad after the Siege" ("Leningrad posle blokady") and "Zoological Museum on the Tip of the Vasilievsky island" ("Zoologicheskii muzei na strelke Vasil′evskogo ostrova").

The unprejudiced individual cringes at the mountain of bodies that gave birth to the mouse of vers libre. He cringes even more deeply at the demand during less dramatic times, in periods of population explosion, to make this mouse a sacred cow.[43]

Even when Brodsky conceded that free verse had the right to exist, he added a special condition: "In my opinion, in order to use free verse, the poet must come to it in the same way that English letters came to it. That is, in miniature, within the limits of his own life, the poet should repeat the path taken before him by literature, to go through formal schooling. Otherwise, the unit weight of the word in a line of verse might turn out to be zero."[44]

Nevan Poems is a book of recollections. It features a poem about Anna Akhmatova ("Anna Akhmatova in Komarovo"), a poem in memory of the writer and Sinologist Boris Vakhtin ("Descendant of the Decembrist" ["Potomok dekabrista"]), a poem about the Imaginist poet Anatoly Mariengof ("The Last Years of Anatoly Mariengof" ["Poslednie gody Anatoliia Mariengofa"]), and a poem about Dmitri Shostakovich ("Shostakovich at the Dacha in Komarovo" ["Shostakovich na dache v Komarovo"]). In addition to "Friend's Illness," it also includes a number of "small memoirs" from the life of the poet and his family: "Father Leaves to the Finnish War" ("Otets uezzhaet na finskuiu voinu"), "Child's Drama" ("Detskaia drama"; about the theft of bread ration coupons), "Mother's Grave" ("Mogila mamy"). The overarching recurrent themes of the book are loss, death or a threat of death (see "Flood in the Zoo" ["Navodnenie v zooparke"]), and being outcasts or pariahs: see the lines "все мы/ вечные/ жиды" ("we all are/ eternal/ Yids") in the poem "Gypsy Encampment in Ozerki" ("Tsyganskii tabor v Ozerkakh"), which echo Marina Tsvetaeva's verses.[45] The traditional St. Petersburg theme, white nights, is here rendered through metaphors linked to death and murder ("White Nights" ["Belye nochi"]).

---

43 Joseph Brodsky, "Poetry as a Form of Resistance to Reality," tr. and adapted by Alexander Sumerkin and Jamey Gambrell, *PMLA* 107, no. 2 (March 1992): 220–225; cf. the Russian text in Iosif Brodskii, *Sochineniia*, 7 vols., ed. I. A. Gordin, comp. V. P. Golyshev, E. N. Kasatkina, V. A. Kulle, vol. 7 (St. Petersburg: Pushkinskii fond, 2001), 119.

44 Iosif Brodskii, "V mire iziashchnoi slovesnosti. Interv´iu Il´e Suslovu, Semenu Rezniku i Diku Beikeru," *Amerika* (May 1992). Reprinted in *Brodskii Iosif. Kniga interv'iu*, comp. V. Polukhina, 3rd ed. (Moscow: Zakharov, 2005), 661–662.

45 Shraer-Petrov, *Nevskie stikhi*, 39.

"Peter's Oak" ("Petrovskii dub") mentions "мои утраты и обольщения" ("my losses and seductions")[46] and elaborates the motif of an imaginary return "к заброшенному пепелищу" ("to the abandoned [past turned to] ashes").[47] It ends with the lines:

роняй листы
летите
облака и тучи
с силуэтами листов
я возвращаюсь[48]

("drop the leaves [sheets]/ fly/ clouds and storm clouds/ with silhouettes of sheets/ I'm coming back")

Yet the return is illusory: it is not by chance that Shrayer-Petrov incorporates into the text of his poem "Peter and Paul Fortress" ("Petropavlovskaia krepost'") a quote from Brodsky's "December in Florence": "Есть города, в которые нет возврата" ("There are cities one won't see again").[49]

---

46 Ibid., 55.
47 Ibid., 56.
48 Ibid., 57.
49 Ibid., 37. This quote is a part of the poetic dialogue between David Shrayer-Petrov and Joseph Brodsky. Shrayer-Petrov dedicated to Brodsky his long poem *Flying Saucers* (*Letaiushchie tarelki*, 1976), written in the USSR. He had a chance to read this poem in public, even though it could only be published after his emigration to the United States in 1987. Its fifth part, "Mists of Birches" ("Tumany berez"), contains the following lines: "Мой друг, твой кораблик свои паруса размочил./ Чтоб их просушить, надо в гавань войти по реке,/ Четыре моста миновать. Ты мосты различил/ В тумане, что стелется по-над Невой вдалеке?" ("My friend, your little vessel has got its sails wet./ To dry them it must enter the harbor down the river,/ To pass four bridges. Have you made out the bridges/ In the fog that stretches along over the Neva?"). In his literary memoirs of Brodsky, Shrayer-Petrov quotes Brodsky's poem "December in Florence" ("Dekabr' vo Florentsii"): "Есть города, в которые нет возврата. / Солнце бьется в их окна, как в гладкие зеркала. То/ есть, в них не проникнешь ни за какое злато./ Там всегда протекает река под шестью мостами" ("There are cities one won't see again. The sun/ throws its gold at their frozen windows. But all the same/ there is no entry, no proper sum./ There are always six bridges spanning the sluggish river"; Russian text is from Iosif Brodskii, *Chast' rechi* [Ann Arbor: Ardis, 1977], 113; tr. Joseph Brodsky, English text is from Joseph Brodsky, *Collected Poetry in English*, ed. Ann Kjellberg [New York: Farrar, Straus and Giroux, 2000], 132). Shrayer-Petrov comments: "In a striking fashion, my own verses, also written in 1976 and dedicated to Brodsky, form a dialogue with these lines of Brodsky's"; see David Shraer-Petrov, *Druz'ia i teni: Roman s uchastiem avtora* (New York: Liberty Publishing House, 1989), 282–283.

David Shrayer-Petrov's poem "Friend's Illness" in particular and his *Nevan Poems* in general represent an original experience of embodying the St. Petersburg/Leningrad theme, an experience that runs contrary to the literary tradition. The "disintegration of the meter," the "disintegration of syntax," and the loss of the texts' punctuation represent a tragic situation of "post-culture" and "post-literature" (including "post-St. Petersburg poetry"), with a corresponding temporal rupture—the break with the past, with the classical tradition. But at the same time, the "disintegration of meter" and the "disintegration of syntax" compel the reader to search for connections with tradition: to discover pretexts, to reconstruct syntactic connections, to restore and reconstruct the foundation of the meter.

Translated, from the Russian, by
Daria Sadovnichenko and Maxim D. Shrayer

Works Cited

Baevskii, V. S., A. I. Ibraev, S. I. Kormilov, and B. L. Sapogov, "K istorii russkogo svobodnogo stikha." *Russkaia literatura* 3 (1975): 89–102.

Brodsky, Joseph [Iosif Brodskii]. *Chast' rechi*. Ann Arbor: Ardis, 1977.

———. "Poetry as a Form of Resistance to Reality." Translated and adapted by Alexander Sumerkin and Jamey Gambrell. *PMLA* 107, no. 2 (March 1992): 220–225.

———. *Collected Poetry in English*. Editd by Ann Kjellberg. New York: Farrar, Straus and Giroux, 2000.

——— [Iosif Brodskii]. *Sochineniia*. Edited by I. A. Gordin. Compiled by V. P. Golyshev, E. N. Kasatkina, V. A. Kulle. Vol. 7. St. Peterburg: Pushkinskii fond, 2001.

———. "V mire iziashchnoi slovesnosti. Interv´iu Il´e Suslovu, Semenu Rezniku i Diku Beikeru." *Amerika* (May 1992). Reprinted in *Brodskii Iosif. Kniga interv´iu*, compiled by Valentina Polukhina, 661–662. 3rd ed. Moscow: Zakharov, 2005.

Bukhshtab, B. Ia. "Ob osnovakh i tipakh russkogo stikha." *International Journal of Slavic Linguistics and Poetics* 16 (1973): 96–118.

Chernikova, G. F. *Poetika russkogo verlibra vtoroi poloviny XX veka*. Dissertatsiia na soiskanie uchenoi stepeni kandidata filologicheskikh nauk [PhD equivalent thesis]. Astrakhanskii gosuderstvennyi universitet, 2005.

Esenin, Sergei. *Stikhotvoreniia i poemy*. Introduction by I. S. Eventov, compiled and edited by I. S. Eventov and I. V. Aleksakhina, commentary by I. V. Aleksakhina. Leningrad: Sovetskii pisatel´, 1986.

Etkind, Efim. *Razgovor o stikhakh*. Moscow: Detskaia literatura, 1970.

Gasparov, M. L. *Ocherk istorii russkogo stikha: Metrika. Ritmika. Rifma. Strofika*. 2nd ed. Moscow: "Fortuna Limited," 2000.

———. *Russkii stikh nachala XX veka v kommentariiakh*. 4th ed. Moscow: "Fortuna Limited," 2001.

Ioann Damaskin. *Tochnoe izlozhenie pravoslavnoi very*. St. Petersburg: Izdanie knogoprodavtsa I. L. Tuzova, 1894.

Kholshevnikov, V. E. *Osnovy stikhovedeniia: Russkoe stikhoslozhenie. Uchebnoe posobie. Dlia studentov filologicheskikh fakul´tetov*. 4th ed. St. Petersburg: Filologicheskii fakul´tet SPbGU; Moscow: Izdatel´skii tsentr "Akademiia," 2002.

Kviatkovskii, Aleksandr. "Russkii svobodnyi stikh." *Voprosy literatury* 12 (1963): 60–77.

Lermontov, M. Iu. *Stikhotvoreniia i poemy, 1837–1841*. Vol. 2 of *Polnoe sobranie stikhotvorenii*. 2 vols. Introduction by D. V. Maksimov, compiled and commentary by E. E. Naidich. Leningrad: Sovetskii pisatel´, 1989.

Lotman, Iu. M. *Struktura khudozhestvennogo teksta*. Moscow: Iskusstvo, 1970.

———. "Lektsii po struktural´noi poetike." In *Iu.M. Lotman i tartusko-moskovskaia semioticheskaia shkola*, 10–257. Moscow: Gnozis, 1994.

Mandel´shtam, Osip. *Polnoe sobranie stikhotvorenii*. Introduction by M. L. Gasparov and A. G. Mets, compiled and commentary by A. G. Mets. St. Petersburg: Akademicheskii proekt, 1995.

Orlitskii, Iurii. "Gennadii Alekseev i peterburgskii verlibr." *Novoe literaturnoe obozrenie* 14 (1995): 284–292.

———. *Stikh i proza v russkoi literature*. Moscow: RGGU, 2002.

Ovcharenko, Ol´ga. *Russkii svobodnyi stikh*. Moscow: Sovremennik, 1984.

Pasternak, Boris. *Polnoe sobranie stikhotvorenii i poem*. Introduction by V. N. Al´fonsov, compiled and commentary by V. S. Baevskii and E. V. Pasternak. St. Petersburg: Akademicheskii proekt, 2003.

Tolstoi, A. K. *Polnoe sobranie stikhotvorenii i poem*. Introduction, compiled, and commentary by I. G. Iampol´skii. St. Petersburg: Akademicheskii proekt, 2004.

Uspenskii, F. B. "Habent sua fata libellulae: k istorii russkikh literaturnykh nasekomykh." *Vestnik PSTGU*, seriia 3: "Filologiia" 2 (2008): 60–80.

———. *Tri dogadki o stikhakh Osipa Mandel´shtama*. Moscow: Iazyki slavianskoi kul´tury, 2008.

Shapir, M. I. "O predelakh dliny stikha v verlibre (D. A. Prigov i drugie)." *Philologica* 6, nos. 14–16 (1999–2000): 117–142.

Shestov, Lev. *Sochineniia*. 2 vols. Introduction and edited by A. V. Akhutin, commentary by A. V. Akhutin and E. V. Patkosh. Moscow: Izdatel´stvo "Nauka," 1994.

Shraer, Maksim D. [Maxim D. Shrayer], and David Shraer-Petrov [David Shrayer-Petrov]. *Genrikh Sapgir. Klassik avangarda*. 3rd ed. Ekaterinburg: Ridero, 2017.

Shrayer-Petrov, David [David Shrayer-Petrov]. *Druz´ia i teni: Roman s uchastiem avtora*. New York: Liberty Publishing House, 1989.

——— [David Shrayer-Petrov]. *Villa Borgeze. Stikhotvoreniia*. Holyoke, MA: New England Publishing, 1992.

——— [David Shrayer-Petrov]. *Forma liubvi. Izbrannaia lirika*. Moscow: Izdatel´skii dom "Iunost´," 2003.

——— [David Shrayer-Petrov]. *Nevskie stikhi*. Edited by Maksim D. Shraer. St. Petersburg: Ostrovitianin, 2011.

Tanakh: A New Translation of the Holy Scriptures According to the Traditional Hebrew Text. Philadelphia: Jewish Publication Society, 1995.

Veidle, Vladimir. "Peterburgskaia poetika." In Vladimir Veidle, *Umiranie iskusstva*. Compiled and afterword by V.M. Tolmachev, 308–320. Moscow: Respublika, 2001.

Zhovtis, A. L. "Granitsy svobodnogo stikha." *Voprosy literatury* 3 (1966): 113–124.

David Shrayer-Petrov and Genrikh Sapgir: Feasts of Friendship*

Evgeny Ermolin

It is hard to define with a short formula what connects David Shrayer-Petrov and Genrikh Sapgir. But Shrayer-Petrov, coming to our rescue, once did it himself in just one phrase. Already in his relatively recent American years, an interviewer asked Shrayer-Petrov who his "partner in letters" ("друг по цеху") was. And he received an answer, perhaps unexpected for an exterior observer, but natural for someone well familiar with the context: "I keep in touch even more with those who live in Russia. A particularly striking representative of such interpersonal commerce was Genrikh Sapgir." And later, in a rather candid interview, Shrayer-Petrov elaborates: "I would like to conclude this text simply with my grateful memory of him, because he showed both me and my son how you can work for many years and write prolifically, despite the fact that no one knows you and [they] don't even let you publish."[1]

---

* Copyright © 2021 by Evgeny Ermolin. English translation copyright © 2021 by Daria Sadovnichenko and Maxim D. Shrayer.
   Unless noted otherwise, all translations from the Russian are literal. The original title, "David Shraer-Petrov and Genrikh Sapgir: piry druzhby," probably hints at *Pir*, the common Russian title of Plato's Συμπόσιον (*The Symposium*; sometimes translated into English as *The Banquet*).

1 David Shraer-Petrov and Gennadii Katsov, "Ia dumaiu, chto my vse drug druga chemu-to nauchili," RUNYweb, May 17, 2011, http://www.runyweb.com/articles/culture/literature/david-shayer-petrov-interview.html, accessed January 31, 2020.

Thus, Sapgir for Shrayer-Petrov is not a gold standard of creativity, nor an object of emulation—he just set an example of how a poet can live and create, and remain a poet without the air of publicity. This is actually an incredibly difficult task, the weight of which, in our time, in the era of the all-pervasive public online presence, very few remember and almost no one understands in its fatality.

Now, when reading David Shrayer-Petrov's memoirs of Sapgir as well as his book about Sapgir, written in collaboration with his son, Maxim D. Shrayer, one experiences the continuous and everlasting dialogue between two poets rejected by their epoch (by its official Soviet public discourse). In this dialogue, there is neither compulsion nor pressure, but a sense of creative consonance found quickly and forever. Their acquaintance and friendship go back to the late 1950s. They were near contemporaries, but Sapgir was older—and this might have mattered. But not to the effect of creative dependence. Shrayer-Petrov and Sapgir could meet often or go for a while without seeing each other; they could talk ecstatically about poetry or else stay silent in each other's company. But behind their many years of friendly communication there stood the theme of artistic survival; the theme of the artist's resistance to the cotton-wool atmosphere of the late Soviet era; the theme of gaining internal freedom as a prerequisite of the creative act.

Theirs was a consonance above and beyond the private circumstances of daily living; they both rode the wave of outcasts and lived out the biographies of artistic untouchables (this despite Sapgir's relative success as a children's author, the status of which only made him feel ever more sharply his own extremely dubious compromise with the harsh reality of Soviet society). Both of them experienced an acute falling out with officially sanctioned literature. For Sapgir, this discord did not wane, while for Shrayer-Petrov, it perhaps even increased, leading to an uncompromising conflict with the regime and society. Their friendship was a consonance of the Jewish melody in the souls of Russian poets, which was in different ways transformed in their work. And, finally, theirs was a consonance of spiritual, creative freedom, the more palpable and, probably, the more desirable, the less room it left both to negotiate with the authorities and to dwell comfortably in the Soviet literary milieu, accustomed to the censored manner of half-speaking, half-muttering.

To this, I would also add that the poets' mutually creative echoes of each other, as seen in their dedications to each other and in their quest for the maximally free (adequate) form for the maximally concrete content. This state of searching, of renewing meanings, was once expressed by Shrayer-Petrov in "Dahl's Dictionary" ("Slovar′ Dalia," 1990), a poem dedicated to Sapgir:

Бродить блукать плутать блуждать
Брести высокою травою
Брести глубокою водою
Броженье слова пробуждать.[2]

("To wander to stroll to roam to stray/ To plod through tall grass/ To plod through deep waters/ To awaken the word's fermentation.")

This poem may be called programmatic, but it is certainly not a directive. Its infinitives convey not the task, but rather the state that unites the poets. The title of the poem refers to the free verbal element that is, perhaps, most adequately represented in Dahl's dictionary of the "living great Russian language." "Living" is the key term here.

David Shrayer-Petrov's first notes about Sapgir date to the middle 1980s. This is his preface to Sapgir's book *Pushkin's Drafts* (*Chernoviki Pushkina*).[3] About the same time, Sapgir very perceptively wrote about Shrayer-Petrov and his collection *Nevan Poems* (*Nevskie stikhi*; see also Andrei Ranchin's essay in this volume). Along the way, Sapgir compared Shrayer-Petrov with the biblical King David, noting the victorious dance and, of course, the psalms, which Sapgir had transformed into a whole book of modern Russian poetry.[4] The latest, updated edition of Shrayer-Petrov's book *Genrikh Sapgir: The Avant-Garde Classic*, came out in 2017. There, one finds the statement that "Sapgir studies are rapidly developing."[5] But, let us note *à propos*, its most essential and significant developments were only made possible by the relentless efforts of Shrayer-Petrov.

It so happened that the evidence of creative commerce between the two poets is presented to us, *a posteriori*, rather as Shrayer-Petrov's perspective on Sapgir, the view of the poet, memoirist, and researcher. David Shrayer-Petrov is an observer, as well as an interested co-participant,

---

2 David Shraer-Petrov, *Villa Borgeze* (Holyoke, MA: New England Publishing, 1992), 64.
3 Maksim D. Shraer and David Shraer-Petrov, *Genrikh Sapgir. Klassik avangarda*, 3rd ed. (Ekaterinburg: Ridero, 2017), 227–230.
4 G. Sapgir, "Iz predisloviia k 'Nevskim stikham' D. Shraera-Petrova," *Chernovik* 5 (1991): 35.
5 Shraer and Shraer-Petrov, *Genrikh Sapgir. Klassik avangarda*, 130.

an eyewitness-friend. The intimate aura of reminiscences is coalesced with the rigorous analysis of the critic and the literary scholar, bringing one subject under two different optics at once.

The striking fidelity of Shrayer-Petrov's investigations to a literary theme should not surprise us after what has been said about his literary brotherhood with Sapgir. This is, of course, more than just a research interest. This is both a creative affinity and the sense of sailing in the same vessel of Russian poetry, a memory of a journey undertaken together. And this is also a loyalty to friendship, with its obligations and pledges.

David Shrayer-Petrov wrote the best eyewitness accounts and friend's memoir of Sapgir; and the bulk of it was written while Sapgir was still alive.[6] Sapgir read the first version of Shrayer-Petrov's memoir-novel *The Gold-Domed Moscow* (*Moskva zlatoglavaia*, 1994) in manuscript form and responded to it in a 1993 letter to Shrayer-Petrov (which included many different assessments of the memoir's other characters and a conclusive summary):

> So let's leave to literary historians all of those along with the sentimental Bulat [Okudzhava]. After all, life flows and does not stop at "what has been achieved." But in your kind memoirs, I repeat, there is a place for them. Because this is a novel, a story, and as individuals they are amusing, touching, and curious, although they don't fly very high. That is to say, you as a scientist know that an artist must be able to think with his heart, to create new things, but they are for the most part too feeble for that [То есть ты, как ученый, должен знать, что художник должен уметь думать сердцем, рождать новое, а им по большей части слабо]. This is how it's turned out, I'm even tougher, even pickier, because all of this applies to me in full measure. This is why I write a lot. Like you, as I can see. One hope . . . [. . .] From the artistic perspective, I have no critical comments on the text—it should be printed as a novel.[7]

The reminiscences germinated gradually. After the death of Genrikh Sapgir in 1999, Shrayer-Petrov added a section about their meetings in Paris and Moscow after emigration to his long memoiristic essay that had been written in America. This is a unique example of co-creation and loyalty. The

---

6   David Shraer-Petrov, "Tigr Snegov (Genrikh Sapgir)," in his *Moskva zlatoglavaia* (Baltimore: Vestnik, 1994), 18–63.

7   Genrikh Sapgir—to David Shrayer-Petrov, June 5, 1993, quoted in Shraer and Shraer-Petrov, *Genrikh Sapgir. Klassik avangarda*, 246. The original is in the papers of David Shrayer-Petrov. (tr.)

quest for important words was under way. The latter versions[8] sparkle with new experiences and new insights. However, a comparative analysis of the different versions lies beyond my task in this essay.

At the same time, David Shrayer-Petrov (together with his son) has the honor of returning Sapgir to the reader in our century. I am referring to the creation of the first academic edition of his poetic works, together with an extensive introductory essay about Sapgir and a detailed commentary to his longer and shorter poems. (I do not think that without Shrayer-Petrov's labors, Sapgir would have been honored with the laurels of the thick tome published in the authoritative canon of "New Poet's Library" back in 2004.) And there is, finally, an honorary guard: the first book about Sapgir as the new literary classic.[9]

* * *

Sapgir is abundant; the context of his work is too rich to take it all in one sitting. This is the reason why at home Sapgir is often read too generally, too approximately. David Shrayer-Petrov reads and remembers with no haste. As a person and as an investigator, he is passionate about solving Sapgir's mystery, analyzing his "formula" in detail. "Sapgir's note. The voice of Sapgir. The breath of Sapgir. The silence of Sapgir . . ."[10]

No less significant is the fact that it was largely on David Shrayer-Petrov's instigation that Genrikh Sapgir's place in modern letters was defined, and his extraordinary status was clearly determined. It was an act of great responsibility and great timeliness. One must acknowledge that in post-Soviet Russia avant-gardists unrecognized by Soviet officialdom found themselves in a precarious position: either they occupied the literary margins, or they became relics of an era now of little interest to the majority. In the new century, Sapgir is not so much forgotten as still remembered disproportionately, rarely, and semi-randomly outside a narrow circle of connoisseurs and admirers.

---

8   David Shraer-Petrov, "Tigr Snegov. Genrikh Sapgir," in his *Vodka s pirozhnymi. Roman s pisateliami*, ed. Maksim D. Shraer (Saint Petersburg: Akademicheskii proekt, 2007), 177–217; David Shraer-Petrov, "Vozbuzhdenie snov. Vospominaniia o Genrikhe Sapgire," in Shraer and Shraer-Petrov, *Genrikh Sapgir. Klassik avangarda*, 199–267.
9   First edition: Maksim D. Shraer and David Shraer-Petrov, *Genrikh Sapgir. Klassik avangarda* (St. Petersburg: Dmitrii Bulanin, 2004).
10 Shraer and Shraer-Petrov, *Genrikh Sapgir. Klassik avangarda*, 3rd ed., 42.

Meanwhile, I cannot but agree with David Shrayer-Petrov that Sapgir occupies a unique place in the Russian poetry of the second half of the twentieth century. Sapgir is a remarkable poet, highly characteristic of his period. He responded to the putrid smoke and delusion of the epoch. His poems powerfully resonated with the time's most important content. Sapgir is indeed more interesting and significant than many officially sanctioned Soviet poets, but even in his unsanctioned milieu he is one of a kind. Possibly, the leader of the generation and the main Moscow poetic genius of his time (here I am reiterating David Shrayer-Petrov's point). For me personally, Shrayer-Petrov's reflections on Sapgir have been an important analytical experience for over fifteen years; a source of inspiration. I start from him—and I often agree with him.[11]

It was David Shrayer-Petrov (along with Viktor Krivulin and two or three other contemporaries) who began to separate the wheat from the chaff, who tried to highlight and bring into sharp relief Sapgir's unique *face*, and this meant removing him from a cohort of poets of the "unsanctioned Russian literary avant-garde," of which Shrayer-Petrov (and his son) on the first page of their study counted a baker's dozen.[12]

An "avant-garde classic," he says about Sapgir. An unexpected definition, quaint at the first glance, practically an oxymoron. What does this beautiful title mean? That a recent literary outcast, an explorer and experimenter, has received public recognition? Or that his quest has become in a way a norm of new Russian poetry, having entered its corpus as a foundational something? Or a different meaning? How to combine the incompatible? Is it possible?

At the same time, David Shrayer-Petrov's definition is very precise, based on a profound understanding of Sapgir's role in Russian poetry, in the global contexts of Russian modernism, and in Russian history. Sapgir's modernism is a free and open quest, an intensive conquest of the newly discovered verbal horizons. What for the early modernists of the beginning of the twentieth century was a sudden test of their creative audacity (and often predetermined the agony and pathos of disaster in their later work), for Sapgir represents a gloomy, grim routine with no possible alternatives from which to spark a new meaning of poetry. Work and play with the word become a parallel reality, opening the prospect of leaving the barracks,

---

11 Evgenii Ermolin, "Koster v ovrage," *Novyi mir* 4 (2005): 173–178.
12 Shraer and Shraer-Petrov, *Genrikh Sapgir. Klassik avangarda*, 3rd ed., 3.

of emigration without leaving. It is opposed to the barracks spirit of the Soviet epoch: military housing, prison camp, communal enslavement of the individual, which had its own analog in literature—the normativism of socialist realism. Sapgir's poetry is a quite spontaneous creative breakthrough, which has learned the lessons of the revolutionaries of the first half of the century yet is free from their revolutionary enthusiasm, from the rebel's anxiety.

It is telling that in this creative overpowering of the epoch, Sapgir uses the literary tradition as his ally. He becomes a "classic" in the sense that David Shrayer-Petrov so persuasively advances: he undertakes an authorial synthesis of the tradition and goes through the entire path of literary development; he "captures the poetry of two adjacent centuries and looks into the twenty-first,"[13] as he furthers "along with language (and sometimes instead of language) the development of literature as the supreme self-expression of the poet's face."[14]

Sapgir's interactions with the early Russian avant-garde is a station on this path, a very important one for understanding his work (and underlining his connection with Velimir Khlebnikov, early Vladimir Mayakovsky, and Nikolai Zabolotsky[15] is not at all superfluous). But this is only one of the stations. Shrayer-Petrov adroitly brings to the fore the poet's meditation on how he differs from the so-called "Moscow conceptualists." He highlights the freedom of the author's "I" unhindered by a specific formal agenda and focused on self-revelation.

Sapgir's avant-garde poetics is, perhaps, a phenomenon that should not be discussed strictly in connection with the traditions of the first half of the twentieth century. He sang like a free bird. He wanted to sing his own song, and sing it in his own way. The artistic pursuits of his epoch were refracted in his creative work. And at the same time, his poems transcended the limits of his own lifetime. He is unique. In his poems there is something that makes them current and contemporary today. And I think, this will also make keep them current tomorrow. These qualities are traditionally defined as *classic*. And as befits a modern classic, Sapgir is an artist of a great synthesis, neoclassically oriented not so much toward fashion as toward the peaks of poetry. There are a number of such peaks in Russia, so Sapgir's creative synthesis turned out to be amazingly multifaceted and—sometimes—even

---

13 Shraer-Petrov, *Vodka s pirozhnymi. Roman s pisateliami*, 204.
14 Ibid., 205.
15 Shraer and Shraer-Petrov, *Genrikh Sapgir. Klassik avangarda*, 3rd ed., 5.

harmonious; David Shrayer-Petrov correctly discerned in Sapgir's literary career both Pushkin's will for harmony and Pushkin's proteanism.

Shrayer-Petrov expresses a common theme of Sapgir studies: Sapgir was constantly changing, "absorbing formal trends and literary fashions," "passing through himself—like oxygen and like the smoke of a campfire and of cigarettes—the avant-garde quests of its contemporaries or followers."[16] But this formula of a sponge-like poet is ambiguous, and Shrayer-Petrov himself does not insist on it, further noting that somehow "Sapgir managed to remain himself."[17] Perhaps Sapgir remained himself to such an extent that he hardly changed *essentially*—only expressing this essence in a variety of ways. This is a poet of not so much a path as of a condition.

The infinite variability, the will to renew that Sapgir exbibits is, first of all, a free-flowing spirit that is not satisfied with anything that is static. Against the dark backdrop of Soviet stagnation, with such an apparent lack of agreeable historical perspective, during the barrack-and-garrison halt—Sapgir's is a merry impulse for what is new and unprecedented, for new means of expressing new content, for the discovery of something that has not yet been SO named, SO defined. This is individual myth-making, drawing differently from the depths of authentic existence.

Indeed, the trick is that Sapgir retained that rarest ability of creative movement, of renewal. Everyone knows that. He was ever fresh, ever new. Uneven. As if he was born just yesterday. He was ready to go on an unprecedented path. Ready to start over, from scratch. Who else in Moscow showed so much freshness in those deafening times? I do not know. All around him are more local, more artistically covetous. All of the ones who deserve love. He resembles another Muscovite, Boris Pasternak, with his pathological freedom and animal grace. Do you not agree? Against the background of mummified contemporaries and pseudosuccessors, he embodies the poetic experience of fountaining novelty.

But this is not following trends, not living after the formula "from fashion to fashion, the rest to the dumpster." This is hardly a reaction to the undercurrent changes in the tastes and priorities of the intelligentsia. This is not a juggling of intellectual inventions or a random playful change of roles and masks. Accurate in detail but still incorrect in the larger sense is Viktor Krivulin, who wrote:

---

16 Ibid., 41.
17 Ibid.

Sapgir had many roles, at least several different literary masks: an official children's poet and playwright; an underground versifier-avant-gardist who was the first to turn to the living speech practice of the new Moscow; a surrealist who used the experience of modern visual arts and film in creating poetic texts; a neoclassicist who dared to "revise" Pushkin's drafts; a visionary metaphysician concerned with the sublime search for God through poetry; an author of mocking nursery rhymes and chants that entered folklore (such as "Я хочу иметь детей/ От коробки скоростей" ["I desire to have kids/ with my car's clutch plate"]). All of this is Sapgir. His verbal masks are Mardi Gras, holiday disguises . . .[18]

What we call a "role," what we call a "mask," in our case would be more correctly described as facets of a romantic persona, which are not satisfied with the narrow limits of existence, a "гриМАСКА боли" ("griMASK of pain" or "GRIMask of pain"), as David Shrayer-Petrov puts it.[19] I think there is little doubt that in Sapgir's poetry there is a unified, albeit difficult to define, personal core. The will of renewal is not a dispersion of the creative personality or—even more so—the loss of it.

Different themes and perspectives of Sapgir's work, noted by David Shrayer-Petrov, have at different times evoked my response. Thus, David Shrayer-Petrov often revisits the idea of the *jouissance* at the core of Sapgir's texts. In the commentary Sapgir's book *Terverses of Genrikh Bufarev* (*Tertsikhi Genrikha Bufareva*), Shrayer-Petrov correctly noticed Sapgir's kindship with the great Portuguese modernist Fernando Pessoa, who created several heteronymous poets; this phenomenon of the heteronym in Sapgir is explained as "playing with classics and at classics."[20] Around fifteen years ago, when I was mastering Shrayer-Petrov's corpus of texts about Sapgir for the first time, I was critical of the self-sufficiency of *jouissance* in poetry. But today, I would not separate *jouissance* and verbal creation. There is no need to consider Sapgir's heteronymy as an expression of depersonalization, a clinical case of the collapse of the author's "I" in the manner of Luigi Pirandello. In both cases, with Pessoa and Sapgir, there is, more likely, an attempt to explore new resources of self-knowledge, to objectify the subjective-personal nature of creativity.

---

18 Viktor Krivulin, "Golos i pauza Genrikha Sapgira," http://sapgir.narod.ru/talks/mono/mono01.htm, accessed January 31, 2020.
19 Shraer-Petrov, *Vodka s pirozhnymi. Roman s pisateliami*, 205.
20 Shraer and Shraer-Petrov, *Genrikh Sapgir. Klassik avangarda*, 3rd ed., 106.

Or in another perspective, defined by David Shrayer-Petrov: it is the polyphony, the polyreflexivity of Sapgir's free verse[21]—and the polyphonic nature of his personality. He belongs to futurism as well as to OBERIU.[22]

I also always found very appealing David Shrayer-Petrov's ability to detect seriousness and depth in Sapgir, as well as his unwillingness to perceive Sapgir (as is often the case with critics) as a something of a superficial optimist and lover of life.

Sapgir, perhaps, is not a Russian fool, nor a prophet or a court jester. And not a tzaddik. But who is he? Who else can a poet be? "Была ему звездная книга ясна,/ и с ним говорила речная волна . . ." ("The star book was clear to him,/ and the river wave spoke to him . . ."), Baratynsky once wrote about Goethe.[23] An echo! That is who he is. A fountain of being. But above all else, not an echo of other poets, but an echo of Being. From its very depths, noises and sounds rush toward him. And the music of the spheres. It was rare for anyone to hear it, to hear even a small bit of it. Even with two words. And Sapgir could do it with whole phrases, without inertia and routine, outside of ready-made, dormant forms . . . But he was also sociable, democratic in his choices of company, even with a touch of undiscernment, giving his word to everything and everyone. At least, that is what so many believed . . .

In general, in the twentieth century not many natural springs remained, not a lot of room for *naive* poetry. Sapgir has a lot of cultural oddities, exquisite finishes and luster; he created figuratively and with formal sophistication; both naively and artfully. Another thing is that for him, culture was like nature. He took it as it belonged to no one. Like unforecasted rain.

It seems to me that the second half of the twentieth century was not the most fruitful time for creative flights. With a keen desire for perfection and a clearly stated intention to relate himself to the most significant contemporaries and respond to their challenge, Sapgir, unfortunately, lacked a sense of his own mission and faith in the power of the word. He shared this lack of belief with Joseph Brodsky—his antipode, a friend of

---

21 Shraer-Petrov, *Vodka s pirozhnymi. Roman s pisateliami*, 200.
22 OBERIU is the abbreviation for Ob"edinenie real′nogo iskusstva ("Association of Real Art"), a short-lived group of Russian (Soviet) artists, founded in 1928 by Daniil Kharms and Aleksandr Vvedensky (tr.).
23 This is from Evgeny Baratynsky's poem "On the Death of Goethe" ("Na smert′ Gete," 1833).

the Leningrad/St. Petersburg poetic youth of David Shrayer-Petrov. But to Sapgir, one may say, this lack of faith was applicable to a lesser extent. His later poems are free of (Brodsky's) graveside coldness; they possess a vast amount of attention to and tenderness for a person, sometimes to such a degree that they become a sentimental paroxysm. And overall, he is less ironic than anyone else (how easily he waved off this much too infectious disease of the late twentieth century!). He is much more genuine, sublime, moving . . . And he surprises us with this combination of freedom and loftiness.

Collected in such detail and with so much love in the "New Poet's Library" volume, Sapgir doubly amazes: with his dual unity, a synthesis of metaphysics and everyday living, eternity and the present moment, play and depth. What might have seemed an accidental whim of inspiration fell into place and became a part of some generalized poetic teleology—an incomprehensible but apparent Design.

Psalmist ("псалмопевец"; *psalmopevets*)—this is how Shrayer-Petrov (and his son and co-author) define Sapgir in the title of their introductory essay in "New Poet's Library." This is an important reference to the Jewish roots of Sapgir's creative work. The breadth of his cultural associations and interests should not obscure the biblical source of his inspiration, that great wave of Jewish traditions that carried him. This salt cured and saturated Russian letters; but exactly how it did so remains to be food for thought. And if I had to try, at least briefly (thinking along with David Shrayer-Petrov), to highlight the essence of Sapgir's authorial originality, the meaning and otherness of his worldview, then I would first like to mention two more features.

On the one side, there is the irreducible significance of personal presence. Sapgir's human subject does not merely *exist* as a *fact*; he is *irreplaceable* as a unique *concentrate* of Being. And the poet's meeting with his human subjects often yields an acute existential experience, accompanied by a spiritual thrill from recognizing a big and important truth about human existence. (And does not our own encounter with Sapgir himself occur in the same manner? Such is David Shrayer-Petrov's encounter with Sapgir.) This is visible almost everywhere in the poet's work, but it is especially prominent in the book *Three Lives* (*Tri zhizni*), composed during the last year of his life. There this human presence reaches the fierce sharpness of approaching death. With an aching tenderness, Sapgir sang out his swan song.

But there is also another side, the painful experience of having been abandoned by God. Empty is this world—abandoned, godless, overgrown, empty. And it has been this way from the very beginning; this is where Sapgir's *Voices* (*Golosa*) come from, and this is what the early *Women's Village* (*Bab´ia derevnia*) is about. "Man is pitiful."[24] Sapgir, however, does not judge, leaving this mission to God. Except for referencing in his own familiar way a dubious fellow-writer. He is not inclined to dwell in elegiac melancholy. He casually places a quote from Brodsky into a new context: "Оглядываюсь: руины —/ весёлые результаты"[25] ("I'm looking around: ruins—/ amusing results).[26] Yet Sapgir spent his entire life mostly building his poetic home in the midst of these ruins. Breaks and losses, pauses and sighs, a permanent *non finito* and the paradoxes of language slurring and getting lost amid three Pushkinian pines—this is Sapgir's building material, for which not only he is responsible, but his time as well.

A philosopher of the ancient paradigm, an indolent reveler and drinker, Sapgir kept walking past the gray and boring epoch that was fading before his eyes. But in Sapgir's later poems, his own authorial presence already seems optional to him. "'Всё обойдётся'—думаю/ И в самом деле терпимо/ мир обошёлся с нами/ мир обойдётся без нас"[27] ("'We'll do just fine'—I think/ And is actually tolerable/ the world has done us a favor/ the world will do without us"). By the end of the century, Sapgir's world has become a wild-grown space, where something cemetery-like begins to emerge. See his poem about a "deserted club:" "Зеркала/ без актёров умерли/ Тень/ ночью скрадывает весь театр/ складывает в чемодан/ для декораций/ и уносит в тень акаций"[28] ("Mirrors/ without actors

---

24 Genrikh Sapgir, *Stikhotvoreniia i poemy*, ed. David Shraer-Petrov and Maksim D. Shraer (St. Petersburg: Akademicheskii proekt, 2004), 405.
25 Ibid., 413.
26 Cf. Brodsky's "Letters to the Roman Friend" ("Pis´ma rimskomu drugu"): "Вот и прожили мы больше половины./ Как сказал мне старый раб перед таверной:/ 'Мы, оглядываясь, видим лишь руины'./ Взгляд, конечно, очень варварский, но верный" ("Here we've spent—I swear it—more than half our lifetimes./ As a slave— now white-haired—told me near the tavern:/ 'When we look around us, all we see is ruins.'/ A barbarian perspective, though a true one"). Russian text from: Iosif Brodskii [Joseph Brodsky], *Sochineniia*, comp. G. F. Komarov, vol. 2 (St. Petersburg: Pushkinskii fond, 1992), 285. English text from: Joseph Brodsky, *Collected Poems in English*, ed. Ann Kjellberg (New York: Farrar, Straus and Giroux, 2000), 59.
27 Sapgir, *Stikhotvoreniia i poemy*, 413.
28 Ibid., 421.

died/ Shadow/ at night conceals the entire theater/ puts it in a suitcase/ for the sets/ and takes it under the shadow of acacia trees") ...

Where Sapgir started out, they now produce yoghurt. "Скажут: сентябрь не скажут: Господь"[29] ("They will say: September they won't say: Lord").

But nevertheless, life folds inwardly toward God, to whom one can turn with the hope of being heard. Like this:

> Верни нам наивных ангелов
> Верни примитивных демонов
> Верни нам Себя чтоб узрели—
> и в Библии и в саду
> [...] Верни нам таких как видел
> на деревенской северной
> иконе — белой кистью
> все перышки
> И пусть нам будет художник—
> не тот — подражатель прежних
> "Хвала им и слава — в Вышних..."
> а тот которого видел
> в Софронцево на Мологе
>   — костер ещё жгли в овраге
>   — юродствующий дурачок[30]

("Give us back naive angels/ Give back primitive demons/ Give back Yourself for us to see—/ both in the Bible and in the garden/ [...] Give back to us as the ones you saw/ on a Northern village/ icon—in white brush/ each feather accounted for/ And let us have an artist—/ not that one—imitator of former ones/ 'Praise to them and glory—in the Highest...'/ but the one whom I saw/ in Sofrontsevo on the Mologa/—and a fire was burning in the ravine/—a little fool who acts holy")

This is one of the climaxes of Sapgir's privileged theme, the artist and the angels...

No matter what some skeptics may say about the untimely nature of Genrikh Sapgir, his poems became not only a necessary fact of the cultural experience of the poet's inner narrow circle of professionals and admirers,

---

29 Ibid., 453.
30 Ibid., 414.

but also an important part of the literary baggage of many readers who have preserved an interest in Russian poetry. This is in part due to the efforts of David Shrayer-Petrov, who even said that some of Sapgir's works "will enter folklore;"[31] they have not yet, and we are still waiting.

* * *

Let us return to the biographical circumstances that resulted in the bond between Sapgir and Shrayer-Petrov. There are wonderful memoirs about Sapgir. But *Tiger of Snows* (*Tigr Snegov*) and *Awakening of Dreams* (*Vozbuzhdenie snov*)—David Shrayer-Petrov's prose works about Sapgir—are among the very best. The most important aspect of Shrayer-Petrov's reflections about Sapgir is their connection to his own personal impressions, the personal experience of their meetings and communication. Indeed, as I have already noted, we need to look carefully into the friendship between these two writers, because it is a special, extremely rare and valuable phenomenon.

Shrayer-Petrov makes a poignant observation: Sapgir is a nonbinary ("неполярный") person. A mutual friend, as it may seem. Everyone remembers him as a friend, even those who have seen him just once. And it is also a gift to get into the memory of others so that they would consider you a friend after only a brief moment of acquaintance; you need to have a great personal talent for this. But one must also have the ability to portray Sapgir the way David Shrayer-Petrov, a fortuitous participant of Sapgir's life, portrayed him.

When they first met back in 1958 (Sapgir was thirty years old, Shrayer-Petrov was twenty-two), they discovered that they had something important in common. Decades later, Shrayer-Petrov would recall:

> Of course, he complimented me on something. Those poems where I would bear naked the formal devices: "Космос или косметику — что завоюешь ты?/ В резиновой арифметике болтвецки болтались болты" ["Cosmos or cosmetics—what will you conquer?/ In rubber arithmetic bolts bolted like boltmen"]. He approved: "Spoken in the manner of Khlebnikov." He could talk endlessly about Velimir Khlebnikov. [. . .] I immediately registered his blood kinship with Khlebnikov. Exposure of the formal devices. Word creation.

---

31 Shraer-Petrov, *Vodka s pirozhnymi. Roman s pisateliami*, 206.

The use of word as a living material for a line of verse—"corporealness of the word." I was struck by Genrikh's comfortable Jewishness.[32]

And they did not lose each other. They saw each other now often, now rarely, as it happens with poets. In 1985–1987—very often: this is the period of their greatest closeness. They have shared a great life together.

Sapgir has a sonnet, titled "Grasshoppericus" ("Kuznechikus," middle 1980s) and dedicated to David Shrayer-Petrov. The poem is included in his playful book, *Terverses of Genrikh Bufarev* (*Tertsikhi Genrikha Bufareva*); it is a playful poem, light, levitating, and it deals with metamorphoses, with the reincarnation of the world by the efforts and means of poetic inspiration:

> Оретикус моретикус кантарус! —
> Свою латынь теперь изобрету
> Я над любой фонемой ставлю парус
>
> Жив еретик вживлением в ничту
> Как ариель взбежал на звездный ярус
> Кричу судьбе: огнем его! ату!
> И сам себя хватаю на лету
>
> Жгу в ярости! — На сцене — пыль и старость
> Беру ваш мир — и этакий макарус
> Из стеклодранок строю аппаратус
> Кузнечикус — и зинзивер икарус!
>
> Не звездомер не время-акробатус
> Сам-сон лечу и нет пути обрауунс
> Пусть солнце попадает в точку! в ту![33]

("Oreticus moreticus kantarus!—/ I will now invent my own Latin/ I put a sail over any phoneme/ The heretic is alive through grafting onto nothingness/ Like ariel ran up to the tier of stars/ I scream to fate: use fire on him! go!/ I catch myself on the fly/ I burn in rage!—On the stage—dust and old age/ I take your world—and some kind of a focus-pocus/ From shards of glass I build an apparatus/ Grasshoppericus—and a zinziver icarus!/ Not a starmeasurer nor time-acrobaticus/ Together with the dream I fly and there is not waybackus/ Let the sun hit the spot! that very one!")

---

32 Ibid., 179. The quotation comes from Shrayer-Petrov's early poem "Still Life" ("Natiurmort," 1956). (tr.)
33 Sapgir, *Stikhotvoreniia i poemy*, 258.

In her study of this poem, Darya Domnina finds the poem to be "mysterious" "in terms of author's innovations"[34] and his allusions to Khlebnikov. She also cites David Shrayer-Petrov as a memoirist. The connection to Khlebnikov is self-evident. But to me, Sapgir's slightly oblique actualization of Khlebnikov's *zinziver* ("зинзивер"; the great tomtit of the Russian folk imagination—tr.), surrounded by biblical, Shakespearean, and ancient associations, and augmented by the OBERIU poets' interest in the unadorned existence of insects, shows a free parallel to the long story of Sapgir's literary friendship with Shrayer-Petrov—a friendship that began (and continued) with a mutual affinity for Khlebnikov (remember Shrayer-Petrov's story of his first meetings with Sapgir in 1958).

That very union of poets rhymes with the sensation of flight, with the pathos of inner freedom and imagination uncontrolled by any regimes. Here is the basis of a mutual intimacy, which comes to the fore in Shrayer-Petrov's long poem *Grasshopper* (*Kuznechik*). This poem, dedicated to Sapgir, was also written in the middle 1980s. It consistently articulates the antithesis of the grasshopper, which is associated with the theme of inspiration and creativity (with bright erotic details), and the "крепыши" (*krepyshi*), the "strong-armed" prohibitors, who are, apparently, eternal in Russia, so much so that Shrayer-Petrov's poem has acquired a desperately relevant meaning in the recent years:

Гола, гола
кричите
под мостом
я укрываюсь
чем не храм
и свод
и реки купель
гола, гола
галактики капель
не оросит асфальт
владений ваших
не будет проку
от заводов и от пашен

---

34 D. V. Domnina, "Okkazional′nye slova kak pokazateli nesovershenstva okruzhaiushchego mira (na materiale tsikla Genrikha Sapgira 'Tertsikhi Genrikha Bufareva')," in *Aktual′nye problemy sovremennogo slovoobrazovaniia. Sbornik nauchnykh statei*, ed. E. S. Denisova (Kemerovo: Kemerovskii gosudarstvennyi universitet, 2011), 535–536.

> вы прокураторы
> тюремного стола
> изгадили души и тела
> храмы
> вы хамы
> но ваша территория
> мучительна мала
> Я брат Кузнечика
> кро
> кровь капает
> из правого крыла.[35]

("o naked, naked,/ you scream/ under the bridge/ I'm sheltering/ isn't it like a temple/ and a vault/ and the river's baptismal font/ o naked, naked,/ galactic downpour/ won't water the asphalt/ of your properties/ it won't do any good/ from factories and pastures/ you're procurators/ of a prison table/ you've mucked up souls and bodies/ temples/ you're boors/ but your territory/ is painfully small/ I am Grasshopper's brother/ blo/ blood drips/ from the right wing.")

Cross-pollination, mutual creative fertilization is the brightest sign of their literary friendship.

Among the most essential things that Shrayer-Petrov captures in his memoirs—and that bound him with Sapgir—is the special atmosphere of literary life in the Soviet 1960s–1980s. The literary empire had a difficult relationship with the Soviet regime. However, the poets had a sense that they were chosen in a special way by virtue of belonging to the great literary tree. And also because they shared the spiritual aristocratic pathos of tranquil lightness: the weight of burdensome social tasks rested on their shoulders easily, carelessly. Sapgir as depicted by Shrayer-Petrov is completely free of the social directive, is outside of the Soviet officialdom; as if the latter did not exist at all. This lifestyle, this "thirst for literary interpersonal commerce"[36] is a sort of antithesis to the leaden disgraces of the Soviet era. Sapgir has succeeded in deceiving not only his contemporaries, but also his descendants: from the outside, it seems that his life was easy, that he managed, rather effortlessly, to adjust himself to his epoch. Relying on a vast experience of personal communication, David Shrayer-Petrov dispels

---

35 David Shraer-Petrov, "Kuznechik," *Chernovik. Al'manakh* 5 (1991): 32–34.
36 Shraer-Petrov, *Vodka s pirozhnymi. Roman s pisateliami*, 179.

this myth and demonstrates with remarkable depth what lay underneath Sapgir's "lightness." Sapgir's feasts and banquets, drinking parties accompanied with reading poems out loud, the lustrousness of everyday routine, unformulaic interactions with others, the cheerful gastronomy of life, the whole vibrancy and flavor of literary friendships, partly strange and surprising, are exercises in freedom that united the poets at the freedom's feasts and banquets. This is the art of being free and of merging as much as possible with the freedom that revealed itself in the poetic word.

Everything that David Shrayer-Petrov wrote on this subject in his memoirs of Genrikh Sapgir is also his own faithful self-portrait.

Translated, from the Russian, by
Daria Sadovnichenko with Maxim D. Shrayer

Works Cited

Brodsky, Joseph. [Iosif Brodskii]. *Sochineniia*. Compiled by G. F. Komarov. Vol. 2. St. Petersburg: Pushkinskii fond, 1992.

———. *Collected Poems in English*. Edited by Ann Kjellberg. New York: Farrar, Straus and Giroux, 2000.

Domnina, D. V. "Okkazional´nye slova kak pokazateli nesovershenstva okruzhaiushchego mira (na materiale tsikla Genrikha Sapgira 'Tertsikhi Genrikha Bufareva')." In *Aktual´nye problemy sovremennogo slovoobrazovaniia. Sbornik nauchnykh statei*, edited by E. S. Denisova, 534–538. Kemerovo: Kemerovskii gosudarstvennyi universitet, 2011.

Ermolin, Evgenii. "Koster v ovrage." *Novyi mir* 4 (2005): 173–178.

Krivulin, Viktor. "Golos i pauza Genrikha Sapgira." http://sapgir.narod.ru/talks/mono/mono01.htm. Accessed January 31, 2020.

Sapgir, Genrikh. "Iz predisloviia k 'Nevskim stikham' D. Shraera-Petrova." *Chernovik* 5 (1991): 35.

———. *Stikhotvoreniia i poemy*. Introduction, complied, and edited by David Shraer-Petrov and Maksim D. Shraer. St. Petersburg: Akademicheskii proekt, 2004.

Shrayer, Maxim D. [Maksim D. Shraer], and David Shrayer-Petrov [David Shraer-Petrov]. *Genrikh Sapgir. Klassik avangarda*. Saint Petersburg: Dmitrii Bulanin, 2004.

———. *Genrikh Sapgir. Klassik avangarda*. 3rd ed. Ekaterinburg: Ridero, 2017.

Shrayer-Petrov, David [David Shraer-Petrov]. "Kuznechik." *Chernovik. Al´manakh* 5 (1991): 32–34.

——— [David Shraer-Petrov]. *Villa Borgeze*. Holyoke, MA: New England Publishing, 1992.

——— [David Shraer-Petrov]. "Tigr Snegov (Genrikh Sapgir)." In David Shraer-Petrov, *Moskva zlatoglavaia*, 18–63. Baltimore: Vestnik, 1994.

——— [David Shraer-Petrov]. "Vozbuzhdenie snov. Vospominaniia o Genrikhe Sapgire." *Tallinn* 21–22 (2001): 3–36.

——— [David Shraer-Petrov]. "Tigr Snegov. Genrikh Sapgir." In David Shraer-Petrov [David Shrayer-Petrov], *Vodka s pirozhnymi. Roman s pisateliami*, edited by Maksim D. Shraer, 177–217. St. Petersburg: Akademicheskii proekt, 2007.

——— [David Shraer-Petrov]. "Vozbuzhdenie snov. Vospominaniia o Genrikhe Sapgire." In Maksim D. Shraer and David Shraer-Petrov,

Genrikh Sapgir. Klassik avangarda, 199–267. 3rd ed. Ekaterinburg: Ridero, 2018.

Shraer-Petrov, David, and Gennadii Katsov. "Ia dumaiu, chto my vse drug druga chemu-to nauchili...." RUNYweb.com, May 17, 2011. http://www.runyweb.com/articles/culture/literature/david-shayer-petrov-interview.html. Accessed June 3, 2020.

Part Three

David Shrayer-Petrov's Refusenik Novels

David Shrayer-Petrov's *Aliyah* Novels and the Epistemology of the Jewish-Soviet Cultural Revival*

Klavdia Smola

In his study of cultural memory, Jan Assmann describes some culturally established landscapes as topoi that can regain their symbolic character and, consequently, their topicality under certain circumstances: "[. . .] they are elevated [. . .] to the status of a sign, i.e. semiotized."[1] In this essay, I will show how certain strata and places of cultural tradition are re-semiotized in the prose of *aliyah* (or exodus) writers in the period of the late Soviet Jewish renaissance. I will also investigate the relationship between this collective reconsideration of Judaism and the Jewish traditional paradigm of remembrance. In doing so, I will analyze one of the most striking examples of the still relatively unstudied genre of *aliyah* literature: the first two parts of David Shrayer-Petrov's trilogy of refusenik novels, *Doctor Levitin* (*Doktor Levitin*, 1979–1980) and *Cursed Be You... Just Don't Die* (*Bud′ ty prokliat! Ne umirai…*, 1982–1984).[2]

---

* Copyright © 2021 by Klavdia Smola.
1 Jan Assmann, *Das kulturelle Gedächtnis. Schrift, Erinnerung und politische Identität in frühen Hochkulturen* (München: Beck, 1992), 60.
2 Maxim D. Shrayer describes the history of the novel's publication as following: "In 1984 the manuscript of Part One and Part Two was clandestinely photographed by a trusted photographer, and the negatives were smuggled out of the USSR to the West. [. . .] In 1986 an abridged text of Part One appeared in Jerusalem under the title *V otkaze*

Indeed, political implications of the Jewish underground culture in the late Soviet Union, which was marked by the struggle for emigration and by idealism about the state of Israel, exemplify Assmann's concept of "hot memory," called upon to bring about "break, change and upheaval."[3] Early biblical history, the Judaic myth of the Holy Land, the Exodus story, the destroyed Temple in Jerusalem and the *galut* suddenly gain a tremendous explosive power in the secular present of the Soviet Jews. Remote or mythical past becomes politically volatile, moreover, it becomes a source of identity and prepares the longed-for future. In this context, the agenda of collective memory assumes the status of a historical event as understood by the German historian Lucian Hölscher: "Historical interpretations, as they are made in memories and expectations, are themselves historical events."[4]

David Shrayer-Petrov's refusenik trilogy is highly representative of the literary production brought forth by Zionist aspirations and the Jewish revivalist movement during the Soviet 1970s and 1980s. It is also remarkable for its poetics and its philosophical orientation. Together with other exodus texts such as *Jacob's Ladder* (*Lestnitsa Iakova*, 1984) by Efraim Baukh, *The Third Temple* (*Tretii khram*, 1975) and *The Tenth Hunger* (*Desiatyi golod*, 1985) by Eli Lyuksemburg, *The Gates of Our Exodus* (*Vrata iskhoda nashego*, 1980) by Felix Kandel, and *Story Embellishment* (*Priskazka*, 1978) by David Markish, Shrayer-Petrov's refusenik trilogy of novels is both an example of Jewish-Soviet unofficial literature and a unique historical document. As a part of the Soviet dissident culture, these novels contributed to the creation of the counter-canon of Russian literature. Moreover, it also made an important contribution to the Zionist literature in different countries and languages, the beginnings of which reach far back to *Shire Tsion*, the *Zion Songs* of Yehuda Ha-Levi (1075–1141).[5]

(*Being a Refusenik*), in a volume of the same title, comprised of writings by and about refuseniks and published by Biblioteka-Aliia ("*Aliyah* Library") (Maxim D. Shrayer, "About the Text of Doctor Levitin," in David Shrayer-Petrov, *Doctor Levitin: A Novel*, ed. and with notes by Maxim D. Shrayer, tr. Arna B. Bronstein, Aleksandra Fleszar, and Maxim D. Shrayer [Detroit: Wayne State University Press, 2018], 278). The third novel of the trilogy, *The Third Life* (*Tret′ia zhizn′*), was written and published following Shrayer-Petrov's emigration to the United States in 1987.

3   Assmann, *Das kulturelle Gedächtnis*, 70.
4   Lucian Hölscher, "Geschichte als 'Erinnerungskultur,'" in *Generation und Gedächtnis. Erinnerungen und kollektive Identitäten*, ed. K. Platt and M. Dabag (Opladen: Springer, 1995), 166.
5   Both Shrayer-Petrov's novel and *aliyah* prose as a whole inherited the tradition of the early Russian "Palestine" prose of the *halutzim*, prominently represented in Mark Egart's novel *The Scorched Land* (*Opalennaia zemlia*, 1933–1934).

Aside from the trilogy's cultural, historical, and spiritual heritage, I will focus on the hybrid character of its texture. Shrayer-Petrov's refusenik trilogy of novels brings together opposing modes of prose writing. On the one hand, this text has an affinity with documentary and journalistic discourse, while on the other, it contains elements written in a lyrical and confessional mode. Its strong essayistic quality enables a unique blending of voices, and allows the author to combine and conflate different genre conventions such as psychological and adultery novel, diary, memoir, and crime and political thriller. As a result, Shrayer-Petrov's refusenik trilogy is artistically more complex than its more conventional "relatives" on the orbits of Jewish-Russian *aliyah* literature, such as the documentary novel *The Sheremetyevo Airport* (*Shetemet´evo*, 1988) by Grigory Voldman or the brilliant satirical novella *The Merry-Go-Round* (*Karusel´*) by Yuz Aleshkovsky (1979).

The poet and prose writer David Shrayer-Petrov was a refusenik for over eight years. As a result of his application to emigrate, he lost his senior academic position as a research microbiologist, was expelled from the Union of Soviet Writers and was subjected to severe harassment by the Soviet regime. Shrayer-Petrov's *aliyah* prose is partly based on autobiographical experiences. With the dawn of perestroika in the spring of 1987, Shrayer-Petrov and his family were given permission to leave and emigrated to the USA.[6]

Apart from his refusenik status, other significant elements of Shrayer-Petrov's biography also appear in the novel. Its protagonist, Doctor Herbert Anatolyevich Levitin, is a physician, just like Emmanuil Kardin, the central character in Efraim Baukh's *Jacob's Ladder*. Like Doctor Kardin—and like thousands of other members of the Jewish-Soviet intelligentsia—Doctor Levitin is a descendant of religious *shtetl* Jews; this world of traditional Jewish life in the former Pale of Settlement had already become alien to his parents. The historical path from traditional Judaism to assimilation and secular studies—often in the field of medicine—highlights a pivotal period in Doctor Levitin's family history and in Jewish-Soviet history as a whole, the exploration of which is crucial for *aliyah* authors and their concepts of identity. In the 1930s, Levitin's father moved with his young wife from a remote Belarusian *shtetl* to Moscow to study medicine in the "New World" ("в новый мир"): they "could no longer confine themselves to the old environment, rife as it was with ornate disputations, doubts, and

---

6 My conversations with David Shrayer-Petrov in December 2012 in Ramat-Gan and in December 2018 in Boston helped me to visualize the atmosphere of "отказ" ("refusal"), its dramatic long-term effect on the author's family and the period when the novel was written.

the odor of mothballs"⁷ ("не могли оставаться в старой, пропахшей словопрениями и сомнениями, пронафталиненной среде"⁸). Here, the topoi of the early Soviet modernisation discourse, enthusiastically adopted by many Jews of the former Russian Empire, are reproduced. The above-quoted description of the *shtetl* world—critical to the point of disdain—echoes a tradition of writing about the *shtetl* as antiquated and obsolete. Similar repudiatory images, often laden with olfactory associations, appear in the poetry of Eduard Bagritsky and Iosif Utkin, as well as earlier autobiographical prose of Osip Mandelstam. This intertextual passage is a meaningful historical link, which helps to understand the narrated present of the novel, that is, the Jewish revival in late Soviet Russia. Doctor Levitin is raised in a family of Moscow intelligentsia, for whom their Jewishness is merely a family *back*ground, a "thin identity" in an internationalist Soviet multiethnic state. In the "black year" of 1949, Doctor Levitin's father is suspended from his military hospital duties without any plausible cause. In early 1953, he is arrested in the course of the so-called "doctors' plot." Unable to cope with the humiliation and the open state-sponsored antisemitism, Doctor Levitin's father dies shortly after his rehabilitation. At the start of the novel, Doctor Levitin's own outward Jewishness is largely limited to the annual visit to the Moscow Choral Synagogue on the day of his father's yahrzeit. However, when he is there, he always feels an inner, albeit transient, bond with his Jewish ancestors:

> это было временное, закономерно возвращающееся, как память о родителях, приобщение себя к понятию еврейства. То есть он, оставаясь русским интеллигентом, внезапно, но совершенно определенно открывал в себе еще одну важную черту — еврейское происхождение.⁹

> It was more temporary, naturally determined—like the memory of his parents—his return or reattachment to the notion of Jewishness. That is, as a member of the Russian intelligentsia, he would suddenly yet very tangibly rediscover in himself another prominent quality: his Jewish heritage.¹⁰

Doctor Levitin's first impulse to leave the country comes at the very beginning of the text, as his family is harshly confronted with

---

7   Shrayer-Petrov, *Doctor Levitin*, 39.
8   David Shraer-Petrov, *Gerbert i Nelli* (Moscow: Knizhniki, 2014), 39.
9   Ibid., 43.
10 Shrayer-Petrov, *Doctor Levitin*, 36.

state-sponsored antisemitism. The Levitins' only son, Anatoly, fails the entrance examinations to the medical school where his father is a full professor of medicine. This occurs, just as his Jewish father and his Russian mother anticipated, due to his Jewish origin, which the examiners instantly detect and act upon. As a result, Anatoly suffers a severe nervous breakdown. Meanwhile, more and more friends and acquaintances of the Levitin family emigrate on Israeli visas.

Shrayer-Petrov depicts the exclusion of Jews in the late Soviet Union as a multi-layered phenomenon. The whole variety of Judeophobic attitudes can be found here: from the almost biological aversion on the part of the otherwise honest and humane non-Jewish-Soviet citizens all the way to the ideological targeting of Jews as potential "enemies of the people" and "Zionists" by the party officials and the KGB. In the attitude of Levitin's own father-in-law, Vasily Matveevich, towards the Jews, the centuries-old mistrust of simple villagers towards strangers[11] is mixed with political suspicion on the part of a Soviet citizen loyal to the regime, who has internalized the formulas of Communist propaganda. Vasily Matveevich is, as Shrayer-Petrov's narrator explains, not an antisemite, but "he didn't love Jews"[12] ("он не любил евреев"[13]). Grandfather Vasily Matveevich uses anti-Jewish clichés, which are expressed in singular pejorative expressions (for example, he calls Levitin "long nose") and prejudices (he is surprised that Levitin, as a Jew, has no practical sense and has not managed to find a way out of his son's predicament).

Strikingly, in his own nuclear family, Levitin encounters old collective phobias that go beyond the political and the stereotypical and culminate in notes of racial prejudice. His Russian wife Tatyana, for example, finds the idea of emigration to Israel scary and fears that the typical Semitic physical traits of her husband—"elongated cranium," "kinky hair," "dark eyes," "beaked nose"—may have been transmitted to her. Doctor Levitin's physical alterity, which his son Anatolii inherits, is considered a stigma. The fact that this otherness is also perceived suspiciously by one's own close family members marks the tragic insurmountability of ethnic divisions and highlights the long traditions of Russian ethno-religious xenophobia,

---

11 It finds its biological expression in the well-known Russian proverb "The goose is no friend of the pig" ("Гусь свинье не товарищ").
12 Shrayer-Petrov, *Doctor Levitin*, 26.
13 Shraer-Petrov, *Gerbert i Nelli*, 33.

which largely draws its vitality from the poor education of the broad strata of the country's population.

The desire to leave the country and the awakening of Jewish self-awareness of the male protagonists trigger, in Shrayer-Petrov's and in Efraim Baukh's novels, the Judeophobic moods of their non-Jewish wives. In *Jacob's Ladder*, Kardin's wife Lena is of Cossack descent, which is no coincidence in the context of the novel: the Cossacks are depicted as proverbial enemies of the Jews. The more Kardin turns to Judaism, the greater the abyss between him and his wife. Similar to Tatyana Levitina, Lena Kardina also tries to shake off the "pernicious" influence of the Jewishness: "И опять рассказывает еврейские анекдоты в компании, и сквозит в этом болезненное желание приобщиться к 'своим', доказать, что не совсем ожидовилась"[14] ("Yet again she tells jokes about Jews to her friends, and one notices in it a painful desire to be closer to 'her owns', to prove that she is not yet completely 'Jewified'").

The passionate revelation of antisemitism becomes one of the most important components of *Doctor Levitin*, augmenting its affiliation with the late Soviet culture of Jewish protest. The power of reflection as well as the effect of the political invective increase because the flow of *Doctor Levitin*'s fictional narrative is repeatedly interrupted by autobiographical digressions of the authorial first-person narrator. The impression of authenticity in these digressions evokes the conventions of documentary narrative genres such as memoirs and diaries, further complicating the textual structure. The narrator, a Jewish-Russian writer, analyzes his existence as a Soviet Jew in fragments from his childhood to the present—"историю больших и малых обид"[15] ("a story of offenses large and small"[16]). He reconstructs a private encyclopaedia of discrimination, the confession of an outcast.[17] From this double narration, a thematically multidimensional structure emerges

---

14 Efrem Baukh, *Lestnitsa Iakova* (Jerusalem: Moriia, 2001), 297.
15 Shraer-Petrov, *Gerbert i Nelli*, 97.
16 Shrayer-Petrov, *Doctor Levitin*, 86.
17 Irina Grekova's novel *Svezho predanie* (*The Legend's Fresh*, 1962, pub. 1997) was one of the first works of fiction to offer a comprehensive indictment of Soviet antisemitism. Written by a non-Jewish author, it anticipated the Jewish revival in Russia by a number of years. In its incredibly candid depiction of the persecution of Jews in the Soviet Union, this text by far surpasses the novel *Life and Fate* (*Zhizn' i sud'ba*) by Vasily Grossman, written three years earlier than Grekova's novel and published in 1988. The more recent Russian prose trend against antisemitism culminates in the post-Soviet novel *The Confession of A Jew* (*Ispoved' evreia*, 1993) by Aleksandr Melikhov.

in a network of similarities and allusions, a play with personal proximity and fictional distance. Parallels arise between Doctor Levitin's fate and that of the authorial narrator as a victim of Judeophobia. The excerpt from the 1961 indictment of Adolf Eichmann by the Israeli Attorney General illustrates similarities between German National Socialism and the postwar Soviet Communism: ("... торговля свободой еврея стала отныне отныне официальной политикой рейха"[18] ("Trading in Jewish freedom was from that time onward the official policy of the Reich"[19]). Finally, the journey to Trakai, which Anatoly and his beloved Natasha undertake during a visit to Lithuania so as to see what has remained of Trakai's Karaite community, becomes the pretext for the authorial narrator to deploy a travelogue of his own similar journey.[20] As a historical reference, Anatoly and Natasha's excursion to Trakai testifies to the renewed interest in Jewish culture among young people in the late Soviet Union. At the same time, the narrator's metareflection gives the novel an opportunity to report on the fate of the Karaites as part of the tragic Jewish-Soviet history. The old Karaites of Trakai, whose religion had branched off from Judaism, conceal their affinity to the Jews and do not want to be associated with or even mistaken for Jews for fear of persecution. For this reason, the questions posed by the probing narrator sound perilous and harassing to them, and they react in a defensive and unfriendly fashion. The narrator tries to penetrate their secrecy and the resulting oblivion by further investigating the history of the Karaites, visiting their synagogue (*kenesa*) and the museum in Trakai. At the same time, the narrator believes that he can hypothesize about the Semitic ancestry of the beloved Russian poet Alexander Pushkin:

---

18   Shraer-Petrov, *Gerbert i Nelli*, 139.
19   Shrayer-Petrov, *Doctor Levitin*, 127.
20   In the nonconformist Jewish-Soviet literature, the place of repressed or hidden Jewish religious observance or culture is often the Soviet periphery, or Soviet republics: the *shtetl* once abandoned by the protagonist, Lithuania, Caucasus, or Central Asia. Since the Jewish traditions had been preserved to a greater extent in the borderlands, the peripheral often appears as a space where meaning is produced, a space of living memory and of the last remnants of tradition. Charged with living memories, the geographic edge of the empire reflects *ex negativo* the empty space of the center. So Baukh's Kardin travels to his home town to experience this journey as a revelation and a literal return to his own roots. Eli Lyuksemburg, who grew up in Uzbekistan, portrays in *The Tenth Hunger* the Central Asian Jewry of Bukhara. In Markish's *Story Embellishment*, the place of exile—Kazakhstan—is regarded as a substitute Palestine: a space of freedom, which functions as the site of Zionist self-education and precursor of *aliyah*.

> Пушкин получил свои поэтические гены от Давида и его сына Соломона, поскольку род Ганнибалов восходит к династии эфиопских царей через Соломона и царицу Савскую [...]. Прослеживается чёткая генеалогическая и потому — генетическая линия: Давид — Соломон — Христос — Пушкин.[21]

> Pushkin received his poetic genes from David and his son Solomon. The ancestors of Pushkin's mother—the Hannibals—descended from the Abyssinian royal dynasty through King Solomon and the Queen of Sheba. [...] A defined genealogical, and therefore a genetic, lineage may be traced: David—Solomon—Christ—Pushkin.[22]

Like other spiritually awakened protagonists of *aliyah* prose, among them Markish's Simon Ashkenazi, Lyuksemburg's Yoshua, and Baukh's Kardin, as well as the lyrical narrators in Felix Kandel's and Semyon Lipkin's prose, Shrayer-Petrov's narrator seeks to uncover the hidden Jewish layers of a cultural Russian *palimpsest*. The reflection of Russian (cultural) history against the backdrop of Jewish culture is telling here. A particular concept of historicity emerges, one which questions the continuity and homogeneity, the ideological content, even the claim to existence of a grand national historical narrative that overwrites or even erases the concerns and aspirations of the minorities, in particular the Jewish one.[23]

Guided by the passion to rescue through memory the genealogies and links fallen into oblivion, Shrayer-Petrov's narrator, and, together with him, the implied author become a historian of his culture. The history of the Levitin family thus becomes part of the great history of the Jewish people in the Eastern European and especially in Soviet diaspora. The fate of the Karaites, the mention of the poet Ilya Selvinsky with his early crown of sonnets about Bar-Kokhba, and the discussion of then recent research on the history of the Khazars: all of this conveys the intellectual zeitgeist and self-reflexively points to the real circumstances that led to the birth and creation of Shrayer-Petrov's novel. In this respect, the text becomes a sort of a testimonial (non-)fiction, an autobiographically and critically

---

21 Shraer-Petrov, *Gerbert i Nelli*, 189.
22 Shrayer-Petrov, *Doctor Levitin*, 174–175.
23 This goes so far that the reader sometimes detects an authorial desire to attribute an primordial mystical meaning to the Jewish component in Russian culture and to rewrite the cultural "high achievements" of the Russian nation as Jewish contributions.

substantiated research into Jewish history and culture with the elements of Jewish education and ethnography.[24]

At the center of *Doctor Levitin* and David Shrayer-Petrov's entire refusenik trilogy lies one of the most striking facts of the Jewish-Soviet protest movement—the destiny of the refuseniks ("отказники"). The life of the Levitin family changes rapidly after they have applied for permission to emigrate to Israel. Doctor Levitin is forced to give up his work as an academic and a professor. In a detailed and realistic manner, the narrator depicts the harassments that fell onto the heads of those Jews and their families who declared their desire to leave the country. For instance, Levitin needs a special paper from his place of employment in order to submit the visa application at the OVIR (Section of Visas and Registrations). However, once his intention to leave the country becomes known at his medical school (and this happens very quickly), Doctor Levitin, now branded a dangerous Zionist, becomes the object of hatred and open ostracism. The required prerequisite for issuing the required document is his voluntary resignation. Doctor Levitin's nomenclature boss Professor Baronov, the department chair of general internal medicine at the medical school, calls Levitin "nothing but a typical ungrateful Jew, who was given everything here: education, respect, ideas. Even your wife you got from Russia, and now you spit on that which is most holy!"[25] ("просто-напросто типичный неблагодарный еврей, который получил здесь все, что возможно: образование, почет, идеи, даже — жену — получил из России, а теперь плюет на все самое святое!"[26]). The justification for having been refused his visa, which Doctor Levitin struggles and strains to get out of the authorities, shows the blatant arbitrariness of power and the opacity of the emigration policy of the Soviet state. The capitalised words "ПРИЁМНАЯ" ("waiting room") and "ОЧЕРЕДЬ" ("queue") in the OVIR become symbolic topoi of the bleak everyday life of refuseniks and Jewish diaspora. Crowded together in the queue are Jews for whom waiting for the permission to emigrate has become a way of life:

Никогда ещё Герберт Анатольевич не слышал подряд такого разнообразия еврейских фамилий. По этому перечню можно было, как

---

24 A subtle ethnographic undertone appears in the novel when, for example, the story behind the Hanukkah celebration is told in detail or Jewish customs are described and explained.
25 Shrayer-Petrov, *Doctor Levitin*, 52.
26 Shraer-Petrov, *Gerbert i Nelli*, 61.

> по этнографическому путеводителю, проследить историю и географию еврейской диаспоры.²⁷

> Never before had Herbert Anatolyevich heard such a great variety of Jewish last names recited in a row. One could use this list as an ethnographic guide, tracing the history and geography of the Jewish Diaspora.²⁸

The subsequent long list of Jewish surnames and their etymological commentary again tells the story of the origin, migration, and adaptation of the people living in the *galut* (exile): Jewish history in the light of hope for exodus and homecoming.

The documentary dimension of the novel increases again and again when the second, autobiographical level of narration is continued. The fictional narrative becomes a direct parallel to the events experienced by the author as well as to the petitions, visa applications, and open letters documenting the Jewish emigration in the 1970s and 1980s:

> Я — отказник, пария, бесправный гражданин имярек. Меня лишили естественной возможности самовыражения: работать по специальности, а потом отняли писательское удостоверение. Всё, что я пишу, наверняка пропадёт, затеряется.²⁹

> I'm a refusenik, a pariah, a disenfranchised citizen. They first deprived me of the natural means of self-expression—to work in my field—and then they took away my writer's identification card. Everything that I write will most probably be lost, disappear.³⁰

Contemporary facts are also reflected in the novel as the authorial narrator mentions the emigration of the writer Vassily Aksyonov and critiques the indifferent attitude of the poet David Samoylov towards refuseniks. The decisive question of the connection of Soviet Jews to their origins is raised: What is it that holds together people standing in the queue of the OVIR—"[н]еужели только кровь наших загубленных предков?"³¹ ("Is it only the blood of our slaughtered ancestors?").³²

---

27 Ibid., 229.
28 Shrayer-Petrov, *Doctor Levitin*, 211.
29 Shraer-Petrov, *Gerbert i Nelli*, 232–233.
30 Shrayer-Petrov, *Doctor Levitin*, 215.
31 Shraer-Petrov, *Gerbert i Nelli*, 234.
32 Shrayer-Petrov, *Doctor Levitin*, 216.

For the still inexperienced refusenik Doctor Levitin, the rejection is a pure shock, while the reasons for the refusal (отказ) appear obscure. Medical, biological, and life science-related metaphors convey the impenetrable border between the existence of the family before and after the rejection—a kind of narrative essentialization of the cognitive and social processes, which are also characteristic of the excessive tropes in works by other *aliyah* authors: "[. . .] вся жизнь [. . .] сжималась, сокращалась, как тельца одноклеточных животных, превращающихся в цисту, чтобы сохранить самую основу жизни [. . .]"[33] ("Their lives [. . .] were contracting, becoming smaller, like tiny bodies of single-celled animals forming a cyst in order to preserve the mere foundation of life. [. . .]").[34]

The tragedy strikes when Anatoly is drafted to serve in Afghanistan and is killed in action. The family disintegrates, Tatyana dies of grief and guilt (for her infidelity and for not having been able to rescue her son), Doctor Levitin becomes a mentally broken person and is disfigured beyond recognition after a fire: a symbolic stigma of alterity and martyrdom incised onto his body. The fire is set by Doctor Levitin himself: out of desperation, he takes revenge on the old woman, whom he phantasmagorically regards as simultaneously a dispenser of mysterious powders in the homeopathic pharmacy and a receptionist in the OVIR. Plagued by a growing paranoia, the professor half-imagines the old woman as a disgusting gray owl. For Levitin, the Owl embodies the evil of this world, as the usurious old pawnbroker did for Rodion Raskolnikov in Dostoevsky's *Crime and Punishment*. The motif of madness, latent at first, becomes explicit in the finale of the first part of Shrayer-Petrov's refusenik trilogy, when Doctor Levitin recognizes in the OVIR waiting room the organized activity of dark mystical forces, and his thinking ceases to be sober, rational, and scientific. In this key episode, the discourse of a *psychic and metaphysical border*—a reflection of the geographical border (exit, escape, emigration)—is introduced, crucial for *aliyah* prose as a whole. Particularly in the prose by Eli Lyuksemburg, the insanity of the male protagonists blurs the boundary between the reality and the spiritual realm. Levitin's last vision before the outbreak of the fire is followed by poetic lines from Psalm 21 (of David; Psalm 22 in the Christian tradition), steeped in the deep tragedy of being abandoned by God and in the psalmist's despair:

---

33 Shraer-Petrov, *Gerbert i Nelli*, 221.
34 Shrayer-Petrov, *Doctor Levitin*, 204.

> Я пролился, как вода; все кости мои рассыпались; сердце моё сделалось, как воск, растаяло посреди внутренности моей! Сила моя иссохла, как черепок; язык мой прильнул к гортани моей, и Ты свёл меня к персти смерти, ибо псы окружили меня; скопище злых обступило меня; пронзили руки мои и ноги мои.[35]

> My life ebbs away:
> all my bones are disjointed;
> my heart is like wax,
> melting within me;
> my vigor dries up like a shard;
> my tongue cleaves to my palate;
> You commit me to the dust of death.
> Dogs surround me; a pack of evil ones closes in on me,
> like lions they maul my hands and feet.[36]

In the second part of the novel, *Cursed Be You... Just Don't Die*, Levitin dives deeper into the refusenik milieu and experiences a great love for the younger Nelli. But the finale delivers the last failure: the death of his beloved and the return of the phantasmagorical Owl, whom Doctor Levitin attempted to kill at the end of part one, in the episode which epitomizes Levitin's final mental breakdown.

As a particular version of ethnically (Jewish) rooted emancipatory literature, or minority literature, the *aliyah* novel recursively uses real, historical figures, and at the same time evokes their legendary biblical prototypes, which ultimately fulfil a symbolic function in the Zionist teleology. The telos of return, which gains a universalist philosophical meaning and a metaphysical dimension, is expressed in passages like this one: "[. . .] нынешнее существование Герберта Анатольевича, жизнь его витающей над землёй души, было направлено только в один мир, одну вселенную — Эрец Исраэль"[37] ("[. . .] the present existence of Herbert Anatolyevich, the life of his soul hovering above the earth, was aimed toward a single world, toward a single universe—to Eretz Israel"[38]). Furthermore, Doctor Levitin's seventy-five year old uncle Moisey

---

35 Shraer-Petrov, *Gerbert i Nelli*, 295–296.
36 Shrayer-Petrov, *Doctor Levitin*, 274.
37 Shraer-Petrov, *Gerbert i Nelli*, 357.
38 Here and hereafter my literal English translations from the Russian of *Cursed Be You... Just Don't Die* (K.S.).

(Moses), a socialist and an idealist, fled to Palestine at the age of sixteen and, together with the other *halutzim*, helped build the Jewish state. For Levitin, Uncle Moisey embodies the strong, new Jew, whose courage only emphasizes the sluggishness and insecurity of his mentally shrunken descendants, the Soviet Jews, by his own example of life: "[. . .] Герберт Анатольевич тянулся к дяде Моисею, как тянется чахлый росток к солнцу — в надежде выжить и включиться в цикл божественной энергии, эманации, перелиться во вселенную родного народа"[39] ("[. . .] Herbert Anatolyevich yearned for his uncle Moisey like a stunted sprout yearns to reach the sun—hoping to survive and to enter into the cycle of divine energy, an emanation, and to be included into the universe of his own people"). Doctor Levitin's uncle, named after the central figure of the biblical Exodus, enriches the parallelism structures in the novel by infusing the fundamental opposition "Russian-Soviet" versus "Jewish-Israeli" with a historical and a legendary dimension. Indeed, according to some refusenik characters in the novel, humility was a genuinely Russian and Christian trait. It had been implanted in the Jews in the course of assimilation and contradicted the primordial paradigm of Judaism: "Эта покорность противоречит иудаизму"[40] ("This humility contradicts Judaism"). The celebration of Jewish holidays in the milieu of the spiritually awakened Jews also contributes to the network of associations based on biblical models and references—such as the celebration of Hanukkah, which evokes the history of the Maccabees uprising.[41] Dudko, a top OVIR official, is referred to as the "dictator" who tried to "suppress the rebellious slaves who wanted to taste the air of freedom" ("подавляя восставших рабов, пожелавших глотнуть воздух свободы"[42]). When contextualized this way, this reference creates a historical continuity that spans two thousand years: "Ничего не изменилось, хотя прошло две тысячи лет"[43] ("Nothing has changed, although two thousand years have passed").

Shrayer-Petrov's exodus novel envisions Israel simultaneously as a real and a biblical space by transferring the expectations of salvation from the religious to the historical level. Paradoxically in the Zionist context, the novel follows the long Jewish literary tradition of the "poetic settlement"

---

39 Shraer-Petrov, *Gerbert i Nelli*, 357.
40 Ibid., 369.
41 Ibid., 375–376.
42 Ibid., 482.
43 Ibid.

of the Holy Land, "poetically inhabiting *makom*,"[44] which Amir Eshel describes as follows: "Indeed, Jewish writers across the generations of exile were not so much obsessed with the urge to return to Zion—a notion many of them regarded as messianic—but were motivated by the desire to inhabit their dwelling place poetically."[45] The centuries-old *deteritorializing*[46] model of the Jewish homeland, which has emerged in the diaspora,[47] is reinforced again in the late Soviet dissident environment: "The homeland was [. . .] removed from geography into a spiritual category."[48]

In his recurrent digressions and detours from the main plot, the narrator references the destinies of numerous refuseniks in Doctor Levitin's circle of acquaintances so as to illuminate the extent and the specifics of a collective phenomenon hidden from the Soviet public. The object of a focused depiction is the academic underground elite: the author, himself a medical scientist and writer, describes the achievements of the researchers (both real and fictional) who are detained, punished, and belittled in the Soviet Union. These disenfranchised Jews have to survive by working menial jobs: such is the case of the biochemist Volf Izrailevich Zeldin or of Aleksandr Efimovich Khasman, ethnographer and expert on the old Kingdom of Khazaria. The detailed description of the refusenik milieu enhances the realistic-documentary and the political dimensions in Shrayer-Petrov's writing. This factual, politically underpinned authenticity

---

44 *Makom* in Judaism means the holy place, the "good" place, the place of the presence of G-d, and, at the same time, one of his names.

45 Amir Eshel, "Cosmopolitanism and Searching for the Sacred Space in Jewish Literature," *Jewish Social Studies* 9, no. 3 (2003): 124–125.

46 The term "deterritorialization" became one of the key notions in the philosophy of the twentieth and the twenty-first centuries, developed, for example, in the works by Gilles Deleuze, Félix Guattari, and Arjun Appadurai. In the field of cultural anthropology it generally means a decoupling of cultural production from the (original) place.

47 Sidra DeKoven Ezrahi also writes about "textual repatriation" as "alternative sovereignty" in the Jewish poetics of exile: "In its most radical form, this is an imaginative license that has no geographical coordinates: it is an affirmation and reconfiguration of the Jewish word as nomadic exercise and Jewish exile as a kind of *literary* privilege" (see her *Booking Passage. Exile and Homecoming in the Modern Jewish Imagination* [Berkeley: University of California Press, 2000], 10). The eternally postponed return and redemption of the diasporic existence and the tradition of the *written*, symbolic home as *makom*—Jacob's Beth-El, house of God—thus become an indispensable source of literary inspiration in Judaism (ibid., 10–15).

48 Ursula Zeller, "Between goldene medine and Promised Land: Legitimizing the American Jewish Diaspora," in *Diaspora and Multiculturalism: Common Traditions and New Developments*, ed. M. Fludernik (Amsterdam: Anglia, 2003), 5.

is even further amplified by episodes such as the celebration of Jewish holidays, meetings outside the Moscow Choral Synagogue during the Simchat Torah celebration, and controversial debates about the fate of the *aliyah* conducted in private homes (the proverbial Soviet kitchens as places of dissent). In their kitchens, refuseniks discuss the typical topics of their milieu: for example, they talk about the passivity of the assimilated and oppressed Soviet Jews and doubt their ability to assimilate the values of their "home" state Israel. This documentary, journalistically accurate descriptions are typical of testimonial literature, which seeks to capture and preserve forbidden layers of history and culture.

Like some other important novels of the time (David Markish's *Story Embellishment* is a good example), David Shrayer-Petrov's refusenik trilogy is a new version of the Bildungsroman. Like Baukh's *Jacob's Ladder* or Lyuksemburg's *The Third Temple*, it also draws on the Russian "роман прозрения" ("novel of insight"): the hero's development is a dolorous spiritual revelation, similar to that described by Fyodor Dostoevsky, Lev Tolstoy, and (in the form of the short story) Anton Chekhov.[49] Besides these powerful plot structures, the genre of Bildungsroman is supported by the novel's focus on books, which are read and discussed by the refuseniks: they literally constitute an "*aliyah* library" (Russian: "библиотека алии") and represent a mimetic reference to the *intertextually lived Jewish history*.[50] The library with the Russian translations of books by Isaac Bashevis Singer, Vladimir (Ze'ev) Zhabotinsky, Hayim Nachman Bialik, Leon Uris and Natan Alterman is a metonymic sign of spiritual belonging and political solidarity, of Soviet Jewish intellectualism, and of common suffering. However, when this list is recited by one of Doctor Levitin's refusenik friends, Mikhail Gaberman, Doctor Levitin notes: "Но я еще и Герцена перечитываю. Очень полезное чтение для нас"[51] ("But I also read Herzen again and again. It is *a very useful read for us*"). This comment can be interpreted

---

[49] Some well known examples of such "переоценка ценностей" (literally: "reevaluation of values"), which follows a character's mental crisis, include Tolstoy's Pierre Bezukhov (*War and Peace*) and Ivan Ilyich (*The Death of Ivan Ilyich*), but also Dostoevsky's Rodion Raskolnikov (*Crime and Punishment*) and Chekhov's Nadia in his novella "The Bride."

[50] Biblioteka-Aliia ("*Aliyah* Library") is the name of the Russian-language Zionist-oriented book publishing house founded in Israel in 1972, which, among other things, published the essential texts of the late Soviet exodus literature. Some of the books of Biblioteka-Aliia were smuggled into the Soviet Union and thus known to the Soviet Jewish reader.

[51] Shraer-Petrov, *Gerbert i Nelli*, 367, my italics.

as a latent critique of the one-sided, sometimes narrow-minded Zionist or Jewish self-education in the circles of the *aliyah* movement. The mention of Alexander Herzen's autobiography is an allusion to the beginning of the radical movement in Russia and to its bitter historical disillusionments. Apparently, Doctor Levitin has doubts about the future of emigration, which is remarkable in a novel saturated with a passionate plea for Jewish homecoming.

The novel could be seen as a nodal point of Shrayer-Petrov's reflections on Jewish history and culture, which are the focus of many of his texts. A powerful example of such wandering topics—also typical of other *aliyah* authors—is Jewish self-concealment and mimicry: a version of the above-mentioned palimpsest trope, which is epitomized in Shrayer-Petrov's prose and lyrical poetry in numerous material and human metaphors. Thus, the Jews themselves become the site of neglect and oblivion as they adopt Russian and Ukrainian names in the course of assimilation or deny their Judaism out of fear. Here, the theme of cultural and religious traces, confined and recorded in a multilayered memorial structure, covered and yet preserved in the form of remains, merges with the theme of crypto-Judaism, mimicry, and the Jewish underground.

In Shrayer-Petrov's short story "White Sheep on a Green Mountain Slope" ("Belye ovtsy na zelenom sklone gory," 2003) the first-person autobiographical narrator visits Azerbaijan. A group of fellow Soviet writers and performers are treated to an elaborate dinner the home of one Suleiman, a local apparatchik, in a mountain village near the border with Daghestan. The dinner conversation compels the narrator to inquire whether the host's family is related to the well-known surgeon Gavriil Ilizarov. After a pause that no one dares to break Suleiman replies that this is not the case because they are Azeris, while Ilizarov is a Mountain Jew. After dinner, Suleiman unexpectedly leads the narrator to a remote room in the cellar, which is located behind several locked doors in a second, concealed underground room. This small space turns out to be a secret oval prayer room with a "small pedestal draped in a white silk cover, which was adorned along the edges with dark stripes and silk tassels, like those of a *tales*. Resting on the cover was a thick opened leather-bound tome with silver clasps. Behind the Book there stood a silver menorah with blown-out candles." Suleiman reveals to the narrator that his family was descended from Mountain Jews and was once forced to convert to Islam. "Но мы все равно остались евреями,"⁵² he states ("But we still remained Jews"⁵³). In the idyllic setting of Suleiman's house, Shrayer-Petrov's narrator envisions poetic landscapes of ancient Canaan from the time of Abraham, believing as he does that "our forefather Abraham sacrificed [the white sheep] to the Almighty so that one day He would reconcile Abraham's two sons, Ishmael and Isaac."⁵⁴

---

52 David Shraer-Petrov, *Karp dlia farshirovannoi ryby. Rasskazy* (Moscow: Raduga, 2005), 297.
53 David Shrayer-Petrov, *Dinner with Stalin and Other Stories*, ed. Maxim D. Shrayer (Syracuse: Syracuse University Press, 2014), 41.
54 Ibid., 45.

Works Cited

Assmann, Jan. *Das kulturelle Gedächtnis. Schrift, Erinnerung und politische Identität in frühen Hochkulturen.* München: Beck, 1992.

Eshel, Amir. "Cosmopolitanism and Searching for the Sacred Space in Jewish Literature." *Jewish Social Studies* 9, no. 3 (2003): 121–138.

Ezrahi, DeKoven Sidra. *Booking Passage. Exile and Homecoming in the Modern Jewish Imagination.* Berkeley: University of California Press, 2000.

Hölscher, Lucian. "Geschichte als 'Erinnerungskultur.'" In *Generation und Gedächtnis. Erinnerungen und kollektive Identitäten*, edited by Kristin Platt and Mihran Dabag, 146–168. Opladen: Springer, 1995.

Shrayer, Maxim D. "About the Text of Doctor Levitin." In David Shrayer-Petrov, *Doctor Levitin: A Novel*, edited and with notes by Maxim D. Shrayer, translated by Arna B. Bronstein, Aleksandra Fleszar, and Maxim D. Shrayer, 277–280. Detroit: Wayne State University Press, 2018.

Shrayer-Petrov, David [David Shraer-Petrov]. *Gerbert i Nelli.* Moskva: Knizhniki, 2014.

———. *Doctor Levitin: A Novel.* Edited and with notes by Maxim D. Shrayer, translated by Arna B. Bronstein, Aleksandra Fleszar, and Maxim D. Shrayer. Detroit: Wayne State University Press, 2018.

Zeller, Ursula. "Between goldene medine and Promised Land: Legitimizing the American Jewish Diaspora." In *Diaspora and Multiculturalism: Common Traditions and New Developments*, edited by M. Fludernik et al., 1–43. Amsterdam: Brill, 2003.

Doctor Levitin by David Shrayer-Petrov and the Theme of Jewish Revenge *

Joshua Rubenstein

Doctor Levitin is the first in David Shrayer-Petrov's trilogy of novels about refuseniks and Jewish emigration to be published in English translation.[1] As I read *Doctor Levitin* and reached its dramatic and violent climax, I understood how much the destruction of Levitin's family by a system he had once benefited from spoke to a long, simmering urge for revenge on his part, a yearning fueled by decades of cruelty and repression. A highly regarded doctor and a professor of medicine, Herbert Anatolyevich Levitin enjoys his career in a prestigious Moscow clinic, treating his patients, attending conferences, studying new areas of medical research in Western scientific journals. But his career and the life of his family are disrupted when they decide to apply for visas to emigrate from the USSR to Israel and then are denied permission—turned into that category of pariahs that came to be called "refuseniks"; he is fired from his job, shunned by friends and longtime colleagues, set loose from the privileges that had once supported the life of his family in the Soviet capital. Slowly, gradually, Doctor Levitin, fueled by one episode after another of betrayal, loss, and grief, finds a rage within

---

* Copyright © 2021 by Joshua Rubenstein.
1 David Shrayer-Petrov, *Doctor Levitin*, ed. and with notes by Maxim D. Shrayer, tr. Arna B. Bronstein, Aleksandra I Fleszar, and Maxim D. Shrayer (Detroit: Wayne State University Press, 2018).

himself, a rage that had once driven him to be much more aggressive as a younger man than the mild-mannered, gifted physician he became (and we initially encounter). As David Shrayer-Petrov emphasizes about his hero, "he was not among the ten bravest to begin with."[2] But by the close of the novel, Doctor Levitin's complacency is destroyed, then overcome by an insistent, violent urge for justice and revenge against an arbitrary and cruel regime. He will avenge the anti-Jewish discrimination directed against him, his family and other refuseniks by targeting at least some of the perpetrators, and demonstrate that a cornered Jew, however outnumbered or seemingly intimidated, has the strength and courage to fight back.

There was, of course, an earlier, historical example of Jewish revenge in Soviet history; that was against the Germans. After the Nazi invasion of Soviet territory on June 22, 1941, which led to devastating defeats of the Red Army and the eventual occupation of an enormous portion of Soviet territory, the Nazi leadership initiated a campaign of mass murder directed against the country's Jews. Between 1941 and 1944, mobile shooting units, joined by police forces and local militias, with the assistance of the Wehrmacht, slaughtered an estimated two and a half million Soviet Jews.[3] Unlike in Western and Eastern Europe, where the victims were taken to killing centers like Auschwitz and Treblinka, here the killers descended on their victims, carrying out open-air massacres in cities and towns throughout the Baltic republics, Ukraine, Belorussia, and Russia itself. Thousands of massacre sites came to disfigure the landscape: at the Ninth Fort outside of Kaunas; at Ponary outside of Vilnius; at Rumbula outside of Riga; at Drobitsky Yar outside of Kharkov; and most famously at Babi Yar on the outskirts of Kiev, to name a handful of the most infamous examples. Like locusts descending on a wheat field, the Nazis rounded up every Jew they could find, then murdered them by firing squad or with mobile gas vans—trucks whose tailpipe vented through the floor into the rear cabin. Only a portion of Jews were shipped off to Poland to be murdered there in death camps. It was not until the Red Army turned back the Wehrmacht at Stalingrad in early 1943 that it began pushing the Germans out of the country, and then finding massacre site after massacre site, liberating Eastern Europe, including concentration and death camps like Majdanek and Auschwitz in Poland, before reaching Berlin itself in May of 1945.

---

2   Ibid., 92.
3   See Yitzhak Arad, *In the Shadow of the Red Banner: Soviet Jews in the War Against Nazi Germany* (New York: Gefen Books, and Jerusalem: Yad Vashem, 2010), 525.

Soviet Jews played a significant role in the defense of their country. There were hundreds of Jewish generals and admirals in Soviet forces. Over 450,000 Jewish soldiers and officers served in the Red Army where they earned a disproportionately high number of medals—as to the Jewish population—for bravery at the front. As many as 150,000 fell in battle or were summarily executed after being captured.

In a turning point of the war, General Friedrich Paulus, who commanded the German 6th Army, surrendered at Stalingrad to Lieutenant Colonel Leonid Vinokur. Vinokur, who was Jewish, was second in command of the 38th Separate Mechanized Brigade of the 64th Army. *Eynikayt* (*Unity*), the Yiddish-language newspaper of the Jewish Anti-Fascist Committee, proudly reported on the encounter between Paulus and Vinokur in the following way:

> At dawn on January 31 . . . Vinokur's soldiers neared the central department store building where the headquarters of the German 6th Army were located, the headquarters of Field Marshal von Paulus. . . . At 6:40 a.m. the department store was surrounded and the brigade command proposed the Germans surrender. . . . Lieutenant Colonel Vinokur went into the basement where the 6th Army headquarters was located, accompanied by Major Yegorov . . . and a few soldiers with submachine guns. The large courtyard was filled with German soldiers and there was a machine gun at every door. Major General Roske [the commander of the surrounded German force, who was in charge of what was left of the German 71st Infantry Division, which defended the army's headquarters] accompanied the Soviet Lieutenant Colonel to a large, semi-dark room, its walls covered with carpets and its floor with cigarette butts and scraps of paper. As soon as they entered, an unshaven man with a gray face rose from a bed lying near the wall and stood up. "Heil," he greeted Vinokur. . . . For a moment they face one another silently, the Soviet officer, Vinokur, the Jewish boy from Odessa, broad-shouldered and strong, and the defeated German Field Marshal in his wrinkled general's uniform. . . . At nine in the morning on January 31, the battles in the center of Stalingrad stopped.[4]

---

4   Cited in Arad, *In the Shadow of the Red Banner*, 59–60. It is a common mistake to refer to him as von Paulus; he was not a member of the German nobility. Hitler had promoted him to the rank of Field Marshal in the final days of the Stalingrad battle with the hope that the promotion would encourage Paulus to commit suicide rather than surrender, as he eventually did.

Two of the most widely followed Soviet wartime journalists were Ilya Ehrenburg and Vasily Grossman, who both wrote for *Krasnaia zvezda* (*Red Star*), the most important newspaper on the Eastern Front because it was the main paper for the Soviet armed forces. They joined their fellow Russian writers, Konstantin Simonov and Aleksey Tolstoy, who were also particularly prominent voices in the Soviet press. But Ehrenburg was the most influential.[5]

Ilya Ehrenburg had a regular column in *Red Star*. Having spent most of his adult life in Western Europe, he had reported on the rise of fascism for the Soviet press, seen the Nazis in Berlin, and witnessed the triumph of Franco's forces in Spain. A convinced anti-Fascist, Ehrenburg understood that the Soviet people were not ready for this conflict, that they believed they were facing another civilized people like themselves, like the Germans they had fought in World War I. Ehrenburg knew better. He knew they were facing Nazis, not civilized Germans, and that in order to defeat them they would have to hate them. In two thousand articles over the course of the war Ehrenburg repeated this theme again and again, urging the troops to hate and to kill. His articles were often read to the troops before battle. They were set to music and sung at concerts in Moscow. Molotov once said that Ehrenburg was worth a division and Hitler promised to hang Ehrenburg in Red Square once he captured the Soviet capital. But if resistance to the invaders was his principal theme, the right of Jews to seek revenge was his second.

As early as August 24, 1941, just two months after the German invasion, Ehrenburg was among a group of leading Jewish cultural figures to call on Jewish communities in the West, primarily in England and the United States, to join the fight against Nazi Germany and specifically to ensure justice for Nazi crimes against the Jews. England was already in the war, but America was still a neutral nation, at least officially. As Ehrenburg defiantly declared,

> I grew up in a Russian city. My mother tongue is Russian. I am a Russian writer. Like all Russians, I am now defending my homeland. But the Hitlerites have reminded me of something else: my mother's name was Hannah. I am a Jew. I say this with pride. Hitler hates us more than anything. And this hate adorns us. . . .

---

5   See Joshua Rubenstein, *Tangled Loyalties: The Life and Times of Ilya Ehrenburg* (Tuscaloosa: University of Alabama Press, 1999).

My country, the Russian people, the people of Pushkin and Tolstoy, are standing up to the challenge. I am now appealing to the Jews of America as a Russian writer and a Jew. There is no ocean to hide behind. Listen to the sound of weapons around Gomel! Listen to the cries of tormented Russian and Jewish women in Berdichev! Do not block up your ears or close your eyes! The voices of Leah from the Ukraine, Rachel from Minsk, Sarah from Belostok [Białystok] will intrude on your still comfortable dreams—they are crying over their children who have been torn to pieces. Jews, wild animals are aiming at you! Our place is in the front line. We will not forgive the indifferent. We curse anyone who washes his hands. Help everyone who is fighting this rabid enemy. To the assistance of England! To the assistance of Soviet Russia! Let each and every one do as much as he can. Soon he will be asked: What did you do? He will have to answer to the living. He will have to answer to the dead. He will have to answer to himself.[6]

As the German offensive continued, turning the Eastern Front into an unimaginable war of attrition, Ehrenburg sensed the necessity to respond to rumors that the Jews were not bearing their share of the fighting, that, as the antisemitic canard expressed it, "Ivan is at the front while the Jews are in Tashkent." Such longstanding prejudice was directed against them, leading Ehrenburg to highlight the heroic actions of several Jewish soldiers in a famous article entitled "Jews" ("Evrei") in *Red Star* on November 1, 1942. The battle of Stalingrad had already begun. Ehrenburg deliberately chose a group of Jewish heroes whose civilian backgrounds seemed to match the stereotype of an enfeebled intellectual:

> Falkovich was over forty. He was a philologist and had spent his life at a desk. Germans lick their lips over such types: catch and hang them. Cut off from his unit, he pulled eighteen soldiers together. They confronted an enemy company. Falkovich ordered: "Attack!" Eighteen brave souls captured thirty-five fritzes. The philologist killed eight Germans with his own hands.[7]

Another, much younger soldier, seventeen-year-old Hayim Dyskin, had been a student of literature in Moscow before the war. He distinguished himself as an artilleryman, destroying tanks at Mozhaysk: "Fourteen

---

6 Tr. Joshua Rubenstein, in *An Anthology of Jewish-Russian Literature: Two Centuries of Dual Identity in Prose and Poetry*, ed. Maxim D. Shrayer (Armonk, NY: M. E. Sharpe, 2007), vol. 1, 532–533. The original appeared in *Izvestia* on August 26, 1941. (tr.)

7 Ibid., 533.

separate wounds on his body, a gold star on the chest of this hero, five disabled German tanks—this is the story of the seventeen-year-old Hayim."[8]

Recounting such bravery, Ehrenburg could not help but invoke Biblical imagery, an unheard-of reference for the Soviet press: "How could we not recall the ancient legend of the giant Goliath and the young David with his sling?" he wrote. "There was a time when the Jews dreamed of the promised land. Now the Jew has a promised land: the front line. There he can take revenge on the Germans for the women, for the elderly, for the children."[9]

Ehrenburg sustained his commitment to writing about Jewish suffering and Jewish heroism throughout the war. He did not let up. In late April 1944 he wrote a startling profile of the Yiddish poet Abram Sutzkever who had survived the Vilna Ghetto and became a leader of a unit of Jewish partisans. "Three hundred Jews in the ghetto obtained weapons. The Germans were blowing up houses with dynamite. The daring three hundred broke out of the ghetto and joined Lithuanian partisans. The poet Sutzkever was among them."[10]

In August, after the liberation of Majdanek outside of Lublin, Ehrenburg wrote the article "On the Eve" ("Nakanune"). Majdanek was first active killing center to be liberated, and its horrors were covered in the Soviet press and then around the world. With Soviet troops approaching German territory, Ehrenburg focused on the fate of the Jews. In his long, angry article published in *Pravda*, Ehrenburg cited town after town, city after city, where Jews had been slaughtered: "It is not revenge that is leading us, but a longing for justice. . . . We want to march through Germany with a sword so that the Germans will never forget their love of a sword. We want to go to them so that they will never again come to us."[11] For Ehrenburg it was not enough to insist that the Germans get the punishment they deserved. With the ultimate victory of the Allies now assured, it was equally important that the Germans understand that they were never again to engulf Europe in war.

To return to Shrayer-Perov's *Doctor Levitin*, this first part of the trilogy was completed in the autumn of 1980 while he was still living as a refusenik in the former USSR. An abridged edition appeared in Israel in 1986, and three complete Russian editions have since appeared in post-Soviet Russia.

---

8   Ibid.
9   Ibid., 533–534.
10 Ibid., 535–538.
11 Erenburg, "Nakanune," *Pravda* August 7, 1944. English translation in Harriet Murav and Gennady Estraikh, eds., *Soviet Jews in World War II: Fighting, Witnessing, Remembering* (Boston: Academic Studies Press, 2014), 50–51.

The publication of the novel's English translation puts it in conversation with two other novels published recently in the United States to recount how Soviet Jews, at least in an imaginary fable, take their revenge against a heartless regime. With the collapse of the Soviet Union and the emigration of over a million Jews to Israel and the West, it is the regime that now appears vulnerable, while the Jews, who were targets of campaign after campaign, managed to escape, then re-established their lives in more democratic societies.

Paul Goldberg (b. 1959) was born and raised in Moscow before immigrating to the United States as a teenager in 1973. After writing two books on the Soviet human rights movement he turned his attention to fiction; his first novel, *The Yid*, appeared in 2016. Set in Moscow in February 1953, during the frightening weeks that followed the announcement of the notorious "doctors' plot"—a contrived medieval-like accusation that Jewish doctors were part of a conspiracy involving imperialists and Zionists to murder Soviet leaders using their medical expertise—the novel plays against the widely believed fear among Soviet Jews that they were to be rounded up and banished, exiled without trial, to Siberia or other remote areas of the vast country. It is a raucous, often hilarious tale of improbable Jewish heroes who decide to put an end to a looming nationwide pogrom against Soviet Jews that Joseph Stalin is planning to carry out.

But the dictator's plan is thwarted when a small gang of unlikely conspirators, including an elderly but nimble actor from the Yiddish theater—Solomon Shimonovich Levinson, a leading Jewish surgeon, an African-American engineer, and a young woman with reasons of her own, band together, inveigle their way into the Kremlin, and kill Stalin himself, putting an end to his murderous plot. Levinson is the story's central figure; we first meet him when three KGB men come to arrest him in his apartment, but before they can take him into custody he dispatches them with a thrust from a concealed sword. Right away, in the opening pages of *The Yid*, we know we are dealing with a tale of Jewish revenge, like the Jewish Red Army men whose stories Ehrenburg celebrated in the official Soviet press, only now they are not directing their fire against marauding Nazis but against their own hardly less menacing political leaders.

The Yid is an entertaining cartoon with a real-life backdrop that every Soviet Jew from that era remembers in her or his bones: the tsunami of antisemitic propaganda in the Soviet press directed against Jewish medical professionals, against Zionism, against the Jewish Joint Distribution

Committee which was said to be at the heart of the "doctors' plot," even against Israeli Prime Minister David Ben-Gurion after an incendiary device was thrown into the grounds of the Soviet legation in Tel Aviv in early February 1953, a provocative action by right-wing Jewish militants meant as a violent protest against the "doctors' plot." The Kremlin blamed the Israeli government and quickly cut off diplomatic relations with the Jewish state. Ben-Gurion was furious, not wanting to disrupt relations with a powerful country where millions of Jews still lived, however precariously. In addition, without a legation of its own in Moscow, Israel would lose its own presence, its own listening post, in the Soviet capital. The bombing which caused property damage and minor injuries to several Soviet personnel, including the wife of the ambassador, was certainly a real-life act of revenge by Jews in Israel but one that left Soviet Jews all the more exposed to the Kremlin's anger. *Pravda* itself invoked its usual, demagogic rhetoric, declaring that "The pack of mad dogs from Tel Aviv is loathsome and vile in its thirst for blood."[12] The incident compounded the Kremlin's fury and the vulnerability of Soviet Jews to official and popular reprisals. But when Stalin suddenly collapsed with a stroke on Sunday, March 1, 1953—coincidentally, on the Jewish holiday of Purim, which commemorates how the Jews of Persia were saved from an evil conniving antisemite, then took revenge on myriad enemies—and died on March 5, the machinery of repression against the Jews, at least at that point of history, came to an abrupt end. *The Yid* imagines another more entertaining and more satisfying conclusion. But it was providence, not the hands of an assassin, that put an end to Stalin's nightmarish reign.

A second, recent novel brings us closer to our historical era. *On the Sickle's Edge* by the American author Neville Frankel (b. 1948) follows three generations of the same family who are trapped in the USSR. The background to the story is loosely based on Frankel's own family history. Like Lena, a central figure in the novel, Frankel was born and raised in South Africa. Frankel immigrated to the United States as a teenager while Lena is taken to Russia before the 1917 revolution by her father only to find herself unable to leave. Lena and other members of the family experience the full brunt of Soviet history, including the dislocations of war and revolution, of violent terror, and the more stable but still repressive atmosphere of

---

12 Iurii Zhukov, "Terroristicheskii akt v Tel´-Avive i fal´shivaia igra pravitelei Izrailia," *Pravda*, February 14, 1953, 4.

the post-Stalin years. Darya, Lena's granddaughter and a true believer in Communism, initially benefits from the system, but she gradually becomes disillusioned with the regime and resentful of a powerful and abusive secret police official, Grigory Yanov, who has taken her as his lover. The novel even imagines the existence of a violence-prone underground resistance movement—a take-off on the Soviet human rights movement—that seeks to attack the regime head-on. Grigory Yanov, it turns out, has one glaring vulnerability: he adores Lena's handmade ice cream even while he is terrorizing her family. In an act of courageous self-defense and revenge Lena prepares a batch especially for him, mixing in a lethal dose of ground glass; as he gorges himself on ice cream he quickly suffers a gruesome death.

Unlike *The Yid* and *On the Sickle's Edge*, *Doctor Levitin* is not a fable or a grotesque cartoon. Shrayer-Petrov's *Doctor Levitin*, which is almost entirely set in Moscow, has a sharp focus on one family and its tragic fate. When we meet Doctor Herbert Anatolyevich Levitin at the outset of the novel, we are told that "restraint was perhaps Herbert Anatolyevich's main character trait."[13] Experienced, mature, confident in his abilities, he enjoys his work as a clinician and a researcher. But as the novel progresses, we learn with some surprise that unlike Doctor Levitin, his creator was not always so mild-mannered.

As if to prepare us for what is to come, the authorial narrator recounts in one of the novel's autobiographical digressions that as he reached puberty in postwar Leningrad he grew increasingly self-conscious of his Jewish origins, convinced that he was beginning "to look more and more Jewish":

> I began to take heed of casual conversations: in school, in a tram, in a store. Even a slight allusion to my non-Russian lineage wounded my self-esteem. I was taking on the role of the persecuted. . . . Together with my friend, the illegitimate son of a Jewish man and a Russian village girl, who had come to Leningrad from the Luga region before the war to find work, we scoured the outlying streets and decaying parks of the Vyborg Side. We craved fistfights, so that the pain and the blood would wash away the shame of our torturous otherness. We feared no one. . . . Yet little by little, everything fell into place. The other kids around us no longer talked about our Jewishness. We had scorched that pestilence out of our land. And we began to forget old wrongs.[14]

---

13 Shrayer-Petrov, *Doctor Levitin*, 48.
14 Ibid., 83.

More adventures are still to come in the authorial digressions, which prepare the reader for the transformation of Doctor Levitin into a Jewish avenger. As a seventh or eighth grader he attends a dance with his friends and they are quickly drawn to one girl in particular. But though the author's young self dances with her and feels confident about their mutual liking for each other, another boy, Soplov, the son of a party official, attempts to coerce her attention. "It was dangerous to turn down that fellow," the author remembers. "They say that he never turned up at parties without his blade."[15] But that did not deter the author's young self:

> "Get lost!" I said, quickly and rudely, and my friend nodded in support of my words. Soplov, of course, knew us both, knew of our reputations as reckless fighters and truth-seekers; he knew that many charges had been filed against us at the juvy hall of the local police precinct, and also that we never turned away from an honest fight. But the girl was so wonderful; she looked with such great interest at the boys ready to rip each other apart for her, so that for Soplov to step away, to chicken out, would mean to lose her forever. He was used to never losing anything.
>
> "Take a hike, the both of you, right to your native Palestine," Soplov said loudly, and continued to hold our girl's hand tightly. In those days of the British Mandate, they called Jews "Palestinians" as an insult. We both hit Soplov at the same time. I punched him in his right eye, right in the corner where the tear duct showed its scarlet flesh. My friend hit his left jaw, which was still slightly open, as the last sounds of Soplov's loathsome words slid out with poisonous saliva. We saw Soplov crashing, but just before he hit the ground, blood gushed out of his mouth.

The young author and his friend make a quick get-away with the help of relatives and neighbors who lie to the police about their whereabouts as the boys flee Leningrad on an early morning train. This serves as a culminating incident of his growing up in Leningrad during the late Stalin years. "One could write a whole book," he recounts, "a story of offenses large and small, inflicted deliberately or by accident—by people we had not been acquainted with or by supposed friends—at work, at the stadium, in the metro or during a dinner party. You do not get used to discrimination, the way a Negro cannot get used to the black shell given to him by God,

---

15 Ibid., 85.

as punishment for some unknown, nonexistent transgressions."[16] And the author of *Doctor Levitin* does not become inured to such incidents. Soviet life has its own way of continuing to slap him in the face, especially after he and his family applied for exit visas to Israel and became refuseniks.

Through the authorial reflections on antisemitism and the position of Jews in Soviet society, Shrayer-Petrov infuses the novel with autobiographical references. The autobiographical narrative quickly brings us to another dramatic incident; the author has graduated from medical school and is now finishing mandatory service in the army. He is a lieutenant in the medical corps on military exercises in Belarus. Invited to go hunting for starlings with other officers, they together bag dozens of small birds, collect them off the fields, then bring them back to camp where a military cook, a fellow drafted from a small town outside Vinnitsa, in Ukraine, prepared the carcasses in a stew with lots of potatoes. The cook was "terribly shy by nature, and his shyness was exacerbated by the fact that he grunted his *r*'s, misrolling them in the manner associated with a 'Jewish accent,' and lisped on almost all the Russian consonants." In short, a vulnerable Jew whose verbal tics make him all the more prone to ridicule if not abuse. Another officer soon takes offense at his cooking, blaming the Jewish cook for a carcass in the stew whose feathers had not been sufficiently plucked. Holding out the offending bird, the officer berates the cook. "So, you little bastard, this is how you decided to make fools of Russian officers?" "Fohgive me, comhade senioh lieutenant," uttered the terrified cook, stepping back.

Before the others could react the officer "skewered the ill-starred starling [on an iron rod] and smeared it across the soldier's face." "You dirty kike," he shouted at him. "I'll show you how to mock a Russian officer."

The young Jewish lieutenant barely hesitates:

> It was either run away into the forest, to the river, throw myself under a train barreling in the distance. Or take revenge. I ripped the iron rod out of the hand of the HQ lieutenant. I hit him in the solar plexus with my left hand, and when he doubled over and turned up his face with its pencil thin mustache, his mouth contorted with rage and pain, I slashed him across the cheek with the rod, the way Cossacks during the pogroms used to slash defenseless Jews with their sabers and ramrods, the way his own grandfathers slashed unarmed students and workers.

---

16 Ibid., 86.

"You want a court marshal? [sic] You defender of Jews?" wheezed the HQ guy, hunched over, clutching the deep wound on his cheek.

But for some reason the affair was hushed up, and soon I was honorably discharged to the reserves.[17]

The authorial narrator's willingness to act without restraint in such private encounters contrasts with a time when he was still living at home with his parents during the frightening weeks of the "doctors' plot" in early 1953. He is a senior in high school when a teacher reads aloud an anti-Jewish article from the official press, the kind of article that was designed to provoke hatred in the broader population and fear among the Jews. The young narrator is in no mood to object, to fight back:

> I sat there curled up into a ball from insult and shame, and from not knowing what to do. Mother made me promise that I wouldn't utter a sound, no matter what they said in front of me about Jews. She was afraid for me; I had the reputation of a brazen fighter. But I had promised mother I would be silent, and silent I was. . . . I kept silent because our lives were hanging in the balance; I was graduating from high school and applying to university.[18]

Even at home, in the communal kitchen they share with other families, they are subjected to casual abuse. A neighbor, a retired school teacher who had distinguished herself in the war, feels perfectly comfortable uttering "I wish they'd exile all these Jews to Birobidzhan soon," as she stirs a pot of soup. "I was silent, because mother bit her pillow at night, so I wouldn't hear her sobs. We were both silent, as were all other Soviet Jews in those days."[19] But then Stalin suddenly collapses on March 1, then dies on March 5. Whatever he was planning as the culminating act of the "doctors' plot" died with him. Within a month Stalin's heirs publicly disavowed the entire conspiracy, released the doctors, and blamed a high-ranking security official for the whole rotten business.[20] Inspired, Shrayer-Petrov's authorial narrator decides then and there to become a doctor, a gesture of solidarity and defiance. Many other young Jews his age made the same choice at the

---

17 Ibid., 88–89.
18 Ibid., 128.
19 Ibid., 129.
20 See Joshua Rubenstein, *The Last Days of Stalin* (New Haven: Yale University Press, 2017).

time, and the decision to become a physician connects the real Doctor Shrayer-Petrov to the fictional Doctor Levitin.

The travails that engulf Herbert and his family actually begin before they apply for exit visas. His son, Anatoly, dreams of following his father into medicine. Even though he is an accomplished student, the examiners for his medical school entrance examination trip him up and give him far lower than the grade he deserves—as they do with other Jewish students—compelling him to attend a far-less-desirable evening program. Herbert's wife, Tatyana, is not Jewish, which makes it possible for their son to be listed as "Russian" on his internal passport, a not altogether successful way to mask his Jewish origins and avoid discrimination. Soon after, under acute nervous strain, Anatoly suffers a breakdown.

The family's decision to seek an exit visa precipitates a series of disasters: Doctor Levitin has to tell the chair of his department, Professor Baronov, a Soviet apparatchik with a KGB past, about his plans. Baronov quickly denounces him with a tirade of antisemitic invective: "Didn't you have everything here? . . . What sheer ingratitude. Actually, what else could one expect from your kind." Levitin remains calm, "trying not to scream from anger, insult, humiliation." But his boss cannot restrain himself. "You're nothing but a typical ungrateful Jew, who was given everything here: education, respect, ideas. Even your wife you got from Russia, and now you spit on that which is most holy!"[21]

From then on Doctor Levitin, like the biblical Job, endures one disaster after another: Tatyana's father, who lives with them, collapses and dies after a frustrating encounter with a Soviet bureaucrat; Anatoly is kicked out of medical school, making him liable for the draft at a time when Soviet soldiers are bogged down in a hopeless war in Afghanistan; Anatoly is eventually drafted and Tatyana, out of desperation to save her son, calls on an old flame from her youth, Pavel Teryokhin, an officer who works on the draft board; Tatyana gives herself to him, an act of intimacy and betrayal with the hope that Pavel will intervene to spare Anatoly. But Pavel, too, like Herbert Anatolyevich's boss, ends up angry with Tatyana for not telling him they were refuseniks, leaving him vulnerable in his own office when he tried to help Anatoly only to learn the full truth of their situation. For many of the ethnic Russians in *Doctor Levitin*, when they face an uncertain

---

21 Ibid., 52.

situation involving a Jew, their instinct is to lash out with ugly words and phrases:

> You were afraid for your kike, worried sick for your little kikeling, and you used me like small change. And I . . . I could've ruined my whole life because of you. And still there's no telling how this will all end for me and for my family. You know whom I went to see about your son? Do you know what they told me there? Do you have any idea what I had to do so they would forget I ever asked? You . . . you hid your dirty Jewish tricks from me.[22]

Herbert Anatolyevich cannot and will not take it any longer. His son and wife both gone, he abandons all moral restraint and turns into a cold-hearted killing machine. His first victim is Tatyana's old flame, Pavel Teryokhin himself, whom Doctor Levitin blames for not having prevented the dispatching of his son Anatoly to Afghanistan. Following Anatoly's death and Tatyana's subsequent death out of grief for her son, Doctor Levitin invites Teryokhin to a wake on a late afternoon, an encounter that concludes with Herbert Anatolyevich planting a fatal dose of poison in Pavel's glass. Reading this passage I could not help but think of the "doctors' plot" when the Kremlin falsely accused Jewish doctors of conspiring to murder Soviet leaders using their medical expertise. Mocking this medieval claim, Shrayer-Petrov throws the accusation back at his readers, as if to say that "there was no Jewish conspiracy against Soviet power, but don't think, dear reader, that we did not dream of such a thing for our enemies. For good measure here is what it could have looked like!"

But Doctor Levitin is nowhere near done. Earlier in the novel, he had faced dispiriting encounters with two women: an abrupt bureaucrat at OVIR, the notorious visa section where Herbert Anatolyevich, like many Soviet Jews in real life, including our author David Shrayer-Petrov and his family, learned they were not being allowed to leave and became refuseniks, and a second, equally cold-hearted clerk who handles prescriptions at a nearby homeopathic pharmacy. For Doctor Levitin these two predatory vultures, whose voluminous files, full of information about the lives of Soviet Jews, have come to symbolize the life or death fate of thousands, are now the closest he can come to destroying a hateful regime. The two women overlap in Doctor Levitin's imagination, transmogrified into the vicious old Owl who controls the lives of Jewish refuseniks. When Doctor

---

22 Ibid., 246.

Levitin thinks to attack the first ominous old woman but finds her office closed, he quickly sets off to kill the second, destroying her and her hated card file in a fire of vengeance that also burns him beyond recognition. Like the Biblical Samson, Doctor Levitin can only destroy the pillars of a corrupt temple by sacrificing himself.

Works Cited

Arad, Yitzhak. *In the Shadow of the Red Banner: Soviet Jews in the War Against Nazi Germany*. New York: Gefen Books; Jerusalem: Yad Vashem, 2010.

Erenburg, Il'ia. "Evrei." *Krasnaia zvezda* November 1, 1942.

———."Nakanune." *Pravda* August 7, 1944.

Murav, Harriet, and Gennady Estraikh, eds. *Soviet Jews in World War II: Fighting, Witnessing, Remembering*. Boston: Academic Studies Press, 2014.

Rubenstein, Joshua. *Tangled Loyalties: The Life and Times of Ilya Ehrenburg*. Tuscaloosa: University of Alabama Press, 1999.

———. *The Last Days of Stalin*. New Haven: Yale University Press, 2017.

Shrayer, Maxim D., ed. *An Anthology of Jewish-Russian Literature: Two Centuries of Dual Identity in Prose and* Poetry. 1801-2001. 2 vols. Armonk, NY: M. E. Sharpe, 2007.

Shrayer-Petrov, David. *Doctor Levitin*. Edited and with notes by Maxim D. Shrayer, translated by Arna B. Bronstein, Aleksandra I. Fleszar, and Maxim D. Shrayer. Detroit: Wayne State University Press, 2018.

Zhukov, Iurii. "Terroristicheskii akt v Tel´-Avive i fal´shivaia igra pravitelei Izrailia." *Pravda*, February 14, 1953, 4.

On Literary Tradition and Literary Authority in David Shrayer-Petrov's *Doctor Levitin* *

Brian Horowitz

Readers of *Doctor Levitin*, the first in David Shrayer-Petrov's trilogy of novels about refuseniks, must inevitably come to the conclusion that, despite the author's affiliation with nonconformist literature, this particular novel is saturated with the Russian literary tradition and Russian-Jewish culture.[1] Although nonconformist has many dimensions, it requires a demarcation: the nonconformity declares his/her rejection of official literature and adopts an alternative literary identity, including alternative literary predecessors and influences. Despite what we might expect from the nonconformist (one thinks of him/her as avant-garde or experimental—or else ideologically or spiritually subversive), this novel has a tonality that links it to two essentially conservative traditions: the great Russian literary tradition of the nineteenth century and the Russian-Jewish

---

* Copyright © 2021 by Brian Horowitz. An early version of this paper was read at Refusenik Literature: A Symposium at Boston College, April 16, 2019, https://www.bc.edu/content/dam/files/schools/cas_sites/slavic_eastern/pdf/RefusenikSymposiumProgram2019LetterSize.pdf.

1 On David Petrov-Shrayer and nonconformism, see Roman Katsman, "Parallel´nye vselennye Davida Shraera-Petrova," *Wiener Slawistischer Almanach* 79 (2017): 255–256.

cultural tradition. Therefore, rather than throwing tradition off the ship, as Vladimir Mayakovsky proclaimed, Shrayer-Petrov clings to and utilizes literary norms of high Russian culture as a plot tool and a means of expression and characterization. The voice of the narrator, who often (in and outside the authorial digressions) sounds similar to his main protagonist, Doctor Herbert Levitin, reflects a language and culture of discernment, intelligence, honor, and tradition. The novel features a personal tragedy at its core (the death of Levitin's son and wife and Levitin's own self-sacrificial vengeance), but the tragedy is also ideological—culture cannot survive in a world to which it is alien.

"Nonconformist" in Soviet parlance has a specific meaning that should not be conflated with a particular mode of writing.[2] Indeed, *Doctor Levitin* is traditional in many respects. For example, not only does the narrator at times use Herbert Levitin's voice (the deployment of *erlebte Rede*); the narrator also sounds like the novel's protagonist Doctor Levitin: a middle-aged, picture-perfect Russian *intelligent*, whose values resemble those of Russia's literary tradition with its emphasis on truth and justice, the betterment of mankind, and its valorization of culture. The novel also looks to the Russian classical tradition on the subject of family, love, the role of the state, and the Jewish question. It also treats the subject of literary doubles—so famously portrayed by Golyadkin in Fyodor Dostoevsky's *The Double*—and thereby raises questions about the relation of art to life.

At the same time, composed for the desk drawer in 1979–1980, as Shrayer-Petrov became a refusenik and banished Soviet academic and writer, *Doctor Levitin* is a novel of its time, and encapsulates aspects of that historical moment.[3] The plot takes a happy man, Herbert Anatolyevich Levitin, a Jewish intellectual, a doctor and professor, middle-aged, who, as the story begins, is at point A. Doctor Levitin will arrive at point B much changed.[4] He will come to realize that his brilliance, erudition, and diligence give him little advantage in the game of emigration from Soviet Russia.

---

2 Ibid., 255.
3 Maxim D. Shrayer describes the trajectory of his father's biography in "Afterword: Voices of My Father's Exile," in David Shrayer-Petrov, *Autumn in Yalta: A Novel and Three Stories*, ed., co-tr., and with an afterword by Maxim D. Shrayer, Library of Modern Jewish Literature (Syracuse: Syracuse University Press, 2006), 206–229; See also Maxim D. Shrayer's essay in this volume.
4 For classic narratological theory of the plot, see Vladimir Propp, *Morphology of the Folktale* (Austin, TX: University of Texas Press, 1958). Propp's study was originally published in Russian in 1928.

Once Doctor Levitin announces his desire to leave, he and his family will be vulnerable in ways he had not expected or calculated.

What is life in Moscow like in the late 1970s? Despite what Americans believe, in many cases the Homo Sovieticus was not unhappy. He or she had things many of us lack here in the "West": Herbert Anatolyevich had a good creative job, a fine apartment in the capital city, a beautiful and loving wife, Tatyana, and a healthy and talented son, Anatoly. However, the author predicts the coming storm:

> Moscow Jews had already been awakened by the wave of Jewish emigration rolling in from the provinces, yet this ever-growing wave had somehow bypassed Doctor Levitin and his family. They had a good enough life, and Doctor Levitin rejected the herd mentality both in social and scientific affairs.[5]

What would motivate the man who does not bend easily to the crowd? Ostensibly he wants to save his son from the draft and the prospect of fighting in Afghanistan and dying a meaningless death. But in time, the reader understands that there is more to it; Herbert Anatolyevich cannot exist without individual dignity—ethnic, professional, spiritual, and that is a rare commodity in Soviet Russia.

The novel begins in medias res in 1979. We might stop to remember that Jews and Russia did not meet for the first time that year, but had had a long and painful history (from the Jewish side, at least). Despite fearful precedents, the late Brezhnev era appears prosaic. Antisemitism, both state-sponsored and popular, is real, but one can navigate it. Earlier repressions in Budapest and Prague repel any humanist, but perhaps the Soviet Union does a measure of social and educational good—even if at a price to itself and the countries within its sphere of influence—in Cuba, Africa, and parts of Asia. The quotidian is not all bad; there is basic food in the stores of the Soviet capital, cosmonauts on rockets, and while Moscow cannot afford a Paris lifestyle, it beats Khabarovsk by a long shot.

Humiliation plays a large role in the plot's dynamic. The Levitins are insulted that they lack the connections ("протекция"; "блат") first to

---

5 David Shrayer-Petrov, *Doctor Levitin: A Novel*, ed. and with notes by Maxim D. Shrayer, tr. Arna B. Bronstein, Aleksandra I. Fleszar, and Maxim D. Shrayer (Detroit: Wayne State University Press, 2018), 2. The original Russian first edition was published in 1986 in Israel in abridged form; three complete editions have since been published in Russia, most recently in 2014.

ensure that their half-Jewish son is admitted to the day college at the medical school where Doctor Levitin is a full professor—which, in turn, would ensure an exemption from active duty as a soldier. Pride might be unintelligible to many of their fellow Soviets, but to the Levitins, husband and wife, it is completely clear; they feel entirely middle-class. If the state wants use of their valuable talents, it must provide concrete evidence, such as exempting their son from the draft or at least from being sent to the slaughter. Attempts to save their son from military duty will complicate the plot and drive a huge wedge between Doctor Levitin and his attachment to Russia.

The desire to free one's scion from military service does not in itself constitute anti-Soviet or even anti-patriotic activity. The Levitins were members of the academic establishment, members of which had their own conceptions of what privileges they should have. Of course, the quantity and quality of these privileges cannot be calculated on an absolute measure, but rather in comparative terms; in comparison with party elites and moneyed Soviet folks able to bribe officials. In the novel the Levitins hope that they will manage to free their son of military service; they have a number of options to get their way, although, admittedly, some lower them to depravity (Doctor Levitin's wife sleeping with an ex-boyfriend).

To define the Levitins' ideological allegiance, one might hedge and say that the desire to avoid military service reflects, at minimum, an ideological skepticism; Levitin does not feel himself obligated to fulfill every collective demand, especially one as useless as being drafted and fighting in Afghanistan for dubious advantages to the Soviet state. So even before any refusenik scandals arise, the Levitins are potentially subversive in the way that an urban intellectual under certain circumstances can turn anti-Soviet.

Additional complications arise from Doctor Levitin's Jewish background. Thanks in part to the pressure exerted on the USSR under the terms of the Jackson-Vanik Amendment of 1974,[6] large numbers of Jews could leave the Soviet Union in the 1970s. And yet Herbert Anatolyevich Levitin still feels himself foreign to others who flash their Jewish identity. The author contrasts Doctor Levitin to the sternly religious Jew from

---

6 See William E. Pomeranz, "Legacy and Consequences of Jackson-Vanik: Reassessing Human Rigbhts in 21st Century Russia," Kennan Institute, Wilson Center Publication. https://www.wilsoncenter.org/publication/the-legacy-and-consequences-jackson-vanik-reassessing-human-rights-21st-century-russia-0, accessed February 23, 2020. For more information on the Jewish emigration from the USSR, see in Maxim D. Shrayer's notes to the English translation of *Doctor Levitin*.

Tashkent and the maniacal Zionist from Berdichev. The Moscow doctor does not wear his Jewish background on his sleeve. Prior to becoming a refusenik, such "Jewish" Jews appear to Doctor Levitin as too traditionally Jewish—perhaps as uncouth, uncultured, and unsuccessful in their careers.

On the surface, Doctor Levitin's Jewish identity at the start of the novel seems "thin," in the definition of Zvi Gitelman, who performs a dichotomy between Jews who observe religion and maintain social practice and those who do so less or not at all.[7] After all, Doctor Levitin is a cosmopolitan. His wife, Tatyana, is ethnically Russian and comes from a village in the Pskov Province, and their son, born of a non-Jewish mother, is Halachically not Jewish. In any case, Doctor Levitin is a university man, a doctor of medicine; he likely scoffs at belief in a personal divinity. He is loyal above all to knowledge, reason, and hard work. His ideals—justice, free expression, talent, and tolerance—might seem Jewish, but are they not the ordinary values of the urban intelligentsia in any Western democracy? However, the rules on emigration do not make judgments on beliefs, but only on ethnicity, following the Soviet decision of an earlier aspect to include the so-called "пятый пункт" ("fifth line" in a Soviet passport, reserved for indicating ethnicity—"nationality" in Soviet parlance). If it says "еврей" (ethnic Jew in Soviet terms), that person has the right to emigrate, full stop. A multitude of issues related to those who hid their Jewish ethnicity could be discussed, the many problems caused by both concealments and misrepresentation in passports are displayed in the novel. However, the content of Jewishness, a huge theme in the novel, is admittedly given dramatic depiction rather than a dictionary definition.

The Jewish theme is further complicated by the fact that the author depicts Doctor Levitin as a Russified Jew. One should note that "Jew" and "Russian" are hardly polar opposites. Levitin speaks and uses high standard literary Russian, which portrays him as a man of culture. The overlapping and intersecting attributes of Soviet and Russian complicates any transparent definition of identity. However, one should acknowledge that by 1980, many Jews in the Soviet Union were either fully assimilated or well on their way. They identified themselves as Russian, and felt themselves to be Russian. The author, Dr. Shrayer-Petrov, uncannily expressed the same sentiment in the epigraph to the novel: "We know we are Russians; You

---

7   Zvi Gitelman, "The Decline of the Diaspora Jewish Nation: Boundaries, Content, and Jewish Identity," *Jewish Social Studies* 4, no. 2 (Winter 1998): 112–132.

consider us Jews."[8] That the Jew often played the role of loyal patriot in European empires—in contrast to the role of minority in a nation-state—is well documented in the scholarly literature.[9] In the novel the authorial narrator (in his digressions) and Hebert Anatolyevich, the protagonist, reflect pensively on this Jew, Herbert Levitin's, love for Russia:

> But most of all he loved simple peasants and dignified retirement-age workers, particularly those that came from afar, where the dialect was different than in Moscow. A Jew himself, he didn't spend too much time in the Jewish milieu. He loved the Russian peasants for their patience and lack of affectation, and also for their tolerance of human frailties. He loved their speech that flowed like rivers through a valley—slow sinuous, and penetrating to the depths of your soul. That peasant Russian speech is fitted with a multitude of interjections, epithets, prefixes and suffixes, which, like an oven fork, flip a word or a phrase to make the meaning and feeling shine ever more brightly.[10]

The Russians in Shrayer-Petrov's refusenik novel, who are they? Hardly monolithic, they range from the feckless professor-boss-functionary in the medical school, to the surly officials in OVIR (Section of Visas and Registrations), to the rude KGB officers who come with unpleasant truths. Doctor Levitin's department chair, Ivan Ivanovich Baronov, hardly a *baron*, a bureaucrat who is indifferent to science, gets into a heated argument with Levitin and asks the practical, painful questions: "You will not get the required letter for the Visa Section until you resign—that's one. Put that in your Jewish pipe and smoke it. And here's one more thing: your son will be kicked out of the medical school right after winter finals. We'll make sure of that. Have you weighed all the consequences, Levitin?"[11] There are other Russians, too. Tatyana's former boyfriend takes advantage of her desire to save her son and to reconnect with her Russian native village past. However, the author draws Tatyana as a polyvalent figure who fails morally because her emotional health has broken down after the family's application is refused. In a word, she is portrayed as a pained victim rather than a malevolent actor.

---

8   Shrayer-Petrov, *Doctor Levitin*, 8.
9   See Marsha Rozenblit, *The Jews of Vienna, 1867–1914: Assimilation and Identity* (New York: SUNY Press, 1984), 85-104.
10 Shrayer-Petrov, *Doctor Levitin*, 30.
11 Ibid., 54.

Returning to our analysis of the plot, we might think we know how the story will end in a traditional novel—refuseniks experience many surprises, but few details matter in comparison with the final result. Some Jews are permitted to leave, but for many others it is shades of bad, worse, and still worse. There is no middle ground—to apply for an exit visa, one must entirely cut oneself off. A formerly "normal" life inevitably turns into a prison, as real life is elsewhere, and one cannot reach that place. Shrayer-Petrov depicts that new consciousness with great precision; instead of an explanation, one feels the absence of one. Consider the scene of the final meeting with colleagues at the Levitin home; Levitin's Jewishness or otherness is poignantly felt, and the Russian language as it was formerly used is no longer serviceable:

> They sat there for a little bit longer. Some sort of a spring that had previously held together their relationship had snapped. Now, neither shared academic interests nor a table set for a celebration could hold them together. That's why in the hallway they were talking in a forced, unnatural way, as though they were escorting their guests out, rather than seeing them off. This unnaturalness was totally natural; that is, it was at the very core of the Levitin family predicament and Herbert Anatolyevich's colleagues saw it and weren't upset with him. Herbert Anatolyevich stood there lost in his thoughts, saying goodbye to Semyon Antipov and to Alik Volkovich, telling them they should come again, without waiting for special invitations, and they promised to stop by soon and kissed him goodbye, and through all this they understood that if there should be an occasion to see each other, it would be an unusual occasion, a difficult one, because the normal, natural course of life was forever taking them in different directions.[12]

The break with colleagues is the first step that begins the path to catastrophe.

Much of the novel is about the descent from the ordinary into a world for which the refuseniks were unprepared. Doctor Levitin never contemplated what it would mean to focus all his energies into a single battle with the state. In time, he is beaten into despair. Shrayer-Petrov conveys the pain that resides in his protagonist's cranium:

> This appeals office was, as Herbert Anatolyevich reckoned, the last available option, the final line, a dead zone separating the real life for which he had

---

12 Ibid., 139.

prepared himself as well as he knew how, and a life controlled by dark, otherworldly powers. [. . .] Feeling totally crushed, Herbert Anatolyevich sat there for another two or three hours, talking to no one and taking no interest in what Dudko and Anishkina said to those who already had their interviews. He had come to a final realization that one could draw no analogies and find no common patterns between so-called real life and the will of dark secret powers. This had nothing to do with laws of natural sciences or social sciences; no cruel truth of logic here, nor crafty truth of philosophy. Even religiosity—a belief in the supernatural, idealism and pantheism as its extreme version representing an indifference to the individual fates of the human species—any forms of worshiping of a unified idea were alien and foreign to this bacchanalia of principles and deeds. Even the implacable doctrine of monotheism or the childish nimbleness of pagan beliefs was closer to the human soul, and at least erected temples for communicating with the gods. None of this could be in any way compared to the surrogates of ethnics, law and justice, created in the image of the appeals office.[13]

This passage—a litany of exotic belief systems, a mosaic of considerations, speculations, and thoughts—provides no framework for understanding. The history of philosophy and religion exemplify humanity's collective wisdom in the face of the unknowable. And yet these and other attempts to overcome suffering, the best that humanity has designed, are unequal to the task. The author's inference here is that the Soviet bureaucracy in its own unique field surpasses the philosophers; it has perfected a process for destroying a human being.

The author shows how the Soviet authorities practiced their craft of oppression. When a chance misspelling or misconstrued document causes the rejection of a visa, the wisdom of the centuries evaporates. However, the absence of practical logic also transforms Doctor Levitin. He forgets himself and becomes one with hundreds of other Soviet Jews waiting endlessly in and outside state offices, ostensibly to appeal the latest rejection of their applications, but some of them, perhaps, to ask for absolution or some other act of flagellation.

Shrayer-Petrov dispenses pearls of life wisdom, including the adage that no matter how little remains, there is always something more to lose. A large part of the novel is devoted to building up the love story of Anatoly, Levitin's son, and his girlfriend, Natasha Leyn, also a child of an ethnic Russian

---

13 Ibid., 223–224.

mother and a Jewish father. Their love exists to be shattered, and the Levitin family must face destruction. How does it happen? Tatyana, Levitin's wife, will betray him by sleeping with her old village sweetheart, who gave her hope—false yet soothing—that he could save Anatoly from military service. In a phantasmagoric finale, Levitin himself attempts revenge. (About Jewish revenge, see Joshua Rubenstein's essay in this volume.)

Having examined that scaffolding of the novel, I suggest a turn to the relationship of this work to the Russian literary tradition with an accent on genre, ideology, and language.

* * *

Is there a genre called the "refusenik novel" with its own genre conventions? Maybe. *Doctor Levitin* has three endings. One is Levitin's demise. Levitin starts a fire by throwing petrol on an old woman clerk at the OVIR office and her thousands of files and settling them ablaze. The narrator remarks, "Herbert Anatolyvich's last sensation was the joy of revenge."[14] In other words, he assassinated an enemy of Jewish refuseniks but also extinguished himself. Another ending is the demise of the family. Shrayer-Petrov draws on Psalm 22: "Dogs surround me; a pack of evil ones closes in on me,/ like lions they maul my hands and feet."[15] The second ending mocks Doctor Levitin and his fate. His son's girlfriend, Natasha, pregnant with Anatoly's baby, agrees to marry an older man, an American Jewish academic, Stanley Fisher. She alone gets to leave Russia for good:

> Stanley Fisher was returning home to the United States with his young wife. The customs officers treated Natasha with utmost politeness, and her filled-out figure even freed her from a private examination in a gynecology chair. Stanley was a bit nervous, which was totally understandable, if we recall all the events of this most difficult year. There were plenty of reasons for worry up until the moment they announced boarding. Then, for the last time, Natasha turned to look at her parents and followed her husband onto the airplane.[16]

This last ending, which promises a future life in the USA for at least one character, is deeply ironic. Perhaps it is more ironic than the previous

---

14 Ibid., 274.
15 Ibid.
16 Ibid., 274–275.

example of personal apocalypse because in fact Natasha represents success. She is bringing Anatoly's baby to the United States, and the Levitin DNA will survive in the land of liberty; there will be more Levitins, albeit with the name Fisher. What's really important, the DNA or the child's name? However, the irony is not only the dissolution of the Levitin family, the death of Anatoly, Tatyana, and Doctor Levitin himself, all of whom will never see Natasha's baby. The ultimate irony is that Natasha, who comes from a family of official Soviet intelligentsia, emigrates and it has little to do with Jewish identity or Soviet-American politics. She succeeds thanks exclusively to the well-worn but much simpler method of improving one's lot: a marriage of convenience.

Is there a close relationship between Shrayer-Petrov's novel and other nonconformist works? Here I hesitate. Maxim D. Shrayer, the author's son and a literary scholar, doubts that a strong case can be made that *Doctor Levitin* is genetically related to other works of émigré and nonconformist Russian literature.[17] *Doctor Levitin* has the most in common with classical Russian literature and twentieth-century Russian novels inspired by the classics. For example, if the title includes "doctor" and is set in the Soviet period, a comparison with *Doctor Zhivago* is perhaps unavoidable. Themes of individuality and dignity undergird both novels. In both works, the doctor protagonists are at odds with their epoch and the repressive state because their values reflect bourgeois humanism. However, the last name of Yuri Zhivago associates Pasternak's protagonist not merely with the root *zhi-* and its derivatives "жив"; "жизнь" ("live"; "life") but more specifically with "[…] Христос, сын Бога Живаго" ("[…] Christ, the son of the living God," see Matthew 16:16 and John 6:69), while Levitin's last name comes from Levi(te) and marks him as a Jew and a Judean.

If there is any book in the Soviet repertoire, to which *Doctor Levitin* reveals a kinship, it is likely to be Vasily Grossman's *Life and Fate* (*Zhizn' i sud'ba*), where the protagonist, Viktor Strum, debates with himself and others what it means to be a Soviet Jew.[18] Like Levitin, Strum is a Jew of talent, a scientist, who until the end is unsure whether he will get full credit

---

17 Shrayer, "Afterword," 224–225.
18 For additional information on Shrayer-Petrov's view of Grossman as a Jewish writer, see Maxim D. Shrayer and David Shrayer-Petrov, "A Fictional Model of the Former USSR: Part 1 of a 3Part Conversation," Jewish Book Council, https://www.jewishbookcouncil.org/pb-daily/a-fictional-model-of-the-former-ussr-part-1-of-a-3-part-conversation, accessed June 20, 2020.

for his contributions to the war effort. *Life and Fate*, much like *Doctor Levitin*, is a meditation on the place of the Jew in Soviet-Russian society and the alternating feelings of appreciation and rejection experienced by a member of the scientific profession.

Shrayer-Petrov uses descriptive Jewish markers to endow the protagonist with identity. The author describes Doctor Levitin when Anatoly comes to share that he has been drafted into the army and his girlfriend is pregnant: "Anatoly came home and immediately went to see his father. Herbert Anatolyevich, who had lost more weight and become even more stooped, was sitting over his books with the look of tsaddik withdrawn from this world."[19] Misery makes Doctor Levitin appear more Jewish. The narrator's own Jewish identity is further underscored in the next paragraph:

> When the Germans broke into the house of my maternal grandfather, an old rabbi, he was reading the sacred books, a tallis draped over his shoulders, swaying and rocking, like a Bedouin nomad between a camel's humps. A Bedouin nomad reading a sacred book of the desert with verses of the oases, rhythms of water springs, and refrains of sand dunes. The Germans shot the old rabbi, and stomped on and burned the sacred books.[20]

Shrayer-Petrov employs *erlebte Rede* in which it is hard to tell whose speech is present (the narrator is speaking, but it also feels like Levitin's own voice); the Holocaust story underscores the Jewish feeling of the book while also highlighting a larger historical context for the refusenik experience.[21]

Part of the novel's message is to examine the change that goes through the Jewish-Russian relationship at a time of the exodus of Jews from the USSR. One perceives the turn from a desire to integrate into Soviet society to demands for exodus. One might presume that such a change would transform a person. However, Doctor Levitin is not transformed in his soul (so to speak), and yet he is transformed; he remains a Russian *intelligent*, but now he is also a Jewish refusenik, having felt the pain of oppression directed towards himself and his family. As a refusenik, he becomes defined more and more by the situation he finds himself in. That means he is involved

---

19   Shrayer-Petrov, *Doctor Levitin*, 243.
20   Ibid., 243–244.
21   Maxim D. Shrayer insightfully compares his father's novel to texts in the Russian tradition, such as by Chekhov and Nabokov. See his "Afterword," 228–229, and his essay in this volume.

with people who care little about his synthetic Jewish-Russian mind. To the OVIR officials and KGB agents, he is just another Jew who wants to leave Russia. He begins to seem out of place to himself as well. He is depersonalized and his battle with Soviet authorities metamorphoses into a quixotic struggle of the Jew against the system. To restate, the Levitin's final act was motivated by revenge and carried out in a calculated fashion. The point perhaps is that the very idea of an act of revenge through fire is not out of the playbook of a Russian classical novel of the sort Lev Tolstoy embodied and Vasily Grossman sought to emulate.

Shrayer-Petrov's protagonist, Doctor Levitin, is endowed with a consciousness saturated with Russian culture. In *Doctor Levitin,* Russian literature holds a special, privileged position. Several themes, such as madness and the destruction of a family, link *Doctor Levitin* and the classical Russian literary tradition of the nineteenth and twentieth centuries. Levitin's madness as a result of the state's torment reminds one of Alexander Pushkin's *The Bronze Horseman,* in which Evgeny's plans to start a family are disrupted by Peter the Great, who, paradoxically, a century before Evgeny's birth, established the capital in a flood zone and thus prepared the events that would destroy this average man's dreams. The madness theme also relates in a general way to those urban intellectuals in the fictional universe of Gogol and Dostoevsky, who act self-destructively when reality collides with their desires. The destruction of the family is another theme that joins *Doctor Levitin* to the Russian tradition. For example, Tolstoy's *Anna Karenina* codifies themes present in Shrayer-Petrov's novel, such as adultery, worrying over a child's future (compare Anna's anxiety for her son and Dolly's concerns for her children), and the misery of a broken man—Karenin (or Herbert Levitin). Critics blame modernity, a change in external values and attitudes, but one cannot ignore the presence of internal, plot-induced stress, which is present in the principal characters of *Doctor Levitin.*

Another theme that links the novel with the Russian tradition is the question of life, texts and the position of the author vis-à-vis his protagonists. I already mentioned *erlebte Rede*, a device that authors use to give voice to the internal life of characters. I recall from David Shrayer-Petrov's autobiographical short novel, *Strange Danya Rayev,* how during World War II he was taken as a child from his Leningrad apartment and spent his formative wartime years in a remote village in the Ural mountains, while his father fought the Nazis on the war front.[22] There in the village Jewish identity meant little, although his black hair and swarthy skin still marked him as different. But like everyone else, the future writer and his mother bought a piglet and fattened it up during the summer to slaughter for meat in the fall. The evacuees returned to Leningrad in the spring of 1944 after the siege was lifted. He made friends with the local riffraff; the bombed-out buildings made an exciting terrain for adventure and fantasy.

As I imagine it, Shrayer-Petrov went to medical school and entered the literary scene during the early Khrushchev years. He was galvanized by the Thaw; the information that dribbled out about the Soviet past awakened hopes that change was approaching. When Brezhnev consolidated control in 1964, Shrayer-Petrov was already a young medical scientist and professional writer. Like most members of the liberal Soviet intelligentsia, he had too much to lose to make a public scene about the invasion of Czechoslovakia. But he and his friends gave the USSR a tongue lashing in their kitchens. Although the timing does not work perfectly, the thought of keeping his then eleven-year-old son, Maxim, out of army service probably stoked Shrayer-Petrov's desire to emigrate when he and his wife first submitted the application in January 1979. In contrast with Levitin, Shrayer-Petrov survived the refusenik crucible and eventually emigrated with his wife and son. He has had a wonderful career in the United States as a scientist and writer.

Nonetheless, I would like to speculate about the construction of this novel, *Doctor Levitin*: Why does an author choose as his protagonists such figures characterized by failures? Why does he choose suicides and arsonists? I am not sure that this is a Russian affectation, but it occurs among Russia's best authors. Take the example of Vladimir Nabokov. The Russian protagonists in his novels *Pnin* and *Zashchita Luzhina* (*Luzhin's Defense*) are prosaic and even shabby in comparison with their multitalented creator. In fact, one of the common devices of those novels is that the author is linguistically light years ahead of his main characters.[23]

The same may be true for Shrayer-Petrov's protagonist. Doctor Levitin has many of Shrayer-Petrov's gifts, but not all of them. He lacks his creator's artistic talent, and that talent (in my reading of it) makes all the difference between the man who buckles under the pressure of *otkaz* (refusal) and

---

22 The English translation of *Strange Danya Rayev* can be found in Shrayer-Petrov, *Autumn in Yalta*, 1–101.
23 Maxim D. Shrayer comments on Nabokov's trace in Shrayer-Petrov's fiction. See "Afterword," 221.

the man who endures it to live another day and ultimately leave the Soviet Union. Of course, many people without literary talent left Russia, but the intellectual refusenik, an individual imbued with pride and dignity, suffered acute pain. That is clear from the novel. Literary survival skills belong to the creator, David Shrayer-Petrov, and not his hero and fictional double. Vladimir Nabokov's comment, this time about the protagonist of his Russian novel *Podvig* (*Glory*), comes to mind: "[. . .] among the many gifts I showered on Martin, I was careful not to include talent."[24]

We expect nonconformist Soviet fiction to break with authority and provide us with models of a free literature that thinks outside the reigning forms in officialdom. However, refusenik literature aims less for freedom in the abstract and asserts its right to attack the state. This literature is bent on war with the state. Now we can ask again: does the genre of the *refusenik novel* exist? I think a case can be made that such a genre exists, but it is not entirely literary, but has one foot in the real world. For example, authority in Shrayer-Petrov's *Doctor Levitin* is not necessary literary. In fact, this novel shows that an enemy of the state, a refusenik, can also conform to the authority of the Russian literary tradition and interact with the Russian-Jewish cultural tradition in intriguing ways. Shrayer-Petrov's refusenik novel therefore pushes us to rethink the notions of "conformism" and "nonconformity" in connection with Soviet and post-Soviet literary culture.

---

24 Vladimir Nabokov, *Glory*, tr. Dmitri Nabokov in collaboration with the author (New York: MacGraw-Hill, 1971), xiii. The comment is from Nabokov's 1970 Foreword to the English translation of the novel.

Works Cited

Gitelman, Zvi. "The Decline of the Diaspora Jewish Nation: Boundaries, Content, and Jewish Identity." *Jewish Social Studies* 4, no. 2 (Winter 1998): 112–132.

Katsman, Roman. "Parallel´nye vselennye Davida Shraera-Petrova." *Wiener Slawistischer Almanach* 79 (2017): 255–279.

Nabokov, Vladimir. *Glory*. Translated by Dmitri Nabokov in collaboration with the author. New York: MacGraw-Hill, 1971.

Pomeranz, William E. "Legacy and Consequences of Jackson-Vanik: Reassessing Human Rights in 21st Century Russia." Kennan Institute, Wilson Center Publication. https://www.wilsoncenter.org/publication/the-legacy-and-consequences-jackson-vanik-reassessing-human-rights-21st-century-russia-0. Accessed February 23, 2020.

Propp, Vladimir. *Morphology of the Folktale*. Austin, TX: University of Texas Press, 1958.

Rozenblit, Marsha. *The Jews of Vienna, 1867–1914: Assimilation and Identity*. New York: SUNY Press, 1984.

Shrayer, Maxim D. "Afterword: Voices of My Father's Exile," in David Shrayer-Petrov, *Autumn in Yalta: A Novel and Three Stories*, edited, co-translated, and with an afterword by Maxim D. Shrayer, 206–229. Library of Modern Jewish Literature. Syracuse: Syracuse University Press, 2006.

———, ed. *Voices of Jewish-Russian Literature: An Anthology*. Boston: Academic Studies Press, 2018.

Shrayer-Petrov, David. *Doctor Levitin: A Novel*. Edited and with notes by Maxim D. Shrayer, translated by Arna B. Bronstein, Aleksandra I. Fleszar, and Maxim D. Shrayer. Detroit: Wayne State University Press, 2018.

Leaving Home Is for the Brave: A Reading of David Shrayer-Petrov's *Doctor Levitin* *

Monica Osborne

In the second episode of *Shtisel* (written and directed by Ori Elon and Yehonatan Indursky), a Netflix-distributed drama that explores the lives of members of an Ultra-Orthodox Jewish community in Israel, one character says of the concept of waiting that it means "to expect something that will never happen." Nowhere has this idea been more dramatically crystallized than in the plight of the Jewish refuseniks of the Soviet Union, a plight revealed in excruciating detail in David Shrayer-Petrov's novel *Doctor Levitin*, written secretly in Soviet Russia and translated into English by Arna B. Bronstein, Aleksandra I. Fleszar, and Maxim D. Shrayer.[1] Following the death of Joseph Stalin in 1953, and in growing numbers after the Six Day War, Soviet Jews began to seek permission to emigrate to Israel. For while certainly the situation for these Jews was not quite as dire in the absence of Stalin, who had launched an antisemitic campaign after the end of World

---

*   Copyright © 2021 by Monica Osborne.
1   An earlier version of this essay appeared in 2019, as a review of *Doctor Levitin*, in the *Los Angeles Review of Books*, February 8, 2019, https://lareviewofbooks.org/article/little-more-than-pariahs-on-david-shrayer-petrovs-doctor-levitin/. Here and hereafter, parenthetical page references to the English translation of *Doctor Levitin* are from David Shrayer-Petrov, *Doctor Levitin*, ed. and with notes by Maxim D. Shrayer, tr. Arna B. Bronstein, Aleksandra I. Fleszar, and Maxim D. Shrayer (Detroit: Wayne State University Press, 2018).

War II, Jewish religious and cultural life in the Soviet Union continued to be suppressed in both direct and indirect ways, and dreams of emigrating from the Soviet Union gave Jews hope.

But in many cases, especially during most of the 1980s, this hope was futile until around 1988-1989, when the Free Soviet Jewry movement, which had worked for decades to place Western pressure on Soviet leaders in an effort to release Soviet Jews from oppression, and the courageous activism of refuseniks within the Soviet Union, finally resulted in an easing of the restrictions on emigration that had held so many hostage for numerous years. Although some Soviet Jews were able to emigrate beginning in the late 1950s and 1960s, and the 1970s saw a rising wave of Jewish emigration, tens of thousands of applications for exit visas were denied.[2] On occasion, Jews were given specific reasons for the denial. Perhaps it was a lack of family members who could receive them in Israel. Or maybe it was because they had at some point allegedly had access to classified state information, an accusation or assumption that was usually untrue and used simply as a fabricated means to deny the applicant's request to emigrate. But in many other instances there was no reason given at all—applications were simply denied with no explanation. Consequently, many Jews spent years resubmitting their applications only to be denied repeatedly. And in the meantime, they were not only disenfranchised by the Soviet regime but also usually shunned by their fellow-citizens who no longer saw their Jewish neighbors as friends and colleagues, but instead as betrayers of their loyalty, ingrates who cared nothing for the homeland that had cared for them, albeit grudgingly and with little support or admiration. Indeed, from the 1940s onward Jews had been experiencing systematic state-sponsored discrimination. However, once they declared intentions to emigrate to Israel (which was, by the way, a legal channel under international conventions, to which the USSR had been a signatory) they became little more than pariahs

---

[2] Brief statistics on the Jewish emigration from the USSR are found in Maxim D. Shrayer, ed., *Voices of Jewish-Russian Literature. An Anthology* (Boston: Academic Studies Press, 2018), 753–756; Shrayer, "Notes on the Text," in Shrayer-Petrov, *Doctor Levitin*, 282. For details, see Mark Tolts, "Demography of the Contemporary Russian-Speaking Jewish Diaspora," in *The New Jewish Diaspora: Russian-Speaking Immigrants in the United States, Israel, and Germany*, ed. Zvi Gitelman (New Brunswick, NJ: Rutgers University Press, 2016), 23–40; idem, "Demography of the Jews in the Former Soviet Union: Yesterday and Today," in *Jewish Life After the USSR*, ed. Zvi Gitelman, Musya Glants, and Marshall I. Goldman (Bloomington: Indiana University Press, 2003), 173–206.

in their homeland, forced to wait in a holding tank that grew smaller and colder each day.

Waiting, in this context, takes on a whole new dimension of meaning. In Shrayer-Petrov's novel *Doctor Levitin*, the reader experiences along with the Levitin family the tragic toll that such waiting takes on a family. It is, oddly enough, a novel very much about emigration, despite the fact that the family at its center—Professor of Medicine Herbert Anatolyevich Levitin, his non-Jewish Russian wife Tatyana Vasilyevna, and their son Anatoly— never actually emigrates successfully from Russia. In fact, their dreams of emigrating become, literally and figuratively, the death of them all. But it is 1979, and in this moment such was the fate of countless Soviet Jews. And while it may seem curious that a novel about emigration involves family that never—at least in this novel—actually emigrates, in fact *Doctor Levitin* is one of a number of texts written between the 1960s and 1980s that, according to Klavdia Smola, represented "a new, late Soviet shaping of Zionist prose."[3] For many of the writers of such texts, Israel is reconceived as a Promised Land of mythical proportions, a symbol of the salvation of which they dream.

The Levitin family, of course, is no exception. Like so many others of their kind, they are not identifiably Jewish in the ways a Western sensibility might expect. Certainly they are nothing like some of the Jews who once inhabited pre-Holocaust *shtetls*, conspicuously different in their religious garb— their long black coats and *shtreimels*, their *kippot* and *tzitzit*, their women's heads covered with wigs and every inch of skin obscured by dark, colorless clothing. For the most part, among Soviet Jews, including the fictional Levitin family, *kippot*, synagogue attendance, and other traditional tell-tale signs of Jewishness were more often than not the residue of dreams deferred.

One would think that for this reason alone Soviet Jews would have been able to fly under the radar more successfully. But one would be unequivocally wrong. To the dismay of those of Jewish descent, the Soviet regime had a remarkable penchant for sniffing out Jewishness even when it was hardly discernible. "We know we are Russians; You consider us Jews," writes Shrayer-Petrov in the prologue—and later, in the narrative's first line: "My Slavic soul in a Jewish wrapping."[4] The latter reflection is also the first line of one of Shrayer-Petrov's most well-known poems, "Moia

---

3   Klavdia Smola, "The Reinvention of the Promised Land: Utopian Space and Time in Soviet Exodus Literature," *East European Jewish Affairs* 45, no. 1 (2015): 79–108.
4   *Doctor Levitin*, 15.

slavianskaia dusha" ("My Slavic Soul"), in which the "Slavic soul" of a Soviet Jew abandons his body, his "Jewish wrapping," and hides in a hayloft.[5]

While characters with what might be called hyphenated identities abound in the literature of the twentieth and twenty-first centuries, there is something distinctive about the way Shrayer-Petrov characterizes the merging of the Russian and Jewish selves. It is not the typical construction of hyphenated identities that one typically finds in literature about immigrants and immigration. There is no sense of having each foot in a different world, the character doomed to experience life as half Jewish and half Russian and subsequently see everything through this dual perspective. Rather, the construction that Shrayer-Petrov outlines in both his poetry and in this particular novel is, on one hand, much simpler, and on another, much more complex. According to Shrayer-Petrov's construction, the Soviet Jew is first and foremost culturally Russian. In fact, he or she identifies almost solely as Russian. One's Jewishness in this regard is perhaps a kind of accoutrement or adornment. Yet we know it is certainly more complex than this. The characters perceive themselves as Russians, even while knowing that Jewishness is an inextricable component of their Russian identity. This particular Jewish component is something that is more or less imposed on them by non-Jewish Russians, through whose eyes the difference in Jews' Russian identity is pronounced. It marks them as less Russian, somehow deficient, and thereby worthy of suspicion. And so the complexity of Soviet Jewish identity has less to do with a sense of inhabiting two worlds simultaneously, and more to do with being seen as something other than what one perceives himself or herself as. A "Slavic soul in a Jewish wrapping" is quite telling in this way. Shrayer-Petrov seems to suggest that for the Soviet Jew, it is the inner Slavic soul that is indicative of the true self, while the Jewish wrapping is an outer shell that can be discarded if necessary.

One wonders, of course, what happens if and when that outer shell is indeed discarded. But this is not a question that is answered in the novel. Instead, it would seem that it is virtually impossible to remove this outer Jewish wrapping from one's self. Early in the novel, the narrator recounts an incident from his childhood. As a Jewish evacuee from Leningrad, he repeatedly wanted to side with the boys who were villagers in the event of

---

5   See Shrayer, "Notes to the Text," in Shrayer-Petrov, *Doctor Levitin*, 282. For the English translation of the poem, see Shrayer-Petrov, "My Slavic Soul," tr. Maxim D. Shrayer, in Shrayer, *Voices of Jewish-Russian Literature*, 831.

a disagreement, but remembers that they would not acknowledge him as "one of their own."⁶ Later, when faced with a new group of Jewish evacuees from Leningrad, he commits an "act of betrayal." He remembers one "dark-haired, swarthy, Middle Eastern looking Jewish boy" that he approached after class in front of other children. He insults the boy and tries to get him to fight, to which the boy responds, "Just look at yourself... You're just the same as I am!" The narrator realizes, then, that he is indeed "just like that Jewish boy, a stranger among them. A wolf cub pulling a dog sled." And for him it is a "terrible revelation," for it suggests, for him at least, that the Jewish shell cannot be removed or obscured.⁷

The multifaceted identity that both characterizes and haunts the existence of the Levitin family becomes further complicated when, after being refused exit visas, they officially become refuseniks. For the place of the refusenik is to be without a place, to float and drift through a space one used to call home—*wants* to call home—but now realizes was always something else entirely. "What was left?" writes Shrayer-Petrov, "To transform themselves into a totally new existence, the existence of refuseniks?" And yet at the same time, becoming a refusenik ushered one into another welcoming, if eternally discouraged, fold: "Thank God, even here, the Levitins weren't alone and starting from scratch [...] such forms of existence, antithetical to normal life, had already been discovered by their misfortunate precursors, the older refuseniks."⁸

And so we see in *Doctor Levitin* that the borders and boundaries between one community and the next are not as fixed as one might imagine. Whereas one day the family is a Russian-Jewish one, when non-Jewish others realize that they wish to leave Russia they become seen as something else entirely, something that belongs nowhere. They are now refuseniks. They are ushered into a new community, a new identity. This is perhaps one of the most troubling realizations of the Levitins' story—that no matter how firmly etched into the framework of a community one imagines himself or herself, one's place is perhaps always tentative, forever dependent upon regularly subscribing to a prescribed set of actions and behaviors. The community in which one sees himself or herself is not always the community that is most accepting. This is a reality that is undoubtedly familiar to diasporic Jews throughout history. Most countries and cultures

---

6   *Doctor Levitin*, 19.
7   Ibid., 20.
8   Ibid., 205.

are divided deeply along ethnic and religious lines, and diasporic Jews have often been one of the greatest casualties in these divisions. Even in the United States in the twenty-first century, American Jews are seen by many as having a sinister agenda at worst, and as much too tribal at least. But while such scenarios are not historically uncommon regardless of the country, what is perhaps different about the situation of Soviet Jews in the refusenik era is in fact that very possibility of becoming a refusenik, of being named as something or someone not to be trusted, as a betrayer of sorts.

The authorial voice of Shrayer-Petrov, whose own real experience as a refusenik no doubt informs this fictional narrative, breaks through the story at many points, often suggesting the author's own ambivalence with regard to his homeland, Soviet Russia: "Those leaving for good—and those seeing them off—had found themselves alone with Moscow: the mother that was weaning her children."[9] In considering the novel's autobiographical context, one should note that in January of 1979, Shrayer-Petrov and his family applied for exit visas. Upon doing so, he and his wife Emilia Shrayer lost their academic jobs. Shrayer-Petrov was additionally expelled from the Union of Soviet Writers and blacklisted.

The family would exist as refuseniks for eight more years, until they finally emigrated in 1987. But already in the first year of this catastrophic new existence, Shrayer-Petrov began to imagine the story of the Levitins. He completed the manuscript of *Doctor Levitin* in the fall of 1980, and over the next three years he finished the second novel in the trilogy: *Cursed Be You... Just Don't Die*. Of course, publishing fiction in the Soviet Union at that time, especially a story of this scandalous nature, would have been impossible. But in 1984 photographs of the manuscript were smuggled to the West and in 1985 the publication of the novel was announced in Israel, resulting in a substantial intensification of the persecution of Shrayer-Petrov by the KGB. Finally, in 1992, with the dissolution of the USSR, the first two novels were published in Russia in a single volume entitled *Herbert and Nelly*. The first print run of 50,000 copies sold out quickly and was followed by two more editions in Russia. An early version of the final novel in the trilogy, *The Third Life*, was published in 2010.[10]

Doctor Levitin is a fairly chronological tale, with numerous memory flashbacks and authorial digressions throughout. But the most conspicuous

---

9   Ibid., 11–12.
10 For details, see Shrayer, "About the Text of Doctor Levitin," in Shrayer-Petrov, *Doctor Levitin*, 277–279.

breaks in the text are the many authorial reflections placed throughout the text. In some cases they are direct commentary on the text, and in others they are philosophical musings that deepen the overall narrative. Just a few pages into the story, the first interjection, only one line, appears: "Why do I write about somebody else and not about myself?"[11] There is something deeply painful about the idea of wanting to write one's own story, but choosing instead—or being forced to choose?—to write the story of someone else. Yet it is also true that fiction can be more real than real, and it is not a stretch to suggest that in this novel Shrayer-Petrov has, through the Levitin family, illuminated his own struggles more effectively than he could have done through nonfiction. Any person reflecting directly on his or her own experience must acknowledge the blind spots that accompany the attempt to tell one's own story. It may be that using fictional means—if partially based on biography—to tell the story diminishes the extent to which blind spots can dominate and complicate a narrative. Many of the reflections in the novel articulate the protagonist's difficulty of ripping himself away from Russia, and some reveal to the reader that the darkness of 1979 is not a new one. Rather, it is one that Doctor Herbert Levitin was born into, that his ancestors and their ancestors were born into. It is predetermined by his ethnicity ("nationality" configured in Soviet terms), was present even when he was a child, and is inescapable—a generational curse that he intuitively understands will be visited on his children and grandchildren.

The twentieth- and twenty-first-century literary world has been arguably dominated by immigrant stories that focus on the promise of something more, of an easier life, one that is not characterized by constant struggle. The earliest writers of American immigrant fiction in the late nineteenth and early twentieth century all tell a similar story of leaving the darkness and difficulty of a past life and coming to America, a land where dreams can become reality. Similarly, nearly all of these texts simultaneously explore the darker reality of life as an immigrant in America—an unexpectedly difficult existence that is characterized by working multiple jobs for very little money and living in squalor in run-down tenements. Likewise, American immigrant fiction of the twenty-first century often explores the idea of America as a safe haven from the violence and terror of war-torn countries, yet it is a haven in which the immigrant soon learns that racism and bigotry are a kind of cultural

---

11 *Doctor Levitin*, 7.

currency.[12] The point is that stories about immigration and emigration are nothing new. But while most novels of this kind explore the struggles attached to realizing these dreams once the protagonist has arrived in the new country, *Doctor Levitin* reveals with painstaking detail the cost not of working toward those dreams in a new country, but rather of even daring to dream such dreams and of thinking even for a moment that they may in fact be possible. The novel reveals the dark side of imagining a better life and of taking steps to transform dreams into a functioning reality. It is not simply the agony of "tearing away from the placenta," from the motherland, that is it at stake.[13] The cost, as we see in the novel, is unbearably high and the losses are profound, particularly when one cannot emigrate and must endure the pain of repression at home. Herbert Anatolyevich, a physician and full professor of medicine, loses his professorship and is ultimately reduced to making house calls for those who will still see him. His non-Jewish wife, Tatyana, born in a Russian village, also pays heavily for marrying a Jew and for expressing the forbidden desire to exchange her homeland for a life in Israel with her family. In fact, one might argue that it is she who pays most dearly. Their son Anatoly, the product of a mixed marriage, is seen only as a Jew whose family harbors plans to leave the Russia that has embraced them, and is first refused entrance into and then expelled from medical school, putting him at risk of being drafted into the military and sent to Afghanistan, another fear that haunts the family throughout the story. And Grandfather Vasily Matveevich (Tatyana's father) meets his own dark fate even though he, of pure Russian descent, and a former Red Army guerilla fighter during the war against Nazi Germany, is merely guilty by association—despite his latent distrust of Jews—and had never cared for his Jewish son-in-law anyway. As dreams disintegrate, the family finds itself sliding backward into desperation instead of moving forward into a better life.

One gets the sense that Jewishness is feared to be contagious in Soviet Russia. But has not it always been? Doctor Levitin's colleagues distance themselves from him; Tatyana watches as even the mail carrier grows uncharacteristically cold in their interactions, which is no doubt especially upsetting to her given that she had retained her Russian and Orthodox

---

12 For more on this topic as well as excerpts of popular American immigrant novels see Holli Levitsky, Monica Osborne, and Stella Setka, eds., *Literature of Exile and Displacement: American Identity in the Time of Crisis* (San Diego: Cognella Academic Publishing, 2016).
13 *Doctor Levitin*, 81.

heritage as a way of remaining separate from the strangeness of her husband, a Jew; Grandfather Vasily Matveevich is demeaned by authorities for allowing his daughter to marry a Jew, despite the fact that the Jew in question is a doctor serving the Russian villagers. While these experiences are agonizing to absorb, have we not seen them before? The novel's references to the Holocaust are subtle reminders that this is a longstanding darkness. Its tentacles reach backward into history, forward into the future. For the Levitin family, daily life carries this reminder. Shrayer-Petrov suggests in the prologue that over the course of the two years accounted for in this story, even the air "scraped the soul with something akin to the barbed wire of concentration camps: hopelessness."[14] He later describes the family's year as all "anxiety and pain, as if somebody kept dragging them through chinks in camp barbed wire."[15] As in all authentic narratives of trauma, there is no happy ending. Near the end of the novel, we learn that everything is "divided into leaving and not-leaving; and life itself was divided in half: before emigration and after emigration."[16] This too is an echo of the way many Holocaust survivors refer to the two different lives that co-exist following an extended trauma: before and after. In both equations, there is no during, only before and after the experience of trauma.[17]

It is not the Holocaust, of course, but what the Levitins endure is certainly a trauma of devastating proportions. And at the end of the story, when we leave the family we have come to know, the trauma is ongoing. Those who are left are still waiting, and we get the impression that their waiting will be eternal. They are, like characters in so many classic plays—think, for instance, of Anton Chekhov's *Three Sisters* or Samuel Beckett's *Waiting for Godot*—waiting for something that will never come. In this sense it is a quintessentially Jewish tale of striving for what may not be obtainable that transcends boundaries of time and place. It is like a Kafkaesque twist on the old Jewish parable about the man who asks his rabbi when the messiah will come, to which the rabbi responds: when he is no longer necessary. In the parable, waiting is productive; it inspires people to work toward creating a

---

14 Ibid., 2.
15 Ibid., 204.
16 *Doctor Levitin*, 182.
17 I explore more fully the question of what constitutes ethical approaches to and representations of trauma in the context of literature in Monica Osborne, *The Midrashic Impulse and the Contemporary Literary Response to Trauma* (Lanham, MD: Lexington Books, 2017).

world worthy of a messiah for whom they wait. But in *Doctor Levitin* the waiting is toxic and destructive: there is no messiah in sight.

Shrayer-Petrov himself, as well as his family, did in reality finally escape to the United States by way of Austria and Italy in 1987. A portion of this story is told by Shrayer-Petrov's son Maxim D. Shrayer in his English-language memoir *Waiting for America: A Story of Emigration* (and also in the third part of the refusenik trilogy). Shrayer-Petrov's *Doctor Levitin* is conversely, of course, just the first novel in a trilogy that tells the story of a family's attempts to emigrate and their ultimate exodus, and so it does not end in a particularly hopeful fashion. It ends, instead, with Natasha, the former girlfriend of Levitin's son Anatoly, boarding a flight to the United States from Moscow, having met and married Stanley Fisher, a Jew and an American citizen. The irony of her departure is pronounced, given that this woman had not dreamed of emigrating even as the entire Levitin family lost everything in their pursuit of that very hope. (On this point, also see Brian Horowitz's essay in this volume.) Instead of leaving him in the throes of joyful exodus, the reader's last encounter with Levitin is one in which he is enraged and experiencing a psychological breakdown. Most telling is the portion of Psalm 22 on the story's second to last page, literally and figuratively one of the most poetical and catastrophic in the novel:

> My life ebbs away:
> all my bones are disjointed;
> my heart is like wax,
> melting within me;
> my vigor dries up like a shard;
> my tongue cleaves to my palate;
> You commit me to the dust of death.
> Dogs surround me; a pack of evil ones closes in on me,
> like lions they maul my hands and feet.[18]

It is this passage that directly precedes the short and final paragraph of the novel that tells of Natasha's departure. While one goes, one stays to die a slow death.

Shrayer-Petrov's novel may have been written over forty years ago, but it is perhaps more timely now than ever. In the wake of wars and violent uprisings that have emerged across the globe in at least the past decade, countless

---

18 *Doctor Levitin*, 274. The English translation uses the Jewish Publication Society version of *Tanakh*. (ed.)

people of all ethnicities and nationalities are leaving their home countries, dreaming of lives that are not characterized by pain and suffering. And with the rise of antisemitism and violent attacks on synagogues in Europe, many Jews are once again wondering whether they will have to uproot themselves and emigrate to countries such as Israel or America. In fact, major news outlets have reported that the situation is increasingly dire.[19] While this may be reminiscent of the situation of Jews in Europe in the 1930s and 1940s, fortunately, there is one pronounced difference. At this point in time, European political leaders are themselves concerned about the rise in antisemitism, and many are doing what they can in order to denounce and work against such bigotry. The question is whether antisemitism will continue to grow, and whether more and more mainstream individuals will embrace it once again. Recent carnivals and parades featuring antisemitic imagery in both Spain and Belgium suggest that this is indeed a possibility, and are a stark reminder that Jews are never fully at home in a country that is not their own. In America, despite the fact that antisemitic incidents are on the rise, Jews still, for the most part, feel safe, and the questions of whether to emigrate are not nearly as prevalent as they are in Europe. But America has its own demons to fight. In an era when Americans in particular are inundated by both real and fake news regarding immigrants crossing our borders, it might be easy to suppose that emigration is simple, that one can in fact leave his or her country of origin any time he or she wants to and set out for a better life in a more welcoming place. One might be tempted to believe that the hardest part is crossing the border of the new country, of finally getting in. *Doctor Levitin* reminds us that the act of leaving home, of transgressing one's own national and cultural borders, carries with it great, abiding pain, and is undertaken only by the brave.

---

19 For example, see Geir Moulson, "Germany Urged to Fight Anti-Semitism to Avoid Jewish Exodus," ABC News, January 26, 2020, https://abcnews.go.com/Politics/wireStory/germany-urged-fight-anti-semitism-avoid-jewish-exodus-68541020; and Yardena Schwartz, "'Things have Only Gotten Worse': French Jews are Fleeing Their Country,'" *National Geographic*, November 20, 2019, https://www.nationalgeographic.com/history/2019/11/french-jews-fleeing-country/.

Works Cited

Levitsky, Holli, Monica Osborne, and Stella Setka, eds. *Literature of Exile and Displacement: American Identity in the Time of Crisis.* San Diego: Cognella Academic Publishing, 2016.

Moulson, Geir. "Germany Urged to Fight Anti-Semitism to Avoid Jewish Exodus," ABC News, January 26, 2020.

Osborne, Monica. *The Midrashic Impulse and the Contemporary Literary Response to Trauma.* Lanham, MD: Lexington Books, 2017.

———. "Little More Than Pariahs: On David Shrayer-Petrov's *Doctor Levitin.*" *Los Angeles Review of Books*, February 8, 2019. https://lareviewofbooks.org/article/little-more-than-pariahs-on-david-shrayer-petrovs-doctor-levitin/.

Shrayer-Petrov, David. *Doctor Levitin.* Edited and with notes by Maxim D. Shrayer, translated by Arna B. Bronstein, Aleksandra I. Fleszar, and Maxim D. Shrayer. Detroit: Wayne State University Press, 2018.

Schwartz, Yardena. "'Things have Only Gotten Worse': French Jews are Fleeing Their Country,'" *National Geographic*, November 20, 2019.

Smola, Klavdia. "The Reinvention of the Promised Land: Utopian Space and Time in Soviet Jewish Exodus Literature." *East European Jewish Affairs* 45, no. 1 (2015): 79–108.

Part Four

Approaches to David Shrayer-Petrov's Prose

Who is Grifanov? David Shrayer-Petrov's Dialogue with Yury Trifonov*

Marat Grinberg

The place of the Jew in official Soviet literature is circumscribed and often non-existent. Considering the historical importance Russian literature played in shaping the social and existential types—what Lydia Ginzburg called "the general historical character"[1]—the absence of such Jewish characters renders the analysis and reconstruction of Soviet Jewish subjectivity and psyche especially difficult. To uncover its presence, one needs to turn to literature written "for the drawer"—concealed and unpublished—described by Klavdia Smola as "Jewish cultural underground [. . .] which was the result of intensive private exchange, limited knowledge, and collectively discovered sources."[2]

A centerpiece of this sociocultural underground Jewish context is the oeuvre of David Shrayer-Petrov. Never shying away from the Jewish allusions and themes, his prose and verse foreground the existential and historical travails of the Soviet Jew and, especially, the experience of refuseniks. Other writers, who worked both in the official and unofficial mode, for instance,

---
* Copyright © 2021 by Marat Grinberg.
  Unless noted otherwise, translations from the Russian are by the author.
1 Lidiia Ginzburg, *O psikhologicheskoi proze* (Moscow: Intrada, 1999), 11.
2 Klavdia Smola, "Communication and Medial Frontier Crossings in the Jewish Underground Culture," *East European Jewish Affairs* 48, no. 1 (2018): 5.

Friedrich Gorenstein, also made Jewishness their principal focus, but what sets Shrayer-Petrov apart is that he is invested in the Jewish question in a particularly positive and dignified manner. This quality, however, does not take away from the ambiguity of his characters, who waver between their Russian and Jewish allegiances, or the complexity of their position. Rather, it allows the writer to formulate Jewishness as both a powerful biological factor, passed on through cultural and familial legacy, and a lived historical experience which draws on Jewish collective memory. In this regard Shrayer-Petrov seems to follow in the footsteps of the iconic German Jewish writer, Lion Feuchtwanger, which is not surprising, considering the enormous significance of Feuchtwanger's novels in sustaining and bolstering Soviet Jewish identity.[3]

This approach to Jewishness is fully developed in the trilogy of novels about refuseniks, arguably Shrayer-Petrov's most important work, its first two parts known to the Russian readers as *Herbert and Nelly*. Written in 1979–1984 and published in Russia for the first time in 1992 (the last part was composed later and came out in 2010), it features Doctor Herbert Levitin, a full-fledged Russian-Jewish protagonist and an epochal Soviet Jewish type. Intimately connected to Russia and its language and, especially, to his native Moscow, Levitin is also deeply cognizant of his Jewishness as the defining element that sets him apart, endowing with a separate history and fate. Through years of the tragedies and struggles of trying to leave the Soviet Union—the last part of the trilogy finds him in the United States—Levitin's sense of Jewishness only intensifies, expressed in his romanticized view of the Land of Israel and rediscovery of Judaic tradition. It becomes abundantly clear to him who he is, "a part of a nation, a nation that had suffered and been persecuted for thousands of years, a nation that was given hope after the 1917 revolution, a hope that was gradually lost."[4] Shrayer-Petrov conceives of Doctor Levitin as the embodiment of the Soviet Jewish experience.

The trilogy's first part is its most lyrical and stylistically complex due to its masterful interweaving of Levitin's story with that of the author. Levitin

---

3 On Feuchtwanger in the Soviet context, see Marat Grinberg, "The Soviet Jewish Scripture: Lion Feuchtwanger and the Soviet Jewish Bookshelf," in *Feuchtwanger and Judaism: History, Imagination, Exile*, ed. Paul Lerner and Frank Stern (Oxford: Peter Lang, 2019), 139–165.

4 David Shrayer-Petrov, *Doctor Levitin: A Novel*, ed. and with notes by Maxim D. Shrayer, tr. Arna B. Bronstein, Aleksandra I. Fleszar, and Maxim D. Shrayer (Detroit: Wayne State University Press, 2018), 16.

is Shrayer-Petrov's "auto-psychological" double, to use Lydia Ginzburg's term, and like his character the writer also comes in contact with his indelible Jewishness. He recalls how seeing another Jewish boy in a Uralian village, where their families were evacuated during the war, made him come to a startling realization that he "was just like that Jewish boy, a stranger among"[5] others. This reclamation of Jewishness does not turn into a burden but becomes a point of pride as well as historical and moral responsibility.

It is this Jewish factor which unexpectedly, but forcefully links him to the grand Russian literary tradition. One of the most powerful sections of the first part is the author's search for what remains of the Karaites in Lithuania. He learns how this once Jewish sect had painstakingly obfuscated and concealed their Jewish roots; this discovery makes him "want to cry from shame and despair."[6] The narrator is fascinated by Karaites, but pained by their erasure of their Jewish origins and past, which is antithetical to the choices he makes. He finds a kindred soul in Russia's greatest poet, Alexander Pushkin, whom he depicts as a proud Jew:

> Над могилой Пушкина в Святогорском монастыре — памятник. На черном мраморе крест и под крестом — звезда Давида. Пушкин был масоном. Звезда Давида была знаком масонской ложи. Но Пушкин был потомком эфиопских царей из [Соломоновой династии], произошедшей от царицы Савской и царя Соломона. [...] Пушкин был первым и едва ли не единственным в русской литературе XIX века (после него Гоголь в «Тарасе Бульбе»), кто осмелился писать и думать вслух о еврействе, его великой истории и жалком существовании во времена поэта. [...] Если принять за аксиому, что гены бессмертны, то Пушкин получил свои поэтические гены от Давида и его сына Соломона, поскольку род Ганнибалов восходит к династии эфиопских царей через Соломона и царицу Савскую. [...] Пушкин испытывал отвращение к трусости тех евреев, которые скрывали свое происхождение или измывались над памятью о своем происхождении. [...] Так вот пушкинским взглядом смотреть на жизнь, видеть караимов, которые заставили себя забыть еврейство, видеть все по-пушкински (исторически и современно),

---

5   Ibid., 20.
6   Ibid., 172.

думать о том, что нынешние шестнадцатилетние тянутся к правде жизни и правде истории, тянутся к родным истокам.⁷

I recalled Pushkin's tomb at the Holy Hills Monastery. There's a cross on the white tombstone, and beneath the cross, a wreath with a Star of David. Pushkin was a Freemason. A hexagram resembling the Star of David was a Masonic symbol. But on his mother's side, Pushkin had descended from Ethiopian (Abyssinian) princes of the Solomonic dynasty—the "Lions of Judah"—that had originated from the Queen of Sheba and King Solomon. [. . .] Pushkin was the first and virtually the only one in Russian literature of the time who dared to write and think out loud about Jewry, about the great history of Jews and their pitiful state in the poet's day. (After him came Gogol in *Taras Bulba*.) [. . .] If one is to accept as axiomatic that genes are eternal, then Pushkin received his poetic genes from David and his son Solomon. [. . .] Pushkin had an aversion to the cowardice of those Jews who concealed their origins or mocked the memory of their ancestors. [. . .] And that's the way one can see life through Pushkin's eyes: to see the Karaites, who forced themselves to forget their Jewishness; to see everything as did Pushkin (with both a historical and a contemporary perspective); to think about the fact that today's sixteen-year-old Jews are seeking truth in life and truth in history as they search for their native roots.⁸

In offering this sui generis *Jewish* version of Pushkin, Shrayer-Petrov creates in his text a Russian-Jewish poetics, wholly explicit as well as wholly nonconformist and defiant of the governing ideology and widespread moods and stereotypes. As Roman Katsman formulates it, "In the works of David Shrayer-Petrov, the fearless utterances of nonconformism indicate transition to the nonvictimary paradigm. The vector of overcoming victimhood appears almost simultaneously (in the early 1970s) with the intensification of the Soviet-Jewish victimhood paradigm itself. Subsequently [. . .] this vector of overcoming victimhood increases right up to the refusenik literature of the early 1980s, particularly, in the novels of Shrayer-Petrov of those years."⁹

---

7   David Shraer-Petrov, *Gerbert i Nelli* (Moscow: Knizhniki, 2014), 188–191; David Shrayer-Petrov, *Doctor Levitin*, 173–177.
8   Ibid., 173–174, 176.
9   Roman Katsman, "Jewish Fearless Speech: Towards a Definition of Soviet Jewish Nonconformism," *East European Jewish Affairs* 48, no. 1 (May 2018): 44. See also Roman Katsman's essay in this volume.

I will argue in this essay that Shrayer-Petrov arrives at this overcoming of victimhood or shame for being a Jew via, on the one hand, a radical reinterpretation of classical Russian literature, specifically Pushkin, and, on the other, a thinly veiled dialogue with the cult author of 1970s—the champion of "city prose" Yury Trifonov (1925–1981). I will trace the links between Shrayer-Petrov and Trifonov as two models of Soviet and, especially, Soviet Jewish nonconformism—explicit and subterranean.

* * *

By the end of 1970s, when Shrayer-Petrov embarked on writing the first two parts of what would become the refusenik trilogy, Yury Trifonov was at the peak of his fame. To many among the Soviet intelligentsia, who were deeply sceptical of the regime, he represented a breath of fresh air; his often despondent urban characters became their alter egos. Though Trifonov did have his share of struggles with the censors, his novels and short stories were officially published largely in the form he desired. Yet to read Trifonov was to engage in "reading between the lines," to recall Leo Strauss' well-known formulation from *Persecution and the Art of Writing*, first published in 1941. According to Strauss,

> the influence of persecution on literature is precisely that it compels all writers who hold heterodox views to develop a peculiar technique of writing; the technique which we have in mind when speaking of writing between the lines. [. . .] Persecution, then, gives rise to a peculiar technique of writing, and therewith to a peculiar type of literature, in which the truth about all crucial things is presented exclusively between the lines. That literature is addressed, not to all readers, but to trustworthy and intelligent readers only. It has all the advantages of private communication without having its greatest disadvantage—that it reaches only the writer's acquaintances. It has all the advantages of public communication without having its greatest disadvantage—capital punishment for the author.[10]

As Strauss explains, "between the lines" component could be a mere phrase, a quotation, a sentence or two, or even a hint at disagreeing with or subverting an official dogma. Thus, "reading between the lines [. . .] starts

---

10 Leo Strauss, *Persecution and the Art of Writing* (Chicago: The University of Chicago Press, 1988), 24–25.

from an exact consideration of the explicit statements of the author [...] the context in which a statement occurs, and the literary character of the whole work as well as its plan, must be perfectly understood before"[11] reading between the lines takes place. This condition leads to the development of two types of readers: the majority, who can access the *exoteric* meaning of the text, and the minority, who can detect its *esoteric* (or philosophic) layer. Strauss's idea should be seen as the quintessential Soviet and specifically Soviet Jewish position and coping mechanism, to which Shrayer-Petrov offers his bold alternative.

Filled with innuendos, intimations, and inseparable from its context, Trifonov's prose called for the "between the lines" type of decoding and reading. His style was equally nuanced, saturated with what the Russians call "недосказанность"—leaving some of the most essential unsaid and only suggesting it—the feature that applies most prominently to Chekhov's poetics, in whose footsteps Trifonov was following. As noted by Trifonov's widow, Olga Trifonova (Miroshnichenko), the collected writings of Chekhov were the most tattered volumes in his bookcase due to constant rereading.[12] (On Shrayer-Petrov and Chekhov, see Klavdia Smola's and Maxim D. Shrayer's essays in part one of this volume.) Thus, Trifonov's literary lineage and inherent stylistic proclivity for subtlety and nuance coincided fruitfully and tragically with the strictures of his time and its demands: the sense of "time and place," as his last novel phrases it. The fear of persecution hung over Trifonov himself and his readers, which meant that both sides needed to be adept at playing the "between the lines" game. The task of a writer, as Trifonov put it in his diary in 1973, was to say what is "outside the book."[13] Trifonov expected that his readers would engage in discreet and subversive reading practices, figuring out not only the story the book tells, but "what it really wants to say."[14]

However, there were also some readers who viewed Trifonov's art not as a restrained and profound form of nonconformism, but precisely the opposite—the compromise of a talented Soviet conformist. A number of fellow writers, who were more transparent in their antagonism toward the system, reproached and even ridiculed him. Andrei Bitov, for instance, even

---

11 Ibid., 30.
12 From my interview with Trifonova at the House on the Embankment Museum in Moscow on July 13, 2019.
13 N. G. Kataeva, ed., *Iurii Trifonov. Otblesk lichnosti* (Moscow: Galeriia, 2015), 368.
14 Ibid.

though he later gained more respect for Trifonov, mockingly referred to his novels as "socialist existentialism."[15] This attitude was exacerbated by the fact that Trifonov, who never considered immigration as a viable option, could travel freely outside the Soviet Union and, as will be discussed below, began his career as a recipient of the Stalin Prize for his first short novel, *Students* (1950). Thus, some questioned the seriousness of his later attempts to come to terms with the horrors of Stalinism and the Civil War period.

Considering the dominance of Trifonov and his texts in the debates of 1970s, it is not accidental that he would be on Shrayer-Petrov's mind, an ostracized writer choosing explicitness over subtext and understatement. Shrayer-Petrov's allusions to Trifonov are largely located in *Cursed Be You... Just Don't Die*, the second part of the trilogy (he is mentioned a couple of times in the third) through the character of the writer Grifanov, Doctor Levitin's friend. Grifanov takes him to dinners at the famed Central House of Writers (TsDL)—where Shrayer-Petrov himself had met Trifonov[16]—and attempts to help him and the main female character, Nelly Shamova, who eventually becomes Levitin's second wife. Grifanov's status and opinions closely resemble Trifonov's. For instance, like Trifonov, he is interested in the German writer Heinrich Böll (Böll was one of Trifonov's favorite authors and knew him personally)—and, like Trifonov, Grifanov visited the United States and met Marc Chagall.[17] The US visit and meeting Chagall in France would be described in Trifonov's last, novel-like collection of stories, *The Overturned House*.

Grifanov's connection with Nelly Shamova is more intricate. It gets at the heart of Shrayer-Petrov's roman à clef metaliterary game. In the novel, Nelly is the daughter of the fictionalized writer Varlam Denisovich Shamov, a Gulag survivor, an unequivocal reference to both Varlam Shalamov and Alexander Solzhenitsyn's *One Day in the Life of Ivan Denisovich*. Nelly's mother, Liya Shamir, was an actress in Solomon Mikhoels's Moscow Yiddish Theater. Thus, like Trifonov, whose father was Russian and mother Jewish (I will turn to this subject below), Nelly is a Russian-Jewish hybrid. Trifonov was cognizant of these two halves of his identity and might have

---

15 Ibid., 153.
16 Shrayer-Petrov does not devote a chapter to Trifonov in his memoirs, *Moskva zlatoglavaia*, about the writers he knew during the Moscow years, but he does mention Trifonov in his memoirs about his life in science and medicine, *Okhota na ryzhego d'iavola. Roman s mikrobiologami*, and in another novel, *Istoriia moei vozliublennoi, ili Vintovaia lestnitsa*, all written after leaving the USSR.
17 Shraer-Petrov, *Gerbert i Nelli*, 402.

been especially drawn to its dilemmas through his close friend Boris Slutsky's poem, "Polukrovki" ("Half-Breeds"), where the Russian-Jewish blood hyphen is presented as an existentially and ontologically tragic sign:

Вот вы и дрожите. Словно листики.
В мире обоюдных нареканий,
Полукровки — тоненькие мостики
Через море — меж материками.

Что ж вам делать в этом мире гнева?
Как вам быть в жестокой перекройке?
Взвешенные меж земли и неба,
Смешанные крови. Полукровки.[18]

("Here you are trembling. Just like tiny leaves. / In the world of mutual recriminations, /Half-breeds—you are tiny narrow bridges/ Thrown over the sea—in between continents. || What are you to do in this world of wrath? / How can you endure in this cruel newly cut mold? / Suspended between the heaven and the earth, / Mixed up bloods you are. Half-breeds.")

The link with Slutsky is also important because, unlike Trifonov, Grifanov is a veteran of World War II, the youngest among the writers of this cohort, of which Slutsky was the key representative.

Perceptively, Shrayer-Petrov presents Grifanov as Shamov's benefactor and protector after Nelly's father returns from the camps. Though the actual Trifonov and the actual Shalamov most likely never met, both were preoccupied with how to represent the trauma of the Stalinist past in literature and bring it to the Soviet reader. Telling in this regard is an episode described by critic Benedikt Sarnov, who recalls how Slutsky read to him and Trifonov his poem "Lopaty" ("Shovels"), which depicted the inmates' morning in a Gulag camp. After Slutsky stopped, "suddenly the big, bulky Yura made a strange sobbing sound, got up and left the room [. . .] One could hear how the water was running in the kitchen or the bathroom. Then Yura came back. Sat on his chair. His eyes were red."[19] One can certainly imagine Trifonov having a similar, deeply emotional, visceral response to Shalamov's *Kolyma Tales*.

18　Boris Slutskii, "Iz literaturnogo naslediia," *Nash sovremennik* 2 (1991): 166.
19　*Boris Slutskii: vospominaniia sovremennikov*, ed. Petr Gorelik (St. Petersburg: Neva, 2005), 246.

Similarly to Shalamov/Shamov, the alliterative play between Trifonov and Grifanov is obvious, but what else does "Grifanov" suggest? It may refer to griffin (in Russian *grifon*), a mythological hybrid animal with the body of a lion and the head of an eagle, which perhaps again hints at Trifonov's and hence Grifanov's Russian-Jewish hyphen. It may also invoke "grif"—a vulture—and portray Trifonov-Grifanov as a creature who feeds on the books of dead authors and cultures, be it of the Stalinist, Civil War, or Tsarist era. Finally, Grifanov brings to mind "грифель"—a stylus—and Osip Mandelstam's "Grifel'naia oda" ("Slate Ode"), where the speaker describes himself as:

> Кто я? Не каменщик прямой,
> Не кровельщик, не корабельщик, —
> Двурушник я, с двойной душой,
> Я ночи друг, я дня застрельщик.[20]

> Who am I? I am not a straight stone mason,
> Neither a shipbuilder, nor a roofer,
> I am a double-dealer, with a double soul,
> A friend of night, and a daymonger. (tr. Ian Probshtein)[21]

The idea of a "double-dealer, with a double soul" may allude yet again to the conflict between Trifonov's Russian and Jewish halves (and Mandelstam's for that matter), but also to his cautious stance vis-à-vis Soviet censors and the regime and, therefore, to the price he has to pay—"a friend of night, and a daymonger"—for remaining within the zone of official Soviet literature and concealing his innermost thoughts. Not incidentally, in Shrayer-Petrov's refusenik novel, Mandelstam is referred to as one of the "heights of the Russian-Jewish genius."[22]

Grifanov's likeness to Trifonov is further revealed in a conversation between Doctor Levitin and a fellow refusenik, Misha Gaberman, in which Gaberman contrasts Grifanov and Vassily Aksyonov, "two completely dissimilar writers." Gaberman tells Doctor Levitin: "We worshipped them. They were our favorites. They expressed the views of the Russian intelligentsia, of its different layers. And now who do we read—Singer,

---

20   Osip Mandel'shtam, *Sochineniia v dvukh tomakh* (Moscow: Khudozhestvennaia literatura, 1990), vol. 1, 150.
21   Osip Mandelstam, "The Slate Ode," tr. Ian Probstein, https://intranslation.brooklynrail.org/russian/the-slate-ode/, accessed Febrary 10, 2020.
22   Shraer-Petrov, *Gerbert i Nelli*, 168.

Jabotinsky, Bialik, David Markish, Malamud, Leon Uris, Natan Alterman, Igal Alon, and many others, published by Biblioteka-Aliia ['*Aliyah Library*']."²³ Shrayer-Petrov is describing here the transformations in what I have called elsewhere the "Soviet Jewish bookshelf," the source of Soviet Jews' makeshift Jewish heritage.²⁴ The books from Israel, mentioned by Gaberman, which include translations from Yiddish, Hebrew, and English; contemporary Russian-language émigré writers; and early Russian Jewish figures, such as Jabotinsky, were smuggled into the Soviet Union and supplanted, at least in Moscow, both the *samizdat* and officially sanctioned literature. Along with the changes in reading tastes came fundamental changes in the Soviet Jews' consciousness and sense of identity, derived from their "limited knowledge and collectively discovered sources."²⁵

Why, as Gaberman insists, are Grifanov and Aksyonov so different? While Grifanov, as well as his prototype Trifonov, represents the "writing between the lines" model and continues to negotiate with the authorities, Aksyonov's path symbolizes an ultimate failure of compromise and presents emigration as the only sustainable option. This juxtaposition is insightful on Shrayer-Petrov's part, considering that one of the main rifts between Trifonov and Aksyonov, whom Shrayer-Petrov knew well since their shared days at the Pavlov First Medical University in Leningrad, turned out to be Trifonov's refusal to participate in the almanac *Metropol* after Aksyonov invited him to contribute to it.²⁶ *Metropol*, which attracted some of the most interesting writers of the time, both dissident and official, was published in *samizdat* in 1978 and in the United States the next year. It is significant that while Gaberman wants to separate fully from Russian literature and the choices it offers, Doctor Levitin, who in this instance seems to speak for the author, cannot do that. He continues to dwell on Grifanov and the Russian

---

23 Ibid., 366–367.
24 See Marat Grinberg, "Reading Between the Lines: The Soviet Jewish Bookshelf and Post-Holocaust Soviet Jewish Identity," *East European Jewish Affairs* 48, no. 3 (December 2018): 391–415.
25 Smola, "Communication and Medial Frontier," 5.
26 See Kataeva, *Iurii Trifonov. Otblesk lichnosti*, 164–174. A number of writers approached by Aksyonov, including Shrayer-Petrov himself, were not prepared to risk their Soviet careers by contributing to the almanac. In the case of Shrayer-Petrov, there is a particular irony in his refusal to participate in *Metropol*: less than two years later he would be expelled from the Union of Soviet Writers for his decision to emigrate. On Shrayer-Petrov, Aksyonov, and *Metropol*, see the chapter about Aksyonov in Shrayer-Petrov's *Druz´ia i Teni*, repr. in *Vodka s pirozhnymi* (St. Petersburg: Akademicheskii proekt, 2007).

literary tradition while dreaming of emigration. As he later explains to Nelly, "We, Jews, are like mushrooms [conks] on trees. We can be transplanted onto another tree—in Israel, America, even Australia. But it is impossible to tear us away and throw to the ground. We'll perish without the trees that nourish us. And, of course, it is this ground, this Russian tree from which we've imbibed and which has allowed us to grow..."[27]

* * *

Shrayer-Petrov engages Trifonov on a number of levels. The importance of Moscow—a character of its own—in the first two parts of the refusenik trilogy makes it vividly akin to the school of city prose ("городская проза"), exemplified by Trifonov. In dialogue with this tradition, Shrayer-Petrov transforms Moscow, but also Leningrad, into Jewish spaces, as he focuses on the Moscow Choral Synagogue and the gatherings of refuseniks near it and describes the impression the Moorish architecture of the Leningrad synagogue made on the young Doctor Levitin. The shifts between Levitin's and the author's plotlines in the first two parts resemble similar devices in Trifonov's novels, particularly *The House on the Embankment* and the posthumously published *Time and Place*. Finally, the investment in history and memory powerfully links the two authors. Both are searching, to use Trifnov's image in *Time and Place*, for "the verb without a name," which signifies that to live invariably means to remember and vice versa.[28] It is no less significant that Shrayer-Petrov suggests Trifonov as one of the main influences on the Soviet Jewish psyche. With his text's explicit Jewishness he challenges Trifonov's attempts to reflect on the Russian Jewish condition and history through sporadic clues and substitutions. Both writers are ultimately interested in the overcoming of victimhood, shame, and fear for their characters. (On the overcoming of the victimary complex, see Roman Katsman's essay in this volume.)

For Trifonov, the Jewish factor was of tripartite nature: biographical, historical, and psychological, with all three elements tightly interlinked. Trifonov's close circle of friends included such important Soviet Jewish figures as the poet Boris Slutsky, the fiction writer Friedrich Gorenstein, and the translator from German and investigator of Nazi crimes Lev

---

27 Shraer-Petrov, *Gerbert i Nelli*, 503.
28 Iurii Trifonov, *Dom na naberezhnoi. Vremia i mesto* (Moscow: AST, 2000), 334.

Ginzburg; there is no doubt that Jewishness was a frequent topic of their conversations and on Trifonov's mind. Though he certainly saw himself as a Russian writer, the "call of Jewish blood," so to speak, was not insignificant to him. Tellingly, there are numerous references to Jews in his journal entries.[29] His comprehension of Jewishness, however, also ran deeper through his awareness of pre-revolutionary and early Soviet Modernist Jewish culture, as represented by his father-in-law, the Russian-Jewish painter Amshei Nyurenberg, a friend in his early years of such Jewish artists as Marc Chagall and Chaim Soutine, when Nyurenberg himself frequently turned to Jewish subjects in his paintings.[30] Trifonov had a complicated relationship with Nyurenberg. There are characters based on Nyurenberg in a number of Trifonov's works, most explicitly in the short story, "A Visit with Marc Chagall," which describes the author's meeting with the great artist, whom Trifonov admired.[31] Grifanov's visit to Chagall, mentioned in Shrayer-Petrov's novel, hints at the Trifonov-Chagall connection. It is also probably not accidental that Nelly's first name and her mother's profession point to Ninel´ Nyurenberg, Amshei's daughter and Trifonov's first wife, who as an opera singer performed under the pseudonym "Ninel´ Nelina."

Furthermore, a son, like Aksyonov, of a Russian father and a Jewish mother, Trifonov was consumed with untangling his parents' legacies and—through them—the Russian-Jewish bind. His father, Valentin Trifonov, a Civil War Hero and prominent Soviet official and top military judge, was arrested in 1937 on the charges of Trotskyism and executed the following year. Trifonov's mother, Evgenia Lurie, came from the family of devout Bolsheviks and was also arrested in 1938; she survived and was released from the Gulag camps in 1945. Trifonov was raised by his Jewish, maternal grandmother, Tatyana Slovatinskaya, an exemplar of fanatical dedication to the revolutionary cause even in the face of Stalin's crimes.

The issue of the Jewish contribution to the revolution and the Soviet project did not escape Trifonov's historic imagination; the biographical and the historical are intertwined in his sparse but loaded commentary on it throughout his oeuvre. In the impassioned biography of his father,

---

29 This is particularly notable in the journal Trifonov kept while touring the United States. Ibid., 681–743.
30 See Nyurenberg's memoirs, Amshei Niurenberg, *Odessa-Parizh-Moskva. Vospominaniia khudozhnika* (Moscow: Gesharim / Mosty kul´tury, 2010).
31 See Yury Trifonov, "A Visit with Marc Chagall," in *Voices of Jewish-Russian Literature: An Anthology*, ed. Maxim D. Shrayer (Boston: Academic Studies Press, 2018), 648–650.

Glares of Fire, published in 1965, he presents the figure of Aron Stolts, an early prominent Bolshevik known as "the party's conscience," his father's confidant and defender, and later an important Soviet jurist. Trifonov's portrait of Stolts is deeply sympathetic, but what is especially striking, especially in the context of unspoken Soviet taboos on Jewish subjects, is how he emphasizes Stolts's Jewishness as the reason he decided to join the Bolsheviks. Jewishness becomes a redeeming factor in Trifonov's attempt to cling to the revolutionary project perverted by Stalin; as far as Trifonov is concerned, at least at this moment in his life, had people like Stolts prevailed in the Party, Stalin and his atrocities would not have been possible. This idea also links him to Shalamov's view of the revolution and again recalls the-fictionalized Shamov in Shrayer-Petrov's refusenik trilogy.

In the later novels, such as *The Old Man* and the unfinished *Disappearance*, which features a character based on Stolts, Trifonov's view of the revolution and Civil War grows more tragic and indeterminate with the representation of the Jewish participation acquiring a greater complexity as well. In *The Old Man*, published in 1978, he is alluding to Babel and offers his own version of the Jewish commissars. Accused by some readers at the time of succumbing to antisemitic stereotypes, Trifonov's take, however, was characteristically subtle and filled with *nedoskazannost'* ("недосказанность"; "understatedness"). He envisioned the Jewish component both as an indelible part of his personal memory and very being *and* an indelible part of the collective historical memory. He yearned to sustain this memory and understand its significance in the face of Soviet erasure of anything Jewish, on the one hand, and the nationalist Russian condemnation of the Jewish involvement, on the other.

Yet, Trifonov's notion of Russian-Jewish historical synthesis transcends debates about Soviet origins and Stalinism. In *The Long Goodbye*, written in 1971 as part of the so-called Moscow cycle of novellas, the protagonist Grisha Rebrov, a failing playwright, who cannot find his place in the conformist Soviet environment and who most resembles the author, responds to a criticism by a fellow playwright Nikolai Smolianov, an epitome of Soviet conformism and his wife's lover, that he is not rooted in any soil. Rebrov cries out impassionedly:

"Какая почва? О чем речь? Чернозёмы? Подзолы? Фекалии? Моя почва — это опыт истории, всё то, чем Россия перестрадала!" И зачем-то стал говорить о том, что одна его бабушка из ссыльных полячек, что прадед крепостной, а дед был замешан в студенческих беспорядках, сослан в Сибирь, что другая его бабушка преподавала музыку в Петербурге, отец этой бабушки был из кантонистов, а его, Гришин, отец, участвовал в первой мировой и в гражданской войнах... и всё это вместе... и есть почва, есть опыт истории, и есть — Россия.³²

"What soil? Black earth? Podzol? Excrements? My soil is my historical experience, everything that Russia has weathered!" And for whatever reason he began to say that one of his grandmothers came from Polish exiled women, that his great-grandfather was a serf whose grandfather was involved in student protests and sent to Siberia, that his other grandmother taught music in Petersburg while her father was from the cantonists; Grisha's own father participated in World War I and Civil War... all of this... is indeed soil, historical experience and Russia itself.

Every detail is meaningful in this generational lineage, but especially telling and daring is the mention of *cantonists*, Jewish children conscripted into the Tsarist army in the first half of the nineteenth century, who had to serve for twenty-five years and were pressured to convert. Cantonists represent one of the harshest episodes in Russia's treatment of its Jews. Many among the Soviet Jewish readers would have recognized this unambiguous Jewish reference; there's no doubt that Shrayer-Petrov and his character Doctor Levitin would have known it as well.³³ With the image of the cantonists, exemplary of the "writing between the lines" method, Trifonov insists that Jews, from persecution to acculturation, are an inherent part of Russian historical experience and his own roots. Like his other character, Sergei Troitsky in *Another Life*, he "searche[s] for threads, connecting past with the more remote past and the future."³⁴ It is not by chance that Rebrov brings up the cantonists since the accusation of rootlessness—the lack of soil ("беспочвенность")—unmistakably carries with it antisemitic overtones and echoes the postwar anti-cosmopolitan campaign, a topic of particular importance for Trifonov. This way the psychological dimension of his Jewish concerns is brought forth.

---

32 Iurii Trifonov, *Izbrannye proizvedeniia* (Moscow: Khudozhestvennaia literatura, 1978), vol. 2, 167.

33 The published English translation of the novel completely misses this reference, using the vague expression "the soldier class" for cantonists. Yury Trifonov, *The Exchange and Other Stories*, tr. Ellendea Proffer, Helen P. Burlingame, Jim Somers, and Byron Lindsey (Evanston: Northwestern University Press, 1991), 120.

34 Trifonov, *Izbrannye proizvedeniia*, 296.

As mentioned earlier, Trifonov's career began with his first novel, *Students*, published in 1950 and awarded a Stalin Prize. Featuring a bad "cosmopolitan" professor, who is rightfully denounced by his student, it fit in perfectly with the spirit of the times, marked by Stalin's assault on Soviet Jews carried out through the infamous campaign. Tellingly, when Ilya Ehrenburg was asked what he thought of this novel, he responded that Trifonov was a talented writer, but he hoped that one day he would feel regret for having written such a book.[35] This indeed would happen—the mature Trifonov would try to distance himself from it as much as possible, wishing that he could have rewritten it, which is what he largely did in *The House on the Embankment*, his most celebrated text, published in 1976. Taking place during the anti-cosmopolitan campaign, it showcases a similar conflict between a student, Vadim Glebov, and his professor, but the commentary Trifonov offers on the conflict now is markedly different.

Jewishness is never explicit in the text, but central between the lines. The professor, Nikolai Ganchuk, a non-Jew, defends his colleague Boris Astrug, who is accused, along with others, of "rootlessness." It is clear, at least again to the attentive readers searching for esoteric meanings, who Astrug is and what his accusers imply.[36] Trifonov also offers a substitution: as the result of his position, and his troubles during the anti-cosmopolitan campaign, Ganchuk becomes for all practical and symbolic purposes a Jew by default. Forced to give a report on what he observed in Ganchuk's apartment, Glebov recalls, in particular, the statues of philosophers standing atop Ganchuk's bookcase, including Spinoza. "Boruch Spinoza [...] is not a true materialist," says one Shireiko, who runs the campaign against Glebov.[37] It is meaningful that he calls the ideologically impure Spinoza by his Jewish name, rather than the accepted "Benedict." This uncovers not only Spinoza's Jewishness, but Ganchuk's as well.[38] Glebov's betrayal of Ganchuk, his mentor and the father of his girlfriend, is predicated on fear, "the most

---

35 See Aleksandr Shitov, *Iurii Trifonov: Khronika zhizni i tvorchestva* (Ekaterinburg: Ural´skii universitet, 1997), 233.
36 The published English translation of the novel makes this reference explicit in a way that is antithetical to Trifonov's "between the lines" method, calling it "rootless cosmopolitanism—a particular disgusting and hypocritical cover for antisemitism." Yuri Trifonov, *Another Life and The House on the Embankment*, tr. Michael Glenny (Evanston: Northwestern University Press, 1983), 307.
37 Trifonov, *Dom na naberezhnoi. Vremia i mesto*, 115.
38 In this case, the English translation omits Boruch and misses the Jewish suggestiveness altogether. See Trifonov, *Another Life and The House on the Embankment*, 303.

elusive and the most mysterious of triggers for human consciousness."[39] For Trifonov, this fear envelops all of Soviet existence under Stalin and beyond. For him, it acquires deeply personal connotations, which invariably touch on the position of the Jew in the Soviet context.[40] How to overcome this fear is Trifonov's main question, which he would continue confronting until his premature death in 1981.[41]

* * *

This biographical, historical, and psychological background is implicitly carried over into Shrayer-Petrov's Grifanov. What Trifonov-Grifanov accomplishes through subtext and veiled allusion, Shrayer-Petrov achieves directly and unambiguously. Fear is precisely what Doctor Herbert Levitin desires to abscond: fear of fate, represented by the phantasmagoric owl-woman, who haunts him and other Jewish refuseniks; fear of the KGB and Soviet authorities, who destroy his family and prevent their immigration; fear of Vovchik, a Russian-Jewish hybrid and a perverse genius, who embodies all the uncleanliness of Soviet life and is instrumental in the murder of Levitin's beloved Nelly. Doctor Levitin, who remains all alone at the end of the trilogy as he faces death, comes out devoid of fears and regrets and truly becomes an epochal Soviet Jewish protagonist: "He did not have to justify himself or explain anything. With his life he paid in full for the mistakes and weaknesses of the Soviet Jewish *intelligent*, born, raised, and educated as a doctor in the experimental totalitarian-socialist system, which now, based on all evidence, was beginning to sink into the dark hole of eternity."[42] This refusal "to justify himself or explain anything" encapsulates Shrayer Petrov's own stance in writing the "refusenik" trilogy. As he explained to his son Maxim D. Shrayer, the key to this liberation

---

39 Trifonov, *Dom na naberezhnoi. Vremia i mesto*, 138.
40 The figure of Spinoza indeed played an important role during the postwar antisemitic campaigns. As recounted by my grandfather, Mikhail Goldis, a law student at Kiev State University at that time, in 1949, at the peak of anti-cosmopolitan frenzy, Vladimir S. Pokrovsky, professor of the history of law, gave a lecture about Spinoza, whom he referred to by his Jewish name Borukh and called "this great son of the Jewish people." News of the lecture quickly spread among the city's Jews, many of whom petitioned the university administration to allow them to attend Pokrovsky's lectures.
41 *Time and Place* describes a similar predicament for its main character, Antipov. He resolves it in a way that is markedly different from Glebov's actions.
42 David Shraer-Petrov, *Tret'ia zhizn'* (Lugansk: Shiko, 2010), 342.

was "in being absolutely honest with oneself. And so if you no longer look back and take cues. [. . .] And as a refusenik I no longer looked back when I wrote. I only took cues from myself."[43]

Finally, the Russian-Jewish synthesis is a central theme of Shrayer-Petrov's oeuvre, which he expresses in the trilogy in the terms that are evocative of Trifonov. In the second part, Doctor Levitin meets with Yury, Trifonov's namesake, a Russian young man who fought in Afghanistan with his son Anatoly and was with him when Anatoly was killed. Doctor Levitin tries to explain to himself what bonded the two boys and imagines that it was their pedigrees. Shrayer-Petrov writes,

> Русский потомственный интеллигент, из дворян, народоволец, декабрист, новиковец по внутренней убеждённости, переданной с варяжской вольной кровью, буйствующей в застенках абсолютизма. И еврейский мальчик, глотнувший воздух свободы и любви и заточённый в колодки тоталитарного режима, избравшего его, живущего по другим внутренним законам, отбирать жизнь у полудиких горцев ради возвышения и распространения той силы, которая поработила его самого.[44]

> Coming from the generations of Russian *intelligentsia*, [Yury came] from the gentry, from the People's Will, from the Decembrists; a proponent of the enlightenment in his inner convictions, transmitted through his Varangian free blood that rebelled in the prisons of absolutism. And the Jewish boy, [his Anatoly], who breathed in the air of freedom and love only to be shackled by the chains of the totalitarian regime, which picked him, even though he lived according to very different inner rules, to take life away from the barely civilized mountain dwellers for the sake of elevating and spreading that very force which had enslaved him.

Similarly to Trifonov in *The Long Goodbye*, Shrayer-Petrov presents a loaded historical genealogy for Yury, which spiritually unites him with Anatoly in their thirst for freedom; recall that one of the most symbolic moments in the trilogy is the scene of a Passover Seder led by Doctor Levitin in Moscow.[45] With their very being Yury and Anatoly are *rooted* in

---

43 Maxim D. Shrayer, "A Russian Typewriter Longs for her Master." *Tablet Magazine*, January 28, 2020, https://www.tabletmag.com/jewish-arts-and-culture/297595/maxim-shrayer-david-shrayer, accessed February 28, 2020.
44 Shraer, *Gerbert i Nelli*, 343.
45 Ibid., 662.

the centuries of Russian and Jewish pasts, confirming Trifonov's dictum, which is also paramount to Judaism, that to live is to remember.

* * *

Trifonov died in 1981 and so in Shrayer-Petrov's refusenik trilogy, Grifanov is also gone, living in Doctor Levitin's memory. Through Grifanov's portrait, nuanced and fragmentary, as is all of Trifonov's prose, Shrayer-Petrov managed to pay a fitting homage to the writer, who became the sign of his times—giving him, to evoke the title of Trifonov's Moscow novel, *another life*. Crucially, he transformed Trifonov's suggestiveness in regard to Jewishness into an overt "Jewish utterance," "a protest against Jewish helplessness, dependence, and secondariness."[46] Trifonov, one hopes, would have appreciated the gesture.

---

46 Katsman, "Jewish Fearless Speech," 51, 47.

Works Cited

Ginzburg, Lidiia. *O psikhologicheskoi proze*. Moscow: Intrada, 1999.

Gofman, Efim. "Varlam Shalamov i Yurii Trifonov: nesostoiavshiisia dialog" in *Shalamovskii sbornik* 5 (2017): 334–355. https://shalamov.ru/research/320/. Accessed February 10, 2020.

Kataeva N. G., ed. *Trifonov, Iurii. Otblesk lichnosti*. Moscow: Galeriia, 2015.

Katsman, Roman. "Jewish Fearless Speech: Towards a Definition of Soviet Jewish Nonconformism." *East European Jewish Affairs* 48, no. 1 (May 2018): 41–55.

Mandelstam, Osip [Osip Mandel´shtam]. *Sochineniia v dvukh tomakh*. Moscow: Khudozhestvennaia literatura, 1990.

———. "Slate Ode." Translated by Ian Probstein. https://intranslation.brooklynrail.org/russian/the-slate-ode/. Accessed February 10, 2020.

Sarnov, Benedikt. "Zanimatel´naia dialektika." In *Boris Slutskii: vospominaniia sovremennikov*, edited by Piotr Gorelik, 236–254. St. Petersburg: Neva, 2005.

Shrayer, Maxim D., ed. *Voices of Jewish-Russian Literature: An Anthology*. Boston: Academic Studies Press, 2018.

Shrayer, Maxim D. "A Russian Typewriter Longs for her Master." *Tablet Magazine*, January 28, 2020. https://www.tabletmag.com/jewish-arts-and-culture/297595/maxim-shrayer-david-shrayer. Accessed February 28, 2020.

Shrayer-Petrov, David [David Shraer-Petrov]. *Moskva zlatoglavaia*. Baltimore: Vestnik, 1994.

——— [David Shraer-Petrov]. *Tret´ia zhizn´*. Lugansk: Shiko, 2010.

——— [David Shraer-Petrov]. *Gerbert i Nelli*. Moscow: Knizhniki, 2014.

———. *Doctor Levitin: A Novel*. Edited and with notes by Maxim D. Shrayer, translated by Arna B. Bronstein, Aleksandra I. Fleszar, and Maxim D. Shrayer. Detroit: Wayne State University Press, 2018.

Slutskii, Boris. "Iz literaturnogo naslediia." *Nash sovremennik* 2 (1991): 163-168.

Smola, Klavdia. "Communication and Medial Frontier Crossings in the Jewish Underground Culture." *East European Jewish Affairs* 48, no. 1 (2018): 5–22.

Strauss, Leo. *Persecution and the Art of Writing*. Chicago: The University of Chicago Press, 1988.

Trifonov, Yury [Iurii Trifonov]. *Izbrannye proizvedeniia*. Moscow: Khudozhestvennaia literatura, 1978.

———. *Another Life* and *The House on the Embankment*. Translated by Michael Glenny. Evanston: Northwestern University Press, 1983.

——— [Iurii Trifonov]. *Otblesk kostra. Ischeznovenie*. Moscow: Sovetskii pisatel', 1988.

———. *The Exchange and Other Stories*. Translated by Ellendea Proffer, Helen P. Burlingame, Jim Somers, and Byron Lindsey. Evanston: Northwestern University Press, 1991.

——— [Iurii Trifonov]. *Dom na naberezhnoi. Vremia i mesto*. Moscow: AST, 2000.

The Birth of the Novel from the Spirit of Contradiction: The Jewish Theologeme in David Shrayer-Petrov's Novel-Fantella *Yudin's Redemption* *

Leonid Katsis

When reading a novel such as David Shrayer-Petrov's *Yudin's Redemption* (*Iskuplenie Iudina*), the immediate question that comes to mind is that of its significance. What does it mean to be reading a book that was conceived and written in the early 1980s in Russia, then revised in the 1990s after the author's emigration, and first published in the mid-2000s?[1] What has

---

* Copyright © 2021 by Leonid Katsis. English translation copyright © 2021 by Anastasia Degtyareva. Unless noted otherwise, all translations of Russian sources into English are by the translator.

1 David Shraer-Petrov, *Iskuplenie Iudina. Istoricheskii roman v piati chastiakh, oboznachennykh sootvetstvenno drevneevreiskim meram dliny: kane "trostnik", amma "lokot'", zeret "piad'", tefakh "ladon'", etsba "palets,"* Mosty 5 (2005): 5–61; 6: 21–116; 7: 11–88. The term "fantella" (Russian "фантелла"), sometimes deciphered as "fantastical novella," is Shrayer-Petrov's own coinage. In the afterword to the final, revised version of the novel, dated 2019, the author himself provides the following timeline: "Following my application for an exit permit, I was expelled from the Union of Soviet Writers and ostracized. My family became refuseniks. I found myself in academic and literary isolation. In 1981, soon after I finished working on *Doctor Levitin*, the first part of my trilogy about refuseniks, I began writing *Yudin's Redemption*. It was completed in 1982.

happened during those years? And what has changed in our collective perception of the destinies of the assimilated Jewish-Russian intelligentsia of the 1950s–1980s?

If one were to look for analogues for this work or attribute it to a particular movement or tradition, we should look toward Thomas Mann's *Joseph and His Brothers*, Lion Feuchtwanger's *The Judean War*, and, possibly, his *The False Nero*[2] as well, and, finally, the more recent novel *The Psalm* (*Psalom*) by Friedrich Gorenstein, written in 1975. If the latter may be considered a chronological predecessor of *Yudin's Redemption*, then even more relevant here is Gorestein's *Redemption* (*Iskuplenie*), which had been completed in 1967. As for Mann's aforementioned *Joseph and His Brothers* and Feuchtwanger's *The Judean War*, in Soviet-published Russian translations both were essential readings for those Soviet Jews who wished to embrace their Jewish roots. (Also see Marat Grinberg's essay in this volume.)

Among all else, note that the annotator of Feuchtwanger's novels in Russian translation was Simon Markish, elder son of murdered Yiddish poet Perez Markish. For the 1960s–1970s generation, the burgundy spines of Feuchtwanger's and the gray spines of Mann's Soviet editions— and occasionally the gilded spines of the Brockhaus and Efron *Jewish Encyclopedia*—were emblematic of both a return to Jewishness and of an acquisition of the beginnings of Jewish national self-identification in Soviet society. Furthermore, two other relevant books come to mind in this connection. The first is the novel *The Mole of History* (*Krot istorii*, 1979) by Vladimir Kormer, and the second is the memoir *In the Land of the Forefathers* (*V kraiu otsov*, 1998) by Yuri Glazov. Thus we are able to

---

It was an incredibly dangerous time, especially for Jewish refuseniks, who were denied the right to emigration and persecuted." The reader of this article should take this chronology into account. See David Shraer-Petrov, "Posleslovie k romanu 'Iskuplenie Iudina,'" in his *Iskuplenie Iudina. Istoricheskii roman v piati chastiakh, oboznachennykh sootvetstvenno drevneevreiskim meram dliny: kane "trostnik", amma "lokot'", zeret "piad'", tefakh "ladon'", etsba "palets"*, ed. Maksim D. Shraer, forthcoming 2021. The author thanks Maxim D. Shraer for providing the text of the yet unpublished afterword.

2   See my article: Leonid Katsis, "Pragmatika i poetika obrashchenii k sovetskim vozhdiam v 1930-e gg. O. Mandel′shtam, B. Pasternak, I. Sel′vinskii, L. Feikhtvanger, Dem′ian Bednyi," in my *Smena paradigm i smena paradigmy. Ocherki russkoi literatury, iskusstva, nauki 20 veka* (Moscow: Izdatel′stvo RGGU, 2012), 158-165. I analyze the two components of Feuchtwanger's work that were especially attractive for members of the Soviet intelligentsia, especially in *The False Nero*, where the anti-totalitarian message merges with the complex subtexts of political life in Germany and the USSR, and also *Moscow, 1937*.

speak of a greater historical and literary context of Shrayer-Petrov's *Yudin's Redemption*.

That said, my premise in this essay is different from both an analysis of the dissident and nonconformist discourse that shaped Shrayer-Petrov's writing[3] or from a critical analysis in the canon of Jewish-Russian literature and refusenik literature, specifically.[4]

I should mention that I have personally experienced life in the Moscow Jewish refusenik environment, which, in my case, was also a religious one, and some of my recollections of it even found their way into print.[5] This experience could serve as an existential context for my own perception of *Yudin's Redemption* and other works of David Shrayer-Petrov. I actually once knew and am still in contact with some of the people who had once surrounded the author. I will therefore pursue a not so traditional approach to the novel *Yudin's Redemption* by regarding it as a kind of Ocean of Solaris (to borrow the title of Stanisław Lem's famous novel of 1961), as, if you will, a cerebral surface of Russian Jewry circa 1950s–1970s, steaming with national and political thought. I will proceed as if by removing the arch of the skull from this ocean in the course of an imaginary cultural autopsy, and in doing so exposing the gyri and intersections of the tuberous mass that reveal themselves during such a procedure. In so doing, I will support my commentary with insights gained throughout my research into the topics addressed in the novel. Given that the author of *Yudin's Redemption* has had a long parallel career in the world of medicine and microbiology, such an approach does not seem too "biologist" or "vivisectionist." As is inevitable in this case, this approach will produce numerous microtome sections that can either break or conceal the most profound cross-level connections. However,

---

3   Its comprehensive description, including in application to the novel discussed in the present article, has been previously provided in Roman Katsman, "Parallel'nye vselennye Davida Shraera-Petrova, *Wiener Slawistischer Almanach* 79 (2017): 255–279. For a further elaboration of the topic, see Katsman's essay in this volume.

4   See Klavdia Smola," O proze russko-evreiskogo pisatelia Davida Shraera-Petrova," in *Russkie evrei v Amerike*, book 15, ed. Ernst Zal´tsberg (Moscow: Giperion, 2017), 135–150; eadem,"Das Martyrium des Otkaz: David Šraer-Petrovs 'Gerbert i Nèlli,'" in her *Wiedererfindung der Tradition Russisch-jüdische Literatur der Gegenwart* (Cologne: Böhlau, 2019), 139–149. See also Klavdia Smola's essays in this volume.

5   Leonid Katsis, "Dlia menia russkoe i evreiskoe sosushchestvuiut v edinom potoke," in *Iudaika dva. Renessans v litsakh*, ed. Galina Zelenina (Moscow: Knizhniki, 2015), 392–418.

for now, I will build from the assumption that I am working not with a microtome but with a modern tomograph.

This approach will immediately allow us to look past the fact that the author transferred the events that had historically unfolded in Palestine, Rome and so forth, which pervaded the history of ancient Jews and Hurrians and other ancient peoples, to the Caucasus and, as it appears in several instances, to Crimea. After all, the author of the novel and his audience are Soviet Jews, the same ones who used to go to such resorts as Gagra and Koktebel so as to relax and ponder—with "awe"—their "Judean concerns" ("трепет его иудейских забот"—to borrow from Osip Mandelstam's text of 1933). In their imagination, Crimea would be naturally conjoined with Osip Mandelstam, and the verses of Mandelstam's *Octaves*, where he admits to being "unmoved" by the "awe" of the very same Judean "concerns," the "awe" ("трепет") still rhymed with early Jewish "chatter" ("лепет"). For instance, consider *The Awe of Judean Concerns*, the title of one of the books by the Jewish activist Aleksandr Voronelʹ.[6] Voronelʹ was the editor of the Israeli Russian journal *22*, which was so close to the heart of Solzhenitsyn, the author of *Two Hundred Years Together*. Even today, Voronelʹ believes that the formula "both together and apart" ("и вместе, и врозь") is still viable. Importantly for the context of this essay, Voronelʹ aptly titled his memoirs, published in Kharkiv in 2013, *The Zero Commandment* (*Nulevaia zapovedʹ*), referring as he does to Deuteronomy 30:19.[7] In this book, Voronelʹ uses a beautiful expression that is incredibly helpful in clarifying the worldview of this circle and generation: "*All of us who came from Russia* still hope to find and determine the 'right' side in the real world. Laughable, isn't it? . . ."[8] It was a remarkable kind of circle where it was considered necessary first to take a deep plunge into everything Russian, Christian, and "Dostoevskian," and then, having survived it, to move to things Jewish. It was this stance that made possible the unsanctioned journal *Jews in the USSR* (*Evrei v SSSR*), where Father Alexander Menʹ, a Jewish-born Orthodox priest and theologian, speculated about fighting Russian religious antisemitism by creating a certain Jewish Orthodox Church of Jacob, led by a Jewish Patriarch. At the time, no one gave much thought to the fact that blood at its purest

---

6   Aleksandr Voronelʹ, *Trepet zabot iudeiskikh* (Jerusalem: Biblioteka-Aliia, 1976).
7   Aleksandr Voronelʹ, *Nulevaia zapovedʹ* (Kharkiv: Prava liudyny, 2013).
8   Ibid., 12.

is generally not the basis of Abrahamic religions (because how else is one to choose such a Patriarch: based on maternal or paternal ancestry, Israel's Law of Return, or by rejecting a fixed belonging to Judaism? . . .). Such a historically predetermined conflation or collision of concepts shaped the poetics, geography, and world of ideas in *Yudin's Redemption*.

To decipher this collision, let us first address the cultural and poetic play in the names of the heroes. It is undoubtedly tempting to begin straight away with an analysis of the protagonist's name, which explicitly contains "Jude," mainly because the text is studded with allusions to Hitler's policies and genocide, allusions no less dense than the novel's hints at the policies under his Soviet counterpart Stalin. However, before attributing to the author everything that we see here, let us pay tribute to the name and character of the blind painter Lazarus (Lazar´). True to the Gospel story, Lazar´ will be touched by the miracles of the character who partially embodies the symbolic image of the Messiah, Jesus Christ. He also hearkens back to Lazarus (El) Lissitzky, an artist who was very much Jewish, as well as German, Russian and, ultimately, Soviet. Still, Shrayer-Petrov is even more subtle: "Странное дело: когда Евсей и Копл пришли в дом Лазаря-художника, никого не было. На столе ждала их кринка молока и каравай хлеба" ("Curious thing: when Evsey [Eusebius] and Kopl entered the house of Lazarus the painter, nobody was home. On the table, a jug of milk and a loaf of bread were waiting for them"). This is undoubtedly an allusion to Velimir Khlebnikov, the poet at the top of Russian avant-garde, a highly significant figure for Shrayer-Petrov's literary generation:

> Мне мало надо!
> Краюшку хлеба
> И капля молока.
> Да это небо,
> Да эти облака! [9]

> ("I don't need much! / A slice of bread,/ And a drop of milk / And this sky,/ And also these clouds!")

Further in the same scene in Shrayer-Petrov's text, one reads:

> Прохладой сочился хуррийский сыр, запеленутый в виноградные листья. Лазарь исчез, он скрывался от братьев.

---

9 Velimir Khlebnikov, *Sobranie sochinenii v 6 tomakh*, vol. 2 (Moscow: Nasledie, 2001), 381.

— Он не захотел, чтобы мы увидели его бессилие, Копл.

— А картины? Разве они не доказательство его силы. Это ли не чудо?[10]

Wrapped in grape leaves, the Hurrian cheese oozed coolness. Lazarus had disappeared; he was hiding from the brothers.
"He did not want us to see him weakened, Kopl."
"And the paintings? Are they not proof of his strength? Is that not a miracle?"

Here, the future miracle of Lazarus could distract the reader from a much more critical discussion:

— Ты прав, Копл. Но прав — правотой человека, которая ограничена предначертанным.

— Потому что я человек. Один из толпы. Я не могу рассуждать иначе. Ты можешь, Евсей?

— Да, пожалуй, брат. Ко мне приходит иногда *это*.

— Что *это*, Евсей?

— Ощущение, что я — Слово, воплощенное в образ человека.[11]

"You are right, Kopl. But you're right from the point of view constricted by providence.
"Because I am a man. One from a crowd. I cannot argue otherwise. Can you, Evsey?"
"Perhaps I can, brother. Sometimes I am struck by *it*."
"What do you mean by *it*, Evsey?"
"The sensation that I am the Word embodied in human form."

The ingenuous invertedness of this phrase, meant to recall the key Gospel passage from "In the beginning was the Word" to "the Word was God," underscores that the speaker is one whose words and actions resemble those of the Antichrist. This character was intimately familiar to the group of fellow seekers described in *Yudin's Redemption*, as the novel's title itself mirrors Lazarus's resurrection (compare "искупление Юдина" and "воскрешение Лазаря" in Russian). Here, as the doubts have been dispelled, it is time to refer to *The Short Tale of the Antichrist* (1901) by

---

10 David Shraer-Petrov, *Iskuplenie Iudina*, *Mosty* 5 (2005): 22.
11 Ibid., 22. I will not be getting into the Russian pun "Евсей"—"ессей" ("Eusebius"—"Essene") and the revival of interest in the Essenes following the discovery of the Dead Sea Scrolls in the late 1940s and early 1950s, which were being actively studied even in the USSR, for instance, by I. A. Amusin.

Vladimir Soloviev—so as to understand these inversions. The receptiveness of late Soviet era Jewish-Russian intelligentsia to Russian religious philosophy was facilitated, among other things, by other writings of Soloviev such as his essay "Talmud" and his open letter "Against the Antisemitic Movement in the Press." In the latter two works he expressed his dreams of not only the unification of the Christian churches, but all Abrahamic religions, and also declared his support of the actual Judeo-Christian sect of Joseph Rabinowitz.[12] In Soloviev's *The Short Tale of the Antichrist*, the Jews rebelled precisely because it was revealed that the already successful unifier of churches and the savior of Jews was actually uncircumcised! That would explain the contradictions with the *brit milah* (Jewish male circumcision ceremony) becoming a central theme of Vladimir Soloviev's story. However, the rebellion there took place in Jerusalem, the only place where it would make sense to see the Temple rebuilt and await the coming of the true Messiah.

Still, what about the significance and echoes of the Jewish-Russian painters' names in Shrayer-Petrov's novel? After all, El, that is, G-d (an abbreviated form of Eliezer that he chose not by accident) Lissitzky and Yudin appear alongside each other. UNOVIS, the highly influential group founded by Kazimir Malevich at the Vitebsk School of Art in 1919, had their very own artist with the last name Yudin, Lev Yudin. Moreover, considering that Shrayer-Petrov's painter also whittled wooden dolls, this

---

12 See the entry on "Joseph Rabinowitz" in *Jewish Encyclopedia*: "Russian missionary to the Jews; born in Orgeyev, Bessarabia, Sept. 23, 1837; died in Kishinef May 12, 1899. He was brought up as a Hasid, but later acquired some secular knowledge and mastered the Russian language. For a time he practised law in the lower courts of his native town, settling subsequently in Kishinef. In 1878 he wrote a long Hebrew article on the improvement of the rabbinate, which was published in Gottlober's 'Ha-Boker Or' (iv., nos. 7-8). This was his only contribution as a Jew to Hebrew literature. In 1882 he founded the sect Novy Israel, and began in a veiled and cautious way to preach a kind of new Christianity to the Jews of Kishinef. Following immediately upon the founding of the Bibleitzy brotherhood by Jacob Gordin at Elizabethgrad, the new movement attracted much attention, and was freely discussed in Russian newspapers. Rabinowitz succeeded for a time in interesting Professor Delitzsch of Leipzig in his movement and in allaying the suspicions of the Russian government, which strictly prohibits the formation of new religious sects. But his open conversion to Protestantism had the natural result of estranging many of his followers. He was baptized in Berlin on March 24, 1885," http://www.jewishencyclopedia.com/articles/12517-rabinowitz-joseph, accessed July 14, 2020.

list would be incomplete without Aleksandr Tyshler, who not only painted Solomon Mikhoels and Anna Akhmatova but also rescued Marc Chagall's "Introduction to the Jewish Theater."

In the end, the plethora of quotes and cultural associations elicited by Shrayer-Petrov's novel betokens a rather representative set of interests for the generations that, in anticipation of Palestine and of the founding of Israel, which arose from the ashes of six million, discussed, with awe and trepidation, their "Judean" concerns and anxieties in the 1920s–1970s on the Black Sea coast of the Caucasus and in Crimea, there where the novel itself is set. If one had to be convinced any further, there appears also an army of "Britons" and a comedian by the name of Arkady with a not at all random nickname Raikin, alluding not to the female name Raika, not to *раёк* (a Russian peep show akin to the French *guignol*) but to another Russian *рай* (Paradise). In this connection, a merry Yiddish joke comes to mind about deriving Filaret, a common Russian monastic name of Greek origin, from the Yiddish name Kopl: Kopl—*gopl*; *gopl*—"вилка" (fork); "вилка"—Fil´ka (a diminutive of Filaret); Fil´ka—Filaret. The author continues to charge the last name of his title character with various other attributes. It turns out that in the novel the Yudins (the title character and his male ancestors) include a philosopher, a veterinarian, a surgeon, a "Joseph" (Osip; Iosif), and even a musicologist!

In this regard, it would be impossible to proceed without acknowledging several well-known bearers of the last name "Yudin." First, there is Pavel F. Yudin (1899–1968), full member of the Soviet Academy of Sciences, philosopher, diplomat, and one of the pillars of Marxist thought during Stalinism. This Yudin was apparently of Russian peasant origin. Then there is professor Sergey S. Yudin (1891–1954), a distinguished Soviet surgeon. Finally, there is the great pianist Maria V. Yudina (1899–1970). The last two figures are especially relevant to this analysis of *Yudin's Redemption*. Surgeon Sergei Yudin distinguished himself in the specific area of my investigation, which is rather far afield from medicine.. According to the most publicly available information about Sergei Yudin, "he was imprisoned from 1948 to 1953: first in Lubyanka, then transferred into solitary confinement in Lefortovo, where he suffered his second heart attack. During his imprisonment he authored a book, *Musings of a Surgeon* [*Razmyshlenia khirurga*]. [. . .] On 18 August, 1951, during an interrogation,

Yudin proclaimed himself an antisemite before the interrogator, then went on to accuse Professor V. S. Levit of 'Jewish nationalism.' Yudin's original sentence, execution, for high treason, was subsequently commuted to ten years of administrative exile in the town of Berdsk in the Novosibirsk Oblast."[13]

The story of Maria V. Yudina is, however, entirely different. Baptized into Orthodoxy by the theologian Father Pavel Florensky, she was a fanatical Orthodox Christian. Furthermore, Yudina was a friend of the wife and widow of Osip Mandelstam, Nadezhda,[14] a fellow Jewish convert to Orthodox Christianity. Let us here suppose that Shrayer-Petrov takes a step quite uncharacteristic for his peers. In constructing and recording other facets of his protagonist's image, the author allows himself to conflate the destiny of professor Sergei Yudin, a survivor of Stalinist repressions who held a particular view of the nationalities question, with the image of Osip Mandelstam, who perished in the camps. It was there that the poet recited *chastushki*, Russian limericks of sorts, to fellow prisoners; this fact would eventually inform the apocryphal part of the famous poem/song lyrics, "Comrade Stalin, you are a great scholar . . ." ("Tovarishch Stalin, vy bol′shoi uchenyi . . ."), by Yuz Aleshkovsky. In the apocryphal quatrain the poet appears reading "Petrarch in front of the bonfire":

Для вас в Москве построен "Дом подарков",
Сам Исаковский пишет оды вам,
А здесь в тайге читает нам Петрарку
Фартовый парень Оська Мандельштам.

---

13 "Sergei Yudin," *Wikipedia*, https://en.wikipedia.org/wiki/Sergei_Yudin_(surgeon), accessed April 12, 2020. Mikhail Nesterov's "Portrait of Sergey Yudin" (1935) adorns the cover of the English translation of *Doctor Levitin*, part one of Shayer-Petrov's refusenik trilogy. See David Shrayer-Petrov, *Doctor Levitin: A Novel*, ed. and with notes by Maxim D. Shrayer, tr. Arna B. Bronstein, Aleksandra I. Fleszar, Maxim D. Shrayer (Detroit: Wayne State University Press, 2018).

14 A. M. Kuznetsov, ed. and comment, "Desiatoe pis′mo N. Ia. Mandel′shtam M. V. Iudinoi," *Nevel′skii sbornik 7* (2002): 24–27; idem, introduction, ed., commentary, "Pis′ma N. Ia. Mandel′shtam k M. V. Iudinoi i V. A. Stravinskoi," *Nevel′skii sbornik 2* (1997): 42–55.

("For you the 'House of Presents' is built in Moscow/ Isakovsky himself writes odes for you,/ And here in the taiga recited Petrarch to us/ that lucky fellow Osʹka Mandelstam.")

Apparently, Yuz Aleshkovsky, the author of the famous "Song about Stalin," did not care for the apocryphal stanza.[15] At the same time, it was known that Nadezhda Mandelstam liked it.[16]

So that even less doubt remains that Osip Mandelstam's widow is alluded to, the novel's next part raises the question of the "Sarmatian Jews" inheriting the uncompromising nature of the ancient Jews. I will not be elaborating here on the possibility that the novel is built around Arthur Koestler's theory of Jewish ethnogenesis, put forth in *The Thirteenth Tribe*[17] (1976); not that the theory was still quite novel at the time and its different versions and editions overlapped with Shrayer-Petrov's writing process. I will only mention in passing that Lev Gumilev's ideas about the Jewish-Khazar chimera, expounded upon in his book in *Ethnogenesis and the Biosphere of the Earth*[18] (1978), were incredibly popular during the period

---

15 See Iuz Aleshkovskii, "'Pesnia o Staline,'" with the added stanza not composed by Aleshkovskii, http://a-pesni.org/bard/alechk/tovstalin.htm, accessed June 24, 2020.

16 "But among the stories, there are also some that aspire to authenticity and are painted in great detail. One such story asserts that Mandelstam died on board of a ship bound for Kolyma, offering further a detailed account of how he was cast into the ocean. Other legends include Mandelstam being murdered by criminals and reciting Petrarch by the fire." See N. Ia. Mandelʹshtam, *Sobranie sochinenii v dvukh tomakh* (Ekaterinburg: Gonzo, 2014), vol. 1, 477–478. On December 22, 1962 A. K. Gladkov, a friend of Nadezhda Mandelstam, wrote in his diary: "Received a letter from N. Ia. Mandelstam. [She] rejoices at a verse of a song sent to her, about a 'fine fellow Osʹka [diminutive form of the name Osip] Mandelstam reciting Petrarch by the camp-fire' (from the famous 'Letter from a Detainee to Comrade Stalin' ['Pisʹmo ot zeka tovarishchu Stalinu'], which grows longer every day)." The author of the song, Yuz Aleshkovsky, commented: "About the verse. Its author, a lucky poet and lyricist—he kicked the bucket long ago—read it to me at the Central House of Writers, and I said that all the lines were arrogant and idiotic, especially 'recited Petrarch, that fine fellow Osya [another diminutive form of the name Osip] Mandelstam.' I asked, what . . . camp-fire, what . . . recital [of poetry], a man was literally driven to insanity by all that foulness . . . and starved to death, and just in general, what is up with that brazen boorishness of yours, asshole, that familiarity in your tone?" See Pavel Nerler, "Petrarka, Mandelʹshtam i Iuz Aleshkovskii," *Novaia gazeta*, July 23, 2015, https://novayagazeta.ru/articles/2015/07/24/65008-petrarka-mandelshtam-i-yuz-aleshkovskiy, accessed July 14, 2020.

17 Arthus Koestler, *The Thirteenth Tribe: The Khazar Empire and Its Heritage* (New York: Random House, 1976).

18 L. N. Gumilev, *Etnogenez i biosfera zemli* (Leningrad: Gidrometeoizdat, 1990).

in question. I will point out, however, that it was Nadezhda Mandelstam who sought to determine whether or not at least a drop of the ancient Judeans' blood had remained in both her and her husband, a drop that warrants one's resilience and resistance against all odds.

At the same time, the description of the non-Jewish, Scythian mother of Osip Yudin (the future Professor Iosif [Joseph] Yudin and the future father of the novel's title character), unkempt, a *papirosa* in her hand, trying to control everything in her son's life, does not appear to refer to the childless Nadezhda Mandelstam. Moreover, the mere idea on my part of drawing a comparison between one of the greatest widows of Russian culture and one of the female characters of *Yudin's Redemption* might ruffle some of the critics' feathers. It is difficult to say whether David Shrayer-Petrov is referencing any specific impressions or information about Mandelstam's widow, or whether this particular image is simply a binary construct, created from juxtapositions such as Jew-antisemite, mother-wife, Russian-Jew etc. Alternatively, it could have been based on something real.

We should not be surprised that something similar to the supposed iteration of Nadezhda Mandelstam in Shrayer-Petrov's novel was preserved in the memoirs of poet Andrei Voznesensky (1933–2010), whose formal quest in the 1960s was close to that of the poetry of the author of *Yudin's Redemption*. ("As I see it, among our contemporaries Andrei Voznesensky is closely related to him," wrote Viktor Shklovsky about David Shrayer-Petrov's poetry in a 1971 recommendation to the Union of Soviet Writers.)[19] The risky tenuousness of this fragment of Voznesensky's recollections compels me to give it from the point of view of Voznesensky's biographer Igor Virabov:

> Voznesensky considered Nadezhda Mandelstam a *sud'baba* [literally, "destinywoman"] one of the sorceresses of the poetic twentieth century. Nadezhda Yakovlevna herself was cold toward Voznesensky. Not long before she passed, she refused to see him when he arrived with an ostentatious bouquet of flowers. She explained her dislike of him only so vaguely: "spoiled brat." [. . .]

---

19 David Shrayer-Petrov, *Vodka s pirozhnymi. Roman s pisateliami*, ed. Maksim D. Shraer (St. Petersburg: Akademicheskii proekt, 2007), 378.

> Once Andrei [Voznesensky] was completely astonished to hear the harrowing account of an Italian acquaintance who was dreaming of meeting the widow of Osip Mandelstam. Mariolina Marzotto, a "refined young Venetian lady, little countess, whose sister-in-law Marta Marzotto was the queen of Roman high society and a close friend of Renato Guttuzo," could not conceal her shock from her first visit with the poet's widow. In *The Destinywomen* (*Sud′baby*), Voznesensky recounts Mariolina's surprising discovery of quietist Nadezhda Yakovlevna's other side:
>
> "An air of scandal hangs in the room when I enter. Like a witch with her gray hair all disheveled, a madwoman shakes the air with four-story obscenities. She turns out to be Nadezhda Yakovlevna herself. She giggles like a she-demon while ripping to shreds and tossing to the floor the manuscripts of young poets. 'Leningrad sh-t,' were the kindest words uttered by this intellectual lady.
>
> She notices me, and her focus shifts away from the young poets.
>
> 'Well, aren't you a beauty,' she says. "Come, then, pretty girl, give me your earrings." Her hands are quick and nimble as she snatches from my ears my mother's heirloom earring. 'I like them,' she purrs and starts taking the diamond rings off my fingers.
>
> I shy away, not knowing what to do, but refuse to give up the rings. Then N.Ya. turns to a pale young poet sitting next to her and screams: "Isn't she pretty? Go on, then, go f--k her, quickly now, f--k her, come on!"
>
> I dashed to the exit . . ."

* * *

In essence, Nadezhda Yakovlevna was only reiterating her version of her late husband's plea: "их [. . .] полухлебом плоти накорми!" ("feed them the half-bread of flesh!"), from the poem Osip Mandelstam had once dedicated to Maria Petrovykh, with whom he was in love.[20]

Naturally, I cannot guarantee that the author of *Yudin's Redemption* had all of this in mind. However, as I said, the approach to analytical reading that I am taking in this essay is rather personal, existential even. I must

---

[20] Igor′ Virabov, *Andrei Voznesensky* (Moscow: Molodaia gvardiia, 2015), 93, https://dom-knig.com/read_184446-93, accessed April 12, 2020. The poem in question is "Masteritsa vinovatykh vzorov . . ." ("She the mistress of guilty stares . . . ," 1934).

note therefore that, following the publication of Nadezhda Mandelstam's *Hope Abandoned* (titled *Vtoraia kniga* [*The Second Book*] in the original Russian), a frustration with her was not an uncommon motif in the accounts of meeting her. As for Shrayer-Petrov's novel, the author can never be held accountable for those meanings that grow far and wide, as Osip Mandelstam used to put it.

To avoid bias and one-sidedness, an opposing perspective on Nadezhda Mandelstam's escapades follows below, one by the Russian-Israeli literary scholar Dmitry Segal:

> [. . .] I can attest that, on the one hand, Nadezhda Yakovlevna tried to embody her hypostasis of a faithful widow, but, on the other, was fully aware of all the limitations and clichés of her position as a widow, with which she dealt with a great deal of self-awareness and irony. Precisely because she was so aware of the tense boundaries of her position as Mandelstam's widow and the scant possibilities of publication of his oeuvres, she decided early on to act outside the boundaries of her Soviet existence and publish Mandelstam abroad. In doing so, she abandoned the status of a "Soviet widow" and became a "widow of the world" and an "international widow." I believe she came to that decision not without the impact the *tamizdat* fate of Pasternak—first, that of his *Doctor Zhivago*,[21] followed by his collected works published in Michigan, and the latter, in my opinion, had been the incentive for preparing an American edition of Mandelstam. That was the gateway to other emblematic campaigns of Nadezhda Yakovlevna that went against the accepted ethics of being a proper Soviet widows. Such [Soviet] ethics entailed the prohibition against personal writing activities, the need to "keep quiet" and not to "rock the boat," keeping out of her late husband's limelight so as not to outshine him [the mother of Osip Yudin in Shrayer-Petrov's novel has a right to do just that—L.K.], being tolerant of the oscillation of political opinion regarding her husband and to bear patiently the censorial intervention and interference with the publication of his works ("at least they printed something"), waiting patiently for one's turn at the editorial matters and all other stages—really, just avoiding confrontation with everyone (except maybe with "alternative

---

21 This is also important for the professional parallel between Yudin in Shrayer-Petrov's novel and Doctor Zhivago in Pasternak's novel. Perhaps, this emphasis on the medical profession creates an allusion to the antisemitic surgeon Sergei Yudin.

widows"). Nadezhda Yakovlevna broke all of those rules mainly because she considered them a direct continuation of the repressions that, in the end, lead to Mandelstam's demise.[22]

Now consider another example of Nadezhda Mandelstam's "antibehavior," this time applicable either to the namesake of either Shrayer-Petrov's title character, or perhaps, his grandmother. The recollection belongs to the art historian Elena Murina:

> Once following a telephone call that I personally witnessed, she [Nadezhda Mandelstam] "complained" to me about M. V. Yudina, who had been pestering her with demands to convince Natasha Svetlova to "give up" Solzhenitsyn, whose first wife refused to give him a divorce even though he already had another family. N. Ya. was categorical in her refusal to support M. V. Yudina's accusatory pathos, based on the Christian dogma of the indissolvability of marriage. N. Ya. found this argument ridiculous and lacking justification for any sort of interfering in the family's complicated situation. Nevertheless, whenever one of her regular guests or even a friend left his wife for a younger female partner, she always took the side of the "offended party" and stopped receiving "the one at fault," even if she cared about him. This happened on more than one occasion, within my recollection (I will, of course, refrain from disclosing any names). It was not just female solidarity that was at work here but also the clear distinction she made between "lechery" and betrayal. Rejecting "morality," she took questions of ethical integrity very seriously, in some sense juxtaposing these two notions.[23]

Undeniably, David Shrayer-Petrov's novel is a complex composition and its protagonist, Yudin, a multilayered, composite instrument of artistic intent. However, I find that the narrative of life in the concentration and labor camps, created in *Yudin's Redemption*, sometimes finds common ground with stories of Osip Mandelstam's life in the GULAG camps that circulated among the Soviet intelligentsia in the 1960s–1970s.

To restore the context of events and of their perception by the circles close to Nadezhda Mandelstam, I will quote a lengthy passage from one

---

22   Dmitrii Segal, "'Smirennaia, odetaia ubogo, No vidom velichavaia zhena': russkie vdovy v dvadtsatom veke," in his *Literatura kak okhrannaia gramota* (Moscow: Vodolei, 2006), 809.
23   Nikolai Podosokorskii, "Elena Murina. O tom, chto pomniu pro N. Ia. Mandelʹshtam," part 3, https://philologist.livejournal.com/9023859.html, accessed April 12, 2020.

of Dmitry Segal's articles. It was reproduced in a footnote in Nina Segal-Rudnik's study, based on Segal's archives and research on Boris Pasternak and Maria Yudina. My own commentary to one part of this passage will follow below:

> The possibility of becoming the new great Russian writer, the very desire, without which there would have been no *Doctor Zhivago*, meant for Pasternak to take Gorky's place after his death in 1936. To do that, he needed to break—within himself—of his self-imposed restrictions, to overcome the well-known Jewish fear of sticking out, and instead to distinguish himself in an alien environment, to participate in Russian history, in the events of political and literary life, and feel like he was fully entitled to it[24].
>
> Just like Mandelstam in *The Noise of Time* before him, Pasternak had to solve this problem for himself, because, despite his well-known attitude to Jewry, he had a certain sense of Jewishness—see, for instance, his meeting with the poet Avrom Sutzkever and [Pasternak's] mention of Yiddish as the language of his parents' home.[25] To some degree, Pasternak's nervous breakdown in the 1930s might have been a consequence of this extreme internal work that cannot be called anything other than a second birth.

---

24 My analysis of the situation surrounding Gorky, Pasternak, and Jewry can be found in Leonid Katsis, "Evreiskie epizody v 'Apelesovoi cherte' i epistoliarii B. Pasternaka," *Vestnik Evreiskogo Universiteta* 11 (2006): 151–194.

25 The context of every other word from here on needs to be annotated, considering that, since the publication of this article, there have been new and exciting developments in the research and archival publications concerning twentieth-century poets, which have significantly altered the perception of their works (although precisely such unannotated texts as this one by D. Segal make it possible to appreciate the aroma of the time when *Yudin's Redemption* was written). About Sutzkever and Pasternak, see Leonid Katsis, "Perets Markish, Avrom Sutskever i Boris Pasternak (k predystorii i istorii perevoda stikhov Peretsa Markisha 'Mikhoelsu—neugasimyi istochnik')," in my *Idish: yazyk i kul′tura v Sovetskom Soiuze* (Moscow: Izdatel′stvo RGGU, 2009), 174–201. Follow up: idem, "Zametki chitatelia istoriko-filosofskoi literatury. XI. Chego ne ulovil 'lokator' P. Mankozu v dele O. Ivinskoi," on Paolo Mancosu, *Moscow Has Ears Everywhere: New Investigations on Pasternak and Ivinskaya* (Stanford, CA: Hoover Institution Press, 2019), *Istoriia. Nauchnoe obozrenie OSTKRAFT* 4 (2019): 182–191. What Russified Yiddish looked like in the Pasternak family can now be seen firsthand: Leonid Pasternak, *Pis′ma Roze—neveste i zhene*, ed. E. V. Pasternak (Moscow: Azbukovnik, 2017); cf. Natal′ia Kostenko and Lazar′ Fleishman, "Iz semeinoi perepiski Pasternakov. Pis′ma O. M. i A. O. Freidenberg k rodnym v Germanii," in *Materialy Pasternakovskoi konferentsii v Stenforde* (Moscow: Azbukovnik, 2015), 6–135. In both cases, the editors needed to refer to a Yiddish specialist. And I am not even getting into Pasternak's parodies of his grandmother's "Odessa" language in his early letters.

What is meant here is not just the poetic cycle bearing this name, but the internal process of transformation. For Pasternak, becoming a writer in Russia meant fusing with its people in blood as well as spirit. Otherwise, it would be impossible to write about the narodniks and *narodnichestvo*,[26] about nationhood and statehood, and, of course, about his new religion. The poet regarded the official act of baptism as a natural culmination of his internal journey toward Russia, its people, and its religion. The problem of nationhood and national belonging could not be resolved for Pasternak without the embodiment of his idea of Russianness and the fulfillment of his full potential. He arrived at what happened with the blessing of Father Nikolai Golubtsov* not just through religious and philosophical turmoil but first and foremost through a creative process.[27]

What follows are well-known declarations, taken from Pasternak's correspondence with Olga Freidenberg, on the subject of the reckoning with all things Jewish and anti-Christian. Nevertheless, and in connection with *Yudin's Redemption*, I find most engaging the commentary which I marked with an asterisk (*), so as to differentiate it from my own comments in the footnotes:

> The text refers to father Nikolai Aleksandrovich Golubtsov (1900–1963), son of a professor at the Moscow Theological Academy, a biologist by training (he was a graduate of the Moscow Timiryazev Agricultural Academy) who became a priest in 1949 and served at the Church of the Deposition of the Lord's Robe on Donskaya Street in Moscow. "A man of remarkable spiritual beauty and a born pastor" (E. B. Pasternak), the Protopriest Nikolai Golubtsov became Maria Veniaminovna Yudina's confessor. His influence made her change her opinion on the Moscow Patriarchate, and she looked back at her time in his congregation as a great blessing (see the manuscript of M. V. Yudina's diary from the personal archives of D. M. Segal). We know of [Father Golubtsov's] pastoral role in the destiny of B. L. Pasternak from M. V. Yudina, who spoke about it during her concerts.[28]

---

26 It is hard not to think of the real Jewish *narodniks*, who did not think much of this necessity to reach the Russian people.
27 Quoted in N. M. Rudnik, *Budushchee v proshedshem*, introduction by I. Z. Serman, *Studi Salvi e Balti Dipartimento di Linguistica Universita degli Studi di Pisa*, Nuova Serie 3 (2001): 65–66.
28 Ibid., 135.

It, therefore, comes as no surprise that this same Russian Orthodox priest played an important part in Father Alexander Men"s decision to become a pastor, as indicated by the author of the article, Dmitry Segal. This is the most real, tangible example of the very complex and ambivalent, if not to say warped, attitude to both the Jewish-Russian and the Judeo-Christian stratum among members of then the liberal, Christian-oriented but not yet Church-aligned, milieu. It exemplifies the essence of the Jewish-Russian "Solaris," from which the style, ideology, theology, and teleology of *Yudin's Redemption* originated.

The theme of androgyny, if not hermaphroditism, permeates Shrayer-Petrov's novel. In one instance, Yudin the surgeon has to excise the female genitalia of the novel's androgynous Messiah, Evsey. In this connection the work of Jewish antisemite Otto Weininger *Sex and Character* (1903) comes to mind, with the feminine Jew as its core idea. Equally unforgettable is the "eternal womanish [вечное бабьё] in the Russian soul" from Nikolai Berdyaev's response to Vasily Rozanov's book on World War I (then titled *The War of 1914 and the Russian Renaissance* [1915]). The excision of the female from the male body is the very metaphor of the emergence of the manful Jew, the metaphor the Christian believer Nadezhda Mandelstam so pondered, and simultaneously the abandonment, in Sarmatia, of the "feminine Russianness" prior to the Jewish community's exodus to Palestine. I will refrain from enumerating other themes, references, and allusions, otherwise the name of Father Pavel Florensky will inevitably come up in connection with *The Jews' Olfactory and Tactile Relationship to Blood* (1914) by Rozanov, where, under the penname "Omega," Florensky proposed nothing short of having the Jews castrated.[29]

Then again, I am reading *Yudin's Redemption* fifteen years after its original publication and almost forty years since the author first started working on it. It is hardly surprising that my own reader's experience unearths aspects of the novel that may have been hidden from Shrayer-Petrov's contemporary audience—or else unearths and makes explicit a scholarly perspective on that which, to quote Osip Mandelstam's "The Slate Ode" ("Grifel′naia oda," 1923), "scribbled, struggled there" in the 1960s–1980s. ("Мы только с голоса поймем,/ Что там царапалось, боролось . . . ," "Only when listening to the

---

29 This arcane surgery already came to my attention. See Leonid Katsis, "Otets Pavel Florenskii v 'Oboniatel′nom i osiazatel′nom otnoshenii evreev k krovi' V. V. Rozanova," in my *Krovavyi navet i russkaia mysl′. Istoriko-teologicheskoe issledovanie dela Beilisa* (Moscow: Gesharim / Mosty kul′tury, 2006), 353–388.

voice will we comprehend,/ What scribbled, struggled there . . ."). Indeed, this is not so much about the sources of Shrayer-Petrov's novel, which one can determine with a greater or lesser accuracy. What is truly important for me here is to determine the fundamental theologeme of the novel—at least, I am convinced there is one.

By way of example, at one point in *Yudin's Redemption*, a discussion takes place whether ongoing events are happening in the modern-day present or in the nearest future of the Six Day War. One would assume that the presence of the Plastunka Mountains (the name "Plastunka" is perhaps a partial anagram of Palestina and hints at the exodus of the Soviet Jews to Palestine-Israel), the Britons (meaning British colonizers), the Security Service ("Sluzhba bezopasnosti"—whether it be the NKVD-KGB or the SD), and the dissidents would be sufficient evidence of the novel's modern frame of reference. However, that is not the point. Anyone who has ever had to deal with protestant preachers, who were never in short supply in the late Soviet era and in post-Soviet Russia, always received a copy of the bilingual (Russian-Hebrew) Bible accompanied by the words "well, that is your—Jewish—book, isn't it?" It did not matter whether it came with or without the New Testament. What was important is that this constituted a path to "Jews for Jesus"!

However, that is precisely the big game in the novel. Suffice it to translate one of the prophetic verses from the Hebrew Bible, let us say, from Isaiah. Due to the presence of the verb forms beginning with the Hebrew letter "waw," this verse can be translated as either "I said I would come, and I shall," or "I said I would come, and I did."[30] Thus, the Judaic "I shall" is

---

30 In Biblical Hebrew, the past and future tenses form a grammatical pair. In this context, a unique phenomenon of "inverted perfect/imperfect" emerged in connection with the use of the conjunction "waw" (vocalized as "ve" and meaning "and"). The Hebrew term is "waw ha-hipuh"—"the waw of reversal," or "waw-conversive." When added to a verb, this conjunction "inverts" the grammatical meaning: the verb refers to the past instead of the future, or the future instead of the past. Most sentences in the Torah begin with this conjunction, even if they are marked by subordination. It often precedes the form of the narrative past, which in appearance is identical to the imperfect: "va-yikra lahem va-yishme'u"—"He called them, they heard." For this reason, the form of the narrative past is often described as an inverted imperfect form. However, in combination with the negative particle "lo" ("no"), the perfect is used: "va-yikra lahem ve-lo sham'u"—"He called them and they did not hear." Thus, the negative particle "lo" neutralizes the effect of "waw ha-hipuh." Along with the inverted imperfect, Biblical Hebrew also possesses the inverted perfect. It is used in dialogues, prophecies, and some other genres, where one encounters a series of sentences describing a sequence of future events: "ve-khatavti"—"and I will write." Again, the negative particle "lo" negates this effect:

easily turned into the Christian "I did." Ultimately, David Shrayer-Petrov chooses another, third option: the future rather than contemporaneity! Or rather, both the past and the future, just as prophecies are meant to be understood in Judaism.

This point is vital. The present can be Jewish, Christian, or Judeo-Christian, but the future is either the First or Second coming of the Messiah (Mashiach). No matter which one happens, the messianic era will be post-Christian—but it will certainly be Judaic. It would do us well to remember that the hero of the last of Vladimir Soloviev's *Three Conversations*, the Antichrist, wanted to end the Christian numbering of years and begin his own—the post-Common—era. However, if in fact the Jews have allowed him to make it happen, the situation has still remained the same: a Judeo-Christian world with an unresolved messianic question.

In Ultra-Orthodox Judaism, some extreme communities did not or still do not recognize Israel because of the non-messianic nature of the Jewish state. Consequently, for the assimilated Soviet Jews whose consciousness was caught in the dual Judeo-Christian mindset, the new exodus could only be rendered meaningful by a Mashiach. Following the ideology of *Jews in the USSR* and *The Awe of Judean Concerns*, he will arise without ever having to resurrect. He will simply appear "not in the sky but on earth" ("За горами, за лесами,/ За широкими морями,/ Не на небе — на земле/ Жил старик в одном селе").[31]

My discussion is about to turn to the field of medicine, pharmacology (as fantastical as it may be in the novel) and, of course, microbiology. In the present case—pace Nietzsche—the author is born not from the spirit of tragedy but from the spirit of microbiology, to which he dedicated many decades of research and also a literary-scientific memoir, *Hunt for the Red Devil: A Novel with Microbiologists* (*Okhota na ryzhego d´iavola. Roman s mikrobilogami*, 2010). The memoir's significance is also distinctly Jewish.

---

when "waw" and "lo" are used together, the perfect usually conveys the past tense. See "Vvedenie v bibleiskii ivrit," https://www.limud-ivrit.com/biblical-hebrew, accessed July 14, 2020.

31 Ths is from Petr Ershov's *The Little Humpbacked Horse* (*Konek-gorbunok*, 1834; complete edition, 1856). Only in one translation one can find this version of the four first stanzas: "Past the woods and mountain steep/ Past the rolling waters deep/ You will find a hamlet pleasant/ Where once dwelt an aged peasant" (sic—L.K.). See Petr Ershov, *The Little Humpbacked Horse*, tr. Louis Zellikoff (Moscow: Foreign Languages Publishing House, 1957). But this edition does not give an exact translation of the stanza to which I referred.

Indeed, according to various popular antisemitic beliefs, it was the Jews who poisoned wells during the plague, and Jews were also metaphorically regarded as a real disease infecting society. By way of analogy, in the case of microbiologist and writer David Shrayer-Petrov, a fairly assimilated Soviet Jew is entering Russian literature, where for many decades people had been fighting against even the smallest particle of the "musk of Judaism" (the title of my 2002 book about Osip Mandelstam)—both those who took the path of Boris Pasternak and those who preached what Vladimir Jabotinsky called "asemitism." To employ a medical metaphor, those who aimed to purge or safeguard Russian literature tried to prevent the Jewish "microbial ingress" by any means available to them.

Furthermore, since my perception of *Yudin's Redemption* is influenced not just by my reader's experience but also my own research, I cannot resist lingering on one episode in the memoirs of David Shrayer-Petrov, where he reminisces about military service in the small Belarusian city of Borisov in 1958–1959.[32] Shrayer-Petrov described the background of this episode as follows: "However, reality proved stronger than fantasy. Instead of the desired graduate school at the department of microbiology, I was sent to serve as a military physician in a tank division, which was stationed on the outskirts of the small Belarusian city of Borisov."[33]

More information can be found in Chapter 5, "Military Doctor":

> Осенью 1959 года поездом я прибыл на место военной службы в Белоруссию. Это был город Борисов. От Борисова до Минска можно было доехать на поезде за несколько часов. Поездов было много: Ленинград — Минск, Москва — Минск, Москва — Минск — Берлин. Поездов было много, и все останавливались в Борисове. По американским масштабам Борисов не так уж мал. Хотя поменьше Провиденса (штат Род Айлэнд) и Нью-Хэйвена (штат Коннектикут), США. Когда-то Борисов был знаменит своими еврейскими традициями: синагоги, еврейские школы, еврейские магазины. Целые кварталы были заселены евреями — торговцами или ремесленниками. Синагоги сожгла Революция. Еврейские школы закрыла Советская власть. А евреев — [почти 10] тысяч — уничтожили немцы. Спаслись только те (немногие), кто успел вырваться и уехать в эвакуацию на Урал, в Сибирь

---

32 David Shraer-Petrov, *Okhota na ryzhego d´iavola. Roman s mikrobiologami*, ed. Maksim D. Shraer (Moscow: Agraf, 2010).

33 Ibid., 28.

или Среднюю Азию, или кто сражался в рядах Красной Армии или ушел в леса, в партизанские отряды. Были и еврейские партизанские отряды. В городе был привокзальный буфет с неизменным разливным пивом «Жигули», ресторан "Березина", в котором весь офицерский корпус напивался каждый месяц в день зарплаты, Дом Культуры, Парк Культуры, школы, медицинское училище, здания городских и партийных властей, два или три кинотеатра, штаб танковой армии, танковые дивизии и отдельный учебный танковый батальон, церковь (костёл и синагога не работали), какие-то заводы и фабрики, в том числе пианинная, спичечная и фарфоровая (с огромным количеством молодых девушек бойкого западно-славянского, а проще, польского типа), два гастронома и книжный магазин.

In the fall of 1959, I arrived by train at my military posting in Belarus. It was the town of Borisov. Borisov was just a few hours' train ride from Minsk. There were many trains: Leningrad—Minsk, Moscow—Minsk, Moscow—Minsk—Berlin. There were many trains, and they all stopped in Borisov. By American standards, Borisov is not that small. But smaller than Providence (Rhode Island) or New Haven (Connecticut), USA. There was a time when Borisov was famous for its Jewish traditions: synagogues, Jewish schools, Jewish shops. Entire quarters were inhabited by Jews—merchants or artisans. The Revolution burned down the synagogues. The Soviet authorities closed the schools. The Germans destroyed the Jews themselves—[almost ten] thousand of them. The few that survived were those who had either managed to escape beforehand and were evacuated to the Urals, Siberia or Central Asia, or fought in the ranks of the Red Army or went into the woods to join the partisans. There were Jewish partisan units as well. In Borisov, there was a train station cafeteria with its immutable draft beer "Zhiguli," the restaurant Berezina, where the entire officer corps got drunk once a month on payday, the House of Culture, the Park of Culture, schools, a medical college, municipal and party buildings, a couple of cinemas, the headquarters of the tank army, tank divisions and a separate training tank battalion, an Orthodox church (both the Catholic church and the synagogue were not functioning), some factories, including ones that manufactured pianos, matches, and china (they were staffed mostly by young women of the boisterous West Slavic—or simply put, Polish—type), two grocery stores and a bookstore.[34]

---

34 Ibid., 29.

This fact would not have drawn my attention had it not been for my own recent investigation of one amusing episode in the life and work of Vladimir Jabotinsky. It could add some depth to this historical picture of a young Leningrad microbiologist and poet arriving into the heart of a virtual Jewish intelligentsia State within the Russian Empire, very few traces of which had remained after the Shoah. Jabotinsky's "Borisov affair" is described in more detail in my recent monograph about him.[35] What needs to be said here is this: in the mid-1900s, Russian Jews took an active part in the movement of communist anarchists, actively participating in the "expropriations" to raise funds for revolutionary activity. Suddenly, several newspapers started printing articles, poems, field reports, all about the city of Borisov, where the local mayor ordered the Jews to gather in the synagogue so that the entire community would curse the Jewish terrorists (that is, impose *herem* on them!).

The town of Borisov was too small to be the subject of nationwide imperial interest, especially since these endless anarchist affairs were coming up everywhere from Odessa (reflected in the works of Babel) to Białystok. Frequently, articles and letters would simply be signed "Borisov," "Borisovsky," and so forth. But in the end, it turned out that it was just Jabotinsky's way of mocking the efforts of the Minsk governor, who actually made similar demands of Minsk Jews.[36] However, this story is important to me not only not because of the alignment of the two Borisovs, one the real destination of Shrayer-Petrov, the other—a myth of Jabotinsky's making. It is important because in literature, as in life, a successful act of turning something on its head allows one to glimpse in the fictional recreations of real historical events that which is hidden from external observation.

In the chronology of Shrayer-Petrov's career, the original version of *Yudin's Redemption* was composed after *Doctor Levitin*, the first part of his trilogy about refuseniks, as the author indicates in the 2019 preface to his novel. In *Cursed Be You… Just Don't Die* (*Bud´ ty prokliat, ne umirai…*), the second part of the refusenik trilogy, Shrayer-Petrov conjures up the fictional Belarusian town of Glebovsk, inviting the reader to recall the inseparable

---

35 Leonid Katsis, *"Russkaia vesna" Vladimira Zhabotinskogo* (Moscow: Izdatel´stvo RGGU, 2019).

36 See my "Kherem evreiskim anarkhistam-ekspropriatoram v 'Borisovskoi' sinagoge ('Rus´' Polesskii, Illiustrirovannoe prilozhenie k 'Rusi' Iorik, 'Svobodnye mysli' Ka-rov, Borisovskii) i peredovitsy 'Svobodnykh myslei' o sude nad pogromshchikami v Belostoke," ibid., 509–511.

Russian saints Boris and Gleb. *Doctor Levitin* carries a remarkable epigraph and author's note, both of which give us considerable insight into the poetics of David Shrayer-Petrov:

> Мы знаем, что мы русские,
> Вы принимаете нас за евреев.
>
> События и персонажи вымышлены.
>
> *Автор*
>
> *We know we are Russians;*
> *You consider us Jews.*
>
> *Names, characters, places, and incidents either are the products of the author's imagination or, if real, are used fictitiously.*[37]

And once again it is possible to connect many of the themes and images of Shrayer-Petrov's novel with some of the protagonists of this essay. And, oddly enough, once again it is Andrei Voznesensky, whose poem "Chagall's Cornflower" ("Vasil'ki Shagala") reads loud and clear:

> Это росло у Бориса и Глеба,
> в хохоте нэпа и чебурек.
> Во поле хлеба — чуточку неба.
> Небом единым жив человек.[38]

("It grew by [Saints] Boris and Gleb,/ in the raucous laughter of NEP and chebureks,/ In a field of wheat—a bit of sky./ Man lives by sky alone.")

The opening line of the refusenik novel, with its first Moscow place name, "On the corner of Meshchanskaya Street and some lane, named after God only knows whom . . . ,"[39] flows naturally from the epigraph of *Doctor Levitin*. Therefore, an interesting parallel can be drawn between the Russian-Jewish or Jewish-Russian impressions of David Shrayer-Petrov and the Russian poet's reflections about the Jewish artist. Likewise, the Palestine of *Yudin's Redemption* clearly resonates with the first name of a character from Shrayer-Petrov's refusenik novel—Fatah (Fatkh, in the Russian), if the eponymous organization has not yet been forgotten. And the correlation

---

37 David Shraer-Petrov, *Gerbert i Nelli* (Moscow: Knizhniki, 2014); cf. Shrayer-Petrov, *Doctor Levitin*, 1.
38 Andrei Voznesenskii, "Vasil´ki Shagala," https://rupoem.ru/voznesenskij/lik-vash-serebryanyj.aspx, accessed June 24, 2020.
39 Shrayer-Petrov, *Doctor Levitin*, 1.

of the Jewish martyrdom of one novel's doctor with the Jewish redemption of the other does not merely mirror Pasternak's *Doctor Zhivago* but counteracts its author's call on Jews to scatter and disperse among other nations. However, this is a separate and complex topic that goes beyond the scope of the Jewish "redemption of Doctor Levitin."

It is this hidden spiritual life, or spiritual torments, of Soviet Russian Jews standing at the religious and historical crossroads, that the author of *Yudin's Redemption* captured in his novel. He did this by dispatching his refusenik Jews to the mythical Hellenic land of the Golden Fleece, to the Tatar Koktebel and other boundary parts of the former USSR, from whence they set off for the genuine Jewish Palestine. And those who chose a different path managed to avoid apostasy in the spiritual sense, and once more opted for *galut* (exile), which Jewish historian Simon Dubnow saw in the ocean that carried away the emigrants of his time. Dubnow regarded this ocean as the desert that would lead the Jews to liberation, to the state of *geula* (redemption).[40]

Translated, from the Russian, by
Anastasia Degtyareva

---

[40] Here is Dubnow's original text in English translation: "The majority of the refugees follow the old route from the Russian Egypt—through the desert of the Atlantic Ocean to the 'promised land,' where one immediately finds freedom, then—after some heavy struggle—a chunk of bread. This continuous stream has been flowing for a quarter of a century; for a quarter of a century, ferries have been roaming the ocean and, in the process, carrying more than a million Jews from a land of slavery to the great American Republic. Yet even now, on the verge of becoming a land of freedom, Russia remains a land of pogroms, so our eternal wanderer follows the same path, across the ocean. Will you hold him back, will you tell him to be patient, to halt his impetuous exodus from Egypt, to wait for the fall of the pharaohs, the death of the 'Black Hundreds' in the waters of the Red Sea, the transformation of a barbaric Egypt into a civilized one?" See Simon Dubnov, *Pis'ma o starom i novom evreistve* (1897–1907) (St. Petersburg: Obshchestvennaia pol'za, 1907), 319.

Works Cited

Aleshkovskii, Iuz. "Pesnia o Staline." http://a-pesni.org/bard/alechk/tovstalin.htm. Accessed June 24, 2020.

Dubnov, Simon. *Pis′ma o starom i novom evreistve (1897–1907)*. St. Petersburg: Obshchestvennaia pol′za, 1907.

Ershov, Petr. *The Little Humpbacked Horse*. Translated by Louis Zellikoff. Moscow: Foreign Languages Publishing House, 1957.

Gumilev, L. N. *Etnogenez i biosfera zemli*. Leningrad: Gidrometeoizdat, 1990.

"Joseph Rabinowitz." *Jewish Encyclopedia*. http://www.jewishencyclopedia.com/articles/12517-rabinowitz-joseph. Accessed July 14, 2020.

Katsis, Leonid. "Evreiskie epizody v 'Apelesovoi cherte' i epistoliarii B. Pasternaka." *Vestnik Evreiskogo universiteta* 11 (2006): 151–194.

———. "Otets Pavel Florenskii v 'Oboniatel′nom i osiazatel′nom otnoshenii evreev k krovi' V. V. Rozanova.'" In Leonid Katsis, *Krovavyi navet i russkaia mysl′. Istoriko-teologicheskoe issledovanie dela Beilisa*, 353–388. Moscow: Gesharim / Mosty kul′tury, 2006.

———. "Perets Markish, Avrom Sutskever i Boris Pasternak (k predystorii i istorii perevoda stikhov Peretsa Markisha 'Mikhoelsu—neugasimyi istochnik'). In Leonid Katsis, editor. *Idish: Iazyk i kul′tura v Sovetskom Soyuze*, 174–201. Moscow: Izdatel′stvo RGGU, 2009.

———. "Pragmatika i poetika obrashchenii k sovetskim vozhdiam v 1930-e gg. O. Mandel′shtam, B. Pasternak, I. Sel′vinskii, L. Feikhtvanger, Dem′ian Bednyi." In Leonid Katsis, editor. *Smena paradigm i smena paradigmy. Ocherki russkoi literatury, iskusstva, nauki 20 veka*, 158–165. Moscow: Izdatel'stvo RGGU, 2012.

———. "Dlia menia russkoe i evreiskoe sosushchestvuiut v edinom potoke." In *Iudaika dva. Renessans v litsakh*, ed. Galina Zelenina, 392–418. Moscow: Knizhniki, 2015.

———. "Kherem evreiskim anarkhistam-ekspropriatoram v 'Borisovskoi' sinagoge ('Rus′′ Polesskii, Illiustrirovannoe prilozhenie k 'Rusi' Iorik, 'Svobodnye mysli' Ka-rov, Borisovskii) i peredovitsy 'Svobodnykh myslei' o sude nad pogromshchikami v Belostoke.'" In Leonid Katsis. *"Russkaia vesna" Vladimira Zhabotinskogo*, 509–511. Moscow: Izdatel′stvo RGGU, 2019.

———. "Zametki chitatelia istoriko-filosofskoi literatury. XI. Chego ne ulovil 'lokator' P. Mankozu v dele O. Ivinskoi." Review of Paolo

Mancosu, *Moscow Has Ears Everywhere: New Investigations on Pasternak and Ivinskaya*. Stanford, CA: Hoover Institution Press, 2019. *Istoriia. Nauchnoe obozrenie OSTKRAFT* 4 (2019): 182–191.

Katsman, Roman. "Parallel´nye vselennye Davida Shraera-Petrova." *Wiener Slawistischer Almanach* 79 (2017): 255–279.

Khlebnikov, Velimir. *Sobranie sochinenii v 6 tomakh.* Vol. 2 Moscow: IMLI "Nasledie," 2001.

Koestler, Arthur. *The Thirteenth Tribe: The Khazar Empire and Its Heritage.* New York: Random House, 1976.

Kostenko, Natal´ia, and Lazar´ Fleishman. "Iz semeinoi perepiski Pasternakov. Pis´ma O. M. i A. O. Freidenberg k rodnym v Germanii." In *Materialy Pasternakovskoi konferentsii v Stenforde*, 6–135. Moscow: Azbukovnikl, 2015.

Kuznetsov, A. M., ed. "Desiatoe pis´mo N.Ia. Mandel´shtam M. V. Iudinoi." *Nevel´skii sbornik* 7 (2002): 24–27.

Kuznetsov, A. M., intr., ed., comment. "Pis'ma N.Ia. Mandel'shtam k M.V. Iudinoi i V.A. Stravinskoi." In *Nevel'skii sbornik. Vypusk 2.* St. Petersburg: Akropol', 1997. 42-55.

Mandel'shtam, N. Ia. *Sobranie sochinenii v dvukh tomakh.* Yekaterinburg: Gonzo, 2014.

Nerler, Pavel. "Petrarka, Mandel´shtam i Iuz Aleshkovskii." *Novaia gazeta*, July 23, 2015. https://novayagazeta.ru/articles/2015/07/24/65008-petrarka-mandelshtam-i-yuz-aleshkovskiy. Accessed July 14, 2020,

Pasternak, Leonid. *Pis'ma Roze—neveste i zhene.* Ed. E.V. Pasternak. Moscow: Azbukovnik, 2017.

Podosokorskii, Nikolai. "Elena Murina. O tom, chto pomniu pro N. Ia. Mandel´shtam." Part 3. https://philologist.livejournal.com/9023859.html. Accessed April 12, 2020.

Rudnik, N. M. *Budushchee v proshedshem.* Introduction by I. Z. Serman. *Studi Slavi e Balti Dipartimento di Linguistica Universita degli Studi di Pisa*, Nuova Serie 3 (2001): 65–66

Segal, Dmitrii. "'Smirennaia, odetaia ubogo, no vidom velichavaia zhena': russkie vdovy v dvadtsatom veke." In Dmitrii Segal, *Literatura kak okhrannaia gramota,* 800–814. Moscow: Vodolei, 2006.

"Sergei Yudin." *Wikipedi*a. https://en.wikipedia.org/wiki/Sergei_Yudin_(surgeon). Accessed April 12, 2020.

Shrayer-Petrov, David [David Shraer-Petrov]. *Iskuplenie Iudina. Istoricheskii roman v piati chastiakh, oboznachennykh sootvetstvenno drevneevreiskim*

meram dliny: kane "trostnik", amma "lokot´", zeret "piad`", tefakh "ladon´", etsba "palets." Mosty (2005) 5: 5–61; 6: 21–116; 7: 11–88.
——— [David Shraer-Petrov]. *Vodka s pirozhnymi. Roman s pisateliami.* Edited by Maksim D. Shraer. St. Petersburg: Akademicheskii proekt, 2007.
——— [David Shraer-Petrov]. *Okhota na ryzhego d´iavola. Roman s mikrobiologami.* Edited by Maksim D. Shraer. Moscow: Agraf, 2010.
——— [David Shraer-Petrov]. *Gerbert i Nelli.* Moscow: Knizhniki, 2014.
———. *Doctor Levitin: A Novel.* Edited and with notes by Maxim D. Shrayer, translated by Arna B. Bronstein, Aleksandra I. Fleszar, Maxim D. Shrayer. Detroit, Wayne State University Press, 2018.
——— [David Shraer-Petrov]. "Posleslovie k romanu "Iskuplenie Iudina." In *Iskuplenie Iudina. Istoricheskii roman v piati chastiakh, oboznachennykh sootvetstvenno drevneevreiskim meram dliny: kane "trostnik", amma "lokot´", zeret "piad´", tefakh "ladon´", etsba "palets."* Revised and corrected edition. Edited by Maxim D. Shrayer. Moscow, forthcoming 2021.
Smola, Klavdia. "O proze russko-evreiskogo pisatelia Davida Shraera-Petrova." In *Russkie evrei v Amerike*, book 15, edited by Ernst Zal´tsberg, 135–150. Moscow: Giperion, 2017.
———. "Das Martyrium des Otkaz: David Šraer-Petrovs 'Gerbert i Nėlli.'" In Klavdia Smola, *Wiedererfindung der Tradition Russisch-jüdische Literatur der Gegenwart*, 139–149. Cologne: Böhlau, 2019.
Virabov, Igor´. *Andrei Voznesenskii. Zhizn´ zamechatel´nykh liudei.* Moscow: Molodaia gvardiia, 2015. https://dom-knig.com/read_184446-93. Accessed April 12, 2020.
Voronel´, Aleksandr. *Trepet zabot iudeiskikh.* Jerusalem: Biblioteka-Aliia, 1986.
———. *Nulevaia zapoved´.* Kharkiv: Prava liudyny, 2013.
Voznesenskii, Andrei. "Vasil´ki Shagalla." https://rupoem.ru/voznesenskij/lik-vash-serebryanyj.aspx. Accessed June 24, 2020.
"Vvedenie v Bibleiskii Ivrit." https://www.limud-ivrit.com/biblical-hebrew. Accessed July 14, 2020.

To Kill the Leader: The Morphology of David Shrayer-Petrov's Novella "Dinner with Stalin"*

Boris Lanin

David Shrayer-Petrov's novella "Dinner with Stalin" (Russian: "Obed s vozhdem," literally "Dinner with the Leader") was composed in 2008 in Boston.[1] An exemplary text, it embodies the classical narratological notions of the form of the novella.

The novella features a limited number of characters—the participants of the dinner party with the visiting Georgian actor, Stalin's double. The action is restricted to one encounter, one dinner party conversation among a group of émigrés from the USSR, all of whom live in a small American city on the East Coast. The historical context is mostly introduced by the characters' direct speech.

The very opening of the novella contains a prompt: multilayeredness. The narrator, endowed with the author's own biographical features, tells historical anecdotes about doubles and doubleness. In the first anecdote,

---

* Copyright © 2021 by Boris Lanin. English translation copyright © 2021 by Maxim D. Shrayer.

[1] See David Shraer-Petrov, "Obed s vozhdem," in D. Shraer-Petrov, *Krugosvetnoe schast´e. Izbrannye rasskazy* (Moscow: Knizhniki, 2016), 196–215. See Maxim D. Shrayer's commentary in David Shrayer-Petrov, *A Dinner with Stalin and Other Stories*, ed. Maxim D. Shrayer (Syracuse: Syracuse University Press, 2014), 241–244.

on the balcony of an opera house, at the end of the 1890s, the memoirist saw Pushkin, as an old man. The memoirist was so struck by this that during the intermission he ran to Pushkin's box to assure the great poet that he had never accepted his death after the duel as real. [...] Just before the memoirist reached the box, someone whispered to him that Pushkin's son Aleksandr, already an old man, was present in the theater.[2]

In the second anecdote, the storyteller attends a poetry reading in the 1980s Moscow:

Looming behind the last row of chairs, like the legendary cop Uncle Styopa sprung from the pages of children's verses, was the tall figure of the chief poet of the Soviet land, Sergey Mikhalkov, author of the lyrics to the Soviet national anthem. What was he doing here among the semi-destitute brotherhood of third-rate literati?[3]

In the first anecdote Pushkin's aged son is perceived as his resurrected father; in the second, Mikhalkov's twin brother suddenly makes an appearance at a public poetry reading and then leaves, satisfied by the effect of false recognition. Mikhail Bakhtin wrote this about doubles and double-voiced discourse:

This transferal of words from one mouth to another, where the contents remains the same although the tone and ultimate meaning are changed, is a fundamental device of Dostoevsky's. He forces his heroes to recognize themselves, their idea, their own words, their orientation, their gesture in another person, in whom all these phenomena change their integrated and ultimate meaning and take on a different sound, the sound of parody or ridicule.[4]

Let us note this forcing of one's "characters to recognize themselves" and proceed with the analysis of Shrayer-Petrov's novella.

The initially declared multilayeredness prevents one from forming a superficial impression about both characters and the depicted event.

---

2 David Shrayer-Petrov, "Dinner with Stalin," tr. Aleksandra Fleszar and Arna B. Bronstein, in *Dinner with Stalin and Other Stories*, ed. Maxim D. Shrayer (Syracuse: Syracuse University Press, 2014), 121.
3 Shrayer-Petrov, "Dinner with Stalin," 122.
4 Mikhail Bakhtin, *Problems of Dostoevsky's Poetics*, ed. and tr. Caryl Emerson (Minneapolis: University of Minnesota Press, 1984), 217; cf. the original in M. M. Bakhtin, *Problemy tvorchestva Dostoevskogo* (Kiev: NEXT, 1994), 118.

It demonstrates how encounters with doubles influence those who, by dint of circumstance, stand in their path.

It is evident that the structure of the novella is linked to its composition and storytelling technique. The first-person narrative is meant to render the narration more authentic, to convince one not only of the verisimilitude, but of the genuine truth of what is being related.

The literary scholar Mikhail Petrovsky (1887-1937), who devoted much attention to the morphological qualities of the novella as genre, identified two framing elements of the kernel of the novella plot: *Vorgeschichte* and *Nachgeshichte*, which he translated as, respectively, plot prologue (*siuzhetnyi prolog*) and plot epilogue (*siuzhetnyi epilog*). The *Vorgeschichte* of "Dinner with Stalin" are the two anecdotes—about Pushkin's son and Mikhalkov's twin brother—which serve to tune the readers attention.

Petrovsky stated that in the novella:

> [...] everything must be directed toward capturing the attention of the listener (or reader) with the narrative flow, so that the impression from the novella be complete and uninterrupted [indeed!—B.L.]. The attention must be captured and strained, like a taut bowstring, and there must be the target which the arrow hits. Only then does the act of straining obtain its meaning and justification.
>
> The hand is the narrator [Рука — рассказчик]. Just how taut is the bowstring of attention and how precisely the narrative "hits" the target.[5]

The narrator in "Dinner with Stalin" exudes self-irony. He denounces the way he is mesmerized by Stalin's entrance to the dinner party: now the narrator wants to stuff Stalin's pipe, now he is so taken with him that he forgets to take care of his own wife and the dinner table. The narrator only briefly digresses to comment on the guests' characteristic behavior. He sticks strictly to the overarching line of the narrative. This line consists in demonstrating that the arrival of "Stalin" provokes the guests at the gathering and unearths their subconscious phobias. According to Petrovsky's observation, "by itself the strained predicament as it is experienced by its participants should appear less strained for the exterior contemplators. The better the contemplator is informed of all the circumstances, the more calm and unbiased his reflection [of the narrative]."[6] This is exactly how the

---

5   M. A. Petrovskii, "Morfologiia novelly," in *Ars Poetica*, ed. M. A. Petrovskii, vol. 1 (Moscow: Gosudarstvennaia akademiia khudozhestvennykh nauk, 1927), 76.
6   Ibid., 88.

narrative works in Shrayer-Petrov's story. In Petrovsky's view, "the unity of perspective [единство аспекта] thus creates a greater dynamics of the story. This way the unity of perspective is the most essential element in the novella's dynamic structure and, besides its natural function also serves as a unifying element."[7]

In the novella "Dinner with Stalin" Stalin functions as the agent provocateur. Actually, Stalin himself could not have been present at a dinner party for a group of Soviet émigrés in America; Stalin has been long dead. However, his double appears there. The situation becomes deliberately complicated. The guests await the arrival of the actor who has successfully transformed himself into Stalin. The host drives to the airport to pick up the guest. When they return from the airport, the guest turns out none other than Stalin himself. Nowhere does it state that this is an actor playing Stalin, a double, in fact. Noteworthy is the servility and toadying, with which the guest and the hosts play up to Stalin. When he enters—understandingly a double—the host, a giant of a man, shrivels up and minces behind him: "Гриша как бы сократился в росте, съёжился. Шажки стали мелкими и голова внаклонку" ("Bristling, Grisha seemed to have shrunk in height. His steps were tiny, and his head was bent down").[8] The double gets drunk, not too keen on the hors d'oeuvres, and mixing the fine Georgian wine "Alazan Valley" with the Grey Goose vodka, even though just a little while back, in the collective imagination of those gathered at the dinner table, he swam "somewhere outside of the realm of that wonderful meal" ("где-то вне реальности прекрасного застолья").[9] He does not feel like getting to know the guests, has no reason to remembered their names—everything will have fallen into place as the dinner party unravels.

But for Stalin's double the dinner party is also an opportunity to ask questions, in essence, to interrogate. The enormous distance between him and the other dinner guests allows him to ask any question. These questions serve as a test of the author's mythological thinking.

A real Stalin invades the body of the actor; he remembers the names of those long deceased, recalls the details and specifics. Quite soon it becomes apparent that the visiting actor from Tbilisi's Marjanishvili Theater has turned doubleness into his main métier. For him being Stalin's double is both a joy and a fine pleasure. The actor remembers the anti-Stalin long poem,

---

7   Ibid., 90.
8   Shraer-Petrov, "Obed s vozhdem," 203; Shrayer-Petrov, "Dinner with Stalin," 125.
9   Ibid.

composed by the narrator back in 1956; he recalls once meeting the couple of artists from among the émigré gathering at a meeting they attended as young people half a century ago; then recollects meeting Zhora's father, a nuclear physicist. He has not just studied and mastered Stalin's biography and his inner and outer circle; the actor has become an ageless portrait of Dorian Gray, and the original, alas, does not share his appearance with Wilde's beautiful protagonist:

> Лицо у него было нечисто выбрито, или так казалось из-за неровной рябоватой кожи — следствия перенесенного фурункулеза или даже оспы. Но усы! Классические усы Вождя. У детей сталинской эпохи остался в памяти портрет Сталина во френче или шинели, маршальской фуражке, с трубкой, на горловину которой упирались усы. Усы любимого Сталина.

("His face was not cleanly shaven, or it seemed that way owing to his uneven, pockmarked skin, the result of having had bad acne or even smallpox. But his mustache! The leader's classic mustache. Children of Stalin's time still remember Stalin's portrait in a military jacket or overcoat, a Marshal's brimmed cap, and a pipe with his mustache pressed against its mouthpiece. Beloved Stalin's mustache.")[10]

In the novella the mustache is glorified as the leader's principal attribute. They become the detail-motif which is given a special place in the end of the novella.

Only two guests pose questions to Stalin, and these questions most of all bespeak the ones asking them. The couple from Erevan, Vlad and Asya, like to ask questions with a psychological seasoning, although, as the narrator puts it, "not without a distinctive Soviet seasoning being detectable in their arguments" ("советская подкладка не отпускала").[11] Their problem is how to solve the Karabakh question by "using psychology" ("психологически"). The same problem preoccupies the hosts, a mixed Armenian-Azeri couple. Psychology, as it were, is not of concern to Stalin; his recipe is to execute the instigators from both sides. But the matter can no longer be contained just to instigators of national conflicts: now Stalin the actor is fiercely attacking the young artists: "Враги и предатели

---

10 Shraer-Petrov, "Obed s vozhdem," 206; Shrayer-Petrov, "Dinner with Stalin," 127–128.
11 Shraer-Petrov, "Obed s vozhdem," 207; Shrayer-Petrov, "Dinner with Stalin," 128.

уничтожили мои портреты и мои скульптуры, чтобы унизить достоинство нашей социалистической Родины! А вы и не попытались защитить и сохранить произведение искусства. Разве я не прав?" ("Enemies and traitors destroyed my portraits and my statues to demean the honor of our socialist Motherland! And you didn't even try to defend and protect a work of art. Am I not right?").[12]

Stalin is the embodiment of the unconscious of the ones gathered at the dinner table; he is their secret idol. Grisha, the party host, imagines himself as a true beneficiary, even though he is nothing but a "butler" at Stalin's benefit performance. And now the lyrical moment has arrived: after Grisha's announcement, the guest from Tbilisi recites a Russian translation of Stalin's poem "Morning," and then the same poem in the original Georgian. Sycophancy grows and soars up to the ceiling, when one of the guests, Elya, retrieves her accordion, and all the others follow and sing "March of the Artillerymen" ("Marsh artilleristov") with its famous refrain "Artillerymen, Stalin ordered you! Artillerymen, our country calls to battle!" And now the culmination: the actor's a toast in praise of the actor himself: "Comrades, let's drink to the Motherland! To Stalin!" Moreover, the emboldened and inebriated actor confronts Mira and Alyosha: "А вам что, особое приглашение?" ("And you, do you two need a special invitation?").[13]

This question, both somewhat obnoxious and haughty, turns out to be fatal for the whole dinner party. Mira, the narrator's wife, asks questions for all the others at once, and her questions become a denunciation:

> —Хватит нам этого маскарада! . . . почему для мира на земле и прогресса человечества понадобилось фабриковать дело кремлёвских врачей-убийц? Зачем было ломать суставы рук и ног моему дяде, знаменитому хирургу, прошедшему всю войну? Ради какой высокой идеи надо было готовить массовое выселение евреев, как это было сделано с немцами Поволжья, крымскими татарами и чеченцами? Зачем, если не для того, чтобы завершить геноцид, начатый Гитлером?

> ("We've had enough of this masquerade! . . . why it is that in order to have peace on earth and humanity's progress it was necessary to fabricate the Kremlin doctors' plot. Why was it necessary to break the joints of my uncle's

---

12 Shraer-Petrov, "Obed s vozhdem," 209; Shrayer-Petrov, "Dinner with Stalin," 130.
13 Shraer-Petrov, "Obed s vozhdem," 213; Shrayer-Petrov, "Dinner with Stalin," 132.

arms and legs, he a famous surgeon who spent the entire four years saving lives at the war front? For the sake of what lofty ideal was it necessary to design mass deportations of Jews, as had been done earlier to the Volga Germans, the Crimean Tatars, and the Chechens? For what, if not to complete the genocide of Jews Hitler had started?")[14]

Mira covers her face with a napkin and sobs. Stalin's double now faces a moment of retribution: for his bravado, for having tried on the leader's effigy, ultimately, for the choice to venerate Stalin. As it turns out, he has nothing to say in response, except for tired propagandistic formulas from Soviet newspapers and perestroika-era antisemiic newspapers.

Mikhail Petrovsky suggested that the "arrow" of the narration may not hit the target at all, but rather hit the target "only flatways."[15] In that case one could not speak of the full realization of the genre, but only of approaches to the genre. As a realization and embodiment of the world, the genre demands a correspondence to specific criteria. If such a correspondence does not occur, then the reader faces a different world, living in accordance to other principles. In the course of his analysis of some of Boccaccio's novellas, Petrovsky notes that one could not call them fully realized novellas; they have remained anecdotes, or, in the best case, "novella-anecdotes." These "novella-anecdotes" lack the point, that which "can hit and penetrate [the target] with the arrowhead, and therein lies the art of the storyteller [искусство рассказчика]. The sharpness of the novella's final effect is its point (arrowhead)—the technical term of the novella's composition."[16]

The pitiful actor from Tbilisi has exhausted his rhetorical arsenal. To quote the leader does not mean to be one, but it does mean to be responsible for the delivered quotations. Alyosha delivers the verdict to Stalin: "Да вы, к сожалению, и сейчас живы! Явились с того света и продолжаете смердеть!" ("But unfortunately you're alive now! You have returned from the other side, and you continue to emit a foul odor.")[17] After these words Alyosha rips a hunting rifle from the wall. Belatedly, the guest from Tbilisi tears off his glued-on mustache, tries to stop Alyosha, but it is too late: a shot is fired.

---

14   Shraer-Petrov, "Obed s vozhdem," 213; Shrayer-Petrov, "Dinner with Stalin," 133.
15   Petrovskii, "Morfologiia novelly," 75.
16   Ibid., 75–76.
17   Shraer-Petrov, "Obed s vozhdem," 215; Shrayer-Petrov, "Dinner with Stalin," 134.

Riddled with pellets, the painting behind Stalin's back bears symbolic significance. The actor plays Stalin against the backdrop of a painting based on Pushkin's narrative long poem *Ruslan and Lyudmila*, and yet this "fairy tale" is the childhood of so many who were executed by bullet. The actor from the Georgian theater played Stalin with delight, with pleasure, and he had lost himself in the act of playing. And thus one more question lingers: Could it be that Stalin had once lost himself in playing Stalin?

Mikhail Petrovsky underscored that both structural elements, *Vorgeschichte* and *Nachgeschichte*, are potentially (implicitly) present in the text: "Only in one case—that of the cohesion of the kernel plot with the death of the hero—can the plot epilogue [*Nachgeschichte*] be consumed by the middle part, the very '*Geschichte*' of the plot."[18] This is what happened in Shrayer-Petrov's novella: the rifle firing at Stalin, the culmination of the "very *Geschichte*," consumes the *Nachgeschichte*. But what actually happens in the novella? Is the actor deadly frightened or killed? Who is deadly frightened or killed, the actor or Stalin? This remains understated. Petrovsky writes: "The effect of an incomplete denouement consists in a retrospective shifting of the center of story's semantic gravity from the *facts* to the *attitude* toward them. *Factually* (plotwise) the knot has not been untied, but *architectonically* (formally) all the components are apparent, except the place of denouement is filled with a special (not factual) semantic content."[19]

So is the actor killed? Is Stalin killed?

Petrovsky makes an important observation regarding the wholesomeness and completeness of the novella: "The *understatedness* of the denouement does not constitute the story's incompleteness, for the completeness of the story is defined by the way it is delivered and by its composition, and not by the completeness of some life-related content, always fictional in an artistic work."[20] In this sense "Dinner with Stalin" is, without a doubt, a complete novella.

When Stalin dropped into the abyss of jokes and became something like Chapayev (the legendary hero of the Civil War and subject of numerous—and largely irreverent—popular Soviet-era jokes), he had thereby gained

---

18 Petrovskii, "Morfologiia novelly," 73.
19 Ibid., 87.
20 Ibid., 87.

a true immortality. Even today in Russia tens of thousands of people still honor the tyrant and long for his authoritarian and willful rule. His "charm" grew out of the base pleasure of hearing a nighttime knock at the neighbor's, and not one's own, door. Before it had gained the quotation marks, this ability to manipulate the emotions of people had been noted by urban folklore.

After the first reading of Shrayer-Petrov's novella the reader is puzzled by its title. Why "Dinner with the Leader," and not "Dinner with Stalin"? (In the English translation, which lent its title to the third translated collection of Shrayer-Petrov's stories, this question is resolved in favor of greater historical clarity.) After all, Grisha returns from the airport with Stalin, and not with the actor, whose real name we would never learn throughout the story. It is precisely the presence of Stalin that renders Grisha, "a man of gigantic height with a bull's unbending neck and head," so pitiful, diminished, mincing. The role of the title is to serve as a tuning fork for the narration, but not only that. The title is also a synecdoche of the novella itself. The willingness to share a dinner table with the leader a priori provokes all the ones present at the dinner, demanding their co-participation in the leader's ethical legitimization. To share a table with him means, to some extent, to forgive and understand the table-mate.

"What does the title of the novella point to?" Petrovsky wonders. And he goes on to explain:

> It must obviously highlight a substantial moment in the story. Any story, in the end, is a story about that which its title announced. [. . .] But the title stands outside the temporal order of the narration. It is not so much at the beginning, as above, over the entire novella. Its significance is not the significance of the opening of the novella, but is commensurate with the novella as a whole. The novella is related to its title in a synecdochic fashion: the title co-implies the novella's content.[21]

Let us recall that in literature the conceptualization of Stalin started after his death. One of the first to turn to the figure of Stalin was Vasily Grossman. Although Stalin had treated Grossman with a lack of trust, he had not had him arrested or punished; however, year after year Stalin personally crossed Grossman's name from the list of candidates for the Stalin Prize. And he added some writers to the list. Stalin crossed Grossman

---

21 Petrovskii, "Morfologiia novelly," 92.

out, but he did not have him arrested, he did not destroy him or dispossess him, and he allowed Grossman to write as the others were allowed to write. The only correction was made in the novel, which Grossman really wanted to title *Stalingrad*. But Mikhail Sholokhov, not a friend of Jews, to put it mildly, stood up and opined: "Is that whom you trusted to write about Stalingrad!" Stalin had his own hierarchy, and Sholokhov's words reached him. According to the recollections of the writer Semyon Lipkin, a close friend of Grossman's, Grossman was told that his novel could not bear such a title.

For Grossman, Stalin is a totally magical figure. Grossman's artistic discovery lay in the fact that his image of Stalin was deprived of psychology. Grossman does not study Stalin's psychology the way Anatoly Rybakov would subsequently attempted to study it in the novel *Children of the Arbat* [*Deti Arbata*], drawing abundantly from various sources. Psychology appeared only in Stalin's actions, whereas Grossman's prose on principle refused to engage in psychological analysis of Stalin's image. Stalin was "something" that did not succumb to psychological analysis. Stalin's actions had *fatal* consequences, *created* fate. They could bring happiness, or could bring unimaginable, unsurmountable misfortune. Grossman depicts Stalin's actions. Stalin sings a little song, and one feels chilled to the bone from a fear of consequences. Stalin affixes his signature to a piece of paper, and entire nations are transferred to such place where no people had lived before. Stalin makes a call to Pasternak, and this call is remembered forever, simply forever. For Grossman Stalin is a symbol of humanity's enslavement. He is one person who has chained millions.

Two short chapters from Grossman's *Life and Fate* are devoted to Stalin. Prior to making an appearance in them, Stalin is reflected in images—like in mirrors—and manifests himself through destinies of the novel's different characters. Stalin is shown through the eyes of people who observe him, follow his every move. The image of the tyrant is woven from fear and adulation, hate and love, loyalty and provocation. He himself had architectured this terrifying life, and for many decades after his death the stable regime sustained it.

In Grossman's last work *Goodness Be To You!* (*Dobro vam!*), published posthumously, a colossal monument to Stalin appears already in the opening pages. Nobody came to meet the writer, who arrived to Erevan in order to translate into Russian a novel by an Armenian writer. A gigantic Stalin, hanging over the city, greeted Grossman upon his arrival. Even a cosmonaut flown in from a distant planet would immediately see and recognize Stalin, towering over Armenia's capital, notes Grossman. Along with the base, the height of the monument was seventy-five meters (almost 256 feet). It looked as though clouds touched the bronze brimmed hat on his head:

> He towers over Erevan, over Armenia, he towers over Russia, Ukraine, over the Black and the Caspian sea, over the Arctic ocean, over the East Siberian taiga, the sands of Kazakhstan. Stalin is the state. [...] All heads bowed before the master, the leader, the builder of the Soviet state. Stalin's state expressed Stalin's character [Государство Сталина выразило характер Сталина]. In Stalin's character was expressed the character of the state he built.[22]

Published in the USA in 1981, the book by Ilya Suslov (the émigré humorist who had founded the popular "12 Chairs Club" in Moscow's *Literary Gazette*), was given the title *Stories of Comrade Stalin and Other Comrades*.[23] The book's foundation was folklore about Stalin captured in the form of *belle-lettres*. According to a review in then the Parisian émigré magazine *Kontinent*,

> the very style of these stories (although they include commonly known jokes and anecdotes), their very style parodies the style of instructive, "hagiographic" slobbery-didactic stories about Lenin or Dzerzhinsky. To put it simply, the style of these stories, precisely parodied by Suslov, [...] unequivocally betrays ideology by showing that it amounts to a creation of religion without God, that such ideology is a parody of religion. Thus I. Suslov's stories are a parody of parody.[24]

Here is an example particularly fitting for the subject of this article:

A Double

Comrade Beria ran over to see Comrade Stalin and said:
"Comrade Stalin, a double of yours is walking around Moscow. Same height, age, voice, and mustache. What are we going to do, comrade Stalin?

---

22   V. Grossman, *Sobranie sochinenii*, ed. S. I. Lipkin, vol. 2 (Moscow: Vagrius, 1998), 151.
23   Il´ia Suslov, *Rasskazy o tovarishche Staline i drugikh tovarishchakh* (Ann Arbor, MI: Hermitage, 1981).
24   Review of Il´ia Suslov, *Rasskazy o tovarishche Staline i drugikh tovarishchakh*, *Kontinent* 33 (1982): 412.

"Shoot him!" comrade Stalin gave a brief answer.
"Perhaps we should shave off the mustache?" comrade Beria pensively asked.
"We could also do that," comrade Stalin agreed.²⁵

The mustache is a constant feature of Stalin's perception. The visiting actor in Shrayer-Petrov's novella disowns his inner Stalin when, upon seeing rifle pointing at him, he tears off the glued-on mustache, that symbols of doubleness.

Suslov's stories about Stalin have been circulated in collections of urban (or "intelligentsia") folklore. They can be found in the collection *USSR in the Mirror of Political Jokes* (*Sovetskii Soiuz v zerkale politicheskogo anekdota*, 1985; expanded edition 1987), edited by Dora Shturman and Sergei Tiktin, or in Yuri Borev's two-volume set *The Staliniad* (*Staliniada*, 1990) and *Phariseia* (*Fariseia*, 1992). Not surprisingly, the collections do not contain references to Ilya Suslov's book. But Suslov himself, in publishing his stories, borrowed them from the legends and jokes he had heard. He was writing about the Soviet tyrant Stalin, but he recreated a Chapayev of popular Soviet jokes.

Anatoly Gladilin's short story "A Friday Rehearsal" ("Repetitsiia v piatnitsu"), written in 1974 prior to Gladilin's emigration but originally published abroad,²⁶ reminded the reader of the possibility of a Stalinist restoration. The story is based on fantastical circumstances: Stalin has been removed from the Lenin Mausoleum yet not buried but rather preserved for a return at an opportune time. In view of an astonished guard Iosif Vissarionovich rises from a comfortable coffin, modified and outfitted for long-term storage and preservation, and leaves his abode. Stalin's appearance at meeting of a regional party economic council sends all those present into a state of trepidation, but only initially. Immediately people come forward who organize a mass adoration of the leader who has returned to service. Rosy-checked Komsomol members organize scientific-technical seminars, sprouting up right there in the foyer of the regional party committee and devoted to Stalin's legacy.

However, nothing is the same in the once mighty and perfectly functioning Stalinist empire. It is impossible even to gather a rally at the town square: the work day is over; those who are not already drunk have gone back home to

---

25 Il´ia Suslov, "Iumor tovarishcha Stalina," *Vremia i my* 1 (1975): 212.
26 Anatolii Gladilin, *Repetisiia v piatnitsu. Povest´ i rasskazy* (Paris: Tret´ia volna, 1978), 3–21. The story was first published in Russia in *Iunost´* magazine (*Iunost´* 2 [1991]).

watch TV, and Stalin is not even allowed to speak on the local station. In fact, a major soccer game is being transmitted live, and the one to interrupt the transmission, even in favor of a political event, would forever become an enemy of the working Soviet people.

But that is not all. The problem runs deeper: the neo-Stalinists who now hold power have asserted a new style of nomenclature. For simpler folks everything has remained unchanged, even though the means of control have grown weaker: even during the work day one can now venture out to a store or to run other errands. The Stalinist mechanism had gradually come undone, and there is no one left who would carry out executions for gathering bread stalks in the fields or arrests for being five minutes late to work. The party elite is no longer interested in reanimating the leader and teacher. The resulting status quo suits everybody, which is why in Gladilin's story Stalin is not allowed to appear on TV and instead is retired to a classified secret base.

During the years of perestroika, the production of the Moscow State University's Student Theater based on Viktor Korkiya's play *A Black Person, or I, Poor Soso Dzhugashvili* (*Chernyi chelovek, ili Ia, bednyi Soso Dzhugashvili*, 1988) enjoyed phenomenal popularity among the Moscow intelligentsia. Following the 20th Congress of the Communist Party (1956) Stalin's writings were no longer reprinted, and the playwright conflated themes from Stalin's epoch with a dotted plotline, enriched with quotations from classical works: *Hamlet*, Pushkin's *Boris Godunov* and *Little Tragedies*, and others.

Thus the post-Stalinist conceptualization of the epoch continued, grew a baggage of new works. However, the absence of final and categorical de-Stalinization was (and has remained) the socio-political backdrop for such a conceptualization. To the present day this serves as a foundation for the appearance of school textbooks of history with the assertion of Stalin's alleged "managerial abilities," for the deliberately lowered numbers of victims of Stalin's regime, for calls "not to demonize" him, for the praise of Stalin's alliance with the Russian Orthodox Church and so on.

The very tradition of the annual laying of flowers at his grave by leaders of the Russian Communist Party, who form a faction of the Russian Federation's Duma, constitutes a shameful trampling of the humanistic foundations of Russian society. A photograph of Aleksandr Prokhanov, one of the leaders of today's Russian "red-browns" (*krasno-korichnevye*), praying on his knees before a bust of Stalin at his grave, has become an icon for the new generation of Stalinists.

The novella "Dinner with Stalin" strikes me as the concluding note in the tradition of Russian-language prose about the mythologization of Stalin. With this note—this shot—David Shrayer-Petrov has succeeded in creating closure in the conceptualization of the recurrent outbreaks of Stalin's cult. One must put an end to them. Not to debate, not to fool around with Stalin's legacy or to tell jokes, not to join dinner parties with Stalin reenactments, and not to play at questions and answers. There will be no honest answers, because there were no interrogations: no one has managed to interrogate Stalin.

Rifle. Shot. Period.

Translated, from the Russian, by
Maxim D. Shrayer

Works Cited

Bakhtin, M. M. *Problemy tvorchestva Dostoevskogo*. Kiev: Next, 1994.

Gladilin, Anatolii. *Repetisiia v piatnitsu. Povest´ i rasskazy*. Paris: Tret´ia volna, 1978.

Grossman, Vasili. *Sobranie sochinenii*. Edited by S. I. Lipkin. 4 vols. Moscow: Vagrius, 1998.

Petrovskii, M. A. "Morfologiia novelly." In *Ars Poetica*, edited by M. A. Petrovskii, vol. 1, 69–100. Moscow: Gosudarstvennaia akademiia khudozhestvennykh nauk, 1927.

Review of Il´ia Suslov, *Rasskazy o tovarishche Staline i drugikh tovarishchakh*. *Kontinent* 33 (1982): 411–413.

Shrayer-Petrov, David. "Dinner with Stalin." Translated by Aleksandra Fleszar and Arna B. Bronstein. In David Shrayer-Petrov. *Dinner with Stalin and Other Stories*, edited by Maxim D. Shrayer, 120–134. Syracuse: Syracuse University Press, 2014.

——— [David Shraer-Petrov]. "Obed s vozhdem." In David Shraer-Petrov, *Krugosvetnoe shchast´e. Izbrannye rasskazy*, edited by Maksim D. Shraer and David Shraer-Petrov, 196–215. Moscow: Knizhniki, 2016.

Shrayer, Maxim D. [Notes to "Dinner with Stalin"]. In David Shrayer-Petrov. *Dinner with Stalin and Other Stories*, edited by Maxim D. Shrayer, 241–244. Syracuse: Syracuse University Press, 2014.

Suslov, Il´ia. "Iumor tovarishcha Stalina." *Vremia i my* 1 (1975): 209–214.

———. *Rasskazy o tovarishche Staline i drugikh tovarishchakh*. Ann Arbor, MI: Hermitage, 1981.

Post Scriptum

"Each writer has his or her own Jewish secret....": A Conversation in Three Parts*

Conducted on the Occasion of the Publication of

David Shrayer-Petrov's Collection

Dinner with Stalin and Other Stories (2014)

David Shrayer-Petrov and Maxim D. Shrayer

Part One: A Fictional Model of the Former USSR

MDS Let's start with a basic question. What are the stories gathered in *Dinner with Stalin* about?

DSP It's not simple or easy to describe a new collection of short stories in a few brief comments. Too many characters ... A multitude of story lines ... Above all else, *Dinner with Stalin* is about the lives of Russian Jews who found themselves abroad, first emigrating and later rooting themselves into, grafting themselves onto the American soil. Some of the stories take place on tropical islands or in Israel, but the key thing is that my characters are already Americans, and they perceive themselves, especially when they are overseas, as Americans—even though here at home in the US they think of themselves as Russian. But if you press them on the subject, "You're Russians? What kind of Russians are you?" they would answer, "Yes, we're Russian. Russian Jews." A very complex predicament. As a writer I'm having

---

*Copyright © 2021 by David Shrayer-Petrov and Maxim D. Shrayer.
The conversation was originally conducted on the invitation of Jewish Book Council and published, in a slightly abridged form, as part of its "Members of the Scribe" series in July 2014.

to weave the fabric of my stories from a number of different balls of yarn: today my characters appear as Americans at work, tomorrow as Russian persons at home, while in fact they have Jewish souls. Which is why my stories are not easy to describe as a whole without being overspecific or drawing on concrete examples.

MDS But if we take as a symbol of the whole collection the title story, "Dinner with Stalin," how does it express the essence of your book?

DSP Here, I would say, the essence of the book doesn't only encapsulate the Jewish question. This group of émigré friends, all of them hailing from the former Soviet Union, get a visit by Stalin who has come from the next world. It is, of course, an actor who masterfully plays the role of Stalin, bringing the whole thing to the point of absurdity, so much so that the audience begins to believe him—the way they temporarily believe the actor playing Hitler in Ray Bradbury's story "Darling Adolf." And so present among this colorful group of émigrés are representatives of a number of nationalities of the former Soviet Union, including Armenians, Azeris, Ukrainians, Russians and Jews. In this group Jews enjoy parity, and because of this the Jewish émigré protagonist and his wife Mira end up asking Stalin the most painful questions simultaneously pertaining to Soviet history and Jewish history. Especially about the years of late, postwar Stalinism. In the title story, "Dinner with Stalin," Mira addresses Stalin. And she's not pleading with him, but rather accusing him, putting him on trial: "But if you really want to know, I will drink under one condition: if you, the genius leader and teacher, explain to us why it is that in order to have peace on earth and humanity's progress it was necessary to fabricate the Kremlin 'doctors' plot' . . . For the sake of what lofty ideal was it necessary to design mass deportation of Jews, as had been done earlier to the Volga Germans, the Crimean Tatars, and the Chechens? For what, if not to complete the genocide of Jews Hitler had started?" The Jewish characters end up asking the most blunt and honest questions at this dinner with Stalin. . .

MDS . . . so in fact this gathering is a fictional model of the former Soviet Union . . .

DSP . . .yes, that's one. And this dinner is also a model of a United Nations session . . .

MDS . . . already in post-Soviet times . . .

DSP . . . yes, exactly, where representatives of different nations of the former Soviet Union testify about Stalinism and other painful aspects of the Soviet past.

MDS Let's go back to the past for brief moment. You started out as a poet and translator of poetry. And even though your earliest attempts at writing short fiction go back to the 1960s, you hadn't become a writer of short stories until the 1980s, when you were almost forty, having already written three novels and two books of non-fiction. Since then the short story has been one of your chosen literary forms. Why do you think you embraced the form and genre of the short story late in your career?

DSP I believe this had to do with what I demanded of myself. I had been regarding the short story, as opposed to a mere retelling of some episode which has occurred with somebody, as a gem that not every writer gets to cut and polish. For me the stories of Zweig, Thomas Mann, Bunin, Nabokov, Chekhov above all, and of the early Soviet writers such as Olesha and Babel, those stories had been examples of truly high mastery. And it had taken me a while before I felt ready to write true short stories. Of course even as a younger writer I had stories to tell, having seen a lot as a Jewish child and young man during the war and in the terrible postwar years. And I had done so in the memoir vein. But to write the short story as a selfsame unique form and genre . . . I hadn't fully fathomed how to write short stories until I became a Jewish refusenik living like a literary hermit, in total isolation from the official Soviet culture. And already as a writer-refusenik I had suddenly understood that there is a magic trick, a device of fiction-making, which one needs to realize in order to compose a short story—to make it up as opposed to merely copying it from so-called real life. This magic fictional quality—that inimitable vibration of feeling—is something Chekhov's stories exhibit in the fullest sense.

MDS If I remember correctly, you had a very early piece of short prose titled "The Sun Fell into the Mine Shaft" ("Solntse upalo v shakhtu") from the early 1960s, which was about a young Russian Jew's realization that he could never be fully integrated into that country's mainstream. So you must have already been contemplating this problem. But you hadn't begun to write short stories about this until we became refuseniks. I find this very intriguing.

DSP The Jewish question had already been a source of much trepidation on my part for a couple of decades before I started writing short stories. As you can imagine, by the 1960s, I had already lived through a lot. The "doctors' plot," when Jews had again experienced a nearing abyss, occurred during my senior year in high school. But then, after medical school, when I was serving in the military [in 1959–1961], I can't say that I experienced much antisemitism there—or more antisemitism than in everyday Soviet life. But nevertheless the Jewish theme had already stung me. It's just that before we had formally applied for exit visas, I had been distancing myself from writing stories about Jews. I had been tying my own Jewish hands, if you will, trying to resist rebellious urges. But I couldn't suppress these urges, and you already know what happened when we became refuseniks.

MDS Your stories, almost all of them, feature main and secondary Jewish characters. Is writing almost exclusively about Jewish characters what makes a writer-Jew a *Jewish* writer?

DSP I think that's important. At least there's a Jewish calculus. If you're a writer of Jewish origin but you never write about Jews—I don't know. And there were such cases in the Soviet Union. Take, for instance, the poet David Samoylov. In everyday life he never specifically avoided Jewish subjects, even though he was also baptized in the Orthodox Church, but he hardly ever wrote about Jews. In contrast to Samoylov, there was Boris Slutsky, who in everyday life, at the dinner table, wasn't particularly inclined to speak of Jewish questions, but who wrote many wonderful poems not just about Jewish people but ones suffused with the pain of Jewish history.

MDS Exactly. And if this is not only a matter of Jewish themes or characters but something else, can one speak of a Jewish poetics—or specifically of the Jewish short story—not only in terms of Jewish themes? What is that *Jewish something else* in writing?

DSP I don't think it's possible to describe this thing. It's a secret, and I don't think you can isolate it simply the way scientists isolate a gene. Otherwise one could take this Jewish something and transfer it onto any material. Luckily, it doesn't work this way. Each writer has his or her own Jewish secret. Babel has his own, and we immediately feel the presence of Babel's Jewish secret. Or take Ilya Ilf and Evgeny Petrov and their great novels *The Twelve Chairs* and *The Golden Calf*. That's an example of a classic Jewish device in fiction. Even though most of the characters in these books are not Jewish, but the authorial grin, the ironic perspective are very Jewish. Or consider Vasily Grossman's *Life and Fate*. Right away we know that a Jewish writer created this book because of the way the author mourns the fate of Jews as he sets it against the backdrop of a devastating fate of the entire country.

MDS Yes, but I also think that in Grossman there's also a distinctly intellectual perspective, a Jewish intellectual commentary on historical events. In any event, I was wondering to what extent is a Jewish writer a child of the millennia of Judaic civilization and to what extent he is a product of his own epoch and language?

DSP To be honest, I'm not a great fan of the notion of genetic memory. I don't believe in such Jewish memory. There are universal human genes, and there are genes which a high prevalence in the Jewish genotype, but I don't think this has much to do with Jewish writing. What does matter is that writers grew up in a Jewish family—even in post-revolutionary Russia—where they were exposed to Jewish conversations and ruminations.

Part Two: A Jewish-Russian Writer as a New Englander

MDS Let's continue with our topic but also change tack. What happens after a Jewish writer emigrates from the Soviet Union to the US? Of the fourteen stories in *Dinner with Stalin*, you wrote thirteen already in America, as an immigrant. What specifically has changed in your creative laboratory?

DSP Well, first of all both the immediate environment and the greater environment have changed. Most of these stories fashion Russian (Jewish-Russian) characters living in America. In this sense I've become an American writer. For instance, take the story "The Valley of Hinnom" ("Ushchel'e Geenny") Even though much of the action is set in Moscow and in Israel, I could have never written this story without knowing that the main characters are former refuseniks living in the US.

MDS Great. One more "American" question, then. A number of your stories in this book are set in New England cities and towns, in Rhode Island and Massachusetts—Providence, Little Compton, Worcester, towns on Cape Cod and so on. And there are also urban, European stories set in Paris, Moscow and Leningrad (St. Petersburg), and scenes of Rome and Jerusalem, composed, as it were, from memory. How have many years of living in New England influenced your stories?

DSP I've lived here for almost twenty-eight years [thirty-three as of 2020]. I think that I've rooted myself in New England. It has become my second—now my main—natural environment. If asked about it, I would now respond without any hesitation that I'm a New Englander, even though I had lived for fifty years in Russia, in Leningrad and Moscow. In this sense I sometimes wonder how I was able to write, so many years later, the short story "The Bicycle Race" ("Velogonki") set in the Leningrad of my youth. I guess I was able to do it because I really wanted to fish out of the depth of memory and to reconstruct the image of the very complex person whose life informed my story. He's called Shvarts in my story, but his prototype was Eduard Chernoshvarts (nicknamed "Chyorny," which literally means "black" in Russian), a Jew, a famous Soviet cyclist. He was a person of Jewish origin who had risen above the masses at the time when there was a strong popular anti-Jewish sentiment. In my story the main character is a great Jewish athlete, but he is hardly a Jew of high moral standing . . .

MDS . . . yes, but to return to the question of being a Jewish writer rooted in New England . . . If we look analytically at your stories, it appears that you write *without estrangement* about today's life in New England (as in such stories as "A Storefront Window of Miracle" or "The House of Edgar Allan Poe") *and* about your youth in Russia (as in "The Bicycle Race" and in "Mimosa Flowers for Grandmother's Grave"). But at the same time you write with a much greater degree of estrangement about your last three Russian decades, especially about the refusenik years.

DSP Yes, I think it's true. In this regard "Mimosa Flowers for Grandmother's Grave," the only story in *Dinner with Stalin* that I had written while still living in Russia, is a case in point. Your English translation of this story had first appeared in *Commentary*, and judging by the reactions of American readers, of American Jews, it touched some chords . . .

MDS . . . I think, the story tapped our shared memory of a Jewish past in Russia. A Jewish family forever broken by turbulent historical events, a *halutz*, love and longing—these are things to which Jewish-American readers must be particularly attuned.

DSP Yes, and I also think that throughout his or her entire life, every Jew is pursued, haunted by some poignant detail of the past . . . one had a grandmother or a great-grandmother who was a traditional Jew in the full sense of this term. And then across countries and languages this image of a Jewish great-grandmother was being passed on from immigrant grandmother to mother to American child. And it has thus survived.

MDS I agree. "Mimosa Flowers for Grandmother's Grave" is the most universally Jewish story in *Dinner with Stalin*. Let's continue with question of Jewish family and marriage. Practically in each of your stories you observe and comment on aspects of love and marriage between Jews and non-Jews. Critics have pointed out that for you as a Jewish storyteller this is a key question. Why?

DSP I have observed many mixed marriages growing up. My uncle, my mother's brother, was married to a Russian woman who was an observant

Orthodox Christian. And there's a family legend that when I was an infant, a five- or six-month-old, she brought me to church. But now who can tell. The very marriage between Russia and Jewry is, I think, a kind of symbol which was supposed to divert the hand of antisemites—and at times it did do that, but at other times it did not, only nurturing false hopes. There were very many mixed Jewish-Russian marriages in Russia, and this resulted in some good things, but also in many complications.

MDS This is a very relevant topic in today's America, and for that reason I think the stories in *Dinner with Stalin* will be of interest to Jewish-American readers.

DSP Yes, but here there's a religious agenda to this problem as one must decide about the religion of one's children. In the Soviet Union such decision-making was less manifest in mixed marriages. But in 1953, the crucial year for Soviet Jews, with genocidal scenarios in the air, there were non-Jewish spouses who, out of fear, sought to dissolve their marriages to Jews. This shameful conduct of some of the non-Jews married to Jews resembles Germany after the Nazis came to power.

MDS To digress for a moment, it's fashionable these days to ask writers about lists of must-reads, so let me ask you for your list of 5 Jewish books which everyone should read—that is, besides *Dinner with Stalin*.

DSP This is a very partial list, but nonetheless, I would recommend: *The Ugly Duchess* by Feuchtwanger, *Heavy Sand* by Rybakov, *Shosha* by Bashevis Singer, *Ravelstein* by Bellow (and given Thomas Mann's Jewish connections, *Death in Venice*), and Ilf and Petrov's dilogy *The Twelve Chairs* and *The Golden Calf*.

MDS May I also add a personal favorite—and may this wish soon come true— your refusenik saga, which has been translated into English and which we are now editing for publication.

Part Three: Crypto-Jews and Autobiographical Animals

MDS My next question in some way stems from the problem of mixed marriages and the issue of suppressed or concealed identity. I want to ask you about crypto-Jews, those who hide their Jewishness either in order to preserve the tradition (as in your story "White Sheep on a Green Mountain Slope" ["Belye ovtsy na zelenom sklone gor"] set in the Caucasus) or in order to preserve themselves and survive (as the Holocaust survivor, the Polish Jew in "Mimicry" ["Mimikriia"]). Why do so many crypto-Jews populate the pages of your stories, and why are there fewer observant, traditional Jews in them?

DSP I think that very many Jews used to try to conceal their Jewishness, at least in their public conduct... and I myself was sometimes guilty of that in pre-refusenik Soviet life.

MDS But crypto-Jewishness as a quality of your stories, your characters. This is making me think of Dostoevsky's fondness of pathological characters, such as Svidrigaylov in *Crime and Punishment*, who is perhaps the most vibrant and alive creature in the novel, as opposed to the devout believer Sonia Marmeladova, who is righteous but flat. That's what I was wondering about when I contrasted your crypto-Jews and your publically observant Jews.

DSP This is true, because devout, observant Jews don't usually stray from their public image or literary stereotype. Such model Jews are a source of my great admiration, but as a fictionist I don't have much to say about them. It's been done a thousand times before by Sholem Aleichem, Bashevis Singer... even Singer was writing about Jews who exhibit a shift of behavior.

MDS Speaking about shifts of behavior, Jewish or otherwise, your stories carry large doses of erotic tension, both open and hidden; "The Bicycle Race" alone is suffused with subtle eroticism. I don't know why, but I keep thinking of *Dinner with Stalin* and of *Dark Avenues*, perhaps the best of Ivan Bunin's books and certainly his manifesto of the love story. Can we speak of your book as a book of love stories?

DSP I would prefer to call it a book of stories about love. In these stories there isn't only love for a woman, but also a hidden, yet very powerful love for a Jew's homeland, for Russia. The homeland of one's native language, the Russian language. And this love for—this love of—one's native Russian language and culture is perhaps even stronger than erotic love, sexual love in my stories.

MDS And what about the love of American culture? I remember from my earliest Moscow childhood the framed photographs of Hemingway and Robert Frost hanging on the walls of your study.

DSP Yes, this is correct. I was fascinated by them, enchanted by them. But they didn't touch me the way first Chekhov and Bunin, and later Nabokov touched me. Even Hemingway doesn't touch me this way today. I don't know what happened... It's also one's age. For example, when I was a young poet in the late 1950s, so many around me were crazy about Anna Akhmatova. At the time I didn't understand what was so remarkable and special about her, whereas I loved the poetry of Nikolai Zabolotsky. I believed at the time that he had expressed with the greatest power that tremendous upheaval of Russian society. And to think that he had written his *Scrolls* (*Stolbtsy*) in the late 1920s, before the war and before the Thaw! To me *Scrolls* were an expression of the poet's tender love of Russia because Zabolotsky laughed at the very things that Russians kept hidden and concealed, were uncomfortable airing in public. He wanted to unearth those things.

MDS I actually think that if one views your stories about Jewish immigrants from the former Soviet Union as a canvas or an artist's whole perspective, one recognizes that Zabolotskian palette—mixing the colors of love and irony.

DSP I think this is true of some stories in the book, most certainly of "Dinner with Stalin," the title story, with its freak show of the former Soviet Union, an immigrant household in Providence, Rhode Island, and Stalin presiding over the dinner table.

MDS During an event at the wonderful Books on the Square in Providence, Rhode Island, in answering a question that came from a Jewish-American journalist of Soviet descent, you stated that everything you write is autobiographical, including your animal characters, be they wild turkeys or hippos. How literally can one take these words, and couldn't they perhaps lead a gullible reader astray?

DSP I don't think so. Autobiographical in the sense that each bird hum or noise or love call, each sigh or roar of the hippopotamus, each tiny vibration of my story lines has its source in me because I've experienced it. And if I haven't literally experienced it, then I thought that I'd lived it. Believe me, in our mind we sometimes live though an imagined life that is as real as the one we experience outside our consciousness. This is especially true of the things we experience in dreams but don't get to experience in reality due to a lack of time or restrictions of space, abilities to travel and so forth.

MDS You've written some forty-five short stories and novellas and you have also written [ten] novels. Going back to the secrets of Jewish story-writing, I want to ask you what distinguishes the short story from the novel—and specifically your short stories from your novels?

DSP As a genre, the short story is more fragile, tender, and vulnerable than the bigger prose form—the novel. First and foremost, the short story does not tolerate falsity or unintended ambiguity. That is to say, shortcomings are immediately exposed on the face of the short story. At the same time, the short story does not agree particularly well with overabundant and continuous depiction of people and their myths—with the so-called realistic-representational mode. Yes, I said depiction of people and of myths. In a successful short story, each line gains the potential to be read and perceived mythologically. For instance, in "Behind the Zoo Fence" ("Za ogradoi zooparka"), which opens this collection, the hippopotamus is mythological in his capacity to send the mystical vibes of healing to a young woman fighting a lethal infection at a nearby hospital.

MDS And finally, I would like to return to the point you made earlier, what you referred to as a fantastical quality of your short stories. This is, of course, a quality of some of the greatest Jewish fiction, from Sholem Aleichem to Bashevis Singer to Malamud (and in Russia, think, for instance, of the early Veniamin Kaverin and of Lev Lunts). What are some of the literary sources of your stories'?

DSP I have always been drawn to the genres of the fairy tale, legend, and myth. This goes back to my childhood, when I spent three wartime years in a remote Russian village hidden in the Ural Mountains. I was drawn to these things, but not so much to what is popularly known as science fiction. In its structural qualities, traditional science fiction is more akin to the detective genre than to deeply lyrical fiction. It took me quite some time to make sense of these distinctions. This self-awareness came to me, gradually, from poetry, and above all from Pushkin's writings, which are both lyrical and mythological. In modern Russian poetry and fiction I have admired works that were simultaneously fantastical tales and stories of social fantasy. Think of the Strugatsky brothers—those Jewish-Russian geniuses of social fantasy.

MDS Please explain what you have in mind when you call some of your short stories "fantellas"? This is your coinage.

DSP From the fabric of prose, grounded in realistic predicaments, I grow elements of what I call *fantellism*. I take these elements beyond the limits of so-called "real life," and I pour them into the vessels naturally equipped to contain fairy tales. I call such a story *fantella*, and it's been recognized as a new term in Russian prose. Now, through translation, my *fantellas* have entered American literature. This may a good moment to say that I'm most grateful to my dedicated translators, among them my beloved wife Emilia Shrayer . . .

MDS . . . who is also my beloved mother and my teacher of English. But could I please ask you to be more specific about your *fantellas*.

DSP There are a number of stories in *Dinner with Stalin*, which can be called *fantellas*. I already mentioned "Behind the Zoo Fence" with its hippo and his mystical healing powers. Let me also mention "Mimicry" (where it's sometimes impossible to separate the magic kingdom of marionettes from the real lives of puppeteers); "Where Are You, Zoya?" ("Gde ty, Zoya?" with its mysterious appearances and disappearances of a wild turkey who bonds with an elderly Soviet émigré, she the widow of a Jewish poet who had perished in the GULAG during the Stalin years); and also the story "Alfredik" (in which the main character, manned by some otherworldly powers of the Soviet secret police, is constantly bifurcating, turning from one antihero into another, being transformed from a customs official at a Moscow airport into a third-rate writer who, most likely, is a KGB informant). And there are other stories to read and think about. But let me stop here because the process of summarizing a new book not only arouses one's interest in the book but also takes away from the pleasure of reading and imagining another life.

David Shrayer-Petrov: A Pictorial Biography *

Curated by Maxim D. Shrayer

Peysakh (Pyotr) Shrayer (front row left), David Shrayer-Petrov's father, with his parents and four siblings. Kamenets-Podolsk, Ukraine, 1924.

---

* Mainly compiled on the basis of the papers and photo archives of David Shrayer-Petrov and Emilia Shrayer; the photo archives of Maxim D. Shrayer and Karen E. Lasser. Additional sources are credited in individual captions.

David Shrayer-Petrov: A Pictorial Biography | 361

Rabbi Chaim-Wolf Broyde (Breydo), David Shrayer-Petrov's maternal grandfather. Polotsk, Belarus, 1930s. During the Polish-Soviet War of 1919–1920 the family had fled Lithuania and settled in Belarus. Rabbi Broyde was murdered in his own home by Nazis and their collaborators.

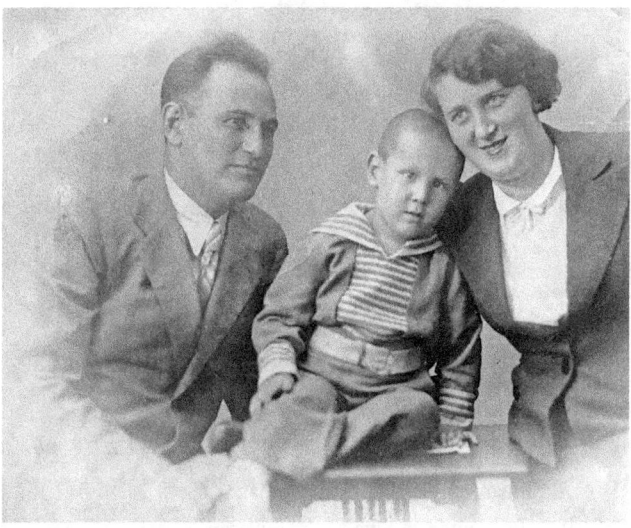

David Shrayer-Petrov with his parents, Bella Breydo and Peysakh (Pyotr) Shrayer. Leningrad, circa 1939–1940.

362 | David Shrayer-Petrov: A Pictorial Biography

Peysakh (Pyotr) Shrayer, captain of the tank troops, Leningrad Front, 1943.

David Shrayer-Petrov and Bella Breydo. Village of Siva, Molotov (now Perm) Province, 1942. Evacuated to Siva in the autumn of 1941 as the Nazi troops closed in on Leningrad, David and his mother spent three years in this remote Uralian village and returned to Leningrad in 1944.

David Shrayer-Petrov: A Pictorial Biography | **363**

7 Engelsa Prospect in St. Petersburg, located at the corner of Novorossiskaia Street and Engelsa Prospect; here seen from Novorossiiskaia Street. Beyond the near corner of this building stood 1 Engelsa Prospect, where David Shrayer-Petrov lived from his birth in 1936 until 1963. Photo by Ekaterina Tsarapkina, summer 2020.

David Shrayer-Petrov, Khmelnik, Vinnitsa Province, Ukraine, summer 1949. Prof. Dr. Izrail' Shrayer, first cousin of Shrayer-Petrov's father, was at the time a professor of medicine at Vinnitsa Medical School and hosted his nephews, among them the future literary scholar Omry Ronen.

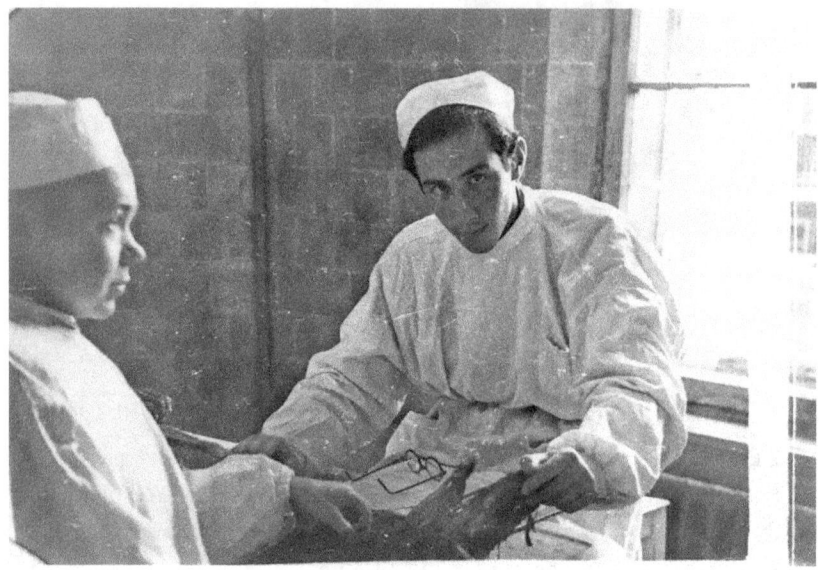

David Shrayer-Petrov (right) with fellow medical student, future pathologist Gennady Khudyakov. Leningrad, 1954.

David Shrayer-Petrov (second from right). Leningrad, 1955. Also captured in the photo are fellow medical students Gennady Khudyakov (second from left) and Aleksandr Muzhetsky (first from right); closest childhood friend Boris Smorodin or "Smoroda" (see Andrey Ranchin's essay in this volume).

David Shrayer-Petrov (third from left) with medical students and instructors. Botkin Hospital, Leningrad, 1958.

David Shrayer-Petrov, submarine training, Baltic Fleet, summer 1958. In part because of the romantic aura of sailing the seas, Shrayer-Petrov had volunteered to serve as a naval doctor and was undergoing naval training in Kronstadt and at sea. However, upon graduation from medical school he was drafted to serve as a military physician in a tank army in Borisov, Belarus.

David Shrayer-Petrov (second row, first from left) with fellow trainees and naval officers, Kronstadt, July 1958.

David Shrayer-Petrov. Drawing by K. K. Inscribed on the back: "To the forever most original of the Shrayers. 14 May 1958. K.K."

David Shrayer-Petrov: A Pictorial Biography | 367

David Shrayer-Petrov. Draft of his well-known poem "Darite devushkam tsvety . . ." ("Give flowers to girls . . ."), here titled "Po Remarku" ("After Remarque") and dedicated to the poet Anatoly Naiman. The bottom part of the page features an ink drawing by the translator and future BBC journalist Efim Slavinsky. Leningrad, 1959.

 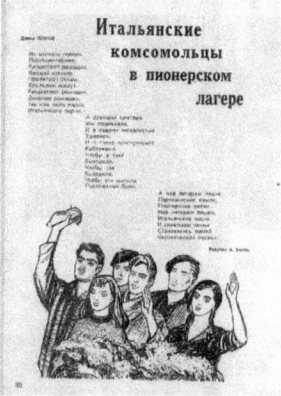

David Shrayer-Petrov's poem "Ital′ianskie komsomol′tsy v pionerskom lagere" ("Italian Young Communists in a Young Pioneer Camp"), May 1959, *Pioner* (*Young Pioneer*) magazine (Moscow). This was the author's first publication in a national magazine. The themes of the poem are illustrated on the front cover (see Stefano Garzonio's essay in this volume).

David Shrayer-Petrov. Outside the Russian Museum, Leningrad, circa 1959. Note an issue of *L'Unità*, newspaper of the Italian Communist party. Newspapers of European Communist parties were available for sale in the USSR, and intellectuals perused them in search of less biased and censored information than what Soviet newspapers had to offer.

David Shrayer-Petrov, MD, lieutenant of the medical corps. Borisov, Belarus, 1960. Shrayer-Petrov served for two years upon graduating from medical school. He briefly returned to Leningrad in December 1960 for his mother's funeral and was discharged from the military in 1961.

David Shrayer-Petrov: A Pictorial Biography | 369

David Shrayer-Petrov (left), Vsevolod Azarov (opposite on left). Outside of Leningrad, 1962. In the middle 1950s, Vsevolod Azarov, poet and playwright, had been one of the officially appointed mentors of the literary seminar (*lito*) at the Palace of Culture of Industrial Cooperation, known as *promka*. He was nicknamed "Lysaya Muza" (The Bald Muse).

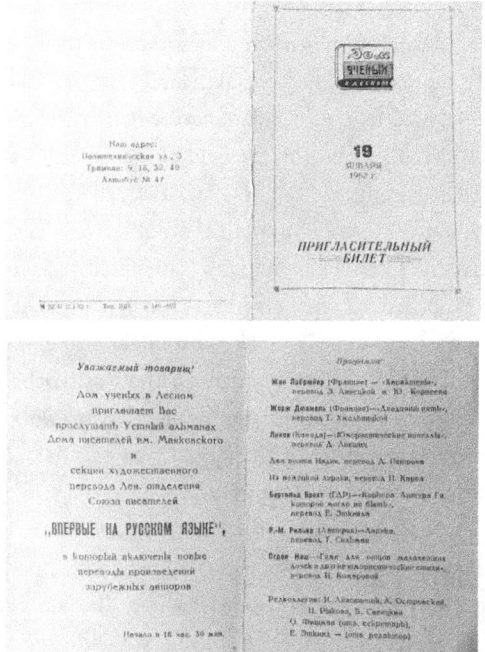

Invitation to an evening of poetry translations as part of the Oral Almanac "First in the Russian Language," curated by the translator and literary scholar Efim Etkind. Leningrad, 19 January 1962. Third on the program is David Shrayer-Petrov with translations of two Indian poets. Sixth on the program is Efim Etkind with the translation of Bertold Brecht's *The Resistible Rise of Arturo Ui*.

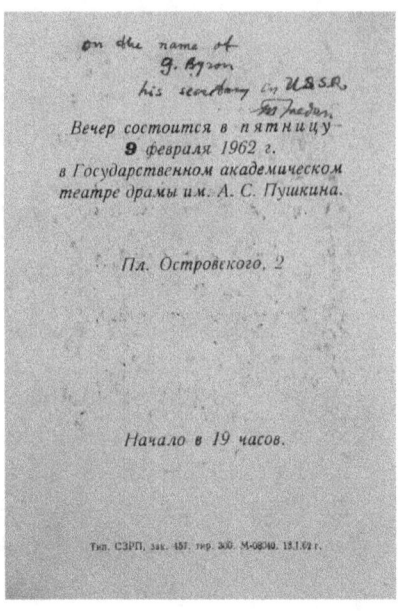

Нет, весь я не умру, — душа в заветной лире
Мой прах переживет...

Invitation to a memorial evening in commemoration of the 125th anniversary of Aleksandr Pushkin's death. A. S. Pushkin State Drama Theater, Leningrad, February 9, 1962. Inscription to David Shrayer-Petrov by Tatyana Gnedich, translator and poet, his mentor in the field of literary translation. Gnedich spent the siege in Leningrad, and in 1942–1943 she served as a military translator for the Leningrad Front and the Baltic Navy. She was arrested in late December 1943 and charged with "attempted treason," "anti-Soviet agitation and propaganda," and "organized activity aimed at committing a counterrevolutionary crime." In 1946 the military tribunal of the NKVD troops sentenced her to ten years of camps. She was rehabilitated in 1956 and was able to return to Leningrad and resume literary work and teaching, while also serving as a mentor to younger literary translators and poets. In his memoir about Gnedich, "A Hermitess from Tsarskoe Selo" ("Otshel′nitsa iz Tsarskogo Sela"; see his books *Druzi′ia i teni* and *Vodka s pirozhnymi*), Shrayer-Petrov described a meeting with Gnedich in the intermission of the 1962 Pushkin memorial evening at the Pushkin Theater. Gnedich related the story of her initial imprisonment, during which in the prison cell she miraculously translated almost seventeen cantos of Byron's *Don Juan*: 17,000 verses of iambic pentameter, about 125,000 words. The inscription, made to Shrayer-Petrov, on the invitation, reads: "In the name of G. Byron his secretary in U.S.S.R. T. Gnedich."

David Shrayer-Petrov: A Pictorial Biography | 371

David Shrayer-Petrov and Emilia Shrayer (née Polyak) on their honeymoon. Crimea, summer 1962. On her father's side, Emilia Polyak's family came from Kamenets-Podolsk, and the families knew each other and were related by marriage. David and Emilia met in Leningrad at the wedding of Eva Bekman and Hillel Butman, future prisoner of Zion. David and Emilia (Mila) were married in Moscow on October 9, 1962 and first lived in Leningrad. They moved to Moscow in 1964.

Poet and playwright Ilya Selvinsky, his daughter, visual artist and poet Tatiana Selvinskaya, David Shrayer-Petrov, poet Yuri Vlodov. Peredelkino outside Moscow, 1966. Selvinsky was and remained one of Shrayer-Petrov's favorite poets.

David Shrayer-Petrov. Moscow, 1967. This photo appeared in the author's first collection of poetry, *Kholsty* (*Canvasses*, Moscow, 1967).

David Shrayer-Petrov with son Maxim D. Shrayer. Beloostrov outside St. Petersburg, at the dacha (summer cottage) of Peysakh (Pyotr) Shrayer, summer 1968.

David Shrayer-Petrov speaking at the Young Scientists Club of the Gamaleya Research Institute of Microbiology of the Academy of Medical Sciences in Moscow. Shrayer-Petrov worked at the Gamaleya Institute in 1967-1978, first as a junior, then a senior research investigator. Here he defended his *doktorskaya* dissertation (habilitation equivalent).

43 Marshala Biryuzova Street, the apartment building where the Shrayers lived in Apt. 73 from 1971 until their emigration in 1987. Photographed in 1998 by Maxim D. Shrayer.

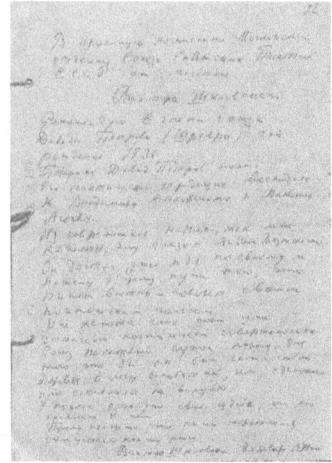

Viktor Shklovsky's recommendation letter for David Shrayer-Petrov's application to the Union of Soviet Writers. Moscow, January 20, 1971. Excerpt: "Comrade David Petrov is a poet. His poetic tradition hearkens back to Vladimir Mayakovsky and Nikolay Aseev. Among contemporary poets, as I see it, Andrei Voznesensky is closely related to him." The admission process to the Union of Soviet Writers dragged on until November 1975. (Original at Russian State Archive for Literature and the Arts [RGALI], f. 631, op. 41; copy among the papers of David Shrayer-Petrov.)

David Shrayer-Petrov in his research laboratory at Gamaleya Institute. Moscow, early 1970s.

David Shrayer-Petrov: A Pictorial Biography | 375

David Shrayer-Petrov with his mother-in-law, Anna Studnits, Maxim D. Shrayer, and Emilia Shrayer, seeing Maxim off to elementary school. Outside their apartment building at 43 Marshala Biryuzova Street. Moscow, September 1, 1974.

David Shrayer-Petrov's membership card, Union of Soviet Writers. Moscow, January 22, 1976. Signed by the writer and functionary Georgy Markov, chairman of the governing board of the Union of Writers. Shrayer-Petrov had applied in 1971 but was only admitted in November 1975 and formally joined in January 1976, after an initial deferral.

David Shrayer-Petrov during one of his 1970s trips to the area of the Baikal-Amur Railroad (BAM) construction. Angarakan, Buryatia, May 1976. At BAM Shrayer-Petrov worked on the treatment of staphylococcal infections among the railroad workers.

26 Taamsaare Street, the apartment building in the Estonian resort of Pürnu, where for many summers in the 1970s and 1980s the Shrayers rented Apt. 36 from Evald Mikkus. Here David Shrayer-Petrov subsequently worked on parts of the first two volumes of the refusenik trilogy and on many other works of prose and poetry. Photographed by Maxim D. Shrayer in the 1990s.

(Left to right.) Poet and translator Vyachelav Kupriyanov, poet Boris Kunyaev, poet Viktor Bokov, poet and translator Nadezhda Maltseva, David Shrayer-Petrov. Vilnius, Lithuania, April 1977. In the 1970s Shrayer-Petrov, whose own family roots on the mother's side were Litvak, became actively involved in translating Lithuanian poetry (see his bibliography in this volume)

Poster for an evening of Lithuanian poetry at the Central House of Writers (TsDL), April 27, 1977. The program lists the moderator, poet and translator Lev Ozerov, and Lithuanian poets: Algimantas Baltakis, Judita Vaičiūnaitė, Justinas Marcinkevičius, Juozas Macevičius, Algimantas Mikuta, Vacys Reimeris. The Moscow poets listed on the program are Larisa Vasilieva, Rimma Kozakova, Yuri Levitansky, David Shrayer-Petrov (as David Petrov), Yuri Ryashentsev, Dmitry Sukharev, Lazar Shereshevsky.

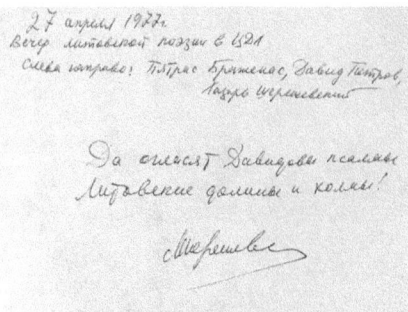

(Left to right.) Literary critic Patras Bražėnas, David Shrayer-Petrov, poet and translator Lazar Shereshevsky. Evening of Lithuanian poetry. Central House of Writers, April 27, 1977. Verse inscription by Shereshevsky on the back: "Да огласят Давидовы псалмы/ Литовские долины и холмы" (Literally: "May the Psalms of David resound/ Over Lithuanian valleys and hills").

David Shrayer-Petrov, Maxim D. Shrayer. Tbilisi, Georgia, June 1977. In the background, the monument to King of Iberia (Eastern Georgia) Vakhtang I Gorgasali. Shrayer-Petrov was in Tbilisi for a month as a visiting researcher at the Research Institute of Vaccines and Serums (presently the Eliava Institute of Bacteriophages, Microbiology and Virology), while also researching the biography of the great microbiologist Félix D'Hérelle, the discoverer of the bacteriophage, who had worked in Soviet Georgia in the 1930s.

(Left to right): David Shrayer-Petrov, pianist Frida Bernstein, art historian Boris Bernstein, Emilia Shrayer, artist Urve Roodes Arrak, Jüri Arrak's first wife. Panga-Rehe, the summer home and studio of the Estonian artist Jüri Arrak. Estonia, summer 1977. The Shrayers and the Arraks became close friends, and visiting Panga-Rehe was an annual ritual for many Estonian summers.

David Shrayer-Petrov, Maxim D. Shrayer, Emilia Shrayer. Panga-Rehe, the summer home and studio of the Estonian artist Jüri Arrak. Estonia, summer 1977.

Emilia Shrayer and David Shrayer-Petrov as refuseniks. The kitchen of the Shrayers' Moscow apartment, 1980.

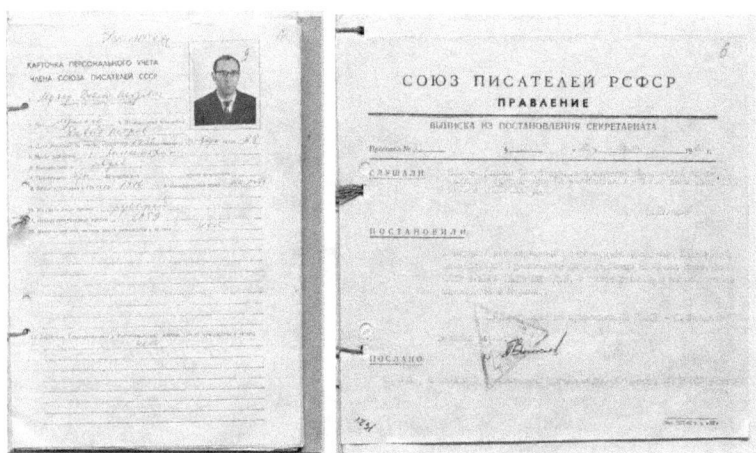

David Shrayer-Petrov's registration file at the Union of Soviet Writer with the handwritten word "исключён" (expelled) at the top of the page. Official resolution of the Secretariat of the Union of Writers of the Russian Federation concerning Shrayer-Petrov's expulsion for "leaving to reside permanently in Israel." July 10, 1980. Signed by Sergey Mikhalkov, writer and functionary, co-author of the lyrics of the Soviet anthem. (Russian State Archive for Literature and the Arts [RGALI], f. 631, op. 41.)

David Shrayer-Petrov: A Pictorial Biography | 381

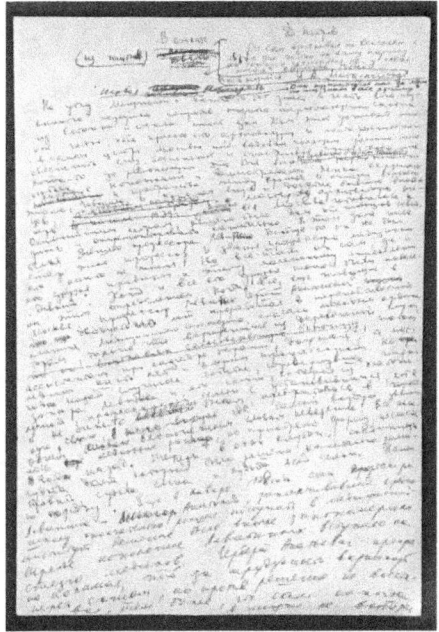

Page 1 of the first, handwritten draft of the future part one of the refusenik trilogy, titled *V otkaze* (*Being Refused*) in the manuscript. 1979.

Jüri Arrak. "Taaveti Lend" ("David's Flight"). 1981. Marker on paper. Collection of David Shrayer-Petrov and Emilia Shrayer.

Jüri Arrak, David Shrayer-Petrov, spaniel Lonni. Panga-Rehe, the summer home and studio of the Estonian artist Jüri Arrak. Estonia, summer 1981.

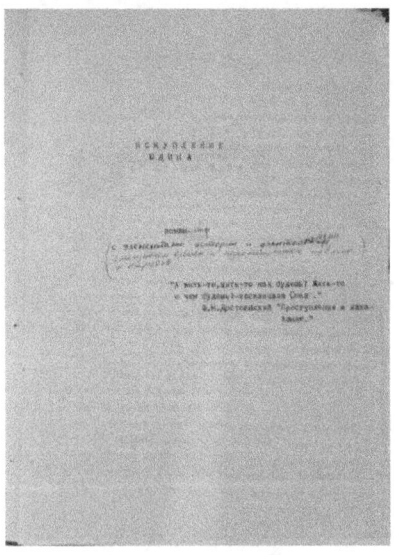

Page 1 of the draft typescript of the novel *Iskuplenie Iudina* (*Yudin's Redemption*) with handwritten corrections. Circa 1982–1983.

David Shrayer-Petrov: A Pictorial Biography | 383

David Shrayer-Petrov, Emilia Shrayer, Maxim Shrayer. The Shrayers' apartment. Moscow, winter 1986. This photo was taken about a month after the worst period of the writer's persecution by the Soviet authorities in November and December 1985.

David Shrayer-Petrov at the celebration of his fiftieth birthday. The Shrayers' Moscow apartment, January 28, 1986. (Left to right.) Jüri Arrak, refusenik Arkady Lakhman, refusenik hero and former prisoner of Zion Vladimir Slepak, David Shrayer-Petrov.

Emilia Shrayer (second from the left) at a demonstration in support of the refusenik hero and prisoner of Zion Yosef Begun. On her left, with the poster "Freedom to my father Yosef Begun," is Boris Begun. February 1987. Moscow, Arbat Street. This photograph by Andrew Rosenthal appeared in *Newsweek* magazine on February 23, 1987. Soon after Begun's release David Shrayer-Petrov composed and read at refusenik gatherings the long poem *Runner Begoon*. (Associated Press.)

Evgeny Reyn, poet and friend of David Shrayer-Petrov's Leningrad youth, and Shrayer-Petrov, sharing a silly moment. Reyn's apartment on Kuusinena Street in Moscow. 1986.

David Shrayer-Petrov: A Pictorial Biography | 385

David Shrayer-Petrov (second from left) with members of an unsanctioned Jewish theater troupe, for whom Shrayer-Petrov wrote a Purimshpil′ (Purim spiel) in the spring of 1987. This is the final performance at the Shrayers' Moscow apartment, April 1987. Directed by Roman Spektor (first from right), featuring Nadezhda Ilyina (second right), Lev Shchyogolev (third from right), Irina Shchyogoleva (second row center), Gennady Milin (first from left). See the complete recording: https://youtu.be/CxW_RNscgTQ.

Emilia Shrayer, Maxim D. Shrayer, and David Shrayer-Petrov, holding exit visas. The Shrayer's Moscow apartment. May 1987, Moscow.

Emilia Shrayer and David Shrayer-Petrov. San Marino, summer 1987. This was a trip to Florence, Bologna, San Marino, and Venice that the Shrayers took while staying in Italy during the summer of 1987 and waiting for their US refugee visas.

Maxim D. Shrayer, Emilia Shrayer, and David Shrayer-Petrov after landing in America. JFK Airport, August 26, 1987.

David Shrayer-Petrov: A Pictorial Biography | 387

Emilia Shrayer and David Shrayer-Petrov on the front porch of their first American home, a first-floor apartment at 379 Morris Avenue on the East Side of Providence, Rhode Island, circa September 1987.

David Shrayer-Petrov with journalist and editor Aleksandr Ginzburg, former editor of *Sintaksis* (*Syntax*) underground magazine, dissident and victim of Soviet repressions. Providence, Rhode Island, autumn 1987. Ginzburg was in Providence to deliver a lecture at Brown University, where Shrayer-Petrov worked as a medical researcher, and stayed with the Shrayers.

David Shrayer-Petrov with artist Vagrich Bakhchanyan, writer Vladimir Solovyov, and publisher Ilya Levkov. Manhattan, autumn 1989. Bakhchanyan designed the cover of Shrayer-Petrov's memoir *Druz´ia i teni* (*Friends and Shadows*), published by Levkov's Liberty Publishing House in the summer of 1989. Solovyov reviewed Shrayer-Petrov's *Friends and Shadows* for *Novoye russkoe slovo*, New York's oldest Russian daily.

(Left to right.) American poet and translator Edwin Honig; Maxim D. Shrayer; David Shrayer-Petrov; Brown professor of Slavic studies, scholar, and translator Victor Terras. Shrayer-Petrov's reading at the International House, Providence, Rhode Island. Circa autumn 1990–winter 1991. At this event Shrayer-Petrov gave the first public reading of his poem *Villa Borghese*, which he had started in Italy and completed in America.

David Shrayer-Petrov at the Golan Heights, Israel, autumn 1994.

(Left to right.) Moses (Munia) Sharir (Shrayer), Shrayer-Petrov's Israeli uncle, former *halutz* who had come to the British Mandate of Palestine in 1924; David Shrayer-Petrov; author and educator Ayala Yiftach-Walbe, first cousin of Emilia Shrayer (on the Polyak side). Tel Aviv, apartment of Munia Sharir, autumn 1994.

David Shrayer-Petrov and Maxim D. Shrayer outside 27 Rue de Fleurus, where Gertrude Stein and Alice B. Toklas lived. Paris, May 1995.

(Left to right.) David Shrayer-Petrov, Emilia Shrayer, poet and Connecticut College professor of German Rita Terras; professor of Slavic languages and literatures, scholar and translator Victor Terras. Little Compton, Rhode Island, late August 1995.

David Shrayer-Petrov: A Pictorial Biography | 391

David Shrayer-Petrov, fishing on Cape Cod. Pocasset, summer 1996.

David Shrayer-Petrov, during his first trip back to Russia since emigration, before his reading at the Central House of Writers in Moscow. In the background is the poster announcing the reading. The poet Genrikh Sapgir moderated the event; the poet Evgeny Reyn, who is also listed as a participant, was unable to attend. Moscow, January 23, 1999.

David Shrayer-Petrov and Genrikh Sapgir at Sapgir's apartment on Novoslobodskaya Street in Moscow. January 1999.

David Shrayer-Petrov and the literary critic Samuil Lurie during Shrayer-Petrov's reading at the Anna Akhmatova Museum in St. Petersburg, Russia. Lurie moderated this event. January 1999.

David Shrayer-Petrov at the grave of his mother Bella Breydo at the Preobrazhenskoe Jewish Cemetery in St. Petersburg, Russia, January 1999. The gravestone of Bella Breydo (1911–1960) carries a verse inscription by David Shrayer-Petrov: "... That the land, where a Jewish Mother/ Raised me in a Slavic way,/ Is our native home, Russia,/ And Russia will forever stand." (Photographed by Maxim D. Shrayer in 2019.)

David Shrayer-Petrov and Emilia Shrayer on the front steps of 110 Overhill Road, their Providence, Rhode Island home in 1990–2007. Here many of Shrayer-Petrov's American works were composed, among them the third part of the refusenik trilogy, the autobiographical novel *Strange Danya Rayev*, and numerous short stories and poems.

(Left to right.) Poet and novelist Dolores Stewart (Riccio); poet and creative writing teacher, Ottone "Ricky" Riccio, veteran of World War II (the Pacific War); Emilia Shrayer; longtime friends Charles and Nathalie Plotkin, at whose Bourne, Cape Cod home the Shrayers stayed many times in the 1990s-2000s; American poet and translator Edwin Honig; David Shrayer-Petrov. The Shrayers' home, Providence, Rhode Island, circa 2000.

David Shrayer-Petrov and writer and feminist theorist, New York University professor Catharine R. Stimpson, who was one of Maxim D. Shrayer's early mentors. The wedding of Maxim D. Shrayer and Karen Elizabeth Lasser, Providence, Rhode Island, August 26, 2000.

Jüri Arrak's cover of David Shrayer-Petrov's novel-fantella *Zamok v Tystamaa* (*The Tõstemaa Castle*, Tallinn, 2001).

David Shrayer-Petrov and Maxim D. Shrayer. Providence, Rhode Island, May 2003. Photograph by Gary Gilbert.

(Left to right.) David Shrayer-Petrov, his daughter-in-law Karen Elizabeth Lasser, a physician, clinician investigator, and professor of medicine at Boston University, Emilia Shrayer, and granddaughters Mira Isabella Shrayer and Tatiana Rebecca Shrayer. Brookline, Massachusetts, circa autumn 2007 or winter 2008.

David Shrayer-Petrov while visiting the Golden Pagoda in Kyoto, Japan, March 2010. Several of the writers' stories, notably "The Love of Akira Watanabe," feature Japanese characters.

(Left to right.) Yosef Begun, David Shrayer-Petrov, and Emilia Shrayer, after Begun's lecture. Boston, April 2010.

David Shrayer-Petrov emailing his wife from a café in Ramat Gan, Israel, near the campus of Bar-Ilan University, January 2012. Shrayer-Petrov was a featured speaker in a panel of Jewish writers at an international conference co-organized by Professor Roman Katsman, one of this volume's co-editors.

David Shrayer-Petrov speaking at the Russian Library of Jerusalem, January 2012.

David Shrayer-Petrov: A Pictorial Biography | 399

A portrait of David Shrayer-Petrov by the Russian-American artist Anatoly Dverin. Pencil on paper, circa 2014. Collection of David Shrayer-Petrov and Emilia Shrayer.

David Shrayer-Petrov and Emilia Shrayer at a rally in support of Israel. Downtown Boston, August 7, 2014.

David Shrayer-Petrov at a joint reading with Maxim D. Shrayer. Books & Arts Russian Bookstore and Gallery, Brookline, Massachusetts. Spring 2016. Shrayer-Petrov is speaking about the 3rd complete Russian edition of *Herbert and Nelly*, parts one and two of the refusenik trilogy.

David Shrayer-Petrov with his granddaughters Mira Isabella Shrayer and Tatiana Rebecca Shrayer holding copies of then the recently published English translation of *Doctor Levitin*, part one of his refusenik trilogy. South Chatham, Cape Cod, summer 2018.

Poster/program for Refusenik Literature, a symposium at Boston College in honor of the publication of *Doctor Levitin*. Devlin Hall, Boston College, April 16, 2019.

"Eye to Eye" (2020), a drawing of David Shrayer-Petrov and Maxim D. Shrayer by the artist Armando Veve. This drawing was commissioned for a story about David Shrayer-Petrov that ran in *Tablet Magazine* on January 28, 2020: https://www.tabletmag.com/sections/arts-letters/articles/maxim-shrayer-david-shrayer.

David Shrayer-Petrov and Emilia Shrayer while sheltering in place at their apartment on Beacon Street in Brookline during the COVID-19 pandemic. Brookline, Massachusetts, April 7, 2020.

David Shrayer-Petrov holding a copy of the July/August 2020 issue of *Stone Soup* magazine, which featured *Searching for Bow and Arrows*, a poetry collection by his granddaughter Tatiana Rebecca Shrayer. The collection won second prize in a 2019 contest and was subsequently released as a separate book. Brookline, Massachusetts, July 2020.

David Shrayer-Petrov
(Давид Шраер-Петров, b. 1936):
A Bibliographyof Works*

Part 1. Books

1A. Fiction in Russian

V otkaze: Roman (В отказе: роман; *Being Refused: A Novel*). In *V otkaze. Sbornik*. Edited by Vladimir Lazaris, 149-242. Jerusalem: Biblioteka-Aliia, 1986 (paperback). [Abridged part one of Shrayer-Petrov's refusenik trilogy; see also in Russian: *Gerbert i Nelli*; *Tret´ia zhizn´* and in English: *Doctor Levitin*.]

Gerbert i Nelli: Roman (Герберт и Нэлли: роман; *Herbert and Nelly: A Novel*). Moscow: GMP Poliform, 1992 (hardcover). [Parts one and two of Shrayer-Petrov's refusenik trilogy; see also in Russian: *V otkaze*; *Tret´ia zhizn´* and in English: *Doctor Levitin*.]

Compiled by Maxim D. Shrayer, with the assistance of Daria Sadovnichenko, and in consultation with David Shrayer-Petrov.

* This bibliography is a work in progress. Within each section, the items are listed chronologically. In its present form, it does not attempt to reflect publications in *samizdat*. It also does not account for all of David Shrayer-Petrov's earliest publications, literary translations or literary translations of his works into foreign languages, his song lyrics and work for the stage, interviews, internet publications and reprintings in online magazines and portals, as well as for all post-Soviet reprintings of Shrayer-Petrov's works. Except for the publications specifically mentioned in the essays, Dr. Shrayer-Petrov's scientific academic publications are not listed in this bibliography. Where both a print and an electronic version of the same publication appeared, only the print version is listed.

David Shrayer-Petrov has published his writings under his birth name, "David Shrayer (Давид Шраер)" and under his pen-names, "David Petrov (Давид Петров)" and "David Shrayer-Petrov (Давид Шраер-Петров)." The vast majority of David Shrayer-Petrov's Soviet-era publications appeared under the penname "David Petrov [D. Petrov]." In the spring of 1980 Shrayer-Petrov was expelled from the Union of Soviet Writers and was subsequently unable to publish his writings in the Soviet Union, save for a few publications that fell through the cracks of censorship. Following his emigration to the USA in 1987, he has been publishing his writings only under the penname "David Shrayer-Petrov."

Frantsuzskii kottedzh: Roman (Французский коттедж: роман; *The French Cottage: A Novel*). Edited by Maksim D. Shraer. Providence, RI: APKA Publishers, 1999 (paperback).

Zamok v Tystamaa: Roman (Замок в Тыстамаа: роман; *The Tõstamaa Castle: A Novel*). Tallinn: Aleksandra, 2001 (paperback).

Eti strannye russkie evrei: Romany (Эти странные русские евреи: романы; *These Strange Russian Jews: Novels*). Moscow: Raduga, 2004 (hardcover). [Contents: *Strannyi Dania Raev*; *Savelii Ronkin*].

Gerbert i Nelli: Roman (Герберт и Нэлли: роман; *Herbert and Nelly: A Novel*). St. Petersburg: Akademicheskii proekt, 2006 (hardcover). [Parts one and two of Shrayer-Petrov's refusenik trilogy; see also in Russian: *V otkaze*; *Tret′ia zhizn′* and in English: *Doctor Levitin*.]

Karp dlia farshirovannoi ryby: rasskazy (Карп для фаршированной рыбы: рассказы; *Carp for the Gefilte Fish: Stories*). Moscow: Raduga, 2010 (hardcover). [Contents: "Za ogradoi zooparka"; "V kamyshakh"; "Uragan po imeni Bob"; "Tsukerman i ego deti"; "Ryzhukha"; "Raschleniteli"; "Osen' v Ialte"; "Molodye evrei i gimnazistki"; "Mimozy na mogilu babushki"; "Mimikriia"; "Karp dlia farshirovannoi ryby"; "Iablochnyi uksus"; "Iona i Sarra"; "Smert' iguany"; "Hände Hoch!"; "Gde ty, Zoia?"; "Staryi pisatel' Forman"; "David i Goliaf"; "Liubov' Akiry Vatanabe"; "Al'fredik"; "Belye ovtsy na zelenom sklone gory"; "Zhurnalist iz 'Vecherki'"; "Krugosvetnoe schast′e"; "Ushchel′e geenny."]

Tret′ia zhizn′: Roman (Третья жизнь: роман; *The Third Life: A Novel*). Lugansk: Shiko, 2010 (hardcover). [Early version of part three of Shrayer-Petrov's refusenik trilogy; see also in Russian: *V otkaze*; *Gerbert and Nelli* and in English: *Doctor Levitin*.]

Istoriia moei vozliublennoi, ili Vintovaia lestnitsa: Roman (История моей возлюбленной, или Винтовая лестница: роман; *The Story of My Beloved, or The Spiral Staircase: A Novel*). Moscow: Vest-Konsalting, 2013 (hardcover).

Gerbert i Nelli: Roman (Герберт и Нэлли: роман; *Herbert and Nelly: A Novel*). Moscow: Knizhniki, 2014 (hardcover). [Parts one and two of Shrayer-Petrov's refusenik trilogy; see also in Russian: *V otkaze*; *Tret′ia zhizn′* and in English: *Doctor Levitin*.]

Krugosvetnoe schast′e: Izbrannye rasskazy (Кругосветное счастье: избранные рассказы; *Round-the-Globe Happiness: Selected Short Stories*). Edited by David Shrayer-Petrov and Maksim D. Shraer. Moscow: Knizhniki, 2016 (hardcover). [Contents: "Belye ovtsy na zelenom sklone gory"; "David i Goliaf"; "Dom Edgara Po"; "German i Lizan′ka"; "Karp dlia farshirovannoi ryby"; "Krugosvetnoe schast′e"; "Lgun′ia Ivanovna v Parizhe"; "Mimozy na mogilu babushki"; "Obed s vozhdem"; "Osen′ v Ialte"; "Trubetskoi, Raevskii, Masha Malevich i smert′ Maiakovskogo"; "Tsukerman i ego deti"; "Ushchel′e Geenny"; "V kamyshakh"; "Velogonki"; "Filosof, getera i mal′chik."]

1B. Fiction in English Translation

Jonah and Sarah: Jewish Stories of Russia and America. Edited and with an afterword by Maxim D. Shrayer, translated by Thomas Epstein; Michael Fine; Dolores Riccio; Emilia Shrayer; Diana Senechal; Margarit Tadevosyan Ordukhanyan. Library of Modern

Jewish Literature. Syracuse: Syracuse University Press, 2003 (hardcover); 2016 (ebook). [Contents: "Preface: To Be Ripped Away"; "Apple Cider Vinegar"; "Rusty"; "The Lanskoy Road"; "Young Jews and Two Gymnasium Girls"; "He, She and the Others"; "Jonah and Sarah"; "In the Reeds"; "Tsukerman and His Children"; "Dismemberers"; "David and Goliath"; "Hurricane Bob"; "Hände Hoch!"; "Old Writer Foreman."]

Autumn in Yalta: A Novel and Three Stories. Edited and with an afterword by Maxim D. Shrayer, translated by Arna B. Bronstein and Aleksandra Fleszar; Margarit Tadevosyan Ordukhanyan; Emilia Shrayer; Maxim D. Shrayer. Library of Modern Jewish Literature. Syracuse: Syracuse University Press, 2006 (hardcover); 2012 (ebook). [Contents: *Strange Danya Rayev*; "Autumn in Yalta"; "The Love of Akira Watanabe"; "Carp for the Gefilte Fish."]

Dinner with Stalin and Other Stories. Edited by Maxim D. Shrayer, translated by Arna B. Bronstein and Aleksandra Fleszar; Margaret Godwin-Jones; Leon Kogan; Margarit Tadevosyan Ordukhanyan; Emilia Shrayer; Maxim D. Shrayer. Library of Modern Jewish Literature. Syracuse: Syracuse University Press, 2014 (hardcover; ebook). [Contents: "Behind the Zoo Fence"; "A Russian Liar in Paris"; "White Sheep on a Green Mountain Slope"; "Round-the-Globe Happiness"; "A Storefront of Memories"; "Mimicry"; "Where Are You, Zoya?"; "Alfredick"; "Dinner with Stalin"; "The Valley of Hinom"; "Momosa Flowers for Grandmother's Grave"; "The House of Edgar Allan Poe"; "Trubetskoy, Raevsky, Masha Malevich, and the Death of Mayakovsky"; "The Bicycle Race."]

Doctor Levitin: A Novel. Edited and with notes by Maxim D. Shrayer, translated by Arna B. Bronstein, Aleksandra I. Fleszar, and Maxim D. Shrayer. Detroit: Wayne State University Press, 2018 (hardcover; paperback; ebook). [Part one of Shrayer-Petrov's refusenik trilogy; see in Russian: *V otkaze*; *Gerbert i Nelli*; *Tret´ia zhizn´*.]

1C. Nonfiction and Memoir

Druz´ia i teni: Roman s uchastiem avtora (Друзья и тени: роман с участием автора; *Friends and Shadows: A Novel with the Participation of the Author*). New York: Liberty, 1989 (hardcover; paperback).

Moskva zlatoglavaia: memuarnyi roman (Москва златоглавая: мемуарный роман; *Gold-Domed Moscow: A Memoir-Novel*). Baltimore: Vestnik, 1994 (paperback).

Vodka s pirozhnymi: Roman s pisateliami (Водка с пирожными: роман с писателями; *Vodka and Pastries: A Novel with Writers*). Edited by Maksim D. Shraer. St. Petersburg: Akademicheskii proekt, 2007 (hardcover). [Contents: *Chast´ Pervaia. V del´te Nevy*: "Lanskoe shosse. Fantaziia o Pushkine"; "Emigrant. Aleksandr Vertinskii"; "Ne khlebom edinym. Vladimir Dudintsev"; "Romanticheskii konstruktivist. Il´ia Averbakh"; "Istopnik Trebnikov. Fantaziia o Klhebnikove"; "Valun v Repino. Dmitrii Bobyshev"; "Serebrianye usiki. Sergei Vol´f"; Belaia staia nad Finskim zalivom. Anna Akhmatova"; "Kuznechik v bashne Vavilona. Aleksandr Kushner"; "Shchetovod iz GULAGa. Zelik Shteinman"; "Lysaia muza. Vsevolod Azarov"; "Komik Arkadii. Fantaziia ob Arkadie Raikine"; "Slomannyi kabluchok. Aleksei Batalov"; "Leningradskie ostzeitsy. Nikolai

Braun. Vadim Shefner"; "Poslednii iz kompanii klassikov. Vsevolod Rozhdestvenskii"; "Vodka s pirozhnymi. Mikhail Dudin"; "Malen´kii Mandel´shtam. Anatolii Naiman"; "Naelektrizovannyi kot. Anatolii Mariengof"; "Iakhta na priviazi. Boris Vakhtin"; "Al'manakh perevodchikov. Efim Etkind"; "Otshel'nitsa iz Tsarskogo Sela. Tat'iana Gnedich"; "Iosif Barbarossa. Iosif Brodskii." *Chast´ vtoraia. Moskvorech´e:* "Tigr snegov. Genrikh Sapgir"; "Gusar s gitaroi. Bulat Okudzhava"; "Ierusalimskii kazak. Boris Slutskii"; "Nochnoi zvonok. Evgenii Evtushenko"; "Terzen´-verzen´-pereverzen´. Viktor Bokov"; "Karaimskie pirozhki. Il´ia Sel´vinskii"; "Tezka. David Samoilov"; "Vitrazhnykh del master. Andrei Voznesenskii"; "Rodivshiisia soldatom. Konstantin Simonov"; "V lodke Kharona. Antokol´skii, Ozerov, Akhmadulina, Ginzburg, Lipkin, Mezhirov, Martynov, L. Smirnov, Iskander, Tarkovskii, Shereshevskii, Levitanskii, Morits, Tsybin, Shostakovich"; "Bronevik avangarda. Viktor Shklovskii"; "Serp i Molot. Igor´ Shkliarevskii i Stanislav Kuniaev"; "Vedro na roiale. Evgenii Rein."]

Okhota na ryzhego d´iavola: Roman s mikrobiologami (Охота на рыжего дьявола: Роман с микробиологами; *Hunt for the Red Devil: A Novel with Microbiologists*). Edited and with afterword by Maksim D. Shraer. Moscow: Agraf, 2010 (hardcover).

1D. Literary criticism

Poeziia i nauka: zametki i razmyshleniia (Поэзия и наука: заметки и размышления; *Poetry and Science: Notes and Reflections*). Moscow: Znanie, 1974 (paperback).

Poeziia o trudovom geroizme (Поэзия о трудовом героизме; *Poetry of Labor Valor*). Moscow: Znanie, 1977 (paperback).

Genrikh Sapgir: Klassik avangarda (Генрих Сапгир: Классик авангарда; *Genrikh Sapgir: Avant-Garde Classic*), with Maksim D. Shraer. St. Petersburg: Dmitrii Bulanin, 2004 (hardcover).

Genrikh Sapgir: Klassik avangarda (Генрих Сапгир: Классик авангарда; *Genrikh Sapgir: Avant-Garde Classic*), with Maksim D. Shraer. 2nd edition. St. Petersburg: BiblioRossica, 2016 (ebook).

Genrikh Sapgir: Klassik avangarda (Генрих Сапгир: Классик авангарда; *Genrikh Sapgir: Avant-Garde Classic*), with Maksim D. Shraer. 3rd, corrected edition. Ekaterinburg: Ridero, 2017 (paperback; ebook).

1E. Poetry

Kholsty (Холсты; *Canvasses*). Foreword by Lev Ozerov. In *Pereklichka*, 116–160. Moscow: Molodaia gvardiia, 1967 (hardcover).

Pesnia o golubom slone: Liubovnaia lirika (Песня о голубом слоне: любовная лирика; *Song of a Blue Elephant: Love Poetry*). Holyoke, MA: New England Publishing Company, 1990 (paperback).

Villa Borgeze: Stikhotvoreniia (Вилла Боргезе: стихотворения; *Villa Borghese: Poems*). Holyoke, MA: New England Publishing Company, 1992 (paperback).

Propashchaia dusha: stikhotvoreniia i poemy, 1987–1996 (Пропащая душа: стихотворения и поэмы, 1987–1996; *Lost Soul: Shorter Poems and Long Poems, 1987–1996*). Edited by Maksim D. Shraer. Providence, RI: APKA Publishers, 1997 (paperback).

Piterskii dozh: Stikhotvoreniia i poema, 1995–1998 (Питерский дож: стихотворения и поэма, 1995–1998; *Doge of Petersburg: Shorter Poems and a Long Poem, 1995–1998*). St. Petersburg: Izdatel'stvo Fonda Russkoi poezii, 1999 (paperback).

Barabany sud′by (Барабаны судьбы; *Drums of Fortune*). Moscow: Argo-risk / Tver′: Kolonna, 2002 (paperback).

Forma liubvi: Izbrannaia lirika (Форма любви: избранная лирика; *Form of Love: Selected Lyrical Poetry*). Moscow: Izdatel′skii dom "Iunost′," 2003 (paperback).

Dve knigi: stikhi (Две книги: Стихи; *Two Books: Poems*). Philadelphia: Poberezh′e, 2009 (paperback).

Linii-figury-tela: Kniga stikhotvorenii (Линии-фигуры-тела: книга стихотворений; *Lines-Figures-Bodies: Book of Poems*). St. Petersburg: Biblioteka Aesthetoscope, 2010 (paperback).

Nevskie stikhi (Невские стихи; *Nevan Poems*). Edited by Maksim D. Shraer. St. Petersburg: Ostrovitianin, 2011 (paperback).

Derevenskii orkestr: shest′ poem (Деревенский оркестр; Шесть поэм; *Village Orchestra: Six Long Poems*). Edited by Maksim D. Shraer. St. Petersburg: Ostrovitianin, 2016 (paperback).

1F. Drama

Vaktsina. Ed Tenner: Tragikomediia v dvukh deistviiakh i shesti kartinakh (Вакцина. Эд Теннер: Трагикомедия в двух действиях и шести картинах; *Ed Tenner: A tragic comedy in two acts and six scenes*). Edited and with an afterword by Maksim D. Shraer. Moscow: Tri kvadrata, 2021 (hardcover).

1G. Edited volume

Genrikh Sapgir. Stikhotvoreniia i poemy (Генрих Сапгир, Стихотворения и поэмы; *Genrikh Sapgir, Shorter and Longer Poems*). Edited, with a foreword and commentary by Maksim D. Shraer and David Shraer-Petrov. Novaia biblioteka poeta. St. Petersburg: Akademicheskii proekt, 2004 (hardcover).

1H. Scientific monograph

[as David Shrayer]. *Staphylococcal Disease in the Soviet Union. Epidemiology and Response to a National Epidemic*. Bethesda, MD: Delphica Associates, 1989.

Part 2. Publications in Periodicals, Anthologies, Collectives, Web Portals etc.

2A. Novels published in periodicals but not in book form

Iskuplenie Iudina: Istoricheskii roman-fantella (Искупление Юдина: исторический роман-фантелла; *Iudin's Redemption: A Historical Novel-Fantella*). *Mosty* 5 (2005): 5–61; 6 (2005): 21–116; 7 (2005): 11–88.

Model´ zhizni: roman (Модель жизни: роман; *Model of Life: A Novel*). *Mosty* 23 (2009): 97–139; 24 (2009): 147–175; 25 (2009): 130–157.

Igra v butylochku: Roman (Игра в бутылочку: роман; *The Kissing Game: A Novel*). Part 1. *Slovo/Word* 97 (2018): 127–148; Part 2 *Slovo/Word* 107-108 (2020): 6-14; Part 3 forthcoming.

2B. Shorter and Longer Fiction (includes serialized novels published in book form)

"V kamyshakh"; "Ryzhukha"; "David i Goliaf." *Vremia i my* 98 (1987): 5–35.
"Iaponskaia kartinka: Fantella." *Chernovik* 2 (1989): 15–23.
"Bulochka i Barzha: Fantella." *Chernovik* 4 (1990): 144–157.
"On, Ona, Drugaia, Drugoi i Podruga." *Vestnik* 3, no. 6 (March 24, 1992): 33–37.
"Molodye evrei i gimnazistki." *Vestnik* 13, no. 4 (December 29, 1992): 37–39.
"Raschleniteli." *Vestnik* 4, no. 4 (25 August 1992): 45–48.
"Iona i Sarra." *Chernovik* 7 (1992): 99–105.
"Osen´ v Ialte." *Poberezh´e* 3 (1994): 235–259.
Iona-strannik: Roman-fantella [early version of *Zamok v Tystremaa*]. *Khimiia i zhizn´* 1 (1994): 97–105; 2 (1994): 92–100; 3 (1994): 97–103.
"Lanskoe shosse." *Panorama* [Los Angeles], February 2–8, 1994.
"Medlitel´naia, kak Gudzon: Fantella." *Poberezh´e* 4 (1995): 140–155.
"Iablochnyi uksus." *Marina* 2 (1995): 10–14.
"Uragan po imeni Bob." *Poberezh´e* 6 (1996): 24–38.
"Karp dlia farshirovannoi ryby." *Interesnaia gazeta* [New York], 27/180 (July 1998); 28/181 (August 1998); 29/182 (August 1998).
"Iablochnyi uksus." *Novoe russkoe slovo*, November 9–10, 1996.
"Gde ty, Zoia?" *Evreiskii mir*, October 11, 1996.
"Ottorzhenie." *Evreiskii mir*, November 8, 1996.
"Osen´ v Ialte." *Neva* 2 (1997): 7–23.
"Fontan zhizni." *Evreiskii mir*, December 12, 1997.
"Za ogradoi zooparka." *Panorama*, June 18–24, 1997; June 25–July 1, 1997.
"Mimozy na mogilu babushki." *Evreiskii mir*, March 21, 1997.
"Tsukerman i ego deti." *Evreiskii mir*, March 24, 1997.
"Ottorzhenie." *Poberezh´e* 6 (1997): 146–150.
"Staryi pisatel´ Forman." *Interesnaia gazeta*, January 24–30, 1998.
"Staryi pisatel´ Forman." *Neva* 12 (1998): 14–21.

"Mimikriia." *Interesnaia gazeta*, April 11-17, 1998.
"Za ogradoi zooparka." *Poberezh´e* 7 (1998): 86-96.
"Iskusstvo—eto politika chuvstv" (Iz romana "Frantsuzskii kottedzh") [excerpt from *Frantsuzskii kottedzh*]. *Al´manakh Kluba russkikh pisatelei* [New York], (1999): 299.
"Lanskoe shosse." *Literaturnyi Rod-Ailend* 1 (1999): 25-27.
"Skandal v dome zhurnalistov." *Evreiskii mir*, December 16, 1999.
"Iona i Sarra." *Forverts*, October 15-21, 1999.
"Kompan´ony." *Evreiskii mir*, August 5, 1999.
"Ryzhukha." *Forverts*, August 27-September 2, 1999.
Zamok v Tystamaa: Roman-fantella. Tallinn 13 (1999): 48-77; 14 (1999): 10-55.
"Liubov´ Akiry Vatanabe." *Forverts*, April 14-20, 2000.
"Staryi pisatel´ Forman." *Forverts*, September 22-28, 2000.
"Mimikriia." *Forverts*, June 2-8, 2000.
"Khende khokh!" ["Hände Hoch"]. *Forverts*, January 14-20, 2000.
"Hände Hoch." *Poberezh´e* 9 (2000): 69-74.
"Fontan zhizni"; "Hände Hoch!"; "Liubov´ Akiry Vatanabe." *Nasha ulitsa* 9 (2000): 82-101.
"Liubov´ Akiro [sic] Vatanabe." *Neva* 12 (2000): 158-163.
"Za ogradoi zooparka." *Mir Paustovskogo* 19 (2002): 95-100.
"Golos gor." *Forverts*, May 24-30, 2002.
"Smert´ iguany." *Poberezh´e* 11 (2002): 25-30.
"Hände Hoch!" *Evreiskaia zhizn´*, January 16, 2002.
"Za ogradoi zooparka." *Russkaia literature / Lettres russes* 30 (2002): 55-61
"Strannyi Dania Raev" [excerpt from *Strannyi Dania Raev*]. *Lekhaim* 6 (June 2003): 77-79.
"Mimozy na mogilu babushki"; "Golos gor." *Russkaia ulitsa* [New York] 4 (2003): 58-73.
"Smert´ iguany." *Kosmopolit* [Boston] 44 (November-December 2003): 20-25.
"Gde ty, Zoia" [abridged]. *Kosmopolit* [Boston] 41 (May-June 2003): 33-36.
"Belye ovtsy na zelenom sklone gory." *Lekhaim* 1 (January 2004): 76-78.
Savelii Ronkin: Roman. Kreshchatik 1[23] (2004): 122-204; 2[24] (2004): 50-41.
"Ushchel´e geenny." *Lekhaim* 8 (August 2004): 66-71.
"Al´fredik." *Put´ domoi* 19 (2004): 27-31.
"Zhurnalist iz 'Vecherki.'" *Poberezh´e* 13 (2004): 129-132.
"Krugosvetnoe shchast´e." *Poberezh´e* 14 (2005): 33-36.
"Sochi." *Evreiskii mir*, November 24-30, 2005; December 1, 2005.
"Hände Hoch!" *Vestnik Rod-Ailenda* 5 (2006): 9-11; 6 (2006): 9-11.
"Za ogradoi zooparka." *Vestnik Rod-Ailenda* 5 (2006): 18-21; 6 (June-July 2006): 16-19.
"Sochi." *Lider. Literaturnoe prilozhenie* [Boston] (Spring 2006): 5-8.
"Velogonki." *Novyi bereg* [Copenhagen] 15 (March 2007): 18-23.
"Mimozy na mogilu babushki." *Evreiskii mir*, July 10 2008.
"Trubetskoi, Raevskii, Masha Malevich i smert´ Maiakovskogo." *Poberezh´e* 17 (2008): 91-96.
"Obed s vozhdem." *Vestnik Rod-Ailenda* 1 (January 2009): 10-11; 2 (February 2009): 10-13.
"Obed s vozhdem." *Reklama i zhizn´* [Philadelphia] 11 (March 18, 2009).

"Obed s vozhdem." *My zdes'* 181 (2008) http://newswe.com/index.php?go=Pages&in=view&id=715.

"Obed s vozhdem." *Krugozor* 11 (November 2008): 16 [beginning; complete text in the online edition].

"Lgun´ia Ivanovna v Parizhe." *Evreiskii mir*, May 12, 2009.

"Obed s vozhdem." *Poberezh´e* 18 (2009): 6–9.

"Al´fredik." *Slovo/Word* 64 (2009): 79–87.

"Krugosvetnoe shchast´e." In *Na poberezh´e. Rasskazy pisatelei russkogo zarubezh´ia*, edited by Igor Mikhalevich-Kaplan, 334-347. Boston: M-Graphics, 2009.

"Obed s vozhdem." *Aesthetoscope* (2010): 42–57.

"Bezhentsev privoziat v Rim" [excerpt from *Tret´ia zhizn´*]. *Nezavisimaia gazeta Ex Libris*, February 11, 2010.

"Lgun´ia Ivanovna v Parizhe." *Slovo/Word* 68 (2010): 93–99.

"Osobniak nad stadionom." *Poberezh´e* 20 (2011): 81–84.

"Byla glubokaia moskovskaia osen´ . . . Iz romana 'Tret´ia zhizn´'" [excerpt from *Tret´ia zhizn´*]. *Evreiskii mir*, January 25, 2011.

"Rancho 'Mirazh.'" *Evreiskii mir*, October 20, 2011.

"Liubov´ Akiry Vatanabe." *Slovo/Word* 70 (2011): 144–148.

"Dom Edgara Po" [excerpt]. *Aesthetoscope* (2011): *Proza*, 47–52.

"Puteshestvie s Lonni." *Paralleli: Russko-evreiskii istoriko-literaturnyi i blibliograficheskii al´manakh* 12 (2012): 258–268.

"Isaak i Bella." *Evreiskii mir*, August 2–9, 2012.

"Evreiskii kamen´." *Evreiskii mir*, October 4–11, 2012; October 11–18, 2012.

"Dom Edgara Po." *Mlechnyi put´* 2 (2012). http://milkyway2.com/shraer.html.

"Volshebnaia vitrina." *Slovo/Word* 73 (2012): 160–166.

Istoriia moei vozliublennoi, ili Vintovaia lestnitsa [roman]. *Kreshchatik* 2 (2012): 85–151; 3 (2012): 10–83; 4 (2012): 11–85.

"Lovlia ryby na pokassetskom molu." *Evreskii mir*, August 15–22, 2013.

"Kak otkazniki vyigrali vyezdnye vizy. Rasskaz-fantella." *Okna. Ezhenedel´noe prilozhenie k gazete "Vesti,"* September 24, 2013.

"Kak otkazniki vyigrali vyezdnye vizy. Iumoiristicheskii rasskaz." *Evreiskii mir*, October 16, 2013.

"Kimono." *Slovo/Word* 74 (2014): 148–157.

"Obed s vozhdem." *Lekhaim* 3 (2016): 123–127.

"Model´ zhizni" [excerpt of *Model´ zhizni*]. In *Sto let russkoi zarubezhnoi prozy. Antologiia*, edited by Gershom Kiprischi, compiled by Vladimir Batshev, vol. 4: *Tret´ia volna emigratsii*, 734–750. Frankfurt: Literaturnyi evropeets, 2020.

2C. Nonfiction, Memoirs, Essays

"Izmenchivost´ vozbuyditelia kholery." *Priroda* 6 (1971): 43–50.

"Antibiotiki prezhde i teper´." *Zdorov´e* 8 (1973): 4–5.

"Lovushka dlia stafilokokka." *Znanie—sila* 10 (1977): 62–64.

"Ispytanie metoda": ocherk." *Severnyi Baikal*, April 16, 1977.
"Gusar s gitaroi." *Vremia i my* 105 (1989): 61–80.
"Karaimskie pirozhki (Sel´vinskii)." *The New Review / Novyi zhurnal* 183 (1991): 107–118.
"Ierusalimskii kazak. Boris Slutskii." *The New Review / Novyi zhurnal* 184–185 (1991): 316–323.
"Vitrazhnykh del master (Voznesenskii)." *The New Review / Novyi zhurnal* 186 (March 1992): 145–157.
"Rodivshiisia soldatom. Konstantin Simonov." *Vestnik* 24 (November 30, 1993): 37–42; 25 (December 14, 1993): 33–35.
"Pamiati Iu. D. Kashkarova." *The New Review / Novyi zhurnal* 195 (1994): 7–10.
"Proshchanie s Brodskim." *Al´manakh Kluba russkikh pisatelei* (1997): 29–30.
"Vozbuzhdenie snov. Vospominaniia o Genrikhe Sapgire." *Tallinn* 21–22 (2001): 3–36.
"Kukla Anechka (Vstrechi s Annoi Akhmatovoi)." *Poberezh´e* 12 (2003): 241–243.
"Kukla Anechka." *Panorama*, May 21–27, 2003.
"From Russia, with Love of Literature," with Maxim D. Shrayer. *The Providence Journal*, April 21, 2004.
"Ierusalimskii kazak" [abridged]. In *Boris Slutskii: Vospominaniia sovremennikov*, edited by Petr Gorelik. St. Petersburg: Zhurnal "Neva," 2005. 456–460.
"Iosif Barbarossa." *Lekhaim* 1 (2006): 38–41.
"Brodskii v N´iu-Iorke." *Nezavisimaia gazeta Ex Libris*, February 2, 2006.
"Brodskii v Pitere i N´iu-Iorke." *Panorama*, March 8–14, 2006.
"Stafilokokk protiv melanomy" [excerpt from *Okhota na ryzhego d´iavola*]. *Khimiia i zhizn´* 10 (2008): 23–27.
"Okhota na 'Ryzhego d´iavola'" [excerpt from *Okhota na ryzhego d´avola*]. *Nauka i zhizn´* 5 (2009): 98–105.
"Vagonetka v lesotekhnicheskom parke." *Nezavisimaia gazeta Ex Libris*, January 28, 2016.

2D. Literary Criticism and Reviews

"Oprokinutaia obydennost´." *Moskovskii komsomolets*, July 29, 1966.
"Klassicheskoe, narodnoe." *Chernomorskaia zdravnitsa*, September 16, 1973.
"Liudi igraiut slovami." *Panorama*, July 21–27, 1993.
"V poiskakh piatogo izmereniia." *Novoe russkoe slovo*, April 31, 1993.
"Zashchita Shteina." *Novoe russkoe slovo*, November 6–7, 1993.
"Poeziia russkikh amerikantsev." *Novoe russkoe slovo*, March 5, 1993.
"Noev kovcheg professora Smita." *Panorama*, September 22–28, 1993.
"Beloi noch´iu na belom kone." *Novoe russkoe slovo*, August 10, 1994.
"Plevat´ na zoloto (molodoi Lev Khalif)." *Panorama*, January 5–11, 1994.
"Vozdushnykh slov okaianstvo." *Panorama*, March 16–22, 1994.
"Poet natury i kollektsioner zaumi." *Panorama*, April 20–26, 1994.
"Pisatel´, kotoryi vsegda s toboi." *Panorama*, August 27–September 2, 1994.
"Iskusstvo kak izlom." *The New Review / Novyi zhurnal* 196 (1994 [1995]): 245–256.

"O poezii Il′i Averbakha." *Poberezh′e* 4 (1995): 207–208.
"Brak s psikhopatom, ili razvod po-emigrantski." *Panorama*, December 14–20, 1996.
"O pol′ze i bespoleznosti russkogo Pen-Kluba." *Novoe russkoe slovo*, October 4, 1996.
"Otkrytoe pis′mo g-zhe Natal′e Solzhenitsinoi." *Evreiskii mir*, November 21, 1997.
"Emigratsii nuzhny svoi poety-pesenniki" [Review of *Liubvi volshebnye napevy* by Boris Vetrov]. *Panorama*, March 19–25, 1997.
"Tragicheskoe na fone komicheskogo." *Evreiskii mir*, February 14, 1997.
"Premiiu im. Bulata Okudzhavy—na berega Gudzona!" *Novoe russkoe slovo*, May 15, 1998.
"Prosypaius′: zdras′te, net sovetskoi vlasti." *Panorama*, September 23–29, 1998.
"I s neba smotrit zheltaia zvezda . . ." [Review of *Apologiia* by Aleksandr Aleinik]. *Evreiskii mir*, June 25, 1998.
"I s neba smotrit zheltaia zvezda . . ." [Review of *Apologiia* by Aleksandr Aleinik]. *Poberezh′e* 7 (1998): 218–220.
"Chto zhe nam delat′ s russkoi literaturoi?" *Interesnaia gazeta*, February 7–13, 1998.
". . . I nichego, chto etot stikh—pechal′nyi . . ." *Panorama*, August 5–11, 1998.
"Pamiati Genrikha Sapgira." *Novoe russkoe slovo*, October 16–17, 1999.
"Pamiati Genrikha Sapgira." *Forverts*, October 22, 1999.
"Krasno-korichnevaia chuma." *Panorama*, July 7–13, 1999.
"Ogurets na vyrez." *Panorama*, March 10–16, 1999.
"Memuary uznits Gulaga." *Panorama*, November 29–December 4, 2000.
"Antologiia, izdannaia 'na arapa.'" *Novoe russkoe slovo*, May 5, 2000.
"Ottsy, deti i al′manakh 'Metropol′.'" *Panorama*, September 27–October 3, 2000.
"Anna Andreevna, Lev Nikolaevich . . ." *Poberezh′e* 9 (2000): 242–243.
"Evridika stanovitsia Evrideem i vliubliaetasia v Orfiku" [Review of *Evridei i Orfika* by Polina Barskova]. *Poberezh′e* 10 (2001): 208–209.
"Stikhi-pis′ma russkikh poetov k zhenshchinam." *Poberezh′e* 11 (2002): 206–209.
"Ia vas liubil . . . Stikhi russkikh poetov, obrashchennye k zhenshchinam." *Panorama*, March 5–11, 2003.
"Genrikh Sapgir (1928–1999): Kratkii obzor zhizni i tvorvchestva," with Maksim D. Shraer. *Wiener Slawistischer Almanach* 53 (2004): 199–258.
"Naslednik impressionistov. K publikatsii al′boma Anatoliia Dverina." *Panorama*, November 29–December 5, 2006.

2E. Poetry

"Fevral′skaia vesna." *Pul′s* [Pavlov First Medical University, Leningrad]. March 19, 1957.
"Ital′ianskie komsomol′tsy v pionerskom lagere." *Pioner* 5 (1959): 30.
"Stikhi o vernosti." *Molodoi Leningrad* (1961): 122.
"Tankisty v kolkhoze." *Neman* 6 (November-December 1961): 10.
"Ital′ianskie komsomol′tsy v pionerskom lagere." In *I snova zovet vdokhnoven′e. Sbornik stikhov*, 79-80. Leningrad: Lenizdat, 1962.
"Na senokos." *Neman* 5 (1962): 109.
"Pokoriteliu vysot." *Ogonek*, August 19, 1962.

"S. N. Konenkovu." *Molodoi Leningrad* (1962): 158.

"Sosny"; "Osen´." *Druzhba. Literaturno-khudozhestvennyi al'manakh* 8 (1962): 99.

"Rozhdenie zherebenka na poligone." *Den´ poezii* (1966): 147.

"Ne prikhodi vo snakh i naiavu . . ." In *Pesn´ liubvi. Lirika russkikh poetov*, edited by Svetlana Magidson and Lev Ozerov, 602. Moscow: Molodaia gvardiia, 1967.

"More"; "Materinskoe serdtse." Introduction by Lev Ozerov. *Moskovskii komsomolets*, January 11, 1967.

"Dozvonis´ v moi lesa!"; "Tanets stroibatovtsev." *Den´ poezii* (1970): 161.

"Syroezhki." *Veselye kartinki* 10 (1970): 5.

"Mikos Teodorakis v Krymu. Avgust 1970." *Moskovskii komsomolets*, November 20, 1970.

"B. Pirogovu—frontoviku, poetu, rybaku." *Komsomol´skaia pravda*, January 8, 1971.

"Ne prikhodi vo snakh i naiavu . . ." In *Pesn´ liubvi. Lirika russkikh poetov XIX i XX vekov*, edited by Svetlana Magidson and Lev Ozerov, vol. 1, 701. 2nd ed. Moscow: Molodaia gvardiia, 1971.

"V karantine." *Den´ poezii* (1972): 115.

"Trevoga." *Meditsinskaia gazeta*, February 23, 1973.

"Billiard v Mikhailovskom"; "Stikhi o sverchke." *Pamir* 6 (1974): 52.

"Gory i palatki"; "Krasnaia ploshchad´"; "Dnevnaia sol´." *Trud*, October 12, 1975.

"Bamskii bog." In *Magistral´. Sbornik stikhotvorenii*, edited by Vladimir Pavlinov, 96. Moscow: Molodaia gvardiia, 1977.

"Vse toboiu, toboiu . . ."; "Zelenye golosa v Palange"; "Kakie u tebia glaza?"; "Litovskii solovei"; "Nad Nemanom." *Komsomol´skaia pravda* [Vilnius], June 2, 1978.

"I kuda ia ni glianu . . ." [song lyrics]. In *Tovarishch pesnia*, vol. 15, edited by Vadim Semernin, 33–34. Moscow: Sovetskii kompozitor, 1980.

"Na ostrove Kikhnu." *Tallin* [sic] 4 (1980): 84–85.

"Monolog Lota." *22* [Dvadtsat' dva] 54 (June/July 1987): 72–73.

"Osennie stikhi"; "Posledniaia muzyka"; "Bol´nichnyi sad"; "Letniaia noch´"; "Otkrovennyi razgovor na Braiton-Biche"; "Iard-Seil." *Novoe russkoe slovo* 24–30 (December 1990).

"Iz tsikla 'Puteshestviia'": "Vishen´e"; "Gadanie pri luchine"; "Moisei: statuia Erzia v Saranske"; "Sobach´i svad´by v Tynde"; "Noch´iu v Sochi"; "Pushkinskii prazdnik na BAMe v 1979 g." *Chernovik* 3 (1990): 66–67.

Kuznechik: Poema. Chernovik 5 (1991): 32–25.

"Iz knigi 'Propashchaia dusha': "V chernoi shali po Vladimirskomu"; "My tantsevali tango v klube"; "Nad Borisovym noch´, nad Rossiei zima"; "Kto tam brodit vkrug kvartala?"; "Banderol´ so stikhami." *Novoe russkoe slovo*, December 27, 1991.

"Devochka-mal´chik"; "Uroki fekhtovaniia"; "Villa Borgeze"; "Otkrovennyi razgovor na Braiton Biche"; "Lesnaia skazka." *Vestnik* 3, no. 13 (June 30, 1992): 26–27.

"Tvoi golubye slezy"; "Ia ustal ia soshel s distantsii"; "V pyl´nom skverike vozle vokzala . . ."; "Domik Chekhova v Gurzufe"; "V metro"; "Garmonicheskie stikhi." *Vstrechi* 16 (1992): 101–103.

Stena placha: Poema. Chernovik 6 (1992): 72–74.

"Nadgrobie Pushkina"; "Var´ete v Talline"; "Uroki fekhtovaniia." *Al´manakh Kluba russkikh pisatelei* (1991): 95–96.

Villa Borgeze. Poberezh´e 1 (1992): 54–55.

"Epidrama. Kazanskie siroty." *Al'manakh Kluba russkikh pisatelei* (1993): 105.

"Staryi vrach"; "Igry na trotuare pered brodveiskim teatrom"; "Proshchal´naia poema"; "Garmonicheskie stikhi"; "Kompozitsiia na Old Silver Biche"; "Vospominanie"; "Korobka iz-pod papiros." *Chernovik* 8 (1993): 125–127.

Letaiushchie tarelki: Poema. Poberezh´e 2 (1993): 98–104.

"Bliuz ianvarskogo snegopada na bulvare chernogo kamnia"; "Bliuz chernoi reki v Providense"; "Idiopaticheskii bliuz"; "Bliuz zheltoi reki v N´iu-Orleane"; "Bliuz evreiskogo muzykanta v tserkvi Garlema." *Chernovik* 9 (1993): 70–74.

Begun: Poema. Klub poetov [New York]. *Al´manakh* (1994): 23–26.

"Belyi gorod"; "Dorogaia moia, dorogaia"; "V roshche pal´movoi . . ."; "Otbolela dusha." *Vstrechi* 19 (1995): 108–110.

Zheltaia zvezda: Poema. Poberezh´e 5 (1996): 352–354.

"Kazhdoe utro ia prosypaius´ poetom." *Klub poetov* [New York]. *Al´manakh* (1996): 21–24.

"Ty govorila: 'Ia tebia liubliu . . .'"; "Mirazh"; "Naberezhnaia reki v Providense"; "Osennii sad"; "Slomannaia stena"; "Poezdom 'Amtrak' iz Providensa n N´iu-Iork." *The New Review / Novyi zhurnal* 203–204 (1996): 46–49.

"Zimniaia pesnia"; "Peizazh bez geroia"; "Ob odnom rasskaze"; "Na predele." *Vstrechi* 20 (1996): 142–144.

"Anna Akhmatova v Komarovo"; "Zhena flotskogo vracha"; "Petropavlovskaia krepost´"; "Nadgrobie Pushkina"; "Vozvrashchenie evenkov s okhoty"; "Osen´ v Novoi Anglii"; "Posledniaia muzyka"; "Poet i narod." *Interesnaia gazeta* 93 (October 1996): 6.

"Novye stikhi": "Mirazh"; "Priiateliu-pessimistu"; "Opasnaia iasnost´"; "Esli pereshchitat´." *Novoe russkoe slovo*, January 2 1996.

"Pered sinagogoi v prazdnik Simkhat-Tora"; "Tsyganskii tabor v Ozerkakh"; "Villa Borgeze." In *Svet dvuedinyi. Evrei i Rossiia v sovremennoi poezii*, compiled by Mikhail Grozovskii, edited by Evgenii Vitkovskii, 442–445. Moscow: "Kh.G.S.," 1996.

"V Leningrade posle blokady"; "Potomok dekabrista." In *Samizdat veka*, edited by Anatolii Strelianyi, Genrikh Sapgir et al., 468. Moscow: Polifakt, 1997.

"Ne govori, moi drug, chto ty ee liubil." *Poberezh´e* 6 (1997): 339.

Zheltaia zvezda: Poema. Bostonskaia nezavisimaia gazeta, February 8, 1997.

"Moia slavianskaia dusha v evreiskoi upakovke . . .": "Bol´nichnyi sad"; "Stikhi iz romana 'Iona-Strannik'"; "Posledniaia muzyka"; "Poet i narod"; "Osen´ v Novoi Anglii"; "Slovar´ Dalia"; "Moi gorod"; "Proshchal´naia poema"; "Otchuzhdennost´"; "Armeniia"; "Sorok chetvertaia ulitsa"; "Staromu emigrantu"; "Vesna v Novoi Anglii"; "Sud´ba-amerikanka"; "Zabroshennaia zheleznodorozhnaia stantsiia na Keip Kode"; "Nostal´giia"; "Poezdom Amtrak iz Providensa v N´iu-Iork"; Osennii sad"; "Smert´ Brodskogo"; "Gody i gady." Introduction by David Gai. *Evreiskii mir*, July 25, 1997.

"Ty zapisyval palindromy . . ."; "Konets XX-go veka"; "Dmitriiu Bobyshevu i Galine Rubinshtein"; "Na koleniakh deda." *Vstrechi* 21 (1997): 107–108.

"Smert' Brodskogo"; "Iz poemy 'Zheltaia zvezda.'" *Al'manakh Kluba russkikh pisatelei* (1997): 30–31.

"Opasnaia iasnost'"; "Otbolela dusha"; "Staromu emigrantu"; "Nad Borisovym noch', nad Rossiei zima"; "My tantsevali tango v klube"; "Osen' v Novoi Anglii"; "Otkrovennyi razgovor na Braiton-Biche." *Interesnaia gazeta* August/September 1997.

"Probuzhdenie v Bostone"; "Moim chitateliam"; "Rannii sneg"; "Zhivoe vremia." *The New Review / Novyi zhurnal* 210 (1998): 114–117.

"Pustynia"; "Vdol' okeana po shosse"; "Na vystavke Pikasso"; "Predzimnii den'." *Vstrechi* 22 (1998): 171–173.

Tenitsy. Poema. Poberezh'e 8 (1999): 351–353.

"Aprel'"; "Serebrianaia priazhka remnia"; "Utrom po doroge na rabotu." *The New Review / Novyi zhurnal* 214 (1999): 76–78.

"Fantelki": "Zhivaia igrushka"; "Bul'varnyi roman"; "Posle smerti"; "Shel po lesu Vanechka"; "Bukhariki." *Novoe russkoe slovo*, April 29–30, 1999.

Tenitsy: Poema. Vyshgorod [Tallinn] 3 (1999): 154–159.

Ukho zemli: Poema. Vestnik 16 (1999): 50–51.

"Stikhi 1998–1999": "Vesna"; "Ne variagi my, a slaviane"; "Zhivaia igrushka"; "V Mar'inoi roshche"; "Na zakhoronenie Romanovykh"; "Posle smerti"; "Letnie dni na poluostrove Keip-Kod"; "Atlantika; "Shel po lesu Vanechka"; "Bukhariki"; "Bul'varnyi roman"; "Moi angliiskii." *Poberezh'e* 9 (2000): 310–311.

"Dm. Bobyshevu i G. Rubinshtein"; "Konets 20-go veka." *Nash Skopus* 18 (2000): 18–19.

"Sobach'i svad`by v Tynde"; "Pushkinskii prazdnik na BAMe v 1979 g." In *Ochen' korotkie teksty: v storonu antologii*, edited by Dmitrii Kuz'min, 224–225. Moscow: Novoe literaturnoe obozrenie, 2000.

"Forel'"; "Siren'"; "Korostel'." *The New Review / Novyi zhurnal* 221 (2000): 70–72.

"Rannie neopublikovannye stikhi": 'Nadoelo'; 'Poedinok'; 'Natiurmort'; 'Il'ia Averbakh stradaet ot liubvi." *Klub poetov* [New York]. *Al'manakh* (2001): 183–185.

"Rannie neopublikovannye stikhi: 'Nadoelo'; 'Poedinok'; 'Natiurmort'; 'Odnazhdy'; 'Napisat' ty mozhesh' gory'; 'Vesna'; 'Ia pisal o sinem nebe'; 'Iazycheskoe'; "Vernost'." *Al'manakh Kluba russkikh pisatelei* (2001): 418–422.

Ukho zemli: Poema. Kreshchatik 3 (2001): 314–316.

Stena placha: Poema. Poberezh'e 10 (2001): 288–289.

"Kolesom kolesa v kolese": "Devochka v solomennoi shliape"; "Vorony v Komarovo"; "Po temnym ulitsam Kronshtadta"; "Belaia noch'" "Abrikosovoe derevo i chinara v Tbilisskom dvorike"; "Oslik po imeni Zhak"; "Moskovskii mart." *Arion* 3 (2001): 24–32.

"Gurman uma." *Novoe russkoe slovo*, March 24–25, 2001.

"Zimnii korabl' (1956–1977)": "Liubimaia ili liubovnitsa"; "Pridi"; "Nochnye golosa"; "Devochka s violonchel'iu"; "V Komarovo"; "Darite devushkam tsvety"; "Zolotye rybiny"; "Kartonnyi kloun." *Poberezh`e* 11 (2002): 276–277.

"Moskovskii mart"; "V bare." *Russkaia ulitsa* [New York] 6 (2002): 91.

"Smert´ Brodskogo," "Ne prikhodi," "Anna Akhmatova v Komarovo." *Novoe russkoe slovo*, October 18-19, 2003.

"Ballada otrazheniia." *The New Review / Novyi zhurnal* 230 (2003): 90-91.

"Nadoelo"; "Poedinok." *Stetoskop/eStethoscope* 36 (2003): 36.

Stikhi 1955-1959 "Nadoelo"; "Pridi"; "Letniaia fantaziia v god razoblacheniia Stalina"; "Iazycheskoe"; "Ty priedesh´"; "Darite devushkam tsvety"; "Skameiki"; "Natiurmort"; "Odnazhdy"; "Vernost´"; "Vesna"; "Shchuch´e ozero"; "Liubimaia ili liubovnitsa"; "Ladozhskii led dvizhetsia po Neve"; "Vospominanie"; "Devushku bili"; "Glukhonemye." *AKT. Literaturnyi samizdat* 8 (January-February 2003): 11-12.

"Liubimaia ili liubovnitsa"; "V Komarovo"; "Kartonnyi kloun"; "Stareiushchie zhenshchiny"; "Uletaiut dozhdi"; "Kakaia muzyka v rebiacheskoi dushe"; "Anna Akhmatova v Komarovo." *Panorama*, August 20-26, 2003.

Avtobus i gory: Poema. Poberezh´e 12 (2003): 316-317.

"Ballada otrazheniia." *Al´manakh Kluba russkikh pisatelei* (2004): 439-441.

"Gorlovina reki"; "Idiopaticheskii bliuz"; "Bliuz nochnogo dauntauna v Providense"; "Esli pereshchitat´"; "Smit-strit"; "Primorskoe shosse"; "Vorony v Komarovo"; "Oslik po imeni Zhak"; "Proshchat´sia poka ne ugasla liubov´"; "Barabany sud´by." In *Osvobozhdennyi Uliss. Sovremennaia russkaia poeziia za predelami Rossii*, edited by Dmitri Kuz´min, 659-663. Moscow: Novoe literaturnoe obozrenie, 2004.

"Vnutrenniaia emigratsiia"; "Amerikanskoe kladbishche"; "Zheny korolia Genrikha." *AKT. Literaturnyi samizdat* 16 (2005): 11.

"Krasnaia solomennaia shliapa: '1. Benzokolonka'; '2. Chuvashskie lapti'; '3. Utro na beregu Meksikansgogo zaliva'; '4. Krasnaia solomennaia shliapa'; '5. Amerikanskii futbol'; '6. Smert´ vraga'; '7. Moskovskie novosti'; '8. Osen´'; '9. Tselitel´'; '10. Bukhariki'; '11. Vanechka'; '12. Nochnye golosa.'" *Poberezh´e* 14 (2005): 365-366.

"Amerikanskoe kladbishche"; "Indian Lake"; "Minuia okrestnosti N´iu-Iorka"; "V evreiskom magazine 'Delikatessen'"; "Garri Konnik (mladshii) i ego bliuzy"; "Amerikanskii student." In *Zapolnenie pustoty. Antologiia russkoi poezii Novoi Anglii*, edited by Mark Chulskii, 186-191. Boston: M-Graphics, 2006.

"Letnie dni na poluostrove Keip-Kod"; "Atlantika"; "Liubimaia ili liubovnitsa"; "Zolotye rybiny." *Poberezh´e* 15 (2006): *Antologiia 1992-2006*, 337-338.

"Nekotoraia stepen' toski po Messii": "Pliaski khasidov"; "Lepet bogov"; "Nekotoraia stepen- toski po Messii"; "Ia—tvoi evrei"; "Zakat"; "Esli"; "Bibleiskie siuzhety"; "Sestry"; "Vernut´sia v Sorrento"; "Zelenye poruchni mosta"; "A mozhet byt´?"; "Novogodnee"; "Ia uzhe nichego ne khochu"; "V restoranchike nad okeanom"; "Puteshestvie so slonom"; "Koldun´ia"; "Muzyka nebes"; "Manernye derev´ia"; "Ulichnyi guliaka"; "Golos"; "Tvar´"; "Nord-Vest"; "Magicheskaia luna"; "Kontsert muzyki Shenberga"; "Vechno prikhodiashchie"; "Zakat na beregu Tirrenskogo moria"; "Mertvoe more"; "Fialki pod zaborom"; "Vnutrennosti sobaki"; "Liubov´ k snegu"; "Zakat nakanune Paskhi"; "Nado li pravit´ teksty?"; "Letnii gorod"; "Vesna v Providense"; "Piatnadtsatiletniaia"; "Moi parikmakher"; "Trio Shostakovicha"; "Pustynnaia doroga"; "Pered grozoi"; "Zhenshchina vesnoi"; "Raskrytaia kniga"; "Davno proshla vesna"; "Grisha Perel´man i Puankare"; "Grisha Perel´man reshaet teoremu Puankare . . ."; "Prosit´ i poluchat´"; "Avtomobil´nyi bliuz." *Poberezh´e* 16 (2007): 305–314.

"Bibleiskie siuzhety"; "Sestry"; "Nado li pravit´ teksty." *Arion* 4 (2007): 11–13.

Avtobus i gory. Poema. Mromm.com Zhurnal stikhoslozheniia, May 26, 2008. http://mromm.com/p/ShrayerDavid-01.htm.

Nekotoraia stepen´ toski po Messii. Sbornik stikhov [see the collection *Dve knigi*]. *Mromm.com Zhurnal stikhoslozheniia*, October 5, 2008. http://mromm.com/p/ShrayerDavid-02.htm.

"Nekotoraia stepen´ toski po Messii": "Golos"; "Nord-Vest"; "Esli"; "Zakat na beregu Tirrensklogo moria." *Krugozor* 4 (April 2009): 34–35.

"Iz ugla v ugol": "Na taburete v bare"; :"Iz Kavafi"; "A mozhet byt´?"; "Novogodnee"; "Ia uzhe nichego ne khochu." *Nezavisimaia gazeta Ex Libris*, July 16, 2020.

"Anna Akhmatova i molodoi poet." *Aesthetoscope/Stetoskop* (2009): 7–8.

"Iz knigi *Linii-figury-tela*: 'Iskusstvo khirurga'; 'Sluchainyi tramvai.'" In *Aesthetoscope. Kontseptsiia prekrasnogo*, edited by Aleksandr Eleukov, 33–34. St. Petersburg: Biblioteka Aesthetoscope, n.d.

"Arkhangel´skoe pod Moskvoi." *Nezavisimaia gazeta Ex Libris*, January 17, 2011.

"Posle pereezda"; "Dirizhabl´." *Arion* 1 (2012): 49–50.

Prishelets. Antiroman. Slovo/Word 76 (2012): 148–155.

"Avtobus i gory." *Aesthetoscope* (2013): *Poeziia*, 85–89.

"Garmonicheskaia povest´." *Kreshchatik* 2 (2015): 290–291.

"Natiurmort"; "Osen´ u moria"; "Podvig"; "Domik Chekhova v Gurzufe"; "Na voinu"; "Vozvrashchenie iz puteshestviia." In *NashKrym. Antologiia*, edited by Igor´ Sid, Gennadii Katsov, Rika Katsova, 277–280. New York: KriK Publishing House, 2014.

"Ne posylai menia na krai zemli. Stikhi o novoi i staroi zhizni": "Smit-Strit"; "Slomannaia stena"; "Stolbtsy Pokassetskoi reki"; "Ty govorila: Ia tebia liubliu"; "Nostal´giia"; "Zimniaia pesnia"; "Podnimi menia"; "Esli pereshchitat´"; "Poslednie rozy"; "Osennii sad." *Etazhi*, January 28, 2016. https://etazhi-lit.ru/publishing/poetry/231-ne-posylay-menya-na-kray-zemli.html.

"Villa Borgeze"; "Bol´nichnyi sad"; "Stikhi iz romana 'Iona-Strannik'"; "Tret´ia volna"; "Posledniaia muzyka." In *Sto let russkoi zarubezhnoi poezii. Antologiia*, edited by Gershom Kiprischi, compiled by Vladimir Batshev, vol. 3: *Tret´ia volna emigratsii*, 540–543. Frankfurt: Literaturnyi evropeets, 2017.

"Ia—tvoi evrei"; "Esli"; "Magicheskaia luna"; "Villa Borgeze." In *70—mezhdunarodnaia poeticheskaia antologiia, posviashchennaia 70-letiiu Izrailia*, edited by Rika Katsova and Gennadii Katsov, 289–294. New York: KRiK Publishing House, 2018.

"Popytka vykhoda iz karatnina." *Coronaverse: Stikhi koronavirusnogo vremeni*. April 14, 2020. https://coronaviruspoetry.com/david-shrayer-petrov/.

2C. Drama

Ed Tenner: Tragikomediia v dvukh deistviiakh i shesti kartinakh (Эд Теннер: Трагикомедия в двух действиях и шести картинах; Ed Tenner: A tragic comedy in two acts and six scenes) [see also 2021 book edition, *Vaktsina. Ed Tenner*]. *Mromm.com Zhurnal stikhoslozheniia*. January 23, 2009. http://mromm.com/p/ShrayerDavid-03.htm.

2D. Literary Translations by David Shrayer-Petrov

"Lesnaia basnia," by Andrey Aleksandrovich. Translated from Belarusian. *Zor´ka* [Minsk]. October22, 1960.

"Svoboda"; "Optimizm"; "Zhemchuzhina"; "Vospominan´e o tebe"; "Pirushka"; "Vinocherpii," by Dhani Ram Chatrik. Translated from Punjabi. In Dkhani Ram Chatrik, *Tsvetok shafrana*, edited by Natal´ia Tolstaia, 26–27; 36–39. Leningrad: Gosudarstvennoe izdatel´stvo khudozhestvennoi literatury, 1962.

Pesn´ kukushki: Poema, by Subramania Bharati. Translated from Tamil. In Subramania Bharati, *Stikhotvoreniia*, edited by N. Smirnova, 117–145. Leningrad: Gosudarstvennoe izdatel´stvo khudozhestvennoi literatury, 1963.

"Bliuz Luizianskoi tiur´my," by Erskine Caldwell. Translated from English with Emilia Polyak [Shrayer]. *Literaturnaia gazeta*, October 13, 1966.

"Ispaniia, so mnoi tvoi skorbnye peizazhi . . . ," by Hugh MacDiarmid. Translated from English. *Literaturnaia gazeta*, August 9, 1967.

"Son," by Fikret Goja. Translated from Azerbaijani. *Literaturnaia Rossiia*, October 2, 1970.

"Moi Azerbaidzhan," by Suleiman Rustam. Translated from Azerbaijani. *Literaturnaia gazeta*, October 30, 1970.

"Nochnoi razgovor Moskva-Tbilisi," by Karlo Kaladze. Translated from Georgian. In Karlo Kaladze, *Na kholmakh Gruzii. Stikhi i poemy*, 43–45. Moscow: Sovetskii pisatel´, 1971.

"Videl mir ia v radosti i gore . . . ," by Aleksei Pysin. Translated from Belarusian. *Literaturnaia gazeta*, January 6, 1971.

"Lirika etogo goda": "Ottsovskaia kuznitsa"; "Khmel´"; "Molcha sosredotochit´sia," by Ellen Niit. Translated from Estonian. *Druzhba narodov* 12 (1972): 150–151.

"Turkmenskoe solntse," by Dondok Ulzytuev. Translated from Buriat. *Literaturnaia gazeta*, September 30, 1972.

"Ia smotriu na ruku svoiu . . ."; "V avguste," by Aleksandar Popovski. Translated from Macedonian with D. Tolovski. *Znamia* 7 (1973): 112–113.

"Slezy schast´ia"; "Malen´kii zabroshennyi maiak," by Radovan Zogović. Translated from Montenegrin with D. Tolovskii. *Znamia* 7 (1973): 114.

"Rakushka," by Dragutin Tadijanović. Translated from Croatian with D. Tolovskii. *Znamia* 7 (1973): 115.

"Liubliu tebia"; "Pokhvala gazeli"; "Slezy," by Bobo Khodzhi. Translated from the Tajik. In *Poklon zemle rodnoi. Stikhi tadzhikskikh poetov*, compiled by Sh. Niiazi, edited by S. Lipkin, 283–284. Moscow: Khudozhestvennaia literatura, 1974.

"Ulybka tsvetov"; "Ruch´i," by Ashur Safar. Translated from the Tajik. In *Poklon zemle rodnoi. Stikhi tadzhikskikh poetov*, compiled by Sh. Niiazi, edited by S. Lipkin, 337–338. Moscow: Khudozhestvennaia literatura, 1974.

Belaia dolina. Roman, by Simon Drakul. Translated from Macedonian with D. Tolovskii. *Literaturnaia Gruziia* 7 (1975): 30–44; 8 (1975): 36–51.

"I den´ i noch´, svershaia trudnyi put´ . . . ," by Il'ia Devin. Translated from Mordovian. *Literaturnaia Rossiia*, December 19, 1975.

"Slova"; "Gostepriimstvo"; "Odinokii krest"; "Osvobozhdenie Tsvety Andrich. 1945"; "Broshennyi kamen´," by Desanka Maksimović. Translated from Serbian. In *Desanka Maksimovich. Izbrannoe*, edited by O. Kutasova, 64; 79; 83; 113; 119–124. Moscow: Khudozhestvennaia literatura, 1977.

"Nuzhna eshche mudrost´"; "Veter i gora"; "Ia—kosmos," by Mirsaid Mirshkar. Translated from Tajik. In Mirsaid Mirshakar, *Izbrannoe*, 54–57; 58. Moscow: Khudozhestvennaia literatura, 1977.

"Kogda minuet etot chas," by Slobodan Rakitić. Translated from Serbian. *Literaturnaia ucheba* 4 (1978): 6.

"Zemliu—slovno iabloko zlatoe . . ."; "Pamiatnik loshadi"; "Monolog mostovoi"; "Van Gog. 'Podsolnukhi'"; "Operatsionnaia. Belyi angel"; "Prebyvanie v gostiakh"; "Tishina"; "Snegir´"; "Grom," by Vladas Rudokas. Translated from Lithuanian. In *Antologiia litovskoi sovetskoi poezii*, edited by R. Trimonis, 314–321. Vilnius: Vaga, 1980.

"Iz chuzhdoi, broshennoi planety . . ."; "Net menia na poliakh . . ."; "Na vokzale"; "Iz 'Poemy Zhvirgzhde,'" by Mykolas Karčiauskas. Translated from Lithuanian. In *Antologiia litovskoi sovetskoi poezii*, edited by R. Trimonis, 493–495. Vilnius: Vaga, 1980.

"Kak serdtse"; "Proshchanie s morem"; "Tebe"; "Sokhrani nas . . . ," by One Baljukonite. Translated from Lithuanian. In *Antologiia litovskoi sovetskoi poezii*, edited by R. Trimonis, 544–546. Vilnius: Vaga, 1980.

"Zdeshnee nebo navislo . . ."; "Vstuplenie"; "Neiasno, chto uzh tam sluchilos´ . . ."; "Vozvrashchenie solntsa," by Juozas Marcinkevičius. Translated from Lithuanian. In *Antologiia litovskoi sovetskoi poezii*, edited by R. Trimonis, 537–540. Vilnius: Vaga, 1980.

"Tebe"; "Proshchanie s morem," by One Baljukonite. Translated from Lithuanian. *Litva literaturnaia* 1 (1980): 85–86.

"Zheltyi list," by Chaim Beider. Translated from Yiddish. In Khaim Beider, *Moia pogoda*, 80. Moscow: Sovetskii pisatel', 1985.

"Opasnoe bezvremen´ie," by Robert Frost. Translated from English. In *Strofy veka-2. Antologiia mirovoi poezii v russkikh perevodakh XX veka*, edited by Evgenii Vitkovskii, 830. Moscow: Polifakt, 1998.

"Tsygan," by Mateja Matevski. Translated from the Macedonean. In *Strofy veka-2. Antologiia mirovoi poezii v russkikh perevodakh XX veka*, edited by Evgenii Vitkovskii, 830. Moscow: Polifakt, 1998.

"Sonetchka," by Maxim D. Shrayer. Translated from English with Emilia Shrayer. *Poberezh´e* 12 (2003): 24–27. Reprinted in *Tallinn* 1 (2004): 34–32; in *Na poberezh´e. Rasskazy pisatelei russkogo zarubezh´ia*, edited by Igor Mikhalevich-Kaplan, 327–333. Boston: M-Graphics, 2009; "Sonetchka," by Maxim D. Shrayer. Translated from English with Emilia Shrayer. Revised translation. *Lekhaim* 3 (2017): 112–115.

"Moi Babel´," by Maxim D. Shrayer. Translated from English with Emilia Shrayer. *Poberezh´e* 13 (2004): 56–65; *Mosty* 4 (2004): 204–222. Reprinted in *Poberezh´e: Antologiia, 1992–2006* (Philadelphia: The Coast, 2006), 166–173.

"Rim, otkrytyi gorod," by Maxim D. Shrayer. Translated from English with Emilia Shrayer. In Maksim D. Shraer, *V ozhidanii Ameriki*, 72–99. Moscow: Al´pina non-fikshn, 2013. Reprinted in Maksim D. Shraer, *V ozhidanii Ameriki*, 72–99. 2nd ed. Moscow: Al´pina non-fikshn, 2018.

"Sudnyi den´ v Amsterdame," by Maxim D. Shrayer. Translated from English with Emilia Shrayer. *Poberezh´e* 14 (2005): 90–96. A revised translation in *Lekhaim* 10 (2016): 111–118.

"Ishcheznovenie Zalmana," by Maxim D. Shrayer. Translated from English with Emilia Shrayer. *Lekhaim* 10 (2015): 117–124.

"Sudnyi den´ v Amsterdame"; "Lovlia foreli v Virdzhinii"; "Sonetchka"; "Ishcheznovenie Zalmana," by Maxim D. Shrayer. Translated from English with Emilia Shrayer. In Maksim D. Shraer, *Ishcheznovenie Zalmana. Rasskazy*, 15–44; 141–191; 221–236; 237–288. Moscow: Knizhniki, 2017.

Part 3. Literary translations of David Shrayer-Petrov's works

3A. Into English (also see books in Part 1)

Fiction and Nonfiction

"Rusty." Translated by Maxim D. Shrayer and Thomas Epstein. *Providence Sunday Journal Magazine*, October 22, 1989, 21–23.

"The Towering Stranger Read On and On." Translated by Emilia Shrayer-Polyak. *Brown Alumni Monthly* 12 (1989): 64.

"David and Goliath." Translated by Maxim D. Shrayer and Thomas Epstein. *Midstream* (February/March 1990): 38–41.

"Joseph Barbarossa: Joseph Brodsky in Leningrad." Translated by Maxim D. Shrayer. *Midstream* (June/July 1990): 29–32.

"Felix d'Herelle in Russia." Translated by Emilia Shrayer. *Bull. Inst. Pasteur* 94 (1996): 91–96.

"Apple Cider Vinegar." Translated by Maxim D. Shrayer and Victor Terras. *Marina* 2 (1995): 14–18.

"In the Reeds." Translated by Maxim D. Shrayer and Victor Terras. *The Massachusetts Review* (Summer 1999): 175–183.

"Dismemberers." Translated by Maxim D. Shrayer and Victor Terras. *Southwest Review* 85, no. 1 (2000): 68–73.

"Jonah and Sarah." Translated by Maxim D. Shrayer. *Bee Museum* 1, no. 1 (Spring 2002): 9–20.

"Hände Hoch!" Translated by Maxim D. Shrayer. In *An Anthology of Jewish-Russian Literature: Two Centuries of Jewish Identity in Prose and Poetry*, edited by Maxim D. Shrayer, vol. 2, 1062–1070. Armonk, NY: M. E. Sharpe, 2007; reprinted in *Voices of Jewish-Russian Literature: An Anthology*, edited by Maxim D. Shrayer, 833–842. Boston: Academic Studies Press, 2018.

"Alfredick." Translated by Emilia Shrayer. *Slovo/Word* 64 (2009): 79–87.

"Ivanovna the Liar in Paris." Translated by Emilia Shrayer. *Slovo/Word* 68 (2010): 93–99.

"The Love of Akira Watanabe." Translated by Emilia Shrayer. *Slovo/Word* 70 (2011): 148–152.

"A Storefront Window of Miracles." Translated by Margaret Godwin-Jones. *Slovo/Word* 73 (2012): 160–166.

"Kimono." Translated by Emilia Shrayer. *Slovo/Word* 74 (2014): 148–157.

"Mimosa Flowers for Grandmother's Grave." Translated by Maxim D. Shrayer. *Commentary* 173, no. 3 (March 2014): 39–44.

Poetry

"Monologue of Lot to His Wife." Translated by Maxim D. Shrayer [Leaflet: Supplemental Haggadah Readings]. *National Conference on Soviet Jewry/Coalition to Free Soviet Jews*, Spring 1987.

"Villa Borghese." Translated by Dolores Stewart and Maxim D. Shrayer. *Salmagundi* 101–102 (Winter/Spring 1994): 151–153.

"Lot's Monologue to His Wife"; "Anna Akhmatova in Komarovo"; "Early Morning in Moscow." Translated by Egwin Honig and Maxim D. Shrayer. In *A Glass of Green Tea—with Honig*, edited by Susan Brown, Thomas Epstein, and Henry Gould, 238–241. Providence, RI: Alephoe Books, 1994.

"Edwin Honig as Translator of Russian Verse." Translated by Maxim D. Shrayer. In *A Glass of Green Tea—with Honig* edited by Susan Brown, Thomas Epstein, and Henry Gould, 236–238. Providence, RI: Alephoe Books, 1994.

"Winter Morning"; "Fall at the Seashore"; "Early Morning in Moscow." Translated by Maxim D. Shrayer and Edwin Honig. *Enlygnion* 1 (Spring 1995): 10–13.

"Five Poems." Translated by Edwin Honig and Maxim D. Shrayer. *Nedge* 2 (Spring 1995): 39–43.

"I Can't Take This Torment Any Longer." Translated by Edwin Honig and Maxim D. Shrayer. *Parnassus of World Poetry* (1997): 47.

"My Slavic Soul"; "Fall at the Seashore"; "I Can't Take this Torment Any Longer"; "Winter Morning." Translated by Edwin Honig and Maxim D. Shrayer. *Bee Museum* 3 (2005): 27–31.

"Chagall's Self-Portrait with Wife"; "My Slavic Soul"; "Early Morning in Moscow"; "Villa Borghese." Translated by Edwin Honig, Maxim D. Shrayer, and Dolores Stewart. In *An*

Anthology of Jewish-Russian Literature: Two Centuries of Jewish Identity in Prose and Poetry, edited by Maxim D. Shrayer, vol. 2, 1058–1061. Armonk, NY: M. E. Sharpe, 2007.

"Birch Fogs (from *Flying Saucers*)"; "Petersburg Doge." Translated by Maxim D. Shrayer. In Valentina Polukhina, *Brodsky through the Eyes of His Contemporaries*, vol. 1, 195–197. 2nd ed. Boston: Academic Studies Press, 2008.

"Fall at the Seashore"; "Still Life"; "Winter Morning"; "My Slavic Soul"; "Chagall's Self-Portrait with Wife"; "Early Morning in Moscow"; "Birch Fogs (from *Flying Saucers*)"; "I Can't Take this Torment Any Longer"; "Anna Akhmatova in Komarovo"; "To Shostakovich at His Summer House in Komarovo"; "Lot's Monolog to His Wife"; "Villa Borghese"; "Petersburg Doge." Translated by Edwin Honig, Maxim D. Shrayer, and Dolores Stewart. *Four Centuries: Russian Poetry in Translation* 12 (2012): 15–26.

"Runner Begoon." Translated by Maxim D. Shrayer. *Four Centuries: Russian Poetry in Translation* 7 (2014): 54–59.

"Snow on the Ground": "Wild Turkeys in Boston"; "Blimp in the Clouds"; "Poets of the Past Century"; "Snow on the Ground"; "Off to War." Translated by Maxim D. Shrayer. *Four Centuries: Russian Poetry in Translation* 11 (2015): 18–22.

"Arkhangelskoe outside Moscow." Translated by Maxim D. Shrayer and Carol V. Davis. *Four Centuries: Russian Poetry in Translation* 15 (2016): 24–27.

"Chagall's Self-Portrait with Wife"; "My Slavic Soul"; "Villa Borghese." Translated by Edwin Honig, Maxim D. Shrayer, and Dolores Stewart. In *Voices of Jewish-Russian Literature: An Anthology*, edited by Maxim D. Shrayer, 830–833. Boston: Academic Studies Press, 2018.

"Lift Me Up": "Nostalgia"; "A Broken Wall"; "The Pocasset River Scrolls"; You Told Me: 'I love you'"; "Winter Song"; "If We Were to Compute"; "Lift Me Up"; "Last Rosas"; "The Autumn Garden." *Four Centuries: Russian Poetry in Translation* 24 (2020), forthcoming.

3B. Into other languages

French

[David Schraer-Petrov.] "Derrière la grille du Zoo." Translated by Richard Roy. *Russkaia literatura / Lettres russes* 30 (2002): 23–29.

Japanese

"Watanabe Akira no koi" ["Liubov' Akiry Vatanabe"]. Translated by Yuri Nagura. In *Vesna v Khongo / The Spring in Hongo*, edited by M. Numano, K. Mouri, and Y. Nagura, 22–33. Tokyo: The University of Tokyo, Department of Contemporary Literary Studies / Department of Slavic Languages and Literatures, 2011.

Croatian

[David Šrajer-Petrov.] "Smrt Brodskog." Translated by Irena Lukšić. In *Poezijom ususret noviom Tisućljeću [International Poetry Festival 2000, Zagreb]*, 1280. November 16–10, 2000.

"Mimikrija." Translated by Irena Lukšić. *Forum* 1–3 (2002): 158–168. Reprinted in *Treći val*, edited by Irena Lukšić, 309–321. Zagreb: Hrvatsko filološko društvo, 2004.

"Josif Barbarossa." Translated by Irena Lukšić, 43–50. In *Brodski! Život, Djelo (1940–1996)*, edited by Irena Lukšić. Zagreb: Hrvatsko filološko društvo; Zadar, 2007.

"Tigar snegova. Genrih Sapgir." Translated by Irena Lukšić. *Književna smotra* 152 (2009): 149-155.

Macedonian

"Sledam mravka"; "Kachen na zmej"; "Kolku bi bilo ubavo." Translated by Aleksandar Popovski. *Razgivor* 5 (January 1, 1975): 24.

Lithuanian

[Davidas Petrovas.] "Kazeivio našlės daina"; "Žali Pajūrio balsai"; "Mano gerumas." Translated by Antanas Drilinga. *Tiesa*, May 20, 1978.

"Trys Marikjos." Translated by Rimgaudas Graibus. *Vienybė* [Akmenė], May 25, 1978.

Hebrew

"Nafshi ha-slavit"; "Vila Borgeze" ("My Slavic Soul"; "Villa Borghese"). Translated by Roman Katsman. *Megaphone*, November 14, 2013. http://megafon-news.co.il/asys/archives/186500.

4. Selected Interviews

Amurskii, Vitalii. "Beseda s Davidom Shraerom-Petrovym." *Radio France Internationale-RFI. Rédaction russe*, February 26, 2005.

Belaia, Mira. "Vselennaia—eto chelovek." *Panorama*, June 7–13, 2006.

Karoian, Marina. "Vtoroe dykhanie." *Panorama*, December 24-30, 2003.

Katsov, Gennadii. "Ia dumaiu, chto my vse drug druga chemu-to nauchili." RUNYweb.com, May 17, 2011. Available in *Entsiklopedia russkoi Ameriki*, https://www.youtube.com/watch?v=XkwiKg9gjN0.

———. "David Shraer-Petrov. Glavnaia liniia moego romana—liubov´ vo vremia totalitarnogo sotsializma." *RUNYweb.com*, July 19, 2013.

Lukšić, Irena [Irena Lukshich]. "'Moia slavianskaia dusha v evreiskoi upakovke. . . .' Interv´iu s Davidom Shraerom-Petrovym." *Vestnik Rod-Ailenda* 12 (December 2000): 10–12.

———. "'Razgovor': David Šrajer-Petrov. Život u tri dimenzije." Translated by Irena Lukšić. *Vijenac* [Zagreb], May 20, 1999. Reprinted in *Treći val*, edited by Irena Lukšić, 456–458. Zagreb: Hrvatsko filološko društvo, 2004.

Malykhina, Svitlana. "Interview with David Shrayer-Petrov," *Russian in Boston*, Boston University, [2019]. http://sites.bu.edu/russianchat/interviews/interview-david-shrayer-petrov/.

Naroditskaia, Evgeniia. "Interview s pisatelem Davidom Shraerom-Petrovym." *Vestnik Rod-Ailenda* 9 (November 2005): 3–5.

Polukhina, Valentina. "Interview. 28 September 2003, London." In Valentina Polukhina, *Iosif Brodskii glazami sovremennikov*, vol. 2: *1996–2005*, 151–167. St. Petersburg: Izdatel′stvo zhurnala "Zvezda," 2006.

———. "He Was a Universal Poet. An Interview with David Shrayer-Petrov. 28 September 2003, London." Translated by Emilia Shrayer. In Valentina Polukhina, *Brodsky through the Eyes of His Contemporaries*, vol. 1, 180–195. 2nd ed. Boston: Academic Studies Press, 2008.

Shrayer, Maxim D. "Dinner with Stalin: A 3-Part Conversation with David Shrayer-Petrov." *Jewish Book Council / My Jewish Learning*, July 8–10, 2014. https://www.jewishbookcouncil.org/pb-daily/crypto-jews-and-autobiographical-animals-part-3-of-a-3-part-conversation.

———. "Evreiskii sekret. David Shraer-Petrov o dragotsennom kamne rasskaza, vibratsii chuvstva i upornoi liubvi k rodine" *Nezavisimaia gazeta Ex Libris*, September 11, 2014.

———. "Menia vsegda tianulo k zhanru skazki . . ." *Lekhaim* 10 (2014): 83–84.

———. "Krugosvetnoe shchast′e. K iubileiu Davida Shraera-Petrova." *Reklama i zhizn′* [Philadelphia], February 3, 2016.

———. "Nepovtorimaia vibratsia chuvstva." *Runyweb.com*, January 15, 2016.

———. "A Russian Typewriter Longs for Her Master." *Tablet Magazine*, January 28, 2020. https://www.tabletmag.com/sections/arts-letters/articles/maxim-shrayer-david-shrayer.

Tashkov, O. "I v budushchem godu—chitaite!" *Vechernii N′iu-Iork*, December 31– January 2, 1998.

Tukh, Boris. "Legko li byt′ russkim pisatelem v Amerike?" *Vesti* [Tallinn], January 22, 1999.

Vais, Svetlana. "K iubileiu. David Shraer-Petrov. 'Chuvstvo otkaza postepenno otpuskaet . . .'" *RUNYweb.com*, January 28, 2011.

Vol′tskaia, Tat′iana. "Mertsanie zheltoi zvezdy." Radio Liberty/Radio Svoboda, January 28, 2016, http://www.bigbook.ru/articles/detail.php?ID=25001, accessed June 3, 2020.

INDEX

A
Abramovitsh, S. Y., 86
Aizman, David, 64
Akhmadulina, Bella, 138
Akhmatova, Anna, 32, 112, 177, 192, 312, 356
Aksyonov, Vasily, 6, 31-32, 49, 98, 109-110, 138, 230, 293-294, 296
Aleshkovsky, Yuz, 313-314
    The Merry-Go-Round (*Karusel'*, 1979), 223
Aliagrov Roman, (penname of Roman Jakobson), 141-142
Aliyah Library *see* Biblioteka-Aliia
aliyah literature, ix, 222n5, 222-223, 228
aliyah (immigration to the Land of Israel and the State of Israel), 3, 5, 7-8, 13-14, 33, 38, 44, 123
Alon, Igal, 294
Alterman, Natan, 235, 294
Altshuller, Isaak, 75
America *see* United States
American jazz, 110
antisemitism, 4-5, 8-9, 66n6, 73-74, 224-226, 249, 257, 280, 299n36, 308, 352
anti-cosmopolitan campaign, 98
anti-Soviet activity, 69, 124
Arguments and Facts (*Argumenty i fakty*) newspaper, 7
Arrak, Jüri, 122, 379, 381-383, 395
Arrak, Urve Roodes, 379
Aseev, Nikolai, 145, 374
Assmann, Jan, 221-222
Averbakh, Ilya, 9, 31, 98
Auschwitz (Poland), 240
Austria, 72, 279
Azarov, Vsevolod, 98, 369

B
Babel, Isaac, 297, 351-352
    "Pan Apolek," 164
    Red Cavalry (*Konarmiia*), 164

Babi Yar (Kiev), 240
Bakhchanyan, Vagrich, 388
Bagritsky, Eduard, 224
Baikal-Amur railroad (BAM), 66, 376
Bakhtin, Mikhail, 36, 333
Baltakis, Algimantas, 377
Baratynsky, Evgeny, 133, 207
Batyushkov, Konsantin, 157
Baukh, Efrem, 5
    Jacob's Ladder (*Lestnitsa Iakova*, 1984), 222-223, 225, 227, 235
Beckett, Samuel
    Waiting for Godot, 278
Begun, Josef, 7, 34, 123, 384, 397
Bekman, Eva, 371
Belarus (Belorussia), 7, 66, 85, 99, 240, 249
Bellow, Saul
    Ravelstein, 355
Ben-Gurion, David, 246
Berdyaev, Nikolai, 321
Berlin, 76, 240, 242, 311n12
Bernstein, Frida, 379
Bernstein, Boris, 379
Bialik, Hayim Nachman, 235, 294
Biblioteka-Aliia, 33, 68, 235, 294
Bildungsroman, 45, 235
Bitov, Andrey
    Pushkin House (*Pushkinskii Dom*), 14
Blok, Alexandr, 132, 148, 186n22
    The Twelve (*Dvenadtsat'*), 109-110, 132-133
Bokov, Viktor, 377
Bradbury, Ray
    "Darling Adolf," 350
Brecht, Bertold, 43, 369
Brezhnev, Leonid, 267
Breydo, Bella, 361-362, 393
Broyde (Breydo) Chaim-Wolf, 361
Brodsky, Joseph, 27, 30, 32, 34, 119, 191-192, 207, 209

"December in Florence" ("Dekabr' vo
    Florentsii"), 193
"On the Death of a Friend" ("Stikhi na
    smert' druga), 177
"On the Death of Zhukov" ("Na smert'
    Zhukova"), 177
Bobyshev, Dmitry, 6, 32, 98, 191
Bogliasco, Italy, 61-62, 64
Bokstein, Ilia, 30
Böll, Heinrich, 291
Boston, 15, 64, 126, 332
Boston College, 50, 100
Bražėnas, Patras, 378
Brown University, 72, 104
Bryusov, Valery, 148
Budapest, 257
Bulgakov, Mikhail, 104
Bunin, Ivan, 61, 75, 84, 351
    Dark Avenues (*Temnye allei*), 356
    "Genrikh," 79
Butman, Hillel, 371

C

Canada, 9, 34
cantonists, 298
Caucasus, 117, 227n20, 308, 312, 355
Central Asia, 227n20
Central House of Writers (TsDL, Moscow),
    the, 15, 142n37, 291, 314n16
Chagall, Marc, 291, 296, 312
Chaikovskaya, Irina, 108
Chapayev, Vasily, 339, 343
Chekhov, Anton, 3, 15, 17-18, 59-61, 64,
    70-72, 74-76, 78-81, 84, 104, 235, 290,
    351, 356
    "A Man Encased" ("Chelovek v
        futliare"), 20
    "Belated Flowers" ("Tsvety
        zapozdalye"), 75
    "Enemies" ("Vragi"), 19
    "Gooseberries" ("Kryzhovnik"), 149
    "The Grasshopper" ("Poprygun'ia"), 79
    "Grisha," 10
    "Ionych," 75
    Ivanov, 20, 75
    "Kashtanka," 70
    "Lady with a Lapdog" ("Dama s sobach-
        koi"), 72, 74, 76-77
    "Mire" ("Tina"), 75
    "My Life" ("Moia zhizn'"), 75
    "Pecheneg," 20
    "Rothschild's Fiddle" ("Skripka
        Rotshil'da"), 18, 75
    "Steppe" ("Step'"), 75
    The Cherry Orchard (*Vishnevyi sad*), 74
    "The Duel" ("Duel'"), 19
    Three Sisters (Tri sestry) 74, 278
    "Ward 6" ("Palata № 6"), 72
Chernoshvarts, Eduard, 354
Christianity, 27, 46, 48
Christmas, 12
Chudakov, Aleksandr
    *A Gloom Is Cast upon the Ancient
        Steps* (*Lozhitsia mgla na starye
        stupeni*), 10
Chukovsky, Korney, 132
Churchill, Winston, 59
Communism, 21, 227, 247
Communist Party of the Soviet Union, 97, 344
Crimea, 59, 308, 312
Cuba, 257

D

Daniel, Yuly, 81
Dar, David, 31, 110
Deleuze, Gilles, 30
Derzhavin, Gavriil
    "Bullfinch" ("Snegir'"), 177
D'Hérelle, Félix, 378
"doctors' plot" of 1952-1953, 98
Domnina, Darya, 213
Dostoevsky, Fedor, 15, 111, 235, 266
    Crime and Punishment (*Prestupleniue i
        nakazanie*), 356
    Idiot (*Idiot*), 111
Drobitsky Yar (Kharkov), 240
Dubnow, Simon, 328
Dudintsev, Vladimir, 49
Dverin, Anatoly, 399

E

Easter, 12
Baukh, Efraim, 222
Ehrenburg, Ilya, 242-244, 299
    Stormy Life of Lazik Roitschwantz
        (*Burnaia zhizn' Lazika Roitsh-
        vantsa*), 14
Eichmann, Adolf, 227
Elon, Ori, 270
England, 34, 242-243
Eremin, Mikhail, 6, 32, 98
Erevan, Armenia, 341
Ermilov, Vladimir, 138
Ermolin, Evgeny, ix, 99
Etkind, Efim, 32, 101, 369
Europe, 4, 18, 20, 59, 77, 240, 242, 244, 280

Evangelical Baptist Church, 33
Evtushenko, Evgeny, 138

F
Fet, Afanasy, 133
Feuchtwanger, Lion, 286
  The False Nero, 306
  The Judean War, 306
  The Ugly Duchess, 355
Florence, Italy, 164
Florensky, Pavel, Father, 313, 321
France, 34, 291
Frankel, Neville, 246
  On the Sickle's Edge, 246
Freidenberg, Olga, 320
Frieden, Ken, 86
Frost, Robert, 356

G
Gamaleya Research Institute of Epidemiology and Microbiology, Moscow, 66, 80, 104, 373-374
Gans, Eric, 25, 29, 51
Garin, Erast, 72
Garin-Mikhailovsky, Nikolai
  Tyoma's Childhood, Pupils, University Students (Detstvo Temy, Gimnazisty, Studenty), 71
  Engineers (Inzhenery), 72
Garzonio, Stefano, ix, 7, 100
Gasparov, Mikhail, 187, 190
Genoa, Italy, 61-65
Georgia, 49, 101, 157
Germany, 9-10, 71, 242, 244, 277, 306n2, 359
Ginzburg, Aleksandr, 387
Ginzburg, Lidiya, 26, 285, 287
Ginzburg, Lev, 294
Gitelman, Zvi, 259
Gladilin, Anatoly
  "A Friday Rehearsal" ("Repetitsiia v piatnitsu"), 343
Glazov, Yuri
  In the Land of the Forefathers (V kraiu otsov), 306
Gnedich, Tatiana, 32, 101, 370
Gnedov, Vasilisk, 142
  "The Poem of the End" ("Poema kontsa"), 142
Gogol, Nikolai, 13, 64, 144, 266
Goldberg, Paul, 245
  The Yid, 245, 247
Goncharov, Ivan
  Oblomov 16

Gorenstein, Friedrich, 9, 286, 295
  Redemption (Iskuplenie), 306
  The Psalm (Psalom), 306
Gorky, Maxim, 75
Grekova, Irina
  The Legend's Fresh (Svezho predanie), 226n17
Grossman, Vasily, 242, 340-341
  Goodness Be To You! (Dobro vam!), 341
  Life and Fate (Zhizn' i sud'ba), 226n17, 264, 352
GULAG (Gulag) camps, 292, 296, 318, 359
Gumilev, Lev, 112
  Ethnogenesis and the Biosphere of the Earth (Etnogenez i biosfera zemli), 314

H
Ha-Levi, Yehuda
  Zion Songs (Shire Tsion), 222
Haskalah (the Jewish Enlightenment), 4
Hellenism, 108
Hemingway, Ernest, 89, 356
  The Sun Also Rises (Fiesta), 89
Herzen, Alexander, 236
Hitler, Adolf, 242, 309, 350
Holocaust *see* Shoah
Hölscher, Lucian, 222
Honig, Edwin, 88, 388, 394
Horowitz, Brian J., ix

I
Ilf, Ilya and Petrov, Evgeny
  The Twelve Chairs (Dvenadsat' stul'ev), 352, 355
  The Golden Calf (Zolotoi telenok), 352, 355
Ilyina, Nadezhda, 385
Indursky, Yehonatan, 270
Institute of World Literature of the Soviet Academy of Sciences (IMLI), Moscow, 137
Iraq War, 127
Isakovsky, Mikhail, 129
Israel, 17, 19-20, 28, 33, 35, 44, 101, 245-246, 270-271, 275, 286, 294, 312, 349, 353
Italian themes and motifs, ix, 157-158
Italy, 54, 72, 138, 156-158, 165, 279
Ivanova, Natalia, 27

J
Jackson, Robert Louis, 71
Jackson-Vanik Amendment of 1974, 258

Judaic culture, 6
Judaism, 21, 48, 108, 169, 223, 309, 323
Judeomania, 18
Judeophobia, 12, 137, 225, 227
Jerusalem, 68, 222, 311, 353
Jewish assimilation, 4
Jewish culture, 3, 9, 227-229, 296
Jewish customs, 14, 229n24
Jewish community, ix, 64, 85, 270, 321
Jewish diaspora, 4, 229
Jewish emigration, 17, 72, 124, 230, 239, 258n6, 271
Jewish Encyclopedia, Brockhaus and Efron, 306
Jewish history, 3, 229-230, 235-236, 350, 352
Jewish identity, ix, 5, 17, 25, 31, 33, 66, 135, 258-259, 264-265, 267, 273, 286
Jewish refusenik (otkaznik), *see* refusenik
Jewish revenge, ix, 68, 240, 245
Jewish-Russian culture, vii-ix
Jewish-Russian identity, 73
Jewish-Russian intelligentsia *see* Russian-Jewish intelligentsia
Jewish-Russian literature, vii, 7, 61, 140, 307
Jewish *samizdat*, 32
Jewish-Soviet diaspora, 3
Jewish theme(s), 7, 33, 38, 43, 120, 259
Jewishness, ix, 4, 12, 75, 89, 289, 296, 299, 302, 355-356
Jews in the USSR (*Evrei v SSSR*), journal, 308, 323

K

Kaddish, 39, 122-123
Kafka, Franz
   "The Metamorphosis", 77
Kandel, Felix, 5, 228
   The Gates of Our Exodus (*Vrata iskhoda nashego*, 1980), 222
Karabchievsky, Yury, 5, 14, 32
Karaite community, 17, 75, 227-228, 287
Kassil Lev, 13
   Konduit and Shvambrania (*Konduit i Shvambraniia*), 13
Katsis, Leonid, ix
Katsman, Roman, ix, 67, 104, 186, 288, 398
Kaverin, Veniamin, 358
Khazanov, Boris, (Gennady Faibusovich), 5
Khlebnikov, Velimir, 143, 189, 204, 213, 309
   "I don't need much" (Mne malo nado!") 309

Khrushchev's Thaw, 65, 110, 267, 357
Khudyakov, Gennady, 364
KGB, viii, 44, 68-69, 97, 225, 245, 251, 260, 275, 322, 359
Klyuev, Nikolay, 97
Knipper-Chekhova, Olga, 75
Koestler, Arthur
   The Thirteenth Tribe, 314
Kontinent, magazine, 342
Korkiya, Viktor
   A Black Person, or I, Poor Soso Dzhugashvili (*Chernyi chelovek, ili Ia, bednyi Soso Dzhugashvili*), 344
Kormer, Vladimir
   The Mole of History (*Krot istorii*, 1979), 306
Kozakova, Rimma, 377
Kozhinov, Vadim, 137-138
Krasnaia zvezda (*Red Star*), newspaper, 242
Krivulin, Viktor, 30, 203, 205
Kruchenykh, Aleksey, 142
Kunyaev, Boris, 377
Kuprin, Alexandr, 13, 75
Kupriyanov, Vyachelav, 377
Kushner, Aleksandr, 6, 31-32
Kuzmin, Mikhail, 186n22
   Alexandrian Songs (*Aleksandriiskie pesni*), 105, 110

L

Lanshchikov, Anatoly, 138
Lacan, Jacques, 42
Lahusen, Christian, 45
Lakhman, Arkady, 383
Lanin, Boris, ix, 90
Lasser, Karen Elizabeth, 395-396
Latour, Bruno, 50
Lem, Stanisław, 307
Leningrad (St. Petersburg) viii, 6, 10, 12-13, 31-32, 34-35, 60, 65-66, 73, 95, 126, 164, 190, 208, 247-250, 266, 326, 353, 362-365
Leningrad Institute of Tuberculosis, 66, 99
Lermontov, Mikhail, 177
   "Death of a Poet" ("Smert' poeta"), 177
   "Both bored and sad . . ." ("I skuchno i grustno . . ."), 177
Lerner, Aleksander, 34
Levinson, Solomon, 245
Levitansky, Yuri, 150, 377
Levkov, Ilya, 388
Lianozovo school, 98
Lipkin, Semyon, 228, 341
   Decade (*Dekada*), 17

literary seminar (*lito*)
  of the First Leningrad Medical School, 31
  of the Palace of Culture of Industrial Cooperation (*lito Promkooperatsii*, or Promka), 6, 31, 98, 369
Literary Gazette (*Literaturnaia Gazeta*), weekly, 101, 342
Lithuania, 67, 101, 227, 287
Lotman, Yuri, 186
Lunts, Lev, 358
Lurie, Evgenia, 296
Lurie, Samuil, 392
Lyubimov, Yuri, 46
Lyuksemburg, Eli, 5, 228
  The Tenth Hunger (*Desiatyi golod*, 1985), 222
  The Third Temple (*Tretii khram*, 1975), 222, 235

M

Macevičius, Juozas, 377
Majdanek (Lublin), 240, 244
Malamud, Bernard, 89, 294, 358
  The Assistant (1957), 89
Malevich, Kazimir, 311
Mallarmé, Stéphane, 133
Maltseva, Nadezhda, 377
Mandelstam, Nadezhda, 313-315, 317-318, 321
  Hope Abandoned (*Vospominaniia*), 317
Mandelstam, Osip, 39, 97, 103, 109, 114, 142, 144, 157, 164, 224, 308, 313-314, 317-318, 324
  "After the long-fingered Paganini…" ("Za Paganini dlinnopalym…"), 115
  "Ariosto" ("Ariost"), 162
  "I came back to the city familiar to the point of tears . . ." ("Ia vernulsia v moi gorod, znakomyi do slez … "), 183
  Octaves (*Oktavy*), 308
  "Rome" ("Rim"), 162
  "Slate Ode" ("Grifel´naia oda"), 293, 317-318, 321
Mann, Thomas, 84, 351
  Death in Venice, 355
  Joseph and His Brothers, 306
Marcinkevičius, Justinas, 377
Mariengof, Anatoly, 192
Markish, David, 5, 235, 294
  Story Embellishment (*Priskazka*, 1971), 12, 222, 228
  Dog (*Pes*, 1984), 17

Markish, Perez, 306
Markish, Simon, 306
Markov, Georgy, 375
Matusovsky, Mikhail, 129
Maupassant, Guy de, 84
Mayakovsky, Vladimir, 134, 138, 148, 204, 256, 374
Medvedkov, Yuri, 34
Melikhov, Aleksandr, 5, 13
  The Confession of A Jew (*Ispoved´ evreia*), 226n17
Men', Alexander, Father, 308, 321
Metropol, almanac, 32, 294
Metter, Izrail', 5
Mezhirov, Aleksandr, 149-150
Mikhailov, Eduard, 103
Mikhalkov, Sergey, 380
Mikhoels, Solomon, 291, 312
Mikuta, Algimantas, 377
Milin, Gennady, 385
Molotov, Viacheslav, 242
Moscow, 6, 15, 32-33, 38, 43, 65-67, 68n10, 70-72, 97, 99, 104, 157, 162, 190, 201, 245, 257, 294-295, 353
Moscow Art Theater, 75
Murina, Elena, 318
Mussolini, Benito, 162
Muzhetsky, Aleksandr, 364
mythopoesis, 29

N

Nabokov, Vladimir, 19, 61, 72, 76-81, 84-85, 143, 157, 168, 267, 351, 356
  "Jubilee" ("Iubilei"), 106
  Lolita, 83
  Pnin, 83, 267
  Glory (*Podvig*), 157, 268
  "Spring in Fialta" ("Vesna v Fial´te"), 76-77, 79
  The Gift (*Dar*), 83
  Luzhin's Defense (*Zashchita Luzhina*), 267
Naiman, Anatoly, 6, 32, 98, 367
Nature (*Priroda*), magazine, 80
Neman, magazine, 98
Nervi, Italy, 63-65
New England, 19, 72, 77, 128, 139, 157, 353-354
Nietzsche, Friedrich, 323
Ninov, Aleksandr, 98
Ninth Fort (Kaunas), 240
nonconformism, ix, 26-30, 36-37, 44, 46, 52, 288, 290

Jewish nonconformism, 26, 30, 289
Nyurenberg, Amshei, 296

O

OBERIU, group, 97, 207, 213
Okudzhava, Bulat, 16, 163
Olesha, Yuri, 351
Orlitsky, Yuri, 187-188
Osborne, Monica, ix
OVIR (Section of Visas and Registrations), 35, 67, 104, 229, 260
Ozerov, Lev, 31, 37, 66, 99, 101, 155, 377

P

Palestine, 33, 164, 227n20, 233, 308, 312, 321-322, 327-328
    see also Israel
Paris, 76, 201, 257, 353
Pärnu, Estonia, 122
Pasternak, Boris, 31, 103, 105, 109, 146, 177, 205, 319-320
    Doctor Zhivago, 264, 319, 328
    "Spring has been simply you ..." ("Vesna byla prosto toboi ..."), 180, 185
Paulus, Friedrich, General, 241
Pavlov First Medical School, Leningrad, 66, 98, 294
People's Friendship (*Druzhba narodov*), magazine, 101
Peretz, I. L., 86
Pessoa, Fernando, 206
Petrov, Evgeny *see* Ilf, Ilya and Petrov, Evgeny
Petrovsky, Mikhail, 334-335, 338-340
    Petrovsky, "Morphology of the Novella" ("Morfologiia novelly"), 334
Picasso, Pablo, 141-142
Pilnyak, Boris
    "A Story about the Writing of Stories" ("Rasskaz o tom, kak sozdaiutsia rasskazy"), 85
Pirandello, Luigi, 206
Pleshcheev, Aleksey, 60
Poland, 86, 240
Plotkin, Charles, 394
Plotkin, Nathalie, 394
Ponary (Vilnius), 240
Prague, 257
Pravda, newspaper, 246
Pristavkin, Anatoly
    (*Nochevala tuchka zolotaia* (*A Golden Cloud Spent the Night*), 10

Probstein, Ian, ix, 158, 186
Prokhanov, Aleksandr, 344
Providence, Rhode Island, 60, 72, 85, 106, 158, 353, 357
Pulse (*Pul's*), newspaper of the Pavlov First Medical University, 98
Purim, 36, 246
Pushkin, Alexandr, 13, 114, 146-147, 157, 177, 227, 287-289, 358, 370
    Boris Godunov, 344
    Eugene Onegin (*Evgenii Onegin*), 109, 115
    Little Tragedies (*Malen'kie tragedii*), 344
    Ruslan and Lyudmila (*Ruslan i Liudmila*), 339
    The Bronze Horseman (*Mednyi vsadnik*), 266
Pushkinskiye Gory (Pushkin Hills), 146

R

Rabinowitz, Joseph, 311
Radio Liberty (Radio Svoboda), 4
Ranchin, Andrei, ix, 104
Rapoport, Alek, 27, 30
Red Army, 240-241, 245, 277, 235
refusenik(s) (otkaznik[i]), viii, 3, 7, 15, 25, 34-36, 43-44, 49, 67, 69-70, 80, 104, 123, 223, 255, 265, 268, 270, 285, 306, 351-353
Reimeris, Vacys, 377
Reyn, Evgeny, 6, 32, 98, 384, 391
Riccio, Ottone "Ricky," 394
Rome, 106, 157, 162, 308, *353*
Ronen, Omry, 363
Roosevelt, Franklin D., 59
Roziner, Felix
    A Certain Finkelmayer (*Nekto Finkel'maier*, 1975), 16-17
Rozanov, Vasily
    The Jews' Olfactory and Tactile Relationship to Blood (*Oboniatel'noe i osiazatel'noe otnoshenie evreev k krovi*), 321
    The War of 1914 and the Russian Renaissance (*Voina 1914 goda i russkoe vozrozhdenie*), 320
Rubenstein, Joshua, ix
Rumbula (Riga), 240
Russia, 3, 28, 33, 64, 69, 77, 80, 121, 125, 136, 138, 147, 163, 165, 236, 275, 305, 340, 353, 356-357
Russian avant-garde, ix, 40, 102, 110, 141-142, 146, 204, 309

Russian émigré literature, 4
Russian futurism, 141-143, 207
Russian intelligentsia, 43, 45, 293
Russian Jewry, 4, 307
Russian Jews, 20, 349
Russian-Jewish culture, 255
Russian-Jewish intelligentsia, 3, 75, 103, 306, 311
Russian-Jewish urban culture, 12
Russian Orthodoxy, 27
Russian Orthodox Church, 344
Russian rock, 26
Russianness, ix, 320-321
Ryashentsev, Yuri, 377
Rybakov, Anatoly,
    Children of the Arbat (*Deti Arbata*), 341
    Heavy Sand (*Tiazhelyi pesok*), 355

S
samizdat, 27, 33, 37n60, 98, 294
Samoylov (Kaufman), David, 98, 150, 230, 352
Sapgir, Genrikh, ix, 15, 32, 40, 42, 99, 102-103, 123, 144, 189, 198-215, 391-392
    "Grasshoppericus" ("Kuznechikus"), 212
    Pushkin's Drafts (*Chernoviki Pushkina*), 200
    Preface to *Nevan Poems* by David Shrayer-Petrov
    Samizdat of the Century (*Samizdat veka*), 102, 123
    Terverses of Genrikh Bufarev (*Tertsikhi Genrikha Bufareva*), 206, 212
    Three Lives (*Tri zhizni*), 208
    Voices (*Golosa*), 209
    Women's Village (*Bab´ia derevnia*), 209
Sarnov, Benedikt, 292
Savitsky, Stanislav, 28
Segal, Dmitry, 319, 321
Segal-Rudnik, Nina, 319
Selvinskaya, Tatiana, 371
Selvinsky, Ilya, 228, 371
Sevela, Efraim, 14
Schweitzer, Albert, 147
Shalamov, Varlam, 291
    Kolyma Tales (*Kolymskie rasskazy*), 292
shestidesyatniki, 97
Shereshevsky, Lazar, 377-378
Shestov, Lev
    On Job's Balance (*A Wandering across Souls*) (*Na vesakh Iova* (*Stranstvovanie po dusham*)), 181-182

Sholem Aleichem, (Shalom Rabinovitz), 14, 63-65, 86, 356, 358
Shmukler, Yulia, 5
Shoah (Holocaust), 9, 17-18, 26, 31, 38, 84, 86, 114, 169, 265, 272, 278, 326, 355
Shchyogolev, Lev, 385
Shchyogoleva, Irina, 385
Shklovsky, Viktor, 66, 101, 133, 141, 315, 374
    "Art as Device" ("Iskusstvo kak priem"), 115
    "Art as Fracture [or 'Rupture']" ("Iskusstvo kak izlom"), 115, 121, 141, 150
Sholokhov, Mikhail, 341
Shostakovich, Dmitry, 141, 192
    "Young Lady and Hooligan" ("Baryshnia i khuligan"), ballet, 120
Shrayer, Emilia, 9, 37, 66, 105, 100, 123, 275, 371, 375, 379-381, 383-387, 389-390, 394, 396-397, 399, 402
Shrayer, Izrail', 363
Shrayer, Maxim D., ix-x, 3, 33, 102, 128, 175, 189, 199, 256n3, 265n21, 267, 270, 279, 290, 300, 372, 375, 378-379, 385-386, 388, 390, 395-396, 400-401
    Waiting for America: A Story of Emigration, 279
Shrayer, Mira Isabella, 396, 400
Shrayer (Sharir), Moses (Munia), 389
Shrayer, Peysakh (Pyotr), 65, 175, 360-362, 372
Shrayer, Tatiana Rebecca, 396, 400
Shrayer-Petrov, David, works
    "A Donkey Named Jacques" ("Oslik po imeni Zhak"), 117
    "A Storefront Window of Miracle" ("Vitrina chudes"), 354
    "Alfredik," 359
    "Anna Akhmatova in Komarovo" ("Anna Akhmatova v Komarovo"), 132, 145, 191
    "Apple Cider Vinegar" ("Iablochnyi uksus"), 71
    "Art as Fracture [or 'Rupture']" ("Iskusstvo kak izlom"), 115, 121, 141, 150
    "Autumn in Yalta" ("Osen´ v Ialte"), 17, 65-66, 73, 75-77, 79-80, 84-85, 90
    Awakening of Dreams (*Vozbuzhdenie snov*), 211
    "Behind the Zoo Fence" ("Za ogradoi zooparka"), 71, 358-359

Being a Refusenik (V otkaze), 68
"Biblical Plots" ("Bibleiskie siuzhety"), 158
Canvasses (Kholsty), 7, 66, 99, 101, 155-157
Carp for the Gefilte Fish (Karp dlia farshirovannoi ryby), 9, 84-86, 89-90
"Chimney Sweep" ("Trubochist"), 122
"Come Back to Sorrento" ("Vernut´sia v Sorrento"), 158, 165
"Coolidge Corner," 125
"Cottage of Yanka Kupala" ("Domik Ianki Kupaly"), 100
Cursed Be You... Just Don't Die (Bud´ ty prokliat! Ne umirai...), 68, 221, 232, 275, 291, 328
"Dahl's Dictionary" ("Slovar´ Dalia"), 200
Dinner with Stalin, ix, 69, 90, 332-345, 350-359
Doctor Levitin (Doktor Levitin, 1979-1980), viii-ix, 5, 17, 68, 70, 90, 221, 226, 228, 239, 242, 247, 255, 270, 326-327
"During a Flood in Leningrad in the Late Fifties" ("Vo vremia navodneniia v Leningrade v kontse piatidesiatykh"), 96
"Drums of Fate" ("Prayer Wheels"), (*Barabany sud´by*), 109, 115, 118, 150
"Early Morning in Moscow" ("Ranee utro zimoi," literally "Early Morning in Winter"), 38, 87-88
"Exploit"; "Act of Heroism" ("Podvig"), 157-158, 168-169
"Fencing Lessons" ("Uroki fekhtovaniia"), 145
Flying Saucers (Letaiushchie tarelki), 6, 122
Form of Love (Forma liubvi), 158
"Friend's Illness" ("Bolezn' druga"), 175-190
Friends and Shadows (Druz´ia i teni), 35, 83, 176
Genrikh Sapgir: The Avant-Garde Classic (Genrikh Sapgir: Klassik avangarda), 200
"Girl in a Straw Hat" ("Devochka v solomennoi shliape"), 115
Gold-Domed Moscow (Moskva zlatoglavaia), 101, 201

Grasshopper (Kuznechik), 213
"Gypsy Encampment in Ozerki" ("Tsyganskii tabor v Ozerkakh"), 39
"Hände Hoch!", 84
Herbert and Nelly (Gerbert i Nelli), 33, 35, 42-43, 69n10, 275, 286, 400
see also refusenik trilogy
"Hospital Garden" ("Bol´nichnyi sad"), 105
Hunt for the Red Devil (Okhota na ryzhego d´iavola), 6, 34, 104, 323
"Idiopathic Blues" ("Idiopaticheskii bliuz"), 110, 120
"In Front of the Synagogue at Simchat Torah" ("Pered sinagogoi v prazdnik Simkhat-Tora"), 97
"In Leningrad after the Siege" ("V Leningrade posle blokady"), 179
"In the Bar" ("V bare"), 116
"Ivan Terekhin Returns from the Front to the Village of Siva, Molotov Province in 1943" ("Ivan Terekhin vozvrashchaetsia s fronta v selo Siva Molotovskoi oblasti, 1943 god"), 96
Jonah and Sarah: Jewish Stories of Russia and America, 83, 89-90
"Lift Me Up" ("Podnimi menia"), 108
Lost Soul (Propashchaia dusha), 105, 108, 116, 157
"Members of the Italian Komsomol in a Young Pioneer Camp" ("Ital´ianskie komsomol´tsy v pionerskom lagere"), 100, 156
"Memories of Eastern Siberia" ("Vospominaniia o Vostochnoi Sibiri"), 126
"Mimicry" ("Mimikriia"), 18, 355, 359
"Mimosas for My Grandmother's Grave" ("Mimozy na mogilu babushki"), 66, 354
"Moscow March ("Moskovskii mart"), 125
"Moses—Erzia's Sculpture in Saransk" ("Moisei — skul'ptura Erzia"), 141
"Mother's Grave" ("Mogila mamy"), 39, 122
My Slavic Soul (Moia slavianskaia dusha), 6, 38, 67, 87, 101, 272-273
"My Soul Is Done Aching" ("Otbolela dusha"), 108

Nevan Poems (*Nevskie stikhi*), 35, 38, 103, 122, 175, 179, 186, 190-194
"New Year Poem" ("Novogodnee"), 150
"New World" ("Novyi svet"), 157
Oddities (*Strannosti"*), 96
"On Our Way to Serve" ("Edem sluzhit´," 100
"Once in Petersburg" ("Kogda-to v Pitere"), 116, 125
"Peter's Oak" ("Petrovskii dub"), 41, 191, 193
"Poems about Loyalty" ("Stikhi o vernosti"), 100
Poetry and Science: Notes and Reflections (*Poeziia i nauka: Zametki i razmyshleniia*), 50, 101
Purim spiel (Purim play), 36-37, 104
"Pushkin's Gravestone" ("Nadgrobie Pushkina"), 132, 141-142, 144-146
refusenik trilogy, ix, 5-6, 8, 33, 35, 39, 42, 45, 49, 51-52, 68, 176, 222-223, 229, 231, 235, 279, 289, 295, 297, 300, 302, 312n13, 326, 376, 381, 394, 400
  see also Herbert and Nelly
"Return from a Journey" ("Vozvrashchenie is puteshestviia"), 127
Round-the-Globe Happiness (*Krugosvetnoe schast´e*), 10
Runner Begoon (*Begun*), 6, 104, 123
Savely Ronkin (*Savelii Ronkin*, 2004), 9, 14-15, 17
Shadowmaidens (*Tenitsy*), 148
"Shostakovich at the Dacha in Komarovo" ("Shostakovich na dache v Komarovo"), 141
"Six American Blues on Russian Themes" ("Shest´ amerikanskikh bliuzov na russkie temy"), 105, 108-109
"Skating on the Ice of the Gulf of Finland in a Finnish Sledge" ("Katanie po l´du Finskogo zaliva na saniakh"), 102-103
Some Degree of Longing for the Messiah (*Nekotoraia stepen´ toski po Messii*), 104, 120
Song of a Blue Elephant (*Pesnia o golubom slone*), 108, 147, 157
"St. Isaac's Cathedral" ("Isaakievskii sobor"), 191
Staphylococcal Disease in the USSR, 66

Strange Danya Rayev (*Strannyi Dania Raev*), 5, 9-10, 13, 36, 60, 65, 73, 80, 84, 267
"Sunset at the Shore of the Tyrrhenian Sea" ("Zakat na beregu Tirrenskogo moria"), 158, 166-168
"Synagogue in Tbilisi" ("Sinagoga v Tbilisi"), 117-118
"Tbilisi", 157
Tiger of Snows (*Tigr Snegov*), 211
"The Bicycle Race" ("Velogonki"), 60, 353-354
"The Blues of a Jewish Organist in a Harlem Church" ("Bliuz evreiskogo organista v garlemskoi tserkvi"), 114
"The Blues of the Yellow River in New Orleans" ("Bliuz zheltoi reki v Novom Orleane"), 112
"The Concert of Schoenberg's Music" ("Kontsert muzyki Shenberga"), 120
"The Crowd in Boston" ("Tolpa v Bostone"), 127
"The Form of the Soul" ("Forma dushi"), 125
The French Cottage (*Frantsuzskii kottedzh*), 49, 60, 80-81, 83
The Gold-Domed Moscow (*Moskva zlatoglavaia*), 17
"The House of Edgar Allan Poe" ("Dom Edgara Po") 354
"The Love of Akira Watanabe" ("Liubov´ Akiry Vatanabe"), 84
"The Old Writer Forman" ("Staryi pisatel´ Forman"), 17
"The Shifted World" ("Sdvinutyi mir"), 126-127
The Story of My Beloved, or the Spiral Staircase (*Istoriia moei vozliublennoi, ili vintovaia lestnitsa*), 46, 49
"The Sun Fell into the Mine Shaft" ("Solntse upalo v shakhtu"), 351
"The Valley of Hinnom" ("Ushchel'e Geenny"), 353
These Strange Russian Jews (*Eti strannye russkie evrei*), 9
"Tolstoy, Dostoevsky, Chekhov," 120
"To My [Old] Female Friend" ("Moei podruzhke"), 108

"To Part before Love Has Faded Away" ("Proshchat′sia poka ne ugasla liubov′"), 116
Travels from the Banks of the Neva (*Puteshestviia ot beregov Nevy*), 96, 142
"Trio of Shostakovich" ("Trio Shostakovicha"), 120
"Tsukerman and His Children" ("Tsukerman i ego deti"), 19
Two Books (*Dve knigi*), 158
Vaccine. Ed Tenner (*Vaktsina. Ed Tenner*), 35, 48-50, 52
"V sadakh iuga" ("In the Orchards of the South"), 157
"Variety Show in Tallinn" ("Var'ete v Tallinne"), 145
Villa Borghese (1987–1990), 6, 105-108, 157-164, 168
Village Orchestra (*Derevenskii orkestr*), 158
Vodka and Cakes (*Vodka s pirozhnymi*), 101
"Wanderings across the Urals" ("Bluzhdaniia po Uralu"), 96
Winter Ship (*Zimnii korabl′*), 34, 67, 101-102, 157
"Where Are You, Zoya?" ("Gde ty, Zoya?"), 359
"White Night" ("Belaia noch′"), 116
"White City" ("Belyi gorod"), 108
"White Sheep on a Green Mountain Slope" ("Belye ovtsy na zelenom sklone gory," 2003), 42n76, 236, 355
"Wild Turkeys in Boston" ("Dikie indeiki v Bostone"), 128
"Winter Song" ("Zimniaia pesnia"), 108
Yellow Star (*Zheltaia zvezda*), 119
"You said: I love you" ("Ty govorila: Ia tebia liubliu"), 108
Yudins Redemption, (*Iskuplenie Iudina*), ix, 35, 46, 48-49, 52, 305-328
Yuri the Long-Armed (*Iurii Dolgorukii*), 121
Shrovetide, 12
Shteynman, Zelik, 98
Simonov, Konstantin, 15, 242
Sinani, Isaak, 75
Singer, Isaac Bashevis, 84, 86, 235, 293, 356, 358
   Enemies: A Love Story (1966), 86
   Collected Stories (1982), 86
   Shosha (1974), 86, 355
Sintaksis, magazine, 27
Simchat Torah, 45
Sinyavsky, Andrey, 81
skaz, 40
Slavic literature, 3
Slavinsky, Efim, 367
Slepak, Vladimir, 7, 34, 383
Slovatinskaya, Tatyana, 296
Slutsky, Boris, 65, 97, 150, 295, 352
   "Half-Breeds" ("Polukrovki"), 292
   "Shovels" ("Lopaty"), 292
Smirnova-Sazonova, Sofia, 76
Smorodin, Boris, 364
Smola, Klavdia, viii-ix, 42, 285, 290
Smola, Oleg, ix, 158
Smorodin, Boris, 176-177
Soloviev, Vladimir, 388
   "Against the Antisemitic Movement in the Press," 311
   "Talmud", 311
   The Short Tale of the Antichrist (1901), 310-311
   Three Conversations, 323
Solzhenitsyn, Alexander
   One Day in the Life of Ivan Denisovich (*Odin den' Ivana Denisovicha*), 291
   Two Hundred Years Together (*Dvesti let vmeste*), 308
Song of Songs, 108
Sosnora, Viktor, 6, 98
Soutine, Chaim, 296
Soviet authorities, viii, 7, 26, 35, 42, 262
Soviet culture, 34, 268, 351
Soviet immigrants, 84
Soviet Jewish intelligentsia, ix, 223
Soviet Jews, 4, 39, 208, 246, 271, 273, 275, 294, 299, 306, 308, 323-324, 355
Soviet Jewry, 13, 74, 271
Soviet literature, 26-27, 31, 46, 49, 286
Soviet nonconformism, 25
Soviet unofficial or nonconformist literature, 25
Soviet regime, 123, 213, 223, 271-272
Soviet system, 26
Soviet Union, the, 3, 7, 34, 47, 65, 68, 72, 74, 84, 156-158, 163, 165, 222, 225, 245, 258, 270-271, 275, 286, 350-351, 353, 355, 357
Spanish Jews, 42
Spektor, Roman, 385
Spinoza, Boruch, 299, 300n40
St. Petersburg *see* Leningrad

Stalin, Joseph, 37, 59, 65, 98, 245-246, 250, 270, 296, 299-300, 309, 340-341, 350
Stalingrad, 13, 240-241, 243, 341
Stewart (Riccio), Dolores, 394
Stimpson, Catharine R., 395
Strauss, Leo
    Persecution and the Art of Writing, 289
Strugatsky brothers (penname of Arkady and Natan Strugatsky), 358
Sukharev, Dmitry, 377
surrealism, 17, 112, 142
Suslov, Ilya, 343
    Stories of Comrade Stalin and Other Comrades (Rasskazy o tovarishche Staline i drugikh *tovarishchakh*), 342
Sutzkever, Abram, 242
Svirsky, Grigory, 9
Svyatogorsky Monastery ("The Holy Mountains" cloister) *see* Pushkinskiye Gory (Pushkin Hills)
Switzerland, 64

T
Taganka Theater, 46
Talmud, 27, 181n14
tamizdat, 81, 317
Thaw-era hipsters (*stiliagi*), 26
Tel Aviv, 246
Terras, Rita, 390
Terras, Victor, 105-106, 388, 390
Tillich, Paul, 30
Tolstoy, Aleksey N., 242
    The Hyperboloid of Engineer Garin (*Giperboloid inzhenera Garina*, 1927), 72
Tolstoy, Aleksey K.
    "Where the vines bend over the whirlpool . . ." ("Gde gnutsia nad omutom lozy . . . "), 182
Tolstoy, Lev, 15, 111-112, 235, 243
    Anna Karenina, 266
    Boyhood (*Detstvo*), 10
Trakai, Lithuania, 227
Treblinka (Poland), 240
Trifonov, Yuri, ix, 289-302
    Another Life (*Drugaia zhizn'*), 298
    Disappearance (*Ischeznovenie*), 297
    Glares of Fire (*Otblesk kostra*), 297
    Students (*Studenty*), 291, 299
    Time and Place (*Vremia i mesto*), 295
    The House on the Embankment (Dom na naberezhnoi), 295, 299
    The Long Goodbye (*Dolgoe proshchanie*), 297, 301
    The Old Man (*Starik*), 196
    The Overturned House (*Oprokinutyi dom*), 291
Trifonova (Miroshnichenko), Olga, 290
Trinity Sunday, 12
Tsvetaeva, Marina, 39, 106, 192
    Poem of the End (*Poema Kontsa*, 1924), 136, 149
Turgenev, Ivan, 133
Tvardovsky, Aleksandr, 129
Tynyanov, Yuri
    Kyukhlya, 13
Tyshler, Aleksandr, 312
Tyutchev, Fyodor, 132, 147

U
Uflyand, Vladimir, 98
Ukraine, 80, 240, 249, 342
Ulitskaya, Lyudmila, 5
United States of America, the, viii, 3, 7, 9, 15, 19-20, 34-35, 61, 64, 68n10, 71-72, 80, 84, 86, 89, 105, 125, 134, 139, 157, 165, 168, 201, 223, 245-246, 275-276, 279, 286, 291, 294, 349, 353, 357
Union of Soviet Writers, the, viii, 7, 32-33, 38, 66-68, 101-102, 110, 157-158, 275, 375, 380
UNOVIS, 311
Urals, the, 10, 36, 65, 73, 95, 266, 358
Uris, Leon, 235, 294
USSR, vii-ix, 27, 48, 61, 68n10, 80, 89, 110, 134, 155, 246, 265, 267, 271, 328
Utkin, Iosif, 224

V
Vakhtin, Boris, 32, 192
Vaičiūnaitė, Judita, 377
Vasilieva, Larisa, 377
Veidle, Vladimir, 191
Vilnius, Lithuania, 38, 67, 377
Vinokur, Leonid, 241
Virabov, Igor, 315
Vitebsk School of Art, 311
Vlodov, Yuri, 373
Voldman, Grigory
    The Sheremetyevo Airport (*Sheremet'evo*), 223
Volf, Sergei, 6, 98, 109
Voloshin, Maximillian, 157
Voltskaya, Tatyana, 4
Voronel', Aleksandr

The Awe of Judean Concerns (Trepet zabot iudeiskii), 308
The Zero Commandment (Nulevaia zapoved'), 308
Voznesensky, Andrei, 66, 101, 138, 315, 327
  "Chagall's Cornflowers ("Vasil'ki Shagalla"), 327

W

Waife-Goldberg, Marie, 64
  My Father, Sholom Aleichem, 64
Wehrmacht, 240
Weininger Otto
  Sex and Character (1903), 321
Williams, William Carlos, 104
World War I, 64, 242
World War II, 35, 73, 97, 156, 266, 270, 292

Y

Yalta, 59-61, 74-76, 80-81
Yalta Conference, 59
Yesenin, Sergei
  The Black Man (*Chernyi chelovek*), 177, 185
Yiftach-Walbe, Ayala, 389
Young Communist League (Komsomol), 99
Young Pioneer (*Pioner*), magazine, 7, 98
Yudin, Lev, 311
Yudin, Pavel F., 312
Yudin, Sergey S., 312
  Musings of a Surgeon (*Razmyshlenia khirurga*), 312
Yudina Maria V., 312, 319
Yurchak, Alexei, 26
Yushkevich, Semyon, 64

Z

Zabolotsky, Nikolai, 189, 204, 357
  Scrolls (*Stolbtsy*), 357
Zaichik, Mark, 5
zaum', 120
Zhabotinsky Vladimir (Ze'ev), 235, 294, 326
Zionism, 6, 8, 38, 42, 46, 75
Zolotussky, Igor, 138
Zweig, Stefan, 351

Contributors

Authors

Evgeny Ermolin is professor and chair of the Department of Journalism and Publishing at K. D. Ushinsky Yaroslavl State University in Yaroslavl, Russia. A literary and art scholar, and a critic and a blogger, he has taught the history of world and Russian culture, modern literature and art, and journalism in Moscow, Yaroslavl, Arkhangelsk, and Tashkent. Ermolin has served as deputy editor of *Kontinent* and presently serves as editor of the electronic journal *Kontinent* (e-continent.de). He has authored books about Russian culture in the vein of dialogical personalism and critical essays about contemporary culture and leading contemporary writers. His books about literature include *Mediums Outside Time. Literature in the Postmodern Epoch, or Trans-Avantgarde* (2015), *The Last Classics. Russian Literature of the Last Third of the Twentieth Century: Peaks, Principal Texts and Landscape* (2016), *Existence and Multiauthorship. The Origin and Essence of Literary Blogging* (2018*)*, *The Zeroing-Out of the Obvious: The Crisis of Reliable Truths in Literature and Essayism of the Twentieth Century* (2019). Ermolin's literary prizes include Antibuker-Luch sveta (2000). In 2010 he was named "Stationmaster" of the I. P. Belkin Literary Prize.

Stefano Garzonio is professor of Slavic studies (Russian language and literature) at Pisa University in Italy. In 1999–2009 he was the President of the Italian Association of Slavists (AIS). He presently serves as Vice President of the Executive Committee of the International Council for Central and East European Studies. Garzonio is the author of many books, articles and other publications about the theory and history of Russian verse, Russian literature of the eighteenth century, the poetry of the Russian Silver Age, and the history of Russian emigration in the twentieth century, including the Russian cultural presence in Italy. He is the editor of two comprehensive anthologies *Poesia Russa* (2004) and *Lirici Russi dell'Ottocento* (2011), and the author of two collections (2017; 2020) of his own verse originally written in Russian and published in Russia under the pseudonym Stepan Fryazin. Stefano Garzonio has translated and annotated works by Lermontov, Turgenev, Fet, Dostoevsky, Mayakovsky, Georgy Ivanov, and other Russian authors, including contemporary émigré writers. In 2010 he was awarded the literary prize Globus (Moscow).

Marat Grinberg emigrated from the former USSR in 1993, studied at the Jewish Theological Seminary, and received his PhD from the University of Chicago. A scholar of Jewish and Russian literature and culture, and of cinema, he is an associate professor of Russian and humanities at Reed College in Portland, Oregon. Grinberg is the author of *"I am to Be Read not from Left to Right, but in Jewish: from Right to Left": The Poetics of Boris Slutsky* (2011, to be published in Russian in St. Petersburg in 2021), *Aleksandr Askoldov: The Commissar* (2016), and co-editor of *Woody on Rye: Jewishness in the Films and Plays of Woody Allen* (2013). Marat Grinberg's most recent essays have appeared in *Tablet Magazine*, *Mosaic*, *Los Angeles Review of Books*, *Cineaste*, and *Commentary*. He lectures widely on topics ranging from Shoah literature and film to Jewish-Russian poetry. Grinberg's current book project, to be published by Brandeis University Press, is *The Soviet Jewish Bookshelf: Jewish Culture and Identity Between the Lines*.

Brian J. Horowitz holds a PhD from Berkeley and is professor of Jewish studies and the Sizeler Family chair at Tulane University. One of the pioneers of the study of Jewish-Russian culture and intellectual history, Horowitz is the author of numerous scholarly essays and five books, among them *Vladimir Jabotinsky's Russian Years* (2020), *Russian Idea—Jewish Presence* (2013), *Jewish Philanthropy and Enlightenment in Late-Tsarist Russia* (2009), and *Empire Jews* (2009). He has won numerous awards for his works, including fellowships in Israel, Germany, and the United States. His presently writing a history of Jewish historiography in Eastern Europe that will feature the development of Jewish nationalism as it moved from Russia to Poland, the United States, and Israel. He is also preparing a volume of Abba Achimeir's writings. Achimeir was the founder of Brit ha-Biryonim (Group of Hoodlums) in Palestine in the two decades before the outbreak of World War.

Leonid Katsis received his doctoral habilitation from the Russian State University for the Humanities in 2002. From 2002 he has been a professor at the Russian-American Center for Bible and Jewish Studies at the Russian State University for the Humanities. In 2019 he became the Director of Scientific and Scholarly Center for Bible and Jewish Studies at the Russian State University for the Humanities, where he is Head of the Department of Theology of Judaism, Bible and Jewish Studies and Head of the MA Program "Holocaust and Genocides: International Consulting" (jointly with Ilya Altman). Leonid Katsis's books include: *Vladimir Mayakovsky: A Poet in the Intellectual Context of the Epoch* (2002; 2nd enlarged edition 2004), *Osip Mandelstam: Musk of Judaism* (2002), *The Blood Libel and The Russian Thought: Historic and Theology Study of the Beilis Trial* (2006); *"The Russian Spring" of Vladimir Jabotinsky: Attribution, Bibliography, Autobiography* (2019), and others.

Roman Katsman was born in the USSR and has lived in Israel since 1990. He is a professor in the Department of Literature of the Jewish people of Bar-Ilan University. Katsman is the author of number of books and articles about Hebrew and Russian literature, particularly about Jewish-Russian and Russian-Israeli literature and thought. He has worked on the theoretical problems of mythopoesis, chaos, nonverbal communication, sincerity, alternative history, and humor. His most recent books, *Elusive Reality: A Hundred Years of Russian-Israeli Literature (1920–2020)* (2020, in Russian) and *Nostalgia for a Foreign Land* (2016, in English), examine the Russian-language literature in Israel. Other major publication include *Laughter in Heaven: Symbols of Laughter in the Works of S.Y. Agnon* (2018, in Hebrew), *Literature, History, Choice: The Principle of Alternative History in Literature* (2013), *At the Other End of Gesture. Anthropological Poetics of Gesture in Modern Hebrew Literature* (2008), *The Time of Cruel Miracles: Mythopoesis in Dostoevsky and Agnon* (2002), and others.

Boris Lanin, born in Baku to a Jewish-Russian family, served as professor and director of reading pedagogy in the Academy of Education of Russia in 1999–2015 and is now professor of Russian literature at the State Institute of Theatre Arts (GITIS) in Moscow. His first book on Vasily Grossman was published in 1996, and since then he has published extensively on Jewish-Russian literature and Russian émigré literature. Boris Lanin's works have been published in nine languages. His textbooks of literature are widely used at secondary schools in the Russian Federation, with about one million copies sold to date. Lanin served as a visiting professor at the Kennan Institute, the Woodrow Wilson Center (Washington, DC), the Institute for Advanced Studies (Paris), Alfried Krupp Wissenschaftskolleg, the Swedish Collegium for Advanced Studies (Uppsala), and as NEH distingiushed visiting professor at the State University of New York (Potsdam). Lanin's most recent book is *The Prose of the Third Wave of Emigration*, 2nd edition (2018).

Monica Osborne is a writer and former professor of literature and cultural studies. She holds a PhD in modern and contemporary Jewish thought from Purdue University. Osborne is the author of *The Midrashic Impulse and the Contemporary Literary Response to Trauma* and the co-editor (with Holli Levitsky and Stella Setka) of *Literature of Exile and Displacement: American Identity in a Time of Crisis*. She has written for *The New Republic, The Chronicle of Higher Education, The Jewish Journal* (where she is a regular columnist), *The Los Angeles Review of Books, Religion and Literature, Multi-Ethnic Literatures of the US*, as well as other magazines, academic journals, and edited collections. Her journalistic writing has dealt with issues including trauma and violence, immigration, the #MeToo movement, the TSA, racism and antisemitism, and the ethics of Holocaust and 9/11 comedy. She was an Andrew W. Mellon fellow at UCLA 2008–2010, and has taught at Purdue University, Pepperdine University, Loyola Marymount University, and the 92nd Street Y in New York City.

Ian Probstein, professor of English at Touro College in New York City, is a bilingual Russian-American poet, scholar, and translator of poetry. A native of Minsk, he has published twelve books of poetry in Russian, one in English, translated more than a dozen poetry volumes; and has compiled and edited more than thirty books and anthologies of poetry in translation. His essays, poems in English and translations of poetry into English have been published in such journals as *Atlanta Review, The International Literary Quarterly, Brooklyn Rail: In Translation, Four Centuries of*

Russian Poetry in Translation, International Poetry Review, Metamorphosis and many anthologies, including *An Anthology of Jewish-Russian Literature*. His most recent books are, in English, *The River of Time: Time-Space, Language and History in Avant-Garde, Modernist, and Contemporary Poetry* (2017), and in Russian, the complete annotated edition of *T. S. Eliot's Poetry and Plays* (2019) and the edition/translation of Charles Bernstein's *Sign Under Test: Selected Poems and Essays* (2020).

Andrei Ranchin, professor of philology at Moscow State University, is the author of over seven hundred publications on the history of Old Russian literature and Russian literature from the seventeenth to the twentieth centuries. Among his interests are the Old Russian lives of the saints, writings of Mikhail Lomonosov, Edokiya Rastopchina, Nikolai Gogol, Lev Tolstoy, Nikolai Leskov, the poetry of Joseph Brodsky, and the poetics of Aleksandr Solzhenitsyn. He has published commentaries to Russian writers' works, textbooks, and children's tales. He had been the recipient of the Yury Tynyanov Prize (1994), Arkady Belinkov Prize (1995), the Novyi Mir Prize (2013) and other prizes. Ranchin's books include *Essays on Old Russian Literature* (1999), *Joseph Brodsky and Russian Poetry of the Eighteenth–Twentieth Centuries* (2001), *A Garden of Golden Words: Old Russian Book Culture Through Interpretations, Analyses and Commentaries* (2007), *A Guide to Afanasy Fet's Poetry* (2010), *About Brodsky: Reflections and Analyses* (2016), *The Tale of Igor's Campaign: A Guide* (2019) and others.

Joshua Rubenstein, Boston-based author and scholar, was on the staff of Amnesty International USA from 1975 to 2012 as the Northeast regional director. He is also a long-time associate of the Davis Center for Russian and Eurasian Studies at Harvard University In the spring of 2015, Mr. Rubenstein became associate director for Major Gifts at the Harvard Law School. Working as an independent scholar, Rubenstein is the author of many books, including *Soviet Dissidents, Their Struggle for Human Rights* and *Tangled Loyalties: The Life and Times of Ilya Ehrenburg*. He is the co-editor of *Stalin's Secret Pogrom: The Postwar Inquisition of the Jewish Anti-Fascist Committee* (recipient of a National Jewish Book Award in the category of East European Studies). He is the co-editor of *The KGB File of Andrei Sakharov* and of *The Unknown Black Book, the Holocaust in the German-Occupied Soviet Territories*. Rubenstein contributed a concise interpretive biography of Leon Trotsky to the Jewish Lives series at Yale University Press. His most recent book, *The Last Days of Stalin* (2016), has been translated into nine languages.

Maxim D. Shrayer, translingual author, scholar, and translator, was born in Moscow and emigrated in 1987 with his parents, David Shrayer-Petrov and Emilia Shrayer. He is professor of Russian, English, and Jewish studies at Boston College and Director of the Project on Russian and Eurasian Jewry at the Davis Center, Harvard University. Shrayer is the author and editor of nearly twenty books of criticism and biography, fiction and nonfiction, and poetry. His books include *The World of Nabokov's Stories, Russian Poet/Soviet Jew, Yom Kippur in Amsterdam, Bunin and Nabokov: A History of Rivalry* (which was a bestseller in Russia), *Leaving Russia: A Jewish Story*, and, most recently, *Antisemitism and the Decline of Russian Village Prose* and *Of Politics and Pandemics: Songs of a Russian*

Immigrant. He is the editor of *An Anthology of Jewish-Russian Literature* and *Voices of Jewish-Russian Literature*. Shrayer is a Guggenheim Fellow and the winner of a National Jewish Book Award. His works have appeared in ten languages.

Klavdia Smola, a Moscow-born scholar, is professor and chair of Slavic literatures and cultures at the Department of Slavic studies, University of Dresden (Germany). She obtained her PhD at the University of Tübingen, taught at the University of Greifswald, and was research fellow at the universities of Jerusalem, Moscow, Barcelona, Constance, and Cracow. She authored the books *Types and Patterns of Intertextuality in the Prose of Anton Chekhov* (2004, in German) and *Reinvention of Tradition: Contemporary Russian-Jewish Literature* (2019, in German). Smola co-edited *Jewish Underground Culture in the Late Soviet Union* (Special Issue of *East European Jewish Affairs*, 2018); *Russia—Culture of (Non-)Conformity: From the Late Soviet Era to the Present* (special issue of *Russian Literature*, 2018, with Mark Lipovetsky); *Postcolonial Slavic Literatures after Communism* (2016, together with Dirk Uffelmann); *Jewish Spaces and Topographies in East-Central Europe: Constructions in Literature and Culture* (2014, in German, together with Olaf Terpitz), and *Eastern European Jewish Literatures of the 20th and 21st Centuries: Identity and Poetics* (2013).

Oleg Smola, author and literary scholar, was born in Georgievsk, Stavropol Region and graduated from Moscow State University. He holds a *kandidat nauk* (PhD equivalent) and *doktor nauk* (habilitation equivalent) degrees in philology. He worked as an editor at the journal *Voprosy literature* (*Questions of Literature*) and, from 1973-1995, as a researcher at the Institute of World Literature of the Russian Academy of Sciences. Oleg Smola's work has focused on the study of poets and poetry. In his own words, "perhaps this has to do with the fact that Pushkin and Lermontov has each visited my native town twice. Pushkin stayed at the building with an annex, which a century later would become School no. 3, where I studied for the first four years." Oleg Smola is the author of numerous articles about Andrei Voznesensky, Velimir Khlebnikov, Aleksandr Blok, Vladimir Mayakovsky and other poets. His books included: *Vladimir Mayakovsky: Life and Work* (1977), *Nikolay Aseev's Lyrical Poetry* (1980), *"Black evening. White snow . . .": The Creative Story and Destiny of Blok's Long Poem* The Twelve (1993), *"If words ache . . ."* (co-authored with Klavdia Smola, 1998).

Translators

Anastasia Degtyareva holds a degree in linguistics from Lomonosov Moscow State University. She has been working as a freelance translator since 2015 and specializes in the fields of humanities and social sciences. She lives in Moscow.

Dobrochna Fire was born in Łódź, Poland, and grew up in the United States. She holds a PhD from Harvard University in Slavic languages and literatures. Her translation credits range from articles to books, children's literature to scholarly works and include Edward Kopówka's *Jews in Siedlce: 1850–1945* and Szymon Zakrzewski's *Yoke of the Night: Along* the Trail of the Bowed, both from Polish. Her copyediting credits include *The Staszów Yizkor Book* and Maxim D. Shrayer's *Of Politics and Pandemics*.

Daria Sadovnichenko, a native of Moscow, graduated from the Russian State University for the Humanities. She will receive an MA in Russian literature at Boston College in 2021. As Maxim D. Shrayer's research assistant, she had worked on a number of research projects, including a cultural history of the 1943 Krasnodar Trial and Russian émigré poetry. She has also translated Russian poetry into English.

Maxim D. Shrayer (see above).

Praise for *The Parallel Universes of David Shrayer-Petrov*

"This fascinating collection provides many insights into one of the finest poets and an outstanding writer, David Shrayer-Petrov, who made a significant contribution to Russian and Jewish cultures. This multi-facing study explores many topics—from Shrayer-Petrov's life, his variety of themes, genres, and styles to textual and cultural sources of his poems, short stories, and novels. Many essays illuminate the brilliant mind and the innovations of David Shrayer-Petrov. The bibliography compiled by his son Maxim D. Shrayer is a vital contribution to this book and helps to appreciate the outstanding achievements this poet, writer and translator. The *Parallel Universes of David Shrayer-Petrov* the best thing written about the writer and an essential reading for all who are not indifferent to literature and culture."

- Valentina Polukhina, University of Keele; author of *Joseph Brodsky: A Poet for Our Time* and *Brodsky Through the Eyes of His Contemporaries*

"The book contextualizes, analyzes, and celebrates the work of a nonconformist writer who for several decades explored the thought, the feel, and the fantasy of Russian-Soviet-Jewish, Jewish-refusenik, and Jewish-immigrant-American experience. The studies collected in this volume discuss the ways in which the hyphenated literary identity of David Shrayer-Petrov enters an interface with a variety of intellectual communities without catering to their biases or expectations."

- Leona Toker, the Hebrew University of Jerusalem; author of *Gulag Literature and the Literature of Nazi Camps: An Intertextual Reading* and *Nabokov: The Mystery of Literary Structures*

"This book, devoted to the prose and poetry of the brilliant Jewish-Russian writer David Shrayer-Petrov, both from his Soviet and his American periods, is more than a collection of essays. The first book devoted to the works of Shrayer-Petrov, it is a thoroughly conceived and impressively structured full-length study of Shrayer-Petrov's literary exploration of Russian and Soviet Jewry. The nuanced psychological reflection, sharp socio-historical vision and high aesthetic qualities of Shrayer-Petrov's literary works make them of significant interest both to those who self-identify with the refuseniks' worldview and to those who oppose it on political or ethical grounds. The same is true of *The Parallel Worlds of David Shrayer-Petrov*. Bringing together a powerful group of scholars, among them some of the leading students of Russian-Jewish culture, this is an outstanding study which is bound to attract the attention of different audiences, with diverse personal experiences, worldviews, and convictions."

- Dennis Sobolev, University of Haifa; author of the novel *Jerusalem* and *The Split World of Gerard Manley Hopkins: An Essay in Semiotic Phenomenology*

www.ingramcontent.com/pod-product-compliance
Lightning Source LLC
Chambersburg PA
CBHW052041220426
43663CB00012B/2398